T0321927

Handbook of Research on Emerging Trends and Applications of Machine Learning

Arun Solanki
Gautam Buddha University, India

Sandeep Kumar
Amity University, Jaipur, India

Anand Nayyar
Duy Tan University, Da Nang, Vietnam

A volume in the Advances in Computational Intelligence and Robotics (ACIR) Book Series

Published in the United States of America by
    IGI Global
    Engineering Science Reference (an imprint of IGI Global)
    701 E. Chocolate Avenue
    Hershey PA, USA 17033
    Tel: 717-533-8845
    Fax: 717-533-8661
    E-mail: cust@igi-global.com
    Web site: http://www.igi-global.com

Library of Congress Cataloging-in-Publication Data

Names: Solanki, Arun, 1985- editor. | Kumar, Sandeep, 1983- editor. |
  Nayyar, Anand, editor.
Title: Handbook of research on emerging trends and applications of machine
  learning / Arun Solanki, Sandeep Kumar, and Anand Nayyar, editors.
Description: Hershey, PA : Engineering Science Reference, [2020] | Includes
  bibliographical references. | Summary: "This book examines the role of
  machine learning in various applications such as data mining, natural
  language processing, image recognition, and expert systems"-- Provided
  by publisher.
Identifiers: LCCN 2019005483 | ISBN 9781522596431 (h/c) | ISBN
  9781522596455 (eISBN) | ISBN 9781522596448 (s/c)
Subjects: LCSH: Machine learning. | Data mining. | Natural language
  processing (Computer science)
Classification: LCC Q325.5 .H357 2020 | DDC 006.3/1--dc23
LC record available at https://lccn.loc.gov/2019005483

This book is published in the IGI Global book series Advances in Computational Intelligence and Robotics (ACIR) (ISSN: 2327-0411; eISSN: 2327-042X)

British Cataloguing in Publication Data
A Cataloguing in Publication record for this book is available from the British Library.

All work contributed to this book is new, previously-unpublished material. The views expressed in this book are those of the authors, but not necessarily of the publisher.

For electronic access to this publication, please contact: eresources@igi-global.com.

Advances in Computational Intelligence and Robotics (ACIR) Book Series

Ivan Giannoccaro
University of Salento, Italy

ISSN:2327-0411
EISSN:2327-042X

MISSION

While intelligence is traditionally a term applied to humans and human cognition, technology has progressed in such a way to allow for the development of intelligent systems able to simulate many human traits. With this new era of simulated and artificial intelligence, much research is needed in order to continue to advance the field and also to evaluate the ethical and societal concerns of the existence of artificial life and machine learning.

The **Advances in Computational Intelligence and Robotics (ACIR) Book Series** encourages scholarly discourse on all topics pertaining to evolutionary computing, artificial life, computational intelligence, machine learning, and robotics. ACIR presents the latest research being conducted on diverse topics in intelligence technologies with the goal of advancing knowledge and applications in this rapidly evolving field.

COVERAGE

- Cognitive Informatics
- Adaptive and Complex Systems
- Intelligent control
- Computational Logic
- Fuzzy Systems
- Algorithmic Learning
- Neural Networks
- Agent technologies
- Evolutionary Computing
- Brain Simulation

IGI Global is currently accepting manuscripts for publication within this series. To submit a proposal for a volume in this series, please contact our Acquisition Editors at Acquisitions@igi-global.com or visit: http://www.igi-global.com/publish/.

Titles in this Series

For a list of additional titles in this series, please visit: https://www.igi-global.com/book-series/advances-computational-intelligence-robotics/73674

Avatar-Based Control, Estimation, Communications, and Development of Neuron Multi-Functional Technology Platforms
Vardan Mkrttchian (HHH University, Australia) Ekaterina Aleshina (Penza State University, Russia) and Leyla Gamidullaeva (Penza State University, Russia)
Engineering Science Reference • © 2020 • 355pp • H/C (ISBN: 9781799815815) • US $245.00

Handbook of Research on Fireworks Algorithms and Swarm Intelligence
Ying Tan (Peking University, China)
Engineering Science Reference • © 2020 • 400pp • H/C (ISBN: 9781799816591) • US $295.00

AI Techniques for Reliability Prediction for Electronic Components
Cherry Bhargava (Lovely Professional University, India)
Engineering Science Reference • © 2020 • 330pp • H/C (ISBN: 9781799814641) • US $225.00

Artificial Intelligence and Machine Learning Applications in Civil, Mechanical, and Industrial Engineering
Gebrail Bekdaş (Istanbul University-Cerrahpaşa, Turkey) Sinan Melih Nigdeli (Istanbul University-Cerrahpaşa, Turkey) and Melda Yücel (Istanbul University-Cerrahpaşa, Turkey)
Engineering Science Reference • © 2020 • 312pp • H/C (ISBN: 9781799803010) • US $225.00

Virtual and Augmented Reality in Education, Art, and Museums
Giuliana Guazzaroni (Università Politecnica delle Marche, Italy) and Anitha S. Pillai (Hindustan Institute of Technology and Science, India)
Engineering Science Reference • © 2020 • 385pp • H/C (ISBN: 9781799817963) • US $225.00

Advanced Robotics and Intelligent Automation in Manufacturing
Maki K. Habib (The American University in Cairo, Egypt)
Engineering Science Reference • © 2020 • 357pp • H/C (ISBN: 9781799813828) • US $245.00

Language and Speech Recognition for Human-Computer Interaction
Amitoj Singh (MRS Punjab Technical University, India) Munish Kumar (MRS Punjab Technical University, India) and Virender Kadyan (Chitkara University, India)
Engineering Science Reference • © 2020 • 225pp • H/C (ISBN: 9781799813897) • US $185.00

701 East Chocolate Avenue, Hershey, PA 17033, USA
Tel: 717-533-8845 x100 • Fax: 717-533-8661
E-Mail: cust@igi-global.com • www.igi-global.com

Editorial Advisory Board

List of Contributors

Table of Contents

Detailed Table of Contents

Chapter 1
Method to Rank Academic Institutes by the Sentiment Analysis of Their Online Reviews 1
> *Simran Sidhu, Central University of Punjab, India*
> *Surinder Singh Khurana, Central University of Punjab, India*

A large number of reviews are expressed on academic institutes using the online review portals and other social media platforms. Such reviews are a good potential source for evaluating the Indian academic institutes. This chapter aimed to collect and analyze the sentiments of the online reviews of the academic institutes and ranked the institutes on the basis of their garnered online reviews. Lexical-based sentiment analysis of their online reviews is used to rank academic institutes. Then these rankings were compared with the NIRF PR Overall University Rankings List 2017. The outcome of this work can efficiently support the overall university rankings of the NIRF ranking list to enhance NIRF's public perception parameter (PRPUB). The results showed that Panjab University achieved the highest sentiment score, which was followed by BITS-Pilani. The results highlighted that there is a significant gap between NIRF's perception rankings and the perception of the public in general regarding an academic institute as expressed in online reviews.

Chapter 2
Machine Learning in Higher Education: Predicting Student Attrition Status Using Educational
Data Mining 27
> *Garima Jaiswal, Indira Gandhi Delhi Technical University for Women, India*
> *Arun Sharma, Indira Gandhi Delhi Technical University for Women, India*
> *Reeti Sarup, Indira Gandhi Delhi Technical University for Women, India*

Machine learning aims to give computers the ability to automatically learn from data. It can enable computers to make intelligent decisions by recognizing complex patterns from data. Through data mining, humongous amounts of data can be explored and analyzed to extract useful information and find interesting patterns. Classification, a supervised learning technique, can be beneficial in predicting class labels for test data by referring the already labeled classes from available training data set. In this chapter, educational data mining techniques are applied over a student dataset to analyze the multifarious factors causing alarmingly high number of dropouts. This work focuses on predicting students at risk of dropping out using five classification algorithms, namely, K-NN, naive Bayes, decision tree, random forest, and support vector machine. This can assist in improving pedagogical practices in order to enhance the performance of students predicted at risk of dropping out, thus reducing the dropout rates in higher education.

The importance and growth of the digital IC have become more popular because of parameters such as small feature size, high speed, low cost, less power consumption, and temperature. There have been various techniques and methodologies developed so far using different optimization algorithms and data structures based on the dimensions of the IC to improve these parameters. All these existing algorithms illustrate explicit advantages in optimizing the chip area, maximum temperature of the chip, and wire length. Though there are some advantages in these traditional algorithms, there are few demerits such as execution time, integration, and computational complexity due to the necessity of handling large number of data. Machine learning techniques produce vibrant results in such fields where it is required to handle big data in order to optimize the scaling parameters of IC design. The objective of this chapter is to give an elaborate idea of applying machine learning techniques using Bayesian theorem to create automation tool for VLSI 3D IC design steps.

#### Chapter 4

With the advent of Kinect and other modern-day sensors, gesture recognition has emerged as one of the most promising research disciplines for developing innovative and efficient human-computer interaction platforms. In the present work, the authors aim to build an interactive system by combining the principles of pattern recognition along with the intelligent application of Kinect sensor. Involving Kinect sensor has served the purpose of collecting skeletal data, and after processing the same, the extracted relevant features have been fed to principal component analysis for dimensionality reduction phase. Finally, instead of using a single classifier for detection, in this chapter, an ensemble of k-nearest neighbor classifiers has been chosen since an ensemble algorithm is always likely to provide better results than a single classifier. To justify the efficacy of the designed framework it is implemented for interpretation of 20 distinct gestures, and in each case, it has generated better performances as compared to the other existing techniques.

Personalized treatment (PT) is an emerging area in healthcare that provides personalized health. Personalized, targeted, or customized treatment gains more attention by providing the right treatment to the right person at the right time. Traditional treatment follows a whole systems approach, whereas PT unyokes the people into groups and helps them in rendering proper treatment based on disease risk. In PT, case by case analysis identifies the current status of each patient and performs detailed investigation of their health along with symptoms, signs, and difficulties. Case by case analysis also aids in constructing the clinical knowledge base according to the patient's needs. Thus, PT is a preventive medicine system enabling optimal therapy and cost-effective treatment. This chapter aims to explore how PT is served in works of literature by fusing machine learning (ML) and artificial intelligence (AI) techniques, which creates cognitive machine learning (CML). This chapter also explores the issues, challenges of traditional medicine, applications, models, pros, and cons of PT.

Chapter 6

Arun Solanki, Gautam Buddha University, India
Rajat Saxena, Gautam Buddha University, India

With the advent of neural networks and its subfields like deep neural networks and convolutional neural networks, it is possible to make text classification predictions with high accuracy. Among the many subtypes of naive Bayes, multinomial naive Bayes is used for text classification. Many attempts have been made to somehow develop an algorithm that uses the simplicity of multinomial naive Bayes and at the same time incorporates feature dependency. One such effort was put in structure extended multinomial naive Bayes, which uses one-dependence estimators to inculcate dependencies. Basically, one-dependence estimators take one of the attributes as features and all other attributes as its child. This chapter proposes self structure extended multinomial naïve Bayes, which presents a hybrid model, a combination of the multinomial naive Bayes and structure extended multinomial naive Bayes. Basically, it tries to classify the instances that were misclassified by structure extended multinomial naive Bayes as there was no direct dependency between attributes.

Chapter 7

Vibha Verma, University of Delhi, India
Neha Neha, University of Delhi, India
Anu G. Aggarwal, University of Delhi, India

Software firms plan all development and management activities strategically to provide the best products and solutions to their user. IT professionals are involved in the process of studying the bugs reported and assign severity to make decisions regarding their resolution. To make the task fast and accurate, developers use automatic methods. Herein, the authors have used feature selection-based classification technique to decide about the severity of reported bugs. TF-IDF feature selection method is used to select the informative terms, determining the severity. Based on selected terms the support vector machine and artificial neural network classifiers are used for classification. A number of performance measures have been used to test the performance of classification. The bug reports of Eclipse project for JDT and platform products were collected from Bugzilla. The results show that classifying bugs on the basis of severity can be effectively improved by feature selection-based strategy.

    Anand Kumar M., Department of Information Technology, National Institute of Technology
        Karnataka, Surathkal, India
    Shivkaran Singh, Arnekt Solutions, Pune, India
    Praveena Ramanan, Quantiphi Inc, Bangalore, India
    Vaithehi Sinthiya, Karunya Institute of Technology and Sciences, Coimbatore, India
    Soman K. P., Amrita School of Engineering, Amrita Vishwa Vidyapeetham University, India

In recent times, paraphrase identification task has got the attention of the research community. The paraphrase is a phrase or sentence that conveys the same information but using different words or syntactic structure. The Microsoft Research Paraphrase Corpus (MSRP) is a well-known openly available paraphrase corpus of the English language. There is no such publicly available paraphrase corpus for any Indian language (as of now). This chapter explains the creation of paraphrase corpus for Hindi, Tamil, Malayalam, and Punjabi languages. This is the first publicly available corpus for any Indian language. It was used in the shared task on detecting paraphrases for Indian languages (DPIL) held in conjunction with Forum for Information Retrieval & Evaluation (FIRE) 2016. The annotation process was performed by a postgraduate student followed by a two-step proofreading by a linguist and a language expert.

    Tamanna Sharma, Department of Computer Science and Technology, Guru Jambheshwar
        University of Science and Technology, Hisar, India
    Anu Bajaj, Department of Computer Science and Engineering, Guru Jambheshwar
        University of Science and Technology, Hisar, India
    Om Prakash Sangwan, Department of Computer Science and Technology, Guru
        Jambheshwar University of Science and Technology, Hisar, India

Sentiment analysis is computational measurement of attitude, opinions, and emotions (like positive/ negative) with the help of text mining and natural language processing of words and phrases. Incorporation of machine learning techniques with natural language processing helps in analysing and predicting the sentiments in more precise manner. But sometimes, machine learning techniques are incapable in predicting sentiments due to unavailability of labelled data. To overcome this problem, an advanced computational technique called deep learning comes into play. This chapter highlights latest studies regarding use of deep learning techniques like convolutional neural network, recurrent neural network, etc. in sentiment analysis.

    Nimmi K., National Institute of Technology, Tiruchirappalli, India
    Varun G. Menon, SCMS School of Engineering and Technology, India
    Janet B., National Institute of Technology, Tiruchirappalli, India
    Akshi Kumar, Delhi Technological University, India

Recent years have witnessed an exponential rise in the number of connected wireless devices. This number is expected to rise at an unprecedented rate leading to severe challenges in user demands and network infrastructure. With the fusion of artificial intelligence (AI) technologies, these devices have become more smart and intelligent. Using machine learning, efforts are being carried out to artificially train these networks to determine the optimum system requirements automatically. With these intelligent networks generating an enormous volume of data along with the demand for high data rate, machine learning has found its few limitations. Deep learning techniques have emerged as one of the most impressive tools to solve many of these problems. The primary objective of this chapter is to provide insights into deep learning and the applications of deep learning in next-generation inventive wireless networks. The chapter also presents the issues, challenges, and future directions in this research area.

Chapter 11

Ashok Suragala, JNTU Vizianagaram, India
PapaRao A. V., JNTU Vizianagaram, India

The exponential surge in healthcare data is providing new opportunities to discover meaningful data-driven characteristics and patterns of diseases. Machine learning and deep learning models have been employed for many computational phenotyping and healthcare prediction tasks. However, machine learning models are crucial for wide adaption in medical research and clinical decision making. In this chapter, the authors introduce demystifying diseases identification and diagnosis of various disease using machine learning algorithms like logistic regression, naive Bayes, decision tree, MLP classifier, random forest in order to cure liver disease, hepatitis disease, and diabetes mellitus. This work leverages the initial discoveries made through data exploration, statistical analysis of data to reduce the number of explanatory variables, which led to identifying the statistically significant attributes, mapping those significant attributes to the response, and building classification techniques to predict the outcome and demystify clinical diseases.

Chapter 12

P. Victer Paul, Indian Institute of Information Technology, Kottayam, India
Harika Krishna, Vignan's Foundation for Science, Technology, and Research, India
Jayakumar L., Vel Tech Rangarajan Dr. Sagunthala R&D Institute of Science and
Technology, India

In recent years, a huge volume of data has been generated by the sensors, social media, and other sources. Researchers proposed various data analytics models for handling these data and to extract insight that can improve the business of various domains. Data analytics in healthcare (DAiHC) is recent and attracted many researchers due to its importance in improving the value of people's lives. In this perspective, the chapter focuses on the various recent models proposed in DAiHC and dissects the works based on various vital parameters. As an initial part, the work provides comprehensive information on DAiHC and its various application illustrations. Moreover, the study presented in the work categorizes the literature on DAiHC based on factors like algorithms used, application dataset utilized, insight type, and tools used for evaluation of the work. This survey will be helpful for novice to expert researchers who works in DAiHC, and various challenges in DAiHC are also discussed which may help in defining new problems associated with the domain.

#### Chapter 13

Machine learning (ML) is prevalent across the globe and applied in almost all domains. This chapter focuses on implementation of ML with real-time use cases. Day-to-day activities are automated to ease the task and increase the quality of decision. ML is the backbone of the perfect decision support system with a plethora of applications. The use case described in this chapter is ML & Security, which is implemented in R Script. Adversaries took advantages of ML to avoid detection and evade defenses. Network intrusion detection system (IDS) is the major issue nowadays. Its primary task is to collect relevant features from the computer network. These selected features can be fed into the ML algorithms to predict the label. The challenge in this use case is what type of feature to consider for intrusion and anomaly detection (AD). This chapter focuses on end-to-end process to get insight into the stream of data from the network connection with priority given to forecasting mechanism and prediction of the future. Forecasting is applied to the time series data to get sensible decisions.

#### Chapter 14

Information is second level of abstraction after data and before knowledge. Information retrieval helps fill the gap between information and knowledge by storing, organizing, representing, maintaining, and disseminating information. Manual information retrieval leads to underutilization of resources, and it takes a long time to process, while machine learning techniques are implications of statistical models, which are flexible, adaptable, and fast to learn. Deep learning is the extension of machine learning with hierarchical levels of learning that make it suitable for complex tasks. Deep learning can be the best choice for information retrieval as it has numerous resources of information and large datasets for computation. In this chapter, the authors discuss applications of information retrieval with deep learning (e.g., web search by reducing the noise and collecting precise results, trend detection in social media analytics, anomaly detection in music datasets, and image retrieval).

#### Chapter 15

Game consoles that use interactive interfaces have drawn users' attention as they reduce the total cost and are user-friendly too. This chapter introduces an interactive game to aid motor rehabilitation applicable to patients belonging to all age groups. In the system, the users receive some audio instructions regarding the action they have to perform next. According to that instruction, the user tries to complete the 'Fruit-to-Basket' game as soon as possible by dropping all the fruits into the basket. Kinect sensor placed in front of the user detects their motions using skeletons containing three-dimensional coordinates of 20 body joints. The speeds of the movements are detected by the accelerometer. After extracting the required features from skeleton and speed, the use of principal component analysis is proved to be effective for feature space reduction. Then support vector machine is used efficiently to recognize the action. The experimental result indicates that the proposed algorithm is best suited in this domain and a very promising one.

Chapter 16
Janjanam Prabhudas, VIT-AP University, India
C. H. Pradeep Reddy, VIT-AP University, India

The enormous increase of information along with the computational abilities of machines created innovative applications in natural language processing by invoking machine learning models. This chapter will project the trends of natural language processing by employing machine learning and its models in the context of text summarization. This chapter is organized to make the researcher understand technical perspectives regarding feature representation and their models to consider before applying on language-oriented tasks. Further, the present chapter revises the details of primary models of deep learning, its applications, and performance in the context of language processing. The primary focus of this chapter is to illustrate the technical research findings and gaps of text summarization based on deep learning along with state-of-the-art deep learning models for TS.

Chapter 17
Dragorad A. Milovanovic, University of Belgrade, Serbia
Zoran S. Bojkovic, University of Belgrade, Serbia
Dragan D. Kukolj, Faculty of Technical Sciences, University of Novi Sad, Serbia

Machine learning (ML) has evolved to the point that this technique enhances communications and enables fifth-generation (5G) wireless networks. ML is great to get insights about complex networks that use large amounts of data, and for predictive and proactive adaptation to dynamic wireless environments. ML has become a crucial technology for mobile broadband communication. Special case goes to deep learning (DL) in immersive media. Through this chapter, the goal is to present open research challenges and applications of ML. An exploration of the potential of ML-based solution approaches in the context of 5G primary eMBB, mMTC, and uHSLLC services is presented, evaluating at the same time open issues for future research, including standardization activities of algorithms and data formats.

Chapter 18
Neha Garg, Manav Rachna International Institute of Research and Studies, India
Kamlesh Sharma, Manav Rachna International Institute of Research and Studies, India

This chapter provides a basic understanding of processes and models needed to investigate the data posted by users on social networking sites like Facebook, Twitter, Instagram, etc. Often the databases of social networking sites are large and can't be handled using traditional methodology for analysis. Moreover, the data is posted in such a random manner that can't be used directly for the analysis purpose; therefore, a considerable preprocessing is needed to use that data and generate important results that can help in decision making for various areas like sentiment analysis, customer feedback, customer reviews for brand and product, prevention management, risk management, etc. Therefore, this chapter is discussing various aspects of text and its structure, various machine learning algorithms and their types, why machine learning is better for text analysis, the process of text analysis with the help of examples, issues associated with text analysis, and major application areas of text analysis.

Chapter 19

Utsha Sinha, Netaji Subhas University of Technology, India
Abhinav Singh, Netaji Subhas University of Technology, India
Deepak Kumar Sharma, Netaji Subhas University of Technology, India

Currently, machine learning and artificial intelligence technology is one of the fastest growing trends all over the world, especially in the medical industry. The rise in the machine learning applications in the healthcare domain is giving substantial hope to the human race for achieving greater abilities to diagnose and treat illness. Machine learning is not only used in the diagnosis of the disease but also its prognosis. From discovering a compound as a drug to the marketing as well as monitoring of the potential drug, machine learning plays a vital role in each stage. Nearly, all the major companies in the medical space are moving towards machine learning and its potential applications in the medical industry. This chapter explains the concept of machine learning and its working as well as the applications in the medical industry. While it describes the basic concepts of machine learning in the medical industry, it also proposes future challenges for the aforementioned subject.

Chapter 20

Jayakumar Kaliappan, Vellore Institute of Technology, Vellore, India
Karpagam Sundararajan, Spectrum Info Tech, India

Machine learning is a part of artificial intelligence in which the learning was done using the data available in the environment. Machine learning algorithms are mainly used in game development to change from presripted games to adaptive play games. The main theme or plot of the game, game levels, maps in route, and racing games are considered as content. Context refers to the game screenplay, sound effects, and visual effects. In any type of game, maintaining the fun mode of the player is very important. Predictable moves by non-players in the game and same type of visual effects will reduce the player's interest in the game. The machine learning algorithms works in automatic content generation and nonpayer character behaviours in gameplay. In pathfinding games, puzzle games, strategy games adding intelligence to enemy and opponents makes the game more interesting. The enjoyment and fun differs from game to game. For example, in horror games, fun is experienced when safe point is reached.

Chapter 21

Diwakar Tripathi, SRM University, Amaravati, India
Alok Kumar Shukla, G.L. Bajaj Institute of Technology and Management, Greater Noida, India
Ramchandra Reddy B., SRM University, Amaravati, India
Ghanshyam S. Bopche, SRM University, Amaravati, India

Credit scoring is a process to calculate the risk associated with a credit product, and it directly affects the profitability of that industry. Periodically, financial institutions apply credit scoring in various steps. The main focus of this study is to improve the predictive performance of the credit scoring model. To improve the predictive performance of the model, this study proposes a multi-layer hybrid credit scoring model. The first stage concerns pre-processing, which includes treatment for missing values, data-transformation, and reduction of irrelevant and noisy features because they may affect predictive performance of model. The second stage applies various ensemble learning approaches such as Bagging, Adaboost, etc. At the last layer, it applies ensemble classifiers approach, which combines three heterogeneous classifiers, namely: random forest (RF), logistic regression (LR), and sequential minimal optimization (SMO) approaches for classification. Further, the proposed multi-layer model is validated on various real-world credit scoring datasets.

Chapter 22

Hemanta Kumar Palo, Siksha O Anusandhan(Deemed), India
Lokanath Sarangi, College of Engineering, Biju Patnaik University of Technology, India

Machine learning (ML) remains a buzzword during the last few decades due to the requirement of a huge amount of data for adequate processing, the continuously surfacing of better innovative and efficient algorithms, and the advent of powerful computers with enormous computation power. The ML algorithms are mostly based on data mining, clustering, classification, and regression approaches for efficient utilization. Many vivid application domains in the field of speech and image signal processing, market forecast, biomedical signal processing, robotics, trend analysis of data, banking and finance sectors, etc. benefits from such techniques. Among these modules, the classification of speech and speaker identification has been a predominant area of research as it has been alone medium of communication via phone. This has made the author to provide an overview of a few state-of-art ML algorithms, their advantages and limitations, including the advancement to enhance the application domain in this field.

Chapter 23

Pooja Jha, Amity University, Jharkhand, India
K. Sridhar Patnaik, Birla Institute of Technology, Mesra, India

Human errors are the main cause of vehicle crashes. Self-driving cars bear the promise to significantly reduce accidents by taking the human factor out of the equation, while in parallel monitor the surroundings, detect and react immediately to potentially dangerous situations and driving behaviors. Artificial intelligence tool trains the computers to do things like detect lane lines and identify cyclists by showing them millions of examples of the subject at hand. The chapter in this book discusses the technological advancement in transportation. It also covers the autonomy used according to The National Highway Traffic Safety Administration (NHTSA). The functional architecture of self-driving cars is further discussed. The chapter also talks about two algorithms for detection of lanes as well as detection of vehicles on the road for self-driving cars. Next, the ethical discussions surrounding the autonomous vehicle involving stakeholders, technologies, social environments, and costs vs. quality have been discussed.

#### Chapter 24

Due to the advent of Web 2.0, the size of social media content (SMC) is growing rapidly and likely to increase faster in the near future. Social media applications such as Instagram, Twitter, Facebook, etc. have become an integral part of our lives, as they prompt the people to give their opinions and share information around the world. Identifying emotions in SMC is important for many aspects of sentiment analysis (SA) and is a top-level agenda of many firms today. SA on social media (SASM) extends an organization's ability to capture and study public sentiments toward social events and activities in real time. This chapter studies recent advances in machine learning (ML) used for SMC analysis and its applications. The framework of SASM consists of several phases, such as data collection, pre-processing, feature representation, model building, and evaluation. This survey presents the basic elements of SASM and its utility. Furthermore, the study reports that ML has a significant contribution to SMC mining. Finally, the research highlights certain issues related to ML used for SMC.

#### Chapter 25

Social media is used to share the data or information among the large group of people. Numerous forums, blogs, social networks, news reports, e-commerce websites, and many more online media play a role in sharing individual opinions. The data generated from these sources is huge and in unstructured format. Big data is a term used for data sets that are large or complex and that cannot be processed by traditional processing system. Sentimental analysis is one of the major data analytics applied on big data. It is a task of natural language processing to determine whether a text contains subjective information and what information it expresses. It helps in achieving various goals like the measurement of customer satisfaction, observing public mood on political movement, movie sales prediction, market intelligence, and many more. In this chapter, the authors present various techniques used for sentimental analysis and related work using these techniques. The chapter also presents open issues and challenges in sentimental analysis landscape.

Tool wear is a major factor that affects the productivity of any machining operation and needs to be controlled for achieving automation. It affects the surface finish, tolerances, dimensions of the workpiece, increases machine down time, and sometimes performance of machine tool and personnel are affected. This chapter deals with the application of artificial neural network (ANN) models for tool condition monitoring (TCM) in milling operations. The data required for training and testing the models studied and developed are from live experiments conducted in a machine shop on a widely used steel, medium carbon steel (En 8) using uncoated carbide inserts. Acoustic emission data and surface roughness data has been used in model development. The goal is for developing an optimal ANN model, in terms of compact architecture, least training time, and its ability to generalize well on unseen (test) data. Growing cell structures (GCS) network has been found to achieve these requirements.

#### Chapter 27

Millions of people in this world can't understand environment because they are blind or visually impaired. They also have navigation difficulties which leads to social awkwardness. They can use some other way to deal with their life and daily routines. It is very difficult for them to find something in unknown environment. Blind and visually impaired people face many difficulties in conversation because they can't decide whether the person is talking to them or someone else. Computer vision-based technologies have increased so much in this domain. Deep convolutional neural network has developed very fast in recent years. It is very helpful to use computer vision-based techniques to help the visually impaired. In this chapter, hearing is used to understand the world. Both sight sense and hearing have the same similarity: both visual object and audio can be localized. Many people don't realise that we are capable of identifying location of the source of sound by just hearing it.

Foreword

Since its first appearance, Artificial Intelligence has gained more and more momentum and affected all fields of modern life. Although it was used along scientific and academic research studies in early times, need for running effective and efficient solution techniques for complex real-life problems have allowed that field to break all borders and be used within every field of the life. That is remarkable that especially revolutionary developments in surrounding technologies such as electronics, computer, and communication have increased the speed of rising for Artificial Intelligence. After the start of the 21st century, use of intelligent systems in daily life has become almost a common thing, and we all started to worry about if the future of Artificial Intelligence will be dangerous or not for the existence of the humanity. Now, another vital question to ask here should be "How Artificial Intelligence is such good on adapting itself to every kind of problem from different fields?" The answer may be with two different perspectives: One is the Mathematics and Logic shaping the background of Artificial Intelligence. The other one is Machine Learning, which is a sub-field of Artificial Intelligence that can learn from known samples to derive solutions for newly encountered states of target problem(s). Although there are alternative sub-fields such as Swarm Intelligence, which gather intelligent optimization algorithms to solve advanced optimization problems iteratively, and Cybernetics, which is focused more on combining biological and robotics oriented systems in one hand to solve or improve control oriented problems of especially living organisms, Machine Learning is known as the most essential sub-fields of the Artificial Intelligence. By running different leaning paradigms like Supervised Learning (Classification/Regression), Unsupervised Learning (Clustering), and Reinforcement Learning, every problem that can be modeled over data can be solved with Machine Learning techniques. The literature of the Machine Learning is full with different, remarkable techniques such as Artificial Neural Networks, Support Vector Machines or Decision Trees and currently that sub-field includes Deep Learning, which is another type of Machine Learning, which is more robust against problems requiring using an enormous amount of complex data. Since the scientific community is too busy with solving different problems via Machine Learning, it is important to learn most new uses and make that happen by analyzing remarkable research works from different fields.

This book you are currently reading is an excellent source for giving many answers to the question that I have pointed in last parts of the previous paragraph. Titled as 'Handbook of Research on Emerging Trends and Applications of Machine Learning,' that book project by the editors: Dr. Solanki, Dr. Kumar, and Dr. Nayyar provide a recent, comprehensive enough source for opening our eyes for understanding how Machine Learning is designing the current world and also shaping our future. When you are reading every chapter of that book, you will be informed about different features or mechanisms of Machine Learning techniques, which allowing them to be used in a flexible way within different problems. You will also be informed about essentials of Machine Learning and be able to derive ideas about which Machine Learning can be used for a problem you have been thinking for a while and which kind of solution model (i.e. using single technique or building a hybrid system) can be used accordingly. All these aspects are main factors making that book an exact, competitive handbook for the scientific literature.

Forgiving more idea about how that book is incredibly comprehensive, I would like to talk briefly about some of the chapters: In the early chapters of the book, you can see examples of using Machine Learning in the field of education.In this context, you can take a look at to the Chapter 1, and the Chapter 2 for learning about research works employing Machine Learning in order to improve evaluation of educational quality and analyze better about students' attrition. Following them, a remarkable work for 3D IC Physical Design using Machine Learning optimization was provided in Chapter 3, for the interested readers.

As HCI is among trendy topics nowadays (because the concept of interaction between us and the computer systems often receives revolutionary developments), Chapter 4 comes with a remarkable work about Gesture Recognition done with Kinect and Machine Learning collaboration. Next, Chapter 5 is about fascinating survey research regarding precision treatment for humans, thanks to Cognitive Machine Learning. From Chapter 6 to 9, you can taste a collection of research works focused on remarkable topics such as text analyze and software management. Especially anyone interested in use of Deep Learning for sentiment analysis may refer to Chapter 10.

As you know, the future of communication is improved and made more practical with wireless technologies. Moving from that, Chapter 11 gives a good focus for running Deep Learning within Next Generation Inventive Wireless Networks. Including remarkable multidisciplinary applications so far in the book, chapters from Chapter 12 to Chapter 19 are generally associated with use of Machine Learning in healthcare, communication, and data analysis including especially text data. You can read Chapter 17, in order to learn triggering roles of Machine Learning in new 5G technology and its effective use within the medical industry.

The industry of video games is another remarkable field in which Machine Learning has already been using accordingly. In this context, Chapter 20 gives an excellent work to learn some about it. If you heard lately about some innovations by Artificial Intelligence in speech data, you could read Chapter 21 to be informed about an example for using Machine Learning towards classification of speech signals. Following to that chapter, Chapter 22 hits the bulls-eye and focuses on a remarkable topic: self-driving cars, by considering Machine Learning.

You know social media is a key environment where everybody can derive some ideas about people's interests, behaviors, or future habits. As that requires some adequate data analyze procedures, Machine Learning has been already using for different research objectives. As some early chapters already cover similar data analysis works, Chapter 23 explains recent trends with Machine Learning, in order to run some sentiment analysis from Social Media data. Next to that chapter, you can read Chapter 324 for a hybrid application aiming Skin Melanoma segmentation.

Chapter 25 revisits the topic of sentiment analysis, but this time with the concept of Big Data. Anyone interested in recent use of social media data for sentiment analysis may get the most recent information with that chapter. As an interesting research topic, Chapter 26 considers Tool Condition Monitoring done with Machine Learning. The book is ended with Chapter 27 combining Computer Vision and Deep Learning for supporting Visually Impaired and Blind people.

As you can see, the book is an excellent collection of multidisciplinary applications done with Machine Learning. While discussing multidisciplinary applications, it is a common disadvantage that reference works may give more emphasis to some specific fields. However, that book seems to ensure the right balance for different fields and different applications, in order to learn better about how Machine Learning is flexible for all kinds of problems from real life.

As my final words, I would like to thank the editors: Dr. Solanki, Dr. Kumar, and Dr. Nayyar for their significant contribution to the scientific literature. I believe that the 'Handbook of Research on Emerging Trends and Applications of Machine Learning' will give opportunity to everyone interested in applied Machine Learning to understand more about current and future state of that sub-field of Artificial Intelligence, and even increase their awareness on the related research topics for specific areas of the modern world. Furthermore, that book will enable students and independent researchers stepping into the world of Artificial Intelligence first time to get enough knowledge about how Machine Learning systems are developed and used in a multidisciplinary manner. Now, take a cup of coffee and enjoy your journey through cutting-edge applications of Machine Learning!

Utku Kose received the B.S. degree in 2008 from computer education of Gazi University, Turkey as a faculty valedictorian. He received M.S. degree in 2010 from AfyonKocatepe University, Turkey in the field of computer and D.S. / Ph. D. degree in 2017 from Selcuk University, Turkey in the field of computer engineering. Between 2009 and 2011, he has worked as a Research Assistant in AfyonKocatepe University. Following, he has also worked as a Lecturer and Vocational School - Vice Director in AfyonKocatepe University between 2011 and 2012 and as a Lecturer and Research Center Director in Usak University between 2012 and 2017. Currently, he is an Assistant Professor in SuleymanDemirel University, Turkey. He has more than 100 publications including articles, authored and edited books, proceedings, and reports. He also serves as Associate Editor, Book Series Editor, and Editorial Board Member for reputable institutions-publishers such as IEEE, CRC Press, University of Cambridge Press, and IGI Global. His research interest includes artificial intelligence, machine ethics, artificial intelligence safety, optimization, chaos theory, distance education, e-learning, computer education, and computer science.

Utku Kose
Suleyman Demirel University, Turkey
August 2019

Preface

Machine learning is a subfield of AI. This field primarily focuses on the structure of data and matches that data into models. These models are understood and utilized by individuals. Machine Learning allows the machines to create data-driven selections instead of being expressly programmed for concluding a particular task. These programs or algorithms are designed in a method that machine learn and improve over time as exposed to new knowledge. Machine learning facilitates computers in building models from sample knowledge to alter decision-making processes with supported data inputs. Any technology used these days have benefitted from machine learning like optical character recognition (OCR) technology converts pictures of text into movable sort, recommendation engines, steam-powered by machine learning, recommend what movies or TV shows to watch with user preferences, self-driving cars.

Machine Learning program is trained using a training data set which is used to develop a model. When a data set is introduced to the program, then the model makes a prediction. The prediction is evaluated for accuracy, and if the accuracy is suitable, the Machine Learning program is deployed. If the accuracy is not acceptable, the Machine Learning program is trained once again. It will be more accurate with an increased trained data set. This is simply a high-level example, as there are several factors and different steps concerned. There are mainly Supervised,

Unsupervised and Reinforcement Machine Learning techniques.

SUPERVISED LEARNING

In supervised learning, a dataset works as a teacher who trains the model. Once the model gets trained, it begins creating a prediction and improves itself once new knowledge is found. This technique has the labeled classes of the dataset.

UNSUPERVISED LEARNING

In unsupervised learning, the model learns through observation and finds structures in the dataset. The model creates the cluster of the same patterns and finds a relationship between the clusters. The dataset is unlabeled in this machine learning technique.

Figure 1.

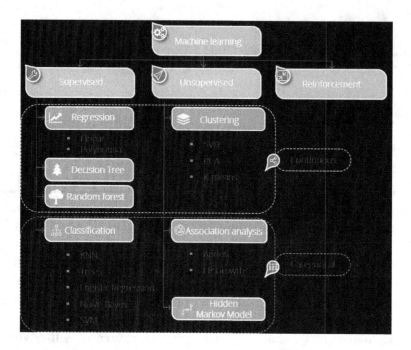

REINFORCEMENT LEARNING

In reinforcement learning, an agent interacts with the environment and find out the best solution. This technique follows the concept of hit and trial method. The agent is rewarded or penalized with a point for a correct or a wrong answer, and based on the positive reward points gained the model trains itself. After the training, the agent gets ready to predict the new data presented to it.

The contents of the book are organized as follows:

CHAPTER 1: METHOD TO RANK ACADEMIC INSTITUTES BY THE SENTIMENT ANALYSIS OF THEIR ONLINE REVIEWS

This chapter aimed to collect and analyze the sentiments of the online reviews of the academic institutes and ranked the institutes based on their garnered online reviews. Lexical based Sentiment analysis of their online reviews is used to rank Academic Institutes. Then these rankings were compared with the NIRF PR Overall University Rankings List 2017. The outcome of this work can efficiently support the overall university rankings of the NIRF ranking list to enhance NIRF's public perception parameter (PRPUB). The results showed that Panjab University achieved the highest sentiment score, which was followed by BITS-Pilani. The results highlighted that there is a significant gap between NIRF's perception rankings and the perception of the public in general regarding an academic institute, as expressed in online reviews.

CHAPTER 2: MACHINE LEARNING IN HIGHER EDUCATION: PREDICTING STUDENT ATTRITION STATUS USING EDUCATIONAL DATA MINING

In this chapter, educational data mining techniques are applied over a student dataset to analyze the different factors causing an alarmingly high number of dropouts. This work focuses on predicting students at risk of dropping out using five classification algorithms, namely, K-NN, Naive Bayes, Decision Tree, Random Forest, and Support Vector Machine. This can assist in improving pedagogical practices in order to enhance the performance of students predicted at risk of dropping out, thus reducing the dropout rates in higher education.

CHAPTER 3: MACHINE LEARNING OPTIMIZATION TECHNIQUES FOR 3D IC PHYSICAL DESIGN

The importance and growth of the digital IC have become more popular because of five parameters such as small feature size, high speed, low cost, less power consumption, and temperature. There have been various techniques and methodologies developed so far using different optimization algorithms and data structures based on the dimensions of the IC to improve these parameters. All these existing algorithms illustrate clear advantages in optimizing the chip area, the maximum temperature of the chip and wire length. Though there are some advantages in these traditional algorithms, there are few demerits such as execution time, integration and computational complexity due to the necessity of handling a large number of data. Recently, Machine Learning techniques produce vibrant results in such fields where it is required to handle big data in order to optimize the scaling parameters of IC design. The objective of this chapter is to give an elaborate idea of applying Machine Learning techniques using Bayesian theorem to create automation tool for VLSI 3D IC design steps.

CHAPTER 4: A NOVEL APPROACH TO KINECT-BASED GESTURE RECOGNITION FOR HCI APPLICATIONS

In this chapter, authors build an interactive system by combining the principles of pattern recognition along with the intelligent application of the Kinect sensor. Involving Kinect sensor has served the purpose of collecting skeletal data, and after processing the same, the extracted relevant features have been fed to principal component analysis for dimensionality reduction phase. Finally, instead of using a single classifier for detection, in this paper, an ensemble of k-nearest neighbor classifiers has been chosen since an ensemble algorithm is always likely to provide better results than a single classifier. This work is implemented for interpretation of 20 distinct gestures. In each case, it has generated better performances as compared to the other existing techniques.

CHAPTER 5: A SURVEY ON PRECISION TREATMENT FOR HUMANS USING COGNITIVE MACHINE LEARNING TECHNIQUES

Personalized Treatment (PT) is an emerging area in healthcare which provides personalized health. Personalized, targeted, or customized treatment gains more attention by providing the right treatment to the right person at the right time. Traditional treatment follows a whole systems approach, whereas PT unyokes the people into groups and helps them in rendering proper treatment based on disease risk. In PT, case by case analysis identifies the current status of each patient and performs a detailed investigation of their health along with symptoms, signs, and difficulties. Case by case analysis also aids in constructing the clinical knowledge base according to the patient's needs. Thus, PT is a preventive medicine system enabling optimal therapy and cost-effective treatment. This chapter aims to explore how PT is served in works of literature by fusing Machine Learning (ML) and Artificial Intelligence (AI) techniques, which relinquish Cognitive Machine Learning (CML). This chapter also explores the issues, challenges of traditional medicine, applications, models, pros, and cons of PT.

CHAPTER 6: TEXT CLASSIFICATION USING SELF STRUCTURE EXTENDED MULTINOMIAL NAIVE BAYES: TEXT CLASSIFICATION USING SSENM

This chapter proposes Self Structure Extended Multinomial Naïve Bayes, which presents a hybrid model, a combination of the Multinomial Naive Bayes and Structure Extended Multinomial Naive Bayes. It tries to classify the instances that were misclassified by Structure Extended Multinomial Naive Bayes as there was no direct dependency between attributes.

CHAPTER 7: APPLICATIONS OF MACHINE LEARNING FOR SOFTWARE MANAGEMENT

This chapter used feature selection based classification technique to decide about the severity of reported bugs. TF-IDF feature selection method is used to select the informative terms, determining the severity. Based on selected terms, the Support Vector Machine and Artificial Neural Network classifiers are used for classification. Several performance measures have been used to test the performance of classification. The bug reports of Eclipse project for JDT and Platform products were collected from Bugzilla. The results show that classifying bugs based on severity can be effectively improved by feature selection based strategy.

CHAPTER 8: CREATING PARAPHRASE IDENTIFICATION CORPUS FOR INDIAN LANGUAGES – OPENSOURCE DATA SET FOR PARAPHRASE CREATION

In recent times, paraphrase identification task has got the attention of the research community. The paraphrase is a phrase or sentence which conveys the same information but using different words or syntactic structure. The Microsoft Research Paraphrase Corpus (MSRP) is a well-known openly available paraphrase corpus of English language. There is no such publicly available paraphrase corpus for any

Indian Language (as of now). This paper explains the creation of paraphrase corpus for Hindi, Tamil, Malayalam & Punjabi language. This is the first publicly available corpus for any Indian language. It was used in the shared task of Detecting Paraphrases for Indian Languages (DPIL) held in conjunction with the Forum for Information Retrieval & Evaluation (FIRE) 2016. The annotation process was performed by a postgraduate student followed by 2-step proofreading by a linguist and a language expert.

CHAPTER 9: DEEP LEARNING APPROACHES FOR TEXTUAL SENTIMENT ANALYSIS

Sentiment analysis is a computational measurement of attitude, opinions, and emotions (like positive/ negative) with the help of text mining and natural language processing of words and phrases. Incorporation of machine learning techniques with natural language processing helps in analyzing and predicting the sentiments in a more precise manner. However, sometimes, machine learning techniques are incapable of predicting sentiments due to unavailability of labeled data. To overcome this problem, advanced computational technique called deep learning comes into play. This chapter highlights latest studies regarding use of deep learning techniques like a convolutional neural network, recurrent neural network, etc. in sentiment analysis.

CHAPTER 10: DEEP LEARNING FOR NEXT GENERATION INVENTIVE WIRELESS NETWORKS – ISSUES, CHALLENGES, AND FUTURE DIRECTIONS

The primary objective of this chapter is to provide insights into deep learning and the applications of deep learning in next-generation inventive wireless networks. The Chapter also presents the issues, challenges, and future directions in this research area.

CHAPTER 11: DEMYSTIFYING DISEASE IDENTIFICATION AND DIAGNOSIS USING MACHINE LEARNING CLASSIFICATION ALGORITHMS – DEMYSTIFY MEDICAL DATA WITH MACHINE LEARNING ALGORITHMS

In this chapter, the authors introduce demystifying diseases identification and diagnosis of various disease using machine learning algorithms like Logistic Regression, Naive Bayes, decision tree, MLP classifier, Random forest in order to cure Liver disease, Hepatitis disease, and diabetes mellitus. This work leverages the initial discoveries made through Data exploration, statistical analysis of data, reduce the number of explanatory variables led to identifying the statistically significant attributes, mapping those significant attributes to the response and build classification techniques to predict the outcome and demystify clinical diseases.

CHAPTER 12: EVOLUTION OF DATA ANALYTICS IN HEALTHCARE – EVOLUTION OF DATA ANALYTICS IN HEALTHCARE

This chapter focuses on the various recent models proposed in DAiHC and dissect the works based on various vital parameters. As a first part, the work provides comprehensive information on DAiHC and its various application illustrations. Moreover, the study presented in work categorizes the literature on DAiHC based on factors like Algorithms used, Application DataSet utilized, Insight type and Tools used for evaluation of the work.

CHAPTER 13: IMPLEMENTATION OF MACHINE LEARNING IN NETWORK SECURITY

This chapter focuses on the end to end process to get insight into the stream of data from the network connection with priority given to forecasting mechanism and predict the future. Forecasting is applied to the time-series data to get sensible decisions.

CHAPTER 14: INFORMATION RETRIEVAL IN CONJUNCTION WITH DEEP LEARNING

This chapter discusses the applications of information retrieval with deep learning, e.g., web search by reducing the noise and collecting precise results, trend detection in social media analytics, anomaly detection in music datasets and image retrieval, etc.

CHAPTER 15: INTERACTIVE GAME-BASED MOTOR REHABILITATION USING HYBRID SENSOR ARCHITECTURE

This chapter introduces an interactive game to aid motor rehabilitation applicable to patients belonging to all age groups. In our system, the users receive some audio instructions regarding the action they have to perform next. According to that instruction, the user tries to complete the 'Fruit-to-Basket' game as soon as possible, by dropping all the fruits into the basket. A Kinect sensor placed in front of the user detects their motions using skeletons containing 3-dimensional coordinates of twenty body joints. The speed of the movements is detected by the accelerometer. After extracting the required features from skeleton and speed, the use of Principal Component Analysis is proved to be useful for feature space reduction. Then Support Vector Machine is used efficiently to recognize the action. The experimental result indicates that the proposed algorithm is best suited in this domain and an auspicious one.

CHAPTER 16: LEVERAGING NATURAL LANGUAGE PROCESSING APPLICATIONS USING MACHINE LEARNING – TEXT SUMMARIZATION EMPLOYING DEEP LEARNING

The enormous increase of information along with the computational abilities of machines created innovate applications in Natural Language Processing by invoking Machine Learning models. This chapter will project the trends of Natural Language Processing by employing Machine Learning and its models in the context of Text Summarization. This chapter is organized to make the researcher understand technical perspectives regarding Feature representation and their models to consider before applying on language-oriented tasks. Further, the present chapter revises the details of primary models of Deep Learning, its applications, and performance in the context of language processing. The primary focus of this chapter is to illustrate the technical research findings and gaps of Text Summarization based on Deep Learning along with state-of-the-art Deep Learning models for TS.

CHAPTER 17: MACHINE LEARNING IN 5G MULTIMEDIA COMMUNICATIONS – OPEN RESEARCH CHALLENGES AND APPLICATIONS

This chapter presents open research challenges and applications of ML. An exploration of the potential of ML-based solution approaches in the context of 5G primary eMBB, mMTC, and uHSLLC services are presented, evaluating at the same time open issues for future research, including standardization activities of algorithms and data formats.

CHAPTER 18: MACHINE LEARNING IN TEXT ANALYSIS

This chapter provides a basic understanding of processes and models needed to investigate the data posted by users on social networking sites like Facebook, Twitter, Instagram, etc. Often the databases of social networking sites are large and cannot be handled using traditional methodology for analysis. Moreover, the data is posted in such a random manner that can't be used directly for the analysis purpose, therefore a considerable preprocessing is needed to use that data and generate essential results that can help in decision making for various areas like sentiment analysis, customer feedback, customer reviews for brand and product, prevention management, risk management etc. Therefore, this chapter is discussing various aspects of text and its structure, various machine learning algorithms, and their types, why machine learning is better for text analysis, the process of text analysis with the help of examples, issues associated with text analysis and major application areas of text analysis.

CHAPTER 19: MACHINE LEARNING IN THE MEDICAL INDUSTRY

This chapter explains the concept of Machine Learning, and it is working as well as the applications in the Medical Industry. While it describes the basic concepts of Machine Learning in the Medical Industry, it also proposes future challenges for the above subject.

CHAPTER 20: MACHINE LEARNING IN VIDEO GAMES

Machine learning is a part of Artificial Intelligence, in which the learning was done using the data available in the environment. Machine learning algorithms are mainly used in game development to change from prescripted games to adaptive play games. The main theme or storyplot of the game is the game levels, maps in route. The racing games are considered as contents and context refers to the game screenplay, sound effects, and visual effects. In any games, maintaining the fun mode of the player is very important. Predictable moves by non-players in the game and same type of visual effects will reduce the player's interest in the game. The machine learning algorithms work in automatic content generation and Nonpayer Characters behaviors in gameplay. In pathfinding games, puzzle games, strategy games adding intelligence to enemy and opponents make the game more interesting. The enjoyment and fun differ from game to game. For example, in horror games fun is experienced when safe point is reached. Overcoming a level after repeated failures in a quiz or knowledge-based games.

CHAPTER 21: MULTI-LAYER HYBRID CREDIT SCORING MODEL BASED ON FEATURE SELECTION, ENSEMBLE LEARNING, AND ENSEMBLE CLASSIFIER – MULTI-LAYER HYBRID CREDIT SCORING MODEL

This study proposes a Multi-layer Hybrid credit scoring model. First stage concerns about Pre-processing, which includes treatment for missing values, data-transformation and reduction of irrelevant and noisy features because they may affect predictive performance of model. The second stage applies various ensemble learning approaches, such as Bagging, Adaboost, etc. At last layer, it applies Ensemble classifiers approach which combines three heterogeneous classifiers namely: Random Forest (RF), Logistic Regression (LR) and Sequential Minimal Optimization (SMO) approach for classification. Further, the proposed multi-layer model is validated on various real-world credit scoring datasets.

CHAPTER 22: OVERVIEW OF MACHINE LEARNERS IN CLASSIFYING OF SPEECH SIGNALS

Machine Learning (ML) remains a buzzword during the last few decades due to the requirement of a vast amount of data for adequate processing, the continuously surfacing of better innovative and efficient algorithms and the advent of powerful computers with enormous computation power. The ML algorithms are mostly based on data mining, clustering, classification, and regression approaches for efficient utilization. Many vivid application domains in the field of speech and image signal processing, market forecast, biomedical signal processing, robotics, trend analysis of data, banking and finance sectors, etc. benefits from such techniques. Among these modules, the classification of speech and speaker identification has been a predominant area of research as it has been alone medium of communication via phone. This has made the author provide an overview of a few state-of-art ML algorithms, their advantages, and limitation, including the advancement to enhance the application domain in this field.

CHAPTER 23: SELF-DRIVING CARS – ROLE OF MACHINE LEARNING

The chapter discusses the technological advancement in transportation. It also covers the autonomy used according to The National Highway Traffic Safety Administration (NHTSA). The functional architecture of self-driving cars is further discussed. The chapter also discusses two algorithms for detection of lanes as well as detection of vehicles on the road for self-driving cars. Next, the ethical discussions surrounding the autonomous vehicle involving stakeholders, technologies, social environments, and costs vs. quality has been discussed.

CHAPTER 24: SENTIMENT ANALYSIS ON SOCIAL MEDIA – RECENT TRENDS IN MACHINE LEARNING

This chapter studies recent advances in machine learning (ML) used for SMC analysis and its applications. The framework of SASM consists of several phases, such as data collection, pre-processing, feature representation, model building, and evaluation. This survey presents the essential elements of SASM and its utility. Furthermore, the study reports that ML has a significant contribution to SMC mining. Finally, the research highlights specific issues related to ML used for SMC.

CHAPTER 25: SOCIAL BIG DATA MINING – A SURVEY FOCUSED ON SENTIMENT ANALYSIS

Nowadays, social media is used to share the data or information among a large group of people. Numerous forums, blogs, social networks, news reports, e-commerce websites, and many more online media play role in sharing individual opinions. The data generated from these sources is vast and in unstructured format. Big data is a term used for data sets that are large or complex, and that cannot be processed by traditional processing system. Sentimental analysis is one of the significant data analytics applied to big data. It is a task of Natural Language Processing to determine whether a text contains subjective information and what information it expresses. It helps in achieving various goals like the measurement of customer satisfaction, observing public mood on political movement, movie sales prediction, market intelligence, and many more. In this paper we present various techniques used for sentimental Analysis and related work using these techniques. The chapter also presents open issues and challenges in sentimental analysis landscape.

CHAPTER 26: TOOL CONDITION MONITORING USING ARTIFICIAL NEURAL NETWORK MODELS

This chapter deals with the application of Artificial Neural Network (ANN) models for tool condition monitoring (TCM) in milling operations. The data required for training and testing the models studied and developed are from live experiments conducted in a machine shop on a widely used steel, medium carbon steel (En 8) using uncoated carbide inserts. Acoustic emission data and surface roughness data have been used in model development. The goal is for developing an optimal ANN model, in terms of compact architecture, least training time and its ability to generalize well on unseen (test) data. Growing Cell Structures (GCS) network has been found to achieve these requirements.

CHAPTER 27: COMPUTER VISION-BASED ASSISTIVE TECHNOLOGY FOR HELPING VISUALLY IMPAIRED AND BLIND PEOPLE USING DEEP LEARNING FRAMEWORK

Millions of people in this world cannot understand environment because they are blind or visually impaired. They also have navigation difficulties which lead to social awkwardness. They can use some other way to deal with their life and daily routines. It is challenging for them to find something in unknown environment. Blind and visually impaired people face many difficulties in conversation because they cannot decide whether the person is talking to them or someone else. Nowadays use of computer vision-based technologies is increased so much in this domain. The especially deep convolutional neural network is developed very fast in recent years. It is beneficial to use computer vision-based techniques to help visually impaired. In this paper, Hearing sense to understand world around them want to use. Both sight sense and hearing sense have the same similarity: both visual object and audio can be localized. Many peoples do not realize that we are capable enough of identifying location of source of sound by just hearing it.

Chapter 1
Method to Rank Academic Institutes by the Sentiment Analysis of Their Online Reviews

Simran Sidhu
Central University of Punjab, India

Surinder Singh Khurana
Central University of Punjab, India

ABSTRACT

A large number of reviews are expressed on academic institutes using the online review portals and other social media platforms. Such reviews are a good potential source for evaluating the Indian academic institutes. This chapter aimed to collect and analyze the sentiments of the online reviews of the academic institutes and ranked the institutes on the basis of their garnered online reviews. Lexical-based sentiment analysis of their online reviews is used to rank academic institutes. Then these rankings were compared with the NIRF PR Overall University Rankings List 2017. The outcome of this work can efficiently support the overall university rankings of the NIRF ranking list to enhance NIRF's public perception parameter (PRPUB). The results showed that Panjab University achieved the highest sentiment score, which was followed by BITS-Pilani. The results highlighted that there is a significant gap between NIRF's perception rankings and the perception of the public in general regarding an academic institute as expressed in online reviews.

INTRODUCTION

A sentiment (Kaur and Solanki, 2018) in generic terms refers to a feeling, an attitude, an opinion or an emotion expressed by a person. Sentiments cannot be termed as facts as they may vary from person to person. Hence, sentiments can be labeled as subjective impressions. Having given a text written by a

DOI: 10.4018/978-1-5225-9643-1.ch001

person we need to understand the sentiment that it conveys. This comprises of sentiment analysis. Sentiment analysis is also referred to as opinion mining. Sentiment analysis being an interdisciplinary field of study covers various fields like artificial intelligence, text mining and natural language processing.

In today's digital age, online reviews, comments and critiques about various entities like consumer product reviews, movie reviews, tweets, university reviews and college reviews are found on numerous web portals. Sentiment analysis is the process of extracting sentiment from the text. The text can be in the form of online customer reviews, Tweets, blogs, news clips or any piece of text that people write to express their opinions about varied things or even about populist events. These reviews that are written by the public express opinions about the aforementioned articles and hence they help in swaying the mind of a new user in buying or rejecting a product. Sentiment analysis deals with understanding the sentiments behind those reviews..

Given the wide range of review websites available online, we needed a method to make sense of these vast available online review data of the Indian academic institutes. This required a method that could automatically analyze the sentiments of the reviews and thus help the students in making a conscious decision about the choice of institute they should join for further study. This method can efficiently augment the rankings as ranked by the NIRF and help it in adding to it the real sentiments of the people regarding an academic institute over a longer period of time. This research aimed to analyze and perceive the online reviews of the various different Indian academic institutes collected from a wide range of online review portals of universities and colleges. The data was analyzed by text categorization tools, natural language processing tools and the sentiment analysis approaches to determine the sentiment of people towards a particular academic institute of India. The results of which were used to rank the academic institutes. Furthermore, these ranks shall be compared with the yearly standardized rankings of the institutes that are issued annually NIRF namely, the NIRF Rankings 2017.

According to a review of research on Sentiment analysis as of 2017 (Mäntylä, et. al., 2018), Sentiment analysis is a field of research that is one of the fastest growing fields in computer science.

But, most of the work done in the field of sentiment analysis has been in context with social media like Twitter, Facebook and other domains of micro blogging which express movie and product reviews. Little has been done in the application of sentiment analysis to the reviews posted about the academic institutes like universities and colleges of India. This online data comprising of university and college reviews that is available on multiple websites needs to be harnessed to its full potential so that the public opinion and perception about these academic institutes of India comes to the fore.

SENTIMENT ANALYSIS USING SEMANTIC ANALYSIS APPROACH

In this approach a predefined lexicon/dictionary is used. This lexicon is full of words that have already been assigned a polarity value i.e. some words have been assigned negative polarity values while the others have been assigned positive polarity values. Firstly, pre-processing tools are applied on the text that we want to analyze and these tools segregate the full text into words/tokens after the initial pre-processing steps. These pre-processing steps comprise of normalization of the text with lemmatization and stemming of the text. After the whole of the text has been converted into words/tokens these are matched with the entries of the lexicon. If a match is found of that word in the lexicon, then the polarity values are assigned to each of these words. Then the aggregate polarity of the whole text is ascertained by adding up the polarity values of the words that comprise the text.

Figure 1. showing the popularity of sentiment analysis based upon worldwide searches on Google from 2004 to 2017

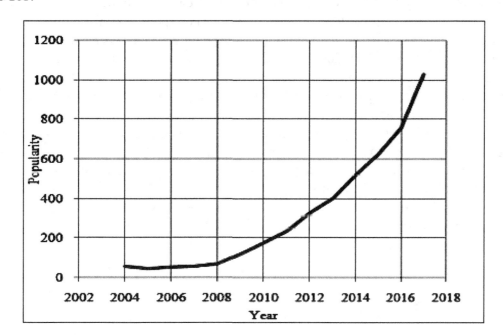

INDIAN INSTITUTE RANKINGS FRAMEWORK

National Institutional Ranking Framework (NIRF) is an MHRD ranking framework that ranks the all the major Indian educational institutes annually based on five major parameters. It was first launched by MHRD in September 2015 and the first ranking list was released in April 2016. The second rankings list was released for 2017 which included the same five major parameters but there were some changes made regarding the sub parameters.

Parameters Used for NIRF Ranking:

The five major parameters and their subsequent underlying parameters that the NIRF ranking system used to assign a rank to the Institute were the following:

1. Teaching, Learning and Resources
2. Research and Professional Practice
3. Graduation Outcomes
4. Outreach and Inclusivity
5. Perception: Peer Perception: Employers and Research Investors (PREMP), Peer Perception: Academics (PRACD),
6. Public Perception (PRPUB), Competitiveness (PRCMP)

Focusing mainly on the fifth parameter 'Perception' involved in the NIRF ranking framework we see that the data collected by MHRD in this field was mainly done by the following two methods: online perception system and the online feedback system. The Online Perception System was open for the peers, the employers and also for the public. It was an online perception system that operated for 23 days, which is too less a time to gauge the perception towards a particular academic institute. Also the people's perceptions may change over time. Although MHRD mentions in its annual report that a large number of individuals had submitted their perceptions but there is no exact number or statistics that accompany this claim. Moreover, it is a possibility that the peers of the participating academic institutes perceived their own institute in a good way so based on this perception parameter the rankings may have been biased.

Whereas the Online Feedback System was specifically to get feedback from the general public; it was an online feedback system that operated only for 10 days starting from 1st February 2017 to 12th February 2017, which is again a very short period of time to make an opinion regarding an institute based upon limited data which further may be biased. The people were not asked to give a general feedback or a review but they were asked to give feedback only on the data pre-submitted by the applicant organizations by answering some set questions.

SENTIMENT ANALYSIS: LITERATURE REVIEW

The sentiment analysis techniques have been applied in various different fields in the previous research works:

All the known word net methods and approaches that were used to develop them were formulated in 1990, under a study (Miller et.al, 1990). It included word nets in various languages from around the world. It summarized the word net methods.

A comparison of the different sentiment analysis techniques was presented (MD, Sunitha& Ganesh, 2016). It compared and analyzed the Machine learning approach, Rule Based sentiment analysis approach and the Lexical Based sentiment analysis approach. It demonstrated that using each of these approaches of sentiment analysis would yield different results. Comparing the accuracy, performance and efficiency of these three approaches it concluded that the machine learning approach provided the best overall results surpassing the Rule based approach and the Lexical based approach. It further analyzed the various machine learning approaches used in sentiment analysis such as Support Vector Machine (SVM), N-gram Sentiment Analysis, Naïve Bayes (NB) method, Maximum Entropy (ME) Classifier, k-Nearest Neighbors (kNN) Method, Weighted kNN method, Multilingual sentiment analysis, Feature driven sentiment analysis. Upon considering the advantages and disadvantages of these approaches it was concluded that SVM method works best when the training set is vast and the NB approach is efficient only for a small training set. Max Entropy is a computationally complex approach but can handle vast datasets whereas Feature driven SA is not efficient for small datasets. The kNN approach is demonstrated as a computationally efficient approach. Multilingual SA is specifically used when the dataset comprises of different languages and can handle up to 15 different languages.

Sentiment analysis has been extensively used for the micro-blogging website Twitter. One of the earliest popular works in this field was attempted using distant supervision technique (Go, Bhayani &Huang, 2009). The tweets were classified as positive and negative based on the happy or sad emoticons used in the tweets. The research demonstrated that the SVM and NB classifiers were the most efficient and readily beat the MaxEnt classifier.

Using the same technique of distant supervision technique but additionally adding the neutral class for tweets based on the emoticons (Pak & Paroubek, 2010). Hence, a three-way classification of tweets was performed. TreeTagger was used over tweets collected related specifically to news for POS-tagging. The classifier used was SVM, CRF and the multinomial NB classifier. The multinomial NB classifier yielded the best performance. Comparing the unigram approach, bigram approach and the trigram approach they received the highest performance with the bigram approach as the bigrams provided the requisite balance between the unigrams and the trigrams. The unigram approach provided the best requisite coverage whereas the trigram approach provided the best capturing of the sentiment expression, so the bigram approach provided the requisite mix of the two approaches giving the best performance.

Sentiment analysis on movie review data was presented and the classification was done based on SVM, NB and Maximum Entropy Classifier (Pang, Le & Vaithyanathan, 2002) using the movie reviews dataset collected from IMDB. It uses a three-fold cross validation scheme. Feature selection was based on the unigram and the bigram approach. SVM emerged as the best classification algorithm and NB fared the worst. Also the unigram approach performed better than the bigram approach in capturing the sentiment of the reviews.

Sentiment analysis of movie reviews was carried out using labeled movie reviews from IMDB (Sokolov Aleksey, 2015). It specifically aimed at analyzing the quality of the word to vector representation which is used in sentiment analysis. The most accurate results were yielded by using the random forest algorithm in combination with the tf-idf model while using the random forest approach with the bag of words approach was the least accurate. It was concluded that this accuracy primarily depended upon the methods that are used for feature extraction.

Sentiment analysis of movie reviews using the Naïve Bayes model and the n-grams method was carried out. Also a novel optimized version of the Naïve Byes Model was proposed (Uan Sholanbayev, 2016). Using the trigram approach yielded an accuracy of 74% whereas while using the trigram and the bigram approach together, the accuracy levels fluctuated around 78% and could not reach the level of precision that it was expected to reach. Using the basic Naïve Byes Model yielded elevated the accuracy up to 82%. The optimized version of the basic Naïve Bayes model used a filtering operation that filtered out the redundant data keeping only the informative text of the movie reviews passing out its output to the machine learning classifier that worked in the same way as the basic version did. Naïve Bayes's way of assigning the same weights to all the features works against it and hence to have an increased degree of accuracy in NB the weights should be assigned differently to different features.

An in-depth comparison of the three popular machine learning classifiers for the classification of movie review data was presented (Cheng-Tao, Takahashi &Wang, 2017). The three machine learning classifiers used for the study were Maximum Entropy (MaxEnt), Support Vector Machine (SVM) and the Decision Tree (DT). The movie review data used was the same as that used by Pang, Le & Vaithyanathan (2002). Taking the 1000 positive and 1000 negative reviews of movies, POS (Parts-of-Speech) Tagging was applied on it, from which further the features were extracted. The two feature selection algorithms used were: Fisher Score and the Singular Value Decomposition (SVD). The experiments conducted on the data to find the sentiment of the reviews used a combination of the two feature selection methods and the three machine learning classifiers. In all the cases the accuracy of classification of reviews was always higher for positive reviews than the negative ones. Also when fewer features are selected the classification accuracy of the positive reviews improves while at the same time the accuracy levels of the negative reviews degrade. Overall the MaxEnt classifier classification accuracy was 82.6% while the SVM stood at the same accuracy of 82.6% when 28680 features are used. The DTs performed rather poorly with an accuracy of 61.1%.

A novel method that is adaptable and used a fine grained approach was used to generate summary of the Naver movies dataset (Amplayo & Song, 2017). This approach proved that using natural language processing in conjunction with the machine learning procedures yielded better results than using a single-level classifier. It uses a word n-gram SVM classifier and a character n-gram SVM classifier approach for using multilevel sentiment classification. The classifier tool they use outperforms the LingPipe classifier, the Standford Core NLP and also the ASUM classifier. The ASUM classifier fared lowly because it uses short review texts only which are not effective in judging the sentiment analysis of a text. The novel classification method used is an adaptable sentiment extraction algorithm as it can be used over datasets in different languages and across different domains. It uses multiple datasets like the Rotten Tomatoes dataset for English movies, the Amazon movie reviews dataset also for English movies, the Douban dataset for Chinese movies and the Naver dataset for Korean movies. It further ranks the movies based on the reviews collected from the Naver dataset and compares these ranks with the ranks obtained by the same movie in the Blue Dragon Film Awards. It demonstrated that the movies that won awards were also the ones that got a higher score based on aspect sentiment.

Research on sentiment analysis in Hindi has also been carried out successfully (Narayan et. al., 2002) was the first step towards developing a Hindi Senti Word Net. The Indo-word net was though nascent in its approach paved a way for further study in developing a proper Hindi Senti word net. Karthikeyan et al. in their 2010 thesis for IIT Bombay, proposed an efficient way of English-Hindi WordNet Linking.

A Fall-back Strategy for Sentiment Analysis in Hindi was proposed (Joshi et al. in 2010). Taking inspiration from the English SentiWordNet, this research built the first version of H-SWN (Hindi-SentiWordNet). It used two known lexical resources for building the same. The two resources were the existing English SentiWordNet and along with it, it also made use of the English-Hindi WordNet Linking developed (Karthikeyan et al). Making use of this WordNet linking the words in the existing English SentiWordNet were successfully replaced with their equivalent Hindi words. The result was the first Hindi SentiWordNet (H-SWN). This paper paved the way for research in Hindi sentiment analysis. This research work was the first one known for sentiment analysis in Hindi language.

Other English sentiment analysis approaches include, a sentiment topic recognition model called the STR Model was presented to compute the Air Quality Rating (AQR) of three major airline companies namely, AirTran Airways, Frontier and SkyWest Airlines (Adeborna &Siau, 2014). This model was based on the algorithm called Variational Expectation-Maximization (VEM) and also on Correlated Topics Models (CTM). The AQR was calculated per 1000 tweets. Because of the limited number of tweets used the results were of a commendable accuracy.

A paper which focused on analyzing the Twitter data for the sentiment analysis and opinion mining of the tweets about the airlines of the United States of America was presented (Yuan, Zhong, & Uang, 2015). The dataset comprised of 14640 tweets which were split into 80% and 20% for training and testing respectively. For each of the tweets, n-grams of each of the letters were taken and the words of the tweets were used as features. These features were stored in a sparse matrix. Four approaches were further used namely, Lexicon-based Sentiment Classification, Multinomial Naïve Bayes (Multinomial NB), Linear Support Vector Machine (Linear SVM), Convolutional Neural Networks (CNN)(Pandey and Solanki, 2019). The overall accuracy for the sentiment classification task was highest for Linear SVM at 0.796, Convolutional Neural Networks stood at an accuracy level of 0.790. Multinomial Naïve Bayes achieved an accuracy of 0.712 and the Lexicon based approach achieved an accuracy of 0.652. Here, Multinomial Naïve Bayes runs faster than SVM due to its inherent model simplicity.

Sentiment analysis has been applied to the feedback of the airline passengers that has been obtained from the airline forum (Venu, Annie & Mohan, 2016).The machine learning algorithms that are used are Linear Support Vector and Multinomial Naïve Bayes. The dataset used for training the same include 1217 reviews that are positive in nature and 955 reviews that are negative in nature. The testing dataset comprises of 868 reviews. The outcomes of the study are represented in the form of a bar graph. Linear Support Vector model yielded an accuracy of 88.59% and the Multinomial Naïve Bayes model fared slightly lower than the Linear Support Vector model, with an accuracy of 84.56%. The study also presented the runtime analysis of the two models with runtime in seconds. Overall in terms of accuracy levels the Linear Support Vector fared better than Multinomial Naïve Bayes but based on the runtime results it was concluded that Multinomial Naïve Bayes fared better than the Linear Support Vector model.

Twitter data pertaining to the Indian election was analyzed to see the effect the micro blogging website Twitter has on the way the elections in the Indian states and the whole nation turns out (Wani & Alone, 2015). The main election tweets that this model analyzed was the Maharashtra state assembly election. The proposed model makes use of trend and volume analysis in addition to the sentiment analysis of the tweets. Firstly the tweets are cleaned by using the Porter Stemmer algorithm then the tweets are clustered using the K-Means Clustering algorithm then finally the Naive Bayes algorithm is used to do the three way sentiment classification of tweets as negative, positive and neutral tweets. The hash tag based tweet count was also graphically analyzed.

An analysis of the Twitter network pertaining to the 2014 Indian election was carried out (Lu, Shah, & Kulshrestha, 2014). Each of the 15.5 million user accounts that were analyzed were taken as nodes in the network. The followers of these accounts were taken as the edges of the network and these were up to 5000 for each of the nodes under study. The total tweet dataset comprised of 10,595,729 tweets which is approximately 7GB of data. The sentiment analysis of these showed that the NDA, the party that won the 2014 election had very less negative tweets compared to its arch rival UPA. The volume of tweets increased substantially in the months proceeding to the election with April and May having a chunk of the tweets. A new algorithm was devised using the augmented contagion model. Retweet analysis and the Supporter Strength analysis was also carried out to reach the final outcome. The final outcome of NDA against every metric was far above the UPA ones which ultimately led to the win of the NDA against the UPA.

A review paper regarding the various techniques used in predicting the outcome of the elections was presented (Salunkhe, Surnar, &Sonawane, 2017). The various strategies discussed in the outline of the paper were ideological learning via the political tweets, user graph analysis, linguistic behavior, re-tweeting trends etc. Overall this paper gave a bird's eye view of the trends in election prediction via Twitter.

An application of sentiment analysis to classify the users as pessimists or optimists based on their IMDB comments was proposed (Garcia-Cumbreras, Montejo-Raez and Diaz-Galiano, 2013). It advocates for the improvement of the sentiment analysis by looking for similarities between the user's comments and the entire user community in general. This approach is particularly useful for sentiment analysis based recommendation systems. It generates a new corpus from the Internet Movie Database (IMDB) comprising of 80,848 movie opinions based on the user critical comments and ratings and categorizes all the users based on their comments into two classes; as optimists or pessimists and then performs experiments on how these can be used efficiently in collaborative filtering methods by combining them with opinion mining approaches. The approaches used were SVM and kNN. The kNN approach used the Euclidean distance. 10-fold cross validation using stratified sampling technique along with the Root Mean Square Error (RMSE) and the Mean Square Error (MSE) estimators were used for evaluation. It was demonstrated that SVM approach clearly improves upon the kNN approach. A more accurate result was obtained when only the users were classified as pessimists or optimists and the predication of the sentiment when these user orientations were applied to the whole community in general resulted in lesser accuracy.

A fine grained social analytics fuzzy ontology methodology on the customer reviews was adopted (Lau, Li & Liao, 2014). This methodology used a semi-supervised fuzzy learning approach for the fine grained extraction instead of the coarse-grained extraction used previously. The approach used for sentiment analysis is context sensitive and it does not presume that the polarity of a text can only be two fold or it can be same for all different product domains. A seven step LDA based aspect oriented sentiment analysis methodology was applied to the customer's product reviews to gauge the product ontology automatically. It also provided an extension of the LingPipe to make way for a novel Gibbs approach that was used as a sampling algorithm using a WD (Word Divergence) measure to measure the strength of polarity of the words occurring in the customer reviews. ProdOntLearn was the novel algorithm developed that computationally facilitated the learning of the product ontology automatically based on the customer review corpus in this proposed OBPRM system.

Sentiment analysis for evaluating the German Universities using Twitter was presented (Tummel, &Richert, 2015). 16488 tweets pertaining to nine German Universities were collected for the duration of one semester via the Twitter API. Out of these 5000 randomly chosen tweets were then segregated into positive and not positive tweets and were fed into the NB classifier which gave an accuracy of 73.6%. A Python script using the NLTK library was used to create a tool to rank the nine Institutes based on the percentage of positive and not positive Twitter reviews. The word frequency analysis was also carried out which showed the most frequently used words in the university tweets.

INSTITUTION RANKING: AN APPLICATION OF SENTIMENT ANALYSIS

Sentiment analysis was applied to know the tone of the online reviews. The steps of the methodology that were used to perform the sentiment analysis on the online reviews of the selected academic institutes of India were as follows:

1. Designed a dataset comprising of the Institute review corpus of fifteen academic institutes of India.
2. Preprocessed the reviews.
3. Performed the sentiment analysis of the initially processed reviews.
4. Ranked the institutes according to the sentiment score of their garnered reviews.
5. Compared and analyzed the rankings as obtained by the method with the rankings of the Institutes as per NIRF rankings of 2017.

Phases of Methodology

The technique used for performing the sentiment analysis of the academic institutes was the lexicon based sentiment analysis. The Lexical based technique of sentiment analysis was chosen over the machine based technique because the review dataset was not a balanced one i.e. it contained more of positive reviews than the negative ones.

Phase 1: Data Collection: In phase 1, the datasets comprising of the reviews of the academic institutes were created. The academic institutes chosen for the research were the ones that featured in the top 100 overall ranking list of NIRF 2017. Firstly, the institute whose ranks were a multiple of three was picked. Their reviews were searched online. If sufficient number of their reviews were available then that institute was chosen, if not so, then the next one in the list was chosen. Hence, the institutes with their ranks that were chosen for the study were, IISc Bangalore (Rank 1), IIT-Bombay (Rank 3), JNU Delhi (Rank 6), IIT-Roorkee (Rank 9), Jadavpur University (Rank 12) was skipped along with ranks 13, Anna University and rank 14, University of Hyderabad as not a wide variety of their reviews were available online, so University of Delhi (Rank 15) was the next to be picked. Rank 18, Savitribai Phule Pune University again didn't have many reviews online, so it was skipped and rank 19, Aligarh Muslim University was chosen. Rank 21, BITS-Pilani was chosen next. The other universities that were randomly chosen pertained to the availability of many reviews regarding them online as in, IIM-Ahmedabad (Rank 17), Vellore Institute of Technology (Rank 22), IIM-Bangalore (Rank 25), Osmania University (Rank 38), Panjab University (Rank 54), ISM-Dhanbad (Rank 53), Thapar University (Rank 75), NIT-Warangal (Rank 82). All these ranking were from the Overall Rankings list of NIRF 2017.Approximately three hundred reviews per institute were collected for seven universities and for the rest of the eight institutes approximately two hundred reviews per institute were collected. Total reviews collected were 3695 reviews.

Phase 2: Data Analysis of the Collected Data Sets: Data analysis was performed on the collected reviews to know the length of the reviews for each institute. Maximum, minimum and average length of the reviews of each institute was calculated depending on the number of words contained in each of those reviews. The average and the maximum length of the reviews were gathered in a tabular form.

Phase 3: Manual Annotation of the Reviews: Each of the 3695 collected reviews were read and analyzed and tagged (annotated) manually as ''Pos'' or ''Neg'' considering whether they were positive or negative reviews. This manual annotation was done so that the annotation done by the method can be compared with the manual annotation and checked for its accuracy.

Phase 4: Initial Pre-processing of the Review Data: Phase 3 involved writing a script in Python langauge that performs the initial preprocessing of the collected reviews. The script performed all the three initial preprocessing steps on each of the reviews..

Phase 5: NLTK Processing of the Reviews: After all the reviews had been initial pre-processed, the next step involved using the Natural Language Tool Kit (NLTK) of Python for the pre-processing of the reviews. All the three of the most popular NLTK pre-processing steps were carried out in this *work*, namely:

- Tokenization of the Reviews
- Lemmatization
- Parts-of-Speech (POS) tagging of the words contained in the Reviews

Phase 6: Tagging and Calculating the Sentiment Score of the Reviews: The same NLTK script also comprised of the code to get the Sentiment Score for each of the Reviews and for the tagging of the reviews. The reviews were tagged by the Python script as 'Pos' (Positive) or 'Neg' (Negative Review) depending upon their Sentiment Scores. The sentiment scores were calculated based on the synsets of the words contained in the review. After the sentiment score of the review was computed by the method, further the tagging of the reviews was done based on the total sentiment score that the review has gained. The reviews were annotated with a Positive tag or a Negative tag depending on the sentiment score of the review.

The lexical resource used for the sentiment analysis was SentiWordNet 3.0 (Baccianella et. al. 2010) which has automatically annotated all the possible WordNet synsets in three categories namely, their degree of neutrality, positivity and their degree of negativity.

Phase 7: Ranking the Academic Institutes: The sentiment scores of all the reviews of any particular institute were added to get their cumulative effect. Then the total sentiment score was divided by the total number of reviews of that particular institute to get the sentiment score per review. The academic institutes were then ranked based on the sentiment scores per review.

Phase 8: Comparing the Ranks of the Institutes with NIRF Ranks: The ranks of the academic institutes based on their sentiment scores were compared to the ranks garnered by the academic institutes in the NIRF overall university rankings list 2017.

Phase 9: Analyzing the results: The ranks of the academic institutes based on their sentiment scores were compared to the average length of the reviews and also only the sentiment scores of the uniform Google reviews were compared.

Phase 10: Documenting the Results: Each and every result pertaining to each phase of the *work* was documented accordingly.

PARAMETERS RECORDED

The parameters that were recorded were:

1. Total Number of Positively Tagged Reviews by the method
2. Total Number of Negatively Tagged Reviews by the method
3. Sentiment Scores of each of the reviews as computed by the method
4. Total Sentiment Score of the Academic Institute, which was the additive effect of all the sentiment scores of all the reviews pertaining to an academic institute.
5. Total correctly annotated reviews by the Method: The annotated reviews by the method were compared to the manually annotated reviews to check the total number of correctly annotated reviews by the method
6. Total number of incorrectly annotated reviews by the Method: The annotated reviews by the method were compared to the manually annotated reviews to check the total number of incorrectly annotated reviews by the method

Table 1. Number of reviews collected of each academic institute

Sr. No.	Academic Institute	Total Number of Reviews Collected
1	IIT-Bombay	300
2	IISc Bangalore	300
3	IIM-Ahmedabad	299
4	BITS-Pilani	300
5	JNU Delhi	300
6	IIM-Bangalore	199
7	Vellore Institue of Technology (VIT)	200
8	IIT-Roorkee	299
9	Delhi University	300
10	Panjab University	200
11	Aligarh Muslim University	200
12	Thapar University	200
13	Osmania University	200
14	ISM Dhanbad	200
15	NIT-Warangal	198
	Total Reviews	**3695**

7. Finally the accuracy of the sentiment analysis method was computed as per the formula: Accuracy of the Sentiment Analysis method for each institute = (Correctly Annotated Reviews / Total Number of Reviews of that academic institute) * 100

SOFTWARE TOOLS USED

- Python software: Python Version 3.5.4 Release Date: 2017-08-08 (Freeware)
- Natural language toolkit: NLTK Version 3.2.5 (Freeware)
- SentiWordNet Version 3.0 (Freeware)
- MS Office (Pre-packaged in the Windows OS)

RESULTS

Online reviews pertaining to fifteen academic institutes were collected. These fifteen academic universities were the ones that featured in the Overall Rankings top 100 list of NIRF 2017. Out of those 100 academic institutes, only those institutes were chosen whose reviews were readily available online. Approximately 300 reviews per institute were collected for seven academic institutes and approximately 200 reviews per institute were collected for the other eight institutes as in Table 1. The reviews collected were stored in excel spreadsheets.

Table 2. Sources of the collected reviews

Sr. No.	Source	Review Count
1	Google	2674
2	Glassdoor	551
3	Careers 360	153
4	Shiksha	101
5	MouthShut	79
6	Indeed	45
7	CollegeBol	26
8	GetMyUni	23
9	CollegeDunia	23
10	Youtube	16
11	Quora	3
12	CollegeSearch	1
	Total Reviews	**3695**

Table 3. Table showing the sources of the reviews of every academic institute

Source of Review / Academic Institute	Google	Glassdoor	Careers 360	Indeed	Youtube	Shiksha	Get My Uni	Mouth Shut	College Dunia	College Search	College Bol	Quora	Total Number of Reviews
Panjab University	200	0	0	0	0	0	0	0	0	0	0	0	200
BITS-Pilani	204	30	0	0	0	66	0	0	0	0	0	0	300
NIT Warangal	118	0	54	0	0	0	0	0	0	1	26	0	198
IIM- Bangalore	199	0	0	0	0	0	0	0	0	0	0	0	199
IIT-Roorkee	218	39	23	0	0	19	0	0	0	0	0	0	299
Thapar University	136	33	22	0	0	0	0	9	0	0	0	0	200
ISM Dhanbad	200	0	0	0	0	0	0	0	0	0	0	0	200
Aligarh Muslim University	200	0	0	0	0	0	0	0	0	0	0	0	200
IIM- Ahmedabad	169	29	34	0	16	13	17	12	9	0	0	0	299
Vellore Institute of Technology	200	0	0	0	0	0	0	0	0	0	0	0	200
JNU Delhi	219	8	17	0	0	3	6	30	14	0	0	3	300
Osmania University	200	0	0	0	0	0	0	0	0	0	0	0	200
Delhi University	182	54	0	36	0	0	0	28	0	0	0	0	300
IIT-Bombay	108	192	0	0	0	0	0	0	0	0	0	0	300
IISc Bangalore	122	166	3	9	0	0	0	0	0	0	0	0	300
Total	**2674**	**551**	**153**	**45**	**16**	**101**	**23**	**79**	**23**	**1**	**26**	**3**	**3695**

Table 4. Maximum, minimum and average length of the reviews of each academic institute

Academic Institute	Minimum length of Review [Number of Words]	Maximum length of Review [Number of Words]	Average Length of Reviews
BITS Pilani	1	732	68.4466667
NIT Warangal	1	561	56.57575758
IIM-Ahmedabad	1	1161	55.95986622
IIT Roorkee	1	781	46.69899666
JNU Delhi	1	600	43.75
Delhi University	1	436	42.1566667
IISc Bangalore	1	191	38.4766667
IIT Bombay	3	154	35.6066667
Vellore Institute of Technology	1	660	32.385
Thapar University	1	203	30.985
Osmania University	1	410	26.46
Aligarh Muslim University	1	517	24.345
ISM Dhanbad	1	416	19.01
Panjab University	1	200	17.5
IIM-Bangalore	1	128	12.70854271

The review data for the *work* was collected manually from varied online review portals as in Table 2. The 3695 reviews that were collected were primarily Google Reviews The total number of reviews that were collected was 3695 reviews, which comprised of 2674 Google Reviews i.e. approximately 72% of the reviews used in this study were Google Reviews. Google reviews were shorter in length as compared to the reviews from other online review portals like Glassdoor and Careers 360. The reviews were collected from twelve online review portals Table 2.

In, Table 3, the number of reviews collected from each of the different websites pertaining to each of the different academic institutes is tabulated. As can be seen in Table 3, in case of each of the academic institutes, the most number of reviews collected were from Google, namely they were the Google Reviews. The other two online review websites that significantly added up to the review collection were Glassdoor and Careers 360. Google Reviews were relatively shorter in length as compared to the other review portals.

The collected reviews were analyzed to find the minimum, maximum and the average length of the collected reviews. The lengths of the reviews were based on the number of words in the reviews. The minimum length of most of the academic institute reviews was one word. BITS Pilani had the highest average length of the review at 68.44 words per review and IIM-Bangalore had the lowest average at 12.655. The length of the longest review was of IIM-Ahmedabad which comprised of 1161 words. The academic institutes are ranked based on their average length of their reviews in Table 4.

The graphical plots comparing the maximum and the average lengths of the reviews of each of the academic institutes are shown in Figure 2 and Figure 3.

Figure 2. Plot comparing the maximum length of the reviews of the academic institutes

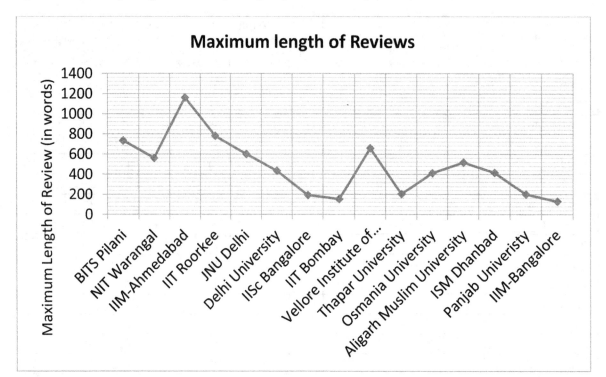

Figure 3. Plot comparing the average length of the reviews of the academic institutes

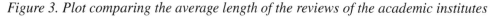
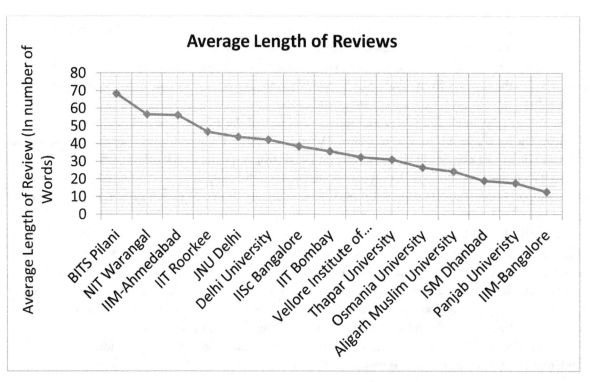

Table 5. Total number of positive and negative reviews of each academic institute (as annotated by the method)

Academic Institute	Total Number of Positive Reviews (As annotated by the Method)	Total Number of Negative Reviews (As annotated by the Method)	Total Number of Reviews
NIT-Warangal	191	7	198
BITS-Pilani	287	13	300
IIT-Roorkee	281	18	299
Thapar University	190	10	200
IIM-Ahmedabad	284	15	299
Panjab University	188	12	200
IIM-Bangalore	183	16	199
IIT-Bombay	290	10	300
ISM Dhanbad	187	13	200
Aligarh Muslim University	185	15	200
JNU Delhi	279	21	300
Delhi University	270	30	300
Vellore Institute of Technology	180	20	200
IISc Bangalore	280	20	300
Osmania University	189	11	200
Total	**3464**	**231**	**3695**

Sentiment Analysis of the Reviews

The sentiment analysis was carried out fifteen academic institutes that featured in the top 100 list of NIRF 2017 and the reviews were given sentiment scores and were tagged as 'Pos' or 'Neg' reviews. Total Number of Positive Reviews (As annotated by the Method) and the Total Number of Negative Reviews (As annotated by the Method) for each of the academic institute is provided in Table 5.

Out of the total 3695 reviews, according to the annotation done by the method, 3464 were positive reviews and 231 were negative reviews. It is concluded that according to the method, 93.74% of the total collected reviews were positive reviews and 6.25% of them were of a negative nature. As can be seen in Table 6, the highest by the percentage of positively tagged reviews method belonged to IIT-Bombay whose 96.67% of the total 300 reviews were annotated a 'Pos' tag. NIT-Warangal followed a close second with the percentage of positively tagged reviews method being 96.46%. The academic institute with the lowest percentage of positive reviews belonged to Vellore Institute of Technology with 90% positive reviews and 10% negative reviews.

Table 6. Percentage of positive and negative reviews of each academic institute

Academic Institute	% of Positive Reviews	% of Negative Reviews
IIT-Bombay	96.67	3.33
NIT-Warangal	96.46	3.54
BITS-Pilani	95.67	4.33
Thapar University	95.00	5.00
IIM-Ahmedabad	94.98	5.02
Osmania University	94.50	5.50
Panjab University	94.00	6.00
IIT-Roorkee	93.98	6.02
ISM Dhanbad	93.50	6.50
IISc Bangalore	93.33	6.67
JNU Delhi	93.00	7.00
Aligarh Muslim University	92.50	7.50
IIM-Bangalore	91.96	8.04
Delhi University	90.00	10.00
Vellore Institute of Technology	90.00	10.00

Figure 4. Showing the percentage of positive and negative reviews of each academic institute as an-notated by the method

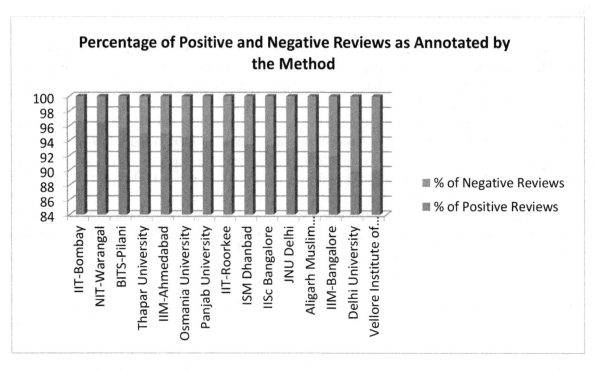

Table 7. Total number of correctly and incorrectly annotated reviews by the method and the Accuracy of the method for each academic institute

Academic Institute	Total Number of Reviews [N]	Total corrected annotated reviews by the method [TC]	Total incorrectly annotated reviews by the method [TI]	Accuracy of the Method [(TC/N)*100]
NIT-Warangal	198	193	5	97.47%
BITS-Pilani	300	287	13	95.67%
IIT-Roorkee	299	288	11	96.32%
Thapar University	200	197	3	98.50%
IIM-Ahmedabad	299	289	10	96.65%
Panjab University	200	195	5	97.50%
IIM-Bangalore	199	184	15	92.46%
IIT-Bombay	300	294	6	98.00%
ISM Dhanbad	200	194	6	97.00%
Aligarh Muslim University	200	186	14	93.00%
JNU Delhi	300	291	9	97.00%
Delhi University	300	297	3	99.00%
Vellore Institute of Technology	200	185	15	92.50%
IISc Bangalore	300	285	15	95.00%
Osmania University	200	191	9	95.50%
Total	**3695**	**3556**	**139**	**Overall Accuracy 96.23%**

Accuracy of the Sentiment Analysis Method

Figure 4 shows the graphical form of the percentage of Positive and Negative Reviews of each Academic Institute as Annotated by the Method. The tags annotated by the method were then compared with the tags annotated manually to each of the reviews and the total number of correctly annotated reviews by the method [TC] and the total number of incorrectly annotated reviews by the method [TI] were computed as shown in Table 7. The accuracy of the sentiment analysis method was computed for each of the academic institutes based on the following formula:Accuracy of the Sentiment Analysis method for each institute = (Correctly Annotated Reviews / Total Number of Reviews of that academic institute) * 100. In this research, the accuracy of the method in tagging the reviews correctly was computed using the formula, [(TC/N)*100] where TC was the total number of correctly annotated reviews and N was the total number of reviews under consideration of that particular academic institute.

Delhi University reviews managed to gain the top slot here with an accuracy of 99% by the method correctly annotating 297 out of the total 300 reviews while IIM-Bangalore's reviews were the ones that fared the lowest with an accuracy of 92.46%, so the accuracy of the method in annotating the reviews correctly as 'Pos' or 'Neg' was 96.238%. As shown in Table 7, where the results of the academic institutes are stored based on the sentiment analysis method's accuracies for the tagging of their reviews, it can be seen that out of the total 3695 reviews that were collected for fifteen academic institutes, 3556

Figure 5. Percentage of Correctly and Incorrectly annotated reviews by the method

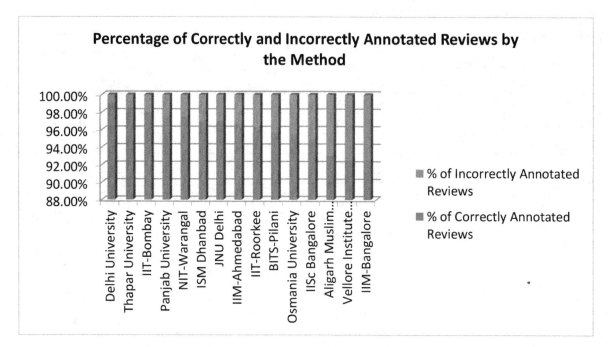

Table 8. Total Sentiment Scores and Sentiment Score per Review of each academic institute

Ranks based on Sentiment Score per Review	Academic Institute	Total Sentiment Score (TSS)	Total Number of Reviews Used (N)	Sentiment Score per Review (SSR) [(TSS*100)/N]
1	Panjab University	26.8949496	200	13.4474748
2	BITS-Pilani	39.6310579	300	13.2103526
3	NIT Warangal	25.9704581	198	13.116393
4	IIM- Bangalore	24.9942405	199	12.5599198
5	IIT-Roorkee	36.5325477	299	12.2182434
6	Thapar University	24.3426583	200	12.1713291
7	ISM Dhanbad	22.6407291	200	11.3203646
8	Aligarh Muslim University	22.5779751	200	11.2889876
9	IIM- Ahmedabad	31.077702	299	10.3938803
10	Vellore Institute of Technology	18.688773	200	9.34438648
11	JNU Delhi	26.7892957	300	8.92976523
12	Osmania University	16.6372043	200	8.31860217
13	Delhi University	23.498462	300	7.83282067
14	IIT-Bombay	21.5477502	300	7.18258338
15	IISc Bangalore	19.7376616	300	6.57922053

Figure 6. Sentiment Score per Review (SSR) of each academic institute

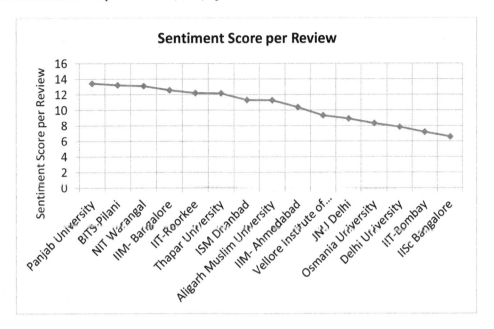

were correctly annotated by the method and 139 reviews were incorrectly annotated, which makes the overall accuracy of the method as 96.23%. The graph showing the percentage of correctly and incorrectly annotated reviews by the method is shown in Figure 5.

Sentiment Analysis of all the Reviews

Along with the tags of 'Pos' and 'Neg' that were annotated by the method to each of the collected reviews, the sentiment score of the reviews was also computed. For each of the fifteen academic institutes, each of its reviews' sentiment scores was added and the summation of the sentiment scores of all the reviews of a particular academic institute was calculated. This was termed as the Total Sentiment Score (TSS). To compare the TSS values of all the institutes, the TSS score was multiplied by 100 and then divided by the total number of reviews for which the TSS was calculated as shown in Table 8. The outcome was the sentiment score per review (SSR). Panjab University topped the list by scoring 13.44 as the Sentiment Score per Review, which was followed by BITS-Pilani with a sentiment score per review of 13.21.

Surprisingly, the institute that topped the NIRF 2017 overall list based on the public perception factor fared the worst in the research by gaining a sentiment score per review of 6.57. The graph showing the SSRs of the fifteen academic institutes is presented in Figure 6.

Results of the Sentiment Analysis of the Google Reviews

To check if the varied nature and lengths of the reviews that were collected from twelve varied online portals had any effect on the results of sentiment analysis. The sentiment analysis method was carried out only on the Google Reviews so that the reviews are uniform. The results of the same are tabulated in Table 9.The results showed that NIT-Warangal secured the highest Sentiment Score per Review (SSR)

Table 9. Sentiment Score per Review of each institute based on Google Reviews

Academic Institute	Total Sentiment Score [Only Google Reviews]	Total Number of Google Reviews	Sentiment Score per Review [SSR] [(TSS*100)/N]	Ranks based on SSR
NIT-Warangal	21.60332494	117	18.46438	1
BITS-Pilani	35.42220079	204	17.363824	2
IIT-Roorkee	33.0495258	218	15.160333	3
Thapar University	19.8983206	136	14.631118	4
IIM-Ahmedabad	23.81189526	169	14.089879	5
Panjab University	26.89494957	200	13.447475	6
IIM-Bangalore	24.99424046	199	12.55992	7
IIT-Bombay	12.549821	108	11.620205	8
ISM Dhanbad	22.64072914	200	11.320365	9
Aligarh Muslim University	22.57797512	200	11.288988	10
JNU Delhi	23.25851768	219	10.620328	11
Delhi University	17.58187207	182	9.6603693	12
Vellore Institute of Technology	18.68877297	200	9.3443865	13
IISc Bangalore	10.99237998	122	9.0101475	14
Osmania University	16.63720433	200	8.3186022	15

Figure 7. Sentiment score per review of Google reviews of each institute

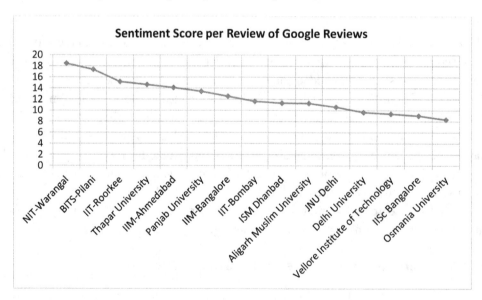

Table 10. Comparing the average length of the reviews with the ranks garnered

Academic Institute	Average Length of Reviews	Ranks According to Sentiment Score per Review
BITS Pilani	68.4466667	2
NIT Warangal	56.57575758	3
IIM-Ahmedabad	55.95986622	9
IIT Roorkee	46.69899666	5
JNU Delhi	43.75	11
Delhi University	42.1566667	13
IISc Bangalore	38.4766667	15
IIT Bombay	35.6066667	14
Vellore Institute of Technology	32.385	10
Thapar University	30.985	6
Osmania University	26.46	12
Aligarh Muslim University	24.345	8
ISM Dhanbad	19.01	7
Panjab Univeristy	17.5	1
IIM-Bangalore	12.70854271	4

at 18.46. BITS-Pilani managed to retain its second position that it had secured when the reviews from all platforms were taken into consideration. The NIRF 2017 PR second ranker IISc-Bangalore still fared lowly managing a rank of 14 out of the 15 academic institutes under study. The graph portraying the SSRs of the academic institutes is shown in Figure 7.

Effect of Average Length of the Reviews on the Sentiment Scores

Now, considering the SSRs computed for all the reviews irrespective of the source of the reviews, the academic institutes were ranked based on the SSRs and their garnered ranks were compared with the average length of their reviews of all the fifteen academic institutes, to see the effect of the lengths of the reviews on the relative ranks of the institutes. The results are given in Table 10. It can be seen from the table while comparing the average length of the reviews with the ranks accorded to the institute based on the sentiment score per review (SSR) that the average length of the reviews does not depend significantly on the sentiment score per review of the institute, as the rank 1 institute, Panjab University has an average length of 17.5 words per review while the rank 2 institute BITS, Pilani has an average length of 68.44 words per review, which is also the highest amongst all the institutes. Similarly the ranks and the average lengths of the reviews do not seem to follow any set pattern.

Table 11. Ranks based on NIRF 2017 versus the sentiment analysis ranks based on the method

Academic Institute	NIRF PR Rank 2017 [From NIRF Overall Ranking 2017]	Relative NIRF PR Ranks 2017	Ranks According to Sentiment Analysis score per Review (SSR)
IIT-Bombay	1	1	14
IISc Bangalore	2	2	15
IIM-Ahmedabad	7	3	9
BITS-Pilani	8	4	2
JNU Delhi	9	5	11
IIM-Bangalore	12	6	4
Vellore Institute of Technology	14	7	10
IIT-Roorkee	15	8	5
Delhi University	16	9	13
Panjab University	36	10	1
Aligarh Muslim University	41	11	8
Thapar University	55	12	6
Osmania University	63	13	12
ISM Dhanbad	97	14	7
NIT-Warangal	106	15	3

Comparison of the NIRF ranks with the ranks based on Sentiment Analysis

The actual NIRF PR in the Overall rankings list of NIRF 2017 is tabulated in Table 11. The NIRF PR ranks of 2017 are taken from this list for the fifteen academic instates under study and their relative ranks are computed with IIT-Bombay topping the rank list and NIT-Warangal at the fifteenth spot. These NIRF PR 2017 ranks were compared with the ranks garnered by the institutes based on their sentiment scores per review (SSR) of all their reviews as in Table 4.11. Panjab University topped the list whereas it had a relative NIRF 2017 rank of being at the 10th place amongst the fifteen academic institutes under study. IIT-Bombay with NIRF 2017 rank 1 stood at the fourteenth place and IISc Bangalore with NIRF 2017 rank 2 stood at the fifteenth place. The results clearly showed that the public perception parameter system adopted by the NIRF rakings does not reflect the public perception as reflected in the reviews about the academic institute posted online by the people.

The reason for the difference between the ranking based on this analysis and NIRF ranking may be due to time lags, change in the public perception. The other reason for the differences may be due to the interpretation of the reviews. The difference between the weightage assigned to different types of sentiments may also be reason for the same.

The results obtained by the sentiment analysis method and the ranking done based on the sentiment score per review of each institute are not consistent with the NIRF rankings 2017. The reason for the same can be understood by the way the 'Perception' parameter works of the NIRF ranking framework. If we tend to focus on the fifth parameter that aimed to perceive the institute involved we can clearly see that the data for perceiving the institute was collected by MHRD by the two methods namely, the online perception system and the online feedback system.

Here we compared the sentiment analysis approach that was used in this research with the approach used by NIRF to get the public perception.

Firstly, the NIRF's Online Perception System was open only for the employers, the peers, and also for the public in general. It was an online perception system that operated for only 23 days, which was too less a time to gauge the actual perception towards any particular academic institute under study. Also the people's perceptions may change over time. In comparison, in this research the reviews that were used ranged several years.

Secondly, although MHRD mentioned in its 2017 annual NIRF ranking report that a large number of individuals had submitted their perceptions online on its online perception system, but it didn't specify the exact number people who participated in that. In this research we collected a total of 3695 reviews.

Thirdly, it is a big possibility that on the online perception system of NIRF the peers of the participating academic institutes could have perceived their own academic institute in a good way so based on this perception parameter the rankings may have been biased or tilted towards a particular institute. Whereas in this research we collected the raw reviews that were posted by the wider range of online users who may or may not have been a part of that institute but who have experienced the good and bad features of the institute. With this we perceived the academic institutes the way the general public perceives them.

Apart from the Online Perception System used by NIRF, another system called the Online Feedback System was used to specifically to get online feedback from the general public. It again had some flaws in it. Firstly, it operated only for ten days starting from 1st February 2017 to 12th February 2017, which is a really short period of time to make a long lasting opinion regarding any academic institute. This research on the other hand collected reviews that ranged over years. Secondly in the Online Perception System used by NIRF, the people were not asked to post a general feedback or a review that was natural but they were asked to give a specified feedback only on the data that was initially pre-submitted by the applicant organizations under study by answering some set questions. Answering some set questions to get the feedback was not as good as looking for feedback pertaining to any or all aspects of the institute, as found in the online reviews that naturally reflect the public opinion that was explored in this *work*, but given the wide range of review websites available online, we needed a method to make sense of these vast available online review data of the Indian academic institutes. This required a method that could automatically analyze the sentiments expressed in those online reviews and thus help the students in making a conscious decision about the choice of institute they should join for further study. This method can efficiently augment and enhance the NIRF rankings and help it in adding to it the real sentiments of the people regarding an academic institute over a longer period of time.

ISSUES AND FUTURE DIRECTIONS

According to an April 2018 poll conducted by Education Times, 73% of the students agreed that the NIRF Rankings would help them choose a particular college or course. Given that the NIRF rankings can sway the public opinion towards a particular academic institute, it must ensure that it strives to take into account all the factors while ranking a particular academic institute. The public perception factor of NIRF was the one that was the most neglected while it was also the most important one. In this chapter an application of sentiment analysis on the online reviews was presented.Aspect based feature extraction can be used for the sentiment classification of reviews and to summarize them based on features like placement, hostel life, academics, extracurricular activities and so on. Some reviews are written on the university review portals in Romanized Hindi. In the future, such reviews can be specifically collected to perform Romanization Transliteration on them and then they can be analyzed to extract their sentiments. This research can be improved upon by inculcating emoticons present in the reviews and the sentiments they express. Further this research also open directions for social science researchers to study the reasons behind differences among the online available public reviews and public perception received for the purposes of NIRF ranking.

CONCLUSION

In this chapter, we discussed various Sentiment Analysis approaches and then applied the same to perform the sentiment analysis of online reviews. This work collected 3695 reviews from online review portals, pertaining to 15 NIRF top 100 ranked academic institutes and performed the sentiment analysis of the reviews using the lexical approach. The method used for the research initially preprocessed the raw reviews by conversion of the review data to lowercase, removing the digits from the data and stripping the punctuation from the reviews. The initial pre-processing of the reviews was followed by the NLTK Pre-processing which included three steps: Tokenization, POS Tagging and Lemmatization of the reviews. After that for performing the sentiment analysis of the reviews, SentiWordNet 3.0 was used as the lexical resource for the research, based upon which the reviews were tagged as 'Pos' or 'Neg' by the method and along with the tagging the sentiment scores of each of the reviews was also computed by the method. These scores were analyzed to get the sentiment score per review of each of the institutes under study. The reviews had also been manually annotated and compared with the ones annotated by the method to check their accuracy- 96.23%. The academic institutes were ranked based on these scores and their ranks were compared with their NIRF ranks. The results showed that the forerunner was Panjab University, followed by BITS-Pilani and NIT-Warangal.

REFERENCES

A Complete Guide to k-Nearest Neighbors with applications in Python and R. (2017). Retrieved from http://www.kevinzakka.github.io/2016/07/13/k-nearest-neighbor/

Adeborna, E., & Siau, K. (2014, July). *An Approach to Sentiment Analysis-the Case of Airline Quality Rating*. PACIS.

Amplayo, R. K., & Song, M. (2017). An adaptable fine-grained sentiment analysis for summarization of multiple short online reviews. *Data & Knowledge Engineering, 110*, 54–67. doi:10.1016/j.datak.2017.03.009

Baccianella, S., Esuli, A., & Sebastiani, F. (2010, May). Sentiwordnet 3.0: an enhanced lexical resource for sentiment analysis and opinion mining. In Lrec (Vol. 10, No. 2010, pp. 2200-2204). Academic Press.

García-Cumbreras, M. Á., Montejo-Ráez, A., & Díaz-Galiano, M. C. (2013). Pessimists and optimists: Improving collaborative filtering through sentiment analysis. *Expert Systems with Applications, 40*(17), 6758–6765. doi:10.1016/j.eswa.2013.06.049

Go, A., Bhayani, R., & Huang, L. (2009). Twitter sentiment classification using distant supervision. CS224N Project Report, 1(12).

Google Trends. (2017, September 20). Retrieved from https://trends.google.com/trends/

Google Trends. (2017, September 27). Retrieved from https://en.wikipedia.org/wiki/Google_Trends

Indeed Reviews. (2017, September). *Reviews from Indeed*. Retrieved from https://www.indeed.co.in/

Introduction to Support Vector Machines. (2017, August 29). Retrieved from http:// www.svms.org/ introduction.html

K-nearest neighbors (k-nn) classification – Intro. (2017, August 29). Retrieved from https:// www.solver. com/k-nearest-neighbors-k-nn-classification-intro

Kaur, N., & Solanki, N. (2018). Sentiment Knowledge Discovery in Twitter Using CoreNLP Library. *8th International Conference on Cloud Computing, Data Science & Engineering (Confluence)*. 10.1109/ CONFLUENCE.2018.8442439

Lau, R. Y., Li, C., & Liao, S. S. (2014). Social analytics: Learning fuzzy product ontologies for aspect-oriented sentiment analysis. *Decision Support Systems*, *65*, 80–94. doi:10.1016/j.dss.2014.05.005

Mäntylä, M. V., Graziotin, D., & Kuutila, M. (2018). The evolution of sentiment analysis—A review of research topics, venues, and top cited papers. *Computer Science Review*, *27*, 16–32. doi:10.1016/j. cosrev.2017.10.002

Miller, G. A., Beckwith, R., Fellbaum, C., Gross, D., & Miller, K. J. (1990). Introduction to WordNet: An on-line lexical database. *International Journal of Lexicography, 3*(4), 235-244.

Multinominal, N. B. (2017, October 20). Retrieved fromhttp://scikitlearn.org/stable/modules/generated/ sklearn.naive_bayes.MultinomialNB.html

Naïve Byes. (2017, August 29). Retrieved from http://www.python-course.eu/naive_byes_classifier_introduction.php

Narayan, D., Chakrabarti, D., Pande, P., & Bhattacharyya, P. (2002, January). *An experience in building the indo wordnet-a wordnet for Hindi*. In *First International Conference on Global WordNet*, Mysore, India.

NIRF Ranking 2018. (2018, April 22). Retrieved from https://www.nirfindia.org/2018/Ranking2018.html

Pak, A., & Paroubek, P. (2010, May). Twitter as a corpus for sentiment analysis and opinion mining. In LREc (Vol. 10, No. 2010, pp. 1320-1326). Academic Press.

Pandey, S., & Solanki, A. (2019). Music Instrument Recognition using Deep Convolutional Neural Networks. International Journal of Information Technology. doi:10.100741870-019-00285-y

Pang, B., Lee, L., & Vaithyanathan, S. (2002, July). Thumbs up?: sentiment classification using machine learning techniques. In *Proceedings of the ACL-02 conference on Empirical methods in natural language processing-Volume 10* (pp. 79-86). Association for Computational Linguistics. 10.3115/1118693.1118704

Parameters. (2017, August 31). Retrieved from https://www.nirfindia.org/Parameter

Reviews from Careers 360. (2017, September). Retrieved from https://www.careers360.com/

Reviews from College Bol. (2017, September). Retrieved from https://www.collegebol.com

Reviews from College Dunia. (2017, September). Retrieved from https://collegeDunia.com/

Reviews from College Search. (2017, September). Retrieved from https://www.collegesearch.in/

Reviews from Get My Uni. (2017, September). Retrieved from https://www.getmyuni.com

Reviews from Glassdoor. (2017, September). Retrieved from https://www.glassdoor.co.in/index.htm

Reviews from Google Reviews. (2017, September). Retrieved from https://www.google.co.in/

Reviews from Mouth Shut. (2017, September). Retrieved from https://www.mouthshut.com

Reviews from Quora. (2017, September). Retrieved from https://www.quora.com

Reviews from Shiksha. (2017, September). Retrieved from https://www.shiksha.com/

Reviews from Youtube. (2017, September). Retrieved from https://www.youtube.com

Salunkhe, P., Surnar, A., & Sonawane, S. (2017). *A Review: Prediction of Election Using Twitter Sentiment Analysis*. Academic Press.

SENTIWORDNET. (2006). *A publicly available lexical resource for opinion mining*. Andrea Esuli and Fabrizio Sebastiani.

Sokolov Aleksey. (2015). *Movie Reviews Sentiment Analysis*. Author.

Tummel, A. A. D. J. C., & Richert, S. J. A. (2015, December). Sentiment Analysis of Social Media for Evaluating Universities. In *The Second International Conference on Digital Information Processing, Data Mining, and Wireless Communications (DIPDMWC2015)* (p. 49). Academic Press.

Uan Sholanbayev. (2016). *Sentiment Analysis on Movie Reviews*. Author.

Venu, S.H., Annie, A.X., & Mohan, V. (2016). *Sentiment Analysis Applied to Airline Feedback to Boost Customer's Endearment*. Academic Press.

Wani, G. P., & Alone, N. V. (2015). Analysis of Indian Election using Twitter. *International Journal of Computer Applications, 121*(22).

Will the NIRF ranking help students choice of courses & colleges? (2018 May 1). Retrieved from http://www.educationtimes.com/article/93/2018041120180411122852781d9010d4f/Will the-NIRF-ranking-help-students-choice-of-coursescollege.html

Yuan, P., Zhong, Y., & Huang, J. (2015). *Sentiment Classification and Opinion Mining on Airline Reviews*. Academic Press.

Chapter 2
Machine Learning in Higher Education:
Predicting Student Attrition Status Using Educational Data Mining

Garima Jaiswal

Indira Gandhi Delhi Technical University for Women, India

Arun Sharma

Indira Gandhi Delhi Technical University for Women, India

Reeti Sarup

Indira Gandhi Delhi Technical University for Women, India

ABSTRACT

Machine learning aims to give computers the ability to automatically learn from data. It can enable computers to make intelligent decisions by recognizing complex patterns from data. Through data mining, humongous amounts of data can be explored and analyzed to extract useful information and find interesting patterns. Classification, a supervised learning technique, can be beneficial in predicting class labels for test data by referring the already labeled classes from available training data set. In this chapter, educational data mining techniques are applied over a student dataset to analyze the multifarious factors causing alarmingly high number of dropouts. This work focuses on predicting students at risk of dropping out using five classification algorithms, namely, K-NN, naive Bayes, decision tree, random forest, and support vector machine. This can assist in improving pedagogical practices in order to enhance the performance of students predicted at risk of dropping out, thus reducing the dropout rates in higher education.

DOI: 10.4018/978-1-5225-9643-1.ch002

INTRODUCTION

In the current information age, there has been an incredible increase in the scope of information technology in solving real-world complex problems. However, along with the establishment of this constantly evolving industrial era, the world also generates humongous volumes of data. Advancements in database management systems have assisted in better storage of data but there is also a dire need of knowledge discovery to be able to analyze and gain useful insights into this vast data for taking wise decisions. It is very cumbersome and inefficient to manually analyze such enormous amounts of data. Thus, data mining can be used to explore the vast volumes of data to discover useful patterns and to draw inferences. In a quest to model intelligent machines which can take rational decisions on their own, the field of artificial intelligence was coined. The discipline of machine learning enables computers to automatically learn from experience. It improves its performance with data and helps in recognizing insightful patterns which further help in making intelligent decisions.

In the education domain, it is vital to understand and interpret the patterns of alarmingly high dropout rates in higher education and their underlying reasons. By utilizing the ability of machine learning, the various factors causing dropouts in higher education can be detected. The results achieved by applying machine learning techniques can further be used to assist in improving student performance thus reducing dropout rates. This chapter elucidates the application of machine learning in education domain to extract and study valuable intricate patterns of the chief factors triggering the high dropout rates in higher education institutes. Various related works as well as the results of the five applied supervised learning techniques, namely, K-NN, Naïve Bayes, Decision Tree, Random Forest and SVM, are discussed and compared in depth in this chapter. Identifying the major factors causing dropout and enhancing the pedagogical practices to overcome them can save time, money and resources of both the student as well as the higher education institutes.

BACKGROUND

Student Attrition in Higher Education

The statistics reported by Ministry of Human Resource Development, Department of School Education & Literacy, New Delhi showed that the percentage enrollment in Engineering & Technology in 2015-16 in India was 15.57%while the percentage of pass out in Engineering & Technology in 2015-16 in India was 13.42% (Ministry of Human Resource Development, 2018). This indicates that the number of students graduating or completing their higher educational studies is getting alarmingly lesser as compared to the number of initial enrollments. The problem of student attrition in higher education is of great concern and it may even discourage the incoming prospective candidates from pursuing higher education courses. When a student leaves a higher education program after getting enrolled, it causes loss of seat, money and time for both the institute and the student. Thus, it is essential to identify the impact of various factors such as parent income, previous scores, gender, demographic details etc. to assist in improving the student's performance. By building a model to predict and assist the students at risk of dropping out, the student retention rates can be improved in higher education programs.

Machine Learning

A widely used definition of machine learning was given by (Mitchell, 2006): "A machine is said to learn from experience E, with respect to some class of tasks T and performance measure P if its performance at tasks in T as measured by P improves with experience E".

Instead of programming the computer to perform a specific set of tasks, machine learning aims at improving the ability of computers to automatically learn from available data and then make useful predictions for unseen new data. The foremost step for creating a machine learning model is collection of a sufficiently large volume of data followed by data preprocessing and feature engineering. Identifying a suitable set of attributes or features is crucial for building a predictive machine learning model.

Though an increase in number of features or dimensions initially improves the performance of machine learning model, however, a further increase in dimensions beyond an optimal number while keeping the training dataset size as constant will generally tend to degradation in performance. Various dimensional reduction techniques such as Principal Component Analysis (PCA) can be used to reduce this curse of dimensionality.

Machine learning can be categorized further into various types. In supervised learning, the model trains over a training set consisting of examples with pre-defined labels which further help in predicting the labels for unseen testing data. Regression and classification are supervised techniques. On the other hand, unsupervised learning does not consist of pre-defined classes or labels. Clustering is an unsupervised learning technique which focuses on grouping parts of data together based on some similarity measures.

An intermediate technique which is provided with partly labeled and partly unlabeled data is known as semi-supervised learning. In addition to these categories, the technique which helps models to learn by working on the principle of feedback in the form of rewards and punishments is known as reinforcement learning.

Applications of Machine Learning

Abundant applications of machine learning strive to simplify and increase productivity of several tasks. From the automatic categorization of an email as spam or not to the voice assistants which can set alarms, navigate through lesser traffic routes or answer the various queries, machine learning applications can be found ubiquitously.

Machine learning algorithms can be used in business intelligence systems to build models which enable computers to extract useful trends and make predictions by exploring and analyzing the available data. Hence, the application of machine learning is widely gaining popularity in various real-life use-cases. For instance, in medical research, the probability of various factors causing a disease can be predicted by applying supervised learning techniques on the available data of current and past patients. The demand and quality for a product can also be analyzed and improved by studying the sentiments of its customer reviews. Ranging from product recommendation systems to handwritten character recognition system and speech to text conversion software, the impact of machine learning is rapidly growing in a large range of applications across a gamut of domains in order to analyze data and make intelligent predictions based on data.

The statistical-computation based field of machine learning can also be used for image processing, computer vision and robotics. By implementing identification systems such as face detection systems, machine learning can also be used for building highly secure features. Many businesses aim to increase

Figure 1. Applications of machine learning

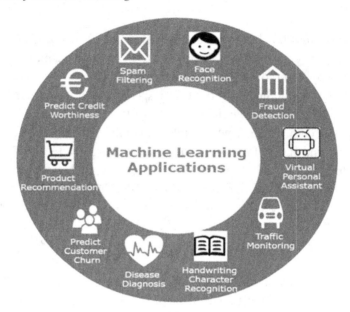

the customer satisfaction for their products by discovering intricate patterns in their customer data. Some major real-world applications of machine learning are depicted in Figure 1.

Machine Learning Applied in Higher Education

Progressing further, machine learning can be utilized similarly in the higher education domain to analyze dataset of students enrolled in a university and then make insightful predictions. It can predict useful trends to improve performance of students as well as reduce the factors of human errors and biases. Since the domain of education still depends on a lot of human dependent tasks, it can be worthwhile to unleash the power of machine learning to enhance the learning and teaching methodologies.

After collection of data, it has to be cleaned by removing noisy and irrelevant data. Data pre-processing is a vital step. Exploratory data analysis for univariate and multivariate analysis can be performed to visualize the available data graphically in form of box plots, bar graphs, pie charts etc. Supervised learning techniques such as classification algorithms can be beneficial in predicting class labels for test data by referring the already labeled classes from available training data set. Various challenges in the current education domain can be solved by providing optimized solutions through application of machine learning techniques on student data. For instance, by applying classification algorithms on the annotated dataset, the rate of dropouts can be predicted and the main factors causing a dropout can be inferred. It can also automate the prediction of final grades of students while customizing learning technologies in order to improve the performance of students. The performance of several classification algorithms can be compared on the student dataset by building the confusion matrix and evaluating each of them on numerous performance metrics such as: Accuracy, Specificity, Recall (Sensitivity), Precision, F1 Score.

Various factors such as scores in various subjects, demographic details, parent's education, early marriage in case of girls, number of study hours etc. can be analyzed for predicting trends such as dropout rates, percentage of students scoring above a threshold score etc. Such an analysis and prediction can facilitate further development of the education system by reforming the pedagogy techniques to provide an enriching learning experience to the students. Since the domain of education is known to produce professionals in almost all domains, it is essential to analyze the hidden trends in the data of students enrolled in universities. Machine learning can aid in revealing the most significant factors which can be controlled to reduce dropout rates and enhance the performance of students.

Hence, as exploration into the field of machine learning continues to expand, the data-intensive domain of education possesses a potential to use optimized learning methodologies by discovering hidden interesting patterns and using predictive machine learning models. The pedagogy practices of education domain can be reformed by automatically learning from experience.

Related Work

(Marquez-Vera, Morales,& Soto, 2013)used various educational data mining techniques such as rule-based classification and decision trees over a dataset for 670 middle school students of Zacatccas, Mexico. To induce rules for predicting failure or non-failure of a student, they considered marks in different subjects as an important factor apart from social, economic and cultural features. Also, since the dataset may contain a much larger proportion of passing students as compared to failed or dropout students, so rebalancing the data and applying cost-sensitive classification helps in improving accuracy of prediction model. The students predicted at risk of failure can then be helped and tutored to improve their performance and prevent failure.

Naive Bayes and Decision tree classifiers were used by (Guarin, Guzman,& Gonzalez, 2015) to predict risk of dropping out applied over two study programs in Colombia. Since the cost of misclassifying a student at risk of failure is higher than misclassifying a student not at risk of failure, so appropriate cost sensitive technique using metaCost algorithm was applied. Best results showed when the previous academic grades were also considered apart from the initial enrollment information and socio-demographic attributes.

Frequent patterns were identified using Apriori algorithm in the research work done by (Angeline, 2013). Thus, association rules were generated for a student dataset consisting of external assessment marks and several internal evaluation metrics including class and lab tests, assignment grades, attendance, extra-curricular scores etc. Student's performance can be improved after predicting it as poor, average or good based on the minimal strong rules generated from the data. The 127 generated rules achieved 100% confidence value and 38.095% support.

(Quadri & Kalyankar, 2010) used a hybrid model consisting of decision tree and logistic regression. A decision tree is built for identifying the major factors leading to a dropout or not. Attributes such as parent income, first child etc. showed higher impact on the dropout feature. Based on these influencing factors as input, the probability of a dropout was then predicted by applying logistic regression.

R-KM is a soft subspace variant of K-Means clustering which was applied by (Iam-On & Boongoen, 2017) over the student database of Mae Fah Luang University. First, the prior academic information, socio-demographic factor and enrollment data were used to predict attrition of students in their first year of enrollment into the university which assisted in suggesting suitable study areas to pursue. Next, the first year academic information was used to form clusters for predicting students at risk of dropping out in their later years of enrollment at university. Results showed that students who previously had good school grades continued to perform well in university and had lower risk of dropout.

Radial Basis Function Network was implemented by (Arora, Singhal, & Bansal, 2014). The output of this network was a linear value which denoted the predicted marks for a target subject. The inputs comprised of marks of those previous semester subjects which are related to the target subject. Performance in related previous semester subjects can affect the performance in target subject, the predicted student performance is categorized as excellent, good, average or poor. By forecasting students' performance, a relevant warning was issued to those students who need to improve their performance in current semester.

An incremental approach was proposed by (Sanchez-Santillan, Paule-Ruiz, Cerezo, & Nunez, 2016) as a more efficient and accurate technique for building predictive classifier models as compared to the lesser accurate traditional total-interaction classifiers. Towards this end, a training course was prepared by dividing it into 11 blocks where each block was evaluated on metrics based on reading the lesson, completing quiz and participating in forum. The accuracy of three algorithms: classification rules, decision tree and Bayesian Network respectively was computed for each incremental block and compared with the total-interaction value obtained in the last block.

(Sri & Muthuramalingam, 2016) proposed threshold-based assessment strategy to analyze and improve performance of students. First, formative assessment was discussed which consisted of continuous evaluation which helps to assist at-risk students at an earlier stage. Next, in summative assessment, the terminal assessment grades were considered. Results illustrated that attendance in lectures is directly proportional to academic performance. The medium of study (English or Tamil) also acts as an influencing factor for performance of students especially in rural regions where communication skills need to be improved.

A simple genetic algorithm and its variant namely Controlled Elitist NSGA-II are applied over the educational dataset of FSKTM, University of Malaya, Kuala Lumpur, Malaysia. (Sheng et al., 2016) proposed an academic planner which stores previous academic records of students and assisted them to achieve a target CGPA (Cumulative Grade Point Average) higher than the current CGPA. It tracked academic performance and used genetic algorithm to recommend various personalized course combinations to each student in order to achieve the target CGPA.

(Almayan & Mayyan, 2016) collected academic, socio-emotional, demographic data through questionnaires and school reports from two schools in Portugal. To predict the academic performance of students as Pass or Fail, the dataset consisted of 33 features which were reduced using dimensional reduction techniques such as Information Gain Ratio attribute evaluation (IGR), Correlation based feature selection (CFS), Symmetrical Uncertainty (SU) and Particle Swarm Optimization Algorithm (PSO). The reduced feature space was then used as input for five classifiers namely feed-forward ANN with MLP, Simple Logistic multinomial logistic model, Rotation Forest, Random Forest ensemble learning technique and decision tree. The accuracy of classifiers for predicting student performance improved with the proposed feature reduction step using PSO.

(De la Pena et al., 2017) focused on assisting e-learning environments using machine learning. The academic scores obtained in various activities were used as attributes in the student dataset extracted from Moodle, an online educational platform. Logistic regression was applied over the academic dataset to predict whether a student will dropout from the course or not. On comparing with other conventional machine learning techniques, logistic regression gave results with higher precision and accuracy.

California State University's academic data for past ten years of enrollment in introductory computer science courses was considered as it experienced high student attrition rates. The progress pattern of students was observed and compared in different computer science courses by (Raigoza, 2017). The work considered those students who were transferred or repeated the courses, passed the courses, failed or dropped out. It helped in predicting the successful graduation chances of students in computer science courses and the estimated degree completion time.

(Roy & Garg, 2017) applied three classification techniques namely Naive Bayes, Decision Tree and MLP using WEKA tool was implemented on educational dataset available at UCI machine learning repository. Previous academic scores, demographic and social factors were considered. Attributes such as parents' qualification level, alcohol consumption etc. were shown to have impact on student's academic performance. From the three classifiers, J48 Decision Tree produced the best results with 73.92% accuracy.

The factors which caused a lower graduation rate in postgraduate programs at a South African higher educational institute despite of an increasing growth in its enrollment rate were analyzed by (Marnewick & Pretorius, 2016). Research portion of the program showed lower performance of students as compared to the lectured units. The various challenges which influenced the successful completion of Engineering Management program were time management, cognitive skills, employment, language barrier and health issues. It was shown that improvement in time management can improve the performance thus leading to successful and timely graduation.

The goal of (Kori, Pedaste, Altin, Tonisson, & Palts, 2016) was to identify the major factors which encouraged the students to pursue Information Technology. The data of 301 students who pursued Information Technology (IT) in Estonia was analyzed. Questionnaires were used to understand the motivating factors for various students who choose IT at beginning of first semester as well as to pursue it after completion of first semester. Factor analysis was performed using principal axis factoring. Factors such as personal development, previous interest in IT, growth opportunities in the reputed field of IT etc. were found to be common motivating factors in students who choose and pursue Information Technology in Estonia.

An intelligent web application system was built by (Devasia, Vinushree, & Hegde, 2016) using Naive Bayes classifier. The system stored previous academic records of students and predicted end-semester examination performance. The data consisted of 700 students of Amrita School of Arts and Sciences, Mysuru. Various attributes such as previous academic scores, gender, income level, parents' education etc. were considered while computing the probabilities in Naive Bayesian classifier. The predicted student performance can be used to provide special assistance and tutoring to students thus reducing failure rate.

(Ktoridou & Epaminonda, 2014) used Holland personalities hexagon to depict the six characteristic personalities: Realistic, Investigative, Artistic, Social, Conventional and Enterprising. They proposed that a student pursuing a major subject which matches his/her personality can lead to better performance and lesser dropout risk.

(Jaiswal, Sharma, & Yadav, 2019) performed a literature survey for predicting dropouts in higher education using machine learning techniques. They stated that freshman students mainly dropout during the starting of the higher studies. They considered the various factors and categorized them in five different categories. Various measures were listed to prevent dropouts.

A project was conducted by (Sanz, Virseda, Garcia, & Arias, 2018) with some students at Spain's National Distance University (UNED). In the project, they applied their proposed effective educational model which integrated technology along with motivating teaching methodologies and continuous evaluations to mentors. Information and communications technology (ICT) was utilized to provide online academic support especially in distance education courses.

A blended learning environment was proposed by (Pardo, Han, & Ellis, 2017) where self-regulated factors were combined with digital learning methods. A study was performed with 145 students who participated in survey to recognize self-regulated behavior like intrinsic motivation, positive or negative self-regulated strategy and self-efficacy. Online learning platform consisted of video lectures, assignments and exercises to be answered. Initially, exploratory factor analysis and principal component analysis were performed to identify most influencing factors for academic performance. Clustering segregates data into groups of students with similar attributes. Multiple regression models were built to show effect of features on academic performance. It was found that students with high performance generally have a more positive self-regulated strategy as compared to the lower performance students.

The major objectives and techniques of the aforementioned related works on prediction of student dropout and educational data mining are summarized in Table 1.

PROPOSED METHODOLOGY FOR STUDENT DROPOUT PREDICTION USING MACHINE LEARNING

Data Description and Features Used

Data is collected for 261 students enrolled in an undergraduate engineering program. The null fields of marks for dropout students have been substituted with 0. Data preprocessing includes encoding of categorical variables and normalization of data. The 19 attributes in the dataset include the following:

1. **Roll No.:** A unique identifier for each student
2. **Gender:** Male/Female
3. **Actual Category:** GEN/OBC/ST/SC
4. **12th Board:** CBSE/ICSE/State Board
5. **12th Agg.%:** Aggregate percentage scored in class 12
6. **12th PCM %:** Cumulative percentage scored in physics, chemistry, math in class 12
7. **Year of Passing 12th:** Year of graduating from class 12
8. **10th %:** Aggregate percentage scored in class 10
9. **First Year Marks:** Percentage scored in first year of engineering
10. **Second Year Marks:** Percentage scored in second year of engineering
11. **Third Year Marks:** Percentage scored in third year of engineering
12. **Fourth Year Marks:** Percentage scored in fourth year of engineering
13. **Marks Obtained:** Cumulative percentage scored in engineering
14. **Placement:** Status of placement, 1 (Placed) or 0 (Not placed)
15. **Higher Studies:** 1 if student enrolled in further higher studies, else 0
16. **No. of Carry Over:** Number of subjects failed
17. **Annual Income:** Annual Income of parents
18. **Parent Occupation:** Father's occupation(Govt. Service/ Private Job/ Business/ Agriculture)
19. **Dropout:** The target class to be predicted, 1 (Dropout) or 0 (Graduated and not dropout)

Data Cleaning and Pre-Processing

Pre-processing and cleaning of data consisted of substituting null value fields with 0 as well as removing features like Roll No. which are not important in classification since each student has a unique Roll No. Also, to apply machine learning models on the data, the values of categorical variables such as Gender,

Table 1. Tabular summary and comparison of related works

Author	Research Area	Features Used	Techniques Used	Results
(Marquez-Vera, Morales,& Soto, 2013)	Predicted failure or non-failure of a student in school	Social, economic and cultural features; Marks in different subjects	Rule-based classification and Decision trees	Marks in different subjects are an important factor in predicting risk of failure.
(Guarin, Guzman,& Gonzalez, 2015)	Predicted risk of dropping out in university	Initial enrollment information and socio-demographic attributes; Previous academic grades	Naive Bayes and Decision tree classifiers along with MetaCost algorithm	Best results showed when the previous academic grades were considered.
(Angeline, 2013)	Predicted student's performance as poor, average or good based on the minimal strong rules generated from the data.	External assessment marks and several internal evaluation metrics including class and lab tests, assignment grades, attendance, extra-curricular scores etc.	Frequent patterns are identified using Apriori algorithm	The 127 generated rules achieved 100% confidence value and 38.095% support.
(Quadri& Kalyankar,2010)	Identified the major factors leading to a dropout or not.	Socio-demographic attributes such as parent income, first child etc.	Hybrid model consisting of decision tree and logistic regression	Attributes such as parent income, first child etc. have shown to cause high impact on the dropout feature.
(Iam-On & Boongoen,2017)	Predicted attrition of students in their first year of enrollment into the university and later years of enrollment at university.	Prior academic information, socio-demographic factor and enrollment data. Next, the first year academic information is used to form clusters for predicting students at risk of dropping out later.	R-KM: a soft subspace variant of K-Means clustering	Students who previously had good school grades continued to perform well in university and also had lower risk of dropout
(Arora, Singhal, & Bansal, 2014)	Categorized student's predicted performance as excellent, good, average or poor.	Marks of those previous semester subjects which are related to the target subject.	Radial Basis Function Network	The output of this network is a linear value denoting the predicted marks for a target subject.
(Sanchez-Santillan, Paule-Ruiz, Cerezo, & Nunez, 2016)	Proposed incremental approach as a more efficient and accurate technique for building predictive classifier models as compared to traditional total-interaction classifiers.	A training course was prepared by dividing it into 11 blocks where each block is evaluated on metrics based on reading the lesson, completing quiz and participating in forum.	Classification rules, Decision tree and Bayesian Network	Accuracy for each incremental block was compared with the total-interaction value obtained in the last block.
(Sri & Muthuramalingam, 2016)	Analyze and improve student's performance.	Formative assessment consisted of continuous evaluation while summative assessment considered the terminal assessment grades.	Proposed threshold-based assessment strategy	Attendance in lectures is shown to be directly proportional to academic performance. Medium of study (English or Tamil) also acts as an influencing factor especially in rural regions.
(Sheng, Mustafa, Alam, Hamid, Sani,& Gani, 2016)	Assisted in achieving a target CGPA (Cumulative Grade Point Average) higher than the current CGPA	Previous academic records of students	Genetic algorithm and its variant namely Controlled Elitist NSGA-II	Recommended personalized course combinations to achieve the target CGPA.
(Almayan & Mayyan, 2016)	Predicted the academic performance of a student as Pass or Fail	Academic, socio-emotional, demographic data collected through questionnaires and school reports	Feed-forward ANN with MLP, Simple Logistic multinomial logistic model, Rotation Forest, Random Forest Ensemble learning technique and Decision tree.	Accuracy of classifiers was shown to improve with the proposed feature reduction step using Particle Swarm Optimization Algorithm (PSO)
(De la Pena et al., 2017)	Assisting e-learning environments in tutoring students by analyzing their performance and identifying their risk of dropout.	Academic scores obtained in various activities are used as attributes in the student dataset extracted from Moodle, an online educational platform	Logistic regression applied to predict whether a student will dropout from the course or not.	On comparing with other conventional machine learning techniques, logistic regression gave results with higher precision and accuracy.
(Raigoza, 2017)	Predicted the successful graduation chances of students in computer science courses	Academic data of ten years of enrollment in introductory computer science courses. It considered students who were transferred or repeated the courses, passed the courses, failed or dropped out.	Progress pattern of students was observed and compared in different computer science courses.	Predicted the estimated degree completion time.
(Roy & Garg, 2017)	Predicted student's academic performance	Previous academic scores, demographic and social factors were considered. Attributes such as parents' qualification level, alcohol consumption etc. were shown to have impact on student's academic performance.	Naive Bayes, Decision Tree and MLP using WEKA tool.	J48 Decision Tree produced the best results with 73.92% accuracy.

continued on following page

Table 1. Continued

Author	Research Area	Features Used	Techniques Used	Results
(Marnewick & Pretorius, 2016)	Recognized factors causing a lower graduation rate in postgraduate programs at a South African higher educational institute	Time management, cognitive skills, employment, language barrier and health issues	Analysis of various influencing factors in research and lectured units	Research portion of the program showed lower performance of students as compared to the lectured units.
(Kori, Pedaste, Altin, Tonisson,& Palts, 2016)	Identified the major factors which encouraged students to pursue Information Technology	Questionnaires were used to understand the motivating factors for various students to choose and pursue IT.	Factor analysis was performed using principal axis factoring. Mann-Whitney U-test and paired sample T-test were also conducted.	Factors such as personal development, previous interest in IT, growth opportunities in the reputed field of IT etc. were found to be common motivating factors in students who pursued Information Technology in Estonia.
(Devasia, Vinushree,& Hegde, 2016)	Predicted end-semester examination performance.	Previous academic scores, gender, income level, parents education etc.	Naive Bayes classifier	Built an intelligent web application system
(Ktoridou & Epaminonda, 2014)	Measured compatibility between major of study and engineering students' personality types	Personalities of students at five universities in Cyprus were identified through questionnaires and matched with the major subject they were pursuing.	Holland personalities hexagon to depict the six characteristic personalities: Realistic, Investigative, Artistic, Social, Conventional and Enterprising.	The lower the computed value, the more suitable is the major subject with the personality. For instance, most successful engineering major students were found to possess investigative personalities.
(Sanz, Virseda, Garcia, & Arias, 2018)	Proposed effective educational model which integrates technology along with motivating teaching methodologies and continuous evaluations to mentor and assess students.	Analysis consisted of a pre-survey which consisted of expectations of participants before the beginning of the project.	Expectations were matched with the post-project evaluations.	Participants of this project were instilled with greater confidence to pass the exams as they found this educational model to be supportive, engaging and motivating.
(Pardo, Han,& Ellis, 2017)	Proposed use of blended learning environment where self-regulated factors were combined with digital learning.	Survey to recognize self-regulated behavior like intrinsic motivation, positive or negative self-regulated strategy and self-efficacy. Online learning platform consisted of video lectures, assignments and exercises to be answered.	Exploratory factor analysis and principal component analysis were performed. Pairwise correlation analysis of variables was observed. Clustering segregated data into groups of students with similar attributes. Lastly, multiple regression models were built.	It was found that higher performance students generally have a more positive self-regulated strategy as compared to the lower performance students.

Figure 2. Correlation matrix

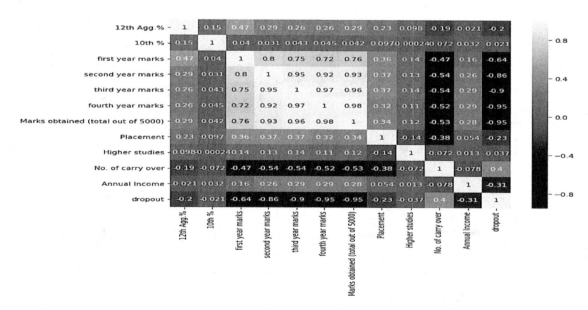

Figure 3. Proposed methodology

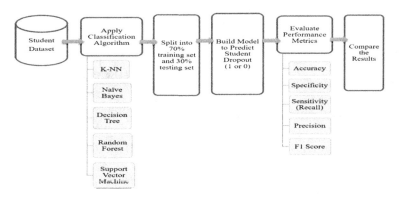

Actual Category etc. are converted to numeric values using label encoding provided by scikit-learn library in Python.

Instead of using label encoding of values in a categorical attribute, one-hot encoding can also be done to split the categorical attribute into multiple columns with binary numeric values (0 or 1). Though accuracy is known to improve with one-hot encoding, it may lead to an increased dimensionality.

Exploratory Data Analysis through Correlation Matrix

Data cleaning and pre-processing is followed by exploratory data analysis for better understanding of the distribution of data in various attributes. Correlation values in the range [-1, +1] are also computed between some attributes as shown in the correlation matrix in Figure 2.

Positively correlated features tend to have correlation values approaching 1 while negatively correlated features tend to have correlation values near -1. Attributes which have no or minimal correlation with each other have values near 0. For instance, 'No. of carry over' and 'first year marks' show negative correlation (-0.47). It signifies that an increase in marks scored in first year is associated with a decrease in the number of subjects failed and vice-versa. On the other hand, '12th Aggregate percentage' and 'first year marks' exhibit positive correlation (0.47) which denotes that a student who scores good in class 12 generally tends to score well in first year of higher education also and vice-versa.

Machine Learning Techniques Applied

Progressing further, five classification algorithms, namely K-NN, Naive Bayes, Decision Tree, Random Forest and Support Vector Machine were applied over higher education student data to predict student attrition or dropout status. As depicted in Figure 3, each classifier is trained on 70% of the dataset while the remaining 30% of data is used as testing data.

Table 2. Confusion matrix

		Predicted Classes		
		Dropout	*Non-Dropout*	*TOTAL*
Actual Classes	*Dropout*	**TP** (True Positives)	**FN** (False Negatives)	*P*
	Non-Dropout	**FP** (False Positives)	**TN** (True Negatives)	*N*
	TOTAL	*P'*	*N'*	*P + N*

K-Nearest Neighbors

K-Nearest Neighbors (K-NN) classification algorithm uses the principle of majority and closeness. It assigns that class label to the test data which occurs the maximum number of times among its k number of closest neighbors in training data. The closeness can be measured through measures like Euclidean distance.

Naive Bayes

Naïve Bayes is a probability-based classification algorithm. It applies Bayes Theorem with the naive assumption of class conditional independence for simpler computations. However, the results may vary because in reality, dependencies can exist between attributes of a dataset.

Decision Tree

Decision Tree classifies the data by creating a tree structure where the internal nodes are the decision nodes which contain the attributes according to which the data is split. The branches define the outcomes of the decision nodes while the terminal nodes contain the predicted classes. Here, decision tree has been implemented considering entropy and information gain.

Random Forest

Random Forest is an ensemble technique that generates many decision trees and combines them to build a more realistic and accurate model. It can be used for classification as well as regression. Using scikit-learn in python, Random Forest can be used to list the relative importance of the features in classifying the target attribute. In this work, a group of 100 decision trees is used in random forest to give a better result. Since the student dropout data is class-imbalanced, so the class_ weight parameter is defined as balanced in Random Forest.

Support Vector Machine

Support Vector Machine (SVM) is a classification technique which uses the concept of a hyperplane to segregate the records of one class from another. It can non-linearly map the existing training set to a higher dimension such that the classes can be split into different sets by a hyperplane. In this research work,SVM model uses radial bias function kernel. In scikit-learn library of Python, it provides the class_weight parameter which can be used to handle class imbalance in data. Cost sensitive classification can thus be used by assigning higher class_weight value to the target minority class to be predicted.

Evaluating Performance Metrics using Confusion Matrix

Since we have to predict dropout using classification, so, let the positive class be 1 (dropout) and negative class be 0 (non-dropout). It is a binary classification as the predicted class will be either 1 or 0. True Positives (TP) is the number of actual positive classes predicted correctly as positive. True Negatives (TN) is the number of actual negative classes predicted correctly as negative. False Positives (FP) is the number of actual negative classes predicted incorrectly as positive. Similarly, the number of actual positive classes predicted incorrectly as negative is represented by False Negatives (FN).

TP, TN, FP and FN can be represented in a 2-column, 2-row tabular arrangement known as confusion matrix where TP and TN are represented on the main diagonal. Using the confusion matrix as shown in Table 2, further metrics can be derived. For instance, Accuracy is the number of correct predictions made by the model out of the total number of predictions.

Precision represents the number of instances that were correctly predicted as positive (TP) out of the total number of instances predicted as positive (TP + FP). Whereas, Recall (also known as Sensitivity) represents the number of instances predicted correctly as positive (TP) out of the total actual positive instances (TP + FN). On the other hand, Specificity represents the number of instances predicted correctly as negative (TN) out of the total actual negative instances (TN + FP). A metric which combines both precision and recall by considering their harmonic mean is known as F1-Score (or F-Score or F-Measure).

$$Accuracy = \frac{TP + TN}{P + N} = \frac{TP + TN}{(TP + FN) + (FP + TN)} \#(1).$$

$$Precision = \frac{TP}{TP + FP} \#(2).$$

$$Recall\,(Sensitivity) = \frac{TP}{TP + FN} \#(3).$$

$$Specificity = \frac{TN}{TN + FP} \#(4).$$

Table 3. Performance evaluation metrics for supervised learning techniques

	Features	Technique	Accuracy	Specificity	Sensitivity (Recall)	Precision	F1 Score
1.	• Gender, • Actual Category, • 12th Board, • 12th Agg.%, • 12th PCM %, • Year of Passing12th, • 10th%	K-NN	94.94%	100%	50%	100%	66.67%
		Naive Bayes	36.71%	32.39%	75%	11.11%	19.35%
		Decision Tree	96.20%	98.67%	50%	66.67%	57.14%
		Random Forest	96.20%	100%	62.5%	100%	76.92%
		Support Vector Machine	27.85%	19.72%	100%	12.31%	21.92%
2.	• 12th Board, • 12th Agg.%, • 12th PCM %, • Year of Passing12th, • 10th%	K-NN	94.94%	100%	50%	100%	66.67%
		Naive Bayes	25.32%	19.72%	75%	9.5%	16.90%
		Decision Tree	96.20%	98.67%	50%	66.67%	57.14%
		Random Forest	96.20%	100%	62.5%	100%	76.92%
		Support Vector Machine	10.13%	0%	100%	10.13%	18.39%
3.	• Gender, • Actual Category, • 12th Board, • 12th Agg.%, • 12th PCM %, • Year of Passing12th, • 10th%, • First year marks	K-NN	94.94%	100%	50%	100%	66.67%
		Naive Bayes	59.49%	57.74%	75%	16.67%	27.27%
		Decision Tree	97.47%	98.67%	75%	75%	75%
		Random Forest	96.20%	98.59%	75%	85.71%	80%
		Support Vector Machine	78.48%	77.46%	87.5%	30.43%	45.16%
4.	• Gender, • Actual Category, • 12th Board, • 12th Agg.%, • 12th PCM %, • Year of Passing12th, • 10th%, • First year marks, • Second year marks	K-NN	96.20%	100%	62.5%	100%	76.92%
		Naive Bayes	94.94%	98.59%	62.5%	83.33%	71.42%
		Decision Tree	97.47%	100%	50%	100%	66.67%
		Random Forest	97.47%	100%	75%	100%	85.71%
		Support Vector Machine	93.67%	95.77%	75%	66.67%	70.59%
5.	• First year marks, • Second year marks, • Third year marks, • Fourth yearmarks, • Marks Obtained	K-NN	98.73%	100%	87.5%	100%	93.33%
		Naive Bayes	98.73%	100%	87.5%	100%	93.33%
		Decision Tree	98.73%	100%	75%	100%	85.71%
		Random Forest	97.47%	100%	75%	100%	85.71%
		Support Vector Machine	98.73%	98.59%	100%	88.89%	94.12%
6.	• Marks Obtained, • Placement, • Higher studies, • No. of carry over, • Annual Income, • Parent Occupation	K-NN	98.73%	100%	87.5%	100%	93.33%
		Naive Bayes	98.73%	100%	87.5%	100%	93.33%
		Decision Tree	100%	100%	100%	100%	100%
		Random Forest	98.73%	100%	87.5%	100%	93.33%
		Support Vector Machine	100%	100%	100%	100%	100%

continued on following page

Table 3. Continued

	Features	Technique	Accuracy	Specificity	Sensitivity (Recall)	Precision	F1 Score
7.	• No. of carry over, • Annual Income, • Parent Occupation	K-NN	93.67%	100%	37.5%	100%	54.54%
		Naive Bayes	94.94%	98.59%	62.5%	83.33%	71.42%
		Decision Tree	97.47%	100%	50%	100%	66.67%
		Random Forest	91.14%	98.59%	25%	66.67%	36.36%
		Support Vector Machine	79.75%	81.69%	62.5%	27.78%	38.46%
8.	• Gender, • Actual Category, • 12th Board, • 12th Agg.%, • 12th PCM % • Year of Passing12th, • 10th%, • First year marks, • Second year marks, • Third year marks, • Fourth yearmarks, • Marks Obtained, • Placement, • Higher studies, • No. of carry over, • Annual Income, • Parent Occupation	K-NN	97.47%	100%	75%	100%	85.71%
		Naive Bayes	98.73%	100%	87.5%	100%	93.33%
		Decision Tree	97.47%	98.67%	75%	75%	75%
		Random Forest	98.73%	100%	87.5%	100%	93.33%
		Support Vector Machine	96.20%	97.18%	87.5%	77.78%	82.35%

$$F1Score = \frac{2}{\dfrac{1}{Precision} + \dfrac{1}{Recall}} = 2 * \frac{Precision * Recall}{Precision + Recall} \#(5)$$

Thus, after applying the supervised learning techniques to build model for predicting student dropout status (1 for dropout or 0 for non-dropout), the performance of classifiers is evaluated and compared based on the metrics: Accuracy, Specificity, Sensitivity (also called Recall), Precision and F1-Score. Since the dropout dataset consists of larger number of negative class (0) instances (non-dropout) as compared to positive class 1 instances (dropout), so metrics such as precision and recall are better evaluators of performance than accuracy for class-imbalanced data.

RESULTS

The performance of five classifiers namely K-NN, Naïve Bayes, Decision Tree, Random Forest and Support Vector Machine is compared in Table 3 over eight different feature subsets from the higher education student dataset for predicting dropout status. Performance of these supervised learning techniques is evaluated using five metrics: Accuracy, Specificity, Sensitivity (Recall), Precision and F1-Score.

DISCUSSION

i) Since it is a class-imbalanced data, thus precision and recall are better indicators of classifier performance as compared to accuracy for predicting student dropout. The high values of accuracy may be caused due to overfitting on class-imbalanced data.

ii) There are techniques to convert class-imbalanced data to balanced dataset using upsampling or downsampling.

    a. Upsampling duplicates instances of minority class to create a balanced dataset with equal number of instances of both classes. Upsampling may lead to overfitting as same instances may be duplicated in training and testing data. Overfitting occurs when a model adjusts to the given data very well but gives poor performance on unseen data. Thus, high accuracy cause by overfitting can be misleading.

    b. On the other hand, downsampling reduces the instances of majority class to match the number of instances of minority class. Though downsampling may avoid overfitting but it may reduce the classifier performance as the amount of data gets reduced to a great extent especially in scenarios where minority class instances are scarcely present as compared to majority class instances.

iii) In order to timely assist students in improving their academic performance; it is more important to ensure correct prediction of a student at risk of dropout as positive. Thus, a model exhibiting higher Recall (Sensitivity) value is preferred in this case, even if a few non-dropout students get incorrectly predicted at risk of dropout.

iv) As observed in Table 3, Support Vector Machine (SVM) using radial bias function kernel achieves highest Recall percentage as compared to other four classifiers on each of the eight feature subsets, thus it can be concluded as a suitable classifier as compared to other four classifiers applied for predicting student dropout.

v) Also, the class-imbalance problem is dealt with SVM to a great extent through cost sensitive classification. Implementing SVM using scikit-learn library of Python, a higher class_weight parameter value is defined for positive class (1) as compared to negative class (0). This tells the algorithm that the misclassification cost of a student at risk of dropout getting incorrectly predicted as a non-dropout is costlier than the cost of misclassifying a non-dropout as dropout.

vi) In order to predict potential dropouts, it is essential to identify the most influential factors causing dropout. The comparison of various metrics in Table 3 provides an insight into the performance of the classifiers over eight different subsets of features. The feature subsets which provided highest recall value for respective classifiers are listed in Table 4.

vii) From Table 3, it can be inferred that all five classifiers achieved their respective highest recall value along with high values of other performance values on the features: Marks Obtained, Placement, Higher studies, No. of carry over, Annual Income, Parent Occupation.

viii) Though Support Vector Machine achieved high recall (sensitivity) values considering only 12th and 10th grade marks also, however, it obtained very less values of accuracy and other performance metrics. Also, on considering only the features: Gender, Actual Category, 12th Board, 12th Agg.%, 12th PCM%, Year of Passing12th, 10th%, First year marks and, Second year marks; all five classifiers achieved lesser than their respectively highest recall values obtained on other feature subsets. So, other features need to be explored to achieve better results.

Table 4.Highest recall value achieved by respective classifiers and corresponding student attributes

	Features used to achieve Highest Recall value		Technique	Highest Sensitivity (Recall) for respective classifiers	Values of other performance metrics
1.	• Gender, • Actual Category, • 12th Board, • 12th Agg.%,	• 12th PCM %, • Year of Passing12th, • 10th%	Support Vector Machine	100%	• Accuracy: 27.85% • Specificity: 19.72% • Precision: 12.31% • F1 Score: 21.92%
2.	• 12th Board, • 12th Agg.%, • 12th PCM %,	• Year of Passing12th, • 10th%	Support Vector Machine	100%	• Accuracy: 10.13% • Specificity: 0% • Precision: 10.13% • F1 Score: 18.39%
3.	• First year marks, • Second year marks, • Third year marks,	• Fourth year marks, • Marks Obtained	K-NN	87.5%	• Accuracy: 98.73% • Specificity: 100% • Precision: 100% • F1 Score: 93.33%
			Naïve Bayes	87.5%	• Accuracy: 98.73% • Specificity: 100% • Precision: 100% • F1 Score: 93.33%
			Support Vector Machine	100%	• Accuracy: 98.73% • Specificity: 98.59% • Precision: 88.89% • F1 Score: 94.12%
4.	• Marks Obtained, • Placement, • Higher studies,	• No. of carry over, • Annual Income, • Occupation	K-NN	87.5%	• Accuracy: 98.73% • Specificity: 100% • Precision: 100% • F1 Score: 93.33%
			Naive Bayes	87.5%	• Accuracy: 98.73% • Specificity: 100% • Precision: 100% • F1 Score: 93.33%
			Decision Tree	100%	• Accuracy: 100% • Specificity: 100% • Precision: 100% • F1 Score: 100%
			Random Forest	87.5%	• Accuracy: 98.73% • Specificity: 100% • Precision: 100% • F1 Score: 93.33%
			Support Vector Machine	100%	• Accuracy: 100% • Specificity: 100% • Precision: 100% • F1 Score: 100%
5.	• Gender, • Actual Category, • 12th Board, • 12th Agg.%, • 12th PCM %, • Year of Passing12th, • 10th%, • First year marks, • Second year marks,	• Third year marks, • Fourth year marks, • Marks Obtained, • Placement, • Higher studies, • No. of carry over, • Annual Income, • Occupation	Naïve Bayes	87.5%	• Accuracy: 98.73% • Specificity: 100% • Precision: 100% • F1 Score: 93.33%
			Random Forest	87.5%	• Accuracy: 98.73% • Specificity: 100% • Precision: 100% • F1 Score: 93.33%

ix) Since many students drop out after first or second year of enrollment in higher education, thus it is important to consider the marks scored in those years to predict dropout status in later years. Three classifiers achieved high recall considering the attributes: First year marks, Second year marks, Third year marks, Fourth year marks and, Marks obtained.

x) All five classifiers have shown to obtain their respective highest recall values when features such as Number of Carry Over, Annual Parent Income and Parent's Occupation were also considered along with total Marks obtained. Thus, considering demographic details of a student along with academic scores is essential to predict students at risk of dropping out. Such students can be assisted in improving their academic performance to prevent dropout.

FUTURE RESEARCH DIRECTIONS

The impact of more demographic attributes can be studied for predicting dropout. More features may be included such as age, marital status, marks in different subjects, residence of student during course etc. In order to achieve better results, deep learning techniques such as recurrent neural networks, convolutional neural network etc. may be performed if an abundant volume of student enrollment and dropout data is available. Since the data has a class imbalance of dropout vs non-dropout students, thus training machine learning models on a balanced data collected for an equal number of dropout and non-dropout instances can help in achieving more realistic and better results.

CONCLUSION

Thus, progressing in the field of educational data mining, five machine learning classifiers were applied in this chapter to predict student attrition or dropout status. This can assist in reducing dropout rates in higher education by enhancing performance through improved pedagogical practices for students predicted at risk of dropping out. Reducing the dropout rate will help in improved graduation rates as well as better utilization of resources, time and money of both the students as well as the higher education institutes.

Among the five classifiers applied on the student dropout dataset, Support Vector Machine using radial bias function kernel achieved the best Recall (Sensitivity) performance value over the eight subsets of features considered. All classifiers achieved their respectively highest Recall values and high values of other performance metrics when apart from total Marks Obtained, other influencing attributes such as Placement, Higher studies, No. of carry over, Parent's Annual Income, Parent's Occupation were also considered to predict student attrition status. Along with academic scores, student's demographic details may also have a significant impact on predicting dropout.

REFERENCES

Almayan, H., & Al Mayyan, W. (2016, October). Improving accuracy of students' final grade prediction model using PSO. In *2016 6th International Conference on Information Communication and Management (ICICM)* (pp. 35-39). IEEE.

Angeline, D. M. D. (2013). Association rule generation for student performance analysis using apriori algorithm. *The SIJ Transactions on Computer Science Engineering & its Applications (CSEA), 1*(1), 12-16.

Arora, Y., Singhal, A., & Bansal, A. (2014). Prediction & warning: A method to improve student's performance. *Software Engineering Notes, 39*(1), 1–5. doi:10.1145/2557833.2557842

De la Pena, D., Lara, J. A., Lizcano, D., Martínez, M. A., Burgos, C., & Campanario, M. L. (2017, May). Mining activity grades to model students' performance. In *2017 International Conference on Engineering & MIS (ICEMIS)* (pp. 1-6). IEEE. 10.1109/ICEMIS.2017.8272963

Devasia, T., Vinushree, T. P., & Hegde, V. (2016, March). Prediction of students performance using Educational Data Mining. In *2016 International Conference on Data Mining and Advanced Computing (SAPIENCE)* (pp. 91-95). IEEE. 10.1109/SAPIENCE.2016.7684167

Guarin, C. E. L., Guzman, E. L., & Gonzalez, F. A. (2015). A model to predict low academic performance at a specific enrollment using data mining. *IEEE Revista Iberoamericana de tecnologias del Aprendizaje, 10*(3), 119-125.

Iam-On, N., & Boongoen, T. (2017). Generating descriptive model for student dropout: A review of clustering approach. *Human-centric Computing and Information Sciences, 7*(1), 1. doi:10.118613673-016-0083-0

Jaiswal, G., Sharma, A., & Yadav, S. K. (2019, July). Analytical Approach for Predicting Dropouts in Higher Education. *International Journal of Information and Communication Technology Education, 15*(3), 89–102. doi:10.4018/IJICTE.2019070107

Kori, K., Pedaste, M., Altin, H., Tonisson, E., & Palts, T. (2016). Factors That Influence Students' Motivation to Start and to Continue Studying Information Technology in Estonia. *IEEE Transactions on Education, 59*(4), 255–262. doi:10.1109/TE.2016.2528889

Ktoridou, D., & Epaminonda, E. (2014, April). Measuring the compatibility between engineering students' personality types and major of study: A first step towards preventing engineering education dropouts. In *2014 IEEE Global Engineering Education Conference (EDUCON)* (pp. 192-195). IEEE. 10.1109/EDUCON.2014.6826089

Marnewick, A., & Pretorius, J. H. C. (2016, October). Master's of Engineering Management: Graduation rates lagging behind growth rate. In 2016 IEEE Frontiers in Education Conference (FIE) (pp. 1-8). IEEE.

Marquez-Vera, C., Morales, C. R., & Soto, S. V. (2013). Predicting school failure and dropout by using data mining techniques. *IEEE Revista Iberoamericana de Tecnologias del Aprendizaje, 8*(1), 7–14. doi:10.1109/RITA.2013.2244695

Ministry of Human Resource Development. (2018). *Educational Statistics at a Glance*. Retrieved fromhttps://mhrd.gov.in/sites/upload_files/mhrd/files/statistics-new/ESAG-2018.pdf

Mitchell, T. M. (2006). *The discipline of machine learning* (Vol. 9). Pittsburgh, PA: Carnegie Mellon University, School of Computer Science, Machine Learning Department.

Pardo, A., Han, F., & Ellis, R. A. (2017). Combining university student self-regulated learning indicators and engagement with online learning events to predict academic performance. *IEEE Transactions on Learning Technologies*, *10*(1), 82–92. doi:10.1109/TLT.2016.2639508

Quadri, M. M., & Kalyankar, N. V. (2010). *Drop out feature of student data for academic performance using decision tree techniques*. Global Journal of Computer Science and Technology.

Raigoza, J. (2017, October). A study of students' progress through introductory computer science programming courses. In 2017 IEEE Frontiers in Education Conference (FIE) (pp. 1-7). IEEE.

Roy, S., & Garg, A. (2017, October). Predicting academic performance of student using classification techniques. In *2017 4th IEEE Uttar Pradesh Section International Conference on Electrical, Computer and Electronics (UPCON)* (pp. 568-572). IEEE. 10.1109/UPCON.2017.8251112

Sanchez-Santillan, M., Paule-Ruiz, M., Cerezo, R., & Nunez, J. (2016, April). Predicting students' performance: Incremental interaction classifiers. In *Proceedings of the Third ACM Conference on Learning@ Scale* (pp. 217-220). ACM.

Sanz, R. A., Virseda, J. A. V., Garcia, R. M., & Arias, J. G. (2018). Innovation in the University: Perception, Monitoring and Satisfaction. *IEEE Revista Iberoamericana de Tecnologias del Aprendizaje*, *13*(3), 111–118. doi:10.1109/RITA.2018.2862721

Sheng, Y. C., Mustafa, M. B., Alam, S., Hamid, S. H., Sani, A. A., & Gani, A. (2016, May). Personal CGPA planning system for undergraduates: Towards achieving the first class CGPA. In *2016 Fifth ICT International Student Project Conference (ICT-ISPC)* (pp. 113-116). IEEE. 10.1109/ICT-ISPC.2016.7519249

Sri, R. L., & Muthuramalingam, S. (2016, December). A Novel Summative Grading Assessment Strategy for Improving Students Performance. In *2016 IEEE 4th International Conference on MOOCs, Innovation and Technology in Education (MITE)* (pp. 311-316). IEEE. 10.1109/MITE.2016.068

Chapter 3
Machine Learning Optimization Techniques for 3D IC Physical Design

Gracia Nirmala Rani D.
Thiagarajar College of Engineering, India

J. Shanthi
Thiagarajar College of Engineering, India

S. Rajaram
Thiagarajar College of Engineering, India

ABSTRACT

The importance and growth of the digital IC have become more popular because of parameters such as small feature size, high speed, low cost, less power consumption, and temperature. There have been various techniques and methodologies developed so far using different optimization algorithms and data structures based on the dimensions of the IC to improve these parameters. All these existing algorithms illustrate explicit advantages in optimizing the chip area, maximum temperature of the chip, and wire length. Though there are some advantages in these traditional algorithms, there are few demerits such as execution time, integration, and computational complexity due to the necessity of handling large number of data. Machine learning techniques produce vibrant results in such fields where it is required to handle big data in order to optimize the scaling parameters of IC design. The objective of this chapter is to give an elaborate idea of applying machine learning techniques using Bayesian theorem to create automation tool for VLSI 3D IC design steps.

DOI: 10.4018/978-1-5225-9643-1.ch003

INTRODUCTION

From Transistor to Integrated Circuit technology

The invention of the first transistor in 1947 was a revolution in the field of semi- conductor technology. Several types of transistors were fabricated in the following years and they were used in variety of applications in the field of Control systems, Military, Medicine, and so on. These transistors were known to be discrete components and number of transistors was connected together on a printed circuit board (PCB) to implement different circuit functions. The planar process was developed in the year 1960, which yielded the famous technology called "Integrated Circuits" as shown in *Figure.1*.

Further enhancement in fabrication and integration technology yielded high density and low cost integrated circuits. Such ICs were designed and fabricated for serving a single application. Numerous logic families such as Transistor- Transistor Logic (TTL), Emitter-Coupled Logic (ECL), and Complementary Metal Oxide Semiconductor (CMOS) had been fabricated in past four decades. Later,1970s the first microprocessor was fabricated by Intel, named Microprocessor 4004,which was a four bit microprocessor capable of manipulating four bit data. From then, the microprocessors and ICs in general have consistently improved, with increase in circuit density, speed, and reliability. This evolution was foreseen by Gordon Moore as, "The Number of transistors integrated on the single chip will double in every 18 months" which is called as Moore's Law.

Limitations of 2D Integrated Circuits

The traditional integrated circuits (ICs) also known as two-dimensional integrated circuits (2D ICs) are constructed up on the single silicon die that comprised of millions of transistors. These large numbers of devices or transistors are integrated on the single layer laterally on a planar structure. When moving to the higher end applications with a bigger circuit, the number of devices to be fabricated on the single layer is increased. If the number of devices and transistors on a single chip is increased the size of the chip, the wire-length required to connect the devices with each other are also increased. These issues predominantly affect the main advantages of the integrated circuits such as small in size, high speed. Also, since the silicon die is heavily integrated with large number of devices, the temperature of the chip is also increased due to the heat dissipation and power consumption. Increased chip size, increased wirelength and increased temperature of the chip severely affect the performance of the system.

From 2D IC to 3D IC Technology

As it is discussed earlier, there exist few limitations in 2D IC technology; a new IC technology was introduced by the researchers, called "Three Dimensional Integrated Circuits" (3D ICs). The 3D IC is designed by stacking several functional device layers vertically instead of mounting devices on a single planar structure like 2D IC and interconnection between these layers is achieved by Through Silicon Via (TSV) techniques, as shown in Figure 2. As expected, Three Dimensional Integrated Circuits (3D ICs) offer promising solutions like reduced chip area and interconnect length/wire length, while improving the electrical performance of the chip. The 3D IC with TSV is optimal finding because of the various advantages. Recently, image sensor chip, shared memory, retinal prosthesis chip, 3D SRAM has been

Figure 1.

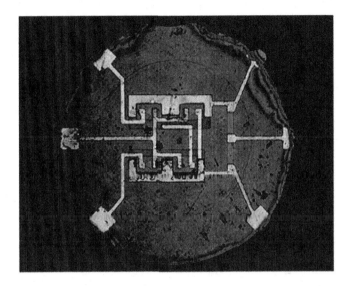

Figure 2.

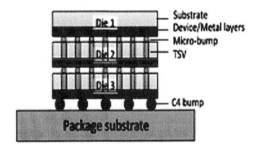

fabricated using 3D IC technology.Some of the 3D IC examples are shown in Figure.4. Also example architecture of heterogeneous 3D SOC is represented in Figure 3.

Design Challenges in 3D Integrated Circuits

Design of Through Silicon Vias

3D IC design can be implemented by arranging the multiple stacked layers and the interconnection between the stacked layers is achieved by means of cylindrical structure TSVs. Therefore, the design and manufacturing technologies of TSV drag high focus in research aspect. TSVs are also known as electrical interconnects that are etched into the silicon wafer. Among different structures of 3D ICs, TSV based 3D-IC is widely used as it imparts some important benefits such as reduced latency; higher speed communications, reduced interconnect length with short vertical connections, lower capacitance and inductance. The entire performance of 3D IC gets reduced, if any one of the TSVs is damaged (Nahid,

Figure 3.

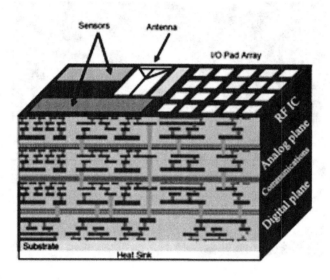

Figure 4.

2018). TSVs may lose their reliability due to fabrication defects, materials used, if there is any short circuit path between TSV and the substrate (Minki Cho & Chang Liu, 2011; Chao Wang & Jun Zhou, 2015).

Hotspot Problem

Thermal management is a challenging task, because of the high integration of the transistors, the circuit complexity gets increased. Due to this, several hotspots will be formed in the 3D IC structure. Thermal dissipation is in lateral direction in the planar silicon chips (2D IC) that yields temperature hike in Si material (Guojie Luo, Yiyu Shi & Jason Cong, 2015) whereas in three dimensional structures, the heat dissipation is in vertical direction. There are different stacking methodologies such as Face to Face, Face to Back and Back to Back exist to arrange layers vertically that helps to reduce the thickness of each layer. Because of the thin chip layers, parallel heat spreading effect is suppressed but it raises the average and peak temperature of the chip. Due to the sustained heat dissipation of hotspots, the chip may get damaged. So the hotspot is considered as a crisis to be alleviated. Jingyan Fu & Ligang Hou (2014) have proposed a technique to resolve the thermal distribution issues by means of inserting the TSVs in the appropriate positions.

CAD Algorithms and Tools

There are number of CAD algorithms and tools invented and found to be promising for the process of physical design automation of 2D IC. But, due to the structural complexity of 3D IC, researchers are still taking efforts to provide optimal solutions to enhance the all the stages of design process. In order to enhance the front-end design process, it is necessary to have an exploratory design procedure. Moreover, the design entry tools should provide a variety of visualization options so that the designer's job will be easy in the design process of complex three dimensional systems. As stated earlier, three dimensional circuits consist of diverse technologies; there is a need of having variety of algorithms that include behavioral models for a larger variety of components. Furthermore, the simulation tool should be powerful to evaluate the entire system efficiently.

Importance of Optimization Algorithms

Though the 3D IC shows hope on various parameters, the introduced third dimension brings some design complexities, as discussed above. The existing optimization algorithm of 2D IC could not be applied directly for 3-D IC design, because of the dimensional variation between them. So, it is mandatory to develop novel optimization algorithms for various steps involved in 3D IC physical design. Machine Learning, an emerging technology in Artificial Intelligence has shown promises in addressing numerous engineering optimization problems, by which the electrical and thermal performance can be maximized in a visible manner, which will be discussed later in this chapter.

THE NEED FOR OPTIMIZATION

Area

In the 3D IC, the footprint area of the chip will be increased, as the number devices to be integrated on the each layer are increased. If the footprint area of the chip is further increasing for the larger circuits, it will become a degrading factor of 3D IC. So, the footprint area of each layer should be minimized as much as possible, by following an efficient floor planning methodology.

Interconnect length/Wirelength

In the aggressive growth of technology scaling of VLSI circuits, interconnect length is one of the significant factors for the delay and power consumption. The 3D IC design has been motivated as a promising candidate to mitigate the interconnect issue. In 3D IC design, as several heterogeneous layers are stacked vertically, it allows the blocks to be placed close to each other; hence the interconnect length can be reduced.

Figure 5.

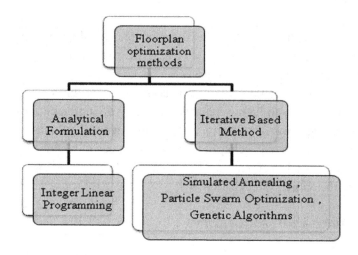

Temperature

The peak and the average temperature of the chip are getting increased, as the designer tries to move from the design of smaller circuits to larger circuits. The temperature issue is a major alarming factor for the 3D IC designers, as it degrades the overall performance of the chip.

Size and Number of TSVs

Through Silicon Via (TSV) is used to transmit the power and data signals between the device layers. Both the size and number of TSVs should be decided during the floorplanning stage itself. Because, when the size and number of TSVs are increased, the footprint area of the chip will be increased. Moreover, too many TSVs will become the obstacles during routing phase. Also, in case of damage in any of the TSVs will yield the serious issue of signal loss. Hence, the main objectives of the floorplanning phase should be to minimize the footprint area of the various layers, to minimize of the interconnection length, to reduce the temperature of the chip and number of TSVs.

Overview of Existing Algorithms for IC design

In recent years the CAD designers have developed numerous optimization algorithms to improve the electrical and thermal characteristics of the IC design. There are number of algorithms such as Deterministic Algorithm (Jai-Ming Lin & Jung-An Yang, 2017), Non Dominated Sorting Genetic Algorithm (NSGA-II) (Ranjita Dash et al,2017) Ant System (AS) Algorithm, Simulated Annealing (SA) Algorithm (Qi Xu & Song Chen, 2016), Adaptive Hybrid Memetic Algorithm (AHMA) (Jianli Chen & Yan Liu 2017) developed to do efficient floorplanning for optimizing various parameters like, temperature, chip area, and wirelength etc,.

Floorplanning optimization methods are classified into two categories (Figure 5), namely Analytical formulation and Iterative based method. In analytical formulation, mathematical programming is applied with objective functions and set of constraints. It is solved by mixed Integer Linear Programming,

Figure 6.

whereas the meta-heuristic methodologies produce optimal solutions. For example, Simulated Annealing (SA) (Sadiq M. Sait, 2016), Particle Swarm Optimization (PSO) and Genetic Algorithms (GA) belong to this category.

Ant Colony Optimization (ACO) (Panayiotis Danassis, 2016), SimPL algorithm (Yu-Min Lee, 2017), Genetic algorithm (Konstantinos Maragos & Kostas Siozios, 2015) are the partitioning algorithms developed to optimize the number of TSVs, to reduce the coupling noise between the TSVs, power consumption and footprint. Some more existing partitioning algorithms are listed in Figure.6.

Yande Jiang (2015) developed an algorithm to optimize the flattened HPWL (Half Perimeter Wirelength) and it is known as partitioning based 3D placement algorithm. They also achieved total run time. Shreepad Panth et al (2016) have designed and analysed a newer methodology that provides trade off between timing, power, testability and 2% reduction in wirelength. Sabyasachee Banerjee et al (2017) found a basic optimization criterion to minimize the wirelength. Their algorithm helped to reduce the wirelength and number of TSVs based area-constraints.

Tiantao Lu, Tiantao Lu, Zhiyuan Yang and Ankur Srivastava, (2016) developed a novel technique and algorithm to optimize the TSV distribution for chip-scale Electro Migration (EM) aware 3D placement. Also they have proposed an heuristic approach to get a desired temperature level which avoids the large global interconnect overhead. Caleb Serafy and Ankur Srivastava (2015), worked on two algorithms which combine coupling-aware TSV placement to acquire large improvement in TSV–TSV coupling.

Also, Gracia.D & S.Rajaram (2013) have done a survey on various algorithms such as Simulated Annealing (Chang Y.C., Chang Y.W., Wu, G.M. and Wu, S.W, 2000), Fast Simulated Annealing (Chen, T-C & Chang, Y-W, 2006), SA in Tau Search (Mao, F., Xu, N. and Ma, Y., 2009), Hybrid Genetic Algorithm (Chen, J. and Zhu, W.,2010), Evolutionary Simulated Annealing (Chen. J. and Chen.J. 2010) and Differential Evolution (Gracia Nirmala Rani.D.& Rajaram, S.,2011) and have produced a comparative analysis on area, wirelength as shown in Table 1,2.

All the above listed algorithms are implemented in high level languages like C, C++ etc., and they have yielded good results in optimization of various parameters in IC design. Recently, Machine Learning shows promising results and solutions in optimization techniques where it is required to handle large

Figure 7.

Benchmark Circuits	Modules No.	Simulated annealing area (mm²) [2]	SA embedded in Tabu search area (mm²)[17]	Evolutionary simulated annealing (mm²) [4]	Hybrid simulated annealing (mm²) [6]	Hybrid genetic (mm²) [5]	Differential evolution area (mm²)[8]
Apte	9	46.92	46.92	49.43	47.12	46.90	46.6339
Xerox	10	19.83	20.08	20.78	20.89	20.03	19.69
Hp	11	8.95	9.16	9.364	9.47	9.08	9.293
Ami33	33	1.27	1.21	1.253	1.21	1.19	1.22
Ami49	49	36.80	36.95	36.74	37.80	37.49	36.22

Figure 8.

MCNC benchmarks		Previous research work				
Circuits	Modules No.	Simulated annealing (mm) [2]	Fast SA (mm)[4]	Hybrid simulated annealing (mm)[6]	Evolutionary simulated annealing (mm)[5]	Differential evolution (mm)[8]
Apte	9	743.281	–	480.0	108.53	357.876
Xerox	10	108.53	–	513	1371.36	59.193
Hp	11	1896.38	–	144.3	205.54	918.228
Ami33	33	347	64.6	61.2	621.05	326.077
Ami49	49	163	753	1020.3	510.24	74.296

number of parameters and data. Different Machine Learning approaches are described in the following sections of this chapter.

Machine Learning

As it is discussed earlier, Machine Learning (ML) (Pandey and Solanki, 2019) is an application of Artificial Intelligence which has established plenty of applications in several science and engineering fields like computer vision, voice recognition, medical diagnosis, robotics, self-driving vehicles, etc. In machine learning technique, a machine will be trained with a large data set. Based on the trained data set the machine can respond to the new data that arrives to the system. The number of applications is also constantly increasing. Also, there are different types of ML technique like supervised, unsupervised and reinforced. According to the problem and the expected solutions, it is the job of designer to choose the suitable technique for their interested task to be solved.

Concept of Machine Learning

Sung Joo Park et al (2017), established a model for Machine Learning concept, with two different phases and three components called 'training phase', 'Execution/Evaluation phase' and task (T), experience (E), performance (P) respectively, as shown in the Figure 7.In Figure 7, "task" represents training and "performance" represents target, whereas "experience" is useful for improving the behavior of target. Recently, Machine learning algorithms have become popular in optimization techniques. These techniques will enable machines to study from the training data set by using programmed algorithms. There are number of techniques available to develop the optimization algorithms.

Among them, one of the most accepted techniques is Bayesian Optimization (BO) (Sung Joo Park, 2017) technique. According to Prof. Ethem Alpaydin (2009), the following is the definition of Bayesian Decision theory.

Figure 9.

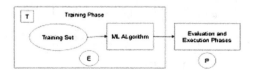

"programming Computers" to make inference from data is a cross between statistics and computer science, where statisticians provide the mathematical framework of making inference from the data and computer scientists work on the efficient implementation of the inference method".(E. Alpaydin, 2009, P.47).

Baye's Rule

Let the observed variables is represented as a vector $x = [x_1, x_2]^T$. The problem is to calculate $P(C|x)$. Using Baye's rule, it is written as,

$$P(C|x) = \frac{P(C)P(x|C)}{P(x)} \tag{1}$$

Prior Probability:

$P(C=1)$ is known as "prior probability" where C takes the value of 1, regardless of the value of 'x'. The value of C is taken before looking at the observables x, satisfying $P(C=0)+P(C=1)=1$.

Class Liklihood:

It is denoted as $P(x|C)$, where C is an event belonging to C and x associated observation value.

Evidence:

$P(x)$, the Evidence is the probability that an observation x is seen, either it is a positive or negative case.

$$P(x) = \sum P(x,C) = P(x|C=1)P(C=1) + P(x|C=0)P(C=0) \tag{2}$$

Posterior Probability:

$P(C|x)$, is the posterior probability, which can be calculated after having seen the observation x.

$$Posterior = \frac{prior \; X \; Liklihood}{Evidence} \tag{3}$$

Figure 10.

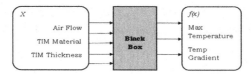

Black Box Optimization:

The goal of black box optimization is to calculate the optimum (the minimum) of an objective function f(x) with less number of total computations. When evaluations of f(x) are costly or need a complex analytical process, Bayesian Optimization (BO) is typically preferred by more number of researchers because it imparts high accuracy with few evaluations,

Sung Joo Park, Madhavan Swaminathan, (2016) shows that the black box functions, where a target output "f(x) is optimized by the input parameter 'x'. For Example, in the case of 3D IC, the black box function *f(x)* will be calculated based on five input parameters (*x*) namely air flow (Heat Transfer Coefficient), TIM (Thermal Interface Material) material, TIM thickness, Under fill Material, PCB material. Maximum temperature, Temperature Gradient and Clock Skew are taken as target parameters as shown in Figure 8.

Black Box Function in 3D IC Partitioning:

The first and foremost step in the physical design of 3D IC is net list partitioning, which involves the splitting the given circuit into smaller parts. The main objectives of circuit partitioning are to lessen the interconnections between the partitions, minimize the delay between partitions, power consumption and chip area. Because, if more TSVs are used between layers of 3D IC, they would consume more chip area and they act as obstacles during placement and routing procedure. Also fabrication cost of TSV is expensive. The black box function can be developed to optimize the above said parameters in partitioning phase as shown in Figure.9.

Using Black Box function in Bayesian Optimization (BO) technique, one can achieve optimization in target output functions, *f(x)* such as, Number of TSVs required between the layers, delay between partitions, power consumption and area of the chip, by choosing input variables *x,* as number of cuts, edges and layers, during partitioning phase. Since, BO can handle large number of input parameters; it will produce the most acceptable results.

Figure 11.

Figure 12.

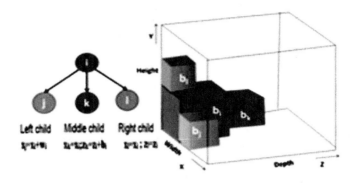

Black Box Function in 3D IC Floor planning:

In physical design of 3D ICs, floorplanning is believed to be a decisive process, since it provides estimation of chip area, total wire length, and cost. Floorplans are classified into two types: slicing and non-slicing floorplans. A slicing floorplan means that it can be obtained through repetitive cuts in the floorplan either in vertical or horizontal direction, whereas a non-slicing floorplan (Figure.10) does not involve in slicing or cutting. The non-slicing floorplan is compatible since it is more flexible and commonly used.

In order to obtain the optimization in the target output *f(x), i.e* fitness function, cost function and temperature of the chip, the designer should select the following input variables *x,*

- Area of the floor plan A(F)
- Total Wirelength of the floorplan W(F)
- Temperature of the floorplan T(F)
- Netlist N

Because, the cost of the floor plan Cost (F) [ ] is given as following equation

$$Cost(F) = \alpha X \frac{A(F)}{A^*} + \beta X \frac{W(F)}{W^*} + \gamma X \frac{T(F)}{T^*} \qquad (4)$$

Where α, β, γ are the control parameters.

In general, for a given floorplan F, the fitness function is represented as given in equation (5).

Figure 13.

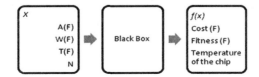

Figure 14.

$$Fitness\left(F\right) = \frac{1}{Cost\left(F\right)} \qquad (5)$$

So the expected black box function will be looking like, in Figure 11.

Black Box Function in 3D Placement:

The goal of the placement stage is to arrange the blocks in such a way that occupies minimum area of the chip while maintaining the interconnections exist between the pins and blocks. The placement stage is considered as more essential because if the placement stage is not giving a desired solution for placing the blocks in efficient manner, then it may cause degraded performance of the chip and may create jamming for the routing task. Hence, an efficient placement technique should be employed to achieve minimum total wire length and less number of TSVs.

The Black Box function as shown in Figure.12 for the placement stage is necessary to obtain the optimization in target output functions $f(x)$, such as total interconnect length, number of TSVs in turn the dead space. With the intention of obtaining this, the x should be the number of blocks and number of layers.

Bayesian Optimization Based on Gaussian Process

Hakki Mert Torun & Madhavan Swaminathan (2017), says that in most of the black box systems, including 3-D ICs, it is not possible directly to access gradient information of f (x) at an arbitrary x. But the gradient information is not required, when using Bayesian Optimization based on Gaussian Processes (GPs). Hence, it is considered as a suitable candidate for black box optimization. BO is a well-known method in the ML approaches and has been primarily used for tuning several parameters (Jasper Snoek, Hugo Larochelle, Ryan P. Adams, 2012).

CONCLUSION

When the number of transistors in 3D IC is getting increased, the associated heat flux and area of the chip may also increase, that degrades the overall system performance. It is necessary to tune the required system parameters such as number of layers, number of TSVs, total interconnect length etc., by means of efficient optimization algorithms as discussed in this chapter. Machine Learning Bayesian (BO) is a popular technique for the black box function optimization which is used to obtain the desired parameters in different design phase is explained in this chapter.

REFERENCES

Alpaydin, E. (2009). *Introduction to Machine Learning* (2nd ed.). Cambridge, MA: MIT Press.

Augarten, S. (1983). *State of the Art: A Photographic History of the Integrated Circuit*. New Haven, CT: Ticknor & Fields.

Banerjee, S., Majumder, S., & Varma, A. (2017). A Placement Optimization Technique for 3D IC. *2017 7th International Symposium on Embedded Computing and System Design (ISED)*. 10.1109/ISED.2017.8303930

Chang, Y. C., Chang, Y. W., Wu, G. M., & Wu, S. W. (2000). B*tree: a new representations for non slicing floorplans. *Proc. ACM/IEEE Design Automation Conf.*, 458–463.

Chen, Liu, Zhu, & Zhu (2017) An adaptive hybrid memetic algorithm for thermal aware non slicing VLSI floor planning. *Integration, 58*, 245–252.

Chen, J., & Chen, J. (2010). A hybrid evolution algorithm for VLSI floorplanning. IEEE Design Automation Conference in Computational Intelligence and Software Engineering (CISE), 1–4. doi:10.1109/CISE.2010.5676951

Chen, J., & Zhu, W. (2010). A hybrid genetic algorithm for VLSI floorplanning. *IEEE Conference on Intelligent Computing and Intelligent Systems (ICIS), 2*, 128–132.

Chen, T.-C., & Chang, Y.-W. (2006). Modern floor planning based on B* tree and fast simulated annealing. *IEEE Transactions on Computer-Aided Design of Integrated Circuits and Systems, 25*(4), 637–650. doi:10.1109/TCAD.2006.870076

Cho, M., Liu, C., Kim, D. H., Lim, S. K., & Mukhopadhyay, S. (2011). Pre-Bond and Post-Bond Test and Signal Recovery Structure to Characterize and Repair TSV Defect Induced Signal Degradation in 3-D System. *IEEE Transactions on Components, Packaging, and Manufacturing Technology, 1*(11), 1718–1727. doi:10.1109/TCPMT.2011.2166961

Danassis, P., Siozios, K., & Soudris, D. (2016). ANT3D: Simultaneous Partitioning and Placement for 3-D FPGAs based on Ant Colony Optimization. IEEE Embedded Systems Letters, 8(2).

Dash, R., Risco-Martín, J. L., & Turuk, A. K. (2017). A Bio-Inspired Hybrid Thermal Management Approach for 3-D Network-on-Chip Systems. IEEE Transactions on Nanobioscience, 16(8).

Fu, J., Hou, L., Lu, B., & Wang, J. (2014). Thermal analysis and thermal optimization of through silicon via in 3D IC. *12th IEEE International Conference on Solid- State and Integrated Circuit Technology (ICSICT) 2014*, 1–3. 10.1109/ICSICT.2014.7021445

Gracia Nirmala Rani. (2013). A survey on B*-Tree-based evolutionary algorithms for VLSI floorplanning optimization. India. *International Journal of Computer Applications in Technology, 48*(4).

Gracia Nirmala Rani, D., & Rajaram, S. (2011). Performance driven VLSI floor planning with B*Tree representation using differential evolution. *Communications in Computer and Information Science, 197*, 456–465. doi:10.1007/978-3-642-22543-7_45

Hossain, Kuchukulla, & Chowdhury. (2018). Failure Analysis of the Through Silicon Via in Three-dimensional Integrated Circuit (3D-IC). *2018 IEEE International Symposium on Circuits and Systems (ISCAS)*.

Jiang, Y., He, X., Liu, C., & Guo, Y. (2015). An Effective Analytical 3D Placer in Monolithic 3D IC Designs. *IEEE 2015 IEEE 11ᵗʰ International Conference on ASIC (ASICON)*. 10.1109/ASICON.2015.7517146

Lee, Y.-M., Pan, K.-T., & Chen, C. (2017). NaPer: A TSV Noise-Aware Placer. IEEE Transactions on Very Large Scale Integration (VLSI) Systems, 25(5).

Lin & Yang. (2017). Routability-Driven TSV-Aware Floor planning Methodology for Fixed-Outline 3-D ICs. IEEE Transactions on Computer-Aided Design of Integrated Circuits and Systems, 36(11).

Lu, T., Yang, Z., & Srivastava, A. (2016). Electromigration-Aware Placement for 3D-ICs. *2016 IEEE 17ᵗʰ International Symposium on Qulaity Electronic Design (ISQED)*.

Luo, G., & Shi, Y. (2015). An analytical placement framework for 3-D ICs and its extension on thermal awareness. *IEEE Trans. Computer Aided Design. Integrated Circuits Systems, 32*(4), 510–523.

Mao, F., Xu, N., & Ma, Y. (2009). Hybrid algorithm for floor planning using B*-tree representation. *IEEE Third International Symposium on Intelligent Information Technology Application, 3*, 228–231.

Maragos, K., Siozios, K., & Soudris, D. (2015). An Evolutionary Algorithm for Netlist Partitioning Targeting 3-D FPGAs. IEEE Embedded Systems Letters, 7(4). doi:10.1109/LES.2015.2482902

Pandey, S., & Solanki, A. (2019). Music Instrument Recognition using Deep Convolutional Neural Networks. *International Journal of Information Technology*. doi:10.100741870-019-00285-y

Panth, S., & Lim, S. K. (2016). Probe-Pad Placement for Prebond Test of 3-D ICs. IEEE Transactions on Components, Packaging and Manufacturing Technology, 6(4). doi:10.1109/TCPMT.2015.2513756

Park & Swaminathan. (2016). Preliminary Application of Machine Learning Techniques for Thermal-Electrical Parameter Optimization in 3D-IC. *IEEE International Symposium on Electromagnetic Compatibility (EMC)*.

Park, S. J., Bae, B., Kim, J., & Swaminathan, M. (2017). Application of Machine Learning for Optimization of 3-D Integrated Circuits and Systems. IEEE Transactions on Very Large Scale Integration (VLSI) Systems, 25(6). doi:10.1109/TVLSI.2017.2656843

Sadiq, M. (2016). Design partitioning and layer assignment for 3D integrated circuits using tabu search and simulated annealing. *Journal of Applied Research and Technology, 14*(1), 67–76. doi:10.1016/j.jart.2015.11.001

Serafy & Srivastava. (2015). TSV Replacement and Shield Insertion for TSV–TSV Coupling Reduction in 3-D Global Placement. IEEE Transactions on Computer-Aided Design of Integrated Circuits and Systems, 34(4).

Snoek, J., Larochelle, H., & Adams, R. P. (2012). Practical Bayesian Optimization of Machine Learning Algorithms. *NIPS Proceedings, Advances in Neural Information Processing Systems, 25*.

Torun & Swaminathan. (2017). *Black-Box Optimization of 3D Integrated Systems using Machine Learning.* School of Electrical and Computer Engineering, Georgia Institute of Technology.

Vasilis, F., Pavlidis, G., & Friedman. (2009). Three Dimensional Integrated Circuit Design. Elsevier Inc.

Wang, C., Zhou, J., Weerasekera, R., Zhao, B., Liu, X., Royannez, P., & Je, M. (2015, January). BIST Methodology, Architecture and Circuits for Pre-Bond TSV Testing in 3D Stacking IC Systems. *IEEE Transactions on Circuits and Systems. I, Regular Papers, 62*(1), 139–148. doi:10.1109/TCSI.2014.2354752

Xu, Q., Chen, S., & Li, B. (2016). Combining the ant system algorithm and simulated annealing for 3D/2D fixed-outline floor planning. *Applied Soft Computing, 40*, 150–160. doi:10.1016/j.asoc.2015.10.045

Chapter 4
A Novel Approach to Kinect–Based Gesture Recognition for HCI Applications

Sriparna Saha
Maulana Abul Kalam Azad University of Technology, West Bengal, India

Rimita Lahiri
Jadavpur University, India

Amit Konar
Jadavpur University, India

ABSTRACT

With the advent of Kinect and other modern-day sensors, gesture recognition has emerged as one of the most promising research disciplines for developing innovative and efficient human-computer interaction platforms. In the present work, the authors aim to build an interactive system by combining the principles of pattern recognition along with the intelligent application of Kinect sensor. Involving Kinect sensor has served the purpose of collecting skeletal data, and after processing the same, the extracted relevant features have been fed to principal component analysis for dimensionality reduction phase. Finally, instead of using a single classifier for detection, in this chapter, an ensemble of k-nearest neighbor classifiers has been chosen since an ensemble algorithm is always likely to provide better results than a single classifier. To justify the efficacy of the designed framework it is implemented for interpretation of 20 distinct gestures, and in each case, it has generated better performances as compared to the other existing techniques.

DOI: 10.4018/978-1-5225-9643-1.ch004

INTRODUCTION

Gesture is an effective non-verbal interactive modality which is embodied by users with an aim to communicate messages. To illustrate further, gestures are characterized as non-verbal body actions associated with the movements of head, hands or face with intent to control specific devices or to convey significant information to the surrounding environment. Gestures can be originated from any human body parts and are expressed by corresponding body part movements (Kendon, 2004).

With the extensive influx of modern day computing and communicative interfaces in the human society, now a day, technology is so deeply embedded in our everyday life that it is practically impossible to imagine any specific task without help of technology. It is quite obvious that with the rapid advancement of technology, the existing interfaces are likely to suffer from limitations in terms of speed and naturalness while exploiting the huge amount of available information. Moreover, the drawbacks of these traditionally used interactive platforms are becoming more and more pronounced with the invent of novel technologies like virtual reality (Burdea & Coiffet, 2003). To address these issues, researchers are investing their valuable resources towards formulating novel algorithms and techniques that facilitate an engaging and effective Human Computer Interaction (HCI) (Dix, 2009). In the present world, HCI is one of the most active research disciplines and it has generated tremendous motivation (Jaimes & Sebe, 2007) for study in the area of pattern recognition and computer vision (Moeslund & Granum, 2001).

A long term attempt of researchers is to migrate the human to human interactive modalities into HCI, gestures are one such non-verbal interactive means capable of expressing a wide range of actions starting from a simple body movement to the more complex ones. It is important to notice that while executing simple body movements the body parts always indicate general emotional states, whereas gestures can add specific linguistic content (Iverson & Goldin-Meadow, 2005) while enacting the same emotional state (Castellano, Kessous, & Caridakis, 2008). In this context, gestures are no longer an ornament of spoken languages rather it is an key element of the language generation process itself. Due to the precision and execution speed, gesture recognition is widely used in developing HCI interfaces and sign language recognition (Liang & Ouhyoung, 1998).

Over the last few decades researchers have proposed numerous techniques of gesture recognition but none of them entirely succeeded in building an efficient HCI interface which motivated us to explore further and come up with novel ideas that addresses the existing limitations (Alzubi, Nayyar, & Kumar, 2018). Osust and Wysocki (Oszust & Wysocki, 2013) have introduced a novel scheme for signed expression detection depending upon the video streams obtained using Microsoft Kinect sensor (Biao, Wensheng, & Songlin, 2013; Lai, Konrad, & Ishwar, 2012; Wang, Yang, Wu, Xu, & Li, 2012), in this case the authors have adopted two variants of time-series, the first one focusing upon the skeletal image of the body and the second one is primarily concerned with extraction of the shape and location of hands as skin colored areas. Malima*et al.* (Malima, Özgür, & Çetin, 2006) has formulated another algorithm for recognizing a predetermined set of static postures which can be utilized for robot navigation purpose and after implementation of the said system it is reported that the concerned algorithm executes the command recognition operation at quite high speed and thus produces relatively lower runtime complexity. Liu *et al.* (Liu, Nakashima, Sako, & Fujisawa, 2003) attempted to develop a new text based input framework for handheld devices with camera embedded in it like video mobile phones etc. and after evaluating the performance of the Hidden Markov Model (HMM) (Rabiner & Juang, 1986) based training algorithms it has been inferred that the developers have attained a fairly good success rate. Lee and Kim have come up with a threshold model following the principles of HMM to address the issues of automatic gesture recognition which is recognized to be an ill-posed issue due to the presence of unpredictable and ambiguous non-gesture patterns (Lee & Kim, 1999).

Kim *et al.* (Kim, Mastnik, & André, 2008) introduced an Electromyography (EMG) (Merletti, Parker, & Parker, 2004) based hand gesture recognition system involving a set of time and frequency based features along with the basic statistical features and using a combination of k-nearest neighbors (k-NN) (Merletti et al., 2004) and Bayesian classifiers (Merletti et al., 2004) at decision level fusion a high recognition rate has been achieved which is truly commendable. Yang *et al.* (Yang, Ahuja, & Tabb, 2002) presented a novel design for decocting and classifying two-dimensional motion from an image sequence depending upon movements, in this work motion patterns are learned using a time delay neural network (Waibel, Hanazawa, Hinton, Shikano, & Lang, 1990) and the designed framework has been tested to recognize a specific number of hand gestures of American sign language (Liddell & Johnson, 1989).

Here, we develop a novel technique towards gesture classification (Solanki & Pandey, 2019) by intellectually exploiting the existing pattern recognition tools. Microsoft's Kinect sensor (Biao et al., 2013; Lai et al., 2012; Wang et al., 2012) serves a key role of generating the three dimensional skeletal coordinates of the 20 body joints accurately while the subjects enact different gestures. In the next step, using elementary mathematical concepts, all possible Euclidean distances between any two body joints have been calculated. The main reason behind incorporating all possible distances is to maintain generality and avoid loss of important information. Now, involving all the combinations introduces a new problem of dimensionality and system complexity, hence to address these issues it is necessary to reduce the dimensions. In these cases principal component analysis (PCA) (Saha, Konar, Bhattacharya, & Nagar, 2015) is found to be the most suitable one and after obtaining the reduced feature set, an ensemble of k-NN classifiers (Athitsos & Sclaroff, 2005; Bhattacharyya, Konar, Tibarewala, Khasnobish, & Janarthanan, 2014; Derlatka & Bogdan, 2015; Kuncheva, Rodríguez, Plumpton, Linden, & Johnston, 2010) has been used to execute the task of unknown gesture recognition.

The later part of the chapter has been segmented in five distinct divisions. Section II describes the different attributes and key features of Kinect sensors, section III recapitulates the elementary concepts and basic postulates that are required to understand the remaining sections of the chapter. Section IV presents the proposed framework in details and section V describes the experimental results obtained while conducting different experiments concerned with the present work. Finally, section VI concludes the chapter the accumulating the findings.

Kinect Sensor

Kinect (Biao et al., 2013; Lai et al., 2012; Wang et al., 2012) is the formal name given to the somatosensory peripheral XBOX360 that had been introduced by Microsoft in June, 2010 (Fig. 1). The term 'Kinect' has been originated due to the association of the device with "kinematics" or facts related to the same. Kinect is a device with an RGB camera, an Infrared (IR) camera, an IR projector and an array of microphones embedded in it which enables the sensor to generate depth images, RGB images and audio signals at the same time. Moreover, Kinect has provisions for speech recognition, dynamic capture, community interaction and so on which can be collectively exploited to develop a dynamic gesture recognition or facial expression detection system. Kinect captures RGB images of any human presented in front of the device at a suitable distance of beyond 1.2 to 3.5m using the RGB camera embedded in it. Further using the IR emitter and receiver, it understands the depth of the subject from the device precisely. It captures the motion of human being by representing the human body as an aggregation of three dimen-

Figure 1. Extraction of 20 joints from RGB image using Kinect sensor.

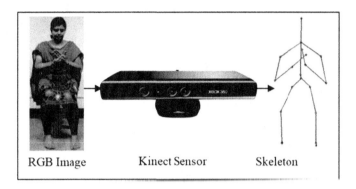

slonal skeletal joint coordinates corresponding to 20 different body joints (Fig. 2). Microsoft released a Kinect Software Development Kit (SDK) (Catuhe, 2012) comprising of a set of efficient algorithm to generate a skeletal model of the subject present in front of the camera in real time. It is important to note that Kinect is chosen over other sensors because of its compatibility, compact architecture, low cost and user friendly framework and above all, it has the ability to collect data 24 hours a day without compromising the precision level, which is a huge advantage itself.

Ryden *et al.* states that the Kinect is a multi-rate system which captures images at 30Hz, updates the visualization at 50Hz and renders the haptic process at 100Hz (Ryden, 2012). Based on this, the software architecture of the Kinect is divided into the following four parts:

i) Communication with the Kinect – In this, the present Kinect frame is captured and from the obtained data, a Cartesian coordinate system can be found.
ii) Visualization – Involves the visualization of the point cloud mainly.
iii) Haptic rendering – Here, a calculation of the forces on the Haptic interfacing point is done in comparison to a proxy position.
iv) Communication with haptic device – The forces are then sent to the Haptic device.

Technical Background

In this section, we emphasize the technicality associated with this chapter in general aspect.

Principal Component Analysis (PCA)

PCA (Saha et al., 2015) (Dong et al., 2018) (Ari, 2019) is a mathematical tool that has been widely used for dimensional reduction purpose, it basically projects the data to a new coordinate system having reduced dimension by Eigen value decomposition with an aim to minimize the redundancy and maximize the variance. To understand mathematically, let us consider that there are N number of d dimensional feature vectors in a matrix F having dimension $N{\times}d$. Using PCA it is possible to build a feature space having reduced dimension of $M{\times}d$, such that ($M{\leq}N$) by projecting the data points onto the principal subspace formed by M number of principal components.

Figure 2. 20 body joints obtained using Kinect sensor.

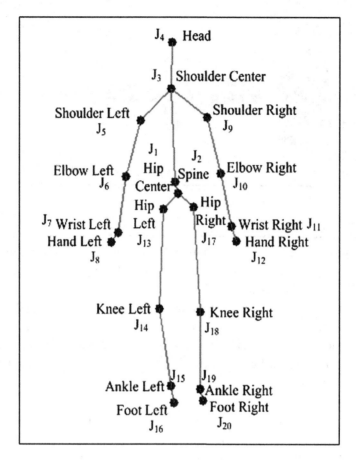

Suppose, the *i*-th feature vector F_i is expressed as $F_i=[f_{i,1}, f_{i,2}, f_{i,3}, \ldots f_{i,d}]$, now normalized vector can be derived as,

$$f'_{i,j} = \frac{f_{i,j}}{\sum_{k=1}^{d} f_{i,k}} \tag{1}$$

Similar procedure is repeated for *i=[1, N]*. In the next step, an empirical mean vector of dimension *N×1* is calculated by,

$$Mn_i = \frac{\sum_{j=1}^{d} f'_{i,j}}{d} \tag{2}$$

After that, the mean adjusted vectors are calculated as,

$$f''_{i,j} = f'_{i,j} - Mn_i \text{ for } i=[1, N] \text{ and } j=[1, d]$$

to normalize the data around zero mean. A matrix F'', containing the mean subtracted vectors, is formed having dimension $N \times d$. Now the covariance matrix C ($N \times N$) is derived using,

$$C = \frac{F'' F''^T}{d-1} \tag{3}$$

After Eigen value decomposition the principal components are found to be the Eigen vectors corresponding to Eigen values sorted in descending order that is the first principal component is nothing but the Eigen vector corresponding to the largest Eigen value. In this way, M principal components each having dimensions ($N \times 1$) is chosen and finally the a reduced feature space is formed by,

$$\theta_i = PC_i^T * F'' \text{ for } i=[1, M] \tag{4}$$

Since M number of principal components are chosen, so the resulting feature space dimension is ($M \times d$).

Ensemble of k-NN Classifiers

An ensemble method (Athitsos & Sclaroff, 2005; Bhattacharyya et al., 2014; Derlatka & Bogdan, 2015; Kuncheva et al., 2010) is actually a supervised classification system comprised of multiple heterogeneous or homogeneous classifiers formally termed as "base learners". In case of high dimensional data it is often found that the training dataset dimensions are very small as analysed to the data dimensionality and as a outcome the classifier is likely to get biased and generate degraded performance, which is extremely undesirable. A method for improving the individual classifier performance is to assimilate multiple classifiers and combine their outcomes using a powerful decision rule; in this case Random Subspace Method (RSM) (Skurichina & Duin, 2002) has been chosen over other popularly used combining techniques. The main purpose of employing ensemble methods is chosen because of the high dimensional data and moreover, the discussed framework has been formulated with an aim to design a real time system, hence it is obvious to alleviate processing time, the training dataset would be low dimensional which makes ensemble methods to be the ideal option to deal with such issues.

In the RSM algorithm, feature subspaces are formed by hapazard choice from the actual feature space and specific classifiers are developed depending upon the prime attributes of the randomly originated feature subspaces. After that, each classifier executes the classification operation separately and finally the ultimate prediction is decided by fusing the outcomes of the individual classifiers based upon a majority voting rule. This algorithm was proposed by Ho (Ho, 1998) and it is extremely suitable for high dimensional data sets.

To illustrate further, let $X=\{X_1, X_2, ..., X_M\}$ is the input from the reduced feature set post the dimensional reduction phase. To obtain a random space ensemble involving t number of classifiers, it is required to extract t number of samples each of size W and these samples are drawn without replacement while maintaining uniform distributions over X. It can be readily seen that this algorithm requires two predetermined parameters, firstly the number of the ensemble size and secondly, the cardinality of subspace.

Figure 3. Classification of unknown data point using kNN.

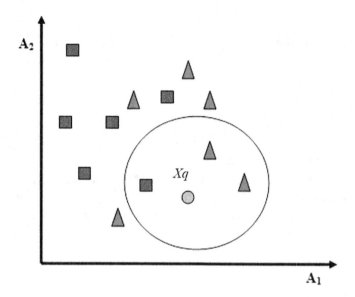

Base Learner:k-NN Classifier

k-NN algorithm (Zhang, Liu, Liu, Huang, & Sun, 2019) (Freitas, Mendes, Campos, & Stevan, 2019) is an instance based or lazy learning algorithm where an object is allotted a particular class label by majority vote of its k nearest neighbours in terms of a specific distance measure like Euclidean distance, Minkowski distance, Mahalanobis distance etc. (Weinberger, Blitzer, & Saul, 2006). For example, given an unknown test sample X_q to be classified and X_1, X_2,...., X_k be the k instances nearest to X_q, then the class that represents the majority of the k instances is returned as the class of X_q. k is a key parameter of the k-NN classifier as the local density of data points is dominated by it and apparantly it is much smaller than the training sample size (Fig. 3). For the proposed work, we have used Euclidean distance measure.

Fig. 4 presents a flowchart of the working mechanism of the ensemble methods classifier. OD denotes the original dataset, from which multiple datasets (MD) are derived using random subspace method, which are fed to the array of classifiers termed as multiple classifiers (MC). Each classifier executes the classification task separately and the final combined classifier (CC) outcome is determined depending upon a majority voting principle.

Proposed Work

The block diagram for the proposed work is presented in Fig. 5. Suppose, we have total G number of distinct gestures and each gesture is performed for Ts duration of time. Thus for a particular gesture, say g ($1 \leq g \leq G$), we have total $d = T \times 30$ frames (as the sampling rate of Kinect sensor for the chosen problem is taken as 30 frames/s). From each frame, say n ($1 \leq n \leq d$), we are calculating N number of features. For a particular feature a ($1 \leq a \leq N$), the representation of feature is done as f_a^n (Fig. 6). As it is not feasible to show all the 171 features in a single figure, four features are depicted using Fig. 7 for better clarification. These features are between hip center (HC) –foot left (FL), spine (S) – knee right (KR), shoulder center (SC) – elbow right (ER), head (H) – hand left (HL).

Figure 4. Ensemble methods.

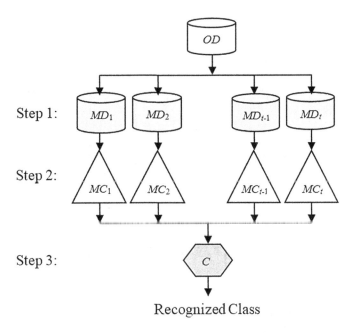

Figure 5. Block diagram for gesture recognition for HCI applications.

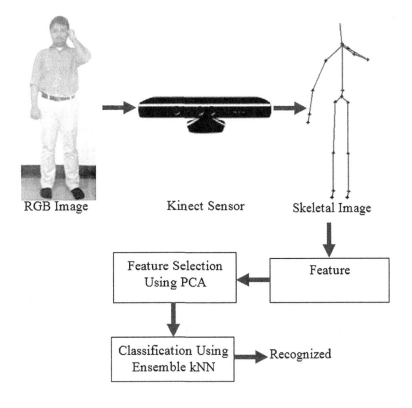

Figure 6. Extracted features for all frames for one particular class.

Class	Frame No.	Feature No.				
		1	...	a	...	d
	1	f_1^1	...	f_a^1	...	f_d^1
	⋮	⋮	...	⋮	...	⋮
g	n	f_1^n	...	f_a^n	...	f_d^n
	⋮	⋮	...	⋮	...	⋮
	N	f_1^N	...	f_a^N	...	f_d^N

Figure 7. Depiction of four arbitrarily selected features.

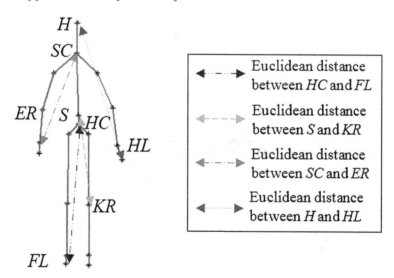

After application of PCA, as a dimensionality reduction tool, the reduced feature space becomes feature space having reduced dimension of $M×d$. This procedure is elaborated in Fig. 8.

For ensemble methods, it works in a simple technique, each classifier operates independently, and finally as the name suggests the final decision is reached by collating the results of each individual classifier following a majority voting rule.

Figure 8. Obtained features after dimensionality reduction using PCA.

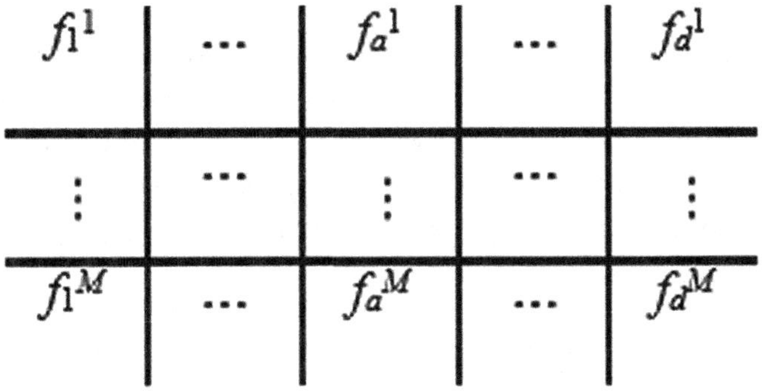

$$
\begin{array}{c|c|c|c|c}
f_1^1 & \cdots & f_a^1 & \cdots & f_d^1 \\
\hline
\vdots & \cdots & \vdots & \cdots & \vdots \\
\hline
f_1^M & \cdots & f_a^M & \cdots & f_d^M \\
\end{array}
$$

Table 1. Details of Training Dataset

	Dataset Number	Subjects		Age
		Male	*Female*	
Jadavpur university scholar	1	35	25	25±3 yrs
	2	25	35	29±5 yrs
	3	30	30	26±4 yrs

EXPERIMENTAL RESULTS

We have taken into account $G=20$ distinct gestures, namely Waving, Answering a call, Stop, Slide, Punching, Picking up an object, Move up, Move down, Move left, Move right, Disgust, Clap, Greeting, Please, Push, Grab, Zoom in, Zoom out, Move front and Move back. Each gesture is enacted for $T=3$s duration, thus $d=3\times30=90$.

The proposed work is implemented using Kinect sensor as the data acquisition device. This sensor can recognize human body using 20 body joints. We have calculated ($^{20}C_2$-19=) 171 Euclidean distances from these 20 body joints (eliminating 19 immovable segments like elbow right–wrist right, hip left–knee right, etc.). Thus $N=171$. Initially for a specific gesture g, the size of the dataset is 171×90. This enormous data has been reduced to 50×90 using PCA, as $M=50$.

Preparation of Dataset

For training purpose, we have accumulated data as given in Table 1. In the present scenario, the datasets have been judiciously partitioned according to sex and different age groups to prove the generality and worth of the discussed scheme in all conditions irrespective of the sex and age-group of the subjects. For testing, we selected discrete 30 subjects (age 30±6yrs with 20 male and 10 female subjects).

Recognicion of Unknown Gesture

The total scheme for identification of an unknown gesture is elaborated in Table 2. Here the RGB and skeletal images for random frame numbers 10, 33, 64 and 86 are shown. As it is not feasible to give all the 171 features, thus only 4 selected feature values are provided. These features are the Euclidean distances as shown in Fig. 7. After performing PCA tool the feature space has been reduced and using ensemble kNN, this unknown gesture is recognized as 'Punching' gesture. Thus our proposed work is able to produce correct results.

Comparison with Existing Literatures

The proposed work is compared with k-nearest neighbor (kNN) (Merletti et al., 2004), support vector machine (SVM) (Suykens & Vandewalle, 1999), binary decision tree (BDT) (Shlien, 1990), ensemble decision tree (EDT) (Banfield, Hall, Bowyer, & Kegelmeyer, 2007) and back propagation neural network (BPNN) (Hecht-Nielsen, 1992). SVM classifier partitions the data using hyperplanes having maximum possible margins with respect to both the classes, both EDT and BDT are predictive models employed for estimating an object's target value from the observations and this estimation is turned into classification when the concluded target value is the class to which the data belongs. BPNN employs a feed forward network topology along with certain weight adaptation rule to classify unknown data.

The performance metrics include precision, recall/sensitivity, specificity, accuracy, F1 score and timing requirement as shown in (5-8) (Hecht-Nielsen, 1992). Here, *TP*, *TN*, *FP* and *FN* are true positive, true negative, false positive and false negative respectively. All the algorithms are performed using Matlab R2012b software running in a Windows 7 PC with 2GB RAM. For timing requirement comparison the unit is taken in second. All the comparison results are given in Fig. 9. From this figure it is prominent that for gesture recognition in HCI domain, ensemble kNN is the best choice.

$$\text{Precision} = \frac{TP}{TP + FP} \tag{5}$$

$$\text{Recall} = \frac{TP}{TP + FN} \tag{6}$$

$$\text{Specificity} = \frac{TN}{FP + TN} \tag{7}$$

$$\text{Accuracy} = \frac{TP + TN}{TP + FN + FP + TN} \tag{8}$$

Table 2. Feature extraction process for unknown gesture

Frame Number			
10	33	64	86
RGB Images			
Skeletal Images			
Four Selected Features			
0.6935	0.7174	0.7203	0.6821
0.3138	0.3145	0.3078	0.3149
0.3120	0.3261	0.1438	0.1094
0.8972	0.9051	0.7398	0.5892

McNemar's Statistical Test

This statistical test is carried out to identify the better algorithm among two competitive ones. Here the reference algorithm (A) is our proposed one, i.e., ensemble of kNN classifiers and any of the other five existing literatures already undertaken in this work is considered as algorithm B. Now, n_{01} is the number of examples misclassified by A but not by B and n_{10} is the number of examples misclassified by B but not by A. The McNemar's statistic Z is calculated as follows(McNemar, 1955)

Figure 9. Comparison of proposed work with existing literatures.

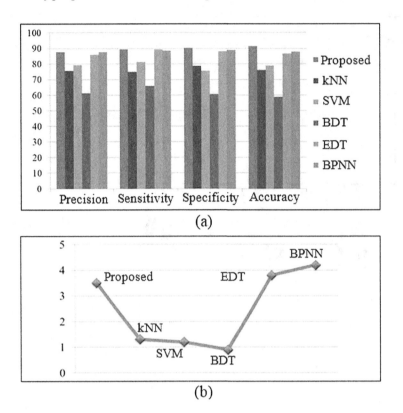

$$Z = \frac{\left(\left|n_{01} - n_{10}\right| - 1\right)^2}{n_{01} + n_{10}} \tag{9}$$

The statistical test has been done for dataset 3 and the results are shown in Table 3. Here, the null hypothesis has been rejected when Z> 3.84, where 3.84 is the critical value of χ^2 for 1 degree of freedom at probability of 0.05 (Dietterich, 1998). It is clear from Table 3 that only for BPNN algorithm, the test is failed but for all the other algorithms the null hypothesis has been rejected.

CONCLUSION AND FUTURE WORK

The present chapter proposes a novel approach for gesture recognition by assimilating the advantages of some of the existing efficient pattern recognition tools. The present work mainly emphasizes on two novel contributions, firstly, deriving simple Euclidean distance based features between all possible dual combinations between 20 concerned body joints to avoid information loss and again introducing dimensionality reduction frameworks to compensate for the computational expense. Secondly, instead of using a single classifier this work implements the usage of ensemble methods to enhance the classification performance. By successful implementation of the proposed framework an average recognition rate of

Table 3. McNemar's Statistical Test

B	A=Proposed			
	n_{o1}	n_{10}	Z	Comment
kNN	4	17	6.8571	Reject
SVM	7	24	8.2571	Reject
BDT	6	25	10.4516	Reject
EDT	4	16	6.0500	Reject
BPNN	6	8	0.0714	Accept

90.12% has been attained which is extremely appreciable for providing motivations of future research works in this research arena.

In this chapter, only an ensemble of homogeneous classifiers has been employed, so the performance is likely to be further improved by employing a heterogeneous variant of the ensemble method classifiers.

REFERENCES

Alzubi, J., Nayyar, A., & Kumar, A. (2018). Machine learning from theory to algorithms: An overview. *Journal of Physics: Conference Series, 1142*, 12012. doi:10.1088/1742-6596/1142/1/012012

Ari, S. (2019). An overview of the research work on multispectral imaging, hand gesture recognition, EEG and ECG signal processing. *CSI Transactions on ICT*, 1–5.

Athitsos, V., & Sclaroff, S. (2005). Boosting nearest neighbor classifiers for multiclass recognition. In *Computer Vision and Pattern Recognition-Workshops, 2005. CVPR Workshops. IEEE Computer Society Conference on* (p. 45). IEEE.

Banfield, R. E., Hall, L. O., Bowyer, K. W., & Kegelmeyer, W. P. (2007). A comparison of decision tree ensemble creation techniques. *IEEE Transactions on Pattern Analysis and Machine Intelligence, 29*(1), 173–180. doi:10.1109/TPAMI.2007.250609 PMID:17108393

Bhattacharyya, S., Konar, A., Tibarewala, D. N., Khasnobish, A., & Janarthanan, R. (2014). Performance analysis of ensemble methods for multi-class classification of motor imagery EEG signal. In *Control, Instrumentation, Energy and Communication (CIEC), 2014 International Conference on* (pp. 712–716). IEEE. 10.1109/CIEC.2014.6959183

Biao, M. A., Wensheng, X. U., & Songlin, W. (2013). A robot control system based on gesture recognition using Kinect. *Indonesian Journal of Electrical Engineering and Computer Science, 11*(5), 2605–2611.

Burdea, G. C., & Coiffet, P. (2003). *Virtual reality technology*. John Wiley & Sons. doi:10.1162/105474603322955950

Castellano, G., Kessous, L., & Caridakis, G. (2008). Emotion recognition through multiple modalities: face, body gesture, speech. In *Affect and emotion in human-computer interaction* (pp. 92–103). Springer. doi:10.1007/978-3-540-85099-1_8

Catuhe, D. (2012). *Programming with the Kinect for Windows software development kit*. Pearson Education.

Derlatka, M., & Bogdan, M. (2015). Ensemble kNN classifiers for human gait recognition based on ground reaction forces. In *Human System Interactions (HSI), 2015 8th International Conference on* (pp. 88–93). IEEE. 10.1109/HSI.2015.7170648

Dietterich, T. G. (1998). Approximate statistical tests for comparing supervised classification learning algorithms. *Neural Computation*, *10*(7), 1895–1923. doi:10.1162/089976698300017197 PMID:9744903

Dix, A. (2009). Human-computer interaction. In *Encyclopedia of database systems* (pp. 1327–1331). Springer.

Dong, X., Xu, Y., Xu, Z., Huang, J., Lu, J., Zhang, C., & Lu, L. (2018). A Static Hand Gesture Recognition Model based on the Improved Centroid Watershed Algorithm and a Dual-Channel CNN. In *2018 24th International Conference on Automation and Computing (ICAC)* (pp. 1–6). IEEE. 10.23919/IConAC.2018.8749063

Freitas, M. L. B., Mendes, J. J. A., Campos, D. P., & Stevan, S. L. (2019). Hand Gestures Classification Using Multichannel sEMG Armband. In *XXVI Brazilian Congress on Biomedical Engineering* (pp. 239–246). Springer. 10.1007/978-981-13-2517-5_37

Hecht-Nielsen, R. (1992). Theory of the backpropagation neural network. In *Neural networks for perception* (pp. 65–93). Elsevier. doi:10.1016/B978-0-12-741252-8.50010-8

Ho, T. K. (1998). The random subspace method for constructing decision forests. *IEEE Transactions on Pattern Analysis and Machine Intelligence*, *20*(8), 832–844. doi:10.1109/34.709601

Iverson, J. M., & Goldin-Meadow, S. (2005). Gesture paves the way for language development. *Psychological Science*, *16*(5), 367–371. doi:10.1111/j.0956-7976.2005.01542.x PMID:15869695

Jaimes, A., & Sebe, N. (2007). Multimodal human–computer interaction: A survey. *Computer Vision and Image Understanding*, *108*(1), 116–134. doi:10.1016/j.cviu.2006.10.019

Kendon, A. (2004). *Gesture: Visible action as utterance*. Cambridge University Press. doi:10.1017/CBO9780511807572

Kim, J., Mastnik, S., & André, E. (2008). EMG-based hand gesture recognition for realtime biosignal interfacing. In *Proceedings of the 13th international conference on Intelligent user interfaces* (pp. 30–39). ACM. 10.1145/1378773.1378778

Kuncheva, L. I., Rodríguez, J. J., Plumpton, C. O., Linden, D. E. J., & Johnston, S. J. (2010). Random subspace ensembles for fMRI classification. *Medical Imaging. IEEE Transactions On*, *29*(2), 531–542. PMID:20129853

Lai, K., Konrad, J., & Ishwar, P. (2012). A gesture-driven computer interface using Kinect. In *Image Analysis and Interpretation (SSIAI), 2012 IEEE Southwest Symposium on* (pp. 185–188). IEEE. 10.1109/SSIAI.2012.6202484

Lee, H.-K., & Kim, J.-H. (1999). An HMM-based threshold model approach for gesture recognition. *IEEE Transactions on Pattern Analysis and Machine Intelligence*, *21*(10), 961–973. doi:10.1109/34.799904

Liang, R.-H., & Ouhyoung, M. (1998). A real-time continuous gesture recognition system for sign language. In *Automatic Face and Gesture Recognition, 1998. Proceedings. Third IEEE International Conference on* (pp. 558–567). IEEE.

Liddell, S. K., & Johnson, R. E. (1989). American sign language: The phonological base. *Sign Language Studies, 64*(1), 195–277. doi:10.1353ls.1989.0027

Liu, C.-L., Nakashima, K., Sako, H., & Fujisawa, H. (2003). Handwritten digit recognition: Benchmarking of state-of-the-art techniques. *Pattern Recognition, 36*(10), 2271–2285. doi:10.1016/S0031-3203(03)00085-2

Malima, A., Özgür, E., & Çetin, M. (2006). A fast algorithm for vision-based hand gesture recognition for robot control. In Signal Processing and Communications Applications, 2006 IEEE 14th (pp. 1–4). IEEE. doi:10.1109/SIU.2006.1659822

McNemar, Q. (1955). *Psychological statistics*. Academic Press.

Merletti, R., Parker, P. A., & Parker, P. J. (2004). *Electromyography: physiology, engineering, and non-invasive applications* (Vol. 11). John Wiley & Sons. doi:10.1002/0471678384

Moeslund, T. B., & Granum, E. (2001). A survey of computer vision-based human motion capture. *Computer Vision and Image Understanding, 81*(3), 231–268. doi:10.1006/cviu.2000.0897

Oszust, M., & Wysocki, M. (2013). Recognition of signed expressions observed by Kinect Sensor. In *Advanced Video and Signal Based Surveillance (AVSS), 2013 10th IEEE International Conference on* (pp. 220–225). IEEE. 10.1109/AVSS.2013.6636643

Rabiner, L., & Juang, B. (1986). An introduction to hidden Markov models. *IEEE ASSP Magazine, 3*(1), 4–16. doi:10.1109/MASSP.1986.1165342

Ryden, F. (2012). Tech to the future: Making a" kinection" with haptic interaction. *IEEE Potentials, 31*(3), 34–36. doi:10.1109/MPOT.2012.2187110

Saha, A., Konar, A., Sen Bhattacharya, B., & Nagar, A. K. (2015). EEG classification to determine the degree of pleasure levels in touch-perception of human subjects. In *2015 International Joint Conference on Neural Networks (IJCNN)* (pp. 1–8). IEEE. 10.1109/IJCNN.2015.7280725

Shlien, S. (1990). Multiple binary decision tree classifiers. *Pattern Recognition, 23*(7), 757–763. doi:10.1016/0031-3203(90)90098-6

Skurichina, M., & Duin, R. P. W. (2002). Bagging, boosting and the random subspace method for linear classifiers. *Pattern Analysis & Applications, 5*(2), 121–135. doi:10.1007100440200011

Solanki, A., & Pandey, S. (2019). Music instrument recognition using deep convolutional neural networks. *International Journal of Information Technology*, 1–10.

Suykens, J. A. K., & Vandewalle, J. (1999). Least squares support vector machine classifiers. *Neural Processing Letters, 9*(3), 293–300. doi:10.1023/A:1018628609742

Waibel, A., Hanazawa, T., Hinton, G., Shikano, K., & Lang, K. J. (1990). Phoneme recognition using time-delay neural networks. In *Readings in speech recognition* (pp. 393–404). Elsevier. doi:10.1016/B978-0-08-051584-7.50037-1

Wang, Y., Yang, C., Wu, X., Xu, S., & Li, H. (2012). Kinect based dynamic hand gesture recognition algorithm research. In *Intelligent Human-Machine Systems and Cybernetics (IHMSC), 2012 4th International Conference on* (Vol. 1, pp. 274–279). IEEE. 10.1109/IHMSC.2012.76

Weinberger, K. Q., Blitzer, J., & Saul, L. K. (2006). Distance metric learning for large margin nearest neighbor classification. In Advances in neural information processing systems (pp. 1473–1480). Academic Press.

Yang, M.-H., Ahuja, N., & Tabb, M. (2002). Extraction of 2d motion trajectories and its application to hand gesture recognition. *Pattern Analysis and Machine Intelligence. IEEE Transactions on*, 24(8), 1061–1074.

Zhang, Y., Liu, B., Liu, Z., Huang, J., & Sun, R. (2019). WristPress: Hand Gesture Classification with two-array Wrist-Mounted pressure sensors. In *2019 IEEE 16th International Conference on Wearable and Implantable Body Sensor Networks (BSN)* (pp. 1–4). IEEE.

Chapter 5
A Survey on Precision Treatment for Humans Using Cognitive Machine Learning Techniques

M. Srivani

 https://orcid.org/0000-0003-3919-4167

College of Engineering Guindy, Anna University, Chennai, India

T. Mala

College of Engineering Guindy, Anna University, Chennai, India

Abirami Murugappan

College of Engineering Guindy, Anna University, Chennai, India

ABSTRACT

Personalized treatment (PT) is an emerging area in healthcare that provides personalized health. Personalized, targeted, or customized treatment gains more attention by providing the right treatment to the right person at the right time. Traditional treatment follows a whole systems approach, whereas PT unyokes the people into groups and helps them in rendering proper treatment based on disease risk. In PT, case by case analysis identifies the current status of each patient and performs detailed investigation of their health along with symptoms, signs, and difficulties. Case by case analysis also aids in constructing the clinical knowledge base according to the patient's needs. Thus, PT is a preventive medicine system enabling optimal therapy and cost-effective treatment. This chapter aims to explore how PT is served in works of literature by fusing machine learning (ML) and artificial intelligence (AI) techniques, which creates cognitive machine learning (CML). This chapter also explores the issues, challenges of traditional medicine, applications, models, pros, and cons of PT.

DOI: 10.4018/978-1-5225-9643-1.ch005

INTRODUCTION

Personalization is a multidisciplinary research topic which triggers the computational intelligence in tailoring specific services to each person. In clinical practice, PT helps in developing treatments that are specific to an individual or group of individuals. PT enhances better patient care and improves healthcare by providing targeted therapy for each person. PT is a case-based model for effective decision making. Tailoring precise treatment to the precise patient at the precise time is the fundamental constituent (Xie Q et al., 2019) of PT. In recent days, AI, ML and Deep Learning (DL) have sparked interest in augmenting medical decision making. ML and AI include brain-inspired algorithms to achieve individual-level clinical predictions. A recent report estimates that a sharp increase of nearly $87 billion in personalized medicine technologies has been expected by 2023 (Aguado et al., 2018). PT treats the patients individually by coupling their genetic information with medical records like Electronic Medical Records (EMR), Electronic Health Records (EHR), and Personal Health Records (PHR). EMR is a computerized version which includes patient's medical history, immunization status, medications, laboratory and test results, diagnoses, progress notes, patient demographics and vital signs. EHR is a comprehensive snapshot of detailed patient's medical history. PHR includes family medical history, prescription records, observations of daily living, chronic diseases, illness, and hospitalizations. Clinically oriented decision-making system is developed for breast cancer patients (Jiang et al., 2019), which provides customized assessments and recommendations by accumulating their health records. This decision support system makes use of Bayesian network architecture and Treatment Feature Interactions (TFI) algorithm to provide optimal and individualized treatment decisions.

A digital oncology platform is created for cancer patients (De Regge et al., 2019) portraying the personalized care path. The care path contains a customized pathway that provides righteous information about treatment options of cancer, pointers to related websites, questionnaires and treatment suggestions from the medication team. Using this care path, doctors can easily personalize and choose the necessary treatment for the patients. A cognitive computing technology-based medical recommender system (Dessi et al., 2019) IBM Watson and Framester performs feature extraction, processes the digitized patient's records and clusters a pile of medical reports. Given, a patient's medical report, the system can detect cohorts of patients with the homologous symptoms. The CML combines the techniques of AI, ML, DL and NLP to provide targeted therapy. CML proves to be an optimal environment for providing PT since it includes the advanced ML and AI techniques. CML helps the doctors for analyzing the massive volume of unstructured medical records efficiently. Doctors usually depend on their experience in diagnosing the illness and the review process is time-consuming, whereas the CML technology saves time by inferring the correct medication from the analysis. Figure 1 depicts the outline of PT for similar cohorts of patients.

Firstly, the CML framework analyzes the patient's records by incorporating the techniques of AI, ML, DL and NLP. Secondly, the framework constructs a clinical database and provides sufficient information about the diseases. Thirdly, the framework involves the identification of cohorts of patients to deliver personalized medications. PT is used to determine the most optimal therapy by an accurate assessment of a patient's condition. This chapter explores the following objectives

- Different approaches in ML and AI for providing personalized patient care.
- How Cognitive Machine Learning (CML) techniques provide an optimal treatment strategy for each patient?
- How PT shapes the future of healthcare?

Figure 1. Outline of personalized medication using cognitive machine learning

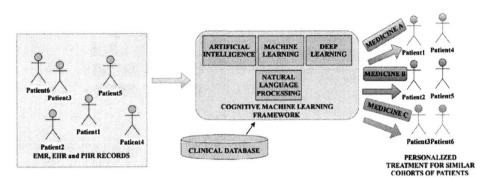

The chapter is designed as follows: background section provides a general overview of AI, ML and CML in PT. The main focus of the chapter section addresses the issues and challenges of traditional treatment. Solutions and recommendations section describes the need for PT, usage of various techniques of AI and ML in PT, the role of CML in PT, applications, pros and cons of PT. Discussion section discusses the major issues and limitations in providing PT. Future research directions and conclusion section concludes the survey by providing future research ideas.

BACKGROUND

ML is a field of study to teach computers without explicit programming. ML deals with task, experience, and performance that is learned from a task, experience with data, and improve the performance. DL or deep structured learning is a family of ML based on neural networks. AI is the science of making intelligent computers. CML is the science of using brain-inspired ML algorithms to develop a cognitive system which can reason, think, judge, solve problems, understand, learn, and decide.

CML is an extension of AI and ML systems that can act intelligently and interact naturally by understanding the human mind. The use of cognitive technology for PT stills in its embryonic stage. The goal of using CML techniques for personalized medication is to render precise treatment to the patients. CML techniques help in pre-diagnosis and preclusion of diseases by taking into account the disease status, disease progression, cohorts identification, and stratification of risky individuals. Substantial research is going on to implement PT using CML techniques. IBM Watson Health (Aggarwal et al., 2016), is a cognitive system which can store, manage access, analyze, and process massive amounts of structured and unstructured data. It helps the cancer people in rural areas by providing them with personalized care and evidence-based treatment. This cognitive system delivers cost-effective therapy with excellent outcomes and offers personalized medication for each person.

Design Cases

PT provides high-quality care at lower costs. For example, PT avoids extraneous diagnostic scan such as Magnetic Resonance Imaging (MRI) for a patient who would not favour from it. By tailoring the favourable treatment to the patient, the use of expensive drugs can be reduced, thereby reducing the

Figure 2. Issues and challenges of traditional treatment

overall costs (Ayer and Chen, 2018). The main design case where the PT is in high demand is cancer. Memorial Sloan Kettering Cancer Center in New York cares for people affected by cancer and proves that people with individualized clinical biomarkers and had targeted therapy survived nearly one year longer than those people without personalized clinical biomarkers and targeted therapy. Another design case is that PT applied for chronic recurrent conditions. A clinically oriented test method called N-of-1 experiment (Xie T and Yu 2017) combines both personalized and randomized clinical trial. It is a cross comparing method which arbitrarily designates each patient to one of the medications and recurrently crosses over two or more therapies. In this method, people's treatment is estimated by the performance of the treatment. So, physicians can quickly determine the best treatment.

A cognitive computing system performs an in-depth analysis of the profile of patients and automatically renders the new actionable and personalized insights within a short period. Watson for Genomics (WG) is a cognitive computing system (Rhrissorrakrai et al., 2016) which tends to provide personalized cancer care. WG examines molecular data and provides evidence-based, clinically actionable insights. Given a patient profile, WG delivers a report with reasonable and actionable insights, which would be helpful for the clinicians to provide personalized evidence-based treatment to the patients. So, these cognitive systems enhance every insight made across different diseases and benefits patients by providing personalized medicine.

MAIN FOCUS OF THE CHAPTER

Issues, Controversies and Problems of Traditional Treatment

Traditional medicine also called as complementary, conventional, and alternative medicine is the oldest form of the healthcare system. Integration of traditional medicine system to healthcare services improves the accessibility to healthcare. Traditional treatment is a "single size matches all" technique. The various issues and challenges of traditional therapy are depicted in the mind map, as shown in Figure 2.

Since clinical data is high dimensional, traditional approaches fail to measure the risk of a medical condition. The various issues and challenges of traditional treatment are

Lack of Privacy

Privacy is a major issue in conventional therapy. Personal data of patients are highly sensitive because it is not just a single person's information but a group of people's information who are in blood relation to that person. So, the privacy of an individual faces a major threat.

Difficulty in Finding the Exact Drug

Exact drug discovery is a major challenge in traditional medication. When people take a particular medication for the first time, they participate in an experiment. Medications prescribed work for some people and don't work for some people. In such situations, doctors using traditional treatment feel very difficult to find a specific drug which is suitable for each patient.

Trial and Error Approach

In trial and error approach, doctor prescribes medication to almost all patients based on the same symptoms and assumptions. These medicines may not be beneficial to all patients and it leads to poor outcomes, adverse side effects, and causes a delay in identifying the disease progression.

Risk Estimation of a Medical Event

It deals with the identification and analysis of future risky events that may cause a negative impact. Traditional treatment fails to analyze the disease risk progression over frequent intervals of time, so risk estimation of a medical event remains to be a significant challenge.

Lack of Specialization Programs for Practitioners

Practitioners, healthcare providers, and patients feel very difficult to understand the traditional treatment concepts, techniques, and methodologies.

Misdiagnosis

In some situations, traditional treatment fails to diagnose the disease correctly. Misdiagnosis increases the healthcare cost since it influences many people to take unnecessary tests, treatment, and therapies.

Reactive Treatment

Traditional treatment is a reactive treatment-based approach. It does not prevent or predicts the disease but detects and reacts to it.

PT overcomes these issues and challenges of traditional treatment with greater precision. Thus, PT is just an extension of traditional treatment. One size fits all approach turns out to be one size no longer fits all approach. Future directions of conventional medicine (Telles et al., 2014) include policy making, standardization, training of researchers regarding traditional treatment concepts and guidelines.

SOLUTIONS AND RECOMMENDATIONS

Need For Personalized Treatment

The main characteristic of PT is that medical treatment is designed based on the individual characteristics of patients. This field plays a decisive role in the prognosis and treatment of medical problems. The promising benefits of PT are extraordinary. PT identifies the progression of the disease and its status at each time intervals thereby decreasing the risk of illness.

Usage Of Machine Learning And Artificial Intelligence Techniques For Personalized Treatment

Nowadays, ML and AI are changing the research methods and personalization of medicine through its advancements. Chronic illnesses such as cancer can be treated using ML and AI techniques within a shorter period. For example, IBM Watson is a cognitive supercomputer which combines ML and AI techniques to prescribe a personalized medication by exploring 20 million cancer research writings in ten minutes. IBM Watson learns continuously from the data and predicts the outcomes more accurately. The various approaches are

Patient Cohort Identification

In medicine, the patient cohort refers to a group of patients who experience similar symptoms over a while. Patient cohort identification plays a major role in providing customized care and medication by unyoking the patients into similar cohorts. The ultimate aim of this method is to determine the patient similarity index and patient cohorts (Wang F, 2015) to provide customized predictions. Adaptive Semi-Supervised Recursive Tree Partitioning (ART) technique performs patient indexing at a large scale and efficient retrieval of clinical patterns from similar cohorts of patients. The overall process involves Kernelized tree construction and Kernelized ART (KART) partitioning algorithms. For efficient retrieval of similar patients, the tree is constructed recursively based on the optimized problem-solving method. The Collaborative filtering method evaluates the clinical similarity of patients. Similarity analytics-based Outcome driven appxroach (Liu H et al., 2017) is used to determine precision cohorts of type 2 diabetes. Patient population data, the clinical outcome of interest, and clinical scenario are used to determine the patient similarity context. After estimating similarity metric and features, segment the patients into groups by clustering. Downstream analytics provides personalized care. So, the overall methodology describes the use of an ML approach finding precision cohorts using outcome driven patient similarity analytics. Ensemble fuzzy models (Salgado et al., 2016) also play a significant role in providing PT by identifying similar cohorts of patients. Fuzzy c-means clustering algorithm groups the patients and develops a fuzzy model for each group. ML makes use of the technologies as mentioned above (Wang F, 2015, Liu H et al., 2017, Salgado et al., 2016) to unyoke the people into similar cohorts.

Personalized Dynamic Treatment Regime

Dynamic Treatment Regime (DTR) encompasses a collection of decision rules for selecting adequate therapies for individual patients. DTR are sequential decision rules with intermediate outcomes observed at each stage. DTR renders optimal therapy to each person based on their response over time. A hybrid approach to merge online learning and regression models such as Q-learning and Augmented Multistage Outcome-Weighted Learning (AMOL) is used in the works of literature to provide DTR. AMOL technique (Liu Y et al., 2016) has been used to fuse outcome weighted learning and Q-learning to determine optimal DTR from Sequential Multiple Assignment Randomization Trials (SMARTs) datasets. ML makes use of Q-learning methodology, to suggest an optimal treatment for the patients.

Deep and Active Learning Approach

Survival Analysis is a statistical technique which analyses and models period until the existence of future events. An effective personalized medication pattern and recommendation approach called Deep learning and Active learning-based Survival Analysis (DASA) framework (Nezhad et al., 2019), compares the relative risks, which correlates with different treatments and assigns the best one. This PT recommendation approach is used to determine the risk ratio of chemotherapy, radiotherapy and surgery. DL improves the performance of survival analysis and provides accurate and PT to the individuals. Deep Treat algorithm (Atan et al., 2018) learns optimal PT from the data using neural networks. This algorithm consists of two stages, namely learning a map-based representation using the auto-encoder system to reduce bias, and construction of efficient treatment techniques using a feed-forward network.

Deep Learning for Image Analysis

DL provides excellent solutions for the problems of medical image analysis, and it is an essential method for many future applications. PT approach stratifies the patients into groups or subgroups or more and more personalized groups by identifying the risk of disease. DL algorithms are useful for providing PT for individuals. A study demonstrated that Convolutional Neural Network (CNN) serves as an emerging technique to act as prognostic aids for a group of classification tasks. CNN (Xie Q et al., 2019) categorized nearly 1,30,000 clinical images of dermatology. Recently, CNN fine-tuned and characterized nearly 1,28,175 diabetic retinopathy images identically as described by the ophthalmologists. DL uses multi-faceted clinical knowledge to integrate classification and prognostic decision support tasks. A novel deep feature learning, selection and representation method (Nezhad et al., 2016) is used to provide PT. This approach makes use of Stacked Autoencoders (SA) based deep architecture to analyze and formulate the crisis attributes for hypertension. This method comprises of three sequential levels namely data remodeling using SA, feature sampling and prognostic modeling. In general DL or Deep ML models abstract input data by using deep architecture with many hidden layers to provide the best PT.

Progression of AI towards Personalized Approach

AI in PT has revolutionized the world. AI helps in the prognosis of diseases and prescribes a more effective treatment for patients. Literature focuses on pretreatment diagnosis. Artificial Neuronal Network (ANN) analysis (Bogani et al., 2019) has been performed to predict the persistence of dysplasia. In the learning phase process, ANN obtains knowledge, intelligence and weights the significance of different Human Papilloma Virus (HPV) genotypes. It also identifies the essential HPV genotypes for pretreatment diagnosis. The risk of developing dysplasia was evaluated using Kaplan–Meier and Cox models. The future of healthcare also relies on AI techniques to diagnose certain diseases and to provide PT. AI has the promising potential to handle vast amounts of structured and unstructured information and provides interactive health solutions to patients. DL based ophthalmology technology (Nik Tehrani, 2018) detects diabetic retinopathy and offers customized treatment to the people.

Optimal Personalized Treatment Rules

Bayesian predictive method (Ma et al., 2019) is a suitable method for the development of PT. This method combines both predictive treatment and diagnostic aspects of a specific disease. This treatment strategy consists of different levels. Given a non-continuous set of well-ordered reaction levels listing clinical outcomes, at the first level "baseline" predictive probability measures are determined based on prognostic characteristics of a specific patient's profile. At the second level, predictive features are integrated to alter the baseline probability measures referring to the successfulness of each treatment option. At the third level, the prognostic effects of a specific disease also alter the predictive features. This proposed method demonstrates improved prognostic values in predicting clinical outcomes. A statistical method has been used to determine optimal ITR (Wang Y et al., 2016) based on certain specific features from medical records of patients. This technique combines mathematical modeling and deep insights about medical domain knowledge with ML processes to provide customized optimal treatment recommendations. A decision tree has been constructed using EHR data for choosing the best-personalized therapy for diabetes patients. An O-learning mechanism has been employed to estimate personalized decision making and optimal ITR. The O-learning mechanism aims to attain individualized medical decision making by determining the optimal and individualized treatment according to the patient's specific characteristics.

Clinical Trial Matching to provide Personalized Treatment

A cognitive computing system called IBM Watson proves to be a promising potential for Clinical Trial Matching (CTM) (Helgeson et al., 2018). Watson CTM enables physicians or clinicians to quickly identify a list of clinical trials for each patient to provide PT. It also analyzes a massive amount of structured, unstructured data from the patient's EHR, mines a useful list of trial options and matches the clinical trials using Natural Language Processing (NLP). Watson CTM also supports proactive patient identification.

Clinical Recommendations for Customized Health

Clinical Decision Support System (CDSS) tailors personalized clinically oriented suggestions to aid clinicians for optimal decision support. Discovery Engine (DE) (Yoon et al., 2017) determines the most relevant patient intricacies for the prognosis of early disease and provides best-personalized treatment regime recommendations for each patient. The DE consists of three processes namely (i) clinical decision dependent feature selection, (ii) relevant feature extraction and (iii) clinical decision recommendation by taking into account the transfer rewards from external knowledge.

These ML and AI techniques play a significant role in building up PT with high precision and accuracy for disease prevention, disease detection, and treatment.

ROLE OF COGNITIVE MACHINE LEARNING IN PERSONALIZED TREATMENT

CML combines processes and analyses the techniques of ML and AI to build up a computerized human model which simulates the human thought process. Since personalized medication orients the treatment towards the individual characteristics of each patient, the CML technology helps in developing a prototype which performs case by case analysis and tailors optimal treatment. It achieves accurate reasoning and decision making by combining the capabilities of NLP, ML, and AI. Figure 3 explains the workflow of PT using CML technology.

Personal Health Records (PHR) and Symptoms

The dataset for analysis consists of the patient's PHR and symptoms. The PHR serves as a tool which collects, shares and maintains the past and current information about each patient. The PHR contains personal identification, emergency contacts, healthcare provider contacts, current medications, dosages, significant illness, surgeries, allergies, family health history, and so on. Symptoms portray the patient's signs, causes, and difficulties of a particular disease. Personal Health Record (PHR) is analyzed using cognitive technologies to provide doctors with the best information to make right and informed decisions.

Identification of Cohorts of Patients

CML makes use of AI in medicine to identify cohorts of patients that is patients who have similar symptoms over a while. AI makes use of PHR to identify better matching patients. Watson CTM (Helgeson et al., 2018) estimates the clinical trials of each patient and identifies the cohorts of eligible patients. Similarity features and similarity metrics are determined by the patients PHR. Patient clustering and patient group characterization are performed to determine similar cohorts of patients.

Case by Case Analysis

Case by case analysis treats each patient as an individual case and renders specific treatment. CML analyzes each patient individually from cohorts of patients. Case by case analysis is performed to investigate the clinical data of patients and to generate deep insights. This analysis provides patient-centered care by honouring patient's virtues, desires and demands. Understanding and flinging back to the needs of an individual is an essential aspect of patient-centered care. For example, the preciseness of hypertension therapy can be increased through case-based clinical trials (Kronish et al., 2019). The medications for Blood Pressure (BP) were selected using a series of N-of-1 experiments approach. BP is measured twice in a day for each patient, and the severity of the disease progression is assessed every day using a computerized questionnaire. The proportion of people who are adherent to self-assessments are determined. The remaining portion of people is adherent to personalized trials. Case by case analysis takes into account the heterogeneity of patient preferences and needs for providing patient-centered care. A neural network based on patient-level sequential modeling (Kang S, 2018) is used to extract various

Figure 3. The workflow of personalized treatment using cognitive machine learning technology

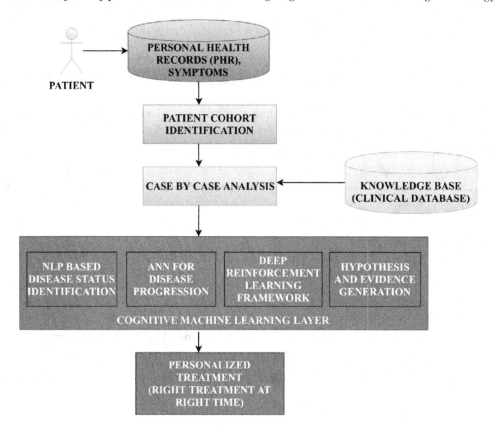

specific patterns of illness. This technique discovers the continuous dependencies encapsulated in the medical records of each patient to relinquish personalized prediction. Case by case personalized ML model identifies different parameters such as response rate, therapeutic measures, biomarker value for each patient based on the various patterns of illness.

Construction of Knowledge Base (KB) (Clinical database)

Clinical database data is the most important resource for healthcare research. It is divided into six major types (i) EHR, (ii) administrative data, (iii) claims data, (iv) patient/disease registries, (v) health surveys and (vi) clinical trial data. An openly accessible critical care database called Medical Information Mart for Intensive Care (MIMIC-III) is a prominent example for the clinical database. MIMIC-III (Johnson et al., 2016) database includes patient's demographics, lab test results, medications, medical reports, survival data, hospital length of stay, observations and medical notes provided by physicians, procedure codes, diagnostic codes and so on. KB has been constructed from medical articles, journals, textbooks related to a particular disease. KB is implemented using concept algebra for CML. Formal concept analysis based on concept algebra (Wang Y and Valipour, 2016) is applied to derive meaningful and useful concepts, objects, and attributes. The different parameters for each patient identified from the case by case analysis are mapped on to the KB.

Cognitive Machine Learning Layer

CML layer

- receives and processes the data from data sources
- application of cognitive learning technique via ML algorithm
- generates the evidence-based optimal result.

CML layer makes use of brain-inspired ML algorithms integrated with big data to perform specific high-level tasks similar to humans. The various processes involved in CML layer are

NLP based Disease Status Identification

Disease status identification is the process of determining the situation or condition of a disease over a series of time intervals. NLP based Cognitive Decision Support System (Alemzadeh and Devarakonda, 2017) is an automated system which determines the disease status from the structured and unstructured medical data of patients. IBM Watson Patient record analytics has been used to analyze the status of disease over intervals of time. The components are sentence segmentation, medical concept annotation, relation detection, medication, and lab vitals extraction. It processes the patient's discharge summaries, medical notes, prescription records, and PHR to identify the disease control targets over the time series. The two main modules are the extraction of evidence from disease status and disease treatment goals. Extraction of evidence from disease status processes the clinical data from the data sources. Disease status is determined from (i) assessment and plan section (example hypertension is well constrained so continue present medications), (ii) laboratory tests or measurement of vital signs (example Blood Pressure (BP) is remaining high), (iii) diagnostic test results (example BP value is 160/80). Disease treatment goals extraction develops a reasoning engine using the data derived from the KB and distills the disease-specific control targets. Transform the targets into a collection of logical conditions based on the patient's demographics and lab test results. The logic rules are then executed by the reasoning engine to identify the status of the disease.

IBM Watson based ML model (Devarakonda and Tsou, 2015) automatically generates a medical problem checklist for each patient. This ML model makes use of NLP techniques to extract the lexical and medical features from the records. It consists of four steps (i) candidate generation, (ii) feature generation, (iii) scoring and weighting, (iv)grouping. Given the structured and unstructured data, the candidate generation step generates clinical factors and Concept Unique Identifiers (CUI). Then the relevant features are generated by using information extraction, text segmentation, and relationship extraction. The scoring/weighting step generates a list of candidate problems. The problems with the highest confidence score are grouped to determine the final list of open-ended problems. The Watson NLP pipeline also summarizes the identified open-ended problems, procedures, medications to provide the physician with a visual summary table (Diomaiuta et al., 2017).

Artificial Neural Networks (ANN) for Disease Onset and Progression

Disease progression explains about the stage by stage worsening of the disease. Progression of the disease is a significant concern for patients, and severe actions should be taken by monitoring the disease and its risk over frequent intervals of time. A computational model is built using ANN to determine the succession of disease and stratification of at-risk individuals. ANN serves as an information processing model and discovers new biomarkers for each disease to identify personalized forecasting of illness. ANN also stratifies the slow progressors as less-risk individuals and fast progressors as high-risk individuals. (Awwalu et al., 2015). For example, continuously monitor the prostate cancer patients for analyzing the disease progression, and provide them with two choices of treatment. The first choice is to take curative treatment immediately with serious complications, and the second choice is to wait until there are signs of disease progression. The PT incorporates the circumstance of the patient and determines the appropriate treatment strategy.

Deep Reinforcement Learning Framework

Deep reinforcement learning framework has been used to determine the optimal DTR (Liu Y et al., 2017) from the clinical data of each patient. This framework establishes a doctor-patient relationship and tailors data and knowledge-driven PT recommendations. It comprises of two steps (i) supervised learning step and (ii) deep reinforcement learning step. In both the steps, the optimal value function is estimated using Deep Neural Network (DNN). This value function estimation is used to provide personalized recommendations. For example, the proposed deep reinforcement learning framework prevents and treats Graft versus Host Disease (GVHD). The framework includes the following processes (i) construction of DNN, (ii) deep Q-learning phase, (iii) cohort retrieval and data preprocessing, (iv) problem definition, (v) possible states and actions, (vi) reward and value functions, and (vii) optimalization techniques for PT.

Hypothesis and Evidence Generation

The essential step in the CML layer is hypothesis and evidence generation. This step consists of three processes, namely hypothesis generation, evidence gathering, and scoring hypothesis. In the first process, for each PT, the hypothesis is generated. This process is responsible for providing many PT recommendations. In the second process, the evidence for each hypothesis is gathered from the KB using ML algorithms. Select the evidence-based hypothesis and reject the evidenceless hypothesis. The third process assigns the degree of confidence to each of the evidence-based hypothesis. Then, calculate the confidence score, and select the PT with the highest confidence score as the optimal PT.

APPLICATIONS OF PERSONALIZED TREATMENT

PT acquires the specific diagnostic tests for each patient, and the most potent treatment is selected based on the test results. PT is an emerging field in healthcare which focuses on each patient's genetic, clinical, and environmental information. The various applications are:

Attention Deficit and Hyperactive Disorder (ADHD)

ADHD is a chronic condition in which the person feels very difficult in paying attention and controlling impulsive behaviors. The children affected by ADHD undergo a two-stage trial for identifying the different intensities of behavioral modifications. Initially, render the children with low dose medication. After two months, the Impairment Rating Scale (IRS) and the Individualized list of Target Behaviors (ITB) (Liu Y et al., 2016) are used to assess the child's response. STAR*D trial method was used for major depressive disorder (MDD) mainly for the children who don't respond to initial treatment. AI focuses on personalized learning, which optimizes the pace of learning and the instructional approach according to the needs of the learner.

Cancer

Cancer is a disease which is defined by cellular alterations. PT for cancer deals with combining genomic and clinical features of each patient to contrive a therapy scheme. DL and active learning are fused and applied to the cancer data for analysis. DL performs deep unsupervised feature learning, and active learning is used to increase accuracy. IBM's Watson For Oncology (WFO) (Somashekhar et al., 2018) is a cognitive computing system which helps the doctors to provide evidence-based and personalized treatment. WFO is an AI-based clinically oriented decision-making system which provides personalized oncological care for breast cancer patients. It consists of a curated KB constructed from at least 300 medical journals, articles, and cancer treatment guidelines. WFO indexes data from patient's medical records, obtain evidence from the curated KB, and inspects the training cases to render the informed decision-based therapy suggestions.

Chronic Kidney Disease (CKD)

CKD is a long-lasting disease of the kidney which leads to renal failure. Literature uses a state-transition microsimulation model for assessing renal tumors. Personalized medication involves identifying the risk factors that worsen CKD (Kang S K et al., 2019). Certain PT strategies were incorporated namely selective ablation, biopsy, watchful waiting and MRI-based surveillance. Personalized decision making has been designed to enhance the treatment of tumors by assessing risk variables.

Autism Spectrum Disorder (ASD)

ASD is a neurodevelopmental disorder, and it has a high impact on how a person perceives, socializes, and interacts with other people. An automated DL based autism prognosis system (Dekhil et al., 2018) makes use of SA and probabilistic Support Vector Machine (SVM) for the prognosis of the disease. The resting-state functional MRI data learns the functional brain connectivity and categorizes the people as autistic or non-autistic by identifying localized abnormalities. The most promising approach is the stratification of biomarkers according to different behavioral modifications, and the PT is provided based on biomarkers.

Diabetes

Diabetes is a severe and lifelong disorder in which the body of the patient is incapable of producing insulin. Computerized clinical decision support system (Donsa et al., 2015) has been designed to personalize diabetes therapy by using ML technology. Fields of ML in personalized diabetes treatment are prediction of blood glucose (non-linear regression problem), hypo-/hyperglycemia detection (classification problem), glycemic variability detection (automated classification task), insulin-based diabetes treatment controller (rule-based and model-based methods) and lifestyle support (automated classification task).

Detailed Case Study for providing PT to the Hypertensive Patients

Hypertension or High BP (HBP) is a chronic condition which raises the pressure of blood against the artery walls. The main aim is to reduce the HBP, thereby preventing the risk of cardiovascular disease and by providing unique and customized treatment to each patient. PT is essential for hypertensive patients because it considers each patient's risk factors, genomic phenotype, pharmacokinetic and other specific features. The process of providing PT includes the following steps

- EMR, EHR and PHR data collection of hypertensive patients
- Cohort Identification
- Identification of New Biomarkers
- Disease Status Identification
- Disease Onset and Progression Modeling
- Evidence-based Personalized Treatment Strategy

The clinical database contains patient's medical history, immunization status, medications, laboratory and test results, diagnoses, progress notes, patient demographics, vital signs, family medical history, diagnostic codes, prescription records, observations of daily living, chronic diseases, illness, and hospitalizations. Patients are stratified, and the cohorts are identified based on the features of the clinical database. Cohort identification deals with feature selection and pre-processing. DL based Stacked Autoencoder algorithm (Nezhad et al., 2016) for feature selection consists of three steps (i) feature partitioning which focuses on representational learning, (ii) feature representation which focuses on unsupervised learning and (iii) supervised learning which focuses on regression and classification. Patient cohort identification deals with the grouping of patients with similar features. Then the biomarkers for hypertension, which indicates the presence or susceptibility to the development of hypertension, are continuously monitored. The biomarkers (Touyz and Burger, 2012), (Shere et al., 2017) are C-Reactive Protein (CRP), Ox-LDL, leptin, TNF alpha, Plasminogen Activator Inhibitor-1, Asymmetric Dimethylarginine (ADMA), Symmetric Dimethylarginine (SDMA) and measures of oxidative stress. Integrate the biomarkers with accurate measurement of BP, and provide meaningful clinical insights for identifying the status of disease and early prognosis. Time series modeling is carried out to estimate the disease status. Determine the progression and onset of hypertension by vascular dysfunction, inflammation and oxidative stress, and predictors. The risk factors for hypertension (Ye C et al., 2019) include gender, age, obesity, stress level, Body Mass Index (BMI), cholesterol, lipoproteins, smoking, and family medical history. Finally, calculate the confidence score for each patient, and determine the various risk categories for classifying the patient as high risk, moderate risk, and low risk. Based on the degree of confidence, render the patient with evidence-based PT.

From these applications, it is clear that PT is applied to all the states of disease development states, risk management, and targeted therapy approaches (Currie and Delles, 2018). With global improvements, PT serves as a battle to fight for the preclusion of chronic diseases.

PT SHAPES THE FUTURE OF HEALTHCARE

PT stimulates early disease prognosis, preclusion, and risk estimation (Mathur and Sutton, 2017). PT enhances the existing traditional treatment based approaches to develop an excellent personalized healthcare system. PT is an innovative prevention based medication system. PT is proved to have a positive and optimal effect in delivering an innovative healthcare system. The highlights of personalized modi cation are target based novel drug development, improved healthcare, optimized treatment selection, biomarker discovery, clinical trials, novel diagnostic and treatment methods, secure patient information, earlier disease detection and optimization of proactive treatment regimes. The other highlights of PT are improved patient outcomes, response to a specific disease, appropriate treatment strategy, disease progression analysis, cost-effectiveness, digitization of healthcare, and novel technology to identify and prioritize disease.

The performance measures of various techniques like AUC (Area Under the ROC Curve), sensitivity, specificity, accuracy, precision, recall, and F-measure, are portrayed. From the Table 1, it can be noted that the deep feature selection approach using Stacked Autoencoders achieved a greater accuracy compared to other techniques.

The various techniques of ML, AI, DL, and NLP showed in Table 1 are explained below:

ML and AI Techniques

SVM, ANN

Application of SVM for treating cardiac diseases provides an accurate classification result of 0.92. Similarly, the application of ANN for treating malignant melanoma, eye problems and different forms of cancer also provides an accurate classification of 0.96.

Multiple Regression

A regression model is developed to establish PT rules through statistical analysis. This technique focuses on the determination of predictive biomarkers to direct the customized therapy selection process based on particular attributes of the illness. This model achieved an accuracy of 0.81.

ART framework

Cohorts of patients who exhibit identical diagnostic clinical or patterns are identified and retrieved efficiently by using the ART technique. The retrieval performance is very high, with a precision of 0.91.

Table 1. ML and AL techniques summary table to provide personalized treatment

Year	Technique	Algorithm	Application	Dataset	Performance Measure
2015	AI techniques (Awwalu et al., 2015)	SVM, ANN	SVM for Cardiac diseases ANN for malignant melanoma, eye problems and different forms of cancer	Real-time dataset	SVM Accuracy – 0.92 F-measure – 0.98 ANN Accuracy – 0.96
2015	ML techniques based on Clinical Decision Support System (Donsa et al., 2015)	Data-driven blood glucose prediction (non-linear regression problem), hypo-/hyperglycemia detection (classification problem), glycemic variability detection (automated classification task),	Diabetes		Non-linear regression problem (ANN with Root Mean Square Error (RMSE)) Accuracy – 0.94 Classification problem (Gaussian SVM) Accuracy – 0.93 Sensitivity – 0.92 Specificity – 0.90 Automated classification (Multilayer Perceptron, Support Vector Regression (SVR) Accuracy – 0.90 Sensitivity – 0.97 Specificity – 0.74
2015	Statistical rule-based methods (Ma et al., 2015)	ITR, multiple regression for randomized clinical trial data, regression model for biomarker discovery	Oncology	Southwest Oncology Group (SOWG)	Accuracy – 0.81
2015	Patient similarity evaluation technique (Wang, 2015)	Adaptive Semi-Supervised Recursive Tree Partitioning (ART) framework	Breast cancer and diabetes	Breast Cancer dataset and Pima Indians Diabetes	Precision – 0.91 F-measure – 0.80
2016	Frequent pattern mining, association rule mining (Kureshi et al., 2016)	SMO, Decision Tree	Non-small cell lung cancer	PubMed database, Catalogue of Somatic Mutations In Cancer (COSMIC) and Estimated Glomerular Filtration Rate (EGFR) Mutations database	SMO Accuracy – 0.76 AUC – 0.76 Precision – 0.77 Recall – 0.77 CART Accuracy – 0.73 AUC – 0.72 Precision – 0.74 Recall – 0.73
2016	Ensemble Fuzzy Models (Salgado et al., 2016)	Fuzzy c-means clustering	Vasopressor administration in Intensive Care Unit (ICU)	MIMIC II and nine benchmark datasets (WBCO, WBCD, WBCP, Glass, Pima, Transfusion, ILPD, Liver, Sonar)	MIMIC II AUC – 0.85 Accuracy – 0.85 Sensitivity – 0.85 Specificity – 0.84 Benchmark datasets AUC – 0.75 Accuracy – 0.79 Sensitivity – 0.78 Specificity – 0.70
2016	Statistical learning methods to estimate optimal ITR (Wang Y et al., 2016)	Classification and Regression Trees in O learning	Diabetes	EHR data from Columbia University clinical data Warehouse	Accuracy – 0.84
2016	Deep Feature Selection (Nezhad et al., 2016)	Stacked Autoencoders	Hypertension and heart disease	African-Americans with hypertension	Accuracy – 0.99
2016	Cognitive Computing approach (Sengupta et al., 2016)	Associative Memory based CML	Cardiac disease	Speckle Tracking Echocardiography (STE) data set	Accuracy – 0.94 AUC – 0.96
2017	Clinical Decision Support (Yoon et al., 2017)	Discovery Engine (DE)	Breast cancer	Patient de-identified database of 10,000 breast cancer patients	Accuracy – 0.90
2018	IBM CTM system (Helgeson et al., 2018)	NLP algorithms to match clinical trials	Breast and lung cancer	Breast and lung cancer at Mayo Clinic	Accuracy – 0.87
2018	Incremental clustering approach (Mulay and Shinde, 2019)	Correlation-Based Incremental Clustering Algorithm (CBICA)	Diabetes	Pathological report of diabetes mellitus	Accuracy – 0.87
2018	Patient-level sequential modeling (Kang, 2018)	RNN	Diabetes	Medical records data from Seoul National University Hospital (SNUH).	Accuracy – 0.88 AUC – 0.87
2018	Optimal PT using neural networks (Atan et al., 2018)	Deep-Treat	Breast cancer	Infant Health and Development (IHDP) dataset and breast cancer dataset.	Accuracy – 0.80
2018	DL technique for image analysis (Xie Q et al., 2019)	CNN	Prostate and breast cancer	Database of 1,30,000 clinical images	Accuracy – 0.89 Sensitivity – 0.96 Specificity – 0.90 AUC – 0.99

Classification algorithms (SMO, Decision Tree)

Decision support and predictive model for personalized therapeutic interventions are developed using frequent pattern mining. The model development comprises of three phases (i) data curation, (ii) association rule detection and (iii) predictive modeling. This model is developed using SMO and decision tree classifiers, which exhibits a classification accuracy of 0.76.

Clustering Algorithm

Fuzzy c-means clustering algorithm renders personalized, prognostic and best treatment guidance to the patients by modeling similar cohorts. The ensemble fuzzy modeling approach achieved a significantly higher performance with an accuracy of 0.85.

Discovery Engine (DE)

DE determines the most relevant features of the patients for presaging the correct prognosis and suggesting the best PT. DE comprises of two algorithms, namely Clinical Decision Dependent Feature Selection (CDFS) and clinical decision recommendation. DE analyzed the de-identified data archive of nearly 10,000 breast cancer patients and achieved an accuracy of 0.90.

Correlation-Based Incremental Clustering Algorithm (CBICA)

An incremental clustering approach CBICA creates clusters from the individualized medical reports of diabetes patients. The various steps of CBICA are pre-clustering, clustering, incremental clustering and post-clustering. This approach takes into account the frequent visits of patients and determines the increase in diabetes level with an accuracy of 0.87.

Deep Learning Techniques

Stacked Autoencoder (SA)

SA based feature selection approach carefully selects the better, appropriate features and provides PT by assessing and prioritizing the risk factors of hypertension. SA approach achieves a better accuracy of 0.99.

DeepTreat

DeepTreat considers the observational data and provides optimal PT using neural networks. This approach consists of two steps (i) bias reduction by representational map learning using an autoencoder network, (ii) construction of effective treatment practices using a feed forward network. This technique is applied in IHDP, breast cancer dataset and achieved a significant improvement in performance with an accuracy of 0.80.

Figure 4. Estimation of accuracy for various algorithms

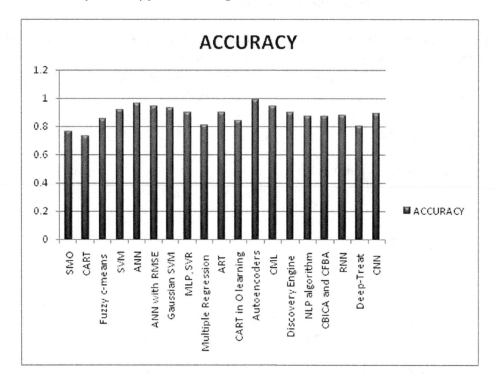

Convolutional Neural Network (CNN)

CNN is an emerging technique which categorizes millions of medical images and provides PT to the patients. CNN categorized nearly 1, 30,000 clinical images of prostate and breast cancer with an accuracy of 0.89. Eight layer deep CNN with ReLu activation function has been used mainly to fit large sized datasets as explained in (Solanki and Pandey 2019).

Recurrent Neural Network (RNN)

Patient-level modeling allows RNN to discover the continuous dependencies encapsulated in the EMR of each diabetes patient to relinquish personalized prediction. This technique achieved a prediction accuracy of 0.88.

Cognitive Machine Learning Techniques

IBM CTM system

IBM Watson CTM system uses NLP techniques to match the patients to clinical trials by analyzing the structured and unstructured data. This cognitive computing system achieved an accuracy of 0.87 when applied to breast trials.

Figure 5. Yearwise development of algorithms for personalized treatment

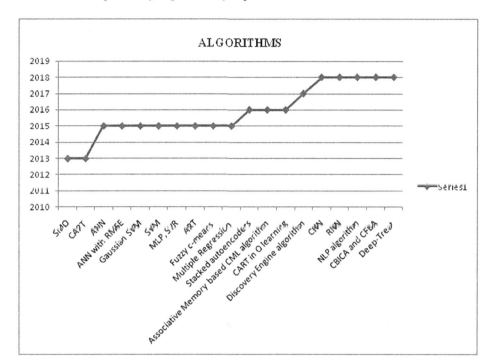

Associative Memory Based CML Algorithm

For learning and recalling patterns from the clinical and electrocardiographic data, Associative Memory Classifier (AMC), a cognitive computing based ML approach observes co-occurrences of predictors under outcomes and designs a set of matrices called associative memories for making predictions. AMC demonstrated a higher accuracy of 0.94.

A bar graph is generated based on the techniques and performance measure, as shown in Figure 4.

The graph, as shown, depicts the different algorithms used for PT along with their accuracy values. The x-axis indicates the algorithms employed for PT and Y-axis indicates the accuracy value of each algorithm. From the graph, it is clear that DL based Stacked Autoencoder (SA) algorithm is very efficient for PT with an accuracy of 0.99. Classification and Regression Trees (CART) is a less efficient algorithm with an accuracy of 0.73.

The graph, as shown in Figure 5, explains the yearwise development of various algorithms from 2013 - 2018 to provide optimal PT. The graph depicts the usage of different algorithms for PT based on ML, DL, and AI techniques, especially in the year 2015 and 2018.

Figure 6. Pros of personalized treatment

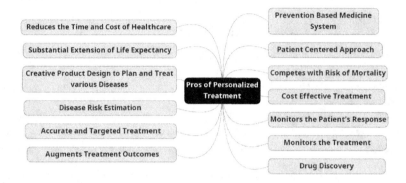

PROS AND CONS OF PERSONALIZED TREATMENT

Pros Of Personalized Treatment

PT is very advantageous in some situations when two persons with the same disease but different symptoms and progress rates respond differently to the same treatment. In such cases, PT is used to predict and manage the differences between patients and provides individualized treatment. The various advantages of PT are depicted in the mind map, as shown in Figure 6.

Reduces the Time and Cost of Healthcare

PT has excellent potential to reduce the time and cost of healthcare. Since many people are worried about their disease risk factors, they undergo costly treatment and tests, but PT predicts the consequences of diseases and provides cost-effective treatment for each patient.

Substantial Extension of Life Expectancy

PT increases the life span of individuals because of the early diagnosis of diseases. When each patient follows the PT prescribed specially for them, their chances of living increases to a greater extent.

Creative Product Design to Plan and Treat various Diseases

Best practices must be established to plan, design, and develop an effective personalized healthcare technology. PT model consists of three stages precise prevention, precise diagnosis, and correct treatment.

Disease Risk Estimation

Using PT, diseases are detected at an early and treatable stage to reduce disease risk. Analyze each patient's patterns of illness and stratify them as less-risk and high-risk patients.

Accurate and Targeted Treatment

PT can make more informed medical decisions and provides more precise treatment for various chronic diseases. PT tends to identify the correct treatment and determine whether the treatment works for the individual or not.

Augments Treatment Outcomes

In PT, patients are proactively involved in treatment decision making. For proactive decision making, use automated reasoning mechanisms. PT is a proactive treatment approach, and it augments the treatment outcomes for optimal treatment.

Prevention Based Medicine System

PT acts as a prevention-based medication because it focuses on prevention of diseases rather than detecting diseases and reacting to them. In prevention based medicine system, focus on healthcare is transformed into predictive and preventive care rather than the treatment of disease.

Patient-centered Approach

PT serves as a patient-centered approach because it provides (i) improved medication, (ii) targeted treatment, (iii) increases patient's confidence, (iv) offers complete satisfaction to patients.

Competes with Risk of Mortality

PT reduces the rate of mortality to a greater extent by some personalized strategies like active surveillance, which monitors the disease risk of patients.

Cost-Effective Treatment

PT provides cost-effective care and treatment to each person. The cost of PT is substantially lower when compared to traditional therapy. PT reduces the cost of care with more informed treatment decisions, and so it becomes cost effective.

Tracks the Patient's Reaction and Therapy

PT continuously follows the patient's response level to individualized therapy to ensure improved treatment outcomes. Disease progression analysis is carried out to categorize slow and fast progressors.

Drug Discovery

Drugs are discovered and developed in a faster and more efficient way by targeting certain diseases rather than the trial and error approach. Analyze the benefits and consequences of each drug to produce safer drugs.

Figure 7. Cons of personalized treatment

CONS OF PERSONALIZED TREATMENT

The implementation of PT faces several challenges in the management of diseases. The most important issue is data standardization and the transition from layered recommendation based techniques to personalized and evidence-based techniques (Currie and Delles, 2018). The various disadvantages of PT are depicted in the mind map, as shown in Figure 7.

Data Storage and Management

Management of massive amounts of data for each patient remains a challenging task in PT. Information from EHR is not standard and interoperable. Specific improvements have to be done in EHR to store huge volumes of patient's data. A hybrid balanced task clustering algorithm (Kaur et al., 2019) serves as an efficient method for large scale data transfer by integrating various tasks with shorter execution time into a single cluster.

Privacy/Security

Privacy/Security is a serious concern to be taken into account in PT. The data about the patients are highly sensitive and therefore deserves special protection. Data sharing practices do not consider privacy issues (Pritchard et al., 2017). Genetic Information Nondiscrimination Act (GINA) has been passed in 2008 to guarantee that the patient's genetic information will not be misused.

Massive Infrastructure Requirement

Healthcare infrastructure is not well equipped for handling enormous amounts of data and information associated with PT. PT requires massive infrastructure, data collection mechanisms, and more time to implement.

Degree of Customization

The main challenge faced while developing personalized medicine is the determination of the degree of customization based on multiple criteria, including patient demographics, clinical need, disease/injury, and cost.

Data Analysis and Interpretation

PT face challenges representing, organizing, and managing large datasets. So, the patient-specific dataset from real-time monitoring needs to be collected and analyzed to provide sufficient insight for an individual patient. Lack of evidence-based, timely, and clinical data analysis and interpretation in PT. Information on PT policies, methods and techniques is insufficient and not available.

Clinical Guidelines and Training

Clinical guidelines and recommendations do not dwell on the recent concepts in PT. The training process for PT is expensive and time- consuming. It is difficult for the patients to have a better intuition of clinical guidelines, technologies, and techniques of PT. Many technologies exist for PT, which leads to confusion. Workforce training for new methodologies is insufficient

DISCUSSION

The most serious issue with customized therapy is the protection of patient details. To overcome this issue, employ patient delegates in the advancement of proactive methods, practices, and policies linked to PT and optimize according to the specific patient characteristics. Another issue is PT is very costly. The cost trend is increased to a greater extent so that the patient's face difficulty in contributing more significant shares for their medical expenses. Coupling the right person with the right drug leads to the formation of significant savings. Inadequate or impractical understanding of PT can be overcome by developing new medical education programs and providing openly accessible educational information and materials. Another major issue is that the healthcare infrastructure and data management are not well equipped. This issue is overcome by making use of existing data, developing proactive practices, standardizing clinical support, developing and implementing user-friendly platforms. PT also helps the doctors as well as patients in choosing the most likely and effective treatment. PT reduces the treatment side effects and avoids the trial and error medicine. PT results in less invasive procedures and results in more control to preclude the diseases.

Blending PT into healthcare using CML technology is a challenging task. There are five principles (Pritchard et al., 2017) for blending PT into healthcare. The first principle states that the patients must have a better intuition of PT ideas, techniques, and technologies. The second principle states that the Schemes related to the protection of patient details must ensure proper approval. The third principle states that best habitudes must be well-established to determine the point of care and clinical utility of PT. The fourth principle states that the enhancement of efficient healthcare infrastructure and data management systems guides clinical decisions. Finally, the fifth principle states that best policies for healthcare delivery approaches, processes and techniques must be enforced. In recent days, PT is moving us near precise, better diagnostics, and effective therapy of diseases, safer and powerful medication (Foroutan, 2015). In future, smart, personalized therapies add up a significant value to the healthcare system.

FUTURE RESEARCH DIRECTIONS AND CONCLUSION

In this chapter, the authors discussed the issues and controversies of traditional treatment and explored the various techniques of AI and ML for providing PT. The workflow of PT using CML techniques to provide an optimal treatment strategy for each patient is visualized. PT serves as an integral part of detecting, managing, and preventing diseases. The overall aim of personalized medicine is that it provides individualized guidelines to the patients for decreasing the health risks based on their personal genetic information. PT provides the ultimate opportunity for Translational Science (TS). It deals with the transfer of preclinical technologies to clinical application. TS makes use of biomarkers, which identifies human disease patterns and reduces failure rates. Management of large repositories remains a challenge towards PT. In the future, to overcome this issue, CML technology combines individual medical information with large scale scientific data, and it allows doctors to determine targeted treatment by immediately accessing all available information. Deep representation in cognitive technology plays a major role in the performance of ML towards PT. This technology allows doctors to identify similar cases of patients and suggest the best PT. Another challenge in PT is the protection of privacy and confidentiality. In the future, develop a personalized medicine workbench for secure storage and sharing of heterogeneous data. To provide evidence-based and customized therapy improve the diagnostic tests which focus on the specific characteristics of each patient. In future, the clinically oriented experiments test the intervention and the stratification rules. To effectively implement PT in clinical practice, the total involvement of the patient is necessary.

REFERENCES

Aggarwal, M., & Madhukar, M. (2017). IBM's Watson Analytics for Health Care: A Miracle Made True. In Cloud Computing Systems and Applications in Healthcare (pp. 117-134). IGI Global. doi:10.4018/978-1-5225-1002-4.ch007

Aguado, B. A., Grim, J. C., Rosales, A. M., Watson-Capps, J. J., & Anseth, K. S. (2018). Engineering precision biomaterials for personalized medicine. *Science Translational Medicine, 10*(424).

Alemzadeh, H., & Devarakonda, M. (2017, February). An NLP-based cognitive system for disease status identification in electronic health records. In *2017 IEEE EMBS International Conference on Biomedical & Health Informatics (BHI)* (pp. 89-92). IEEE. 10.1109/BHI.2017.7897212

Atan, O., Jordon, J., & van der Schaar, M. (2018, April). Deep-treat: Learning optimal personalized treatments from observational data using neural networks. *Thirty-Second AAAI Conference on Artificial Intelligence.*

Awwalu, J., Garba, A. G., Ghazvini, A., & Atuah, R. (2015). Artificial intelligence in personalized medicine application of AI algorithms in solving personalized medicine problems. *International Journal of Computer Theory and Engineering, 7*(6), 439–443. doi:10.7763/IJCTE.2015.V7.999

Ayer, T., & Chen, Q. (2018). Personalized medicine. Handbook of Healthcare Analytics: Theoretical Minimum for Conducting 21st Century Research on Healthcare Operations, 109-135.

Bogani, G., Ditto, A., Martinelli, F., Signorelli, M., Chiappa, V., Leone Roberti Maggiore, U., ... Lorusso, D. (2019). Artificial intelligence estimates the impact of human papillomavirus types in influencing the risk of cervical dysplasia recurrence: Progress toward a more personalized approach. *European Journal of Cancer Prevention*, *28*(2), 81–86. doi:10.1097/CEJ.0000000000000432 PMID:29360648

Currie, G., & Delles, C. (2018). Precision medicine and personalized medicine in cardiovascular disease. In *Sex-Specific Analysis of Cardiovascular Function* (pp. 589–605). Cham: Springer. doi:10.1007/978-3-319-77932-4_36

De Regge, M., Decoene, E., Eeckloo, K., & Van Hecke, A. (2019). Development and Evaluation of an Integrated Digital Patient Platform During Oncology Treatment. *Journal of Patient Experience*.

Dekhil, O., Hajjdiab, H., Shalaby, A., Ali, M. T., Ayinde, B., Switala, A., ... El-Baz, A. (2018). Using resting state functional MRI to build a personalized autism diagnosis system. *PLoS One*, *13*(10), e0206351. doi:10.1371/journal.pone.0206351 PMID:30379950

Dessì, D., Recupero, D. R., Fenu, G., & Consoli, S. (2019). A recommender system of medical reports leveraging cognitive computing and frame semantics. In *Machine Learning Paradigms* (pp. 7–30). Cham: Springer. doi:10.1007/978-3-319-94030-4_2

Devarakonda, M., & Tsou, C. H. (2015, March). Automated problem list generation from electronic medical records in IBM Watson. *Twenty-Seventh IAAI Conference*.

Diomaiuta, C., Mercorella, M., Ciampi, M., & De Pietro, G. (2017, July). A novel system for the automatic extraction of a patient problem summary. In *2017 IEEE Symposium on Computers and Communications (ISCC)* (pp. 182-186). IEEE. 10.1109/ISCC.2017.8024526

Donsa, K., Spat, S., Beck, P., Pieber, T. R., & Holzinger, A. (2015). Towards personalization of diabetes therapy using computerized decision support and machine learning: some open problems and challenges. In *Smart Health* (pp. 237–260). Cham: Springer. doi:10.1007/978-3-319-16226-3_10

Foroutan, B. (2015). Personalized medicine: A review with regard to biomarkers. *Journal of Bioequivalence & Bioavailability*, *7*(06), 244–256. doi:10.4172/jbb.1000248

Helgeson, J., Rammage, M., Urman, A., Roebuck, M. C., Coverdill, S., Pomerleau, K., ... Williamson, M. P. (2018). *Clinical performance pilot using cognitive computing for clinical trial matching at Mayo Clinic*. Academic Press.

Jiang, X., Wells, A., Brufsky, A., & Neapolitan, R. (2019). A clinical decision support system learned from data to personalize treatment recommendations towards preventing breast cancer metastasis. *PLoS One*, *14*(3), e0213292. doi:10.1371/journal.pone.0213292 PMID:30849111

Johnson, A. E., Pollard, T. J., Shen, L., Li-wei, H. L., Feng, M., Ghassemi, M., ... Mark, R. G. (2016). MIMIC-III, a freely accessible critical care database. *Scientific Data*, *3*(1), 160035. doi:10.1038data.2016.35 PMID:27219127

Kang, S. (2018). Personalized prediction of drug efficacy for diabetes treatment via patient-level sequential modeling with neural networks. *Artificial Intelligence in Medicine*, *85*, 1–6. doi:10.1016/j.artmed.2018.02.004 PMID:29482961

Kang, S. K., Huang, W. C., Elkin, E. B., Pandharipande, P. V., & Braithwaite, R. S. (2019). Personalized Treatment for Small Renal Tumors: Decision Analysis of Competing Causes of Mortality. *Radiology*, *290*(3), 732–743. doi:10.1148/radiol.2018181114 PMID:30644815

Kaur, A., Gupta, P., & Singh, M. (2019). Hybrid Balanced Task Clustering Algorithm for Scientific Workflows in Cloud Computing. *Scalable Computing: Practice and Experience*, *20*(2), 237–258.

Kronish, I. M., Cheung, Y. K., Shimbo, D., Julian, J., Gallagher, B., Parsons, F., & Davidson, K. W. (2019). Increasing the Precision of Hypertension Treatment Through Personalized Trials: A Pilot Study. *Journal of General Internal Medicine*, *34*(6), 839–845. doi:10.100711606-019-04831-z PMID:30859504

Kureshi, N., Abidi, S. S. R., & Blouin, C. (2014). A predictive model for personalized therapeutic interventions in non-small cell lung cancer. *IEEE Journal of Biomedical and Health Informatics*, *20*(1), 424–431. doi:10.1109/JBHI.2014.2377517 PMID:25494516

Liu, H., Li, X., Xie, G., Du, X., Zhang, P., Gu, C., & Hu, J. (2017). Precision Cohort Finding with Outcome-Driven Similarity Analytics: A Case Study of Patients with Atrial Fibrillation. In MedInfo (pp. 491-495). Academic Press.

Liu, Y., Logan, B., Liu, N., Xu, Z., Tang, J., & Wang, Y. (2017, August). Deep reinforcement learning for dynamic treatment regimes on medical registry data. In *2017 IEEE International Conference on Healthcare Informatics (ICHI)* (pp. 380-385). IEEE. 10.1109/ICHI.2017.45

Liu, Y., Wang, Y., Kosorok, M. R., Zhao, Y., & Zeng, D. (2016). *Robust hybrid learning for estimating personalized dynamic treatment regimens.* arXiv preprint arXiv:1611.02314

Ma, J., Stingo, F. C., & Hobbs, B. P. (2019). Bayesian personalized treatment selection strategies that integrate predictive with prognostic determinants. *Biometrical Journal. Biometrische Zeitschrift*, *61*(4), 902–917. doi:10.1002/bimj.201700323 PMID:30786040

Mathur, S., & Sutton, J. (2017). Personalized medicine could transform healthcare. *Biomedical Reports*, *7*(1), 3–5. doi:10.3892/br.2017.922 PMID:28685051

Mulay, P., & Shinde, K. (2019). Personalized diabetes analysis using correlation-based incremental clustering algorithm. In *Big Data Processing Using Spark in Cloud* (pp. 167–193). Singapore: Springer. doi:10.1007/978-981-13-0550-4_8

Nezhad, M. Z., Sadati, N., Yang, K., & Zhu, D. (2019). A deep active survival analysis approach for precision treatment recommendations: Application of prostate cancer. *Expert Systems with Applications*, *115*, 16–26. doi:10.1016/j.eswa.2018.07.070

Nezhad, M. Z., Zhu, D., Li, X., Yang, K., & Levy, P. (2016, December). Safs: A deep feature selection approach for precision medicine. In *2016 IEEE International Conference on Bioinformatics and Biomedicine (BIBM)* (pp. 501-506). IEEE. 10.1109/BIBM.2016.7822569

Pritchard, D. E., Moeckel, F., Villa, M. S., Housman, L. T., McCarty, C. A., & McLeod, H. L. (2017). Strategies for integrating personalized medicine into healthcare practice. *Personalized Medicine*, *14*(2), 141–152. doi:10.2217/pme-2016-0064 PMID:29754553

Rhrissorrakrai, K., Koyama, T., & Parida, L. (2016). Watson for genomics: Moving personalized medicine forward. *Trends in Cancer*, 2(8), 392–395. doi:10.1016/j.trecan.2016.06.008 PMID:28741491

Salgado, C. M., Vieira, S. M., Mendonça, L. F., Finkelstein, S., & Sousa, J. M. (2016). Ensemble fuzzy models in personalized medicine: Application to vasopressors administration. *Engineering Applications of Artificial Intelligence*, 49, 141–148. doi:10.1016/j.engappai.2015.10.004

Sengupta, P. P., Huang, Y. M., Bansal, M., Ashrafi, A., Fisher, M., Shameer, K., ... Dudley, J. T. (2016). Cognitive machine-learning algorithm for cardiac imaging: A pilot study for differentiating constrictive pericarditis from restrictive cardiomyopathy. *Circulation: Cardiovascular Imaging*, 9(6), e004330. doi:10.1161/CIRCIMAGING.115.004330 PMID:27266599

Shere, A., Eletta, O., & Goyal, H. (2017). Circulating blood biomarkers in essential hypertension: A literature review. *Journal of Laboratory and Precision Medicine*, 2(12).

Solanki, A., & Pandey, S. (2019). Music instrument recognition using deep convolutional neural networks. *International Journal of Information Technology*, 1-10.

Somashekhar, S. P., Sepúlveda, M. J., Puglielli, S., Norden, A. D., Shortliffe, E. H., Rohit Kumar, C., ... Ramya, Y. (2018). Watson for Oncology and breast cancer treatment recommendations: Agreement with an expert multidisciplinary tumor board. *Annals of Oncology: Official Journal of the European Society for Medical Oncology*, 29(2), 418–423. doi:10.1093/annonc/mdx781 PMID:29324970

Tehrani, N. (2018). How Personalized Artificial Intelligence Is Advancing Treatment Of Diabetes. *International Journal of Scientific and Education Research*, 2, 30–33.

Telles, S., Pathak, S., Singh, N., & Balkrishna, A. (2014). Research on traditional medicine: What has been done, the difficulties, and possible solutions. *Evidence-Based Complementary and Alternative Medicine*. PMID:25013445

Touyz, R. M., & Burger, D. (2012). Biomarkers in hypertension. In *Special issues in hypertension* (pp. 237–246). Milano: Springer. doi:10.1007/978-88-470-2601-8_19

Wang, F. (2015). Adaptive semi-supervised recursive tree partitioning: The ART towards large scale patient indexing in personalized healthcare. *Journal of Biomedical Informatics*, 55, 41–54. doi:10.1016/j.jbi.2015.01.009 PMID:25656756

Wang, Y., & Valipour, M. (2016). Formal Properties and Mathematical Rules of Concept Algebra for Cognitive Machine Learning (I). *Journal of Advanced Mathematics and Applications*, 5(1), 53–68. doi:10.1166/jama.2016.1091

Wang, Y., Wu, P., Liu, Y., Weng, C., & Zeng, D. (2016, October). Learning optimal individualized treatment rules from electronic health record data. In *2016 IEEE International Conference on Healthcare Informatics (ICHI)* (pp. 65-71). IEEE. 10.1109/ICHI.2016.13

Xie, Q., Faust, K., Van Ommeren, R., Sheikh, A., Djuric, U., & Diamandis, P. (2019). Deep learning for image analysis: Personalizing medicine closer to the point of care. *Critical Reviews in Clinical Laboratory Sciences*, 56(1), 61–73. doi:10.1080/10408363.2018.1536111 PMID:30628494

Xie, T., & Yu, Z. (2017). N-of-1 Design and its applications to personalized treatment studies. *Statistics in Biosciences*, *9*(2), 662–675. doi:10.100712561-016-9165-9 PMID:29225716

Ye, C., Fu, T., Hao, S., Zhang, Y., Wang, O., Jin, B., ... Guo, Y. (2018). Prediction of incident hypertension within the next year: Prospective study using statewide electronic health records and machine learning. *Journal of Medical Internet Research*, *20*(1), e22. doi:10.2196/jmir.9268 PMID:29382633

Yoon, J., Davtyan, C., & van der Schaar, M. (2016). Discovery and clinical decision support for personalized healthcare. *IEEE Journal of Biomedical and Health Informatics*, *21*(4), 1133–1145. doi:10.1109/JBHI.2016.2574857 PMID:27254875

Chapter 6
Text Classification Using Self–Structure Extended Multinomial Naive Bayes

Arun Solanki
Gautam Buddha University, India

Rajat Saxena
Gautam Buddha University, India

ABSTRACT

With the advent of neural networks and its subfields like deep neural networks and convolutional neural networks, it is possible to make text classification predictions with high accuracy. Among the many subtypes of naive Bayes, multinomial naive Bayes is used for text classification. Many attempts have been made to somehow develop an algorithm that uses the simplicity of multinomial naive Bayes and at the same time incorporates feature dependency. One such effort was put in structure extended multinomial naive Bayes, which uses one-dependence estimators to inculcate dependencies. Basically, one-dependence estimators take one of the attributes as features and all other attributes as its child. This chapter proposes self structure extended multinomial naïve Bayes, which presents a hybrid model, a combination of the multinomial naive Bayes and structure extended multinomial naive Bayes. Basically, it tries to classify the instances that were misclassified by structure extended multinomial naive Bayes as there was no direct dependency between attributes.

INTRODUCTION

Human civilization has always looked for better ways to carry out their lives. Whether it is a steam engine, electric motor, computers, or the internet, all these things changed the way authors live life. With automation coming in almost all the fields, authors, humans, do not have to do the laborious and repetitive work any longer. When computers came in the 70s and 80s, they brought with them a tide of changes in the way authors work. Programming automated many activities in the 90s. With the advent

DOI: 10.4018/978-1-5225-9643-1.ch006

of Artificial Intelligence, machines can do a lot of decision-making work themselves. Less human involvement means less human errors.

One such task is text classification (Webb, G. et al., 2005) which comes under machine learning. In text classification, this chapter classifies various documents into different known classes. Therefore, it is also known as document classification. Various use cases of text classification are email spam filtering, news article classification, and author prediction of historical texts.

Various algorithms have been developed to automate the task of text classification. Modern-day machine learning algorithms are capable of text classification as accurate as humans. In some cases, computer algorithms can beat the human brain also. Using Deep Learning and Convolutional Neural network, past researchers achieve very high accuracy for text classification. Some of the popular text classification algorithms are listed below. Each one of these has certain advantages as well as disadvantages. Some of these methods are very complex to implement (Jiang, L. et al., 2016).

Past studies used a variant of Bayesian methods for the development of text classification algorithm. Bayesian algorithms use Bayes Theorem at its core. Bayesian techniques give good results, but up to a specific limit. MNB is mostly used for text classification when considering Bayesian classifier. The main disadvantage of Multinomial Naive Bayes (MNB) is that it does not represent the dependency between attributes or features (Jiang, L. et al., 2016). In real life, the words in a document are always interrelated. This interrelation is the prime reason for less accuracy of MNB over another state of the art algorithms. Many authors have tried to overcome this limitation to increase accuracy.

This chapter explored and studied various techniques available for text classification using MNB. The proposed chapter worked on FBIS dataset (Foreign Broadcast Information Service), which consists of 2463 documents, 200 features, and 17 classes. Preprocessing of a dataset is often done to clean it from any outliers present that may deviate the final results. The downloaded dataset was already preprocessed as the words with less than three occurrences were pruned. After that, the algorithm is implemented in the WEKA framework (Witten, I.H. et al., 2011) in JAVA. Finally, the proposed technique is verified by training on the dataset and then tested on new data.

LITERATURE SURVEY

Text classification using MNB (McCallum, A. et al., 1998) assumed that all the attributes or features were independent of each other. However, this assumption was seldom valid in real life. If authors go through any document, the authors found that many words were related to each other in some way or the other. This naive assumption of MNB was the prime reason for it not giving high accuracy. According to it, all the attributes were connected to only the class node and not to each other. However, this limitation can be overcome if try to extend its structure.

Extending the structure allows authors to connect attribute nodes. This could help authors to classify real-life documents and improve accuracy. However, structure extension was challenging if authors have documents that contain a vast number of attributes. An extensive dimensional data can take tremendous time and vast space complexity (Chickering, D.M., 1996).

MNB was a form of a Bayesian network (Pearl, J., 1988), which was a graph consisting of nodes and their connecting arcs. It was also called as a Bayesian structure in which attributes acts as the nodes, and the relationship between attributes was represented through arcs connecting the nodes. These arcs also have arrows, suggesting the direction of a relationship, i.e., an arrow from parent to child indicates that the child was dependent on the parent. To implement the Bayesian network, authors need two things. One was structured learning, and the other was parameter learning. Structure learning means to find the structure of the network, i.e., how were the attributes connected. Authors use structure learning to find which arcs were connected between which attributes. This was often a time-consuming task (NP-Hard), and once authors were done with it, authors have to do parameter learning. Parameter learning was defined as calculating the value of arcs that were present between the attributes. More the value more closely were the attributes related to each other.

Many techniques have been published by authors that aim to improve the accuracy of MNB. One such technique was Frequency Transforming (Amati, G. et al., 2002) (Clinchant, S. et al., 2011) (Ibrahim, O.A.S. et al., 2014) (Madsen, R.E. et al., 2004) (Mendoza, M., 2012) (Norasetsathporn, P., 2002). In this approach, the authors transform the word frequencies. Word frequency was the word count in a document. Transformed word frequencies solve the problem of MNB to some extent. The main equation used for conditional class probability remains the same, but the conditional word probability changes.

Another approach to improve MNB was Instance Weighting (Freund, Y. et al., 1995) (Freund, Y. et al., 1996) (Jiang, L. et al., 2012). In this technique, the authors assign different weights to various documents. Many algorithms have been developed to assign weights to document. The most popular approach was Boosting (Freund, Y. et al., 1995) (Freund, Y. et al., 1996), in which authors have an ensemble of classifiers. Authors determine which documents have been misclassified by the previous classifier and give these documents more weights before classifying again on a new classifier. There may be any number of base classifiers in this approach, which was given by parameter T rounds. (Jiang, L. et al., 2012) presented a new approach for instance weighting called Discriminatively Weighted MNB. In this algorithm, all the documents were discriminately assigned weights according to the conditional probability.

Many other algorithms have been implemented that were hybrid of two or more algorithms to improve the accuracy of MNB. One such approach was called Local Learning (Jiang, L. et al., 2013), (Wang, S. et al., 2015), which combines the K-Nearest Neighbors algorithm with the MNB. The basic idea was to train the documents that were only near to the test data to build the model. Therefore, the whole training dataset was not used to classify; only neighborhood data was used. To find the neighboring points of a test document, authors use k-nearest neighbors algorithm. It was a lazy algorithm, which means that training of the dataset was not done until testing time. These lazy learning methods train the data according to the test data only. The main advantage of this model was that authors do not have to build a classifier model on full training dataset, but only on some data chosen according to k-nearest algorithms. This algorithm was called Locally Weighted MNB (Jiang, L. et al., 2013). For finding the neighborhood of a test data, authors can use many more machine learning algorithms like Decision Tree. (Wang, S. et al., 2015) Used decision tree for this purpose and named the technique as MNB Tree. It builds a decision tree and splits the values into zero and non-zero.

Many authors have also proposed to weight features for increasing the accuracy of MNB. Feature weighting (Lan, M. et al., 2009) (Li, Y. et al., 2012) (Liu, Y. et al., 2009) (Song, S. et al., 2012) (Wang, S. et al., 2014) approaches assign different weights to each attribute. (Li, Y. et al., 2012)(Kim, S.B et al., 2006) Used computing feature weights like information gain, risk ratio, χ^2 static, etc. Initially, only the equation used for classifying documents was used incorporated with weights, but now the conditional probability of words equation also has weights. There was also an approach using Topic Document Model (Kim, S.B et al., 2002) to give weights to attributes.

(Wang, S. et al., 2014) Used correlation-based feature selection (CFS) (Hall, M., 2000) approach to fulfill the same purpose. They first applied CFS to select the best features from the whole dataset and then assigned more weights to the selected ones and fewer weights to others. This technique of assigning weights to features to increase the accuracy was called Feature Weighted MNB (Wang, S. et al., 2014).

Feature selection (Javed, K. et al., 2015) (Yang, Y. et al., 1997) plays a very vital role in text classification. Real-life documents consist of tens of thousands of words. Each of these words acts as features in machine learning algorithms. Now, the problem in Bayesian models was that it would have to do the parameter learning for all these words, which would take very high time complexity. So many authors have proposed techniques to select only essential attributes and build a model only using them. These were various feature selection algorithms like mutual information, CHI square, information gain, and document frequency. According to (Yang, Y. et al., 1997), CHI Square and Information Gain were best approaches for feature selection in text classification as they do not affect the accuracy of the algorithms. A two-stage Markov blanket feature selection method was proposed.

Although many authors have improved, MNB, very few have paid heed towards the feature independence assumption of it. According to this assumption, all the features were independent of each other. However, this was seldom the case because, in real-life documents, most of the words have relation to other words in the document. To solve this issue, One-Dependence Estimators have been discussed (Webb, G. et al., 2005). In One-dependence estimators, authors make a single feature as the parent and all other features as its direct child. This was done one by one for all the features, i.e., all the features become parents precisely one time. Authors consider each feature becoming a parent as one model. So, if there were 1000 features in a dataset, then there will be 1000 models as well. After computing these individual models, authors take their average. This was called as one-dependence estimators because all other features depend on only one feature. Although one-dependence estimators have lousy time complexity, they have given better accuracy as compared to vanilla MNB.

(Jiang, L. et al., 2012) proposed a new technique called a Weighted Average of One-Dependence Estimators. As the name suggests, it has got to do with weights. It assigns weights to all the attributes. When authors were calculating One-Dependence Estimators, at that time, authors include the weight of the parent attribute itself. Moreover, at the time of average, authors take weighted average.

Structure Extended MNB (McCallum, A. et al., 1998) was based on the Weighted Average of One-Dependence Estimators. As discussed by the authors, its accuracy was better than other MNB techniques.

In SEMNB (Jiang, L. et al., 2016), the authors have mentioned that they have transferred some training computations into testing time, which was a proper technique. At the training time, they compute independent class probabilities, conditional word probabilities, and attribute weights. While at the testing time, they calculate the one-dependence estimators for only those words that were present in the test document. This saves many computations and hence, time. If this step had been done at training time, authors would have estimated One-Dependence estimators for all the attributes in the dataset, which was insanely high.

TEXT CLASSIFICATION AND RELATED CONCEPTS

In the era of artificial intelligence, text classification plays a vital role. Machine Learning algorithms being extensively used to do the task of text classification accurately. Naive Bayes was the simplest algorithms used for this task. The Naive Bayes depend on a very classical theorem of mathematics known as

Figure 1. Text classification articles

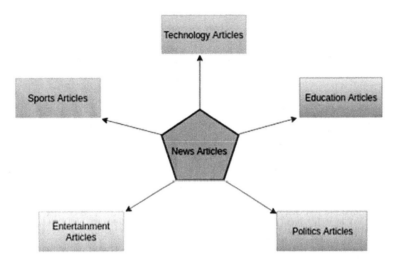

Figure 2. Text classification keywords

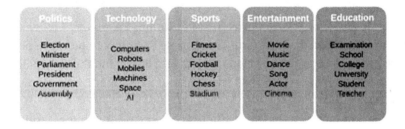

Bayes Theorem. MNB, a type of Naive Bayes, was extensively used in Text Classification. This chapter discusses all these topics in detail.

Text Classification

With the onset of web technology, there have always been discussions about how can authors categorize different digital documents into various categories. Classification of text has various use cases (Rennie, J.D. et al., 2003) like spam filtering, author prediction, news categorization, etc. In the earlier days, most of this digital document classification was done using a static approach. Mostly, an expert was hired who had immense knowledge and experience in the domain field. This expert used to list down various keywords corresponding to different classes. For example, authors can take into consideration the news article categorization, as shown in figure 1. The expert would make a list of keywords for each news category, like politics, technology, sports, and entertainment.

Then this list of keywords was passed to a programmer, who would match these words in various documents and classify them respectively. The more keywords of a particular class matched, the more the probability of the document belonging to that class. Figure 2 shows various keywords for different classes.

Figure 3. Machine learning steps

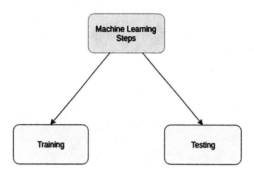

However, with the increase in content, more classes were included. As a result, the keywords increased drastically, and more importantly, the task of domain expert became obnoxious. Hence, a few companies invested in research to automate this task of text classification, as there were various use cases. One of the most compelling use cases was in the history department. Many old texts are unearthed occasionally. Mostly, a part of these texts was discovered, not the full documents. So, it becomes a lot more challenging to find who wrote this magnificent piece of text. Using text classification, authors can find if this text has similarity to some other earlier found text. If the similarity was found, then this text belongs to that particular author, otherwise not.

Another use case of Text classification was Spam Filtering. Yahoo and Google were the first successful companies to introduce emails to ordinary people. With more and more people using emails, there started a problem with spams. The spams are advertising or fraudulent emails, which are of no use to the user. So, these companies developed an automatic spam filtering programs which extensively used text classification.

As authors can see, nowadays, text classification was being used in many fields. It has become an essential concept in Artificial Intelligence. Much intelligent software was inherently using cutting edge text classification techniques to categorize online documents successfully. Furthermore, research was being done to do this classification task in a more optimized manner, i.e., requiring less time to classify.

Machine Learning

(Pandey and Solanki, 2019), discuss the machine learning process with a vast dataset. The machine processes this large dataset and tries to form a pattern. This is called training in machine learning. Then authors provide test data and try to predict an outcome. This is called as testing in machine learning. Machine Learning uses statistical techniques likes probability, inferential statistics, and descriptive statistics to predict outcomes. Machine Learning gives our computers the ability to perform tasks without being explicitly programmed. Figure 3 illustrates the steps involved in a machine learning algorithm.

Around 20% of the current jobs will be replaced by Machine Learning in the future. Many machine learning algorithms have been developed in the past. Significant machine learning algorithms are Naive Bayes, Support Vector Machines, Nearest Neighbor, K-Means, Random Forest, Artificial Neural Networks, Linear and Logistic Regressions, Decision Trees, etc. Each of these algorithms has its application areas. All these techniques are used for data modeling and analysis. Some major domains are Image recognition, Voice recognition, Optical character recognition, etc .

Figure 4. Machine learning types

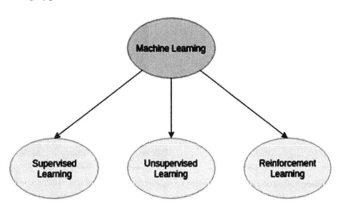

Broadly, there are three types of machine learning algorithms, depending on whether labels or feedbacks are present. Figure 4 shows the different types of ML algorithms (Ahuja, R. et al., 2019), (Solanki, A. and Kumar, A., 2018).

- Supervised Algorithms - In this type of machine learning, authors have classes or labels. This means that each data point belongs to a class or has a label attached to it. Example: News Article Classification. Supervised algorithms are of many types, like classification and regression. Classification is the task of classifying new data point into one of the known classes.
- Unsupervised Algorithms - In this type of machine learning, authors do not have classes or labels. These algorithms cluster the data into various groups. Example: Voice recognition. These algorithms are profoundly used in data clustering and dimensionality reduction. Clustering is the task of grouping the data into two or more categories.
- Reinforcement Learning - In this type of machine learning, authors give scores for every right move. This is similar to a child learning a new game. Authors try different tactics until authors win a game and then learn from that experience. Example: Autonomous Cars and Computer game Alpha-Go.

Bayes' Theorem

Bayes' Theorem (Wang, S. et al., 2014) was a popular probability theorem given by Thomas Bayes in 1763. The following equation represents the statement of Bayes' Theorem. It states that the probability of an event such that authors have some prior knowledge is equal to the inverse probability of that knowledge such that the event has already happened, multiplied by the ratio of the independent probability of occurrence of event A to the total probability of occurrence of event B. The equation 1 is called Bayes' Theorem.

$$P(A|B) = \frac{P(B|A)*P(A)}{P(B)}$$
(1)

Figure 5. Types of Naive Bayes

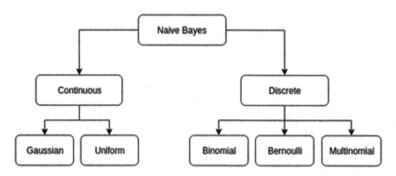

where,

- A and B are events, and P(B) is not equal to zero
- P(A|B) is the Posterior Probability
- P(A) is the Prior Probability of A
- P(B|A) is the Likelihood Probability
- P(B) is the Total Probability of B

The history of Bayes Theorem is quite impressive. As mentioned (Wang, S. et al., 2014), Thomas Bayes wanted to find the chances that God exists such that authors are given some real-life events. He devised this work in his last days. He was never able to publish this mind-blowing work because of his death. This theorem was presented posthumously by his friend Richard Price in the Royal Society in 1763. It was a very significant achievement that even after more than 280 years, this theorem is still being used. Major real-life applications of Bayes' Theorem include drug testing, machine learning, Catalyst tester, medical tests, colonoscopy, etc. In machine learning, all the algorithms that come under the family of Bayesian classifiers use Bayes theorem as their core equations.

Naive Bayes

According to (Li, Y. et al., 2012), Naive Bayes is a machine learning classification algorithm that uses Bayes' theorem to predict the class of test data. It is called as 'naive,' because of its assumption that all the attributes are independent to each other. Therefore, it is sometimes called as idiot Bayes because of this loose assumption. As it is a probabilistic classifier, it depends a lot on the probability density functions. Naive Bayes equations change if the density function is continuous or discrete. Figure 5 classifies different types of Naive Bayes based on probability distributions.

MNB

MNB (McCallum, A. et al., 1998) (Jiang, L. et al., 2016) uses multinomial probability density functions. In these types of density functions, the event is performed multiple times, and the number of outcomes is also more than two. It is ideal for text classification as the number of classes is more than two (outcomes), and there are various documents in training dataset (trials). Word counts can be easily

Table 1. Bag Of Words

Word	Count
Computer	3
Language	2
Long	1
History	2
Pascal	1
First	1
Popular	1
Become	1
Have	1

interpreted through MNB. Therefore, it has extensively been used in text classification domain for a long time. Significant machine learning libraries have MNB functions like sci-kit learn in python and WEKA (Witten, H. et al., 2011) in java.

MNB uses a concept of Bag of Words (Jiang, L. et al., 2016). Authors do not directly process the text documents, and rather authors first convert it into a map of unique words and their corresponding count in that document. This is called the Bag of Words. Table 3.1 shows an example of Bag of Words for the document below.

Computer languages have a long history. Pascal was the first computer language to become popular in the history of computers.

Weka

WEKA stands for Waikato Environment for Knowledge Analysis. It is a JAVA framework for Machine Learning. It has inbuilt algorithms for classification, clustering, associations, attribute selections, attribute weighting, etc. It also has a plug-in manager, through which you can install third-party algorithms and run in WEKA. It is mostly known for its vast set of classification algorithms like Bayesian algorithms, lazy learning algorithms, meta algorithms, tree-based classification algorithms, etc. It is developed by the University of Waikato, New Zealand and is free and open-source software. Figure 6 shows the convenient WEKA Explorer window.

It has six panels, namely Preprocess, Classify, Cluster, Associate, Select Attribute, and Visualize. Preprocess panel is used for loading dataset and preprocessing it using available filters. Here, you may load a .arff, .csv, .json, etc type of files. Classify panel is used for classification and regression algorithms. Some common algorithms present here are Support Vector Machines, Neural Networks, Linear Regression, etc. Cluster panel, as the name suggests, is used for clustering algorithms. Common clustering algorithms included in WEKA are K-means, Fuzzy C- Means, Hierarchical clustering, etc.

The associate panel in the WEKA explorer window is used for forming association rules between various attributes. It is helpful where authors want to find interrelationship between features. Select Attribute panel is used for selecting or filtering attributes. It is also used when authors want to assign

Figure 6. WEKA explorer

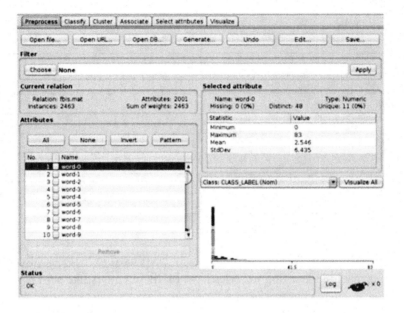

weights to each attribute. The last panel is the Visualize panel, where authors can analyze various scatter plots between various entities like classes and attributes.

DESIGN AND IMPLEMENTATION OF PROPOSED APPROACH

This section introduces the proposed approach Self Structure Extended MNB. It is a hybrid model of MNB and Structure Extended MNB. MNB takes care of the class dependencies of each attribute, and on the other hand, Structure Extended MNB includes the much-needed attribute dependency between each other. The model obtained performs better than the two individual algorithms with almost no increase in time or space complexity. This chapter discusses the design of the proposed approach in detail. Implementation of the algorithm is also stated with corresponding equations.

Self Structure Extended MNB

Figure 7 shows that the design of the Self Structure Extension MNB. The first four models are of Structure Extension MNB, and the last one belongs to the MNB. Together the whole figure is Self Structure Extended MNB. In the first model, the attribute A_1 is the parent while all other are its direct children. In the second model, the attribute A_2 is the parent while all other are its direct children. Similarly, in the third and fourth model, A_3 and A_4 are parents, respectively. In the last model, no attribute is the parent, and all of them depend directly on class.

Figure 7. Self structure extended MNB

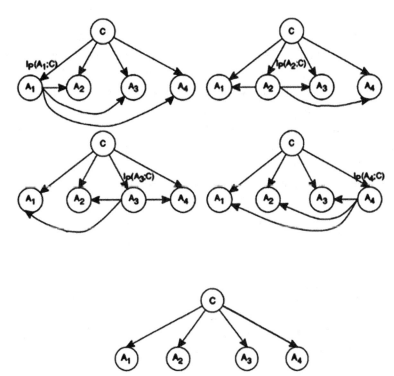

Figure 8. Process flow of SEMNB

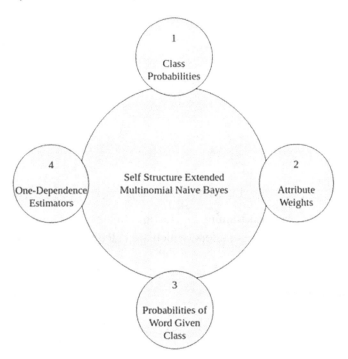

Process Flow

Figure 8 shows the process flow of Self Structure Extended MNB. In step 1, the authors find the independent class probability, which is the prior probability of each class. It tells how many documents of each class are present. In step 2, the authors find the weight of each attribute. Here, authors use the concept of gain ratio. It is the ratio of Information gain to the Split Information. These both are entropy measures and tell the effect of presence and absence of each attribute in the dataset. In step 3, authors find the conditional probability of each word such that a class is given. A particular class can be a label of many documents.

Moreover, a particular word can occur in many documents as well. This is how conditional probability is calculated. In step 4, authors do the most exhaustive calculation to find the One Dependence estimators. In this step, authors start by making a particular attribute as the parent and all other attributes as its child. Finally, authors put all these values in the formula to get the predicted class.

Equations

The following equations are used in Self Structure Extended MNB. Equation 2 represents the hybrid nature of the algorithm as it has two variables a and b. Equation 3 describes the structure extension part. It represents the dependency between attributes. Equation 4 is the actual multinomial part of the hybrid model. It calculates the class dependency of each document.

$$C(d) = \arg \max_{c \varepsilon C} (a+b) \text{-------} \tag{2}$$

$$a = \frac{\sum_{i=1, fw_{i>0}}^{m} W_i P(c) P(w_i \mid c)^{f_i} \prod_{t=1, t \neq 1, f_{t>0}}^{m} P(w_t \mid w_i, c)^{f_i}}{\sum_{i=1, f_{i>0}}^{m} W_i} \tag{3}$$

$$b = P(c) \prod_{i=1}^{m} P(w_i \mid c)^{f_i} \tag{4}$$

Proposed Algorithm

The algorithm is divided into two parts training and testing. In the training part, authors compute all the variables, except the one dependence estimators, which are calculated at the testing time.

I. Training:
    Input: The training dataset D.
    Output: $P(c)$, W_i, $P(w_i \mid c)$
        1. For each class c in D

(a) Calculate independent class probability P(c).

    2.   For each attribute w_i in D

(a) Calculate the weight P (W_i).

    3.   For each attribute w_i in D

(a) For each class c in D

i. Calculate the conditional attribute probability such that class is given P (w_i | c).

II.   Testing:

Input: The test data d, P(c), P (W_i), P (w_i | c).

Output: The predicted class c for test data d.

    1.   For each attribute w_t in d

(a) For each attribute w_i in d and w_t $f-$ w_i

i. For each class c in D

A. Calculate the one dependence estimator P(w_t | w_i, c)

    2.   For each class c

(a) Calculate the conditional class probability c(d) using eq. 2.

    3.   Return the class, which has the maximum value of c(d).

Working of Proposed System

The working of the Self Structure Extended MNB was divided into two components training and testing. Each of the components is discussed in detail below:

Training the Model

In the training component, the authors first task was to calculate the independent class probability for each class in our training dataset. The independent class probabilities represent how many documents exist for each class. The listing 1 shows the independent class probabilities for the FBIS dataset.

The Independent Probability of a Class

Listing 1: Independent Class Probabilities

```
0 0.037535483870967 74
1 0.038306451612903226
2 0.018951612903225806
3 0.15645161290322582
4 0.056451612903225805
5 0.018951612903225806
6 0.049193548387096775
7 0.20443548387096774
8 0.026612903225 80645
9 0.050806451612903224
10 0.14475806451612902
11 0.077016129032258 06
```

120.04838709677419355
130.01895161290322586
140.0197580645161290 3
150.01774193548387096 8
160.0157258064516129 0 2

Authors use MNB to calculate these values. As proposed work had a dataset of 17 classes, therefore the listing 1 has values from 0th class to 16th class. According to listing 1, the class with index 7 has the most number of documents, and the class with index 16 has the least number of documents. If authors predict the class of a new test data according to this probability, then it is called as Baseline classifier. After storing the independent class probabilities in our system memory, authors next go forward to determine the weight of each attribute or feature. The weights determine how valuable a particular attribute is in predicting a class. Listing 2 shows the weights of different attributes of FBIS dataset.

Attribute Weights

0 = 0.6807781133904526
1 = 0.4956431318368632
2 = 0.5800212513450631
3 = 0.33068995745596313
4 = 0.5065394052203063
5 = 0.2720445313481 6176
6 = 0.3625720812598775
7 = 0.5396744828443228
8 = 0.5094923206815277
9 = 0.4295783394986500 4
10 = 0.4471621333574127
11 = 0.2955232612578760 4
12 = 0.4521176315825826 7
13 = 0.42891533448570623
14 = 0.28032239333445
15 = 0.36409150389753564
16 = 0.2857535659602305
17 = 0.27531017001096497
18 = 0.3027806592421311
19 = 0.37976679061198576
20 = 0.2797094436896718

. . .

   . . .

```
1982 = 0.0
1983 = 0.28400939400673 26
1984 = 0.0
1985 = 0.0
1986 = 0.20323987667840956
1987 = 0.0
1988 = 0.0
1989 = 0.0
1990 = 0.26145402731618 82
1991 = 0.18106340193800 93
1992 = 0.0
1993 = 0.19112570178351784
1994 - 0.0
1995 = 0.21544439435547252
1996 = 0.18557344408837223
1997 = 0.0
1998 = 0.0
1999 = 0.0
```

Total Weight = 2 6 7 . 3 0 6 1 6 9 5 4 6 7 7 0 8

Listing 2: Attribute Weights

In SSEMNB, attribute weights play an essential role because authors are using a weighted average approach here. These weights are calculated using information gain values. Information gain is equal to the ratio of entropy to split information. After determining the weights of each attribute, our last component in training is conditional probability of each feature concerning each class. This means that how many words are there for each class across all the documents in the training dataset.

Testing the Model

At the time of testing, authors take one test document at a time and predict a class label for it. The first step involved in the testing is to calculate the One-Dependence estimators for each attribute present in the test document. Here, authors make an attribute as a parent and all other attributes as its children and calculate this probability. After this step, the authors move to the last component of the Self Structure Extended MNB. In this part, authors have to estimate the conditional class probability, which is the probability of each class given the test document. The listing 3 shows the conditional class probability for a single test data for FBIS dataset.

Conditional Class Probability

```
0 3.560967663647893 E-1 5
1 2.367165358228847 3E- 12
2 1.030232290842228 6E-8
```

```
3 1.7 5 4 8 9 5 8 6 4 6 9 5 3 1 3E–23
4 9.8 3 0 6 1 9 6 8 4 4 7 0 3 5 4E–23
5 2.0 8 4 7 5 9 3 6 1 6 0 2 1 9 6E–20
6 1.3 8 5 0 2 6 8 1 3 6 9 4 0 1 1 4E–7
7 1.1 9 8 6 7 6 6 1 9 7 2 5 9 9 9 2E–12
8 4.5 9 4 4 2 0 8 7 9 2 3 5 5 5 6E–10
9 2.2 5 1 4 5 3 1 1 0 3 0 2 5 3 4 7E–19
10 3.3 0 7 1 6 4 8 6 0 7 3 3 0 4 1 4E–11
11 5.7 5 9 4 8 2 8 4 8 9 2 0 3 9 2 5E–24
12 2.6 6 9 9 6 6 6 8 1 9 4 7 2 9 7E–28
13 8.9 3 8 0 2 3 8 2 7 3 4 7 6 9 4E–23
14 1.5 2 1 3 9 0 4 7 1 5 9 2 4 3 9E–8
15 8.8 2 7 9 3 0 1 3 7 9 0 1 4 5 1E–8
16 1.3 9 9 5 0 8 9 7 7 6 2 6 2 1 4 7E–17
```

Listing 3: Conditional Class Probabilities

Conditional class probabilities are the final probability of a class after implementing our model on the test dataset. The higher the conditional class probability, the more is the chance of the test data to belong to that particular class. The equation 4.1 is used for calculating the same. The maximum value of this variable is our predicted class label for the test document. This finishes the working of the Self Structure Extended MNB.

RESULTS AND ANALYSIS

This section discusses the experiments performed and the results obtained in the process. Authors have tried to perform experiments as per the academic level. Authors have made sure that the results are accurate and unbiased. All the results are listed in the subsequent sections. Authors commemorate the authors of various papers who have mentioned the datasets and tools used in their research so that other academicians can also verify and improve their work. The values returned by significant functions in the code are also included in this chapter.

Experiments

In machine learning, experiments play a vital role. Proper tuning of specific major parameters can significantly improve the output results. So, before doing experiments, the authors made sure to study and understand various properties deeply. Most importantly, the data on which authors run our experiments must be clean and without any outliers. Secondly, the tool or framework used must be acceptable to the general academicians. Authors ran our experiments on Intel i3 processor with 4 GB RAM.

Table 2. Dataset properties

Property	Value
Dataset	FBIS
Documents	2463
Words	2000
Classes	17

Figure 9. Header of an ARFF file

```
@RELATION iris

@ATTRIBUTE sepallength  NUMERIC
@ATTRIBUTE sepalwidth   NUMERIC
@ATTRIBUTE petallength  NUMERIC
@ATTRIBUTE petalwidth   NUMERIC
@ATTRIBUTE class        {setosa,versicolor,virginica}
```

Datasets Used

The dataset used by authors is FBIS, which stands for Foreign Broadcast Information Service. It was a US government organization which translated and monitored publicly accessible information and news from sources outside the United States. Authors got this dataset from the University of California, Irvine's website. It has 2463 documents, 200 features, and 17 classes. As this dataset is vast, it ensures the results authors get are unbiased.

The point to be noted is that this dataset is in the format called Attribute Relation File Format (ARFF). It is an ASCII format which has two distinct sections. The first section is called a header section. The header section contains the name of the relation, which is the name of the ARFF file. After the relation name, authors list down all the attribute names and their corresponding data types. Figure 9 represents the header information of the popular iris dataset.

The second part of an ARFF file is called the data section. This is where the actual data mentioned. The lines that begin with % are commented lines which are not processed. The data can either be specified in the rare form or full form. The benefit of using sparse representation is that the resulting dataset file is of minimal size. Figure 10 represents the data section of the iris dataset.

Framework Used

All analysis was done on the machine learning framework in JAVA known as Waikato Environment for Knowledge Analysis (WEKA). It is a Free and Open Source framework (FOSS) developed by the University of Waikato, New Zealand. It is a cross-platform tool, which means that it is operating system independent and can run on any system. With the help of WEKA, authors can efficiently perform the following tasks:

Figure 10. Data of an ARFF file

```
@DATA
5.1,3.5,1.4,0.2,setosa
4.9,3.0,1.4,0.2,setosa
4.7,3.2,1.3,0.2,versicolor
4.6,3.1,1.5,0.2,virginica
5.0,3.6,1.4,0.2,virginica
5.4,3.9,1.7,0.4,setosa
4.6,3.4,1.4,0.3,versicolor
5.0,3.4,1.5,0.2,setosa
4.4,2.9,1.4,0.2,versicolor
4.9,3.1,1.5,0.1,virginica
```

- Data Preprocessing
- Classification
- Clustering
- Attribute Filtering
- Visualization

Figure 11 shows the WEKA interface, which consists of explorer, experimenter, knowledge flow, workbench, and command-line interface. All these tools are beneficial when performing experiments.

Figure 11. WEKA interface

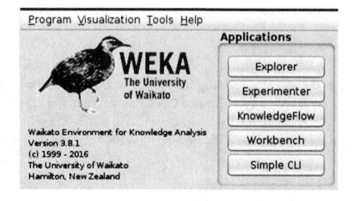

Table 3.

Time taken to build model: 10.1	seconds			
=== Summary ===				
Correctly Classified Instances	2069		84.00	%
Incorrectly Classified Instances	394		16.00	%
Mean absolute error	0.0271			
Root mean squared error	0.1624			
Relative absolute error	15.9867	%		
Total Number of Instances	2463			

Results

In this section, the authors discuss the accuracy achieved by the proposed algorithm and different results that authors got as output from each of primary functions.

Accuracy

=== Run information ===

Scheme: weka.classifiers.bayes.Ssemnb
Relation: fbis.mat
Instances: 2463 Attributes: 2001

=== Classifier model (full training set) ===

Listing 4: Results

Listing 4 describes the overall accuracy after executing each test dataset. 84% of the total instances have been correctly classified, while only 16% are incorrectly classified. The total time taken to build a model on the training data is around 10 seconds. As is evident for the listing 4, there are total 2463 documents in our dataset and 2001 attributes out of which one is the class label. The results also show that the relative absolute error for our algorithm is 15.98%. Total 2069 documents have been correctly classified, whereas 394 documents have been incorrectly classified.

Table 4. Results

Algorithm	Accuracy
MNB	76%
SEMNB	83%
SSEMNB	84%

Figure 12. Comparison with existing techniques

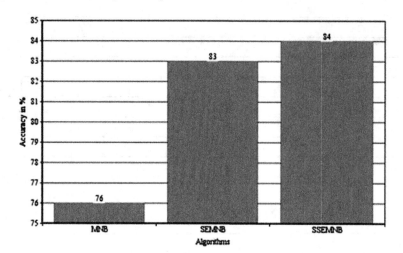

Comparison With Existing Techniques

Table 3 summarizes the accuracy of different algorithms. MNB gives 76% accuracy, followed by SEMNB at 83% and SSEMNB at 84% accuracy. This indicates that SSEMNB can correctly classify more documents than the other two methods. Graph1 also represents the comparison of the accuracy of the three algorithms.

8. Conclusion and Future Work

This chapter concludes that using the benefits of both MNB and structure extended MNB; authors can get better text classification accuracy. The documents where SEMNB was unable to classify confidently because of no parent-child dependency were handled by SSEMNB quite well. There is no extra computational cost and no structure searching as well. One dependence estimators work well where there is a parent-child association to some extent. If there is no such dependency, then the naive Bayes probability factor predicts the results. Authors have various text classification improvements in the pipeline. Authors can use clustering to improve the estimation of results further as it would group similar words and dependency calculations would be more exact. Apart from this, authors can also use techniques like frequency transforming, instance weighting, local learning, feature weighting, and feature selection. These methods are called meta-learning methods and improve the accuracy of any given model.

REFERENCES

Ahuja, R., Nayyar, A., & Solanki, A. (2019). Movie Recommender System Using K-Means Clustering AND K-Nearest Neighbor. In *Confluence-2019: 9th International Conference on Cloud Computing, Data Science & Engineering*. Amity University. DOI: 10.1109/CONFLUENCE.2019.8776969

Amati, G., & Rijsbergen, C. J. V. (2002). Probabilistic models of information retrieval based on measuring the divergence from randomness. *ACM Transactions on Information Systems*, *20*(4), 357–389. doi:10.1145/582415.582416

Chickering, D. M. (1996). *P Learning Bayesian networks is np-complete. In Learning from data* (pp. 121–130). Springer.

Clinchant, S., & Gaussier, E. (2011). Retrieval constraints and word frequency distributions a log-logistic model for ir. *Inf. Retr.*, *14*(1), 5–25. doi:10.100710791-010-9143-7

Freund, Y., & Schapire, R. E. (1995). A decision-theoretic generalization of on-line learning and an application to boosting. *Proceedings of the Second European Conference on Computational Learning Theory*, 23–37. 10.1007/3-540-59119-2_166

Freund, Y., & Schapire, R. E. (1996). Experiments with a new boosting algorithm. In *Proceedings of the 13th International Conference on Machine Learning*. Morgan Kaufmann Press.

Hall, M. (2000). Correlation-based feature selection for discrete and numeric class machine learning. *Proceedings of the 17th International Conference on Machine Learning*, 359–366.

Ibrahim, O. A. S., & LandaSilva, D. (2014). A new weighting scheme and discriminative approach for information retrieval in static and dynamic document collections. *Proceedings of the 14th UK Workshop on Computational Intelligence*, 1–8.

Javed, K., Maruf, S., & Babri, A. (2015). A two-stage Markov blanket based feature selection algorithm for text classification. *Neurocomputing, 157*, 91–104.

Jiang, L., Cai, Z., Zhang, H., & Wang, D. (2013). Naive Bayes text classifiers: A locally weighted learning approach" in J. *Exp. Theor. Artif. Intell.*, *25*(2), 273–286. doi:10.1080/0952813X.2012.721010

Jiang, L., Wang, D., & Cai, Z. (2012). Discriminatively weighted naive Bayes and its application in text classification. *International Journal on Artificial Intelligence Tools, 21*(1).

Jiang, L., Wang, S., Li, C., & Zhang, L. (2016). Structure Extended Multinomial Naive Bayes. *Information Sciences, 329*, 346–356.

Jiang, L., Zhang, H., Cai, Z., & Wang, D. (2012). Weighted average of one-dependence estimators" in J. *Exp. Theor. Artif. Intell.*, *24*(2), 219–230. doi:10.1080/0952813X.2011.639092

Kim, S. B., Han, K. S., Rim, H. C., & Myaeng, S. H. (2006). Some effective techniques for naive Bayes text classification. *IEEE Trans. Knowl. Data Eng.*, *18*(11), 1457–1466. doi:10.1109/TKDE.2006.180

Kim, S. B., Rim, H. C., & Lim, H. S. (2002). A new method of parameter estimation for MNB text classifiers. In *Proceedings of the 25th annual international ACM SIGIR conference on Research and development in information retrieval*. ACM.

Lan, M., Tan, C. L., & Su, J. E. A. (2009). Supervised and traditional term weighting methods for automatic text categorization. *IEEE Trans. Patt. Analy. Mach. Intell.*, *31*(4), 721–735. doi:10.1109/TPAMI.2008.110 PMID:19229086

Li, Y., C., L., & M., C. S. (2012). Weighted naive Bayes for text classification using positive term-class dependency. *Int. J. Artif. Intell. Tools, 21*(1).

Liu, Y., Loh, H. T., & Sun, A. (2009). Imbalanced text classification: A term weighting approach. *Expert Syst. Appl.*, *36*(1), 690–701.

Madsen, R. E., Larsen, J., & Hansen, L. K. (2004). Part-of-speech enhanced context recognition. *Proceedings of the 14th IEEE Signal Processing Society Workshop on Machine Learning for Signal Processing*, 635–643. 10.1109/MLSP.2004.1423027

McCallum, A., & Nigam, K. (1998). A comparison of event models for naive Bayes text classification. In *Working Notes of the 1998AAAI/ICML Workshop on Learning for Text*. AAAI Press.

Mendoza, M. (2012). A new term-weighting scheme for naïve Bayes text categorization. *Int. J. Web Inf. Syst.*, *8*(1), 55–72. doi:10.1108/17440081211222591

Norasetsathaporn, P. (2002). *Automatic Relevant Documents Selection Using Categorization Technique* (PhD thesis). Kasetsart University.

Pandey, S., & Solanki, A. (2019). Music Instrument Recognition using Deep Convolutional Neural Networks. International Journal of Information Technology. doi:10.100741870-019-00285-y

Pearl, J. (1988). Probabilistic Reasoning in Intelligent Systems. Morgan Kaufmann.

Rennie, J. D., Shih, L., Teevan, J., & Karger, D. R. (2003). Tackling the poor assumptions of naive Bayes text classifiers. In *Proceedings of the Twentieth International Conference on Machine Learning*. Morgan Kaufmann.

Solanki, A., & Kumar, A. (2018). *A system to transform natural language queries into SQL queries*. *International Journal of Information Technology*, 1–10. doi:10.100741870-018-0095-2

Song, S., & Myaeng, S. H. (2012). A novel term weighting scheme based on discrimination power obtained from past retrieval results. *Information Processing & Management*, *48*(5), 919–930. doi:10.1016/j.ipm.2012.03.004

Wang, S., Jiang, L., & Li, C. (2014). A cfs-based feature weighting approach to naive Bayes text classifiers. In *Proceedings of the 24th International Conference on Artificial Neural Networks*. Springer. 10.1007/978-3-319-11179-7_70

Wang, S., Jiang, L., & Li, C. (2015). Adapting naive Bayes tree for text classification. *Knowledge and Information Systems*, *44*(1), 77–89. doi:10.100710115-014-0746-y

Webb, G., Boughton, J., & Wang, Z. (2005). Not so naive Bayes: Aggregating one- dependence estimators. *Mach. Learn.*, *58*(1), 5–24.

Witten, I. H., Frank, E., & Hall, M. A. (2011). Data Mining: Practical Machine Learning Tools and Techniques (3rd ed.). Morgan Kaufmann.

Yang, Y., & Pedersen, J. O. (1997). A comparative study on feature selection in text categorization. In *Proceedings of the 14th International Conference on Machine Learning*. Morgan Kaufmann Publishers.

Chapter 7
Applications of Machine Learning for Software Management

Vibha Verma
University of Delhi, India

Neha Neha
University of Delhi, India

Anu G. Aggarwal
ⓘD https://orcid.org/0000-0001-5448-9540
University of Delhi, India

ABSTRACT

Software firms plan all development and management activities strategically to provide the best products and solutions to their user. IT professionals are involved in the process of studying the bugs reported and assign severity to make decisions regarding their resolution. To make the task fast and accurate, developers use automatic methods. Herein, the authors have used feature selection-based classification technique to decide about the severity of reported bugs. TF-IDF feature selection method is used to select the informative terms, determining the severity. Based on selected terms the support vector machine and artificial neural network classifiers are used for classification. A number of performance measures have been used to test the performance of classification. The bug reports of Eclipse project for JDT and platform products were collected from Bugzilla. The results show that classifying bugs on the basis of severity can be effectively improved by feature selection-based strategy.

DOI: 10.4018/978-1-5225-9643-1.ch007

INTRODUCTION

Technological advancements and ease of performing day-to-day chores with lesser time consumption had geared up demand for software products. The wide acceptance of software products is dependent on their quality. Software Industries work systematically to provide the best IT solutions in all domains so that the software faces minimal bugs during its execution period (Humphrey, 1995). Software applications have captured almost all the areas like Banking, Service sector, Health sector, Education, Retail, Manufacturing and Trade, etc. To ensure the effectiveness of the products, firms adopt tactical management activities. Software Management comprises of Development and Maintenance processes (Weinberg, 1993). Development of qualitative Software Systems has become a daunting task for developers because of continuous advances in technology and consumer demands whereas maintenance activities are also very important to maintain the quality of the software system. Maintenance activities are carried out to deal with the bugs faced during the working of the software after its release in the market (Charette, 1989; Humphrey, 1989).

Proper management is possible by adopting the best methods for developing and maintaining the software. Machine Learning (ML) has turned out to be relevant for Software Management (Alzubi, Nayyar, & Kumar, 2018; Michie, Spiegelhalter, & Taylor, 1994). It is the most emerging and acknowledged method used by developers for automatically accomplishing various tasks of estimation, prediction or classification, etc. ML helps to improve task performance based on the training of machines through past data (Alpaydin, 2009; Murphy, 2012). The various domains of Software Management where ML techniques have been employed extensively include:

1. Prediction and Estimation (Wen, Li, Lin, Hu, & Huang, 2012): Various ML Algorithms are applied for predicting and estimating;
    i.   The quality and reliability of a software system
    ii. The appropriate testing time period and hence release time
    iii. The reusability and testability of components/ Modules of a software system
    iv. The development cost and effort and also the maintenance effort required after releasing the software into the market.
    v.   The defects in the software
    vi. The severity of a bug in the software
2. Analyzing the requirements for carrying out a task (Perini, Susi, & Avesani, 2013).
3. ML methods can also be applied to obtain useful information related to entities of software and analyze their vulnerabilities. The model for predicting the same has also been developed (Ghaffarian & Shahriari, 2017).

This chapter deals with the subject of bug severity classification by applying automated ML algorithms and text analytics to process the textual bug reports(Pandey, Sanyal, Hudait, & Sen, 2017). To start with, it is important to first understand bugs and importance of its classification on the basis of severity. A Bug can be interpreted as a flaw or shortcoming in the written program that leads to undesirable consequences, as a result,the software does not perform as intended (Herzig, Just, & Zeller, 2013). These bugs lead to failures (noncompliance with the requirements during execution). A bug may be a result of inadequate testing, inaccurate resource management, unexpected modifications in the code, untrained manpower, dearth of adequate technology, etc. In practice, bugs affect the dependability, availability,

Figure 1. Bug Triaging Process

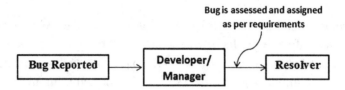

reliability and hence the quality of the software system. To track the bug of their projects, stakeholders maintain a database of bugs through Bug Tracking Systems (BTS).

A large number of bugs are reported every single day both by users and developers on BTS to record the concerns faced during the field operations and testing (Fiaz, Devi, & Aarthi, 2013). These reports are expressed in natural language with all the data in the structured form that helps the developer to understand the cause of failure and accordingly plan for the bug removal. The list of information includes the product component, summary, failure description, version and severity. As this information is shared by the IT community, many suggestions regarding bug are also received through comments.

Jira (https://www.atlassian.com/software/jira), Backlog (https://backlog.com/), Plutora (https://www.plutora.com/), Bugzilla (https://bugs.eclipse.org/bugs/), ReQtest (https://reqtest.com/), Mantis Bug (https://www.mantisbt.org/) are some of the Bug tracking tools used to acquire bug data reports. Some of the bugs received may be invalid or duplicate. Identification of such bugs, in the beginning, is very important to avoid time and effort wastage at the later stages. The above mentioned open-source online repositories built by stakeholders to follow the performance of their products even after release in the market helps to carry out studies on bug triaging process (Fiaz et al., 2013) (Figure 1). In this process, after the bug has been reported the triager i.e. the manager decides about the resolver for the bug based on the description provided. The resolver works on the bug and reports back to triager with the current status of the bug.

One of the criteria used by triager to assign bugs is related to its severity. Bug Severity is more important than the number of bugs present in the system. A critical bug has to be given much more consideration than the other existing bugs in the system and hence those bugs are attended first. As an illustration, Figure 2 shows the various levels of severity defined in the Eclipse projects. When severity classification is carried out normal and enhancement reports are not considered because normal bugs create confusion regarding severity since they lie in the grey zone and enhancement reports are for new features or for updates in existing features. They are not considered to be bugs. By default only most of the bugs are assigned normal severity. This is generally done when the one who reports the bug does not have understanding and knowledge of the technicalities of the system. Each bug level has a different impact on the software during its operation. Quite a few researchers have discussed the need for sever-

Figure 2. Possible severity levels of reported bugs

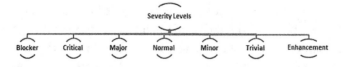

Figure 3. Machine learning process

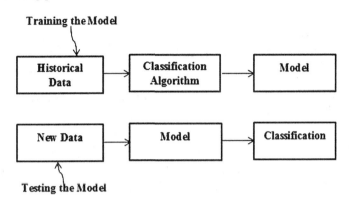

ity assessment and presented automated techniques trained on the textual data obtained from online repositories (Pandey et al., 2017; Xia, Lo, Qiu, Wang, & Zhou, 2014).

There was a need to develop these automated techniques because managing an enormous amount of textual bug data manually to identify each bug's validity is irksome and demands a lot of endeavor on the developer's side. Hence the researchers and practitioners have started adopting automation for defining the severity of bugs (Bowring, Rehg, & Harrold, 2004; Pandey et al., 2017; Xia et al., 2014). Automation is convenient for reasons including:

1. It helps to avoid incorrect decisions
2. The developer can quickly respond to the reported bugs.
3. It makes sure that no critical bug is missed.
4. Less time is consumed in the decision-making process.
5. It helps to assign effort for the activities undertaken by the development unit for mending a bug.
6. It is required so that the allocation of resources can be planned strategically.
7. It prevents time wastage on irrelevant and duplicate reports.

Automation includes the usage of ML algorithms for classifying the reported bugs to designate a priority for fixing it. The process of applying machine learning for classification purpose is shown in Figure 3. A part of bug data is used to train the classifier model and then it is tested for classification on remaining data. Training a model can be referred to as building the model for classification. At first text analytics tools are used to study the textual reports then classifiers are applied for classification. Later accuracy of classification is determined.

Many times irrelevant and duplicate bugs are also reported which need to be sorted out before working on them (Banerjee, Cukic, & Adjeroh, 2012). Hence classification of bugs is a very important step for deciding about which bug to attend first. Priority is attached to a bug on the ground of severity level of the bug. The severity of a bug is defined as an extent up to which it can hamper the working of the software. A complex bug due to its criticality is prioritized first for resolution. A bug with higher severity is allocated higher priority and hence taken up first for rectification. Also, a more severe bug requires more amounts of effort and resources for fixation (Liu, Wang, Chen, & Jiang, 2018; Yang, Chen, Kao, & Yang, 2014).

Figure 4. Feature Selection Based Severity Classification

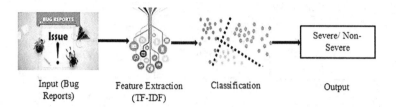

In this chapter, the classifier model is trained based on selected features (terms) using a feature selection technique. The model further classifies severity on the basis of terms fed into the model as critical words that define severity. Figure 4 shows the corresponding research methodology. The Research Objectives fulfilled through this chapter are as follows:

1. To pre-process textual bug reports of a component belonging to JDT and Platform products of Eclipse project extracted from Bugzilla (https://bugs.eclipse.org/bugs/) via Text Mining.
2. To extract top words/terms using a feature selection technique and form a dictionary of critical words that determine severity.
3. To categorise bug reports as Severe or Non-Severe using two Machine Learning Algorithms based on the developed dictionary.
4. To assess the accuracy of the results by testing the model after training the classifiers using extracted features.

From Figure 4 it is clear that the algorithm is implemented in two phases. In the first phase, Term Frequency- Time Inverse frequency (TF-IDF) text mining techniques is used for selection of words or terms shaping the decision after pre-processing of textual reports and then in the later phase Support Vector Machine (SVM) and Artificial Neural Network (ANN) classifiers are used to classify bugs on the basis of severity. This binary classification procedure yields output as either severe or non-severe. The model is executed using Python programming language. The data of bug reports of various components of two eclipse projects namely JDT and Platform have been downloaded from Bugzilla for analysis purpose.

The chapter is divided into five sections; Section two presents a detailed background of the related concepts. Further in section 3, the methodology for severity classification is discussed. Section four presents the implementation of methodology on bug report dataset and the results are discoursed. Later in section 5, threats to validity have been discussed. At last we present conclusions and future work.

RELATED WORK

This section presents a comprehensive review of literature based on the bug severity classification and the techniques used in the text mining for classifying the bug reports. Table 1 shows the summary of the previous studies where the first column indicates the authors and the year in which research has been carried out. The second column shows the datasets collected for implementing the methodology and the last column indicates the methods used to classify the reports.

Table 1. Summary of literature on Bug Severity classification

Authors	Datasets	Techniques
Menzies and Marcus (2008)	NASA's project and Issue Tracking System (PITS)	SEVERityISsue assessment (SEVERIS)
Lamkanfi, Demeyer, Giger, and Goethals (2010)	Eclipse, Mozilla and GENOME	Naïve Bayes
Lamkanfi, Demeyer, Soetens, and Verdonck (2011)	Eclipse & GENOME from Bugzilla	Support Vector Machine, Naïve Bayes, Multinomial Naïve Bayes, K-nearest neighbor
Chaturvedi and Singh (2012a)	NASA from PROMISE Repository	Support Vector Machine, Naïve Bayes, Decision Tree-based J48, Rule-based Repeated Increment Pruning to Produce Error Reduction (RIPPER) and Random Forest
Tian, Lo, and Sun (2012)	Eclipse, Open Office and Mozilla	BM25, SEVERIS, INSPect
Chaturvedi and Singh (2012b)	NASA's PITS, Eclipse, Mozilla and GENOME	Support Vector Machine, Naïve Bayes, Decision Tree-based J48, RIPPER and Random Forest
Zhang, Yang, Lee, and Chan (2015)	Mozilla Firefox & Eclipse	Concept profile based severity prediction
Sharma, Sharma, and Gujral (2015)	Eclipse	Chi-square, Info-gain, Multinomial Naïve Bayes, K-nearest neighbor
Jin, Dashbalbar, Yang, Lee, and Lee (2016)	Mozilla & Eclipse	Multinomial Naïve Bayes
Singh, Misra, and Sharma (2017)	Cross-project bug severity between Mozilla & Eclipse products	TF-IDF, K-nearest neighbor, Naïve Bayes, Support Vector Machine
Liu et al. (2018)	Mozilla & Eclipse	Ensemble Feature Selection algorithm, Multinomial Naïve Bayes
Kukkar, Mohana, Nayyar, Kim, Kang, and Chilamkurti (2019)	Mozilla, Eclipse, JDoss, OpenFOAM, Firefox	Conventional Neural Network, Random Forest with Boosting
Our Proposed Approach	Eclipse (JDT & Platform) from Bugzilla	TF-IDF, Support Vector Machine and Artificial Neural Network

Bug Severity

Several research studies have been carried out to predict bug severity. Menzies and Marcus (2008) introduced an automated method that is SEVERity Issue assessment (SEVERIS); this method assists the software engineer in assigning the severity levels to the gathered bug reports. In SEVERIS, reports are investigated robotically and engineers are alerted if there is any irregularity. For the model validation data has been taken from the NASA and Project & Issue Tracking System (PITS) and results revealed that SEVERIS proved to be an anticipated predictor for the severity.

Lamkanfi et al. (2010) suggested another approach that calculates bug severity by assuming appropriate proportions of training data set. The datasets of textual bug reports, collected from open source community (Mozilla, Eclipse and GENOME) have been classified using Naïve Bayes (NB). Prediction showed that NB provides great accuracy with precision and recall lying in 65% to 75% for Mozilla & Eclipse; 70% to 85% for GENOME.

In a further study, Lamkanfi et al. (2011) used several algorithms for the classification with the help of previous studies and compared the results. The authors selected K Nearest Neighbour (KNN), NB, Multinomial Naïve Bayes (MNB), SVM classifiers for performance evaluation considering GENOME and Eclipse data sets. As a conclusion, MNB showed great prediction as compared to other classifiers in terms of AUC from 59% to 93%.

Chaturvedi and Singh (2012a) proposed prediction models for the bug severity performing NB, k-NN, MNB, SVM, J48 and RIPPER classifiers. Results showed that accuracy varies according to the severity levels, opposing the results of Menzies and Marcus (2008) K-NN provided better accuracy than NB & MNB.

Tian et al. (2012) used duplicate textual data to categorize the features that control the prediction more. To carry out the experiment data was collected from Eclipse, OpenOffice and Mozilla. The study provided reasonable values of precision and recall with precision up to 72%, recall up to 76% and f-measure 74%. Further, this study was also compared with existing studies.

Chaturvedi and Singh (2012b) proposed another study comparing several machine learning algorithms by considering severity prediction performance. SVM, probability-based NB, Decision tree-based J48, RIPPER and Random Forest (RF) was used in investigating the severity levels of the bug reports. The bug reports have been composed of NASA's PITS as closed source and Eclipse, Mozilla and GENOME as open-source projects. For the performance measure, values of F-measure and accuracy were calculated for each severity level and as a conclusion, it has been observed that prediction was better when considering the closed source projects than for open source projects.

Zhang et al. (2015) introduced a concept based classification model for the severity of the bug reports. First concept profile was developed using text mining of the historical bug reports. It was shown that this model gives better precision and recall than KNN, NB, NBM.

Text Mining

Text mining consists of a number of steps as tokenization, stop word removal and stemming to remove the irrelevant and unnecessary information from the textual data set. In literature, it has been applied to various bug reports. Murphy and Cubranic (2004) used machine learning techniques and text categorization to assign the bug to resolver for resolution.

Anvik, Hiew, and Murphy (2006) provided a semi-automated methodology for assigning bug report to software engineers who have the understanding to resolve that particular report. Using Eclipse and Firefox datasets the model achieved a precision of over 50% and reached 64%.

Jeong G., Kim S., Zimmermann T. Jeong, Kim, and Zimmermann (2009) studied the problems or issues due to bug tossing. Bug tossing in a report consumes additional time and effort. In some cases bugs have extensive tossing process i.e., they pass through many developers before actual bug fixation. Therefore authors provided a graph model based on Markov chains that consider bug tossing history to reduce the time consumed in tossing the bugs.

Feature Selection

The data which is collected from the bug repository might contain some correlation among the classes and may cause in misclassification of the instances. Thus to resolve these type of issues we need to select features that are informative and improve the performance of the classifiers. A number of feature selection techniques have been used previously. For example, in software fault prediction models Principal Components Analysis (PCA) has been used widely to select the important attributes of the data (Kumar, Sripada, Sureka, & Rath, 2018). Correlation-based Feature Selection (CFS), Rough Set Analysis, Information Gain Feature Evaluation are also some other techniques that have been used in predicting the fault-prone classes (Kumar et al., 2018; Malhotra & Singh, 2011).

For bug severity classification, features must be selected from the raw data due to the involvement of the textual summary. Some well-adopted techniques for feature selections are Chi-square method, OneR, Gain-Ratio etc. Xu, Lo, Xia, Sureka, and Li (2015) presented a novel approach by considering EFSPredictor. EFSPredictor uses ensemble feature selection on the textual summary of the bug reports. Chi-square, Gain ratio, Relief &OneR has been used to output the selected features. EFSPredictor developed a prediction model based on the ensemble feature selection. They used dataset containing 3,203 bug reports and compared the results with Xia et al. (2014) on bug misconfiguration. This approach is an integrated approach by introducing ensemble techniques for feature selection.

In the urge of making the severity prediction an automatic procedure, Sharma et al. (2015) proposed a different methodology for the severity prediction. In their study, the authors proposed a thesaurus of the critical terms used in the reports with the help of info-gain and chi-square feature selection techniques and used KNN (Ahuja et al., 2019)& MNB for the severity prediction. Apart from these techniques, TF-IDF is one of the most widely used feature selection technique (Lamkanfi et al. (2010), Tian et al. (2012), Zhang et al. (2015), &Chaturvedi and Singh (2012a)). In our study, we have used TF-IDF as a feature selection technique and then performed the classification.

Classifiers

In the literature of the bug severity classification, several classifiers have been considered such as probability-based NB, NBM, SVM, RF, KNN and RIPPER. In our approach, we have used SVM and ANN. SVM and ANN are the most used classifiers in various research areas because of its capability of handling large multifarious data and the other motivation of using these classifiers is that these have not been extensively used for the bug severity prediction.

SVM was first introduced by (Vapnik, Guyon, & Hastie, 1995) and has been implemented a number of times in the software severity classification as well as for fault prediction. Tian et al. (2012) and Chaturvedi and Singh (2012b) considered SVM in severity classification and Erturk and Sezer (2015),Malhotra and Jain (2012)&Mishra and Shukla (2012) used SVM to predict the fault-prone classes of the software system.

There are numerous studies considering ANN in software fault prediction analysis, for example,, Hammouri, Hammad, Alnabhan, and Alsarayrah (2018)&Jaiswal and Malhotra (2018)proposed models assuming different ANN methods as cascade-forward, backpropagation, feed-forward backpropagation, generalized regression neural network and multi-layered perceptron. In our study, we have multi-layered perceptron in classifying the bug reports.

In the above-discussed literature, it is concluded that in maintaining the software system it is necessary to follow a step by step process to resolve the bug reports and for this we have selected the most widely used and appropriate feature selection technique called TF-IDF and for the classification purpose, we have used SVM and ANN classifiers.

Figure 5. Overview of Methodology

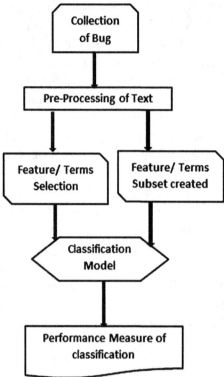

BUG SEVERITY CLASSIFICATION METHODOLOGY

In this section, the step by step method for severity classification used in this chapter has been briefed. The flow diagram in Figure 5 shows the process of how the severity of a newly reported bug is defined automatically through ML techniques.

Now, each step of the methodology is discussed in detail.

Data Acquisition

To put into action the research objectives, data of bug reports is collected for various components of two Eclipse projects publicly available on the Bugzilla website. The two eclipse products considered for this study are JDT and Platform. The data available is in the text form provided by the users, testers or developers. The bug summary of the reports is analyzedfor classification of the bug severity. The reports acquired are presumed to be of good quality (Bettenburg, Just, Schröter, Weiss, Premraj, & Zimmermann, 2008; Yang et al., 2014; Zimmermann, Premraj, Bettenburg, Just, Schroter, & Weiss, 2010) because technical language is used to describe the bug. This promotes the establishment of a subset of well-defined terms for identifying the bug severity level.

Figure 6. Bug classification in BTS

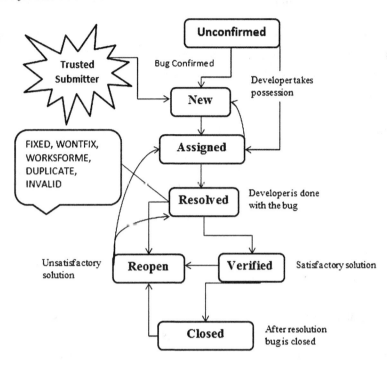

Some advantages of BTS for project stakeholders are:

i.   BTS can record bugs encountered during operation of the software system.
ii.   BTS provides transparency in the software development process.
iii. BTS also helps developers in design planning and resource scheduling.
iv.   It is helpful in the Management of bugs for future releases.
v.   It provides easy access to bug reporters to track their bugs reported.
vi.   BTS also gives free hand to reporters to assign priority to bugs based on their knowledge and experience.
vii. It acts as a hub where information can be shared in the IT community.

All the above benefits help to improve and hence maintain the quality of the software system. In this chapter, data of Eclipse projects is extracted from one of the well-known BTS called Bugzilla. The bug reported here undergoes a process before they are closed or resolved.

The life cycle of bug reported to BTS is represented in Figure 6. The bugs reported are either from a trusted (core team member) or an untrusted (unknown) submitter. On this basis, bugs are classified as new (by trusted submitter) or unconfirmed (by untrusted submitter). After the confirmation about validity and duplicity by the manager, the bug status is moved to new from unconfirmed. Later bugs are assigned to developers for resolution purpose based on its severity and priority. The developers work on the bug after it gets fixed, assignee moves the bug to RESOLVED. Some developers may move the bug to other states, like VERIFIED or CLOSED or REOPEN again. Combination of bug status and resolution denotes the reason for bug resolution. DUPLICATE Bugs, INVALID, WONTFIX and WORKSFORME bugs are considered to be invalid.

Out of the seven bug severity levels, five levels are considered in this study i.e. Blocker, Critical, Major, Minor and trivial. The first three levels i.e. Blocker, Critical and Major are considered to be severe whereas the other two are categorized as non-severe. As already discussed we do not consider normal and enhancement bugs.

Pre-Processing

For bug severity classification; first, we pre-process the extracted data using Natural Language Processing (NLP). This step is performed on the summary of bugs provided (Lamkanfi et al., 2011). Pre-processing details explained by Lamkanfi et al. (2010)includes the three steps on textual reports:

1. Tokenization: Here the description text of bug report in English is broken into the words, phrases, etc. called tokens, basically under this the words present in the text are identified using a space separator and removing the punctuation marks, hyphen, brackets, etc. The remaining text is converted to lower case to make the whole text similar.
2. Stop Word Removal: The often occurring words like prepositions, articles, etc. are removed from the text, repetitive words are also removed. These words do not play any role in determining severity.
3. Stemming: This technique involves mapping of words to its root word. Many words could be expressed into different forms conveying the same meaning and information. These words are converted to their basic form that will represent all the other similar words.

Feature Selection/Terms Extraction

Feature selection is done to obtain the important terms in the summary of the bug reports. Selecting the important terms to form a subset of features helps in effective classification. Also it reduces the dimensionality and complexity of text data. Some of the known feature selection techniques are TF-IDF, Mutual Information, Statistical Dependency, Info Gain, Chi-Square, and Correlation Coefficient.

In this study, feature selection is done using TF-IDF technique. TF-IDF provides the weights related to the importance of the features in determining a bug as severe or non-severe. It provides the importance of a term in the complete dataset. The importance of a term is affected by the frequency of the term in the document. The terms are arranged in descending order of the weights assigned to them. On the bans of importance in defining severity, the top 150 features are extracted from the bug report date. This signifies that these extracted terms play a major role in predicting the severity of bugs. Mathematically TF and IDF are calculated as:

$$TF = \frac{number\ of\ times\ a\ particular\ word\ is\ in\ a\ document}{total\ number\ of\ words\ in\ that\ document} \tag{1}$$

$$IDF = \log\left(\frac{Total\ number\ of\ documents}{total\ number\ of\ documents\ that\ contain\ that\ particular\ word}\right) \tag{2}$$

Table 2. Confusion matrix for bug classification as severe/non-severe

Bug Reports	Classified as Non-Severe Bugs	Classified as Severe Bugs
Non-Severe Bugs	True Negative (t_n)	False positive (f_p)
Severe Bugs	False Negative (f_n)	True positive (t_p)

Using equation (1) and (2) the TF-IDF is obtained as:

$$TF\text{-}IDF = TF*IDF \tag{3}$$

Here equation (3) represents TF-IDF which is calculated as the product of TF and IDF. Thus shows the general importance of the terms in a complete document.

Classifier Building

The training algorithms for classification are written using Python and build the model for classification. The severity of the reduced data has been assessed by two classifiers namely SVM and ANN. For carrying out the analysis, the data is divided into testing and training by using k-fold cross-validation approach where k is determined based on the task and literature. This approach is consistent because the classifier is trained on tested on every data point. The dataset which is used as input to the model is divided into k parts, from which one part is considered for testing while other remaining $k-1$ are considered for training the model. Then this validation is repeated k times considering different part for testing every time. In this way, each part of the data is considered for testing as well as training and the whole data is covered.

Performance Measures

To assess the performance of models, firstly a confusion matrix is built for binary classification of bugs as severe and non-severe as shown in Table 2.

t_p represents the number of severe bugs that were actually classified as severe, f_p signifies the number of bugs that were classified as severe but were not severe. This means the bug was falsely classified. In the same way, f_n is the number of severe bugs that were classified as non-severe and t_n is the number of non-severe bugs that were classified as non-severe bugs. On the basis of the matrix obtained the various performance measures such as precision, recall and F-measure are evaluated. Accuracy of models is based on these three measures. We discuss these measures in detail in Table 3.Table 3 shows the different measures used frequently for the binary classification which are calculated with the help of values obtained by confusion matrix. It also discusses each measure used in this chapter and their corresponding formula has also been provided.

Table 3. Performance measures for binary classification using notations from Table 2 (Sokolova & Lapalme, 2009)

Performance Measure	Formula	Description
Precision	$\dfrac{t_p}{t_p + f_p}$	It is defined as the number of correctly classified bugs among the total number of bugs reported
Recall	$\dfrac{t_p}{t_p + f_n}$	It is defined as the percentage of severe bugs that are correctly classified from the total number of bug reports.
F-measure	$\dfrac{2 \times precision \times recall}{precision + recall}$	It is defined as the harmonic mean of the above two measures.
Accuracy	$\dfrac{t_p + t_n}{t_p + f_p + t_n + t_f}$	It provides the complete influence of the model in classification.

The methodology steps can be summarized as follows:

1. Data Collection: The raw bug reports are obtained from Bugzilla (public repository).
2. The data available is in the text form so to analyze the reports first, we pre-process the data via text mining using NLP.
3. After pre-processing we do feature selection using TF-IDF technique to extract top 150 terms form summary text influencing classification decision.
4. TF-IDF provides the weights related to the importance of the terms. On the bans of importance weights, the terms are arranged in descending order to collect the top 150 terms.
5. The data is divided into training and testing parts using k-fold cross-validation.
6. Then, we train the classifiers based on 150 extracted terms using training data and then test its performance on the remaining testing part of the data.
7. At last, the performance of classifiers is discussed using the most prevalent performance measures like F-measure, Recall, Precision, Accuracy, etc.

IMPLEMENTATION

The discussed methodology is implemented step by step in this previous section. The first step was to acquire the data from BTS. The data we obtained for our study is discussed in detail below:

Figure 7. Home screen of Bugzilla Repository for eclipse bug reports

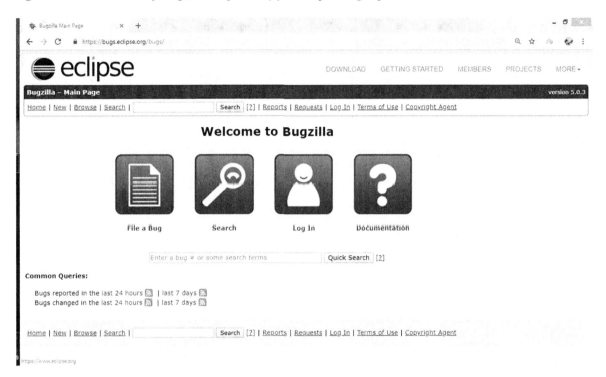

Figure 8. Searching options of bug reports data

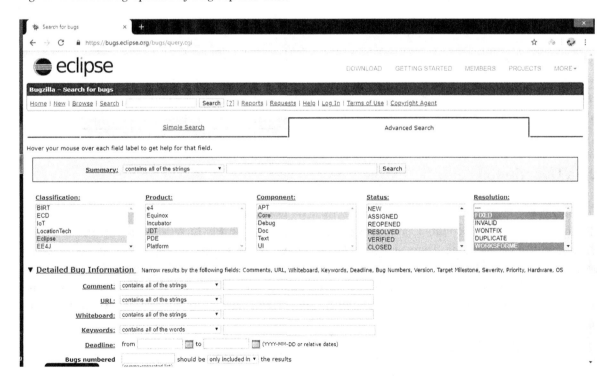

Figure 9. Bug Reports sample for component Core of JDT

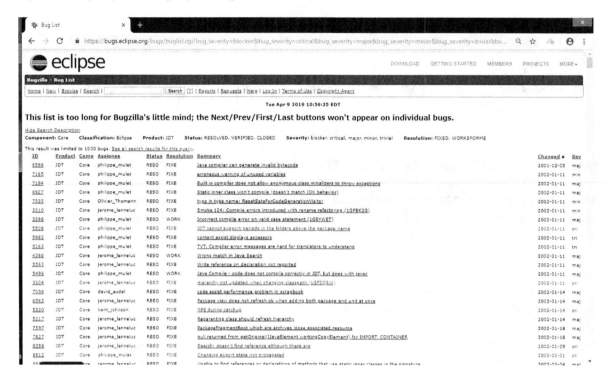

Table 4. Bugs in different severity level for each component of JDT

Components/Severity	Blocker	Critical	Major	Minor	Trivial	Total
Core	94	213	653	298	105	1363
Debug	23	49	182	96	70	420
Text	3	27	182	243	105	560
UI	10	50	279	315	168	822

Data Description

For the model development, the data of two Eclipse products namely JDT and Platform is extracted. In JDT product, four components Core, Debug, Text and UI, and in Platform seven components Debug, Releng, Resource, Runtime, Team, Text and User Assistance are selected. Bugs reported from January 1st, 2005 to April 4th, 2019 have been collected for the studywhere around 45 bugs are being reported on a daily basis. Bugzilla provides the number of bugs reported in the last 24 hours and also the total bugs reported in the last seven days. Figure 7 shows the home screen of the Bugzilla repository for searching bug reports.

Table 5. Bugs in different severity level for each component of platform

Components/ severity	Blocker	Critical	Major	Minor	Trivial	Total
Debug	7	39	175	129	96	446
Releng	84	72	203	85	39	483
Resource	9	42	124	33	18	226
Runtime	26	56	86	18	21	207
Team	14	22	88	55	99	278
Text	6	27	143	142	93	411
User	12	48	197	135	60	452

Table 6. Words selected using TF-IDF for JDT

Components	Words
Core	Hidden, hierarchi, hoc, focus, misc, inf, front, mn, sg, gtk, git, frequent, foo, gdk, jdk
Debug	Invoc, ja, jvm, gle, loc, bin, git, osx, ok, inf, node, overlap, leak, cce, html
Text	Yellow, incl, id, pl, gtk, jme, icu, origin, plug, magnet, ble, ie, xsd, lag, gc
UI	Yet, kb, invert, input, jme, int, nl, lcl, inherit, isk, junk, img, gdxet, doc, jar

Table 7. Words selected using TF-IDF for Platform

Components	Words
Debug	Zh, html, flag, git, jar, log, jvm, jdt, hit, hag, oom, jsr, manifest, adapt, hyperlink
Releng	Ia, jpg, http, isv, dmg, ds, cvs, nest, jgit, juno, npe, ee, dos, oomph
Resource	Ide, hang, invalid, osx, cold, loop, format, build, git, ibm, catalog, byte, adapt, jdk, jdt
Runtime	Flaw, html, gnu, gc, lost, fatal, jvm, jpg, af, arch, linux, bug, mf, break, argument
Team	Hang, host, http, gui, git, grey, gtk, nfe, xp, jni, jar, clash, ca, iw,lib
Text	Git, ie, expand, mess, lf, gc, doc, hyperlink, isc, lose, log, map, group, nls, mislead
User Assistance	Zip, index, img, ic, jdk, git, gif, iw, gui, nl, pdt, loss, node, html, jre

Bugswith status as RESOLVED, VERIFIED & CLOSED and resolution as FIXED & WORKS-FORMEare downloaded for the study (Figure 8) because the summary for these reports will not get changed over time. The sample bug reports corresponding to JDT bug reports is shown in Figure 9.

As already discussed in the previous sections, bugs with five severity levels namely Blocker, critical, major, minor & trivial have been considered for the study. The number of bug reports corresponding to a particular severity level and for different components of both the Eclipse products in shown in Table 4 and Table 5 respectively.

Table 8. Confusion matrix of model 1 & model 2 for jdt

Core					
Model 1			**Model 2**		
Data class	**Classified as Non-Severe**	**Classified as Severe**	**Data class**	**Classified as Non-Severe**	**Classified as Severe**
Non-severe	41	47	Non-severe	53	35
severe	32	221	Severe	66	187
Debug					
Model 1			**Model 2**		
Data class	**Classified as Non-Severe**	**Classified as Severe**	**Data class**	**Classified as Non-Severe**	**Classified as Severe**
Non-severe	24	18	Non-severe	0	42
severe	9	54	Severe	0	63
Text					
Model 1			**Model 2**		
Data class	**Classified as Non-Severe**	**Classified as Severe**	**Data class**	**Classified as Non-Severe**	**Classified as Severe**
Non-severe	66	15	Non-severe	65	16
severe	17	42	Severe	17	42
UI					
Model 1			**Model 2**		
Data class	**Classified as Non-Severe**	**Classified as Severe**	**Data class**	**Classified as Non-Severe**	**Classified as Severe**
Non-severe	79	28	Non-severe	76	31
severe	45	54	Severe	39	60

Numerical Analysis

After obtaining data from the Bugzilla, reports have been downloaded as Comma Separated file (CSV), so that it is usable in the python. Firstly to analyze the textual data we perform the pre-processing steps and select the features/words using TF-IDF technique. The selected features/words for the different data sets are shown in the Tables 6 and Table 7. 15 words out of 150 words that were selected using feature selection technique for each component have been shown for the reference purpose.The words are with respect to the reports received for different components.

For the classification purpose, SVM (Pandey and Solanki, 2019) and ANN classifiers are considered. k-cross validation method has been used to split the dataset into training and testing. In this study k is considered as 10 i.e. $k = 10$, and hence, 90 percent of the data is used in training and 10 percent for testing the trained models. This procedure is repeated 10 times, where each part of the data gets the chance to act as training and testing. After carrying out the procedure for both classifiers SVM (Model 1) and ANN (Model 2), the performance measures values are obtained using the confusion matrix. Confusion matrix shows the classified bug reports as severe and non-severe with respect to the actual severity. In Table 8, the number of severe and non-severe classes has been shown for all the components

Table 9. Performance measures of model 1 and model 2 for JDT

Components	Model 1			components	Model 2		
	Precision	Recall	F-measure		Precision	Recall	F-measure
Core	0.7567	0.7683	0.7683	Core	0.7398	0.7038	0.7163
Debug	0.7409	0.7428	0.7360	Debug	0.3600	0.6000	0.4499
Text	0.7705	0.7714	0.7708	Text	0.7637	0.7642	0.7640
UI	0.6474	0.6456	0.6420	UI	0.6601	0.6601	0.6591

of JDT based on model 1 and model 2 i.e. the confusion matrix for all the components of both the products.. Here, in model 1 for Core, 221 bugs are classified as severe which were actually severe in nature, whereas 47 bugs each of which was non-severe in nature are classified as severe. Further 32 bugs that were severe but classified as non-severe and 41 non-severe bugs were classified as non-severe. Similarly, other models with respect to different component are defined in the Table 8.

Based on the confusion matrix different performance measures such as Precision, Recall and F-measures are calculated. Table 9 represents the performance measures for the four components of the JDT product with respect to Model 1 and Model 2. Here component core has been predicted very well by Model 1, as the precision i.e., the proportion of bug reports that were classified as severe and were actually also severe is higher (0.7567 > 0.7398) for Model 1. Similarly, debug & text have better precision values by Model 1 than Model 2 as the precision values are 0.7409>0.36 & 0.7705>0.7637. But in UI precision is lower than model 2. This implies Model 1 classified more severe classes correctly for core, debug and text, whereas, more severe bugs of UI has been classified correctly by Model 2.

Table 9 also lists the Recall values obtained after running both the models. The recall is the proportion of bug reports that were classified correctly. The values of Recall for core, debug & text components of JDT product are larger for Model 1 than for model 2 but for UI Recall is greater of model 2. Herethe concern is that a severe bug should not be classified as non-severe, since missing a severe bug will of more loss to developers. F-measure has also been calculated for each component for both products (Table 9 and Table 11) which gives an average value of precision and recall to classify the bugs as severe. It is obtained when precision and recall are combined to form a single measure that gives harmonic mean of the two. If either of them hasa low value that mean also results to be a low value and vice-versa.

For product JDT, three components have been classified by model 1 with higher Precision and Recall that implies Model 1 a good classifier. Now we discuss performances of the Model 1 and Model 2 for the second Eclipse product.

Now for the second Eclipse product Platform, Table 10 shows the confusion matrix of the seven components for Model 1 and Model 2. In model 1for debug component 37 bugs are defined as severe which were actually severe and 21 bugs are defined as severe which were actually non-severe in nature. Also, 38 bugs are classified as non-severe which were actually non-severe. And there are 16 severe bugs which were classified as non-severe. Similarly, values of the confusion matrix can be summarized for both the models of different components of the product platform.

Table 11 gives the Precision, Recall and F-measures for seven components of the Platform. Here it can be observed that for component Debug precision and recall are poor by model 2 (0.2239 & 0.4732 respectively) but model 1 describes severity with good values of precision and recall (0.6725 & 0.6696 respectively). For component Releng, model 2 explains severity with more precision as compared to

Table 10. Confusion matrix of model 1 & model 2 for platform

Debug					
Model 1			**Model 2**		
Data class	**Classified as Non-Severe**	**Classified as Severe**	**Data class**	**Classified as Non-Severe**	**Classified as Severe**
Non-severe	38	21	Non-severe	0	59
Severe	16	37	Severe	0	53
Releng					
Model 1			**Model 2**		
Data class	**Classified as Non-Severe**	**Classified as Severe**	**Data class**	**Classified as Non-Severe**	**Classified as Severe**
Non-severe	8	27	Non-severe	12	23
Severe	11	75	Severe	15	71
Resource					
Model 1			**Model 2**		
Data class	**Classified as Non-Severe**	**Classified as Severe**	**Data class**	**Classified as Non-Severe**	**Classified as Severe**
Non-severe	2	11	Non-severe	0	13
Severe	4	40	Severe	0	44
Runtime					
Model 1			**Model 2**		
Data class	**Classified as Non-Severe**	**Classified as Severe**	**Data class**	**Classified as Non-Severe**	**Classified as Severe**
Non-severe	0	6	Non-severe	0	6
Severe	0	46	Severe	4	42
Team					
Model 1			**Model 2**		
Data class	**Classified as Non-Severe**	**Classified as Severe**	**Data class**	**Classified as Non-Severe**	**Classified as Severe**
Non-severe	37	5	Non-severe	38	4
Severe	10	18	Severe	12	16
Text					
Model 1			**Model 2**		
Data class	**Classified as Non-Severe**	**Classified as Severe**	**Data class**	**Classified as Non-Severe**	**Classified as Severe**
Non-severe	42	15	Non-severe	43	14
Severe	24	22	Severe	25	21
User Assistance					
Model 1			**Model 2**		
Data class	**Classified as Non-Severe**	**Classified as Severe**	**Data class**	**Classified as Non-Severe**	**Classified as Severe**
Non-severe	29	20	Non-severe	25	24
severe	15	49	Severe	15	49

Table 11. Performance measures

Components	Model 1			Components	Model 2		
	Precision	Recall	F-measure		Precision	Recall	F-measure
Debug	0.6725	0.6696	0.6697	Debug	0.2239	0.4732	0.3040
Releng	0.6443	0.6859	0.6527	Releng	0.6653	0.6859	0.6727
Resource	0.6814	0.7368	0.6980	Resource	0.5958	0.7719	0.6725
Runtime	0.7825	0.8846	0.8304	Runtime	0.7740	0.8076	0.7905
Team	0.7853	0.7857	0.7812	Team	0.7760	0.7714	0.7623
Text	0.6177	0.6213	0.6146	Text	0.6179	0.6213	0.6123
User	0.6880	0.6902	0.6877	User	0.6511	0.6548	0.6487

Table 12. Accuracy for JDT

Components	Model 1	Model 2
Core	0.7683	0.7038
Debug	0.7428	0.6000
Text	0.7714	0.7642
UI	0.6456	0.6601

Figure 10. Accuracy of model 1 and model 2 for JDT

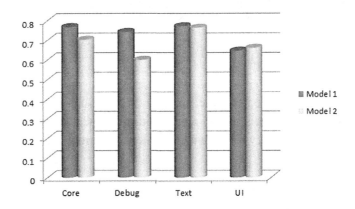

model 1. For components Resource and Runtime, the precision values are higher while model 2 gives a higher proportion of properly classified reports i.e. correctly classified reports for component Resource with a higher value of Recall. Now for components Team & User Assistance, both precision and recall are higher for model 1 than model 2 as precision are 0.7853>0.7760 & 0.6880>0.6511 respectively and recall are 0.7857>0.7714 & 0.6902>0.6548 respectively. For component Text, the severity is better predicted by Model 2 with better recall.

Table 13. Accuracy for platform

Components	Model 1	Model 2
Debug	**0.6696**	0.4732
Releng	0.6859	0.6859
Resource	0.7368	**0.7719**
Runtime	**0.8846**	0.8076
Team	**0.7857**	0.7714
Text	0.6213	0.6213
User Assistance	**0.6902**	0.6548

Figure 11. Accuracy of model 1 and model 2 for platform

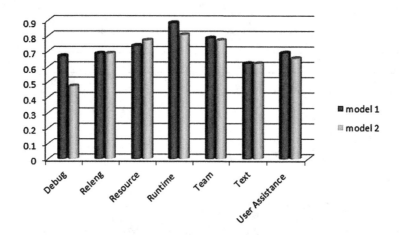

Till now, model performance based on Precision, recall and F-measure for each dataset has been discussed. Based on the different precision and recall values the overall performance of the models is calculated by determining the accuracy for both the products. Accuracy has been discussed in the next sub-section.

RESULT AND DISCUSSION

After discussing precision and recall values, we now analyze the accuracy of both the models for all the components is analyzed. Table 12 shows the respective accuracies for JDT components. The accuracy of both the models has been plotted for each component (Figure 10). Detailed literature study in the previous section suggests that the results of this study are consistent with past work (Lamkanfi et al., 2010). Here, the two classifier models are compared for their classification performance. From Table 12 it is evident that model 1 classified Core, Debug & Text with accuracy 0.7683, 0.7428 & 0.7714 respectively, which are more than the model 2. This implies SVM is a good classifier than ANN for these components. But for component UI, ANN classified with higher accuracy.

Now for Platform product, accuracies for each of the components is shown in Table 13. Here, Debug, Runtime, Team & User Assistance are classified by model 1 with higher accuracy values i.e., 0.6696, 0.8846, 0.7857 & 0.6902 respectively. For components Releng& Text, both models classified it with equal values of accuracy. For component Resource, accuracy is 0.6902 of model 1 which is higher than model 2.

Figure 11 shows the accuracy of both the models for each component of Platform which implies that four components are classified as severe and non-severe by model 1 and two components are equally classified by both the models. Only one component of project Platform has been classified by model 2. The results represent SVM plays a better role in classifying the reports than ANN for different components of the product Platform.

THREATS TO VALIDITY

In this section, the risks that might affect the validity of the obtained results are identified and what steps were taken by us to reduce those risks. Going with the studies presented in the literature (Joachims, 1998; Weng & Poon, 2008) this is organized into four types.

Construct Validity

In this research, the classifiers are trained using component-wise bug data for two eclipse projects. Four components of JDT product and seven products of Platform product of eclipse projects were retrieved from online publicly available Bugzilla repository. The components were selected if a large number of bugs was reported corresponding to it. This data related to a specific component of the product helps to predict better by removing any kind of biasedness that may be involved.

Reliability

The reports categorized under Normal severity and Enhancements were intentionally omitted. A bug categorized as normal creates a confusion related to the correct severity of that bug. Since normal is the default severity assigned to a bug while reporting, it is generally given by the user with less experience and understanding of the software. On the other hand, enhancements are even considered to be a bug as it is related to a request for updates in an existing feature and addition of the new feature.

Internal Validity

Also, it has been considered that all the fields of the dataset have some relationship with the severity of the bug. While training the model using the extracted terms the importance of terms in defining severity was also measured. The use of cross-validation method for dividing the data into training and testing reduces the risk of internal validity of results. But any kind of effort to deal with the imbalance data has not been incorporated.

External Validity

Here, in this study, two products of Eclipse project whose reports are assumed to be of good quality has been considered for the study. This is so because the user base of the Eclipse project mostly consists of developers(Liu et al., 2018). In this study, the bug report summary has been used for bug severity classification instead of the full long description as provided by the bug reporters.

CONCLUSIONS AND FUTURE SCOPE

Any software with complex structure cannot be developed 100% bug-free because testing required to remove every possible bug involves a lot of costs in large projects. Hence to deal with the bugs after release the managers create BTS where the bugs are reported by members of the development team as well as the users. This platform lets the whole IT community interact at a place for suggesting a solution to the reported bugs. On a daily basis, many bugs are reported in a format with summary, description and many other fields to describe the system configurations. This leads to a large amount of textual data which cannot be manually addressed within a reasonable time. The manager needs to assign bugs to resolver based on the severity. The severity level of a bug is defined by the person who is reporting the bug. But it can be determined based on the textual description and the summary provided. Automatic identification saves time and resources spent on the task.

In this chapter, bugs are classified based on the information contained in the summary of eclipse projects. The classification accuracy of Models trained is studied using selected important terms that help to determine severity. In this extent, TF-IDF, a feature extraction technique is used along with ANN and SVM, the two ML classifier has been implemented to tackle the bug severity assessment problems for textual bug reports recorded by the user and developer.

The use of feature selection based classification technique is suggested to improve the classification accuracy of the model. This is because here the model is trained for classification based on the terms that are most informative in defining severity. The terms in the text are an indicator of severity. The lists of terms obtained are different corresponding to different components of the product. The terms are component-specific; hence the severity of a bug is also specific to the component.

Based on results obtained in section 4 we see that the Text component of JDT product has the highest accuracy corresponding to both SVM and ANN classifiers i.e. 0.77 and 0.76 respectively whereas for Platform product, the classification accuracy results to be best for Runtime component for both SVM (0.88) and ANN (0.80). For JDT product ANN classifies better for each component expects for UI, on the other hand for platform product SVM predicts better for three components whereas for two accuracy remains unchanged and ANN predicts better for remaining components.

The results obtained are dataset specific i.e. if a particular classifier predicts better for a component than also it may not give the best accuracy for the other component. This is also visible from past literature. Hence it can be concluded that there is no noticeable difference in the prediction capabilities of these two machine learning algorithms. But it significantly contributes to the automatic prediction of severity for bugs.

This work is significant for enabling automated bug severity classification and improving the efficiency of bug triaging process. It is helpful in expediting the maintenance process carried out by the developers. The chapter correspondingly helps to realize the probable potential of text analytics in enhancing and boosting software maintenance strategies.

In the future, the following research areas can be further explored;

1. Use some additional feature selection techniques (Info gain,) and classifiers (Naïve Bayes, J48, Random forest, k-NN, decision tree, etc.) for building classification models.
2. The model can be validated for products of other projects like Mozilla, Gnome, etc. The bug reports for these open source software are also publicly available.
3. The model can be built to handle the imbalanced class data.
4. Before selecting the features, a study can be carried out to know the optimal number of features that will have maximum impact on determining severity.
5. Instead of keeping the testing and training data form the same project, cross-project validation can also be done.
6. Severity levels ranging from 1 to 5 can be assigned instead of just classifying them as severe and non-severe.
7. In this study, the models were trained on top 150 features and obtained the accuracy. The models can also be compared for the accuracy when the number of features extracted is changed monotonically.

REFERENCES

Ahuja, R., Nayyar, A., & Solanki, A. (2019). Movie Recommender System Using K-Means Clustering AND K-Nearest Neighbor. In *Confluence-2019: 9th International Conference on Cloud Computing, Data Science & Engineering*. Amity University. DOI: 10.1109/CONFLUENCE.2019.8776969

Alpaydin, E. (2009). *Introduction to machine learning*. MIT Press.

Alzubi, J., Nayyar, A., & Kumar, A. (2018). *Machine learning from theory to algorithms: an overview*. Paper presented at the Journal of Physics: Conference Series. 10.1088/1742-6596/1142/1/012012

Anvik, J., Hiew, L., & Murphy, G. C. (2006). Who should fix this bug? *Proceedings of the 28th international conference on Software engineering*.

Banerjee, S., Cukic, B., & Adjeroh, D. (2012). *Automated duplicate bug report classification using subsequence matching*. Paper presented at the 2012 IEEE 14th International Symposium on High-Assurance Systems Engineering. 10.1109/HASE.2012.38

Bettenburg, N., Just, S., Schröter, A., Weiss, C., Premraj, R., & Zimmermann, T. (2008). What makes a good bug report? *Proceedings of the 16th ACM SIGSOFT International Symposium on Foundations of software engineering*. 10.1145/1453101.1453146

Bowring, J. F., Rehg, J. M., & Harrold, M. J. (2004). *Active learning for automatic classification of software behavior*. Paper presented at the ACM SIGSOFT Software Engineering Notes. 10.1145/1007512.1007539

Charette, R. N. (1989). *Software engineering risk analysis and management.* McGraw-Hill.

Chaturvedi, K., & Singh, V. (2012a). *Determining bug severity using machine learning techniques.* Paper presented at the 2012 CSI Sixth International Conference on Software Engineering (CONSEG). 10.1109/CONSEG.2012.6349519

Chaturvedi, K., & Singh, V. (2012b). An empirical comparison of machine learning techniques in predicting the bug severity of open and closed source projects. *International Journal of Open Source Software and Processes, 4*(2), 32–59. doi:10.4018/jossp.2012040103

Erturk, E., & Sezer, E. A. (2015). A comparison of some soft computing methods for software fault prediction. *Expert Systems with Applications, 42*(4), 1872–1879. doi:10.1016/j.eswa.2014.10.025

Fiaz, A., Devi, N., & Aarthi, S. (2013). *Bug tracking and reporting system.* arXiv preprint arXiv:1309.1232

Ghaffarian, S. M., & Shahriari, H. R. (2017). Software vulnerability analysis and discovery using machine-learning and data-mining techniques: A survey. *ACM Computing Surveys, 50*(4), 56. doi:10.1145/3092566

Hammouri, A., Hammad, M., Alnabhan, M., & Alsarayrah, F. (2018). Software bug prediction using machine learning approach. *International Journal of Advanced Computer Science and Applications, 9*(2).

Herzig, K., Just, S., & Zeller, A. (2013). It's not a bug, it's a feature: how misclassification impacts bug prediction. *Proceedings of the 2013 international conference on software engineering.* 10.1109/ICSE.2013.6606585

Humphrey, W. S. (1989). *Managing the software process* (Vol. 1). Addison-Wesley.

Humphrey, W. S. (1995). *A discipline for software engineering.* Addison-Wesley Longman Publishing Co., Inc.

Jaiswal, A., & Malhotra, R. (2018). Software reliability prediction using machine learning techniques. *International Journal of System Assurance Engineering and Management, 9*(1), 230–244. doi:10.100713198-016-0543-y

Jeong, G., Kim, S., & Zimmermann, T. (2009). Improving bug triage with bug tossing graphs. *Proceedings of the the 7th joint meeting of the European software engineering conference and the ACM SIGSOFT symposium on The foundations of software engineering.* 10.1145/1595696.1595715

Jin, K., Dashbalbar, A., Yang, G., Lee, J.-W., & Lee, B. (2016). Bug severity prediction by classifying normal bugs with text and meta-field information. *Advanced Science and Technology Letters, 129*, 19–24. doi:10.14257/astl.2016.129.05

Joachims, T. (1998). *Text categorization with support vector machines: Learning with many relevant features.* Paper presented at the European conference on machine learning. 10.1007/BFb0026683

Kukkar, A., Mohana, R., Nayyar, A., Kim, J., Kang, B.-G., & Chilamkurti, N. (2019). A Novel Deep-Learning-Based Bug Severity Classification Technique Using Convolutional Neural Networks and Random Forest with Boosting. *Sensors (Basel), 19*(13), 2964. doi:10.339019132964 PMID:31284398

Kumar, L., Sripada, S. K., Sureka, A., & Rath, S. K. (2018). Effective fault prediction model developed using least square support vector machine (LSSVM). *Journal of Systems and Software, 137*, 686–712. doi:10.1016/j.jss.2017.04.016

Lamkanfi, A., Demeyer, S., Giger, E., & Goethals, B. (2010). *Predicting the severity of a reported bug.* Paper presented at the Mining Software Repositories (MSR), 2010 7th IEEE Working Conference on. 10.1109/MSR.2010.5463284

Lamkanfi, A., Demeyer, S., Soetens, Q. D., & Verdonck, T. (2011). *Comparing mining algorithms for predicting the severity of a reported bug.* Paper presented at the 2011 15th European Conference on Software Maintenance and Reengineering. 10.1109/CSMR.2011.31

Liu, W., Wang, S., Chen, X., & Jiang, H. (2018). Predicting the Severity of Bug Reports Based on Feature Selection. *International Journal of Software Engineering and Knowledge Engineering, 28*(04), 537–558. doi:10.1142/S0218194018500158

Malhotra, R., & Jain, A. (2012). Fault prediction using statistical and machine learning methods for improving software quality. *Journal of Information Processing Systems, 8*(2), 241–262. doi:10.3745/JIPS.2012.8.2.241

Malhotra, R., & Singh, Y. (2011). On the applicability of machine learning techniques for object oriented software fault prediction. *Software Engineering: An International Journal, 1*(1), 24–37.

Menzies, T., & Marcus, A. (2008). *Automated severity assessment of software defect reports.* Paper presented at the 2008 IEEE International Conference on Software Maintenance. 10.1109/ICSM.2008.4658083

Michie, D., Spiegelhalter, D. J., & Taylor, C. (1994). Machine learning. *Neural and Statistical Classification, 13*.

Mishra, B., & Shukla, K. (2012). Defect prediction for object oriented software using support vector based fuzzy classification model. *International Journal of Computers and Applications, 60*(15).

Murphy, G., & Cubranic, D. (2004). Automatic bug triage using text categorization. *Proceedings of the Sixteenth International Conference on Software Engineering & Knowledge Engineering.*

Murphy, K. P. (2012). *Machine learning: a probabilistic perspective.* MIT Press.

Pandey, N., Sanyal, D. K., Hudait, A., & Sen, A. (2017). Automated classification of software issue reports using machine learning techniques: An empirical study. *Innovations in Systems and Software Engineering, 13*(4), 279–297. doi:10.100711334-017-0294-1

Pandey, S., & Solanki, A. (2019). Music Instrument Recognition using Deep Convolutional Neural Networks. International Journal of Information Technology. doi:10.100741870-019-00285-y

Perini, A., Susi, A., & Avesani, P. (2013). A machine learning approach to software requirements prioritization. *IEEE Transactions on Software Engineering, 39*(4), 445–461. doi:10.1109/TSE.2012.52

Sharma, G., Sharma, S., & Gujral, S. (2015). A novel way of assessing software bug severity using dictionary of critical terms. *Procedia Computer Science, 70*, 632–639. doi:10.1016/j.procs.2015.10.059

Singh, V., Misra, S., & Sharma, M. (2017). Bug severity assessment in cross project context and identifying training candidates. *Journal of Information & Knowledge Management, 16*(01), 1750005. doi:10.1142/S0219649217500058

Sokolova, M., & Lapalme, G. (2009). A systematic analysis of performance measures for classification tasks. *Information Processing & Management, 45*(4), 427–437. doi:10.1016/j.ipm.2009.03.002

Tian, Y., Lo, D., & Sun, C. (2012). *Information retrieval based nearest neighbor classification for fine-grained bug severity prediction.* Paper presented at the 2012 19th Working Conference on Reverse Engineering. 10.1109/WCRE.2012.31

Vapnik, V., Guyon, I., & Hastie, T. (1995). Support vector machines. *Machine Learning, 20*(3), 273–297. doi:10.1007/BF00994018

Weinberg, G. M. (1993). Quality software management. New York: Academic Press.

Wen, J., Li, S., Lin, Z., Hu, Y., & Huang, C. (2012). Systematic literature review of machine learning based software development effort estimation models. *Information and Software Technology, 54*(1), 41–59. doi:10.1016/j.infsof.2011.09.002

Weng, C. G., & Poon, J. (2008). A new evaluation measure for imbalanced datasets. *Proceedings of the 7th Australasian Data Mining Conference-Volume 87.*

Xia, X., Lo, D., Qiu, W., Wang, X., & Zhou, B. (2014). *Automated configuration bug report prediction using text mining.* Paper presented at the 2014 IEEE 38th Annual Computer Software and Applications Conference. 10.1109/COMPSAC.2014.17

Xu, B., Lo, D., Xia, X., Sureka, A., & Li, S. (2015). *Efspredictor: Predicting configuration bugs with ensemble feature selection.* Paper presented at the 2015 Asia-Pacific Software Engineering Conference (APSEC). 10.1109/APSEC.2015.38

Yang, C.-Z., Chen, K.-Y., Kao, W.-C., & Yang, C.-C. (2014). *Improving severity prediction on software bug reports using quality indicators.* Paper presented at the 2014 IEEE 5th International Conference on Software Engineering and Service Science. 10.1109/ICSESS.2014.6933548

Zhang, T., Yang, G., Lee, B., & Chan, A. T. (2015). Predicting severity of bug report by mining bug repository with concept profile. *Proceedings of the 30th Annual ACM Symposium on Applied Computing.* 10.1145/2695664.2695872

Zimmermann, T., Premraj, R., Bettenburg, N., Just, S., Schroter, A., & Weiss, C. (2010). What makes a good bug report? *IEEE Transactions on Software Engineering, 36*(5), 618–643. doi:10.1109/TSE.2010.63

Chapter 8
Creating Paraphrase Identification Corpus for Indian Languages:
Opensource Data Set for Paraphrase Creation

Anand Kumar M.

(iD) https://orcid.org/0000-0003-0310-4510

Department of Information Technology, National Institute of Technology Karnataka, Surathkal, India

Shivkaran Singh

Arnekt Solutions, Pune, India

Praveena Ramanan

Quantiphi Inc, Bangalore, India

Vaithehi Sinthiya

Karunya Institute of Technology and Sciences, Coimbatore, India

Soman K. P.

Amrita School of Engineering, Amrita Vishwa Vidyapeetham University, India

ABSTRACT

In recent times, paraphrase identification task has got the attention of the research community. The paraphrase is a phrase or sentence that conveys the same information but using different words or syntactic structure. The Microsoft Research Paraphrase Corpus (MSRP) is a well-known openly available paraphrase corpus of the English language. There is no such publicly available paraphrase corpus for any Indian language (as of now). This chapter explains the creation of paraphrase corpus for Hindi, Tamil, Malayalam, and Punjabi languages. This is the first publicly available corpus for any Indian language. It was used in the shared task on detecting paraphrases for Indian languages (DPIL) held in conjunction with Forum for Information Retrieval & Evaluation (FIRE) 2016. The annotation process was performed by a postgraduate student followed by a two-step proofreading by a linguist and a language expert.

DOI: 10.4018/978-1-5225-9643-1.ch008

INTRODUCTION

Paraphrases are pair of sentences that express the equivalent meaning using different wording. A paraphrase is a linguistic phenomenon of a language. It has numerous applications in the area of computational linguistics and teaching languages. In language teaching, paraphrasing reveals the amazing inherent power of human language. All the natural languages show their specific nature through their lexicon and syntactic constructions. The use of different forms of words, word-clusters or multi-words, phrases, and sentences reveal a different kind of dictum. If there is an ambiguity in the expression, it can be removed by paraphrasing (i.e. by using the unambiguous expression). Sometimes paraphrasing can reveal the attitude of the speaker or writer. Automatically detecting the paraphrase in Indian languages using the recent machine learning-based methods requires the paraphrase annotated corpora. The research on paraphrase in Indian Languages is less because of the unavailability of corpora.

Paraphrase detection, on the other hand, is the process of detecting a sentence or paragraph which is represented using different words while preserving the same meaning (Fernando, S., & Stevenson, M, 2008). The process of constructing the semantic representation in natural language is called computational semantics. Computational semantics is very important in many fields such as search engines, summarization, machine translation, question answering, etc. Paraphrase detection requires deep semantic understanding. The quality of paraphrases depends on one's understanding of deep semantics. The primary importance of paraphrase is to preserve the meaning while rephrasing it (Bhagat, R., & Hovy, 2013). Paraphrase detection is much useful in text summarization, rewriting tools, evaluating machine translation systems, etc. The automatic plagiarism detection models also employ paraphrase detection techniques. To obtain high accuracy in an automatic paraphrase detection task, deep semantic and syntactic analysis of sentences is needed.

This paper aims to develop the paraphrase corpus for Indian languages as paraphrase corpus for any Indian language is not available as an open-source. This is because of the scarcity of research in paraphrase identification for Indian languages. The objective of this work is encouraging the research community working on Indian languages towards the challenging field of paraphrase identification.

TYPOLOGIES OF PARAPHRASES

A paraphrase is a distinct technique to shape different language models (Barreiro, A., 2009). Linguistically, paraphrases are described in terms of meaning or semantics. According to Meaning-Text theory (Mel'čuk, I. A., & Polguere, A, 1987), in a language, if one or more syntactic construction (sentence formation) preserves semantic equality, those are considered as paraphrases. The agreement of semantic likeness between the source and paraphrased text expresses the range of semantic similarity between them. Paraphrasing is typically associated with synonyms. Various other linguistic units such as semi-synonyms, metaphors, linguistic entailment, and figurative meaning are considered as the components for paraphrasing. It is not only seen at the lexical level. It also found in other levels such as phrasal and sentential level (Zhao, S., Liu, T., Yuan, X., Li, S., & Zhang, Y, 2007). Various levels of paraphrasing reveal the diversified classes of paraphrases and the relationship to its source document. Some of the most common paraphrase types are described below (Barrón-Cedeño, A., Vila, M., Martí, M. A., & Rosso, P, 2013).

Lexical paraphrasing is the major method of paraphrasing found commonly in the literature. For instance (Anand Kumar, M., Singh, S., Kavirajan, B., Soman, K.P, 2018), If a source sentence is, *"The two ships were acquired by the navy after the war"*, then the proper paraphrased variants are: *"The two ships were conquered by the navy after the war"* and *"The two ships were won by the Navy after the war"*. There are still more paraphrases feasible for the given example sentence. The source verb 'acquire' is paraphrased with its synonym words 'conquer' and 'win'. In lexical paraphrases, the source sentence and paraphrased sentence show similar syntactic structural phenomena.

Approximate paraphrases are another popular form found commonly in headlines of newspapers. Approximate paraphrases by different newspapers are: "India and U.S. Prepare to Share Military Logistics" (The American Interest), "India, US agree to share military supplies and fuel" (The Indian Express). Sometimes these kinds of paraphrases reveal the attitude of the speaker.

Sentential level paraphrases are another type of paraphrases which can be easily paraphrased by changing the structure of the source sentence. For source sentence - "All rich countries". Possible paraphrase could be - "All countries that are rich". Similarly for "Hindi speaking people", the possible paraphrase is "The people who speak Hindi". The way of changing the active and passive voice in writing is also considered as paraphrasing. For example, William Shakespeare wrote "The Tragedy of Othello, the Moor of Venice" could be paraphrased as "The Tragedy of Othello, and the Moor of Venice" was written by William Shakespeare.

The addition of extra-linguistic units that do not affect the semantics of a sentence is another kind of paraphrasing. For example: "Hilda helped Tony because of his injury" could be paraphrased as "It was Hilda that helped Tony because of his injury" or "it was Tony that Hilda helped because of his injury" or "It was because of his injury that Hilda helped Tony".

Changing the order from word-level to sentence-level makes paraphrases. For example: "Hilda only helped Tony because of his injury" could be paraphrased as "Hilda helped Tony only because of his injury". Certain types of paraphrases exhibit substantial dissimilarity between the structural level, but they possess the semantic similarities. For example: "The men made a delivery of sandwiches to everyone at the shop before lunchtime" could be paraphrased as "Before lunchtime, the men delivered the sandwiches to everyone at the shop" or "The men gave everyone their sandwiches at the shop before lunchtime".

Phrase level paraphrase is very common in which paraphrases possess phrase-level variations. For example: "His kids click through Web sites" could be paraphrased as "His children are surfing the Web".

Adverbs of Manner can paraphrase easily from "the puppy ran happily towards its mother" to "the puppy ran towards its mother happily". Adverbs can easily paraphrase a sentence into an adverbial phrase. For example: "He completed his coursework with great success" could be paraphrased as "He completed his coursework successfully". Differed linguistic relationships like hypernyms, hyponyms, and antonyms between words can also be used to make legitimate paraphrases. For example: *"Sukumaran has enjoyed the chirps of ruby-throated bulbul at Chinnar"* could be paraphrased as "Sukumaran has enjoyed the chirps of birds at Chinnar". Different nominal entities of the same concepts like medical insurance/health insurance, daycare center/playschool are best examples of paraphrases.

SIGNIFICANCE OF PARAPHRASING

Paraphrasing a sentence can reveal the style of the language used by the speaker. Defining a technical term or semantically non-understandable expression is a sort of paraphrasing indeed. Even translation from the source language to target language can be considered as paraphrasing across languages. Paraphrasing is vital for teaching unknown concepts through known concepts. In the era of information explosion, one need to know things in crisp format due to time constraint. We cannot read all the books, texts, research papers and news items dealing with a particular subject or topic or domain. Paraphrasing comes handy in this context. For example, we need not go through all the newspapers; news summarization helps us from reading all sorts of reading materials. Text summarization is another dimension of paraphrasing. It saves a lot of time. Most people end up reading only abstracts and summaries of certain articles. Paraphrasing has much scope in the field of language processing, but still, this particular linguistic phenomenon is not exploited due to the unavailability of comparable data and the lack of fully developed technologies. To resolve this problem, we should ensure the availability of comparable corpora which reveals the techniques as well as types of paraphrasing.

There are two main issues in paraphrasing: Paraphrase Reorganization (PR) and Paraphrase Generation (PG). Paraphrase Generation (PG) aims at the generation of paraphrases for different domains for specific applications. Automatic Paraphrase Generation is considered one of the most needed areas in language processing research. It has various applications and one such application is Question Answering (QA). QA system can be improved with the help of paraphrasing (Rinaldi, F., Dowdall, J., Kaljurand, K., Hess, M., & Mollá, D, 2003) (Fader, A., Zettlemoyer, L., Etzioni, O., 2013). It can improve the query system as well as the answering system; that is, it can improve the quality of the answer for a given query. Paraphrases can be used for the simplification of texts as a pre-processing technique for machine translation. Paraphrases are useful for the improvement of Machine Translation (MT) system (Callison-Burch, C., Koehn, P., & Osborne M, 2006). The available techniques for MT system evaluation are not suitable for Indian Languages. Automatic paraphrase identification will surely improve the performance of automatic Machine Translation evaluation.

Utilizing paraphrases, one can easily find out the similarity of the meanings of the sentences from a larger set of data. We can easily exploit paraphrasing in Text Summarization too. Automatic Text Summarizer highlights all the significant and influential information from a lengthy document. Abstract summarizer summarizes necessitous information from reviews only. This sort of information is more reliable. This kind of data keeps sophisticated about the original text; it is free from verbose expressions and is much systematic too.

Abstract Summarizer is controlled by the Natural Language Generation (NLG) system. The present NLG system is performed with skillful linguistic rules. These linguistic rules are highly complex. PG can scale down this complexity, which will assist the improvisation of Natural Language Generation. Some European Languages' research communities are working on Recurrent Neural Network (RNN) (Tarasov D. S, 2015) for producing atypical paraphrases, which are utilized for the improvisation of Text Summarization. There is a lot of scope in this area for Indian Languages too. In Natural Language Generation (NLG), paraphrasing can be utilized for the rephrasing of sentences, bring modifications in the style of writing, text simplification, and plagiarism detection. It is also useful for information extraction (IE) and retrieval (IR), Text manipulation, Sentence Alignment, Creation of Grammar Formalism and Paraphrase detection.

Paraphrases and plagiarism retain noteworthy similarities. If a sentence maintains the analogy of vocabulary and style of another sentence, then it's identified as plagiarism. In other words, "Plagiarism is representing someone else's writing as your own original writing" (Barrón-Cedeño, A., Vila, M., Martí, M. A., & Rosso, 2013). A paraphrase means borrowing an idea from another source and re-ordering the idea by means of one's own vocabulary and style. Thus he/she maintains the essence of the source text, but he/she had not copied the vocabulary and style as such as the source text. In general, many kinds of plagiarism are found in common practice, paraphrasing is also a kind of plagiarism. Paraphrasing without a proper citation is also considered as a kind of plagiarism. If we adopt someone's idea and present that in our own words and style, we should make sure that along with our text, correct information about the source must be given. Paraphrase not only gives adequate information about the source text, but it also preserves the idea and meaning of the source text. Paraphrasing skill helps a person to stay away from plagiarism. Developing a paraphrasing skill has become a need of our time.

RELATED WORK AND EXISTING CORPORA

Research in paraphrase detection lacks publicly available corpus. This scarcity hinders research in paraphrase detection. This situation is even worse for Indian languages since there is no openly available paraphrase corpus (to the best of our knowledge).

The most commonly used openly available corpus is the Microsoft Research Paraphrase Corpus (MSRP) developed by Dolan and Brocket (2005) for English. It is labeled manually with binary judgment as to whether the pair consists of a paraphrase or not. It was created automatically using heuristic extraction techniques with a Support Vector Machine classifier.

The WRPA corpus consists of several relational paraphrases extorted using WRPA system from Wikipedia (Vila, M., Rodríguez, H., & Martí, M. A., 2015). WRPA corpus is available in English and Spanish. In English, it is composed of several paraphrases containing person-date of birth relation, person-date of death relation, and person-place of birth relation, etc. In Spanish, it is composed of paraphrase expressing authorship relations, etc.

The P4P (Paraphrase for Plagiarism) is another famous paraphrase corpus (Barrón-Cedeño, A., Vila, M., Martí, M. A., & Rosso, P., 2013). It uses paraphrase typology to label a subset of PAN plagiarism corpus 2010 (PAN-PC-10) with related paraphrase phenomena. This corpus relies on a corpus with plagiarism cases and evaluation measure suited for the automatic plagiarism detection task. Instead of string annotations, linguistic units like words, clauses, and phrases, etc. were annotated. Several other paraphrase corpora available for different languages. Some of these available corpora with domains they address are mentioned in Table 1.

The paraphrase detection can be associated and compared with the sentiment (Munjal, P., Narula, M., Kumar, S., & Banati, H., 2018) and polarity of the sentences. The recent deep learning (Sachin Pandey, Arun Solanki, 2019) and machine learning models provide the extensive solution to the proposed corpora. The more details on bench-mark accuracy of the data set and the best features and inferences are discussed in (Anand Kumar, M., Singh, S., Kavirajan, B., Soman, K.P, 2018).

Table 1. Some of the existing paraphrase corpora

Name	Domain	Pairs	Language
MSRP	News	5,801	English
WRPA	Wikipedia	≈4,000	English
		≈82,000	Spanish
P4P	-	847	English
QA Paraphrase Corpus (Bernhard, D., & Gurevych, I. 2008)	Q-A	7,434	English
Russian Paraphrase Corpus (Pronoza, E., Yagunova, E., & Pronoza, A., 2016)	News	4,758	Russian
Turkish Paraphrase Corpus (Demir, S., El-Kahlout, I. D., Unal, E., & Kaya, H., 2012)	News, Novels, Subtitles	1,270	Turkish

PARAPHRASE CORPORA CREATION FOR INDIAN LANGUAGES

Detecting Paraphrases in Indian Languages (DPIL) shared task conducted in conjunction with the Eighth meeting of the Forum for Information Retrieval and Evaluation (FIRE-2016)[1] at ISI, Kolkata. The task asked the participants to identify whether the given sentence pairs are paraphrases or not in four Indian languages, namely Hindi, Punjabi, Tamil and Malayalam (Anand Kumar, M et.al, 2016) (Anand Kumar, M et.al, 2018). The paraphrase corpora were already used for creating the paraphrase identification system in Indian languages (Bhargava, R., Sharma, G., & Sharma, Y., 2017), (Sarkar, K., 2018), (Praveena, R., Anand Kumar, M., Soman, K.P., 2017), (Tian, L., Ning, H., Kong, L., Chen, K., Qi, H., Han, Z., 2018), (Saini, A., Verma, A., 2018). The collected sentences were paired in three different categories. The dataset comprised of paraphrase, semi-paraphrase and non-paraphrase pairs collected from the headlines of regional newspapers.

The sentence pairs which conveyed the same meaning were named paraphrases. The sentence pairs which partially conveys the meaning or one sentence contains additional information or partial information than the other sentence was named as Semi-Paraphrases or somewhat equal Paraphrases. The sentence pairs that discuss two different topics were labeled as non-paraphrases. The dataset was created from news headlines and articles collected from various available web-based news pages. The exploitation of news articles for the generation of paraphrase corpus is not new (Shinyama, Y., Sekine, S., & Sudo, K., 2002).

The news articles reporting the same event collected from different web-based news sources will generally convey the same meaning with different words. This kind of articles can be further fine-tuned to create paraphrase sentence pairs. However, this fact is not always true. The sentence may contain additional information about the same event. Such cases can be used to our advantage as these cases share the attribute of a semi-paraphrases. There may be some articles which report two different events hence the content is not at all equivalent. The sentences from these articles could be classified as non-paraphrases. However, there are cases when articles don't fall into one or another category. In this case, we can manually fine-tune the sentence according to our requirement.

The creation of paraphrase corpora for various Indian languages began with collecting online news articles and headings from various online web-based news pages. The manually obtained sentence pairs were further cleaned from the noises and unwanted information. After manually removing all the irregularities like spelling corrections and transformations in the text, the sentences were tagged according to

Figure 1. Corpora creation process

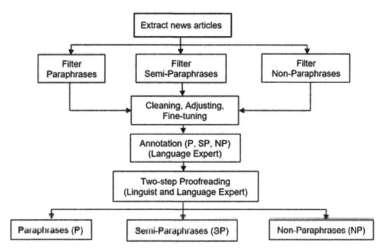

the paraphrase impact (Paraphrase, Non-Paraphrase, and Semi-Paraphrase) and the similarity occurred in each sentence pair. The annotation labels used were Paraphrase (P), Semi-Paraphrase (SP), and Non-Paraphrase (NP). These annotations were initially assigned by the postgraduate students for each language. The initial level tagged corpora were again proofread by a language expert and followed by a linguistic expert. In addition to that, the tagged sentence pairs of each language were converted to the Extensible Markup Language (XML) format. The entire process towards corpora creation is summarized in Figure 1. Figure 2 depicts the sample paraphrase corpora in XML format. The example instances of paraphrase, semi-paraphrase, and non paraphrase sentence pairs are depicted in Table 2 and Table 3.

The example instances of paraphrase, semi-paraphrase, and non-paraphrase sentence pairs for Hindi and Punjabi languages are given in Table 2. Here, H represents for Hindi language and Pu stands for Punjabi language and P, SP and NP are the labels used for Paraphrase, Semi-Paraphrase, and Non-Paraphrase respectively. The English translation for each sentence pairs has also given to understand the meaning by the non-native speakers. It can be observed from the table that paraphrased sentence pair contains the semantically similar sentence, Semi-paraphrased sentence pair captures only the partial meaning and Non-Paraphrase conveys completely diverse meaning. Similarly, Table 3 contains example instances of paraphrase, semi-paraphrase, and non-paraphrase sentence pairs of Tamil language and Malayalam language corpora.

CORPORA ANALYSIS

The paraphrase corpus created was used in the shared task on Detecting Paraphrases in Indian Languages (DPIL) conducted in association with FIRE-2016 at Indian Statistical Institute (ISI), Kolkata, India.

The task concentrates on sentential paraphrase detection of four Indian languages (Hindi, Malayalam, Tamil, and Punjabi). The task is split into subtask-1 and subtask-2:

Figure 2. Sample data format

```
<?xml version="1.0" encoding="UTF-8"?>
<Data version="1.0" name="AmritaCEN_DPIL.TAM.TASK2">
    - <Corpus domain="NEWS">
        <Language>Tamil</Language>
        - <Paraphrase pID="TAM0001">
            <Sentence1>சங்கராபுரம் தொகுதியில் போட்டியிடும் வேட்டுமேல் தலைப்பவதயாக வெல்லு பிரசாரம் செய்தார்.</Sentence1>
            <Sentence2>டி.மு.க., வேட்டாளர் வேட்டுமேல் போட்டியிடும் சங்கராபுரம் தொகுதியில் சின்ன பெல்ல பகுதியில் தலைப்பவதயாக வெல்லு ஓட்டு
            செருக்கார்.</Sentence2>
            <Class>P</Class>
        </Paraphrase>
        - <Paraphrase pID="TAM0002">
            <Sentence1>சேரன மாநில திருகுசிக் கடைமானிக்கல் கோயில் திருவிழா துவங்கியது.</Sentence1>
            <Sentence2>கடைமானிக்கல் கோயில் திருவிழா கோலகலமாக துவங்கியது.</Sentence2>
            <Class>P</Class>
        </Paraphrase>
```

Table 2. Examples for Hindi and Punjabi Language (Anand Kumar, M., Singh, S., Kavirajan, B., Soman, K.P, 2018)

H	मृतका नशि तीन भाई-बहनों में सबसे बड़ी थी। *[The deceased Nisha was eldest of three siblings]* तीन भाई-बहनों में सबसे बड़ी थी मृतका नशि। *[Out of three siblings, deceased Nisha was the eldest]*	P
	उपमंत्री की बेसिक सैलरी 10 हजार से बढ़कर 35 हजार हो गई है। *[The basic salary of deputy minister is increased from 10k to 35k]* उपमंत्री की बेसिक सैलरी 35 हजार हो गई है। *[The basic salary of deputy minister is 35k]*	SP
	जमिनास्टकि में दीपा 4th पोजिशन पर रही थी। *[Deepa came at 4th position in gymnastics]* 11 भारतीय पुरुष जमिनास्ट आजादी के बाद से ओलपिकि में जा चुके हैं। *[Since independence 11 male athletes have been to Olympics]*	NP
Pu	ਕਾਬੁਲ ਦੇ ਹੋਟਲ ਤੇ ਅੱਤਵਾਦੀ ਹਮਲਾ। *[A Kabul hotel was attacked by the terrorists]* ਅੱਤਵਾਦੀਆਂ ਦੁਆਰਾ ਕਾਬੁਲ ਦੇ ਹੋਟਲ ਤੇ ਕੀਤਾ ਗਿਆ ਹਮਲਾ। *[The terrorists attacked a hotel in Kabul]*	P
	ਪੁਲੀਸ ਅਧਿਕਾਰੀ ਮੁਹੰਮਦ ਮੁਤਾਬਕ ਦੋਵੇਂ ਭਰਾਵਾਂ ਵਚਿਕਾਰ ਕਾਰੋਬਾਰ ਨੂੰ ਲੈ ਕੇ ਝਗੜਾ ਸੀ। *[According to the police officer, there was a dispute over trade among two brothers.]* ਦੋਵੇਂ ਭਰਾਵਾਂ ਵਚਿਕਾਰ ਕਾਰੋਬਾਰ ਨੂੰ ਲੈ ਕੇ ਝਗੜਾ ਸੀ। *[There was a dispute over trade between two brothers]*	SP
	ਅਮਰਨਾਥ ਤੇ ਵੈਸ਼ਨੋ ਦੇਵੀ ਯਾਤਰਾ ਨੂੰ ਭਾਰੀ ਬਾਰਸ਼ਿ ਚਲਦਯਿਾ ਰੋਕ ਦਤਿਾ ਗਯਾ ਹੈ। *[Travels to Amarnath and Vaishno devi were stopped because of heavy rain]* ਅਮਰਨਾਥ ਗੁਫਾ ਭਗਵਾਨ ਸ਼ਵਿ ਦੇ ਪ੍ਰਮੁੱਖ ਧਾਰਮਕਿ ਥਾਂਵਾਂ ਵਿੱਚੋ ਇੱਕ ਹੈ। *[Amarnath cave is one of the major religious site of Lord Shiva]*	NP

Subtask 1: Classify the given sentence pairs as paraphrase or non-paraphrase.

Subtask 2: Given the sentence pairs, identify whether the pairs are semantically equivalent (Paraphrases) or not equivalent (Non-paraphrases) or semi equivalent (Semi-paraphrases).

The training and testing corpora statistics for subtask-1 and subtask-2 are shown in Table 4. The train and test dataset has split randomly. The basic similarity between the two subtasks enabled us to use corpus from one subtask into another subtask. As mentioned in the corpora creation section, the

Table 3. Examples for Tamil and Malayalam Language [25]

T	புதுச்சேரியில் 84 சதவீத வாக்குப்பதிவு [84 percent voting in Puducherry] புதுச்சேரி சட்டசபை தேர்தலில் 84 சதவீத ஓட்டுப் பதிவானது [Puducherry assembly elections recorded 84 percent of vote]	P
	அப்துல்கலாம் கனவை நிறைவேற்றும் வகையில் மாதம் ஒரு செயற்கை கோள் அனுப்ப திட்டம் [In order to fulfill Abdul Kalam's dream, planning is to send a satellite per month] ஒரு செயற்கை கோளை அனுப்ப வேண்டும் என்பது அப்துல் கலாமின் கனவு [Abdul Kalam's dream is to send a satellite]	SP
	அறைகளில் இருந்தும் சிலைகள், ஓவியங்கள் கிடைத்தன [Statues and paintings were found from the rooms] மூன்று நாட்கள் நடத்தப்பட்ட சோதனையில் மொத்தம் 71 கற்சிலைகள் மீட்கப்பட்டுள்ளன [A total of 71 stone statues have been recovered in a three day raid]	NP
M	നാളെ തന്നെ അവന്റെ യാത്ര ആരംഭിക്കാന്അവന്പദ്ധതിയിട്ടു [He planned to start his journey tomorrow itself] അവന്റെ യാത്ര നാളെ തന്നെ ആരംഭിക്കാനായിരുന്നു അവന്റെ പദ്ധതി [His plan was to start his journey tomorrow itself]	P
	ഒ. രാജഗോപാല എം.എൽ.എയായി സത്യപ്രതിജ്ഞ ചെയ്തു [O. Rajagopal was sworn in as legislator] കേരളാ നിയമസഭയിലെ ആദ്യ ബി.ജെ.പി എം.എൽ.എ ഒ. രാജഗോപാല സത്യപ്രതിജ്ഞ ചെയ്തു [The first BJP MLA of Kerala Legislative Assembly O. Rajagopal was sworn in]	SP
	ഇന്ത്യയുടെ ദേശീയ ഗാനം രചിച്ചത് രബീന്ദ്രനാഥ് ടാഗോര് ആണ് [India's national Anthem is written by Rabindranath Tagore] രബീന്ദ്രനാഥ് ടാഗോറിന്റെ കൃതിയായ ഗീതാഞ്ചലിക്ക് നോബേല്യേ സമ്മാനം ഭിച്ചിട്ടുണ്ട് [Rabindranath Tagore won the Nobel Prize for his work Gitanjali]	NP

Table 4. Statistics of Training the Testing dataset in pairs (Anand Kumar, M., Singh, S., Kavirajan, B., & Soman, K. P, 2016)

Language		Hindi	Tamil	Malayalam	Punjabi
Subtask 1	Train	2500	2500	2500	1700
	Test	900	900	900	500
Subtask 2	Train	3500	3500	3500	2200
	Test	1400	1400	1400	750

Table 5. An average number of words per sentence for each subtask

Language		Hindi	Tamil	Malayalam	Punjabi
Subtask 1	Sentence 1	16.058	11.092	9.253	19.485
	Sentence 2	16.376	12.044	9.035	19.582
	Pair	16.217	11.568	9.144	19.534
Subtask 2	Sentence 1	17.780	11.097	9.414	20.994
	Sentence 2	16.48	11.777	8.449	19.699
	Pair	17.130	11.437	8.932	20.347

Table 6. Vocabulary (unique words) size for all languages

Language	Task 1-Test	Task 2-Test	Task 1-Train	Task 2-Train
Hindi	8597	13773	7054	10492
Tamil	2808	4358	17266	19889
Malayalam	8614	13122	22433	28899
Punjabi	3283	3284	6744	6820

Figure 3. Vocabulary size for all languages (Anand Kumar, M., Singh, S., Kavirajan, B., & Soman, K. P, 2016)

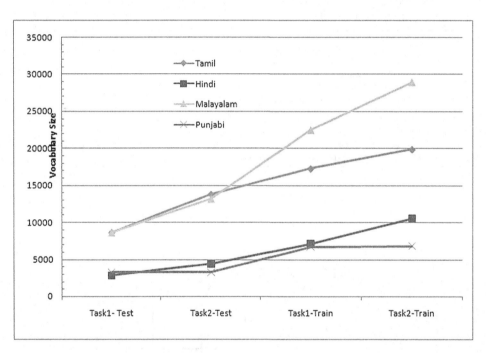

dataset is converted to XML format which is readable by a human as well as a machine. After annotating the paraphrase corpora, to examine the quality of the corpora, we analyzed it for certain parameters such as an average number of words in a sentence for each subtask, an average number of words in a sentence-pair for each subtask, and overall vocabulary (unique words) for each language per task. The more details about the shared task participants and results are found in (Anand Kumar, M., Singh, S., Kavirajan, B., Soman, K.P, 2018).

The average number of words in a sentence along with an average number of words in a sentence-pair for subtask-1 and subtask-2 are given in Table 5.

The remarkable fact in Table 5 is that an average number of words in a sentence for Hindi and Punjabi language is more than the average number of words per sentence for Tamil and Malayalam language. This is because Tamil and Malayalam languages are morphologically rich just like languages such as Kannada and Telugu. The Tamil, Malayalam, Kannada and Telugu languages come under the Dravidian family of languages which are agglutinative in nature (Rekha, R. U, Anand Kumar, M., Dhanalakshmi, V., Soman, K. P., & Rajendran, S., 2012). In other words, a sentence written in Hindi or Punjabi can be expressed in Tamil and Malayalam in fewer words.

The other most important fact about different languages is that they vary in the vocabulary they use. The word order preference used for Hindi, Tamil, Malayalam, and Punjabi is Subject-Object-Verb (S-O-V), which is the most common type of word order preference among all Indian Languages. The percentage of languages in the world which follows $S - O - V$ word order is around 45% followed by the languages which follow $Subject - Verb - Object\,(S - V - O)$ is around 42% (Tomlin, R. S., 2014), (Meyer, C. F. 2010). Though the word order of the languages under consideration for this work is the same, still they vary in the vocabulary they use. This is also because of the phenomena just discussed i.e. morphology. The verb, noun inflections, etc. count for the vocabulary for Dravidian Languages. The vocabulary statistics for subtask-1 and subtask-2 are shown in Table 6 along with a line chart of the same in Figure 3. The line chart for vocabulary size reveals the morphological similarity between Tamil-Malayalam and Hindi-Punjabi.

CONCLUSION

The paraphrase corpus is the first openly available corpus for Indian languages. It can be requested for download from DPIL shared task[2] and Amrita NLP tools website[3]. The scarcity in this research area for Indian languages motivated us to develop the paraphrase copra and conduct the shared task. The corpora creation started with news articles and headlines from various online web-based news resources. These articles were further cleaned and transformed into a syntactically valid form. The annotation process was performed by a postgraduate student followed by 2-step proofreading by a language expert and a linguist. The corpus also points out the morphological similarity between Tamil-Malayalam and Hindi-Punjabi. Since there were several steps involved in the development of the corpus, we believe that there may be some irregularities in the corpus. Any suggestions regarding typos, errors, etc. which we may have missed will be much appreciated. We intend to further improve as well as expand the existing corpus. The similar way can be extended for creating paraphrase corpus for other Indian languages. The further research challenge could be on creating a paraphrase corpora from social media content. The creation of multilingual and cross-lingual paraphrase corpora are the areas which need immediate attention from the research community.

REFERENCES

Anand Kumar, M., Singh, S., Kavirajan, B., & Soman, K. P. (1737). DPIL@ FIRE 2016: Overview of Shared Task on Detecting Paraphrases in Indian Languages (DPIL). *CEUR Workshop Proceedings*, 233–238.

Anand Kumar, M., Singh, S., Kavirajan, B., & Soman, K. P. (2018). Shared Task on Detecting Paraphrases in Indian Languages (DPIL): An Overview. Lecture Notes in Computer Science, 10478, 128-140.

Barreiro, A. (2009). *Make it simple with paraphrases: Automated paraphrasing for authoring aids and machine translation* (Doctoral dissertation). Universidade do Porto.

Barrón-Cedeño, A., Vila, M., Martí, M. A., & Rosso, P. (2013). Plagiarism meets paraphrasing: Insights for the next generation in automatic plagiarism detection. *Computational Linguistics*, *39*(4), 917–947. doi:10.1162/COLI_a_00153

Bernhard, D., & Gurevych, I. (2008, June). Answering learners' questions by retrieving question paraphrases from social Q&A sites. In *Proceedings of the third workshop on innovative use of NLP for building educational applications* (pp. 44-52). Association for Computational Linguistics. 10.3115/1631836.1631842

Bhagat, R., & Hovy, E. (2013). What is a paraphrase? *Computational Linguistics*, *39*(3), 463–472. doi:10.1162/COLI_a_00166

Bhargava, R., Sharma, G., & Sharma, Y. (2017, July). Deep Paraphrase Detection in Indian Languages. In *Proceedings of the 2017 IEEE/ACM International Conference on Advances in Social Networks Analysis and Mining 2017* (pp. 1152-1159). ACM. 10.1145/3110025.3122119

Callison-Burch, C., Koehn, P., & Osborne, M. (2006, June). Improved statistical machine translation using paraphrases. In *Proceedings of the main conference on Human Language Technology Conference of the North American Chapter of the Association of Computational Linguistics* (pp. 17-24). Association for Computational Linguistics.

Demir, S., El-Kahlout, I. D., Unal, E., & Kaya, H. (2012). *Turkish Paraphrase Corpus*. LREC.

Dolan, W. B., & Brockett, C. (2005, October). Automatically constructing a corpus of sentential paraphrases. *Proc. of IWP*.

Fader, A., Zettlemoyer, L., & Etzioni, O. (2013). Paraphrase-driven learning for open question answering. *ACL 2013 - 51st Annual Meeting of the Association for Computational Linguistics, Proceedings of the Conference*, 1, 1608-1618.

Fernando, S., & Stevenson, M. (2008, March). A semantic similarity approach to paraphrase detection. In *Proceedings of the 11th Annual Research Colloquium of the UK Special Interest Group for Computational Linguistics* (pp. 45-52). Academic Press.

Mel'čuk, I. A., & Polguere, A. (1987). A formal lexicon in the meaning-text theory:(or how to do lexica with words). *Computational Linguistics, 13*(3-4), 261–275.

Meyer, C. F. (2010). *Introducing English Linguistics International Student Edition.* Cambridge University Press.

Munjal, P., Narula, M., Kumar, S., & Banati, H. (2018). Twitter sentiments based suggestive framework to predict trends. *Journal of Statistics and Management Systems, 21*(4), 685–693. doi:10.1080/097205 10.2018.1475079

Pandey, S., & Solanki, A. (2019). *Music Instrument Recognition using Deep Convolutional Neural Networks. International Journal of Information Technology.* doi:10.100741870-019-00285-y

Praveena, R., Anand Kumar, M., & Soman, K. P. (2017). Chunking based malayalam paraphrase identification using unfolding recursive autoencoders. *2017 International Conference on Advances in Computing, Communications and Informatics, ICACCI 2017,* 922-928.

Pronoza, E., Yagunova, E., & Pronoza, A. (2016). Construction of a Russian paraphrase corpus: unsupervised paraphrase extraction. In *Information Retrieval* (pp. 146–157). Springer International Publishing. doi:10.1007/978-3-319-41718-9_8

Rekha, R. U., Anand Kumar, M., Dhanalakshmi, V., Soman, K. P., & Rajendran, S. (2012). A novel approach to morphological generator for Tamil, Lecture Notes in Computer Science. LNCS, 6411, 249-251.

Rinaldi, F., Dowdall, J., Kaljurand, K., Hess, M., & Mollá, D. (2003, July). Exploiting paraphrases in a question answering system. In *Proceedings of the second international workshop on Paraphrasing-Volume 16* (pp. 25-32). Association for Computational Linguistics. 10.3115/1118984.1118988

Saini, A., & Verma, A. (2018). Anuj@DPIL-FIRE2016: A Novel Paraphrase Detection Method in Hindi Language Using Machine Learning. Lecture Notes in Computer Science, 10478, 141-152.

Sarkar, K. (2018). Learning to Detect Paraphrases in Indian Languages, Lecture Notes in Computer Science. LNCS, 10478, 153-165.

Shinyama, Y., Sekine, S., & Sudo, K. (2002, March). Automatic paraphrase acquisition from news articles. In *Proceedings of the second international conference on Human Language Technology Research* (pp. 313-318). Morgan Kaufmann Publishers Inc. 10.3115/1289189.1289218

Tian, L., Ning, H., Kong, L., Chen, K., Qi, H., & Han, Z. (2018). Sentence Paraphrase Detection Using Classification Models, Lecture Notes in Computer Science. LNCS, 10478, 166-181.

Tomlin, R. S. (2014). *Basic Word Order (RLE Linguistics B: Grammar): Functional Principles* (Vol. 13). Routledge. doi:10.4324/9781315857466

Vila, M., Rodríguez, H., & Martí, M. A. (2015). Relational paraphrase acquisition from Wikipedia: The WRPA method and corpus. *Natural Language Engineering*, *21*(03), 355–389. doi:10.1017/S1351324913000235

Zhao, S., Liu, T., Yuan, X., Li, S., & Zhang, Y. (2007). *Automatic Acquisition of Context-Specific Lexical Paraphrases* (Vol. 178921794). IJCAI.

ENDNOTES

[1]   http://fire.irsi.res.in/fire/2016/home

[2] http://nlp.amrita.edu/dpil_cen[3] http://nlp.amrita.edu/nlpcorpus.html

Chapter 9
Deep Learning Approaches for Textual Sentiment Analysis

Tamanna Sharma

Department of Computer Science and Technology, Guru Jambheshwar University of Science and Technology, Hisar, India

Anu Bajaj

https://orcid.org/0000-0001-8563-6611

Department of Computer Science and Engineering, Guru Jambheshwar University of Science and Technology, Hisar, India

Om Prakash Sangwan

Department of Computer Science and Technology, Guru Jambheshwar University of Science and Technology, Hisar, India

ABSTRACT

Sentiment analysis is computational measurement of attitude, opinions, and emotions (like positive/negative) with the help of text mining and natural language processing of words and phrases. Incorporation of machine learning techniques with natural language processing helps in analysing and predicting the sentiments in more precise manner. But sometimes, machine learning techniques are incapable in predicting sentiments due to unavailability of labelled data. To overcome this problem, an advanced computational technique called deep learning comes into play. This chapter highlights latest studies regarding use of deep learning techniques like convolutional neural network, recurrent neural network, etc. in sentiment analysis.

INTRODUCTION

Sentiment analysis is a subset of natural language processing used in association with text mining techniques for the extraction of subjective information from social media sources. Collection of documents, reviews, blog posts, data from microblogging sites like tweets from twitter, status and news articles. Basically sentiments are analysed for certain product, domain, people and try to quantify the polarity of

DOI: 10.4018/978-1-5225-9643-1.ch009

that particular information. In other words, Sentiment analysis means mining of text for finding out the actual meaning/essence/attitude behind the text. It is also called as opinion mining. It is both science and art because of its complex context. Correct identification of hidden polarity behind the text is the key of success for any sentiment analysis task. Some of the reasons which make sentiment analysis a tough job in text are:

- Understanding the context of language for human is easy but teaching the same thing to machine is a complicated task.
- Vast variety of languages and grammar usage of every language is different.
- Usage of unstructured text like slangs, abbreviated form of text and grammar nuances make it more difficult to analyse.

Figure 1 shows the general framework of sentiment analysis. With the advent of web and social media lots of information is present for opinion mining like blog posts, data from microblogging sites, news posts etc. Most of this data is in textual form and for computation we need to transform it in to vector form. Natural language processing come up with loads of models like bag of words vector, vector space models, word embedding etc. Mining technique is chosen after that according to application for example if we want to analyse movie reviews we have rating and text as our dataset etc. Correct feature extraction is necessary for the training and testing accuracy of any machine learning model.

Now a days, deep learning models do not required hand coded features but they are data hungry techniques and need loads of data for training. Training is accomplished with the help of labelled data. After that trend or pattern is analysed by machine learning technique called knowledge. At last this knowledge with some mathematical function will be used for predictions of unlabelled data.

Sentiment analysis plays a greater role in gaining the overview of wider public opinion and social media interactive dataset is the best source for it. Gaining deeper insights from dataset make it more useful for forecasting applications like stock market in which correct sentiment identification make it more predictable for investors. Market research for maintaining the quality of product can be accomplished with the help of sentiment analysis. Opinion mining of customer review helps in knowing the current status of our product and its competitors.

Natural language processing (NLP) is one of the promising domain which makes our day to day life easier like keyboard auto completion, speech recognition, dictionary prediction etc. Amalgamation of machine learning with NLP brings awesome results in various applications and sentiment analysis is one of them. Sentiment analysis become talk of the town day by day because of its deep business insights which help in taking further decisions. Sentiment information is taken from customer reviews, posts from microblogging sites like twitter, rediff etc. and computational intelligence based techniques are applied for mining, analysing and forecasting of trend information.

Major limitation in sentiment analysis is the strict classification of polarity in to three buckets called positive, negative and neutral. While human emotions are not so quantifiable every time sometime it is ambiguous and chaotic in nature. While in future researchers are trying to move from one dimensional monotonous scaling of positive to negative to multidimensional scaling. Involvement of deep learning techniques opens a new line of research in sentiment analysis which is described in last part of this chapter. In next section we presented a simple case study of sentiment classifier using Naïve Bayes machine learning algorithm for understanding the general flow of model.

Figure 1. General framework of sentiment analysis

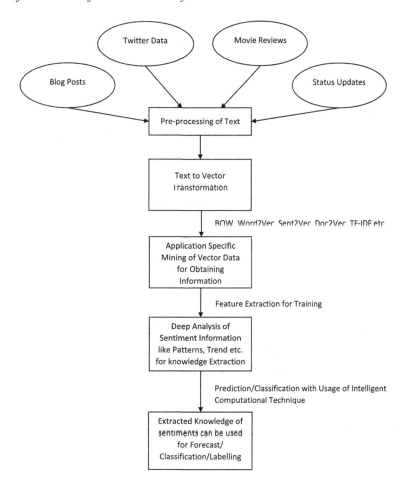

This chapter is arranged as follows. Second section tells about basic machine learning based sentiment analysis with the help of tabular representation. Third section discusses supervised based sentiment classifier. Fourth section is all about revolutionary change bought by next generation of learning (deep) techniques in accuracy of sentiment analysis with the help of existing studies followed by conclusion in the last section.

Case Study Of Naïve Bayes Based Sentiment Classifier

In this small and simple case study our attempt was to make a sentiment classifier based on movie review dataset. In this model firstly we have labelled set of sentiments (positive, negative and neutral) used for training of classifier. After training of classifier unlabelled set of movie reviews are taken for testing. Naïve Baye's model was chosen as classifier for classification task. Let's have some basic idea about Baye's formula first:

$$P[a/b] = [P[b/a]*P[a]]/P[b] \tag{1}$$

Table 1. Most valuable information ten features

Word(unimaginative) = T	n: p =	8.3: 1.0
Word(shoddy) = T	n: p =	6.9: 1.0
Word(schumacher) = T	n: p =	6.9: 1.0
Word(singers) = T	n: p =	6.4: 1.0
Word(turkey) = T	n: p =	6.3: 1.0
Word(suvari) = T	n: p =	6.3: 1.0
Word(mena) = T	n: p =	6.3: 1.0
Word(wasted) = T	n: p =	6.3: 1.0
Word(atrocious) = T	n: p =	5.8: 1.0
Word(justin) = T	n: p =	5.8: 1.0

True = T, Negative = n, Positive = p

Equation 1st is the basic Bayes formula consist of b is the document and a is the class and objective is to find out the probability of class b given by document a. So numerator is composed of likelihood and prior information and denominator consist of normalization constant. Mapping of Bayes algorithm in this problem is followed as: Prior information is original label (L.H.S part) which model come to know at training time and after that testing is done on unlabelled reviews and try to predict the correct labels. Naïve Bayes works on this principle and termed as multinomial Naïve Bayes in text classification problems.

Natural language toolkit was used for importing dataset and further computations. Argmax function was employed which returns probability of polarity with respect to class and help in finding out the class of unlabelled reviews. Trained and fine-tuned model was employed on unlabelled data with best possible parametric setting for this model. Accuracy measure was used for assessment of overall performance. It was observed that seventy to seventy five percent of accuracy was achieved. Top ten words are shown with predicted labels in Table 1.

Accuracy obtained: 82%

It can be concluded that basic machine learning techniques works good but doesn't have brilliant performance. Last three years of research shows a deflection towards NLP with deep learning. It is one of the emerging fields with enormous applications and improving accuracy. In this chapter our aim is to explain the drift of Basic learning based sentiment analysis to advanced learning based sentiment analysis. We tried to explain the power of deep learning based sentiment analysis with the help of detailed review of existing research studies.

MACHINE LEARNING BASED SENTIMENT ANALYSIS

Due to exponential increase in digital world (like social networking sites and online marketing sites) decision making becomes logical. In previous times people use their intution or data was not the biggest power that time. But now prediction becomes easy due to vast availability of data like reviews, blogs etc. Sentiment analysis is one of the major tool in business analytics because it helps in knowing the doamin, needs and trend of target users. Machine learning based approaches plays a great role in classification and analysis of sentiments for example labelling of unstructured reviews with the help of labelled one. Some of the machine learning based sentiment analysis studies are described and summarised with the help of table 2.

DEEP LEARNING BASED SENTIMENT ANALYSIS

Sentiment analysis aim is to analyse people's sentiments or opinions according to their area of interest. Sentiment analysis becomes a hot topic among researchers with the rapid growth of online generated data and equally powerful processing techniques like natural language processing, machine learning and deep learning etc. As we already discussed machine learning techniques in previous section in association with supervised learning based case study. Results are still not satisfactory with basic learning techniques. In this section we will study advance learning techniques called deep learning and studies which accomplished these techniques in sentiment analysis and opinion mining.

Word embedding is one of the crucial step in deep learning based sentiment analysis technique. As described in (Tang et al., 2016) "Word embedding is a representation in which each word is represented as a continuous, low-dimensional and real valued vector". Basic concept behind word embedding is the utilization of context information. For example words like good and bad will be mapped in to same space and beneficial in many NLP applications (POS tagging etc.) but proved to be a disaster in case of sentiment analysis because of their opposite polarity. Therefore, extra information called sentiment embedding is needed for increasing the effectiveness of word context. Semantic embedding is composed of labelled information called sentiment polarity and able to differentiate between words which have opposite polarity. The authors (Tang et al., 2016) uses two neural networks one for prediction (predict polarity of words) and another for ranking (provide real valued sentiment score for word sequence with fixed window size). Empirical study was carried out with three models (Dist + Ngrams, SVM+ Ngrams, SVM + Text Features) on twitter dataset. Effectiveness of sentiment embedding was experimented on three levels word, sentence and lexical. End results concluded sentiment embedding and proved to be a milestone on three levels; word level shows sentiment similarity between words, sentence level for discriminative features and lexical level for sentiment lexicon.

Another approach was proposed by (Chen, Sun, Tu, Lin, & Liu, 2016) for same problem: absence of sentiment information. This approach utilizes the document –level sentiment information which deals with complete information about a product instead of just local level text information. This model was built on hierarchical neural network in association with global user and product based information. Hierarchical long short term memory model was employed to generate sentence and document embedding. Sometime due to vague ratings and complex statement of reviews sentiment analysis degrades its accuracy. At that time user and product information played a significant role in improving the accuracy of model.

Customer reviews is one of the major factor for accessing the opinionated quality of any product. Traditionally it was accomplished with manual steps like lexicon construction, feature engineering etc. But revolutionary change in computation come up with deep learning techniques which reduces the human efforts of feature selection and make this work automated with high demand of large data. Deep learning techniques intrinsically learn mappings from large scale training data. The authors (Guan et al., 2016) proposed a new framework in association with deep learning which is composed of two steps. First one is to learn embedding from rating of customer reviews and second one is the addition of classification layer for supervised fine tuning of labelled sentences. Learning of embedding is based on the

Table 2. Basic learning based sentiment analysis

Reference	Machine Learning Technique Used	Purpose
Neethu & Rajasree, 2013	Naïve Bayes, Support Vector Machine, Maximum Entropy, Ensemble learning	Classification efficiency is improved by using feature extraction technique
Maas et al., 2011	Vector space model, Probabilistic latent topic Model, Linear SVM	Extended unsupervised model with semantic information in association with lexical information
Gautam & Yadav, 2014	Naïve Bayes, Maximum entropy and Support vector machine, Semantic analysis	Naïve Bayes outperform maximum entropy and SVM in classification of reviews with the help of twitter dataset
Mudinas, Zhang, & Levene, 2012	Support Vector Machine, Sentiment strength detection.	Integrates lexicon and learning based approaches and shows better results on CNET and IMDB movie reviews as compared to individual learning or lexicon based models
Tripathy, Agrawal, & Rath, 2016	Stochastic Gradient Descent, Naïve Bayes, Maximum Entropy,	Text conversion in to vector is accomplished with the Combination of count vectorizer and TF-IDF, also compare N-Gram with POS techniques. It was shown that as N increases after two accuracy starts decreasing
Rosenthal, Farra, & Nakov, 2017	Support Vector Machine, word2vec	Cross lingual training was explored with the help of Arabic language and shows improved results in irony and emotion detection
Cambria, 2017	Gated Multimodal Embedding Long short term memory	Use of temporal attention layer proved to be very beneficial in dealing of acoustic and visual noise
Chen, Xu, He, & Wang, 2017	Divide and Conquer, Neural Network	Sentence level sentiment analysis was accomplished with convolutional neural network at sentence level
Appel, Chiclana, Carter, & Fujita, 2016	Naïve Bayes, Maximum Entropy	Semantic orientation of polarity was utilized with the help of NLP based hybrid technique and shows improved results than NB and ME
Kolchyna, Souza, Treleaven, & Aste, 2015	Support Vector machine, Naïve Bayes, Lexicon based ensemble method	Naïve Bayes and SVM outperforms the lexicon based methods
Toh & Su, 2016	Feed forward Neural Network	Two step approach was employed, single layer feed forward network for domain classification, DNN for sequential classification
Kanakaraj & Guddeti, 2015	Decision Tree, Random Forest, Extremely Randomized Trees	Experimented with ensemble based learning which have kind of approaches depend on application and training data provided.
Chalothom & Ellman, 2015	Naïve Bayes, Support Vector Machine, Senti Strength and Stacking	Different flavour of supervised and semi supervised ensemble classifiers was explored in association with lexicons and shows better results than BOW
Dey, Chakraborty, Biswas, Bose, & Tiwari, 2016	Naïve Bayes, K- Nearest Neighbour	Two supervised learning approaches were used by focussing on sentence polarity and subjective style on movie and hotel reviews. Results were application specific.

concept of sentences with same labels are ranked closer while sentences with opposite labels are ranked farther from each other. Weakly supervised deep learning embedding (WDE) was employed with the help of convolutional neural network. Effectiveness of WDE was measured with the help of amazon reviews and it was concluded that framework based on weakly labelled set of sentences outperforms existing baseline models.

Employment of deep learning in sentiment analysis make it easier to extract contextual information from complex short texts like reviews, posts of microblogging sites etc. Joint model was proposed by (Wang, Jiang, & Luo, 2016) was built with convolutional neural network (CNN) and recurrent neural network (RNN). CNN took the advantage of coarse grained local features while RNN learned via long term distance dependencies. Windows of different length and involvement of various weight metrics was employed in CNN and max pooling was used from left to right. Pipeline of framework was composed of word and sentence embedding after that convolutional and pooling layers, RNN layer support with concatenation layer and final output with softmax output. Results was computed on three benchmark datasets 1) Movie Review 2) Stanford sentiment treebank1 (SST1) with all kind of reviews 3) SST2 with binary labels only. This joint model outperforms the CNN and RNN models alone.

One of the best application which exploits deep learning is financial sentiment analysis. Stock price forecasting is of great interest for investors before investing their money. Financial sentiment analysis comes under financial technology also called as Fin Tech (Day & Lee, 2016) is one of the growing research field. Exploration of deep learning for improving accuracy of forecasting make it more interesting for investors. Stock attributes is composed of information like firm specific news articles, public sentiments which affects decision and impact of media information on firms. This means same information may leads to different decisions for different investors. Deep learning model was employed with three non-linear activation functions called Sigmoid, TanH and rectified linear Unit (ReLu). Result shows that inclusion of deep learning techniques proved to be a turning stone in increasing the forecasting accuracy of Fin Tech models.

Deep learning techniques are data hungry and therefore they work best in case of big data analytics. Big investment banks like Goldman Sachs, Lehman Brothers and Salomon brothers uses the financial advice as their backbone. StockTwits and SeekingAlpha is one of the growing social media for investors and stock information. Long short term memory, doc2vec and CNN model was employed by (Sohangir, Wang, Pomeranets, & Khoshgoftaar, 2018) for finding out the hidden knowledgeable patterns from StockTwits network. Performance was evaluated with accuracy, precision, recall, F-measure and AUC. It was concluded from results that CNN outperforms logistic regression, doc2ve and LSTM for StockTwits dataset.

Most of the sentiment analysis models are based on English generated texts, the authors (Vateekul & Koomsubha, 2016) evaluated the deep learning based sentiment analysis on Thai generated twitter data. Two efficient deep learning techniques was employed one is long short term memory (LSTM) and another is dynamic convolutional neural networks (DCNN) except maximum entropy. Effect of word orders was also taken in to consideration of experimental study. LSTM and DCNN outperforms basic machine learning models for Thai based twitter data. Comprehensive experimental study was carried out for parametric adjustments and results as computed on best parametric settings. It was concluded that DCNN followed by LSTM give best results and shuffling of word orders strongly influence sentiment analysis.

In traditional sentiment analysis (around 2005) statistical models used words with their sentiment scores called lexicons, as their features. But now a days due to involvement of word embedding, use of lexicons become invisible and almost obsolete. The authors (Shin, Lee, & Choi, 2016) tried to explore the combination of word embedding with lexicons. Weather it is a useful combination and if it is what is the best path of using both in association. Experimental study was carried out on two datasets SemEval-2016 Task 4 and Stanford sentiment treebank. Word2Vec from google skip-gram model and six types of lexicon embedding was employed. CNN in association with attention vectors (importance of each word and lexicon) was used as deep learning layer. Integration of lexicons with word embedding helps in improving the efficiency of traditional CNN model.

Sarcasm detection is one of the crucial task in sentiment analysis. Sarcasm consist of ambiguous and reversible statements whose polarity can't be classified positive or negative easily. Therefore, powerful NLP techniques are required for analysis of sarcastic statements. CNN based deeper analysis of sarcastic tweets was accomplished by (Poria, Cambria, Hazarika, & Vij, 2016). CNN was used because it doesn't need any hand crafted features and build its global feature set by taking local features which is good for learning context. Macro-F1 was used as efficacy measure and experiments was accomplished on both CNN and CNN-SVM in which extracted features from CNN, fed to SVM for classification.

Similar to sarcasm there is one more information called hate speech detection. It is useful in various business decisions. Hateful tweets are imposed of abusive language and a targeted domain may be product, gender, racism, Gay community etc. Multiple classifiers was employed by (Badjatiya, Gupta, Gupta, & Varma, 2017) in association with three deep learning embedding called Fast Text, CNN and LSTM for detection of hateful sentiments. Comprehensive analysis of numerous embedding was accomplished like TF-IDF values, Bag of words model, GLoVe model and deep learning based embedding. Precision, recall and F1 measure was used as evaluation metrics. It was observed that deep learning based embedding outperform baseline embedding models and gradient boosted decision tree shows best accuracy values.

Composition of sentiment plays an important role in detecting the sentiment polarity. Extended approach of layer-wise relevance propagation was used with recurrent neural network (RNN) (Arras, Montavon, Müller, & Samek, 2017). RNN was employed with one hidden layer of bi-directional long short term memory and five class sentiment prediction. Trained LSTM was compared on two decomposition methods sensitivity analysis and LRP. It was concluded from our experiments, LRP based LSTM supports best classification decision as compared to gradient based decomposition.

Lexical and syntactic features are one of the turning stones in improving the accuracy of sentiments. Unsupervised learning (Jianqiang, Xiaolin, & Xuejun, 2018) was used in association with latent contextual semantic relationship and co-occurrence relationship between tweets. Feature set was obtained through word embedding with n-gram features and polarity score of word sentiments. Feature set was propagated to deep convolution neural network was for training and prediction of sentiment labels. Accuracy and F1 measure on five twitter datasets (STSTd, SE2014, STSGd, SED, SSTd) clearly shows GloVe - DCNN model outperform baseline N-gram model, BoW and SVM classifier.

With the advent of deep learning models traditional approaches become invisible while they also have good computational powers. The authors (Araque, Corcuera-Platas, Sanchez-Rada, & Iglesias, 2018) explores combination of both traditional surface approaches and deep learning. Baseline model was formed with word embedding and linear machine learning approach. Ensemble of (classifiers and features) models was formed from these varied feature set and experimented on six public datasets. Friedman test was used for empirical verification of results and it was observed that ensemble of features and classifiers outperforms basic models.

One of the major issue in sentiment analysis is their language because not all tweets are monolingual, and at that time translation incurs extra cost. Machine learning based approaches needs extra effort of machine translation. Deep learning based models was proposed by (Wehrmann, Becker, Cagnini, & Barros, 2017) which learn latent features from all languages at the time of training. Word level and character level embedding was explored with CNN. Four different language tweets (English, Spanish, Potuguese and German) was analysed. Results was compared with machine translation based techniques with three polarities (Positive, Negative, Neutral) with the help of accuracy and F-Measure. Proposed approach

Table 3. Deep learning in sentiment analysis

Authors	Algorithm	Dataset	Text 2 vec	Efficacy Measures	Language
Tang et al., 2016	Sentiment Embedding+KNN	Twitter Data (SemEval, RottenTomatoes)	WE, SE, word2veec	Accuracy	English
Guan et al., 2016	SVM, SVM+NB, CNN	Amazon Customer Review	Word2vec	Accuracy, Macro F1	English
Wang et al., 2016	CNN, CNN+RNN	Movie Reviews, Stanford Sentiment Treebank (SST1) and SST2	Word2vec	Accuracy	English
Chen et al., 2016	Hierarchical LSTM	IMDB, Yelp 2013, Yelp 2014	Sentence level embedding	Accuracy, RMSE	English
Day & Lee, 2016	Deep neural network with sigmoid, tanH and ReLu function	News data (Now News, Apple Daily, LTN and Money DJ finance)	Lexicon based embedding	ROI Heatmap	Chinese
Vateekul & Koomsubha, 2016	LSTM and DCNN	Thai tweet corpus	Word2vec	Accuracy	Thai
Shin et al., 2017	CNN	SemEval'16 Task 4 and SST	Word2vec, lexicon embedding	F1 score, Accuracy	English
Poria et al., 2017	CNN, CNN-SVM	Sarcastic tweets	Word2vec	F1 score	English
Badjatiya et al., 2017	CNN, LSTM	Hate related tweets	BOWV, N-gram, GloVe, FastText	Precision, Recall, F1 measure	English
Arras et al., 2017	Bi-directional LSTM	SST, movie reviews	Word2vec	Accuracy	English
Jianqiang et al., 2017	Deep convolution neural network	STSTd, SemEval2014, Stanford twitter sentiment gold, SED, SSTd	GloVe, BOW	Precision, Recall, F1 score	English
Araque et al., 2017	Ensemble of classifiers	Microblogging data and movie reviews	Word2vec, GloVe	F1 score	English
Wehrmann et al., 2017	CNN, LSTM	1.6 million annotated tweets	Word and character level embedding	Accuracy, F-measure	English, German, Portuguese, Spanish
Sohangir et al., 2018	LSTM, CNN	StockTwits posts	Doc2vec	Accuracy, Precision, AUC	English

works on character level networks so independent of machine translation technique, word embedding, less pre-processing steps and took only half of memory space. Summary of deep learning techniques used in sentiment analysis is presented Table 3.

CONCLUSION

Sentiment analysis is one of the evolving research area with an ample amount of applications and getting matured day by day. It is concluded from above studies that accuracy of sentiment analysis models are not up to the mark till now. One of the main reason behind lacking of accuracy is complex structure of data. While, it is also observed that drift from machine learning to deep learning techniques with natural language processing shows promising results. Unstructured nature of data is very difficult for training and accuracy achieved by basic machine learning algorithms were very low. Correct feature extraction is the heart of machine learning algorithms. But this problem is very much solved by the use of deep learning algorithms due to automatic selection of features with large availability of data. And it is estimated that understanding the contextual behaviour of data (ratings, reviews etc.) with deep learning and other computational techniques make it more likable for more applications in future.

REFERENCES

Appel, O., Chiclana, F., Carter, J., & Fujita, H. (2016). A hybrid approach to the sentiment analysis problem at the sentence level. *Knowledge-Based Systems*, *108*, 110–124. doi:10.1016/j.knosys.2016.05.040

Araque, O., Corcuera-Platas, I., Sanchez-Rada, J. F., & Iglesias, C. A. (2017). Enhancing deep learning sentiment analysis with ensemble techniques in social applications. *Expert Systems with Applications*, *77*, 236–246. doi:10.1016/j.eswa.2017.02.002

Arras, L., Montavon, G., Müller, K.R., & Samek, W. (2017). *Explaining recurrent neural network predictions in sentiment analysis*. Academic Press.

Badjatiya, P., Gupta, S., Gupta, M., & Varma, V. (2017). Deep learning for hate speech detection in tweets. *Proceedings of the 26th International Conference on World Wide Web Companion*, 759-760. 10.1145/3041021.3054223

Cambria, E. (2016). Affective computing and sentiment analysis. *IEEE Intelligent Systems*, *31*(2), 102–107. doi:10.1109/MIS.2016.31

Chalothom, T., & Ellman, J. (2015). Simple approaches of sentiment analysis via ensemble learning. In Information science and applications. Springer. doi:10.1007/978-3-662-46578-3_74

Chen, H., Sun, M., Tu, C., Lin, Y., & Liu, Z. (2016). Neural sentiment classification with user and product attention. *Proceedings of the 2016 conference on empirical methods in natural language processing*, 1650-1659. 10.18653/v1/D16-1171

Chen, T., Xu, R., He, Y., & Wang, X. (2017). Improving sentiment analysis via sentence type classification using BiLSTM-CRF and CNN. *Expert Systems with Applications*, *72*, 221–230. doi:10.1016/j.eswa.2016.10.065

Day, M. Y., & Lee, C. C. (2016). Deep learning for financial sentiment analysis on finance news providers. *2016 IEEE/ACM International Conference on Advances in Social Networks Analysis and Mining*, 1127-1134. 10.1109/ASONAM.2016.7752381

Dey, L., Chakraborty, S., Biswas, A., Bose, B., & Tiwari, S. (2016). *Sentiment analysis of review datasets using naive bayes and k-nn classifier*. arXiv preprint arXiv:1610.09982

Gautam, G., & Yadav, D. Sentiment analysis of twitter data using machine learning approaches and semantic analysis. In *2014 Seventh International Conference on Contemporary Computing (IC3)*. IEEE. 10.1109/IC3.2014.6897213

Guan, Z., Chen, L., Zhao, W., Zheng, Y., Tan, S., & Cai, D. (2016). *Weakly-Supervised Deep Learning for Customer Review Sentiment Classification*. IJCAI.

Jianqiang, Z., Xiaolin, G., & Xuejun, Z. (2018). Deep convolution neural networks for Twitter sentiment analysis. *IEEE Access: Practical Innovations, Open Solutions, 6*, 23253–23260. doi:10.1109/ACCESS.2017.2776930

Kanakaraj, M., & Guddeti, R. M. R. Performance analysis of Ensemble methods on Twitter sentiment analysis using NLP techniques. In *Proceedings of the 2015 IEEE 9th International Conference on Semantic Computing*. IEEE. 10.1109/ICOSC.2015.7050801

Kolchyna, O., Souza, T. T. P., Treleaven, P., & Aste, T. (2015). *Twitter sentiment analysis: Lexicon method, machine learning method and their combination*. arXiv preprint arXiv:1507.00955

Maas, A. L., Daly, R. E., Pham, P. T., Huang, D., Ng, A. Y., & Potts, C. Learning word vectors for sentiment analysis. In *Proceedings of the 49th annual meeting of the association for computational linguistics: Human language technologies*. Association for Computational Linguistics.

Mudinas, A., Zhang, D., & Levene, M. (2012). Combining lexicon and learning based approaches for concept-level sentiment analysis. In *Proceedings of the first international workshop on issues of sentiment discovery and opinion mining*. ACM. 10.1145/2346676.2346681

Neethu, M. S., & Rajasree, R. Sentiment analysis in twitter using machine learning techniques. In *2013 Fourth International Conference on Computing, Communications and Networking Technologies*. IEEE. 10.1109/ICCCNT.2013.6726818

Poria, S., Cambria, E., Hazarika, D., & Vij, P. (2016). *A deeper look into sarcastic tweets using deep convolutional neural networks.*, arXiv preprint arXiv:1610.08815

Rosenthal, S., Farra, N., & Nakov, P. (2017). SemEval-2017 task 4: Sentiment analysis in Twitter. *Proceedings of the 11th international workshop on semantic evaluation (SemEval-2017)*, 502-518. 10.18653/v1/S17-2088

Shin, B., Lee, T., & Choi, J. D. (2016). *Lexicon integrated cnn models with attention for sentiment analysis*. arXiv preprint arXiv:1610.06272

Sohangir, S., Wang, D., Pomeranets, A., & Khoshgoftaar, T. M. (2018). Big Data: Deep Learning for financial sentiment analysis. *Journal of Big Data, 5*(1), 3. doi:10.118640537-017-0111-6

Tang, D., Wei, F., Qin, B., Yang, N., Liu, T., & Zhou, M. (2016). Sentiment embeddings with applications to sentiment analysis. *IEEE Transactions on Knowledge and Data Engineering, 28*(2), 496–509. doi:10.1109/TKDE.2015.2489653

Toh, Z., & Su, J. (2016). Nlangp at semeval-2016 task 5: Improving aspect based sentiment analysis using neural network features. *Proceedings of the 10th international workshop on semantic evaluation*, 282-288. 10.18653/v1/S16-1045

Tripathy, A., Agrawal, A., & Rath, S. K. (2016). Classification of sentiment reviews using n-gram machine learning approach. *Expert Systems with Applications, 57*, 117–126. doi:10.1016/j.eswa.2016.03.028

Vateekul, P., & Koomsubha, T. (2016). A study of sentiment analysis using deep learning techniques on Thai Twitter data. *2016 13th International Joint Conference on Computer Science and Software Engineering*, 1-6. 10.1109/JCSSE.2016.7748849

Wang, X., Jiang, W., & Luo, Z. (2016). Combination of convolutional and recurrent neural network for sentiment analysis of short texts. *Proceedings of COLING 2016, the 26th International Conference on Computational Linguistics: Technical Papers*, 2428-2437.

Wehrmann, J., Becker, W., Cagnini, H. E. L., & Barros, R. C. (2017). A character-based convolutional neural network for language-agnostic Twitter sentiment analysis. *2017 International Joint Conference on Neural Networks (IJCNN)*, 2384-2391. 10.1109/IJCNN.2017.7966145

Chapter 10
Deep Learning for Next-Generation Inventive Wireless Networks:
Issues, Challenges, and Future Directions

Nimmi K.
https://orcid.org/0000-0003-3609-7978
National Institute of Technology, Tiruchirappalli, India

Varun G. Menon
https://orcid.org/0000-0002-3055-9900
SCMS School of Engineering and Technology, India

Janet B.
https://orcid.org/0000-0001-7030-9634
National Institute of Technology, Tiruchirappalli, India

Akshi Kumar
Delhi Technological University, India

ABSTRACT

Recent years have witnessed an exponential rise in the number of connected wireless devices. This number is expected to rise at an unprecedented rate leading to severe challenges in user demands and network infrastructure. With the fusion of artificial intelligence (AI) technologies, these devices have become more smart and intelligent. Using machine learning, efforts are being carried out to artificially train these networks to determine the optimum system requirements automatically. With these intelligent networks generating an enormous volume of data along with the demand for high data rate, machine learning has found its few limitations. Deep learning techniques have emerged as one of the most impressive tools to solve many of these problems. The primary objective of this chapter is to provide insights into deep learning and the applications of deep learning in next-generation inventive wireless networks. The chapter also presents the issues, challenges, and future directions in this research area.

DOI: 10.4018/978-1-5225-9643-1.ch010

INTRODUCTION

Over these years, tremendous increase has been seen in the number of connected wireless devices. With the introduction of technologies like Internet of Things (IoT) (Ahlgren et al., 2016; Philip et al., 2016; Deshkar et al., 2017; Jacob et al., 2019; Menon et al., 2019; Rajesh et al., 2019) fog computing (Nayyar 2018; Menon & Prathap, 2017, 2018), flying ad hoc networks(Rosati et al., 2016; Cruz 2018), 5G networks, dynamic ad hoc networks(Menon &Prathap 2016, 2017, 2019; Nayyar et al., 2018), cognitive radios etc. this number is rising exponentially. With Artificial Intelligence (AI) (O'Leary, 2013; Murphy, 2018; Jain, 2019; Vinoj, 2019) incorporating adaptive learning and decision-making capabilities, these devices have become smarter and more intelligent. Modern applications thus face a huge task of providing high data rates and better Quality of Service. Handling the huge amount of generated data is yet another challenge in these networks (Yazti & Krishnaswamy, 2014; He at al., 2016; Mengke et al., 2016; Londhe & Rao, 2017; Vijay et al., 2018).

Many technologies have been tried to optimize the performance of the modern wireless networks and to provide better service to users. Machine learning (Xue & Zhu, 2009; Ross et al., 2013; Louridas and C. Ebert, 2016; Alzubi et al., 2018) has been one of the successful methods. Machine learning techniques and approaches have helped the modern applications using intelligent wireless devices to provide better QoS to users. Optimization of network resources, traffic management, routing of data packets, congestion management etc. has been effectively dealt using machine learning approaches. Using various machine learning approaches, most of the devices in the network have been trained with the collected data and knowledge to perform better in future. But with the number of devices increasing at an unprecedented rate, machine learning has found its limitations. This has given way to the rise of deep learning technology (Wang, 2016 2017; Nishani & Çiço 2017, Kauer et al., 2018).

With the use of deep learning computational models composed of several processing layers which are capable of learning data representations with multiple levels of abstraction. Deep learning has been a revolution and has effectively managed various problems faced by modern applications. Many deep learning techniques are being used to improve the performance of the intelligent wireless networks. The research article provides insights into fundamental deep learning concepts with some of its applications in next-generation inventive wireless networks

The organization of the research paper is as follows. The transition from machine learning to deep learning is discussed in section 2. This section presents the advantages of deep learning compared to machine learning approaches. Next section gives a detailed explanation on the various concepts in deep learning. Section 4 presents a summary of the next generation wireless network technologies. The application of deep learning in these inventive wireless networks is discussed in Section 5. Issues and challenges existing in this research area are discussed in Section 6 and we conclude the paper in section 7.

MOVING FROM MACHINE LEARNING TO DEEP LEARNING

This section describes the transition from machine learning to deep learning approaches. As a subset of artificial intelligence, machine learning is widely used for a variety of applications. Machine learning is the art of gaining knowledge from experience and using it for future decisions. The primary objective of Machine learning is the development of computer programs which can access data from the dataset and learn by themselves. The overview of machine learning process is illustrated in Figure 1.

Figure 1. Machine learning

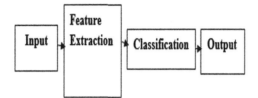

The three categories of machine learning are

- Supervised learning,
- Unsupervised learning
- Reinforcement learning

Supervised Learning

Supervised learning is the learning in presence of a supervisor. The data used for training include both the desired output and input. The input to which the output is known already is used for the training process; the method uses well-labeled data. Supervised learning is fast and accurate. The generalization of results should be there, that is it should analyze the training data and should be able to predict the correct result for the unknown data set. Two categories of supervised learning are classification and regression. Major problem is over fitting

Unsupervised Learning

Unsupervised learning is a training process without any guidance. The dataset is not labeled. The algorithm analyzes the data according to similarity trends or patterns without any prior training of data and finds the hidden structure in unlabeled data. Two categories of unsupervised learning are Clustering and Association:

Reinforcement Learning

Reinforcement learning is a machine learning technique where an agent understands how to behave in an environment through the process of performing some actions. The elements involved in the learning process consist of an actor or agent, an environment, and a reward signal. The agent learns about the environment through the process of interacting with the environment, and receives the rewards based on the action performed by the agent. The manner in which an agent chooses an action is based on a policy. The rewards obtained by the agent can be increased by learning the optimal policy by the process of interacting with the environment. Figure 2 illustrates the reinforcement learning approach.

Exploration and exploitation are the two essential principles in the case of reinforced learning. Exploration is the process of exploring the environment and finding more information about the environment. Exploitation is just following best the apparent path which is gained through previous experience to

Figure 2. Reinforcement learning

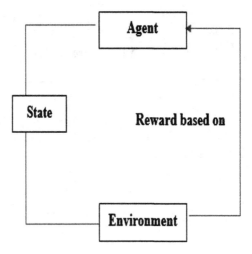

Figure 3. Q learning

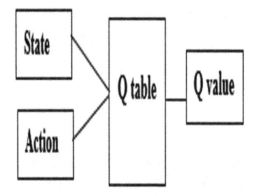

maximize the reward. Figure 3 illustrates Q learning, which is one of the popular reinforcement learning techniques used.

Artificial Neural Network

The human biological nervous system has inspired the neural networks technology. An Artificial Neural Network (ANN) (Uhrig, 1995; Jain et al., 1996; Yao, 1999; Mishra and Srivastava, 2014; Zhang et al., 2018; Liu et al., 2018) is made up of a number of interconnected neurons, also called as nodes which are the processing elements. Inputs, x1, x2,...xn, each multiplied by a specific weight, w1, w2, . . ., wn, is fed to the ANN along with a transfer function fi of the form, $z = \sum xnwn$, i=0 n wi xi, where i is the inputs and wi is the weights.

Figure 4. Deep learning

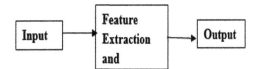

There are many models for the implementations of ANN. According to their connectivity, ANN's can be classified as being feed forward and recurrent. In feedforward, all the nodes are connected to the previous layer, and there is no feedback mechanism used, here nodes are processed in layers. Feedforward network can be a single layer or Multllayer feed forward network. A multilayer perception (MLP)(Yao, 1999) has a minimum of three layers of nodes. Besides the input nodes, all nodes are neurons using a nonlinear activation function. MLP's popularity is decreasing as it has fully connected structure. MLP was used for integrated or more complex architectures. Feedback network has feedback paths, which means the signal, can flow in both directions using loops. Feedback network can be recurrent networks or fully recurrent networks. Boltzmann Machine uses only locally available information. Boltzmann Machine was one of the first neural networks capable of learning internal representations and can represent and solve difficult combinatorics problems.

Neural networks are the base for deep learning techniques. Deep learning refers to deep networks with differing topologies. It is a growing trend to abstract better results when data is large and complex.

Figure 4 illustrates a high level view of deep learning.

GPUs are much advanced than traditional multicore processors. GPU may contain 1,000 - 4,000 specialized data processing cores whereas conventional multicore processors have 4 - 24 general-purpose CPUs. Addition of more layers (adding more functionality) creates more interconnection and weights between and also within the layers. In this circumstance, GPU helps in training and executing these networks effectively than traditional multicore processors.

Figure 5 represents the motivation for deep learning. Deep learning provides better performance compared to all older learning algorithms. Table 1 summarizes some key differences between ML and Deep Learning.

Some of the unique advantages of deep learning are,

- Deep Learning is best suited when the data size is large.
- Deep Learning techniques need reasonable time to train along with high-end infrastructure
- Deep Learning techniques are used when there is a lack of domain understanding.
- Deep Learning is able to solve complex problems.
- The human need not describe the learning process. Data with complicated structure and inner correlations when provided to the Deep learning algorithm, it automatically extracts high-level features.
- Representations learned by deep neural networks are universal across different tasks.

Figure 5. Why deep learning (Collobert&Bengio, 2004)

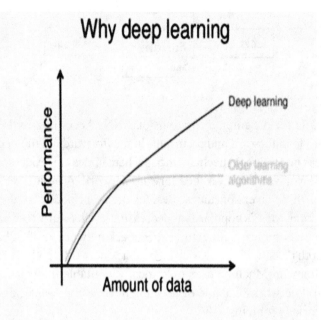

Table 1. Machine learning and deep learning differences

Machine learning	Deep learning
Subset of Artificial Intelligence	Subset of Machine Learning
A method to attain Artificial Intelligence	Efficient technique for implementing machine learning
Algorithms are directed by experts to examine the variables	Algorithms are usually self-directed for analysis of data
Output is normally a numerical value, a score or classification	Output can be a score, text, sound etc.
Few thousand data points used for analysis	Millions of data points used for analysis
Used with lesser sized data sets compared to deep learning	High efficiency in large data sets

DEEP LEARNING: FUNDAMENTAL PRINCIPLES

This section gives an overview of the fundamental principles in deep learning. All the concepts involved in deep learning are discussed in detail.

Figure 6. Q-Learning

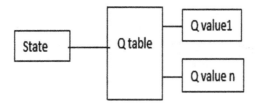

Figure 7. Deep belief network

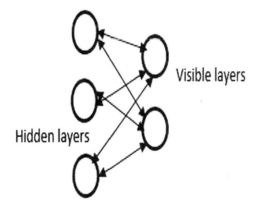

Deep Reinforcement Learning

Deep reinforcement learning (DRL) is the most exciting area of artificial intelligence. Reinforcement Learning problems are solved using DRL that uses deep neural networks. Deep Q Neural Network uses Neural Network by taking the state and approximating Q-values instead of using a Q-table for each action based on that state.

Deep Q Learning

Deep Q learning enables learning the unknown environment by the usage of deep learning and q learning. Both q learning and deep learning are integrated to study the unfamiliar environment. Any object under consideration is called as an agent. The different situations are named as states, and these states are input, and a Q value is estimated to learn policies for high-dimensional and large state-space problems. Q-Learning is an algorithm based on a Q-table which is used by an agent to find the best action to take given a state. Figure 6 presents the Q-Learning approach.

Deep Belief Network

Deep neural network class called DBN. DBN comprises of multiple layers of the graphical mode (Hua et al., 2015) which have directed edges and undirected edges. DBN has numerous interconnected hidden nodes between the layers, and not between nodes within a layer. Layers of Restricted Boltzmann Machines (RBMs) for the pre-train phase, while the fine-tuning phase uses a feed-forward network. Figure 7 illustrates deep belief network.

The Restricted Boltzmann Machine (RBM) is so-called because there is no communication between the layers in the model. An RBM is a reproductive stochastic ANN that can learn a probability distribution over its set of inputs. RBM is useful for filtering, feature learning, classification, and it employs some types of dimensionality reduction to help tackle complicated input.

Recurrent Neural Network

RNN algorithm uses an internal memory and memorizes the inputs thus making it ideal for ML problems with sequential data. In RNN the information cycles through a loop. While taking decisions, it takes into consideration the current input along with the previously learned data. Exploding problems and gradient vanishing and are some of the problems in the traditional RNNs; therefore, training of RNN is difficult (Tran and d'Avila Garcez, 2018).

The original RNN design, "vanilla" network is unable to model long-term sequential dependencies. In contrast, long short-term memory networks (LSTMs) do additive—not multiplicative—updates to the cell state, and therefore avoid vanishing gradients. Thus, the LSTMs [48] are special type of RNNs with memory cells. LSTM performs better than standard RNN in some of the applications like speech recognition.

Convolutional Neural Networks

Convolutional neural networks (CNNs or ConvNets) (Li, 2017) (Pandey & Solanki, 2019) are a type of deep neural network which can extract features. In CNN there are some kernels which are connected locally that capture the correlation between diverse channels. CNNs can learn multiple layers of feature hierarchies automatically (also called "representation learning"), sparse interactions, parameter sharing, and equi-variant representations are achieved using this model.

In Dense Convolutional Network (DenseNet) (Ordóñez, & Roggen, 2016) each layer is connected to every other layer in a feed-forward manner. DenseNet uses fewer layers, and reuses feature maps from every layer, hence, is able to achieve better accuracy as compared to other CNN models (Zoph & Le, 2017).

Auto Encoders

An auto encoder is unsupervised artificial neural network model, used for efficient data encoding. Auto encoders mainly have three layers; an input layer, an encoding layer, and a decoding layer. The four types of Auto encoders are Denoising auto encoder, Sparse auto encoder, Variation auto encoder (VAE), Contractive auto encoder (CAE). Auto encoder along with Global Stacked Auto Encoder (GSAE) and multiple Local SAEs (LSAEs), helps in enhanced input representation(Wang et al., 2017)with reduced model size, and support for application-aware and parallel training.

GAN (GENERATIVE ADVERSARIAL NETWORKS)

GAN (Generative Adversarial Networks) (Zhang et al., 2017) generates data from scratch. GAN is made up of two deep networks named generator and discriminator. ZipNetis found to reduce prediction error. Using GAN a technique has been proposed for mobile traffic analytics using a combination of Zipper Network (ZipNet)and Generative Adversarial Neural Network (GAN) models.

Deep Learning in Future Wireless Networks

This section describes the usage of deep learning in the modern wireless networks. Deep learning is used in many modern applications to optimize various parameters and performance of the network.

Wireless Resource Management

Deep reinforcement learning is implemented to provide solution to resource management problems in Vehicle-to-vehicle (V2V) communications. Vehicle-to-vehicle (V2V) communications play a key role in the improvement of transportation services and road safety. The multi-agent deep reinforcement learning for V2V communications can be used to produce a decentralized resource allocation method by addressing problems of latency. A method has been proposed (Ye & Li, 2018) using a decentralized mechanism of resource allocation for vehicle-to-vehicle (V2V) communications for decision-making and to find out optimal sub-band and the power level for transmission without waiting for global information and with minimum transmission overhead.

Sun et al., 2017 proposed a method for wireless resource management using a learning-based approach. A deep neural network (DNN) was approximated by considering the input and output of resource allocation as unknown non-linear mapping. If DNN learns the nonlinear mapping accurately and effectively, then it can be used for resource allocation in almost real time by using a few simple operations. DNNs can provide high sum-rate performance and low computational complexity.

Mobile Traffic Analysis

This is one of the major areas where deep learning has found its efficient usage. Mobile traffic data is a rich source of wide variety of information. Mobile traffic analyses are categorized into three; social analyses, mobility analyses, and network analysis. Social analyses deal with the process of finding the relationships between a broad set of social features and mobile traffic. Mobility analysis is the extraction of the mobility information from mobile traffic. Network analyses deal with the understanding of the mobile traffic demand and evolving better mobile network infrastructure. The process of extracting fine-grained mobile traffic patterns is very complex as well as expensive. The complexity and expense rely on specialized equipment, intensive post-processing, and substantial storage capabilities. Naboulsi et al. 2016surveyedprevalent mobile traffic analysis methods and suggested dependency of monitoring the cellular traffic with various probe types deployed across cities. Zhang et al., 2017projecteda "mobile traffic super-resolution" (MTSR) technique which extrapolated fine-grain mobile traffic consumption, giving only limited coarse-grained measurement collected by probes. Furno et al., 2017 classified mobile traffic demand network-wide by spatial and temporal dimensions for serving network activity profiling and land use detection profiling.

Network Optimization

Efficient management of network resources is a significant challenge for most of the previously suggested techniques. Deep learning has found a major application in this area. A method was proposed in this direction (Liu et al., 2017) to optimize the network flow and link usage. The method was aimed at predicting if a link will be scheduled through link evaluation. The method also removed any unused link for the network. Many similar works using deep learning have been targeted at optimizing various parameters in the network to improve the efficiency.

Routing

Efficient routing of data packets from the sender to the receiver is a chief area of research for many years. Deep learning has been a major solution to many problems in routing. Many methods have been proposed to improve the efficiency of routing in the network. A method was proposed (Mao et al., 2017) to enhance the efficiency of route computation in high speed core networks. The method used a supervised deep learning system for constructing the routing table and finding out the next optimized route for the data packet in the network. The paper also discussed about the feasibility of the method being integrated into routers. Many similar techniques have been proposed recently to improve the routing performance.

Network Intrusion Detection System (NIDS)

Deep learning has found numerous applications in security of information transferred through the internet (Xin et al., 2018). One of the major applications is in designing efficient Intrusion Detection Systems. Depending on the location where the intrusion detection performs, there are two types; host-based IDS (HIDS) and network-based IDS (NIDS). Network security breaches can be found using the Network Intrusion Detection System (NIDS). The traffic to and from the network can be analyzed and monitored using the network intrusion detection system. According to Javaid et al. 2016, NIDSs are of two classes; Signature (misuse) based NIDS, here intrusion can be detected by pattern matching the preinstalled attack signature. Signature based NIDS (SNIDS) is best suited for known attacks, Anomaly detection-based NIDS(ANIDS), here invasion can be identified by observing a deviation from the regular traffic pattern. Anomaly detection based NIDS helps in identifying new attacks. Developing an efficient and flexible NIDS for unknown future attacks are challenging because of two main reasons, Feature selections for anomaly detection from the network traffic dataset is difficult, and the selected feature may work well for one type of attack and may not work well for another set of attack. Also the labeled traffic dataset is unavailable from real networks for developing a NIDS. Various machine learning techniques like Artificial Neural Network ANN, Support Vector Machine, etc. were used for developing Anomaly detection based NIDS but were not much useful. Deep learning techniques were effective in overcoming the challenges of developing effective NIDS. The deep learning technique can be used to create good feature representation from unlabeled network traffic data collected from various network sources. Salama et al. [60] proposed an anomaly intrusion detection scheme using a RBM-based DBN for feature reduction and SVM based classification.

Network Anomaly Detection

Another major application of deep learning in detection of malwares and anomalies in the network (Salama et al., 2011). Complexity and unpredictability of network traffic changes in the model over time due to continuous evolution of the anomalies are two key challenges while generating the required training data for effective network modeling. Due to changing patterns and techniques for attacking, the prior acquired information regarding how to tell attacks apart from normal traffic may lose their validity. A self-learning system is needed. Anomaly detection systems using semi-supervised techniques with the classifier being trained only with "usual" traffic data such that information about anomalous behaviors might be built and dynamically developed. The Discriminative Restricted Boltzmann Machine (Fiore et al., 2013) can be used to aggregate the expressive ability of generative models with good proficiency for classification accuracy to deduce portion of its knowledge from incomplete training data.

Malware Traffic Classification

Classification of traffic into benign and malware is yet another application of deep learning in network security. Traffic classification methods include port-based, statistical-based, behavioral-based and deep packets inspection (DPI)-based. Wang et al. 2017 introduced a new taxonomy of traffic classification and also proposed a malware traffic classification method by taking traffic data in the form of images and used the convolutional neural network. This application has gained wide popularity due to its efficiency in identifying the malwares spreading in the network.

Software Defined Networking (SDN)

Software Defined Networking (SDN) (Piedrahita et al., 2018) is an upcoming architecture. Its dynamicity, manageability, cost-effectiveness and adaptability make it perfect for modern high-bandwidth and dynamic applications. Numerous deep learning methods have been suggested for improved security in software defined networks. Recently, a method has been proposed for intrusion detection using a Deep Neural Network (Tang et al., 2016)

CHALLENGES AND OPEN RESEARCH PROBLEMS

This section presents some of the challenges existing with deep learning applications in new generation wireless networks,

- Improving the efficiency with large quantities of data

Amount of data that is being generated in modern wireless networks is very huge. Further the numbers of connected wireless devices are also increasing at an exponential rate. This big data needs to be handled in the most efficient way to get the best results. Deep learning approaches face a big challenge in handling this tremendous amount of generated data and also in processing the data to meaningful results.

- Handling the problems related to mismatching of testing distribution and training distribution.

This is another area in deep learning where there is a huge scope for further research and improvement. It is very essential for the new methods proposed with deep learning in modern wireless networks to efficiently handle the testing and training distribution.

- Mobility of devices

Deep learning technologies have been trying hard to provide efficiency to wireless networks even with high mobility of devices. In vehicular networks and highly mobile ad hoc networks it is very essential to handle the high mobility of nodes. Deep learning approaches have to deal with increasing as well as random mobility of these devices in the network.

- Deep learning approaches for geographic data analysis

Research in this direction has gained wide popularity and acceptance. Many methods have been proposed for efficient analysis of environmental data collected from satellites and other sensor devices. But still there is a larger scope for research in this area due to its scalability.

- Information and Network Security

Although many methods have been proposed using deep learning approaches to enhance security features in the networks, there is still wide scope of research in this area. As the cyber-attacks are increasing every day, more efficient deep learning techniques could be developed for improved security of information passed through the network.

CONCLUSION

The research article initially discussed about artificial intelligence and machine learning approaches. The transition from machine learning to deep learning was discussed in detail highlighting the advantages of deep learning. Fundamental principles of deep learning were then discussed in detail. Various approaches and models used in deep learning were then presented. The applications of deep learning in intelligent wireless networks were discussed. Latest applications using deep learning for improving efficiency in wireless networks was discussed in detail. Further, the paper presented the open research challenges and issues existing in this direction. This article would give a thorough and better understanding to researchers involved in designing new applications for new generation wireless networks using latest deep learning approaches.

REFERENCES

Ahlgren, B., Hidell, M., & Ngai, E. C.-H. (2016, November-December). Internet of Things for Smart Cities: Interoperability and Open Data. *IEEE Internet Computing, 20*(6), 52–56. doi:10.1109/MIC.2016.124

Alzubi, J., Nayyar, A., & Kumar, A. (2018, November). Machine learning from theory to algorithms: An overview. *Journal of Physics: Conference Series, 1142*(1), 012012. doi:10.1088/1742-6596/1142/1/012012

Collobert, R., & Bengio, S. (2004). Links between perceptrons, MLPs and SVMs. In *Proceedings of the twenty-first international conference on Machine learning (ICML '04)*. ACM. 10.1145/1015330.1015415

Cruz, E. (2018). A Comprehensive Survey in Towards to Future FANETs. IEEE Latin America Transactions, 16(3), 876-884. doi:10.1109/TLA.2018.8358668

Deshkar, S., Thanseeh, R. A., & Menon, V. G. (2017). A Review on IoT based m-Health Systems for Diabetes. *International Journal of Computer Science and Telecommunications, 8*(1), 13–18.

Fiore, U., Palmieri, F., Castiglione, A., & De Santis, A. (2013). Network anomaly detection with the restricted Boltzmann machine. *Neurocomputing, 122*, 13–23. doi:10.1016/j.neucom.2012.11.050

Furno, A., Fiore, M., & Stanica, R. (2017). Joint spatial and temporal classification of mobile traffic demands. *IEEE INFOCOM 2017 - IEEE Conference on Computer Communications*, 1-9.

He, Y., Yu, F. R., Zhao, N., Yin, H., Yao, H., & Qiu, R. C. (2016). Big Data Analytics in Mobile Cellular Networks. *IEEE Access: Practical Innovations, Open Solutions, 4*, 1985–1996. doi:10.1109/ACCESS.2016.2540520

Hua, Y., Guo, J., & Zhao, H. (2014). Deep belief networks and deep learning. *Intelligent Computing and Internet of Things (ICIT), 2014 International Conference on*, 1-4.

Jacob, S., & Menon, V. (2019). *MEDICO-A Simple IoT Integrated Medical Kiosk for the Rural People*. Preprints.

Jain, A. K., Mao, J., & Mohiuddin, K. M. (1996, March). Artificial neural networks: A tutorial. *Computer, 29*(3), 31–44. doi:10.1109/2.485891

Jain, D. K., Jacob, S., Alzubi, J., & Menon, V. (2019). An efficient and adaptable multimedia system for converting PAL to VGA in real-time video processing. *Journal of Real-Time Image Processing*, 1–13.

Javaid, A., Quamar, W. S., & Alam, M. (2016). A deep learning approach for network intrusion detection system, In *Proceedings of the 9th EAI International Conference on Bio-inspired Information and Communications Technologies (formerly BIONETICS)*, (pp. 21-26). ICST (Institute for Computer Sciences, Social-Informatics and Telecommunications Engineering). 10.4108/eai.3-12-2015.2262516

Kauer, T., Joglekar, S., Redi, M., Aiello, L. M., & Quercia, D. (2018, September/October). Mapping and Visualizing Deep-Learning Urban Beautification. *IEEE Computer Graphics and Applications, 38*(5), 70–83. doi:10.1109/MCG.2018.053491732 PMID:30273128

Li, Y. (2017). *Deep reinforcement learning: An overview*. arXiv preprint, arXiv:1701.07274

Liu, L., Cheng, Y., Cai, L., Zhou, S., & Niu, Z. (2017). Deep learning-based optimization in wireless network. *2017 IEEE International Conference on Communications (ICC)*, 1-6.

Liu, Z., Li, Z., Wu, K., & Li, M. (2018, July/August). Urban Traffic Prediction from Mobility Data Using Deep Learning. *IEEE Network*, *32*(4), 40–46. doi:10.1109/MNET.2018.1700411

Londhe, A., & Rao, P. P. (2017). Platforms for big data analytics: Trend towards hybrid era. *2017 International Conference on Energy, Communication, Data Analytics and Soft Computing (ICECDS)*, 3235-3238. 10.1109/ICECDS.2017.8390056

Louridas, P., & Ebert, C. (2016, September-October). Machine Learning. *IEEE Software*, *33*(5), 110–115. doi:10.1109/MS.2016.114

Mao, B., Fadlullah, Z. M., Tang, F., Kato, N., Akashi, O., Inoue, T., & Mizutani, K. (2017, November 1). Routing or Computing? The Paradigm Shift Towards Intelligent Computer Network Packet Transmission Based on Deep Learning. *IEEE Transactions on Computers*, *66*(11), 1946–1960. doi:10.1109/TC.2017.2709742

Mengke, Y., Xiaoguang, Z., Jianqiu, Z., & Jianjian, X. (2016, March). Challenges and solutions of information security issues in the age of big data. *China Communications*, *13*(3), 193–202. doi:10.1109/CC.2016.7445514

Menon, V. (2019). *Optimized Opportunistic Routing in Highly Dynamic Ad hoc Networks*. Preprints.

Menon, V. G. (2017). Moving from Vehicular Cloud Computing to Vehicular Fog Computing: Issues and Challenges. *International Journal on Computer Science and Engineering*, *9*(2), 14–18.

Menon, V. G. (2019). *Light Weight Secure Encryption Scheme for Internet of Things Network, Encyclopedia*. MDPI.

Menon, V. G., & Prathap, P. M. (n.d.). Moving from Topology-Dependent to Opportunistic Routing Protocols in Dynamic Wireless Ad Hoc Networks: Challenges and Future Directions. In *Algorithms, Methods, and Applications in Mobile Computing and Communications*. IGI Global.

Menon, V. G. (2017). Analyzing the Performance of Random Mobility Models with Opportunistic Routing. Advances in Wireless and Mobile Communications, 10(5), 1221-1226.

Menon, V. G., & Joe Prathap, P. M. (2016). Analysing the Behaviour and Performance of Opportunistic Routing Protocols in Highly Mobile Wireless Ad Hoc Networks. *IACSIT International Journal of Engineering and Technology*, *8*(5), 1916–1924. doi:10.21817/ijet/2016/v8i5/160805409

Menon, V. G., & Joe Prathap, P. M. (2016). Routing in highly dynamic ad hoc networks: Issues and challenges. *International Journal on Computer Science and Engineering*, *8*(4), 112–116.

Menon, V. G., Joe Prathap, P. M., & Vijay, A. (2016). Eliminating Redundant Relaying of Data Packets for Efficient Opportunistic Routing in Dynamic Wireless Ad Hoc Networks. *Asian Journal of Information Technology*, *12*(17), 3991–3994.

Menon, V. G., & Prathap, J. (2018). Vehicular Fog Computing: Challenges Applications and Future Directions. Fog Computing: Breakthroughs in Research and Practice, 220-229.

Menon, V.G., & Prathap, P.J. (n.d.). Opportunistic routing with virtual coordinates to handle communication voids in mobile ad hoc networks. In *Advances in Signal Processing and Intelligent Recognition Systems* (pp. 323-334). Springer.

Mishra, M., & Srivastava, M. (2014). A view of Artificial Neural Network. *2014 International Conference on Advances in Engineering & Technology Research (ICAETR - 2014)*, 1-3.

Murillo Piedrahita, A. F., Gaur, V., Giraldo, J., Cárdenas, Á. A., & Rueda, S. J. (2018, January/February). Leveraging Software-Defined Networking for Incident Response in Industrial Control Systems. *IEEE Software*, *35*(1), 44–50. doi:10.1109/MS.2017.4541054

Murphy, J. (2018, January/February). Artificial Intelligence, Rationality, and the World Wide Web. *IEEE Intelligent Systems*, *33*(1), 98–103. doi:10.1109/MIS.2018.012001557

Naboulsi, D., Fiore, M., Ribot, S., & Stanica, R. (2016). Large-Scale Mobile Traffic Analysis: A Survey IEEE Communications Surveys & Tutorials, 18(1), 124-161. doi:10.1109/COMST.2015.2491361

Nayyar, A. (2018, August). Flying Adhoc Network (FANETs): Simulation Based Performance Comparison of Routing Protocols: AODV, DSDV, DSR, OLSR, AOMDV and HWMP. In *2018 International Conference on Advances in Big Data, Computing and Data Communication Systems (icABCD)* (pp. 1-9). IEEE. 10.1109/ICABCD.2018.8465130

Nayyar, A., Batth, R. S., Ha, D. B., & Sussendran, G. (2018). Opportunistic Networks: Present Scenario-A Mirror Review. *International Journal of Communication Networks and Information Security*, *10*(1), 223–241.

Nishani, E., & Çiço, B. (2017). Computer vision approaches based on deep learning and neural networks: Deep neural networks for video analysis of human pose estimation. *2017 6th Mediterranean Conference on Embedded Computing (MECO)*, 1-4.

O'Leary, D. E. (2013, March-April). Artificial Intelligence and Big Data. *IEEE Intelligent Systems*, *28*(2), 96–99. doi:10.1109/MIS.2013.39 PMID:25505373

Ordóñez, F., & Roggen, D. (2016). Deep convolutional and lstm recurrent neural networks for multimodal wearable activity recognition. *Sensors (Basel)*, *16*(1), 115. doi:10.339016010115 PMID:26797612

Pandey, S., & Solanki, A. (2019). Music Instrument Recognition using Deep Convolutional Neural Networks. International Journal of Information Technology. doi:10.100741870-019-00285-y

Philip, V., Suman, V. K., Menon, V. G., & Dhanya, K. A. (2016). A Review on latest Internet of Things based Healthcare Applications. *International Journal of Computer Science and Information Security*, *15*(1), 248–254.

Rajesh, S., Paul, V., Menon, V. G., & Khosravi, M. R. (2019). A secure and efficient lightweight symmetric encryption scheme for transfer of text files between embedded IoT devices. *Symmetry*, *11*(2), 293. doi:10.3390ym11020293

Rosati, S., Krużelecki, K., Heitz, G., Floreano, D., & Rimoldi, B. (2016, March). Dynamic Routing for Flying Ad Hoc Networks. *IEEE Transactions on Vehicular Technology*, *65*(3), 1690–1700. doi:10.1109/TVT.2015.2414819

Ross, M., Graves, C. A., Campbell, J. W., & Kim, J. H. (2013). Using Support Vector Machines to Classify Student Attentiveness for the Development of Personalized Learning Systems. *2013 12th International Conference on Machine Learning and Applications*, 325-328.

Rosten, E., Porter, R., & Drummond, T. (2010, January). Faster and Better: A Machine Learning Approach to Corner Detection. *IEEE Transactions on Pattern Analysis and Machine Intelligence*, *32*(1), 105–119. doi:10.1109/TPAMI.2008.275 PMID:19926902

Salama, M. A., Eid, H. F., Ramadan, R. A., Darwish, A., & Hassanien, A. E. (2011). Hybrid intelligent intrusion detection scheme. In *Soft computing in industrial applications* (pp. 293–303). Berlin: Springer. doi:10.1007/978-3-642-20505-7_26

Sun, H., Chen, X., Shi, Q., Hong, M., Fu, X., & Sidiropoulos, N. D. (2017). Learning to optimize: Training deep neural networks for wireless resource management. *2017 IEEE 18th International Workshop on Signal Processing Advances in Wireless Communications (SPAWC)*, 1-6.

Tang, T. A., Mhamdi, L., McLernon, D., Zaidi, S. A. R., & Ghogho, M. (2016). Deep learning approach for Network Intrusion Detection in Software Defined Networking. *2016 International Conference on Wireless Networks and Mobile Communications (WINCOM)*, 258-263. 10.1109/WINCOM.2016.7777224

Tran, S. N., & d'Avila Garcez, A. S. (2018, February). Deep Logic Networks: Inserting and Extracting Knowledge From Deep Belief Networks. *IEEE Transactions on Neural Networks and Learning Systems*, *29*(2), 246–258. doi:10.1109/TNNLS.2016.2603784 PMID:27845678

Uhrig, R. E. (1995). Introduction to artificial neural networks. *Proceedings of IECON '95 - 21st Annual Conference on IEEE Industrial Electronics*, 33-3. 10.1109/IECON.1995.483329

Vijay, A., Menon, V. G., & Nayyar, A. 2018, November. Distributed Big Data Analytics in the Internet of Signals. In *2018 International Conference on System Modeling & Advancement in Research Trends (SMART)* (pp. 73-77). IEEE.

Vinoj, P. G., Jacob, S., & Menon, V. G. (2018). Hybrid brain actuated muscle interface for the physically disabled. *Basic & Clinical Pharmacology & Toxicology*, *123*, 8–9. PMID:29345051

Vinoj, P. G., Jacob, S., Menon, V. G., Rajesh, S., & Khosravi, M. R. (2019). Brain-Controlled Adaptive Lower Limb Exoskeleton for Rehabilitation of Post-Stroke Paralyzed. IEEE Access. doi:10.1109/ACCESS.2019.2921375

Wang, J. (2017). Spatiotemporal modeling and prediction in cellular networks: A big data enabled deep learning approach. *IEEE INFOCOM 2017 - IEEE Conference on Computer Communications*, 1-9.

Wang, W., Zhu, M., Zeng, X., Ye, X., & Sheng, Y. (2017). Malware traffic classification using convolutional neural network for representation learning. *2017 International Conference on Information Networking (ICOIN)*, 712-717. 10.1109/ICOIN.2017.7899588

Wang, Y. (2017). Cognitive foundations of knowledge science and deep knowledge learning by cognitive robots. *2017 IEEE 16th International Conference on Cognitive Informatics & Cognitive Computing (ICCI*CC)*, 5.

Wang, Y. (2016). Deep reasoning and thinking beyond deep learning by cognitive robots and brain-inspired systems. *2016 IEEE 15th International Conference on Cognitive Informatics & Cognitive Computing (ICCI*CC)*, 3-3.

Xin, Y., Kong, L., Liu, Z., Chen, Y., Li, Y., Zhu, H., ... Wang, C. (2018). Machine Learning and Deep Learning Methods for Cybersecurity. *IEEE Access: Practical Innovations, Open Solutions*, 6, 35365–35381. doi:10.1109/ACCESS.2018.2836950

Xue, M., & Zhu, C. (2009). A Study and Application on Machine Learning of Artificial Intelligence. *2009 International Joint Conference on Artificial Intelligence*, 272-274. 10.1109/JCAI.2009.55

Yao, X. (1999, September). Evolving artificial neural networks. *Proceedings of the IEEE, 87*(9), 1423–1447. doi:10.1109/5.784219

Yao, X. (1999, September). Evolving artificial neural networks. *Proceedings of the IEEE, 87*(9), 1423–1447. doi:10.1109/5.784219

Yazti, D. Z., & Krishnaswamy, S. (2014). Mobile Big Data Analytics: Research, Practice, and Opportunities. *2014 IEEE 15th International Conference on Mobile Data Management*, 1-2.

Ye, H., & Li, G. Y. (2018). Deep Reinforcement Learning for Resource Allocation in V2V Communications. *2018 IEEE International Conference on Communications (ICC)*, 1-6. 10.1109/ICC.2018.8422586

Zhang, C., Ouyang, X., & Patras, P. (2017, November). Zipnet-gan: Inferring fine-grained mobile traffic patterns via a generative adversarial neural network. In *Proceedings of the 13th International Conference on emerging Networking EXperiments and Technologies* (pp. 363-375). ACM. 10.1145/3143361.3143393

Zhang, D., Han, X., & Deng, C. (2018). Review on the research and practice of deep learning and reinforcement learning in smart grids. CSEE Journal of Power and Energy Systems, 4(3), 362-370.

Zoph, B., & Le, Q. V. (2016). *Neural architecture search with reinforcement learning*. arXiv preprint arXiv:1611.01578

Chapter 11

Demystifying Disease Identification and Diagnosis Using Machine Learning Classification Algorithms:
Demystify Medical Data With Machine Learning Algorithms

Ashok Suragala

https://orcid.org/0000-0002-8431-2479

JNTU Vizianagaram, India

PapaRao A. V.

JNTU Vizianagaram, India

ABSTRACT

The exponential surge in healthcare data is providing new opportunities to discover meaningful data-driven characteristics and patterns of diseases. Machine learning and deep learning models have been employed for many computational phenotyping and healthcare prediction tasks. However, machine learning models are crucial for wide adaption in medical research and clinical decision making. In this chapter, the authors introduce demystifying diseases identification and diagnosis of various disease using machine learning algorithms like logistic regression, naive Bayes, decision tree, MLP classifier, random forest in order to cure liver disease, hepatitis disease, and diabetes mellitus. This work leverages the initial discoveries made through data exploration, statistical analysis of data to reduce the number of explanatory variables, which led to identifying the statistically significant attributes, mapping those significant attributes to the response, and building classification techniques to predict the outcome and demystify clinical diseases.

DOI: 10.4018/978-1-5225-9643-1.ch011

INTRODUCTION

There is a growing need for accurate classification of disease as if the disease is detected earle, then it become easy to cure rather than in the future stages.

The purpose of a medical diagnostic machine learning model research is to find better ways to demystifying diseases identification and diagnosis in patients. The result of diagnostic model research is a diagnostic machine learning model that allows telling with reasonable certainty whether or not the patient has a certain disease, based on a number of variables.

Medical diagnostic model research improves diagnosis by avoiding the need for surgery, thereby making it easier to diagnose disease earlier which substantially improves survival rates. Now how are the diagnostic models calculated? They are calculated using machine learning technology called machine learning classification models.

The idea with this technique is to collect a lot of data from patients with and without the diseases.

Clinicians collect a lot of other information about the patients; information that can be obtained using non-invasive techniques. This can be demographic data, information obtained from ultrasound or other images or any other information that medical researchers suspect might be linked to the true diagnosis. The information obtained non-invasively is the inputs, while the gold standard diagnosis is the output. Both are fed to a classifier which will calculate a model to predict the output from the inputs. This, in the case of diagnostic mobile research, means predicting a patient's diagnosis based on information that was obtained from the patient by non-invasive means. Now, diagnostic model research isn't just a case of running patient data through a classifier. It requires stepping through an entire workflow.

Evaluation of clinical data from different patient cohorts and decision making are significant factors in diagnosis and making prediction of diseases using machine learning classifiers. For this purpose, we first organize this chapter by defining the patient population from different cohorts, identifying phenotypes, perform statistical analysis, apply different feature selection techniques to identify statistically significant features, applying machine learning classification algorithms and validate the model.

In this chapter, we organize our work by defining a study, continue with data collection & data analysis, identifying computational phenotypes, apply classifiers (machine learning models) with significant features (phenotypes) and conclude with validation and model dissemination to predict the outcome and demystify clinical diseases and a tool for valuable clinical decision making.

BACKGROUND

Machine Learning Algorithms are widely used in diagnosis of different clinical diseases. In recent years researchers adopted different machine learning classification algorithms for disease diagnosis and prediction.

Machine Learning Algorithms classified as supervised, Un-supervised and ensembles algorithms aims to focus on making predictions using computers in social media, financial, Medical, Entertainment and building product, movie and song recommendation engine domains. (Jafar Alzubi, Anand Nayyar & Akshi Kumar, 2018). In this chapter, we use various supervised learning algorithms like classification, regression and Ensemble techniques (Jafar Alzubi, Anand Nayyar & Akshi Kumar, 2018) such as Logistic Regression, decision tree, Naïve bayes and Random Forest Algorithms.

We build decision tree Classification algorithms and leaf node signifies final decision (Jafar Alzubi, Anand Nayyar & Akshi Kumar,2018) on various clinical diseases prediction and diagnosis.

We build Naïve Bayes Classifier which classifies based on Bayes theorem (Jafar Alzubi, Anand Nayyar & Akshi Kumar,2018). It is a statistical learning algorithm. It works on one inference that is the effect of an attribute value of a given class is independent of the values of the other attributes.

In this chapter we also build ensembles algorithm Random Forest creates a bunch of decision trees with random subset of samples (Jafar Alzubi, Anand Nayyar & Akshi Kumar,2018) also build variable importance on various clinical diseases for diagnosis and prediction.

Prediction of diabetes disease using Naïve Bayes classifier which performs highest accuracy of 76.30%. (Deepthi Sisodia, Dilip Singh Sisodia 2018).

Prediction of target class using Decision rule taken from prior data uses nodes and internodes for the prediction and Classification. The Root node in decision tree which classifies the instances with different features and leaf nodes represent Classification (Deepthi Sisodia, Dilip Singh Sisodia, 2018). Our work improves the accuracy on diabetes disease classification using decision tree algorithm with 76.95%.

Logistic regression measures the relationship between dependent variable and one or more number of independent variables using probability score as the predicted values of the dependent variable (Hoon jin, Seoungcheon Kim and Kinhong kim,2014) where the probability of class derived based on p-value. When p-value > 0.5 samples belongs to class 0 otherwise it belongs to class 1 (Hoon jin, Seoungcheon Kim and Kinhong kim, 2014). In this we uses the data distribution of each features in ILPD observed (Hoon jin, Seoungcheon Kim and Kinhong kim, 2014), which features not follows normality we apply log transformations on those features. Those differences observed in data exploration and visualization sections.

In spite of that we discussed more elaborately with machine learning classifiers Logistic regression, decision tree, and naïve bayes classifiers and ensembles random forest for diagnosis and prediction of diabetes, Liver and Hepatitis diseases. We emphasis on Bias and variance problems for clinical diseases using Logistic regression.

MAIN FOCUS OF THE CHAPTER

This chapter aims to provide data science pipeline procedure for the analysis of clinical data. To illustrate the proposed steps in this methodological guide, we use Hepatitis, Diabetes and Indian Liver Patient data to show how these steps are applied in practice.

In this chapter introduces Machine Learning Classification Algorithms on medical data to make good predictions in clinical trials (health care domain) with data acquisition, data exploration, statistical analysis and better visualization, feature selection, build predictive modeling and validate models to demystifying disease identification and diagnosis using machine learning classification algorithms.

This chapter introduces using Machine Learning Classification Algorithms to demystify medical diseases diagnosis, detection to predict clinical outcomes.

Step 1: Ask a question
1. How to construct an automated case finding system for predicting disease?
2. How to acquire data from different cohorts?
3. How to analyze Data and make inference?
4. What is the Association between input variables and the outcome variables?

Figure 1. Methodology

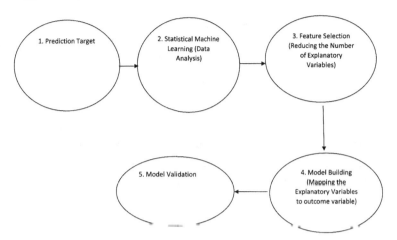

5. How the input variables are distributed?
6. If the input variables not obey normality (distribution not in nature) how to transform it? What type of transformation techniques can we apply?
7. What are the different feature selection techniques apply for selecting the statistically significant features?
8. How to build Machine Learning Prediction Models with relevant features? And How to Validate with new data?
9. How to Evaluating Risk Factors to Save Lives from clinical diseases? Like Hepatitis Disease prediction, Occurrence of diabetes mellitus and liver disease detection and diagnosis?
10. Risk factors are variables that increase the chances of a disease, how well investigate risk factors like Demographic risk factors, Behavioral risk factors, Medical history risk factors and Risk factors from first examination?
11. How to set out to better understand clinical disease?
12. How to understand Physical characteristics, Behavioral characteristics and Test results of the patient?

Step 2:   Do background research

To answer the above questions in the present era of healthcare domain, many numbers of Machine Learning and deep learning models are used for clinical outcome predictions and interventions.

In this chapter the authors focuses on data Acquisition, identify phenotypes, data exploration, statistical analysis and visualization, feature selection, Build predictive modeling and validate models.

In this process data acquisition from different cohorts we take samples and find distribution of samples using histograms, most statistical approaches requires data in one form. So we confirm to the normal distribution, which is most important for statistical testing. We verify this normality and explore individual variables, also measure correlation between two continuous variables and check the significance test to correlations using cor.test().The result shows the statistical significance of the correlation. We also use scatter plots especially to the "relationship between two variables". We use different feature selection techniques for selecting statistically significant features using step wise forward selection and backward elimination techniques. Risk factors are key to successful prediction of any disease. So that we

Figure 2. Computational phenotyping

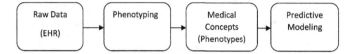

can identify important risk factors using partial search algorithms. We build various machine learning classifiers with all features, with intercept variable and with significant features. We observed various results that are presented below sections. Finally we validate the Model with test data and present the performance metrics like Accuracy, root mean square errors and many more.

Data Acquisition

In order to perform the research experiments reported in the following paper, we used different data cohorts from UCI Machine Learning repository with the name ILPD.

The ILPD data consisted of 583 records/cases and 11 attributes. These 11 attributes are age, gender, total bilirubin, direct bilurbin, Alkaline,sgpt, Alanine Aminotransferase, Aspartate, total Protein, Alb Albumin, A/G ratio Albumin and Globulin ratio and outcome variable i.e. affected by disease or not.

The outcome variable was identified as the predictable attribute with value 0 for patients with liver disease and value 1 for patients with no liver disease.

The Hepatitis dataset download from UCI machine learning data repository. The Hepatitis data consisted of 155 records with 19 attributes.

The Diabetes dataset download from the UCI Machine Learning data repository. This dataset consisting of 768 instances with 8 attributes.

Identify Computational Phenotypes

In the clinical predictive modeling phenotypes are medical concepts which are generated from raw data i.e. demographics data, Data from diagnosis, procedures, medications, lab results and clinical notes deriving research great phenotypes from clinical data using computing algorithms.

Statistical Machine Learning (Informally Data Analysis):

The main Components of Statistical Analysis which includes Data Analysis, Probability distributions and Inference.

Data Exploration, Statistical Analysis and Visualization

Descriptive Statistics and Distributions

Descriptive Statistics is used to summarize data. We use Histograms to visualize distributions (shape, center, range, variation) of continuous variables and also observed Graphical display of the distribution of quantitative variables. We can describe the statistics with measures of central tendency, measures of

Table 1. Correlation outcomes for Hepatitis dataset

Correlation Test Results			
Attribute Name	**Spearman Correlation Coefficient**	**p-Value**	**Number of Samples**
FATIGUE	0.3092691	9.509e-05	155
MALAISE	0.3378593	1.825e-05	155
SPLEEN.PALPABLE	0.2387337	0.00326	155
SPIDERS	0.3983078	4.466e-07	155
ASCITES	0.477882	6.247e-10	155
VARICES	3.41e-06	0.368846	155
BILIRUBIN	2.579e-09	-0.4637524	155
ALBUMIN	2.713e-10	0.5032724	155
PROTIME	7.554e-05	0.4091599	155
HISTOLOGY	1.713e-05	-0.3378561	155

dispersion which gives how data deviate? Finally we are summarizing numerical variables using histograms. Histograms gives better visualization of each input variable. Histogram is the classic way of viewing the distribution a sample. We looked at Histograms and Density Plots to visualize a distribution. We estimate the appearance of Normal Distribution by its bell shape.

Most statistical approaches require data in one form i.e. distribution of variables follows normal distribution, which is most important for statistical testing. If features not follow normality we should apply log transformation and make it into follows normality.

The scatter plots show the relationship between two variables. Data Visualization gives better understanding instead of numerical analysis. We use R and Tableau software for understanding the variable distributions. The resultant Histogram and scatter plots visualized in the Appendix of this chapter.

Correlation Analysis

When we have two continuous features, and look for a link between two features. We can apply a significance test to correlations using cor.test ().

The results show the statistical significance of the correlation

Correlation analysis provides relationship between categorical and numeric variable

We use Spearman's rank correlation assesses monotonic relationship (whether linear or not) between feature and the response variables whether positively correlated or negatively correlated based on p-value. We assess the correlation between explanatory variable and response variable by taking p-value. The features are statistically significant if probability value (p-value) less than 0.05. The resultant correlations for Hepatitis, ILPD disease given in Table 1.

Figure 3: Correlation plot for ILPD dataset

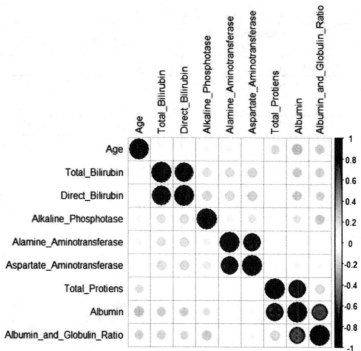

Table 2. Correlation outcomes for Diabetes dataset

Attribute Name	Spearman Correlation Coefficient	p-Value	Number of Samples
Pregnancies	rho = 0.1986887	p-value=2.813e-08	768 samples
Glucose	rho = 0.4757763	p-value < 2.2e-16	768 samples
Blood Pressure	rho = 0.1429207	p-value = 7.047e-05	768 samples
Skin Thickness	rho = 0.08972776	p-value = 0.01286	768 samples
Insulin	rho = 0.06647165	p-value = 0.0656	768 samples
BMI	rho = 0.3097067	p-value < 2.2e-16	768 samples
Diabetes Pedigree Function	rho = 0.1753535	p-value = 1.011e-06	768 samples
Age	rho = 0.3090403	p-value < 2.2e-16	768 samples

Figure 4. Feature selection plots of Hepatitis

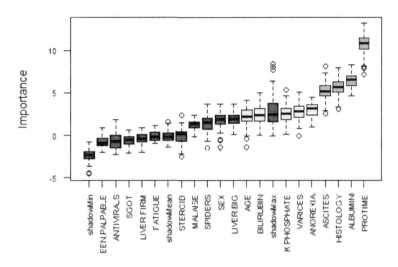

> ##cor.test()used for association/correlation between paired samples. It returns both the correlation coefficient and the significance level (or p-value) of the correlation.
> cor.test (diabetes1$Pregnancies, diabetes1$Outcome, method=c ("spearman"), data=diabetes1)

Step 3:   Construct a hypothesis

Testing of Hypothesis

The Testing of hypothesis play a significant role in decision making in data analysis to determine whether the observed results follows certain assumption (hypothesis).

A definite statement about a population (disease) is known as hypothesis.

To test the hypothesis in data analysis applications to determine whether accept or reject the hypothesis.

The acceptance of hypothesis is defined as Null Hypothesis (H0) if the statistical significant value (p-values) less than 0.05, otherwise we reject the hypothesis which is defined as Alternative Hypothesis (H1)

Feature Selection

The Accuracy or Significance of the machine learning model based on statistically significant features (i.e feature selection).In this chapter the authors use various feature selection techniques such as Partial search algorithms which includes Forward selection, Backward Elimination, Boruta algorithm and Stepwise selection method used along with L1 regularization for optimization.

> boruta_output

Boruta performed 99 iterations in 5.622752 secs.
4 attributes confirmed important: ALBUMIN, ASCITES, HISTOLOGY, PROTIME;

Figure 5. Feature selection plots of Liver Disease

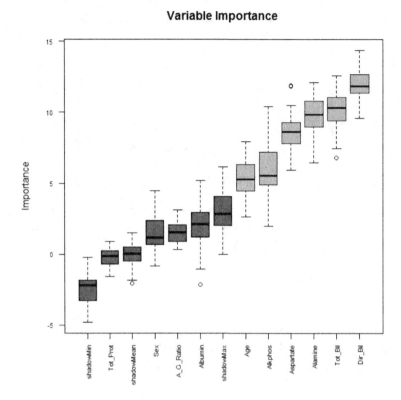

Figure 6. Feature selection plots of diabetes disease

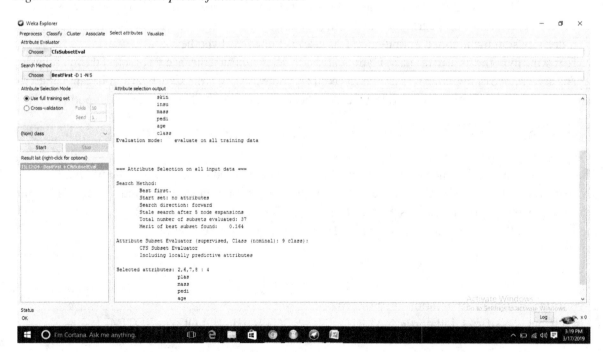

Figure 7. Logistic regression

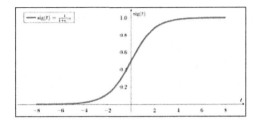

10 attributes confirmed unimportant: ANTIVIRALS, FATIGUE, LIVER.BIG, LIVER.FIRM, MAL-AISE and 5 more;

5 tentative attributes left: AGE, ALK.PHOSPHATE, ANOREXIA, BILIRUBIN, VARICES;

The Final Resultant Feature Selection Visualization Summary

Feature selection plots of Hepatitis, Liver disease and Diabetes Disease

Step 4:   Test your hypothesis by doing an experiment
The main goal of the chapter is to test the hypothesis using various machine learning predictive algorithms on different clinical diseases and achieve better accuracy. In the following, the results obtained by doing experiments on various clinical datasets.

Step 5:   Analyze your data and draw a conclusion

The most important in this chapter is to apply predictive modeling algorithms using Logistic regression, Multiple Logistic Regression, Naive Bayes classifier, decision tree, MLP classifier and nonlinear methods such as random forests.

- Randomly split diseases data into 70% as training dataset and evaluate predictive power on 30% of testing sets
- Use Machine Learning Classification Algorithms on training set to predict whether the patient live or dies with different diseases.

Logistic Regression Results Analysis on Various diseases:

We want binary classifier (mathematical function) which generates Y=0 (not disease) or Y=1(diseased) by taking symptoms as inputs.

Independent Variables: Glucose, Blood Pressure etc.,

Dependent Variables: Zero or One

We are going to design a classifier which give a value between 0 and 1 instead of giving binary values Y=0 or Y=1. We treat this value (p) as the probability of belonging to class 1

$$f\left(\text{glucose}, \text{blood pressure}\right) = p = \frac{1}{1} + e^{-(.\,0+, \,1*\text{glucose}+, \,2*\text{blood pressure})}$$

where e= 2.718 281 828 459

The parameters are selected to

- Predict a high probability for the poor care cases
- Predict a low probability for the good care cases

$$P(y=1)=\frac{1}{1}+e^{-(\theta 0+^2 1*x1+^2 2*x2+^2 3*x3+...+^2 k*xk)}$$

Training Model

- Our aim is to find parameters (thetas) such that for all red points p is nearly one for all black.
- For all points p is nearly zero and for all border cases p is nearly 0.5
- On border: $\theta 0 + \theta 1*$ glucose $+\theta 2*$ blood pressure $= 0$ (Equation of a line: Border points lie on line)

For disease: $\theta 0 + \theta 1 *$ glucose $+\theta 2*$ blood pressure $\gg 0$

For not diseased: $\theta 0 + \theta 1 *$ glucose $+\theta 2*$ blood pressure $\ll 0$

Evaluating Model for Under-Fitting

We evaluating Logistic regression model is good or not using confusion matrix which displays correct and incorrect predictions made by the model on training data values.

We use cut off value 0.5 for constructing this confusion matrix from training data.

And also find overall Error rate in Confusion Matrix.

From this we measure Accuracy of the classifier.

Accuracy = 1- error

We believe that **"Accuracy should more than percentage of majority class"**.

Evaluating Model for Over-Fitting

Error rate in confusion matrix should be same for both Training Data and Test Data.

We consider Values of θs should be reasonably small.

Logistic Regression Model Building with features on Hepatitis Data Set: Logistic Regression model building with all features (Full Model):

> fullmodel = glm(Class~., family=binomial,data=hepa)
> summary(fullmodel)

Table 3. Logistic regression analysis on three diseases with performance metric

Sl. No	Dataset	Design matrix	Associated task	Accuracy (%) with LR and MLR (Training Data)	Accuracy (%) with LR and MLR (Test Data)	Bias and Variance Trade off	Splitting Criterion
1	Hepatitis	155×19	Classification (2 classes)	87.878% albumin, anorexia, ascites, bilirubin, histology and 4 more	86.046%	Error rate in Confusion matrix should be same for both training and test data	70% Training & 30% Testing
2	Liver disease	583x10	Classification	71.077% Age + Dir_Bil + Alamine + Albumin	77.143%	Error rate in Confusion matrix should not be same for both training and test data	70% Training & 30% Testing
3	Pima Indian Diabetes	768x9	Classification	77.281% Glucose + BMI + Pregnancies + Diabetes Pedigree Function + Blood Pressure + Age + Insulin	76.19%	Error rate in Confusion matrix should be same for both training and test data	70% Training & 30% Testing

Call:

glm(formula = Class ~ ., family = binomial, data = hepa)

Deviance Residuals:

Min 1Q Mcdian 3Q Max

-2.936e-05 2.110e-08 2.110e-08 2.110e-08 2.714e-05

Coefficients:

Estimate Std. Error z value Pr(>|z|)

(Intercept) -2.281e+02 1.258e+06 0.000 1.000

AGE 9.430e-01 2.835e+03 0.000 1.000

SEX 1.566e+02 4.121e+05 0.000 1.000

STEROID 8.044e+01 1.243e+05 0.001 0.999

ANTIVIRALS 7.408e-01 1.293e+05 0.000 1.000

FATIGUE 7.624e+00 3.256e+05 0.000 1.000

MALAISE -1.324e+01 2.964e+05 0.000 1.000

ANOREXIA -6.775e+01 1.752e+05 0.000 1.000

LIVER.BIG -8.319e+01 1.322e+05 -0.001 0.999

LIVER.FIRM 3.665e+01 2.819e+05 0.000 1.000

SPLEEN.PALPABLE 2.501e+01 1.087e+05 0.000 1.000

SPIDERS 1.985e+01 8.394e+04 0.000 1.000

ASCITES 4.498e+00 2.245e+05 0.000 1.000

VARICES 3.119e+01 1.667e+05 0.000 1.000

BILIRUBIN -2.760e+01 7.374e+04 0.000 1.000

ALK.PHOSPHATE -3.383e-02 1.146e+03 0.000 1.000

SGOT 8.206e-01 1.354e+03 0.001 1.000

ALBUMIN 1.227e+01 1.603e+05 0.000 1.000
PROTIME 7.724e-01 1.138e+03 0.001 0.999
HISTOLOGY -4.520e+01 1.476e+05 0.000 1.000
(Dispersion parameter for binomial family taken to be 1)

Null deviance: 7.1007e+01 on 79 degrees of freedom
Residual deviance: 6.7558e-09 on 60 degrees of freedom

(75 observations deleted due to missingness)

AIC: 40

Number of Fisher Scoring iterations: 25

Logistic Regression model building with no features (Null Model):

> nullmodel = glm(Class~1, family=binomial,data=hepa)
> summary(nullmodel)

Call:
glm(formula = Class ~ 1, family = binomial, data = hepa)
Deviance Residuals:
Min 1Q Median 3Q Max
-1.7763 0.6801 0.6801 0.6801 0.6801
Coefficients:
Estimate Std. Error z value Pr(>|z|)
(Intercept) 1.3464 0.1984 6.785 1.16e-11 ***

Signif. codes: 0 '***' 0.001 '**' 0.01 '*' 0.05 '.' 0.1 ' ' 1
(Dispersion parameter for binomial family taken to be 1)

Null deviance: 157.86 on 154 degrees of freedom
Residual deviance: 157.86 on 154 degrees of freedom

AIC: 159.86
Number of Fisher Scoring iterations: 4
Logistic Regression model building with significant features(After applying Boruta Feature selection Method):

> finalmodel=glm(Class~ALBUMIN+ASCITES+HISTOLOGY+PROTIME,

family=binomial,data=hepa)

> summary(finalmodel)

Call:

glm(formula = Class ~ ALBUMIN + ASCITES + HISTOLOGY + PROTIME,
family = binomial, data = hepa)

Deviance Residuals:

Min 1Q Median 3Q Max

-2.3733 0.1255 0.1965 0.4199 2.0059

Coefficients:

Estimate Std. Error z value Pr(>|z|)

(Intercept) -3.31462 2.93303 -1.130 0.2584

ALBUMIN 1.07666 0.77154 1.395 0.1629

ASCITES 1.28486 0.92962 1.382 0.1669

HISTOLOGY -1.83891 0.88660 -2.074 0.0381 *

PROTIME 0.03118 0.01916 1.627 0.1037

Signif. codes: 0 '***' 0.001 '**' 0.01 '*' 0.05 '.' 0.1 ' ' 1

(Dispersion parameter for binomial family taken to be 1)

Null deviance: 82.636 on 85 degrees of freedom

Residual deviance: 47.952 on 81 degrees of freedom

(69 observations deleted due to missingness)

AIC: 57.952

Logistic Regression model building with step wise feature selection method on Liver disease dataset (with feature selection):

Stepwise forward selection and backward elimination add statistically significant variables into model and remove insignificant features on Liver disease dataset

```
> stepMod <- step(fullmodel, scope = list(lower = nullmodel, upper = fullmodel), direction = "both",
      trace = 0, steps = 1000)
> stepMod
```

Call: glm(formula = Disease ~ Age + Dir_Bil + Alkphos + Alamine + Tot_Prot +
Albumin, data = liver_data)

Coefficients:

(Intercept) Age Dir_Bil Alkphos Alamine Tot_Prot Albumin

0.4057462 0.0032443 0.0241181 0.0001814 0.0003140 0.0593629 -0.1069797

Degrees of Freedom: 582 Total (i.e. Null); 576 Residual

Null Deviance: 119.2

Residual Deviance: 105.2   AIC: 672.4

Figure 8. Standardized residuals against fitted values

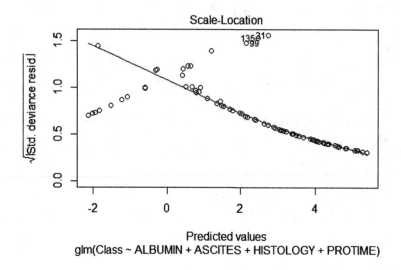

Diagnostic Plots Of Hepatitis Disease With Statistically Significant Features

Figure 9. Residuals against fitted values

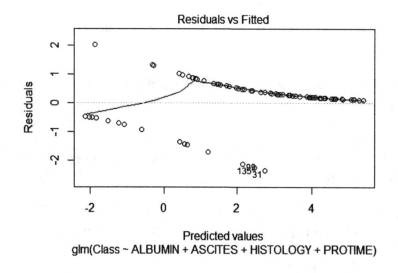

Figure 10. Normal QQ Plot

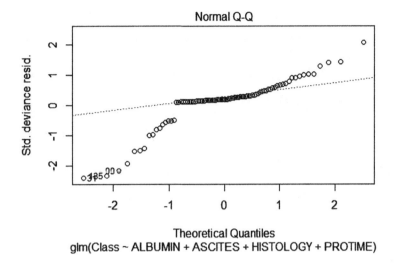

Figure 11. Residuals against leverage values

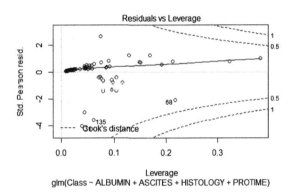

Diagnostic Plots Of Liver Disease With All Features

Figure 12. (Square root) Standardized residuals against fitted values

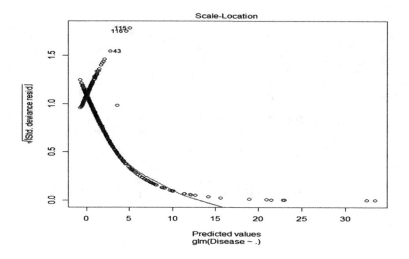

Figure 13. Normal QQ Plot

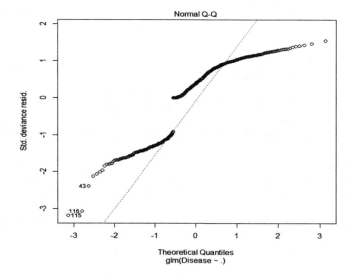

Figure 14. Standardized residuals against leverage

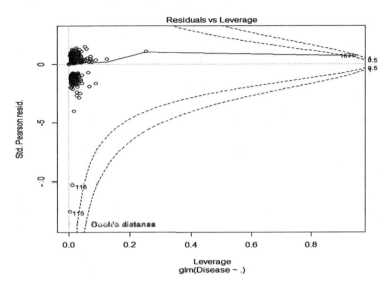

Figure 15. Residuals against fitted values

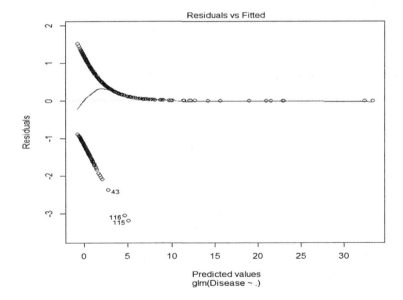

Figure 16. Lasso logistic regression regularization plots of liver disease dataset

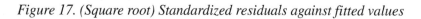

Diabetes Diagnostic Plots Using Logistic Regression

Figure 17. (Square root) Standardized residuals against fitted values

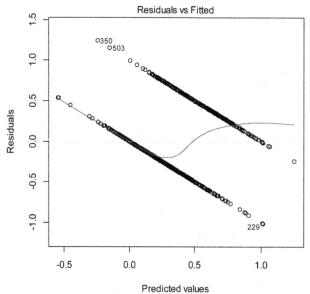

Figure 18. Normal QQ Plot

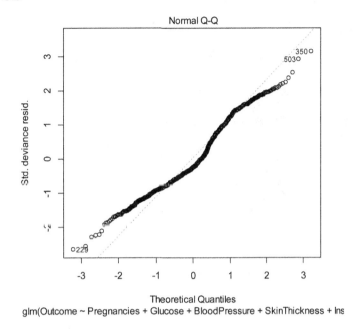

Figure 19. Standardized residuals against fitted values

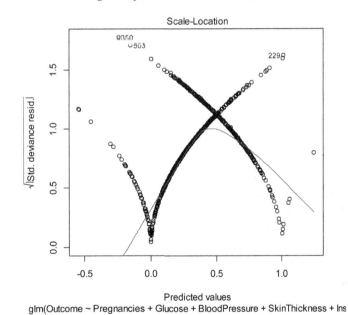

Figure 20. Residuals against leverage values

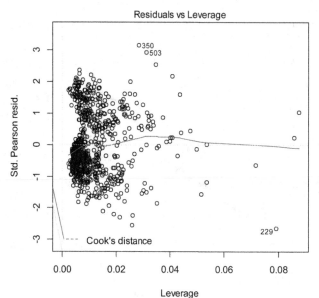

> summary(model)

Call:
   glm(formula = Outcome ~ Pregnancies + Glucose + BloodPressure +
   SkinThickness + Insulin + BMI + DiabetesPedigreeFunction +
   Age, data = diabetes1)
Deviance Residuals:
Min 1Q Median 3Q Max
-1.01348 -0.29513 -0.09541 0.32112 1.24160
Coefficients:
Estimate Std. Error t value Pr(>|t|)
(Intercept) -0.8538943 0.0854850 -9.989 < 2e-16 ***
Pregnancies 0.0205919 0.0051300 4.014 6.56e-05 ***
Glucose 0.0059203 0.0005151 11.493 < 2e-16 ***
BloodPressure -0.0023319 0.0008116 -2.873 0.00418 **
SkinThickness 0.0001545 0.0011122 0.139 0.88954
Insulin -0.0001805 0.0001498 -1.205 0.22857
BMI 0.0132440 0.0020878 6.344 3.85e-10 ***
DiabetesPedigreeFunction 0.1472374 0.0450539 3.268 0.00113 **
Age 0.0026214 0.0015486 1.693 0.09092 .

Signif. codes: 0 '***' 0.001 '**' 0.01 '*' 0.05 '.' 0.1 ' ' 1
(Dispersion parameter for gaussian family taken to be 0.1601684)
Null deviance: 174.48 on 767 degrees of freedom

Figure 21. Random forest results analysis diabetes diseases

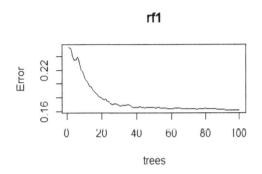

Figure 22. Features importance

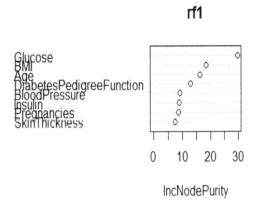

Figure 23. Random forest results analysis on hepatitis diseases

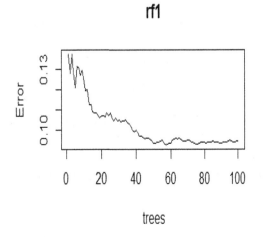

Figure 24. Feature importance on hepatitis diseases

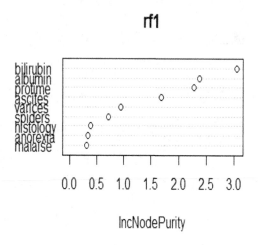

Figure 25. Random Forest Results Analysis on ILPD diseases

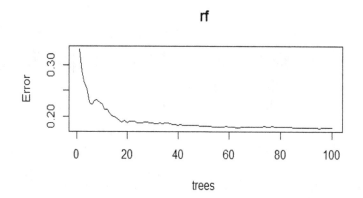

Residual deviance: 121.57 on 759 degrees of freedom

AIC: 783.82

Number of Fisher Scoring iterations: 2

From the above summary of a logistic regression model on diabetes data suggest that relationship between explanatory variable and outcome variable derived with statistically significant features i.e p value < 0.05.

Random Forest Results Analysis on Various diseases:

Random Forest is non linear ensemble classifier; we can apply on various clinical diseases identification and prediction. This algorithm used to reduce problem of over fitting. It consisting of a collection of decision trees, where each tree is constructed by applying an algorithm training dataset with an additional random vector sample.

The prediction of the random forest is obtained by a majority vote over predictions of the individual trees

Figure 26. Feature importance on ILPD diseases

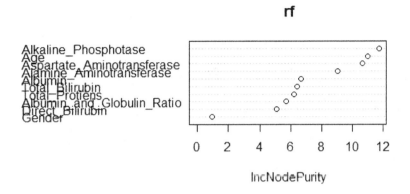

> print(rf1)

Call:
randomForest(formula = Outcome ~ Pregnancies + Glucose + BloodPressure + SkinThickness + Insulin + BMI + DiabetesPedigreeFunction + Age,
    data = traindata, ntree = 100, proximity = TRUE)
    Type of random forest: regression
    Number of trees: 100
    No. of variables tried at each split: 2
    Mean of squared residuals: 0.1623453
    % Var explained: 28.97
> importance(rf1)
IncNodePurity
Pregnancies 8.614510
Glucose 29.758906
BloodPressure 8.952774
SkinThickness 7.342818
Insulin 8.792742
BMI 18.346203
DiabetesPedigreeFunction 12.788080
Age 16.272872
Random Forest Results Analysis on Hepatitis diseases:

> print(rf1)

Call:
randomForest(formula = class ~ albumin + spiders + bilirubin + anorexia + ascites + histology + protime + varices + malaise, data = traindata, ntree = 100, proximity = TRUE)
    Type of random forest: regression
    Number of trees: 100
    No. of variables tried at each split: 3

Figure 27. Decision Tree on Heapatitis

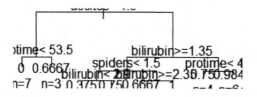

Mean of squared residuals: 0.09429558
% Var explained: 32.64

> importance(rf1)

IncNodePurity
albumin 2.3815297
spiders 0.7213968
bilirubin 3.0404879
anorexia 0.3358385
ascites 1.6913211
histology 0.3919137
protime 2.2766508
varices 0.9417305
malaise 0.3175823
Random Forest Results Analysis on ILPD diseases:

> cf1

Random Forest using Conditional Inference Trees
Number of trees: 50
Response: Disease
Inputs: Age, Dir_Bil, Alamine, Tot_Prot, Albumin
Number of observations: 583
Decision tree construction results on hepatitis:
Tree based Classifiers used to classify the data. The outcome observed at leaf level. But selecting the best Attribute as root node based on the information gain and Entropy.
Decision tree on the hepatitis dataset:
Decision tree build on the training data subset with statistically strong features. We build decision tree with minimum prediction error.

> myformula<-class~albumin+spiders+bilirubin+anorexia+ascites+histology+protime+varices+m
  alaise

train a decision tree

Figure 28. Selected decision tree with minimum prediction error

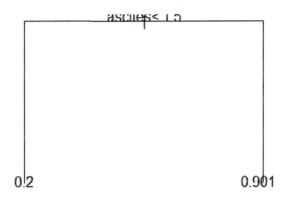

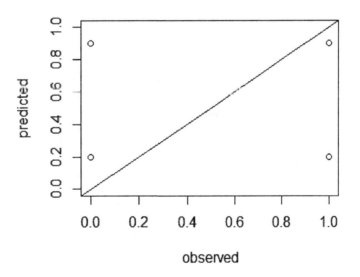

> heparpart<- rpart(myformula,data=traindata,control = rpart.control(minsplit = 10))
> attributes(heparpart)

    $names

[1] "frame" "where" "call"
[4] "terms" "cptable" "method"
[7] "parms" "control" "functions"

Figure 29. Decision tree on liver data

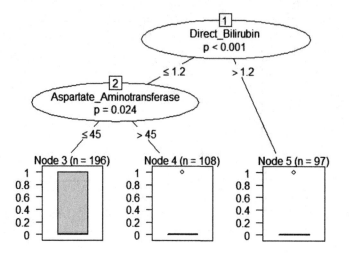

Figure 30. Decision tree (simple style)

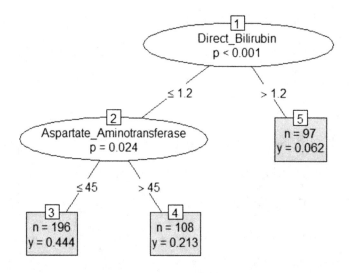

[10] "numresp" "splits" "variable.importance"
[13] "y" "ordered"

    $xlevels
    named list()
    $class

[1] "rpart"
> heparpart$variable.importance

Figure 31.

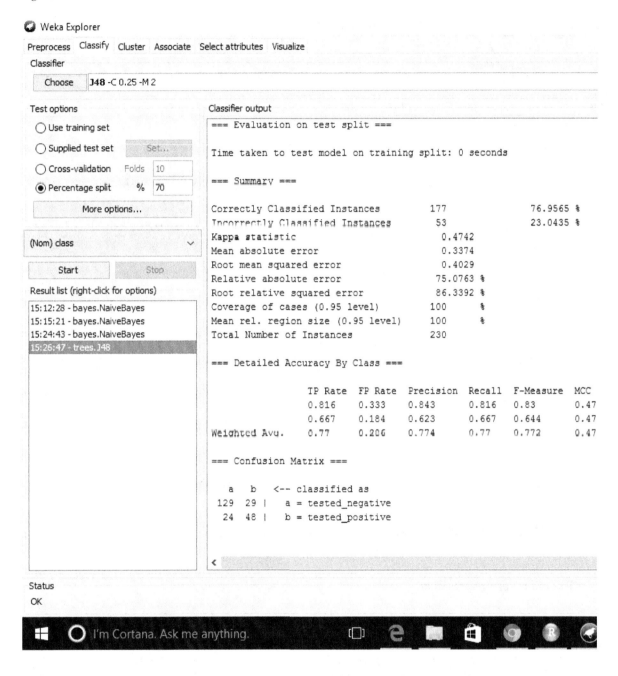

ascites protime bilirubin albumin spiders varices anorexia
4.42872375 2.58172136 2.53407673 1.48009281 0.96047431 0.66895224 0.26194754
malaise histology
0.26194754 0.08080808

> print(heparpart$cptable)

Table 4. Classification Confusion Matrix on diabetes dataset decision tree classifier

Classification Confusion Matrix		
	Predicted Class	
Actual Class	1	0
1	129	29
0	24	48

Figure 32.

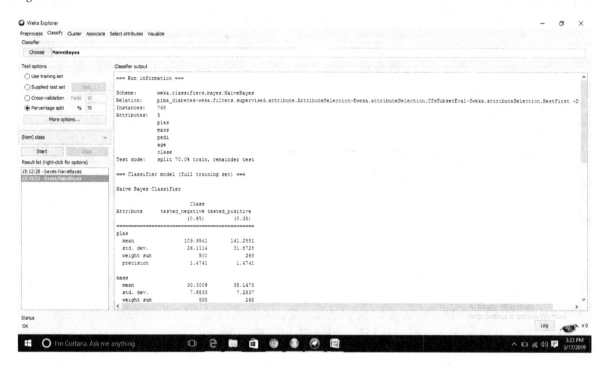

CP nsplit rel error xerror xstd

1 0.31323606 0 1.0000000 1.0197193 0.1797804
2 0.09188655 1 0.6867639 0.8212187 0.1881076
3 0.06793271 2 0.5948774 0.8589004 0.1919099
4 0.06601307 3 0.5269447 0.9158308 0.2026604
5 0.02652311 4 0.4609316 0.9119797 0.2081156
6 0.01714625 5 0.4344085 0.9118665 0.2062632
7 0.01462671 6 0.4172622 0.9263962 0.2053453
8 0.01000000 7 0.4026355 0.9393800 0.2074564

Decision tree construction results on Indian Liver patient dataset:

Figure 33.

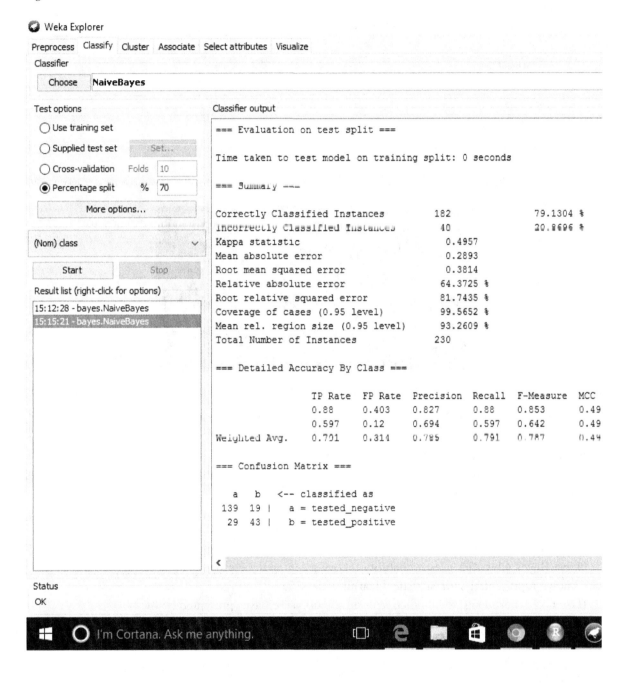

Before Modeling, the ILPD data into 70:30 Splitting criterion. Decision Tree construction on 70% tainting data and validate on 30% test data

Table 5. Classification Confusion Matrix on diabetes dataset with naïve Bayes classifier

Classification Confusion Matrix		
	Predicted Class	
Actual Class	**1**	**0**
1	139	19
0	29	43

Figure 34. Naïve Bayes classifier results on ILPD data

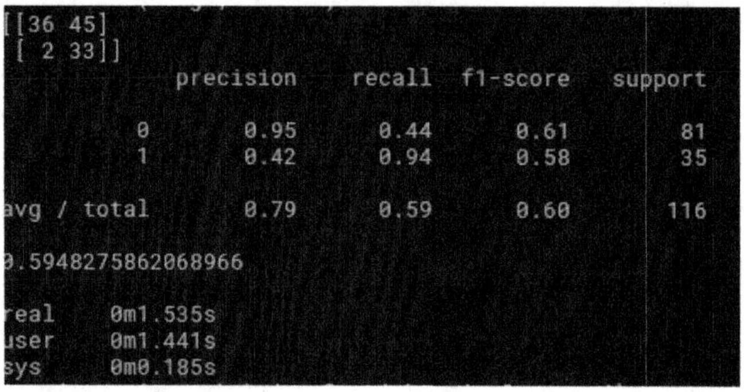

```
[[36 45]
 [ 2 33]]
              precision    recall  f1-score   support

           0       0.95      0.44      0.61        81
           1       0.42      0.94      0.58        35

avg / total       0.79      0.59      0.60       116

0.5948275862068966

real    0m1.535s
user    0m1.441s
sys     0m0.185s
```

Probabilities of Each Instances Falling Into Two Classes

Decision tree construction results on Diabetes data:

We will get correctly classified instances are 177 with 76.9565% and incorrectly classified instances are 53 with 23.0435% Accuracy.

Overall error rate = (29+24)/230 = 0.2304*100 = 23.04

Accuracy= 1-error = 1- (129+48) = 0.77*100 = 77.00

Naïve Bayes Classifier construction results on Diabetes data:

Naive Bayes Classifier uses probability theory as an approach to concept classification. It is most well known representation of Statistical learning classifier.

Based on experiments, the predictive accuracy of Naïve bayes presented below.

We will get correctly classified instances with 65.00% as tested negative instances and incorrectly classified instances with 35.00% Accuracy as tested positive with statistically significant variables such as plas, mass, pedi and age features.

Overall error rate = (29+19)/230 = 0.2086*100 = 20.86

Accuracy= 1-error = 1- (139+43) = 0.7913*100 = 79.13

Naïve Bayes Classifier construction results on ILPD data:

While Naive Bayes performed well with the highest mean sensitivity of 0.9594 and some folds reached a high sensitivity of 1. Naive Bayes fared with a mean specificity of 0.3962 which has the least specificity and also the accuracy of naive Bayes is the least among all with a mean accuracy of 0.5559

In this study we used three types of performance evaluation measures namely Sensitivity, Specificity and Accuracy.

1) **Sensitivity:** Sensitivity is a measure of the ability of a prediction model to select instances of a certain class from a data set. It is commonly called as Recall, and corresponds to the true positive rate. Sensitivity is the probability that a test result will be positive when the disease is present in the body.

   True Positive/True Positive + False Negative
   where
   TruePositive = numbers of true positive predictions for the considered class
   FalseNegative = numbers of false negative predictions for the considered class
   (TruePositive + FalseNegative)= total number of test examples of the considered class

2) **Specificity:** Recall/sensitivity is related to specificity, which is a measure that is commonly used in two class problems where one is more interested in a particular class. Specificity corresponds to the true-negative rate.

   Specificity is the probability that a test result will be negative when the disease is not present in the body.
   True Negative/True Negative + False Positive
   Where
   TrueNegative = numbers of true negative predictions for the considered class
   FalsePositive – numbers of false positive predictions for the considered class
   (TrueNegative + FalsePositive)= total number of test examples of the considered class

3) **Accuracy:** Accuracy is the overall probability that a patient will be accurately classified.

$$T P + T N /(T P + T N + F P + F N)$$

   Where

   TP = TruePositive=numbers of true positive predictions for the considered class;
   TN = TrueNegative=numbers of true negative predictions for the considered class;
   FP = FalsePositive=numbers of false positive predictions for the considered class;
   FN = FalseNegative=numbers of true negative predictions for the considered class;
   (TP + TN + FP + FN) = total number of test examples of the considered class

   Interestingly, naive Bayes has got the highest sensitivity among all other models with a mean sensitivity.
   Step 6: Communicate your results
   In this section, the results are analyzed how predictive modeling is influenced when using Logistic Regression, naïve Bayes, Random Forest, Decision Tree, Multilayer perceptron. This work is implemented in R tool, Anaconda and Weka Tool.

Hypothesis One:

This work leverages the initial discoveries made through Data exploration, statistical analysis of data, led to identifying the statistically significant attributes, mapping significant attributes to the response and build classification techniques to predict the outcome and demystify clinical diseases.

These results communicates that Random Forests, Logistic Regression, Naïve Bayes, Decision Tree consistently outperform across Hepatitis, Diabetes and Liver disease analysis and prediction.

Hypothesis Two:

In Future we go through different Cohorts take into consideration and perform different ensembles, Deep Models and Interpretable Models with strong significant variables and meet help for disease diagnosis and prediction.

SOLUTIONS AND RECOMMENDATIONS

Future Research Directions

In future people with diabetes have increased high risk of developing serious health problems. Consistently high blood glucose levels can lead to heart and blood vessels, eyes, kidneys, nerves and teeth.

In addition, people with diabetes also have a higher risk of developing infections.

In almost all income countries, diabetes is a leading cause of cardiovascular disease, blindness (diabetic Retinopathy), kidney failure, and lower limb amputation.

In Future we go through different Patient Cohorts and Electronic Health Records take into consideration and perform different ensembles, Deep Models and Interpretable Models and propagated through diseases progression markers initiatives and also help for disease diagnosis and predictions in healthcare Domain.

CONCLUSION

In this chapter we merely reporting that Data Acquisition, Data exploration, Statistical analysis of the data, Correlation analysis between data features and outcome variable, feature selection, mapping those e statistically significant features with outcome variables and build machine learning models to demystify clinical diseases. Machine learning classifiers Random Forests, Logistic Regression, Naïve Bayes, Decision Tree consistently outperform disease diagnosis and prediction.

REFERENCES

Alzubi, J., Nayyar, A., & Kumar, A. (2018). Machine learning from theory to algorithms: an overview. *Journal of Physics: Conference*. Retrieved from iopscience.iop.org

Jin, Kim, & Kim. (2014). Decision factors on effective liver patient data prediction. *International Journal of Bio Science and Bio-Technology, 6*(4), 167-178. doi:10.14257/ijbsbt.2014.6.4.16

Sisodia, D., & Sisodia, D. S. (2018). Prediction of Diabetes using Classification Algorithms. *Procedia Computer Science, 132*, 1578–1585. doi:10.1016/j.procs.2018.05.122

APPENDIX

Figure 35.

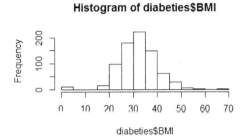 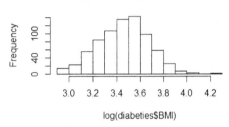

Figure 36.

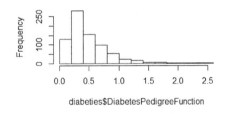 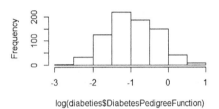

Figure 37.

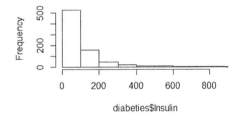 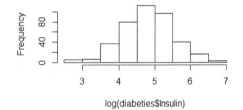

Figure 38.

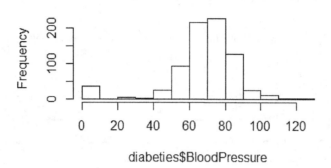

Figure 39.

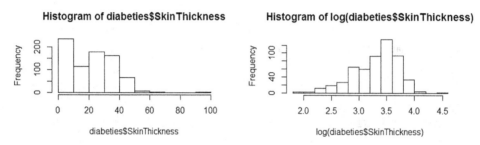

Histogram Plots of Diabetes Disease and Log Transformations

Figure 40.

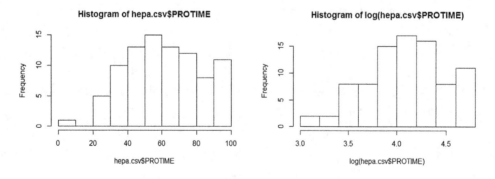

Figure 41.

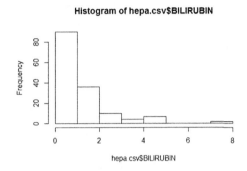

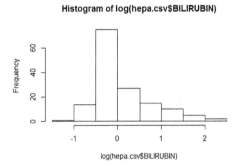

Figure 42.

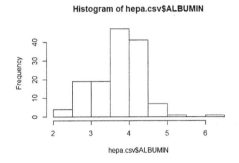

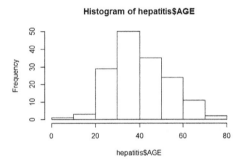

Figure 43.

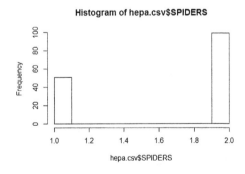

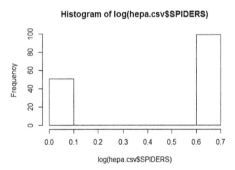

Histograms of Hepatitis Disease With and Without Log Transformations

Figure 44.

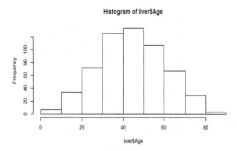 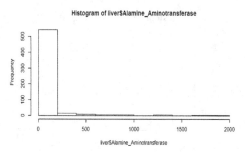

Figure 45.

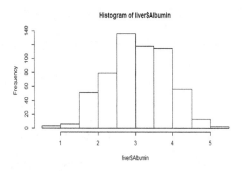 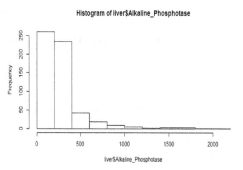

Figure 46.

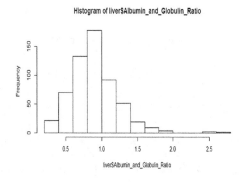 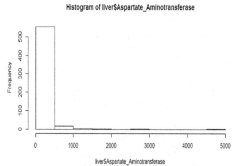

Figure 47.

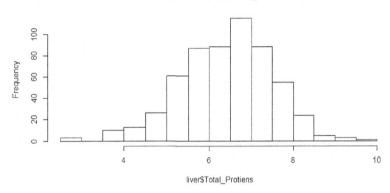

Figure 48.

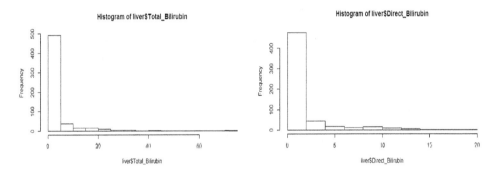

Histogram Plots of ILPD Disease and Log Transformations

Figure 49.

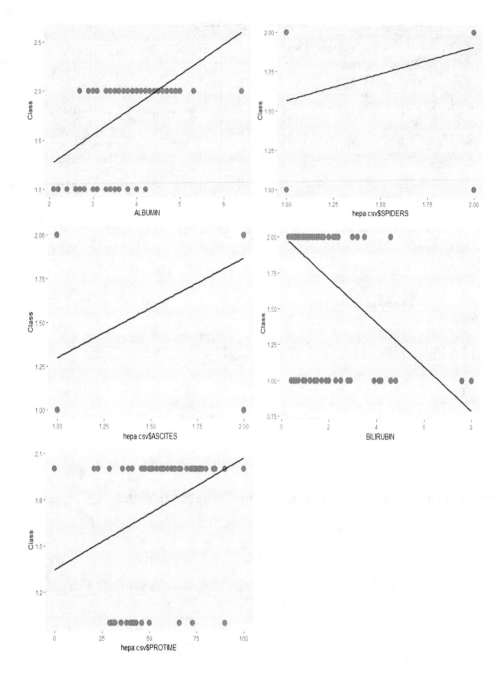

Figure 50.

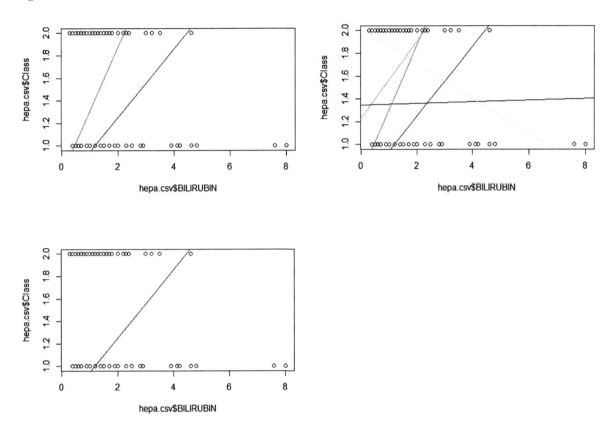

Scatter Plots of Hepatitis Dataset Input Variable and Output Variable

Figure 51.

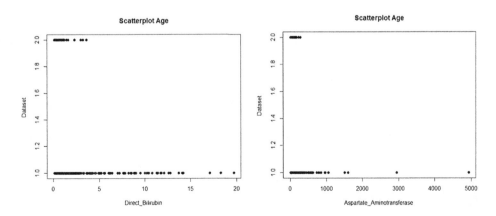

Figure 52.

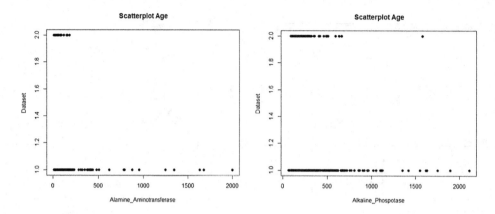

Figure 53.

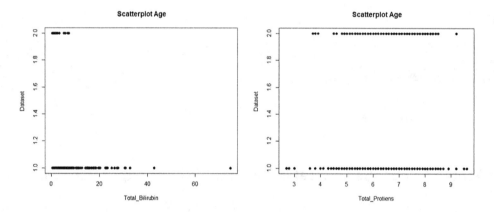

Figure 54.

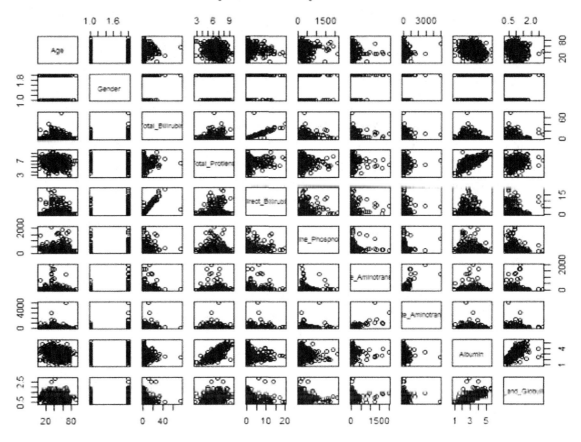

Figure 55.

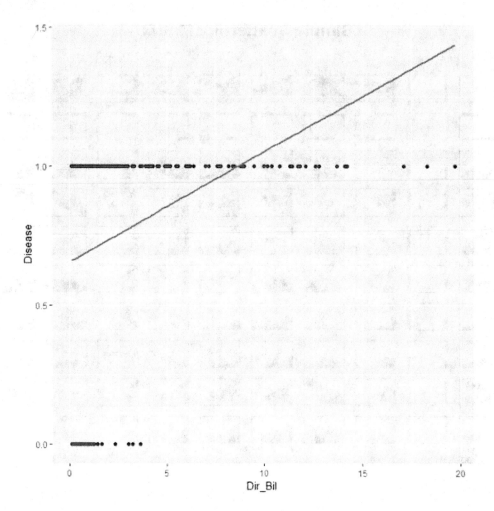

Figure 56.

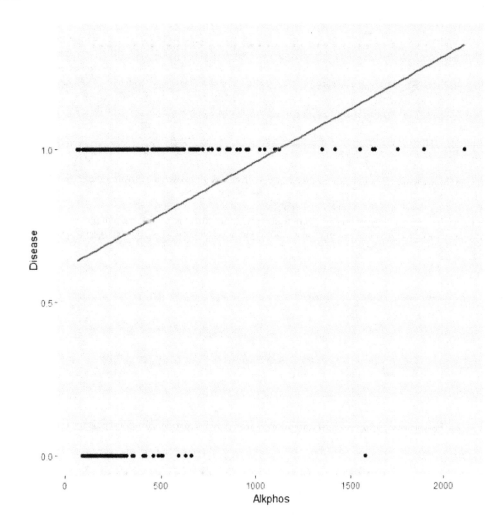

Figure 57.

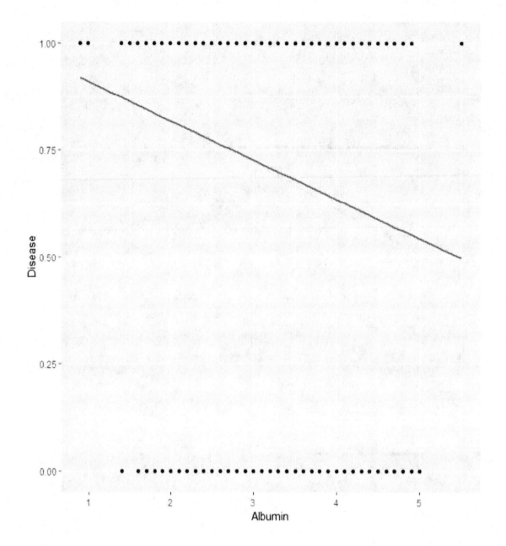

Figure 58.

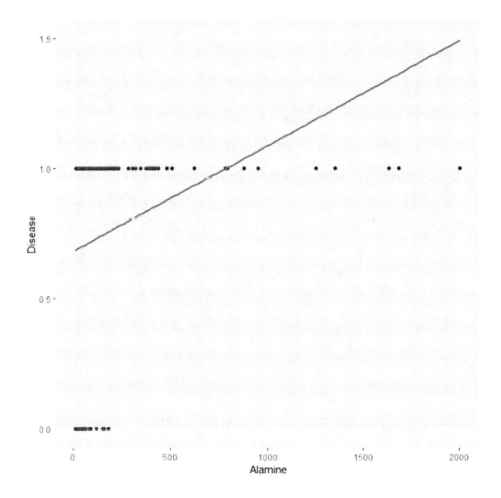

Figure 59.

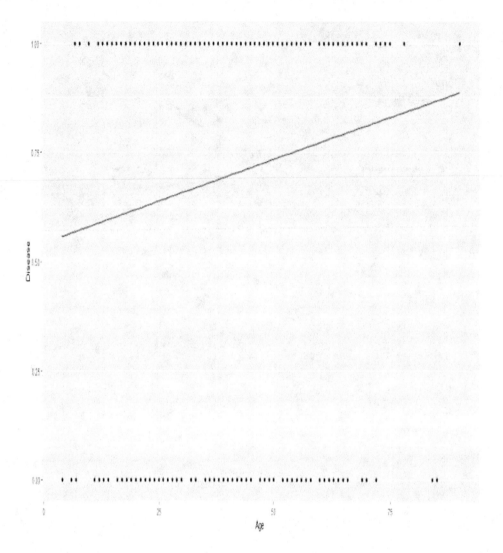

Figure 60.

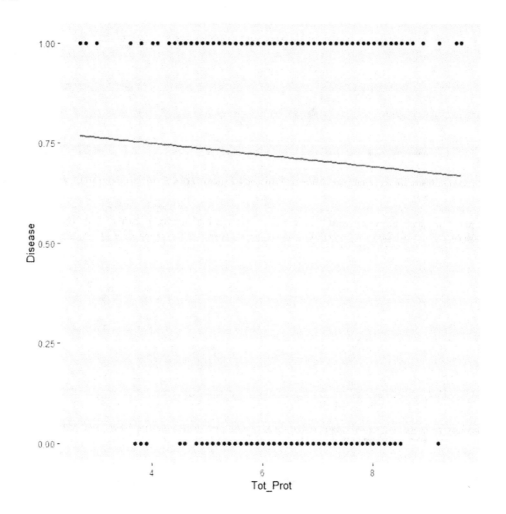

Scatter Plots of ILPD Dataset Explanatory Variable and Outcome Variable

Figure 61.

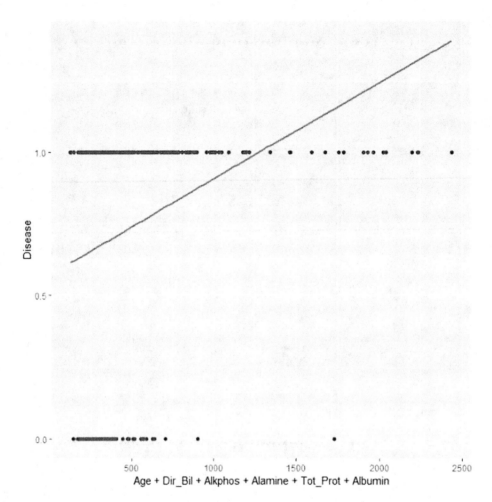

**Scatter Plots of Diabetes Dataset all Explanatory
Variable with Outcome Variable**

Figure 62.

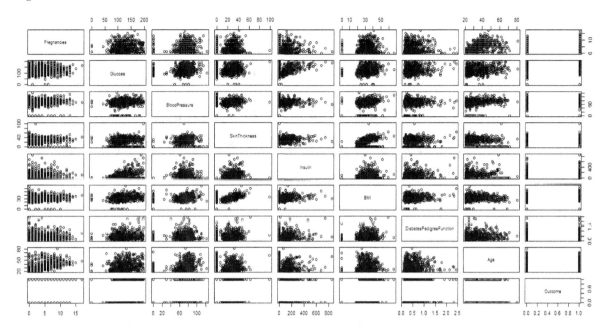

Chapter 12
Evolution of Data Analytics in Healthcare

P. Victer Paul
Indian Institute of Information Technology, Kottayam, India

Harika Krishna
Vignan's Foundation for Science, Technology, and Research, India

Jayakumar L.
Vel Tech Rangarajan Dr. Sagunthala R&D Institute of Science and Technology, India

ABSTRACT

In recent years, a huge volume of data has been generated by the sensors, social media, and other sources. Researchers proposed various data analytics models for handling these data and to extract insight that can improve the business of various domains. Data analytics in healthcare (DAiHC) is recent and attracted many researchers due to its importance in improving the value of people's lives. In this perspective, the chapter focuses on the various recent models proposed in DAiHC and dissects the works based on various vital parameters. As an initial part, the work provides comprehensive information on DAiHC and its various application illustrations. Moreover, the study presented in the work categorizes the literature on DAiHC based on factors like algorithms used, application dataset utilized, insight type, and tools used for evaluation of the work. This survey will be helpful for novice to expert researchers who works in DAiHC, and various challenges in DAiHC are also discussed which may help in defining new problems associated with the domain.

INTRODUCTION

Data analytics are a process of acquiring both subjective, quantifiable models and procedures that can be utilized to improve the business and productivity. Data sets are examined to analyze observable data and patterns in order to produce outcomes as per the organizational needs (DAD, 2019). Data analytics are mainly concentrating and providing solutions for the specific applications like public sector services,

DOI: 10.4018/978-1-5225-9643-1.ch012

Figure 1. Process flow of data analytics

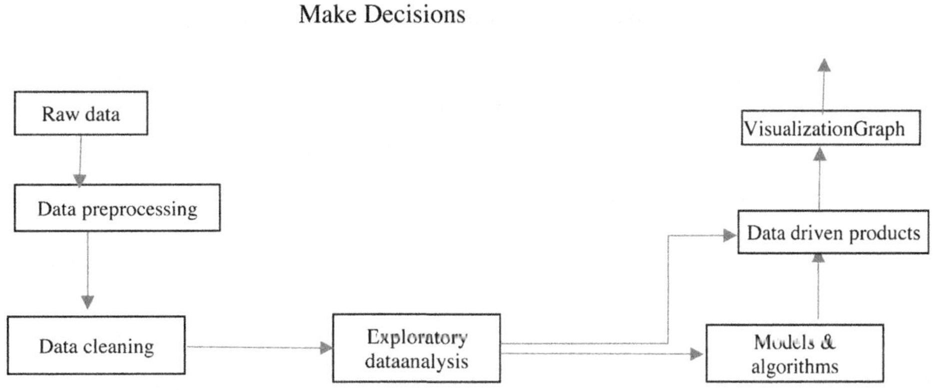

healthcare, social networking and education (DAA, 2019). Recent studies anticipated that enterprise server in the world are processing extensive amount of data in the year 2008 (Kambatla, Kollias, Kumar, & Grama, 2014). Our current output of data is approximately 2.5 quintillion bytes of data per day. Almost over 90% of the data has been produced in the world over the last two years (DAR, 2019). Due to advent of Internet of Things (IoT) and ever increasing number of embedded devices, we can estimate that by every two years the data are getting doubled and in coming years the data is going to be unstable. Most of the large volume of the data is generated from health care providers, retail and enterprise.

Analytics is to use the data and find advantageous patterns to make better decisions and it is one of the BI (business intelligence) techniques to improve the organizational gain. Data analytics are the best way for business people grab the customers 'attention and to get success in business without facing more stress (DAP, 2019). Data analytics models can enhance the businesses by increasing the profits and also operational efficiency. (DAI, 2019). Analytics mainly focused on two vital issues such as the forward motion of the data and value. Currently, data analytics are playing a major role in many organizations by giving useful insights and valid decisions based on their necessities. It is an emerging technique in a recent survey and used as a tool in any industry where data is collected and accessed.

Many more organizations are using data analytics to give qualitative patterns. This data can be used in various circumstances as improving the quality of the organizations, identifying fraud from insights on online and digital information, and improving customer service (AP, 2019). Fig.1 shows the data analytics process, where the knowledge discovery in databases (KDD) is with more clarity. Fayyad and his team members explained the KDD process by performing some operations in which raw data, preprocessing, data cleaning, Exploratory data analysis, models & algorithms, data-driven process, Visualization Graph, decision making (BD,2019). Raw data refer to the primary unstructured data that has been collected based on the use and purpose of the application. Raw data are also known as the source data. The data whatever we collected is unprocessed until it comes in one order. The data coming in one of the manners then only it is easy from the designers. Each of the preprocessing operations performs different tasks in the raw data. It is a method used to eliminate noise from the collected data what we have. We are collecting data from the different locations than it is not realistic to perform analytics (DAI, 2019), (ML, 2019).

Figure 2. Data analytics methods and algorithms

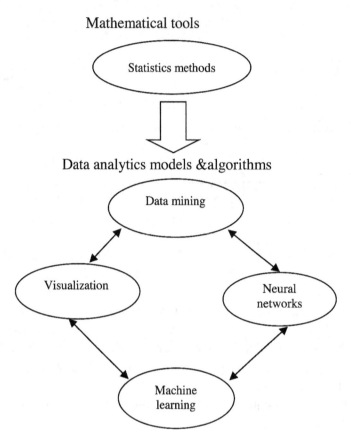

As a starting point, data will be refined by removal of extra and unusable noise & other data, in order to improve processing speed. The primary data analysis was developed by John Turkey to support Statisticians to analyze data and this is a new method of data collection. Analytics may perform various techniques to explore the data and explain the meaning in the data (PE, 2019). Many of the exploratory data analysis (EDA) techniques are represented graphically with some of the quantifiable techniques. By taking the EDA model as the reference only the Data Scientist can verify that may take action on the problem algorithm (Net, 2019). Fig: 2 explains the Data analytics mechanisms and algorithms are categorized into several types that are Statistics, Data mining, machine learning, and visualization methods.

Statistics is the branch of the science that is used to collect the data; organize and display of summarized data. The data analyst segregates a data set (ST, 2019). Descriptive-statistics explains how to view the huge volume of observations. Based on the observations, the user will get a view of the dataset. Descriptive-statistics are useful to review the collection of data using a amalgamation of tabulated depiction, graphical and discussion of the results. There are three popular central tendency methods, mean, median & mode. These are the types of data distribution methods like normal and corresponding standard deviations. Inferential statistics involve drawing the right conclusions that have been coming from one of the studies related to general populations. Inferential statistics will give answers to the population related questions and it is also not done testing on the given experiment.

- **Data Mining**: This includes several methods that are applied to observe useful insights (trends) from data. Data mining has an association rule learning, classification, regression, and clustering analysis. Inferential statistics involve drawing the right conclusions from studies related to general populations. Inferential statistics will provide answers to population-related questions.
- **Machine Learning (ML)**: ML are the prominent field of domain the Artificial Intelligence Techniques that are used to construct an algorithm that will use computers to know behavior based on given data. There are some of the frameworks in ML-like map/reduce, Dryad LINQ and SVM (support vector machine).
- **Neural Network:** The Neural network is useful in many circumstances. Some of the Real-world applications include its techniques such as pattern recognition, image analysis and others.
- **Visualization** makes it easier to understand complex ideas. It is displayed statically through the usage of specific techniques. We can visually see this by creating tables; images and other displayed methods understand data. At present, there are lots of tools available for visualization, making manual graphs and charts obsolete. Visualization of data is in the form the maps, graphs, spreadsheets, and also charts like pie, bar, line and Cartesian graphs (DAD2, 2019).

Data-Driven Products

In order to get the result of raw data, we are using a data-driven process. From the raw data, we have gained useful insights, which lead to better decisions. In business, the data-driven process plays a major role. In any company, this is done based on the data analysis. This approach will help to improve the customers' experience, according to the trends. With the help of the data-driven process, we have the many advantages that are enhancing the point of sale and we can also predict the faults occurring in the business.

At present, the term "Data analytics" has become more popular in business, education, health studies, retail, and many other fields. Data analytics are a technique to explore the large data set for identifying the recent trends in the business and improve the profits of the business (Russo, 2015). Applications of the data analytics are as follows.

Education

Education sector is one of the most used applications for data analytics.Educational institutions hold a very large amount of data associated to students, faculty, and others (EDU2, 2019). Academic analytics will help to improve the resources and workflow of the educational institute by using the academic data (EDU, 2019). At present, in the educationalSystem students' marks, students' behavior and details about students are processing statically. Because of this, analyzing the individual student's performance and improving the quality of education became easy. By performing analytics, we can improve the appropriate learning of the students (EDU3, 2019). However, we perform analytics on the education data it will give the detail about the insight like improving thePerformance of the students, developing the education process flow, and to upgrade the administration process.

Healthcare

Healthcare analytics is a phrase used to explain health care activities.In the health sector, analytics can be performed by data collected from the ElectronicMedical records (EHR), clinical data, imaging data, and pharmaceutical data. DA will Focus on insights into hospital management, diagnosis of the patient's, medical records, and charges of the patients. Based on the data in healthcare, we can perform Analytics like patients who are frequently visiting the hospital (profile analytics), mostly for which disease they are consulting the doctor. We can find the disease outbreak based on the previous data. In the real world, the main reason behind the analytics in healthcare is to improve the value of the healthcare reduces the noise generating from the electronic health records (EHR), and improve the evidence-based healthcare (DAH,2019).

Retail

Data analytics in retail industry takes a vital role in society. The startingpoint of performing analytics is to calculate the store performance based on the data from the store (Fan, & Bifet, 2013). DA in the retail industry will identify the patterns and give the best decision (RET, 2019). Retail analytics are mainly focusing on some areas like customer insights, sales, and brand assessment, inventory or stock of the goods and materials. Cost reduction will improve business gains and profits. It is easy to identify insights and improve the business gains due to performing the data analytics.

Social Network

In recent trends, social networks have become one of the mostexplosive businesses. To perform Social networking analytics data is collected from different social networking websites and that are analyzed by using social networking tools to make the decision. The common social-networking pages like Facebook, LinkedIn and Twitter (Aggarwal, 2011) are the tools for improving communication, sharing and discussing information between thousands of people. Analytics will give information about the total number of users using the network and to know the competitors and this knowledge will help you to give the best ideas (SMA, 2019).

E-commerce

Electronic commerce plays an important role in data analytics in recent years (ECOM, 2019). E-commerce is used to do the transactions through online by selling goods or services. Some of the e-commerce sites are Amazon, eBay or Netflix, LinkedIn. E-commerce analytics give better decisions and business gains. Analytics will focus on increasing customers, improving price model, improving organizations, and activities (supply chain management), maintain the customer care services (BD2,2019)

The remaining sections of the chapter has been organized as follows: Section 2 defines about significances of data analytics in health care. Section 3 comprehensively narrates recent study on data analytics in healthcare in terms of the various categories of discussion. Section 4 and 5 consists of the discussion on the study and the conclusion of the chapter respectively.

DATA ANALYTICS IN HEALTHCARE

Healthcare analytics are spreading throughout the United States (US), it may expect to cross more than $18.7 billion by 2020 (HC, 2019). When compared to the last ten years at present most of the data is in the form of the digital across the healthcare industries (Mehta, & Pandit, 2018).In health care, digital data are stored as Electronic Health Records (EHR). EHR is consists of the patient details, lab data, imaging data and data that are collected from the smart devices. The volume of health-related data is growing high (Kakkanatt, Benigno, Jackson, Huang, & Ng, 2018). Healthcare organizations are looking to maintain the data easily and perform analytics on that data to improve patient's needs and physician's needs. Some of the important gains by performing analytics on health care are the following (BD2, 2019).

- Enhance the quality of the healthcare
- Maintain the evidence based medicine
- Easy to find outbreak of the diseases
- Improve the satisfaction of the patients
- Reduced the cost of the health care
- To reduce the fraud detection in health care

Needs for Data Analytics in Healthcare

Identifying and assessing health care needs is not an easy task. It is very difficult to identify the needs of health care. In the healthcare industry, the process is physician has to listen to patients and give the treatment based on their experience and patient's needs. It is the one process to identify the people who are suffering from the UN health by that the needs of the health care can improve (Wright, Williams, & Wilkinson, 1998) manual process follows like this. One of the major of the data analytics is to enhance the needs in the healthcare.

- To identify the patterns of the diseases in the population.
- How to use the resources effectively and give the quality care to the patients.
- Give the care to people need identify diseases patterns based on the areas, district, stated and countries.
- To no disease outbreak based on the climatic conditions.
- Prediction of the diseases.

These are the some of the basic needs of the health care in the data analytics. By this DA in healthcare there is a benefit to both the health professionals and patients.

Importance of Data Analytics in Healthcare

Healthcare is one of the most data generated sector due to all most all the data as digital EHR (Kakkanatt, Benigno, Jackson, Huang, & Ng, 2018). In healthcare the data collected from the EHR, imaging data, pharmaceutical data, and laboratory data. A report estimating that in the year 2012, the healthcare industry generated more than the 500 pet bytes of the data and after introducing the act. Affordable health care is providing the quality of the healthcare to the patients and reduce the cost to the patients based on their admission to the hospitals.

Healthcare analytics will provide the most efficient services to patients (IHC, 2019). Analytics in health care will maintain the health records of the patients perform the analytics on the records, predict the diseases and give valuable insights that will improve the care of the health care. Healthcare analytics collect and integrate data from different healthcare and perform analytics on that data, and then we can predicate more diseases, it will help the patients and improve their life expectations by giving treatment at the most necessary time.

Health Care Analytics Process Flow: fig. 3 describes how the process flow is going in to healthcare. What are the layers present in the process flow and working on each.

At present in healthcare, often the data are backed in the digital format collected from the different sources like the electronic health record (EHR), lab data, imaging data like (MRI), genomic data, pharmaceutical data, and hospital management data. Like that huge volume and variety of data is generated from the health care. The process flow explains the method of processing the huge volume of data, and at which layer data analytics is performing is explained in the process flow (Ojha, & Mathur, 2016).

As show in the fig: 3 is the process flow of the healthcare it consist of the four layers that are:

Data Connection Layer: In data connection layer at first raw data is gathered fromdifferent sources or places like electronic health records (EHR), hospital information system (HIS), and laboratory information system (LIS). The main problem is managing the large quantity of data collected from various sources. The raw data goes through data sensing, data integration, and data extraction in this layer.

- Data sensing- sensors are fixed on the bodies, that sensors sense the heart beats, blood pressures, and other the sensors can detect the condition of the patients if the condition is not in the correct way then it will give signal to physicians (HP,2019).
- Data integration- Integrating different types of structure & Unstructured data like the sensor data, imaging data, data collected from the HIS, LIS and EHR data. During the data integration, redundant, duplicate data might occur. The performance metric is measured in this layer.
- Data extraction- Extracts the patterns from the integrated data with valuable insights like patients suffering from the same diseases, date of admission, selecting the patients suffering from the same diseases.

Data Storage And Management Layer

This layer will help to store the enormous amount of the heterogeneous data produced from the healthcare. This layer is implemented by using the Google data store, NOSQL, and AMAZON RDS.

Figure 3. Healthcare analytics process flow

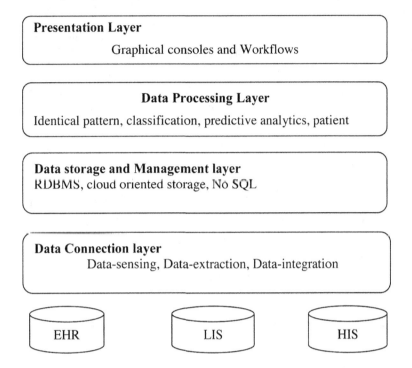

Big Data Processing Layer

At this layer, processing of data which are integrated and stored in the hospital data and EHR. Analytics will be performed by observing the patterns and find out the useful & amp; helpful insights which are helpful to both the patients as well as the doctors. Healthcare analytics will focus on understanding information about the diseases which the patients are consulting a doctor for, we can find disease outbreak based on the previous data.

Presentation Layer

This layer will use tools to display the data in the form of thestatistics. It will display the data by using the dashboards. Dashboards will display the data in an easy way to understand the insights in the healthcare. It is helpful to the physicians to recognize the patterns and also improve the quality of the health care.

Applications

In healthcare analytics, there are several applications that are used to analyze the needs, services, and also help to identify the patterns. Some of the applications of health care are patient profile analytics, the social network for patients, Evidence based medicine, genomic prediction, and epidemiological studies.

Patient-Profile Analysis

Data analytics in a patient profile application will identify the patient details like the name, age, date of admission into the hospital, and diagnosis details (Ward, Marsolo, & Froehle, 2014). On that detail, we, have to perform analytics and predict the insights give benefits to the patients and hospitals. Analytics will provide data about people who are suffering from the same diseases, the number of times that specific patients admitted to the hospitals based on that we can reduce the cost of the patients. Dashboards and control charts are used for visualization (DD, 2019).

Social Network For Patients

(PLM, 2019) patientslikeme.com, The Social network for patients is one of the trending applications in recent years. An example of the social network based is patient's analytics are patients like me. It was started in the year 2006, and data of the patients were shared online and connected and share the details about the disease like medicines, diagnosis, and medical test details. At present, it consists of 17,800 patient details and the details about the 1500 diseases. By looking at the data of the patients, we can identify the patterns and give valuable insights.

Evidence Based Medicine

Evidence-based medicine will give better decision making to the physicians. It will give the optimized and evidence-based medicine in the healthcare. In evidence-based medicine, data is collected for the electronic health record (EHR) it will take less time for the diagnosis of the patients (Chitra & Vijaya 2016) and Clinical Decision Support System (CDSS) is used to enhance the value of the healthcare and improving the efficiency of the diagnosis.

Genomic Analytics

Health care will give the best solutions to the patients by taking evidence as the genomic data. Example identifies the genetic differences in patient and predicates the types of diabetes and controls the diabetic levels in the patients then it will help the patients without affecting the disease (GA, 2019). Genomic analytics will also reduce the cost (GA2, 2019).

Epidemiological Studies

Epidemiology describes the people who belong to a particular area, age group, or gender and this is why this type of study will be known as an epidemiological study. It will specify how a disease will occur based on the people, place & time (Williams, & Wright, 1998). People - People who are suffering from the disease are part of a particular sex, age grouped. Place - People who are living in the same area, state, or country are afflicted with the same disease. Time - people get the disease during a specific season.

Figure 4. Needs of study in Data Analytics

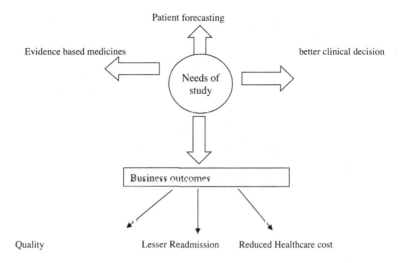

RECENT STUDY ON DATA ANALYTICS IN HEALTHCARE

Need of the Study

At present in society, health care data analytics are placing the major role. Healthcare is in general, most of the data generated unit. In recent trends data generating is fast and most of the data become digitalized in health care. In healthcare, data are stored as the EHR as mentioned in the previous section. Many of the healthcare systems are performing analytics on their health data to know the insights in their health care. There is the huge volume of the data in the healthcare to filter the valuable insights from the noise and redundant data by the some phase's data collecting, data integrating, and data extracting (DAA,2019), (PLM,2019). By this data analytics health care will give efficient outcomes as given at Fig.4.

Data analytics give outcomes, managing and analyzing the data across the different EHR in the healthcare, hospital information system (HIS), laboratory information system (LIS).using analytics we can predicate the diseases. The Main reason to perform analytics in the healthcare is to find the patterns in the patient's details and financial issues in the health care. In recent studies for researches need data based on their research purpose like the all age groups, gender, and people suffering with particular diseases (NSHC, 2019).

Why Should I Need?

- To enhance the models to maintain the value of the healthcare.
- To help at the evaluation of medications, tests, or programs that may not be available outside of research.
- To help to businesses gains.
- To improve the knowledge of the researchers and the scientist.

Table 1. Classification of the recent study in DA in HC

RE NO	Categories of study	Sub classes of the categories of the study	References
1.	Algorithms	Machine learning, Data mining	(Chitra & Vijaya, 2016), (Kakkanatt, Benigno, Jackson, Huang, & Ng, 2018), (Mehta, & Pandit,2018), (Khan, Idris, Ali, Ali, Hussain, Hussain, & Lee, 2015)
2.	Data Set	EHR, Hospitals	(Ojha, & Mathur, 2016), (Chitra & Vijaya 2016), (Ta, Liu, & Nkabinde, 2016),(Kakkanatt, Benigno, Jackson, Huang, & Ng, 2018)
3.	Insight	Descriptive, Predictive, Prescriptive, Diagnostic.	(Kakkanatt, Benigno, Jackson, Huang, & Ng, 2018), (Chitra & Vijaya 2016),(Khan, Idris, Ali, Ali, Hussain, Hussain, & Lee, 2015),(Ojha, & Mathur,2016)
4.	Tools	Structured Data, Unstructured Data, Big data tools, Natural language processing.	(Ojha, & Mathur,2016), (Rao, Suma, & Sunitha, 2015), (Khan, Idris, Ali, Ali, Hussain, Hussain, & Lee, 2015), (Kakkanatt, Benigno, Jackson, Huang, & Ng, 2018)

Categories of the Study

In section the categories of the study in data analytics in healthcare are classified into four types that are algorithms, data sets, insights and tools and subclasses of the categories of the study will be briefly explained in the following section.

Chitra (Chitra & Vijaya 2016) was identified that most of the recent study in DA in healthcare majorly using two types of algorithms like machine learning and data mining. This algorithm is effectively helpful in health care by using the data of the healthcare analytics. This can be done by identifying the faults in health care and improving the effective care and reducing the costs of the patients (Thamizhselvan, Raghuraman, Manoj, & Paul, 2015). In data mining, the algorithms are sub classified into clustering, classification, and association. Machine learning algorithms applied to the high; multidimensional data related to health care (ML, 2019).

Datasets for recent literature is sub classified into EHR & hospital system data. Data is collected from different sources in hospitals like EMR, patient diagnosis details, imaging data, medical data (Chitra & Vijaya 2016). EHR is the collection of the patient details like the name, age, disease type, and diagnosis details. Hospital data are the same as the electronic health record data, but the researcher is collecting data from the direct hospital and performing analytics on that data give valuable insights to health care. As explained in (Kakkanatt, Benigno, Jackson, Huang, & Ng, 2018) (Khan, Idris, Ali, Ali, Hussain, Hussain, & Lee, 2015) (Chitra & Vijaya 2016), gives that the analytics can be classified as vital four types as follows:

- Descriptive analytics - Descriptive analytics will explain the huge volume of data is collected from health care at different time intervals and give insights like what happens before one month and one year etc. For example, how many patients are suffering from the fever in the last month that is answered by the descriptive analytics (DA, 2019).
- Predictive analytics-Predictive analytics will give the solution to what is likely to happen. That is, it will predict what is happening in the future. From the healthcare data, it will find the patterns predicate the problem by this analytics. Example predicting the flu may be coming in the few months (PA, 2019).

Table 2. Classification of models in DA in HC based on the type of algorithm used

Type of Algorithm	Sub-classes of Algorithm Type	Description
Machine Learning Models	Decision trees, Bayesian classifiers, ANN and SVMs	Machine learning is an agglomerate technique to predict the patterns from dataset.
Data Mining Algorithms	Clustering, classification, sequential patterns, association.	Data mining is a collection of models to mine informative outlines from data

- Prescriptive analytics-It will tell about what action to take. It is a combination of both descriptive and predictive analytics. Example patients suffering from some of the diseases, the then doctor will prescribe some of the medicines.
- Diagnostic analytics- This method tells about why something happened. We are using the data mining techniques like the drill down. An example is the diagnoses of the patients and the prescribed medications what they are used for the treatment. Based on that information, we can answer why something is happening (TA, 2019).

Tools that are mainly used in the health data analytics are categorized into the four types. They are structured data, unstructured data, the big data, and NLP tools that are observed in the literature study. Structured tool like MY SQL is used to process the structured data. NO SQL is used to process unstructured data. It used to bridge the gap between the two different languages. Big data tools are used for the storing the large amount of the data and processing that data. Some of the big data tools are the Hadoop, pig, and hive. Natural Language processing will give right solutions to the insights in the health care from the unstructured data. NLP tools are used for the processing and analyzing the data and give the insights as the outcomes this is useful to health care. Today NLP is used in the clinical automated documentation.

Category 1

In this section, the study of recent works on DA in health care is discussed based on the type of algorithm used in the model. Among the various algorithms observed in the literature, the types of algorithms can be broadly classified into two as, Machine learning and Data mining. Table 2 shows the different types of algorithms used in DA in HC. These algorithms are briefly discussed in the following subsection

Machine Learning

ML is a subclass of AI domain which extract patterns from the data based on their behavior by using the methods or algorithms in the ML (Chen, & Zhang, 2014). There is a huge amount of unwanted data in the stored raw data, we have to process and analyze and do an action on the data sets. This is useful for the purpose of transforming the empirical data into the form of knowledge. It has been classified into three types first- improve the prognosis, second-work on the radiologists and anatomical pathologists. Third – improve diagnostic accuracy (Obermeyer,& Emanuel, 2016). The following section contains brief explanations about the subcategories of the machine learning methods and its applications in the recent study on data analytics in healthcare.

Table 3. Classification of models in DA in HC based on the types of machine learning algorithms used.

Methods	Application	References
Decision trees	Evidence Based Health Care System.	(Chitra & Vijaya 2016)
Artificial neural networks	GEMINI: An Integrative Healthcare Analytics System	(Mehta, & Pandit,2018)
Pattern recognition	Consensus of health care & bigdata analysis	(ANAL,2019)

The following is the section consists of brief explanations about the subcategories of the machine learning methods and its applications in a recent study on data analytics in healthcare.

Decision Trees

A Tree has many comparisons and correlations in the real world. It is used for making and analyzing decisions. The Tree has different types of decisions and it can also represent an internal and external representation of the decisions. It has two different types of nodes.

- Every leaf node has the class label, and remaining nodes try reaching that leaf node.
- Each internal node is a question and its branches are answers based on the outcome (NN, 2019).

These methods are used in the previous and initial days of the research started in the data analytics due to increases in the large volume of the data this method are not the most efficient method to diagnosis and prediction.BI have started using the bigdata processing to manage the data and decision support to the prediction (Chitra & Vijaya 2016).

Artificial Neural Networks

The term neural is an adjunct of the neuron and network will describe its structure is formed in the graph. This is also known as the "neural net" systems. The Artificial neural network has many advantages. But this is extracted from the data sets(NN,2019). Applications that are using ANN are predicting the patients who are readmitted into the hospitals after the discharge (Mehta, & Pandit, 2018).

Pattern Recognition

Pattern recognition is extracting the similarities of the images by using the knowledge to know the object which appears in the patterns (Saraladevi, Pazhaniraja, Paul, Basha, & Dhavachelvan, 2015). This method is at present using many of the healthcare applications to improve public health surveillance (ANAL, 2019).

Table 4. Classification of models in DA in HC based on the types of data mining algorithms used

Methods	Applications	References
Clustering	1. Curating and incorporation of user generated health data. 2. GEMINI: An Integrative Healthcare Analytics System. 3. Data Analysis in Healthcare at Hospitals	(Kakkanatt, Benigno, Jackson, Huang, & Ng, 2018) (Chitra & Vijaya 2016) (Ojha, & Mathur,2016)
Classification	1. GEMINI: An Integrative Healthcare Analytics System. 2. Curating and incorporation of user generated health data. 3. Associating Wellness and Health analysis to consider for Personal Decisions	(Chitra & Vijaya 2016) (Kakkanatt, Benigno, Jackson, Huang, & Ng, 2018) (Khan, Idris, Ali, Ali, Hussain, Hussain, & Lee, 2015)
Association	1. Stream Computing in Healthcare using big data analytics. 2. Bigdata analytics: a survey 3. Emerging Technologies for Health Data Analytics.	(Ta, Liu, & Nkabinde, 2016), (Tsai, Lai, Chao, & Vasilakos, 2015), (Lu, & Keech,2015)

Data Mining

Data mining has some methods to extract the knowledge from the data set. Data mining techniques are Clustering, classification, association. Data mining algorithm is playing an important role in data analytics. In the following section, we will discuss these techniques and application related to these techniques used in the health sectors.

Clustering

Clustering is a grouping method to set the data which is with the same similarity is grouped together and remaining are the outliers. Whether the cluster is good or bad this can be defined based on the shape (Paul, Monica, & Trishanka, 2017). Curating the user produced health information from various resources to support health care analytics is the one of the application, in which clustering is used for the stratification groups and profiles resulting from unsupervised clustering. It will separate the patients based on their profiles and highlighted the patients (BMI, T2D type-2 diabetics) (Kakkanatt, Benigno, Jackson, Huang, & Ng, 2018).

Classification

It is the technique applied to classify the data and extract from the data. This method is processed the variety of the data and the regression is growing more important in the recent days(Balaji, Paul, & Saravanan,2017).different methods in the classification algorithms are Naïve Bays, SVM, k-nearest neighbor, ID3.

Classification algorithm algorithms will find the frequent item sets after that certain rules are applied on to the data, then it will get the support and confidences values & analyzing the patient's health conditions extract the disease which is diagnosed by using the data analytics with the evidence based medicines (EBM) (Chitra & Vijaya 2016).

Table 5. Classification of data sets in DA in HC

Datasets	Applications	References
EHR (electronic health record)	1. Curating and incorporation of user generated health data. 2. Associating Wellness and Health analysis to consider for Personal Decisions 3. Evidence Based Health Care System 4. Decision Making in healthcare using analytic hierarchy process	(Kakkanatt, Benigno, Jackson, Huang, & Ng, 2018) (Khan, Idris, Ali, Ali, Hussain, Hussain, & Lee, 2015) (Chitra & Vijaya 2016) (Vijayaraj, Saravanan, Paul, & Raju,2016)
Hospitals	1. GEMINI: An Integrative Healthcare Analytics System. 2. Data Analysis in Healthcare at Hospitals 3. Design of Data Analytics model for Healthcare	(Mehta, & Pandit,2018) (Ojha, & Mathur,2016) (Kuo, Chrimes, Moa, & Hu,2015)

Association

Finding frequent patterns, associations, correlations, is the common methods in the data mining. To store the database, it is easy for the users to find the valuable patterns in the data (ASSO, 2019).

CATEGORIES 2

Data Sets

An association algorithm with the recent application that proposed that find the item sets that are frequently generated and timely finding of adversarial drug measures within population oriented healthcare networks (Ta, Liu, & Nkabinde, 2016).

EHR (Electronic Health Record)

In recent study most of applications, data sets are collected from EHR which contains name, age, disease type, diagnosis, medical tests and prescription details that are stored in the form of the digital instead of the manual papers. EHRs will give the effective results to the users it is the information repository of the health care and give the information to the only authorized users securely (EHR,2019).

An EHR contains the valuable insights in health care that include the following:

- Patient details
- Prescriptions
- Medical histories
- Diagnoses
- Surgical notes
- Admitting & readmitting

Table: 6 EHR (electronic health record) will consist of patient's details like problem list, procedures, major illnesses, family history, medications, and laboratory tests. For instance, the EHR can enhance patient-care by:

Table 6. Sample EHR data type and potential sources (Tansel, 2013)

Data type	Source
Problem list	EHR
Procedures	EHR
Major illnesses	EHR
Provider list potentially linked to problems.	EHR
Allergy data	EHR
Family history	EHR
Social history and lifestyle	EHR
Medication	EHR
Laboratory tests	EHE, commercial lab

Table 7. Number of EHR fields used by hospital system (Jian,Wen, Scholl, Shabbir, Lee, Hsu, & Li, 2011)

Temporary table fields		1	2	3	4	5	6	7	8
Medical encounter	94	102	120	111	98	71	81	99	101
Prescription	201	34	41	20	33	41	26	37	31
Admission note	429	42	57	66	62	47	41	40	39
Progress note	331	33	43	48	31	41	20	33	41
Lab report	458	41	20	33	41	35	33	43	48
Emergency note	453	47	41	40	39	44	30	41	26
Emergency order	343	48	31	41	20	33	42	33	43

Figure 5. Types of the insights in the data analytics in the health care

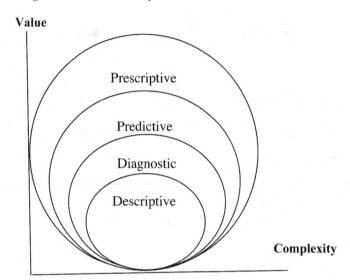

Table 8. Classification of insights in DA in HC based on the type's insight

Insight	Applications	References
Descriptive analytics	1. Curating and incorporation of user generated health data. 2. Associating Wellness and Health analysis to consider for Personal Decisions 3. Physic assault experienced by psychiatric nurses and their intent to leave.	(Kakkanatt, Benigno, Jackson, Huang, & Ng, 2018) (Khan, Idris, Ali, Ali, Hussain, Hussain, & Lee, 2015), (Hanohano, 2017)
Predictive analytics	1. Design of Data Analytics model for Healthcare 2. Curating and incorporation of user generated health data. 3. Evidence Based Health Care System.	(Kuo, Chrimes, Moa, & Hu,2015) (Kakkanatt, Benigno, Jackson, Huang, & Ng, 2018) (Chitra & Vijaya 2016)
Prescriptive analytics	1. Evidence Based Health Care System. 2. From Clinical Intelligence to Inflexible Analytics.	(Chitra & Vijaya 2016) (Van Poucke, Thomeer, Heath, & Vukicevic, 2016)
Diagnostic analytics	1. Decision Making in healthcare using analytic hierarchy process 2. Associating Wellness and Health analysis to consider for Personal Decisions	(Vijayaraj, Saravanan, Paul, & Raju,2016) (Khan, Idris, Ali, Ali, Hussain, Hussain, & Lee, 2015)

- To reduces the faults that are going in health care and improve the accuracy of the patient's records.
- Making the information always available to physicians, reduce the redundancy in the data.
- Improve the quality of the care and give treatment with reducing treatment errors (EHR2, 2019).

Hospitals Systems

In some of the recent lecture study for some of the application data sets are collected from the hospital systems. Suppose, for example, in this application GEMINI: An Integrative Healthcare Analytics System dataset is collected from the National University Health System (NUHS). collect the data set from hospital and perform analytics on that data and give valuable insight & good decision making to the hospitals to improve the quality of the health.

CATEGORIES 3

Insight

In this section, the study of recent works on DA in health care is discussed based on the type of insight used in the model. As we observed in the literature, the types of insight can be broadly classified into four as, descriptive, predictive, prescriptive and diagnostics as shown in Fig. 5. Table 7 shows the different types of algorithms used in DA in HC.

Descriptive Analytics

Descriptive analytics, use the data mining techniques to give insights into the past and give the solution to what has happened? An Example of the descriptive analytics is the how many of the patients were suffering with the fever in the past that gives the solution to the descriptive analytics. There are a lot of statistics that we use in this category. (Think of basic arithmetic, such as amounts, average, percentage changes). Every patient will help with the maintenance of population health management such as identifying benchmark results against diabetes, government expectations, or finding areas to improve clinical quality activities or other factors. Descriptive analytics are performed on the curate data. Here descriptive analytics are patient's population based on the information we have to identify the patterns of T2DM (type 2 diabetes).

Diabetic was segmented into normal, pre diabetics, and post diabetics each event in the health record is first evaluated using the diagnostic criteria to determine if it is a qualifying event for the normal, pre diabetics and post diabetics. On this assumption is made to only allow forward state transition from normal to pre diabetes and from pre diabetes to diabetes. Backward state transition from diabetes to pre diabetes and from pre diabetes to normal. Based on this there event we can provide insight into the past and the answer to what has happened (Kakkanatt, Benigno, Jackson, Huang, & Ng, 2018).

Predictive Analytics

Analytics tells what is likely to happen which the flaming domain in health care analytics. Evidence based ways to decrease redundant costs, productive by exploring the hottest topics related to the health of one of the predictive analytics, the value-based reimbursements are taking advantage of the protection is no longer a gift, and controlling chronic diseases in order to avoid a fine for failing to prevent or avoid the Adverse events (Kuo, Chrimes, Moa, & Hu,2015). Precision analyzes in the work have identified health

Table 9. Classification of tools in DA in HC based on the types tools used

Tools	Applications	References
Unstructured Data	1. Security solutions for healthcare analytics. 2. Stream Computing in Healthcare using big data analytics. 3.Emerging Technologies for Health Data Analytic	(Rao, Suma, & Sunitha,2015), (Ta, Liu, & Nkabinde, 2016), (Lu, & Keech,2015)
Big data tools	1. Data Analysis in Healthcare at Hospitals 2. Correlating Health and Wellness Analytics for Personalized Decision Making. 3. Evidence Based Health Care System	(Ojha, & Mathur, 2016) (Khan, Idris, Ali, Ali, Hussain, Hussain, & Lee, 2015), (DD,2019)
Natural language processing	1. GEMINI: An Integrative Healthcare Analytics System. 2. Curating and incorporation of user generated health data.	(Mehta, & Pandit,2018), (Kakkanatt, Benigno, Jackson, Huang, & Ng, 2018)

care trends, infiltrating infection control to control infections, where data from the hospital system is collected and its data warehouse in the Island Health Authority (VIHA).

Prescriptive Analytics

This defines the probable steps to be taken to eradicate the problem happening in the future. This data is collected from an EHR and also it can helpful to find the diseases with the same properties will be identified in the form of <key, values> pairs. Symptoms and diseases with same similar will be extracted from all the clinical records which are available. The diseases with the highest probability of symptoms are extracted from the patients' data along with this parallel best drug for that particular diseases also recommended based on the data what we have and give actionable perceptions (Chitra & Vijaya 2016).

Diagnostic Analytics

At this stage, the answer to the question of why something happened has been measured in historical data against other data. Drilling down, it is possible to find clues and mark patterns. The health care provider responds to patients' response to promotional campaigns in different areas a retailer sells to subcategories.

CATEGORIES 4

Tools

In this section, the study of recent works on DA in health care is discussed based on the type of tools used in the model. As we observed in the literature, the categories of tools can be broadly classified into three as unstructured data, big data and natural language processing tools. Table 8 shows the different types of tools used in DA in HC. These tools are briefly discussed in the following subsections.

Unstructured Data

Unstructured data is the information as images, text, audios, videos, power point presentations, transaction of the organizations, blogs and the posts in the social networks etc… mainly to process the unstructured data in recent studies they are using the tools like No SQL, Cassandra the tools which are to process the unstructured data. No SQL is the new method for data storing, processing and analyzing and also used to increase the volume, velocity, verity of the data organization. To store and retrieve data stored in forms other than Tubular Relations used in relational databases.

No SQL databases are relative to relational databases, no SQL database Information. It may have multi-level nodes and the complete data model is complicated. Tools can include Secure Socket Layer technique for secure connection, Kerberos for user validation, encryption for data security, and recognition and authority (groups, roles) (Rao, Suma, & Sunitha,2015).

Big Data Tools

The various tools that can be used analyze the big data are, (Tools,2019).

- Hadoop
- Hive
- Pig
- Spark
- HBase

Hadoop

Apache Hadoop is the most commonly used platform for data intensive distributed app (Chen, & Zhang, 2014). This frame runs parallel to the cluster and also possess the ability to allow us to process data in all nodes. In recent applications, HDFS, the distributed file system that appears to be too large for every file is adapted and randomly invasive. The key value layer in a hadoop is for simple key oriented record maintenance activity (Ojha, & Mathur, 2016).

Pig

Apache Pig is a better platform to lessen Hadoop programs for the implementation map. Programming language, programming, optimization opportunities, and extensibility language for Pig Latin and some Pig Technology for Pig (PIG,2019).Data generated from various sources with different vocabulary and schemes .Data Selection Scheme Generates and execute the high query in line with the data selection process. Data generation creates a new dataset based on data selection implementations based on the components of information reform. The Analyst can edit; Data exported or produced by export or data based on its expertise in data analytics and / or target datasets(Ojha, & Mathur,2016), (Hbase,2019), (Cha, Abusharekh, & Abidi,2015).

Natural Language Processing

It uses computer technology for speech, in order to understand and analyze how to use them for various business purposes. NLP takes on various disciplines, including computer science and computational linguistics, Interval between human communication and computer perception(Chitra & Vijaya 2016), (Kakkanatt, Benigno, Jackson, Huang, & Ng, 2018), (Paul, Yogaraj,Ram,& Irshath, 2017), (Cha, Abush-arekh, & Abidi,2015).

Some of the NLP tools such as Medical LEE, CTAKES and Unified-Medical Language System (UMLS) are some of the NLP applications that require a single integrative healthcare analyst system to refer to two aspects, each instance of the institution's practice, for example, and doctors in a particular section do not have a different tradition Version (Mehta, & Pandit,2018).

CONCLUSION

As we are at advent of data analytics, which is the succeeding platform for innovation and productivity. In this survey paper, Data analytics in HealthCare (DAiHC) are recent and attracted many researchers due to its importance in improving the value of people life. In this perspective, the paper focuses on the various recent models proposed in DAiHC and dissect the works based various vital parameters. As an initial part, the work provides comprehensive information on DAiHC and its various application illustrations. Moreover, the study presented in the work categorizes the literature on DAiHC based on factors like Algorithms used, Application DataSet utilized, Insight type and Tools used for evaluation.

In various application domains we are focusing mainly on data analytics in healthcare. Data-analytics in healthcare are also placing a vital role in the society. Here we give overview analytics in healthcare, needs of healthcare analytics, process flow of healthcare analytics, the KDD process is used as the framework for these studies and summarized into four parts and some of the example scenarios in healthcare.

REFERENCES

Aggarwal, C. C. (2011). An introduction to social network data analytics. In *Social network data analytics* (pp. 1–15). Boston, MA: Springer. doi:10.1007/978-1-4419-8462-3_1

Analytics (ANAL). (n.d.). Retrieved from http://pages.cs.wisc.edu/~jerryzhu/cs540/handouts/dt.pdf

Analytics process (AP). (n.d.). Retrieved from https://www.iss.nus.edu.sg/community/newsroom/news-detail/2016/06/24/the-7-step-business-analytics-process

Association (ASSO). (n.d.). Retrieved from https://searchbusinessanalytics.techtarget.com/definition/association-rules-in-data-mining

Balaji, S. N., Paul, P. V., & Saravanan, R. (2017, April). Survey on sentiment analysis based stock prediction using big data analytics. In *2017 Innovations in Power and Advanced Computing Technologies (i-PACT)* (pp. 1-5). IEEE.

Big data (BD2). (n.d.). Retrieved from https://klantenffabriek.nl/wp-cgontent/upload/2017/06/big-data_literature_review.pdf

Big data (BD). (n.d.). Retrieved from https://journalofbigdata.springeropen.com/articles /10.1186/s40537-015-0030-3

Cha, S., Abusharekh, A., & Abidi, S. S. (2015, March). Towards a'Big'Health Data Analytics Platform. In *2015 IEEE First International Conference on Big Data Computing Service and Applications* (pp. 233-241). IEEE. 10.1109/BigDataService.2015.13

Chen, C. P., & Zhang, C. Y. (2014). Data-intensive applications, challenges, techniques and technologies: A survey on Big Data. *Information Sciences, 275,* 314–347. doi:10.1016/j.ins.2014.01.015

Chitra, P., & Vijaya, K. (2016), Evidence Based Health Care System. *Conference on Advances in EEICB.*

Dashboards definition (DD). (n.d.). Retrieved from https://searchcio.techtarget.com/definition/dashboard

Data analytic definition (DAD). (n.d.). Retrieved from https://www.techopedia.com/definition/26418/data-analytics

Data analytics applications (DAA). (n.d.). Retrieved from https://www.simplilearn.com/big-data-applications-in-industries-article

Data analytics (DA2). (n.d.). Retrieved from https://www.kdnuggets.com/2017/07/4-types-data-analytics.html

Data analytics definition (DAD2). (n.d.). Retrieved from https://searchbusinessanalytics.techtarget.com/definition/data-visualization

Data analytics importance (DAI2). (n.d.). Retrieved from https://peterjamesthomas.com/2017/01/10/alphabet-soup/

Data analytics importance (DAI). (n.d.). Retrieved from https://www.digitalvidya.com/blog/ reasons-data-analytics-important/

Data analytics in healthcare (DAH). (n.d.). Retrieved from https://www.healthcareitnews.com/news/5-ways-hospitals-can-use-data-analytics

Data analytics in retail (DAR). (n.d.). Retrieved from https://www.ibm.com/blogs/insights-on-business/consumer-products/2-5-quintillion-bytes-of-data-created-every-day-how-does-cpg-retail-manage-it/

Data analytics purpose (DAP). (n.d.). Retrieved from https://www.quora.com/What-is-the-purpose-of-data-analytics

Descriptive analytics (DA). (n.d.). Retrieved from https://www.investopedia.com/terms/d/descriptive-analytics.asp

Ecommerce (ECOM). (n.d.). Retrieved from https://www.linkedin.com/pulse/role-analytics-ecommerce-industry-gauri-bapat

Education (EDU2). (n.d.). Retrieved from https://dzone.com/articles/how-is-big-data-influencing-the-education-sector

Education (EDU3). (n.d.). Retrieved from https://www.allerin.com/blog/4-ways-big-data-is-transforming-the-education-sector

Education (EDU). (n.d.). Retrieved from https://pdfs.semanticscholar.org/67a4/28c6764c7ece121dcd0c196f9541c7b2d9f2.pdf

EHR2. (n.d.). Retrieved from https://www.cmss.gov/Mediccare/EHealthRecords/index.html

EHR. (n.d.). Retrieved from https://www.techopediaa.com/definitionn/153337/electronic-health-record-ehr

Fan, W., & Bifet, A. (2013). Mining big data: current status, and forecast to the future. *ACM SIGKDD Explorations Newsletter, 14*(2), 1-5.

Genomic analytics (GA2). (n.d.). Retrieved from https://www.intel.in/content/www/in/en/healthcare-it/solutions/documents/genomicanalytics-speed-time-to-insights-brief.html

Genomic analytics (GA). (n.d.). Retrieved from https://www.intel.com/content/www/us/en/healthcare-it/genomic-analytics-overview.html

Hanohano, C. J. O. (2017). *Physical Assault, Perceived Stress, Coping, and Attitudes toward Assault Experienced by Psychiatric Nurses and Their Intent to Leave* (Doctoral dissertation). Azusa Pacific University.

Hbase. (n.d.). Retrieved from https://www.ibm.com/analytics/hadoop/hbase

Health care analytics (HCA). (n.d.). Retrieved from https://www.infosys.com/data-analytics/verticals/Pages/healthcare.aspx

Health care (HC). (n.d.). In *Wikipedia*. Retrieved from https://en.wikipedia.org/wiki/Health_care_analytics

Healthcare process (HP). (n.d.). Retrieved from https://www.omicssonlineq.org/a-hoppital-health-care-system- -2157-7420.1000121.php

Importance of health care (IHC). (n.d.). Retrieved from http://www.keyush.com/blogs/files/ Importance of Analytics 2020 in Healthcare.pdf

Jian, W. S., Wen, H. C., Scholl, J., Shabbir, S. A., Lee, P., Hsu, C. Y., & Li, Y. C. (2011). The Taiwanese method for providing patients data from multiple hospital EHR systems. *Journal of Biomedical Informatics, 44*(2), 326–332. doi:10.1016/j.jbi.2010.11.004 PMID:21118726

Kakkanatt, C., Benigno, M., Jackson, V. M., Huang, P. L., & Ng, K. (2018). Curating and integrating user-generated health data from multiple sources to support healthcare analytics. *IBM Journal of Research and Development, 62*(1), 2–1. doi:10.1147/JRD.2017.2756742

Kakkanatt, C., Benigno, M., Jackson, V. M., Huang, P. L., & Ng, K. (2018). Curating and integrating user-generated health data from multiple sources to support healthcare analytics. *IBM Journal of Research and Development, 62*(1), 2–1. doi:10.1147/JRD.2017.2756742

Kambatla, K., Kollias, G., Kumar, V., & Grama, A. (2014). Trends in big data analytics. *Journal of Parallel and Distributed Computing, 74*(7), 2561–2573. doi:10.1016/j.jpdc.2014.01.003

Khan, W. A., Idris, M., Ali, T., Ali, R., Hussain, S., Hussain, M., . . . Lee, S. (2015, October). Correlating health and wellness analytics for personalized decision making. In *2015 17th International Conference on E-health Networking, Application & Services (HealthCom)* (pp. 256-261). IEEE. 10.1109/Health-Com.2015.7454508

Kumar, S., Sharma, B., Sharma, V. K., & Poonia, R. C. (2018). Automated soil prediction using bag-of-features and chaotic spider monkey optimization algorithm. *Evolutionary Intelligence*, 1–12.

Kumar, S., Sharma, B., Sharma, V. K., Sharma, H., & Bansal, J. C. (2018). Plant leaf disease identification using exponential spider monkey optimization. *Sustainable Computing: Informatics and Systems*.

Kuo, M. H., Chrimes, D., Moa, B., & Hu, W. (2015, December). Design and construction of a big data analytics framework for health applications. In *2015 IEEE International Conference on Smart City/ SocialCom/SustainCom (SmartCity)* (pp. 631-636). IEEE. 10.1109/SmartCity.2015.140

Lu, J., & Keech, M. (2015, September). Emerging technologies for health data analytics research: a conceptual architecture. In *2015 26th International Workshop on Database and Expert Systems Applications (DEXA)* (pp. 225-229). IEEE. 10.1109/DEXA.2015.58

Machine learning (ML). (n.d.). Retrieved from https://www.xenonstack.com/blog/data-science/preparation-wrangling-machine-learning-deep

Machine learning (ML). (n.d.). Retrieved from https://medium.com/@gp_pulipaka/machine-learning-techniques-for-healthcare-data-analytics-part-1-eb5aada5dce5

Mehta, N., & Pandit, A. (2018). Concurrence of big data analytics and healthcare: A systematic review. *International Journal of Medical Informatics*, *114*, 57–65. doi:10.1016/j.ijmedinf.2018.03.013 PMID:29673604

Mehta, N., & Pandit, A. (2018). Concurrence of big data analytics and healthcare: A systematic review. *International Journal of Medical Informatics*, *114*, 57–65. doi:10.1016/j.ijmedinf.2018.03.013 PMID:29673604

Munjal, P., Kumar, L., Kumar, S., & Banati, H. (2019). Evidence of Ostwald Ripening in opinion driven dynamics of mutually competitive social networks. *Physica A*, *522*, 182–194. doi:10.1016/j.physa.2019.01.109

Munjal, P., Narula, M., Kumar, S., & Banati, H. (2018). Twitter sentiments based suggestive framework to predict trends. *Journal of Statistics and Management Systems*, *21*(4), 685–693. doi:10.1080/097205 10.2018.1475079

Need of study image (NSI). (n.d.). Retrieved from http://www.techferry.com/articles/images/outcome.png

Need of study in health care (NSHC). (n.d.). Retrieved from https://www.researchregistry.pitt.edu/files/faqs.pdf

Network (Net). (n.d.). Retrieved from https://itl.nist.gov/div898/handbook/eda/section1/eda11.html

Neural network (NN). (n.d.). Retrieved from https://www.techopediaa.com/definition/55967/artificial-neural-network-ann

Obermeyer, Z., & Emanuel, E. J. (2016). Predicting the future—Big data, machine learning, and clinical medicine. *The New England Journal of Medicine*, *375*(13), 1216–1219. doi:10.1056/NEJMp1606181 PMID:27682033

Ojha, M., & Mathur, K. (2016, March). Proposed application of big data analytics in healthcare at Maharaja Yeshwantrao Hospital. In *2016 3rd MEC International Conference on Big Data and Smart City (ICBDSC)* (pp. 1-7). IEEE. 10.1109/ICBDSC.2016.7460340

Patients like me (PLM). (n.d.). Retrieved fromhttps://www.patientslikeme.com/

Paul, P. V., Monica, K., & Trishanka, M. (2017, April). A survey on big data analytics using social media data. In *2017 Innovations in Power and Advanced Computing Technologies (i-PACT)* (pp. 1-4). IEEE.

Paul, P. V., Yogaraj, S., Ram, H. B., & Irshath, A. M. (2017, April). Automated video object recognition system. In *2017 Innovations in Power and Advanced Computing Technologies (i-PACT)* (pp. 1-5). IEEE.

Perceptual edge (PE). (n.d.). Retrieved from http://www.perceptualedge.com/articles/ie/the_right_graph.pdf

Pig. (n.d.). Retrieved from https://www.javatpoint.com/what-is-pig

Predictive analytics (PA). (n.d.). Retrieved from https://www.sas.com/en_in/insights/analytics/predictive-analytics.html

Rao, S., Suma, S. N., & Sunitha, M. (2015, May). Security solutions for big data analytics in healthcare. In *2015 Second International Conference on Advances in Computing and Communication Engineering* (pp. 510-514). IEEE. 10.1109/ICACCE.2015.83

Retail (RET). (n.d.). Retrieved from https://www.rishabhsoft.com/blog/retail-store-analytics

Russo. (2015). *Big data analytics*. Best Practices Report, Fourth Quarter.

Sakr, S., & Elgammal, A. (2016). Towards a comprehensive data analytics framework for smart healthcare services. *Big Data Research*, *4*, 44–58. doi:10.1016/j.bdr.2016.05.002

Saraladevi, B., Pazhaniraja, N., Paul, P. V., Basha, M. S., & Dhavachelvan, P. (2015). Big Data and Hadoop-A study in security perspective. *Procedia Computer Science*, *50*, 596–601. doi:10.1016/j.procs.2015.04.091

Social media analytics (SMA). (n.d.). Retrieved from https://iag.me/socialmedia/6-important-reasons-why-you-should-use-social-media-analytics

Solanki, A., & Pandey, S. (2019). Music instrument recognition using deep convolutional neural networks. *International Journal of Information Technology*, 1-10.

Spark. (n.d.). Retrieved from https://www.ibmbigdatahub.com/blog/what-spark

Statistics (ST). (n.d.). Retrieved from https://explorable.com/branches-of-statistics

Ta, V. D., Liu, C. M., & Nkabinde, G. W. (2016, July). Big data stream computing in healthcare real-time analytics. In *2016 IEEE International Conference on Cloud Computing and Big Data Analysis (ICCCBDA)* (pp. 37-42). IEEE.

Tansel, A. U. (2013). Innovation through patient health records. *Procedia: Social and Behavioral Sciences, 75*, 183–188. doi:10.1016/j.sbspro.2013.04.021

Thamizhselvan, M., Raghuraman, R., Manoj, S. G., & Paul, P. V. (2015, January). Data security model for Cloud Computing using V-GRT methodology. In *2015 IEEE 9th International Conference on Intelligent Systems and Control (ISCO)* (pp. 1-6). IEEE. 10.1109/ISCO.2015.7282349

Tools. (n.d.). Retrieved from http://bigdata-madesimple.com/top-big-data-tools-used-to-store-and-analyse-data/

Tsai, C. W., Lai, C. F., Chao, H. C., & Vasilakos, A. V. (2015). Big data analytics: a survey. *Journal of Big data, 2*(1), 21

Types of analytics (TA). (n.d.). Retrieved from https://www.scnsoft.com/blog/4-types-of-data-analytics

Van Poucke, S., Thomeer, M., Heath, J., & Vukicevic, M. (2016). Are randomized controlled trials the (g) old standard? From clinical intelligence to prescriptive analytics. *Journal of Medical Internet Research, 18*(7), e185. doi:10.2196/jmir.5549 PMID:27383622

Vijayaraj, J., Saravanan, R., Paul, P. V., & Raju, R. (2016, November). A comprehensive survey on big data analytics tools. In *2016 Online International Conference on Green Engineering and Technologies (IC-GET)* (pp. 1-6). IEEE. 10.1109/GET.2016.7916733

Ward, M. J., Marsolo, K. A., & Froehle, C. M. (2014). Applications of business analytics in healthcare. *Business Horizons, 57*(5), 571–582. doi:10.1016/j.bushor.2014.06.003 PMID:25429161

Williams, R., & Wright, J. (1998). Epidemiological issues in health needs assessment. *BMJ (Clinical Research Ed.), 316*(7141), 1379–1382. doi:10.1136/bmj.316.7141.1379 PMID:9563997

Wright, J., Williams, R., & Wilkinson, J. R. (1998). Development and importance of health needs assessment. *BMJ (Clinical Research Ed.), 316*(7140), 1310–1313. doi:10.1136/bmj.316.7140.1310 PMID:9554906

Chapter 13
Implementation of Machine Learning in Network Security

Bharathi N. Gopalsamy
SRM Institute of Science and Technology, India

Brindha G. R.
School of Computing, SASTRA University (Deemed), India

B. Santhi
School of Computing, SASTRA University (Deemed), India

ABSTRACT

Machine learning (ML) is prevalent across the globe and applied in almost all domains. This chapter focuses on implementation of ML with real-time use cases. Day-to-day activities are automated to ease the task and increase the quality of decision. ML is the backbone of the perfect decision support system with a plethora of applications. The use case described in this chapter is ML & Security, which is implemented in R Script. Adversaries took advantages of ML to avoid detection and evade defenses. Network intrusion detection system (IDS) is the major issue nowadays. Its primary task is to collect relevant features from the computer network. These selected features can be fed into the ML algorithms to predict the label. The challenge in this use case is what type of feature to consider for intrusion and anomaly detection (AD). This chapter focuses on end-to-end process to get insight into the stream of data from the network connection with priority given to forecasting mechanism and prediction of the future. Forecasting is applied to the time series data to get sensible decisions.

INTRODUCTION

ML is the combination of mathematics and statistics. ML algorithms identify patterns in the data from real time. By viewing this it is possible to identify correlations and also to detect anomalies. This chapter provides intuition to the reader about ML and its significant role in the network security. The reader could have basics of ML and design framework for security issues and have the practical skill to implement the

DOI: 10.4018/978-1-5225-9643-1.ch013

Figure 1.

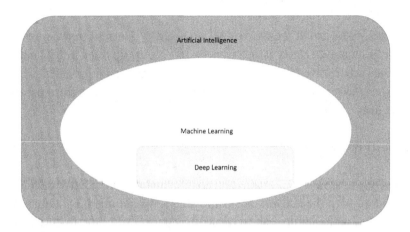

ML algorithms. ML is for learning by experiences. It brings intelligence and adaptable to dynamic data through past data. Being get features of available data and relations among them, it could be possible to predict future outcomes. This could use these tasks: Information mining, and brings the inference and insight from data. Whenever we want to classify the elements, we first extract features from the elements and significant towards the label, which could differentiate between classes. We applied ML algorithms over the labeled data and model parameters are identified. These learned parameters are used to differentiate the unseen data, in the validation phase.

ML seems to be the best solution to cyber security in the large amount of digital era. This chapter focuses on little basics of ML and security. It picturizes the concept of ML in security and it is explained through use cases. The example is going to help the readers to get deep dive into the hands-on part of ML algorithms. It also gives the over view of ML and security state of the art. Key word in this technology world are Artificial intelligence (AI), ML and Deep Learning (DL) given in Figure 1.

AI is the roof; Making things smart by machines and doing human like activities with intelligence. ML is the subset of AI and it learns from experience. ML is having capacity to recognize pattern without program. ML makes decisions based on data not from algorithm.

DL is the techniques for doing ML logics. DL recognizes patterns of pattern.

- Learning [supervised, unsupervised, semi-supervised]
- Supervised (Task driven approach): Classifier, Regression(prediction)
- Unsupervised (Data Driven approach): Clustering
- Semi supervised: combined both supervised and unsupervised
- Ensemble Learning: Extension of Supervised learning. Combining simple models to get best output.
- Reinforcement learning (Environment driven approach): Behavior react on changing environment based on rewards and punishments.
- Active learning: Subset of Reinforcement learning. With teacher correction is possible other than environment changes

ML AND SECURITY- STATE OF THE ART

This section elaborates with current scenario of ML in security. Current trend in research area focused with three major areas such as security issues in network, security issues in IoT and security issues in medicine. These issues are resolved by researchers using several techniques. This chapter concentrates on ML techniques to resolve security issues in these areas. It also discusses three use cases and suggests tool for handling security challenges.

Security Issues in Network

Network plays a vital role in almost all domains and no information can move without it. The data packets which are transmitted through the network are vulnerable [. Mohammed, D., Omar, M., & Nguyen, V. (2018).]. The diffusion of vulnerability can be reduced by packet filtering. In classical network systems the packet filtering is realized with many techniques. For example, deep-packet inspection (DPI) is carried out by inspecting the header/content of the packet to resolve or prevent the network security issues. Similar to DPI several other techniques involve inspection of packets. Inspecting every packet is time consuming and it is inefficient approach. However, the network should be monitored periodically and its report can be analyzed in order to study the regular and abnormal behavior of network [Lin, Z. Yan, Y. Chen and L. Zhang, 2018]. Problem may be reduced to some extent. It can be further reduced if the entire process is automated.

Network monitoring should be used to avoid the security issues like (i) the knowledge of network assets is not clearly defined, hence intruders can attack using unknown device connected to the network (ii) The privileged users become the attackers at some situations (iii) The vulnerability due to newly installing application or software. (iv) Professionals involved in security might be careless enough in checking the network behavior periodically. (v) loosely framed network structure subject to major failure in single attack.

Network monitoring device should possess some intelligence in such a way that it can be trained to recognize and intimate the abnormality in the network [Shone.N, T. N. Ngoc, V. D. Phai and Q. Shi,2018]. That intelligence can be realized with machine learning (ML) algorithms which are used to study the behavioral models and patterns with the data set and rules.

Machine learning is being in progress to adopt in commercial networks for detecting suspicious attacks [Ayoubi.S et al, 2018]. The algorithm generates a predetermined set of rules to govern the behavior of the network. Whenever an anomaly happens, the ML algorithm warns the corresponding data owner to take further action by itself with appropriate authorization. Unlike encryption/signature-based protection ML based algorithms are consuming less processor cycles [Wang.M.et.al.,2018] to resolve the security issues.

Security Issues in Iot Applications

The Internet of Things (IoT) become part of our day to day life. Even unknowingly we are using many devices and completing our works. The heterogeneity of devices is one of the major hurdles in the perspective of security [Kewei Sha.et.al, 2018]. Since IoT market is evolving rapidly, the vendors are promoting their devices before its complete testing and hence the working of the device is limited and more vulnerable to real time attacks [Mauro Conti.et.al.,2018]. In addition to that default passwords are provided with those devices and the end users are not at all aware or lazy enough to change the passwords. It is unprotected situation where the devices are easily compromised in the security aspect.

The IoT framework is also not an exemption for malwares and ransomwares. With a new dimension many malwares are implemented to attack IoT systems rapidly in pace to IoT market or even faster. Most well-known security threat is IoT botnets are targeting the cryptocurrency to get profit in more simple and smarter manner. Data which are private to the users are even traded by large companies. Personal identification data are highly sensitive and can be abused definitely [Mauro Conti.et.al.,2018]. Hence the major requirement of IoT is the security than the development in any other characteristic features of IoT.

IoT devices are always polled for retrieving data by applications reside on mobile phones or cloud platforms. The incoming requests or controls and outgoing response or status are to be monitored to govern the security. IoT security professionals and data scientists are working on various techniques to safeguard the IoT systems efficiently. One such most powerful technique is machine learning (ML) algorithms which can be trained to the IoT bidirectional traffic [Liu.Q,et.al.,2018]. The ML algorithms are configuring the profile of the IoT system based on its normal behavior by monitoring every bits of traffic over a training time period [Al-Garadi.et.al 2018]. Then it is always checked for its normal behavior limits by the machine learning engine and concern the authority about the possible attacks and unsure behavior [Xiao.et.al.,2018].

Security Issues in Medical Domain

The medical diagnosis was becoming easier with the advent of embedded devices and instrumentation. The development of Internet of Things has brought an uprising in medical diagnosis [Nilanjan Dey. et.al.,2018]. Whenever a field is emerging, care should be taken that its usefulness should not be overruled by its shortcomings. Though the development in medical instrumentation is stable, more and more mobile devices are easily prone to heavy security risk [Reddy V. Padmanabha.et.al.,2018]. Embedded devices are more common now a days and medical field is not an exemption to avoid it.

The virtualization of computers and servers as such has its own benefits of connecting remotely and executing applications, but providing a loophole to unauthorized intruding. The security issues are not limited and they are extending with user friendly IT systems and environments along with viruses diffusing social media [Papageorgiou. A.et.al.,2018].

The threatening of security issues disrupts the progress of medical diagnosis [Cárdenas P.et.al, 2018]. However, Implementation of machine learning framework shows a hope in resolving the security issues. The machine learning is initially adopted for progressing flawless diagnosis, monitoring health of patient at low cost, suggesting appropriate medicines, advising revisits and readmissions, recognizing the high-risk patients from their diagnosis reports.

The machine learning algorithms are routinely trained with the data or activities of the system and easily be familiar with the composite patterns [Mukrimah Nawir.et.al.,2019]. later, it will react according to the information dataset given and resolves an intellectual result. It is mainly computing the real and effectual profit of the network performance within networked system. Machine learning can be implemented as either supervised or unsupervised way to categorize the patterns or for new data that is approaching into a network can be classified with the network protocol and according to present network. The advantages to the execution of ML in system are high discovery rates, false caution rates, rational computation, and with less number of messages.

Figure 2.

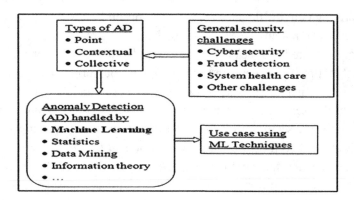

Security challenges and types of anomalies are shown in Figure 2. Wide range of domains like Cyber security, anomaly detection, Intrusion detections, Malware analysis, Spam and web security are to be addressed using ML. ML is applied by both attack defenders and attackers efficiently. Hence it is the real challenge to provide security in digital era. Major application of ML in security domain is categorized as pattern recognition and anomaly detection. A data or group of data that do not have the same pattern or behavior as the majority of the data available, then those data are termed as anomaly data. To detect any such deviations from the normality in the data, anomaly detection is used. ML in security domain is handled by many giant in this era. ML has been used by Google to detect threats in Android mobiles. It also detects and removes it from the handsets. Amazon also applied Macie to resolve s3 cloud issues on cloud storage services. The digital era is facing many security challenges among which anomaly detection is the most widely studied area. AD is used to reveal unusual patterns. It points out the outliers in the system.

Anomalies are related to the activities of any system which does not give assurance of normal activity. The significant and critical part is to detect the anomalies from the available data. The real time problems range from abnormalities in fund transaction to medical images and structural fault of aircraft engines. The picking out outliers provides interesting and significant focus from business perspective. The AD is generally categorized as Point, Contextual and Collective.

Machine learning has vast and influential techniques to handle the AD challenges.

Types of Anomaly

Today's digital world is in need of processing the data to increase productivity and efficiency. Huge data have been created because of the data flow between sensors and devices. The role of data analytics is significant in such situations, which extract the useful information for the purpose of cost reduction, optimization and reduce downtime. To achieve the desired outcome, identification of normal and outlier activities is necessary [Chris McNab,2007, Baron Schwartz, Preetam Jinka, 2016]. The following Figure 4 depicts such anomalies for two-dimensional data.

Figure 3.

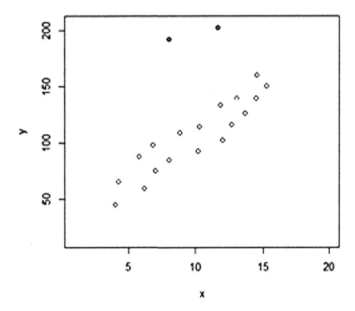

Point anomaly: in a group of data a single entity behaving abnormally, since it is far away in graphical representation for the given data set (Figure 3).

Collective Anomaly

When a group of similar data is anomalies based on the whole data, it is said to be collective anomaly. The member in that group may ne be anomaly, but their presence in the collective group made them anomalies. For example, the identification of 'green' in a geographic location from a satellite image may have low green values. In the group, few points may be with high green value, but since they are surrounded by the group of low green points, they are also considered as anomaly.

The data is described by the characteristics of attributes. The attributes may be contextual or behavioral. Attributes are utilized to identify of similar or related data. Example – In time series analysis, time is the contextual attribute that decides the sequence of instances. Behavioral attributes describe the non-contextual features of an instance.

Contextual Anomaly

For two-dimensional data visualization may be the good approach, but for high dimensional data it is difficult. Hence multivariate statistics such as Gaussian distribution, probability distribution etc can be applied. Data set context decides the anomaly. For example, heart rate 130 is normal for an individual during exercise and running time. But during rest time it is abnormal. Correlation between two or more metrics is used in multivariate model. It uses multiple features to predict the possible outcomes.

Figure 4.

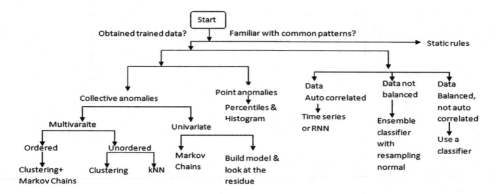

Figure 5.

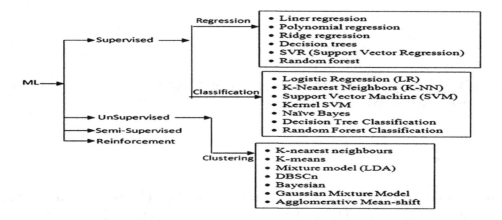

Anomaly Detection Using ML Techniques

The collected from real time should be analyzed earlier to the ML techniques' selection. The nature of data and suitable techniques to be applied are given in Figure 4. Machine Learning techniques available for security problems are given in Figure 5. Generally, the research openings and the real time needs are focused at the point of enhancing the learning part of classification or regression process (Figure 6). By analyzing the working process and intermediate results, the point which lowers the performance can be identified [Harrington, P. 2012, Sammut, C., & Webb, G. I, 2011].

Regression: From the web data attributes, fraudulent actions are predicted and determine the probability.

Classification

Using the historical data of mail with labels spam and ham, model is build to spam mail detector.

Figure 6.

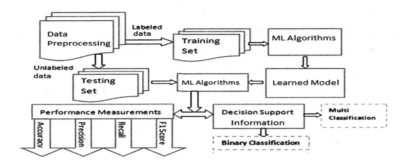

Clustering

Without knowing label, we need to group the data as normal and abnormal which is possible by similarity metrics [Ahuja.R, A.Solanki, 2019]{R. Ahuja, 2019 #18}.

Kernel-Based AD Techniques

The whole test sequence were considered as single element and processed similar to single point- based Anomaly detection. With respect to proximity, using the relevant kernel for the sequence, the anomaly is detected.

Window-Based AD Techniques

The subsequence is termed as 'Window' which is considered as a single element and analyzed at a time in test sequence. The nature whole test sequence is identified with additional step, based on the subsequences of the whole sequence.

Hidden Markov Model-Based AD Techniques

The transformation of the available sequences into hidden positions and the anomalies are detected from the transformed sequences.

Markovian AD Techniques:

Probabilistic model is used to get anomaly rank of the sequence through the probability of each individual symbols. To compute the probability of current symbol, the occurrence of previous symbols is considered.

In literature, various ML techniques have been applied with benchmark data set and the efficiency of the algorithms varies with different attacks [Liu.Q.et.al,2018, Al-Garadi.et.al.2018]. Each method is having its own merits and demerits. Hence researchers are combining two or more different ML technique to form a hybrid technique to improve the performance of IDS. The overall process of ML techniques is depicted in Figure 6. The following sections explain each process.

The expression of input data decides the AD techniques to be applied on the data. For example, to process continuous and categorical data, statistical techniques can be employed. Data collection mode influences the anomaly detection technique. Some data set like special, sequence and graph data are having relation with instances. The nature of data may be either continuous or categorical. Based on this nature, different distance measures are used. Similarity metrics are computed for the collected data features. Given data set is categorized as relation with instances or without relation.

ML is used to design a classifier that could discriminate subjects into two or more classes. Using historical data help the data scientist to design a precise intelligent model. Even the data size is huge, latest Hadoop system framework possible to bring a precise decision. That prediction model is with the following steps.

1. Acquiring data
2. Preprocess the data
   ◦ Extract/Select the features
3. Apply ML
   ◦ Build the model
4. Update the model
5. Generate the DSS

Acquiring Data

Synthetic training sets were designed with equal number of classes. In real time, most of the situations are of imbalanced dataset. (Cancer with a smaller number of samples, non-cancer with large number of samples).

This type of imbalanced data set should be handled specially for building a ML model, classes should be in equal size. If it is not equal then model should apply either up sampling or down sampling. Most classification data sets are not in equal number of samples in each class. Add copies of samples with the less sample size class (Up/Over sampling). Delete copies of samples with the large sample size class (Down/Under sampling).

There are number of methods available to oversample. Most famous technique is SMOT (Synthetic Minority Oversampling Technique). Usually cancer data set, normal cases with more samples, abnormal cases with less samples. To run the dataset, keep the class size balanced one. For over sample, consider the feature space of abnormal case. Select a sample from the dataset and find the k-nearest neighbors from the feature space. For generating synthetic data, take any one of these neighbors' vector point and multiply it with factor x, where x lies between 0 to 1. Insert this synthetic data into data set.

Clustering is the best widely used Under sampling technique. Here this method replaces cluster of samples by its centroid. Hence reduction is possible. Either using SMOT or clustering method imbalanced data set is transformed into balanced one.

Researchers are interested in use of machine learning techniques to critical real-world problems which are having most of the time imbalanced data set.

PREPROCESSING

Principal Component Analysis

The vastly used main technique to reduce the dimensions is Principal Component Analysis [James, Witten, Hastie, Tibshirani,2013]. PCA performs the linear mapping of the data to low dimensional space by maximizing the variance of data. The covariance matrix followed by eigen vectors are computed, the largest eigen values are used to find the variance of the data. Hence the feature space is reduced and retaining the significant variance.

Feature Extraction/ Selection/ Weighting

The data may contain attributes/features which are at various levels of relevancy. To choose appropriate features the traditional methods used are feature extraction, feature selection or feature weighting. Feature selection and weighting is generally used for numeric/ categorical samples and extraction process is added to image and signal samples. First step of these processes obtains the relationship between each feature and the class label through statistical methods such as Mutual information, Information gain, Correlation etc. Secondly, based on certain threshold such as average has been set and the features whose relationship is higher than the threshold value are selected. In feature weighting, the relationship values are used to weight the corresponding sample data.

ML ALGORITHMS

Supervised

The process of supervised learning is initiated using training samples (N) which include features ($X_{j=1..M, i=1..N} = \{(x_1, x_2 ..., x_N)_1, (x_1, x_2 ..., x_N)_2 ..(x_1, x_2 ..., x_N)_M\}$) and their corresponding labels ($Y_j = \{y_1, y_2 ..., y_M\}$). Each Y is generated by $Y = f(X)$, and the classifier find *hypothesis* for the approximation of true function *f*. Here x and y can be any value such as numeric, factor or categorical. Learning is the process of finding well performing hypothesis in the space of possible hypothesis, even for new samples which is not in the training samples. These new samples are used to measure the accuracy/ performance of hypothesis. When Y is set of categorical or factor values, the learning is classification. On the other way, when Y is a numeric value, the learning problem is called regression.

Unsupervised

Using the unlabeled historical data with similarity metrics design a clustering algorithm for feature data is known as unsupervised learning model. ML algorithm is used to predict the label for previously unseen data.

Table 1. Confusion matrix and related measures

	Predicted Yes	Predicted No
Actual Yes	TP	FN
Actual No	FP	TN

Performance Analysis

Output representation of anomaly detection is a challenging issue. Usually scores and labels are used. Scoring based anomaly detection gives score to each data. From the ranking and selection of suitable threshold anomaly is marked. Label based method identifies each record as either normal or anomaly. So, it handles different network attacks such as denial of service, probe, user to root, remote to user. This information is available in KDD data set and all the research papers are based on the ML classifiers using KDD data set with 21 type of attacks grouped into DOS, Probe, User to root and R2L. KDD data has 1,48,753 records.

Intrusion detection system is the great challenge for network administrators. This is handled traditionally with signature-based approach. Currently machine learning becomes new solution for this great challenge and it provide solution and detect attacks and anomalies under the concept of network traffic analytics [Shone.N, T. N. Ngoc, V. D. Phai and Q. Shi,2018, Ayoubi.S et al, 2018]. Major activities like regression classification and clustering are used for this security purpose. Regression is predicting network packet parameters. Based on the predicted value it could be identified as normal or abnormal. Several network attacks are available and this is handled by ML classifiers. Clustering is useful for forensic analysis and anomaly detection. Researchers concentrate on the objective to prepare optimal anomaly detection system. The ML model with low false positive and false negative is the goal of the model builder. Sometimes the feature set selection leads to false alarms and missed alerts. False positive alarms unnecessarily used the time of data analyst to verify the system. In turn it degrades the IDS performance. False negative leads to system collapse. Hence optimal anomaly detector needed to find accurately all intruders without any false alarm and miss alert. Anomaly detection system should get data from the real time in dynamic mode. Seasonality is mainly available in this real time dynamic data. These needs to be addressed in all the real time IDS. Model should adapt with respect to seasonality and trends.

Confusion Matrix

The measures such as accuracy (AC), Precision (PC), Recall (RC) and F1 measure (F1) are calculated as follows from the values of confusion matrix.

$$AC = \frac{TP + TN}{TP + TN + FP + FN}$$

$$PC = \frac{TP}{TP + FP}$$

$$RC = \frac{TP}{TP + FN}$$

$$F1 = \frac{2 \times PC \times RC}{PC + RC}$$

TP: True Positive – Total Number of records anomaly[predicted as anomaly matched with ground truth anomaly]

TN: True Negative – Total Number of record Normal [predicted as normal matched with ground truth normal]

FP: False Positive - Total Number of records anomaly [predicted as anomaly matched with ground truth Normal]

FN: False Negative - Total Number of record Normal [predicted as normal matched with ground truth anomaly]

PROCEDURE

Anomaly Detection with R

In various domain, Anomolus entities are available. This Anomaly detection is having variety of applications in engineering field. These techniques have been required in fraud detection, manufacturing fault detection, and medical device fault detection.

In this Chapter, hands on part of R Script [Nina Zumel and John Mount,2014] is explained with case study concept detect failing servers in a network. Anomaly detection, is starts with visualizing the data at the first step. Servers are characterized by two attributes such as Through-put(mb/s) and Latency(ms) of response of each server. This data set dimension is 307 X 2.

Step 1:   Apply Gaussian model to detect anomaly points in the dataset. Identify the very low probability of data using multivariate normal distribution.

Step 2:   Load the following packages to perform anomaly detection.

For data manipulation, matrix operations, find pseudo-inverse of matrix, for plotting and for pipe the output we need these packages. Magrittr, ggplot2, MASS, caret, reshape2.

Step 3:   Check the data and cross validation data.

Step 4:   Check the count. In this example 9 anamolous and 298 normal servers. Supervised learning is not possible as it is. Try with imbalanced class label techniques to get good prediction.

Imbalanced data problem could be handled by either upsampling or downsampling model.

Step 5:   If the given data set is fit into Gaussian then we do with our analysis. Else apply relevant transformation techniques to get good approximation.

Data=as.data.frame(Data)

names(Data)=c("Latency (ms)", "Throughput (mb/s)")

DataX=melt(Data)

DataX%>%ggplot(aes(x=value,fill=variable,color=variable))geom_density(alpha 0.3)+ggtitle('Distibution of Data')

Step 6: Same work for cross validated data

cval=as.data.frame(cval)

names(cval)=c("Latency (ms)", "Throughput (mb/s)")

ccval = melt(cval)

ccval%>%ggplot(aes(x=value,fill=variable, color=variable))+

geom_density(alpha = 0.3)+ggtitle('Distibution of crossvalidate data')

If the given Data and cross validate are with good approximation, no need to apply transformation technique.

Step 7: Plot the Data points and visualize the attributes Latency and Throughput.

Data%>%ggplot(aes(x=`Latency (ms)`,y=`Throughput (mb/s)`)) + geom_point(color='red')

The output is easily marked the outliers if any. Now we will proceed with Ml algorithm to yield the same output.

Step 8: Apply preprocees function in Caret package to convert given data into preprocessed data.

preprodata <- preProcess(Data,method="center")

ModifiedData <- predict(preprodata,Data)

Step 9: Calculate variance.

ModifiedData = as.matrix(ModifiedData)

variance=diag(var(ModifiedData))

Step 10: Calculate multivariate normal distribution probabilities.

Step 11: Get contour plot of the probabilities and see where the servers with highest probabilities are located.

Normal server points are with higher probability and accumulated near center.

Anomalous points dispersed away from center.

Step 12: Select any classifier. Preprocessed data pass on to the classifier with cross validation.

We have Xtrain and Ytrain split for training . Ytrain with output label either normal server or anomalous server. Xtrain includes predictors.

Step 13: Compute performance metrics using confusion matrix. Measures used here are True positive rate, False positive rate, accuracy, precision, recall and F1 score.

Step 14: Plot AUC and RoC curve for the results.

Step 15: Model predicted accuracy is considered as a measure. We run the data with different classifiers and pick the best model.

Step 16: Compare the visualization graph based anomaly detection outcome with best model outcome.

CASE 1: DETECTION OF TRANSACTION DATA AS FRAUDULENT OR NOT FRAUDULENT USING ML

This case study analyze the transaction data and detect whether the transaction is fraudulent or not. For this, consider the transactions data set with 40,000 data with five features such as account_Age, No_item, Time, payment_method (categorical), Class. Class with 0 – not fraudulent, 1-Fraudulent. Convert categorical into numeric. Install required packages, divide data and apply five classifiers and get performance metrics.

```
# load libraries
library(mlbench)
library(caret)
# load the dataset
# load CSV file example: acc.csv
# prepare training scheme
control <- trainControl(method="repeatedcv", number=10, repeats=3)
# CART
set.seed(7)
fit.cart <- train(Class~., data=acc, method="rpart", trControl=control)
# LDA
set.seed(7)
fit.lda <- train(Class~., data=acc, method="lda", trControl=control)
# SVM
set.seed(7)
fit.svm <- train(Class~., data= acc, method="svmRadial", trControl=control)
# kNN
set.seed(7)
fit.knn <- train(Class~., data=acc, method="knn", trControl=control)
# Random Forest
set.seed(7)
fit.rf <- train(Class~., data=acc, method="rf", trControl=control)
# collect resamples
results <- resamples(list(CART=fit.cart, LDA=fit.lda, SVM=fit.svm, KNN=fit.knn, RF=fit.rf))
results
summary(results)
```

CASE 2: CLASSIFIERS FOR ANOMALY DETECTION

Logistic Regression.

Get the data . In this data n attributes and class label column with two values (Normal and Anomalous)
  Consider Normal as 0 and Anomalous as 1. The data now treated as binary classifier.
  Split the data into training and testing data in the ratio 80,20.

Now X_train is a set with only predictors. Y_train is only the class label with 0 or 1.
Keep 20% of data with X_test and Y_test for validating the model.

```
#logistic regression code
Data=read.csv("server data.csv")
dim(Data) # m entries with n attributes
X-train=Data(:,-class)
Y_train=Data(class)
Fit_lr=glm(Y_train~.,data=Data,family='binomial')
summary(Fit_lr)
p=predict(Fit_lr,X_test)
```

2.   Decision tree

Keep the same X_train and Y_train; X_test,Y_test.

```
#code get data and install rpart package to run decision tree classifier
library(rpart)
dtfit=rpart(Y_train~.,data=Data,method="class")
summary(dtfit)
p=predict(dtfit,X_test)
```

3.   SVM

```
library(e1071)
svmfit=svm(Y_train~.,data=Data)
summary(svmfit)
p=predict(svmfit,X_test)
```

4.Naive Bayes

```
library(e1071)
nbfit=naivebayes(Y_train~.,data=Data)
summary(nbfit)
p=predict(nbfit,X_test)
```

5.   kNN (k- Nearest Neighbors)

```
library(knn)
knnfit=knn(Y_train~.,data=Data,k=2)
summary(knnfit)
p=predict(knnfit,X_test)
```

Figure 7.

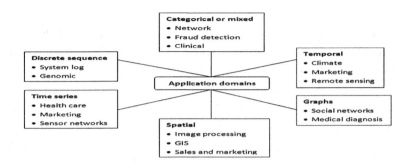

CASE 3: TIME SERIES DATA - ANOMALY DETECTION

Clustering based anomaly detection filter the abnormal data which is not included in any one of the cluster or it is formed as a separate small cluster. It also provides proportion of the outliers present in the given data set. This is calculated as number of outliers. Sequence of observation is considered in the time series model with in uniform interval. If the probability of occurrence is unseen data is negligble then it is labeled as abnormal. Due to trend analysis in time series data, it is possible to detect the abnormalities. But the computational cost will be high. Time series model such as auto regressive moving average (ARMA), generalized auto regressive moving average (GARMA) are example models for IDS. Data types based on applications related to IDS are represented in Figure 7.

```
library(anomalize)
library(tidyverse)
library(coindeskr)
Pri <- get_historic_price(start = "2017-01-01")
Pri_ts <- Pri %>% rownames_to_column() %>% as.tibble() %>%
mutate(date = as.Date(rowname)) %>% select(-one_of('rowname'))
Pri_ts %>%
time_decompose(Price) %>%
anomalize(remainder) %>%
time_recompose() %>%
plot_anomalies(time_recomposed = TRUE, ncol = 3, alpha_dots = 0.5)
Pri_ts %>%
time_decompose(Price, method = "stl", frequency = "auto", trend = "auto") %>%
anomalize(remainder, method = "gesd", alpha = 0.05, max_anoms = 0.2) %>%
plot_anomaly_decomposition()
Pri_ts %>%
time_decompose(Price) %>%
anomalize(remainder) %>%
time_recompose() %>%
filter(anomaly == 'Yes')
```

CONCLUSION

Machine learned model perfectly worked on a training set but performance is degraded in testing set. Common reason is over fit of classification boundary on the training set. The characteristic of the learning data set could not be generalized for other unseen data sets. Proper care should be taken in the designing the classifier model to address over fit and under fit problems. Selection of best classifier algorithm depends upon the nature of the data. Consider the computational complexity, simple implementation and scalability. Here training data construction is another important part of the best model. Cross validation is used to mitigate the over fit problem and helps to get best model parameter. In real time scenario, data set with normal cases examples are larger than abnormal cases. This data set is called imbalanced data set. We need to carefully balance it by up sampling and down sampling technique. Model performance mainly depends on the relevant features selection. The performance of the designed model is evaluated through several metrics which depends on the methods applied and application.

REFERENCES

Ahuja & Solanki. (2019). Movie Recommender System Using K-Means Clustering AND K-Nearest Neighbor. In *9th International Conference on Cloud Computing, Data Science & Engineering*. Amity University.

Al-Garadi, Ali, Mohamed, Al-Ali, Du, & Guizani. (2018). *A Survey of Machine and Deep Learning Methods for Internet of Things (IoT) Security*. CoRR abs/1807.11023

Ayoubi. (2018). Machine Learning for Cognitive Network Management. IEEE Communications Magazine, 56(1), 158-165. doi:10.1109/MCOM.2018.1700560

Cárdenas, P., Theodoropoulos, G., Obara, B., & Kureshi, I. (2018). A Conceptual Framework for Social Movements Analytics for National Security. Lecture Notes in Computer Science, 10860. doi:10.1007/978-3-319-93698-7_23

Conti, M., Dehghantanha, A., Franke, K., & Watson, S. (2018). Internet of Things security and forensics: Challenges and opportunities. *Future Generation Computer Systems*, 78(Part 2), 544–546. doi:10.1016/j.future.2017.07.060

Dey, N., Ashour, A. S., Shi, F., Fong, S. J., & João, M. R. S. (2018). Tavares, Medical cyber-physical systems: A survey. *Journal of Medical Systems*, 42(4), 74. doi:10.100710916-018-0921-x PMID:29525900

Harrington, P. (2012). *Machine learning in action* (Vol. 5). Greenwich: Manning.

Lin, Z., Yan, Z., Chen, Y., & Zhang, L. (2018). Yan, Y. Chen and L. Zhang, "A Survey on Network Security-Related Data Collection Technologies. *IEEE Access: Practical Innovations, Open Solutions*, 6, 18345–18365. doi:10.1109/ACCESS.2018.2817921

Liu, Q., Li, P., Zhao, W., Cai, W., Yu, S., & Leung, V. C. M. (2018). A Survey on Security threats and Defensive Techniques of Machine Learning: A Data Driven View. *IEEE Access: Practical Innovations, Open Solutions*, 6, 12103–12117. doi:10.1109/ACCESS.2018.2805680

McNab. (2007). *Network Security Assesment* (2nd ed.). Academic Press.

Mohammed, D., Omar, M., & Nguyen, V. (2018). Wireless Sensor Network Security: Approaches to Detecting and Avoiding Wormhole Attacks. *Journal of Research in Business. Economics and Management*, *10*(2), 1860–1864.

Nawir, M., Amir, A., Yaakob, N., & Lynn, O. B. (2019, March). Effective and efficient network anomaly detection system using machine learning algorithm. *Bulletin of Electrical Engineering and Informatics*, *8*(1), 46–51. doi:10.11591/eei.v8i1.1387

Padmanabha, Ramnaresh, & Obulakonda. (2018). A Study on Medical Imaging Techniques with Metrics and Issues in Security Cryptosystem *Indian Journal of Public Health Research & Development*, *9*(12), 2544-2549.

Papageorgiou, A., Strigkos, M., Politou, E., Alepis, E., Solanas, A., & Patsakis, C. (2018). Security and Privacy Analysis of Mobile Health Applications: The Alarming State of Practice. *IEEE Access: Practical Innovations, Open Solutions*, *6*, 9390–9403. doi:10.1109/ACCESS.2018.2799522

Sammut, C., & Webb, G. I. (Eds.). (2011). *Encyclopedia of machine learning*. Springer Science & Business Media.

Schwartz, B., & Jinka, P. (2016). *Anomaly Detection for Monitoring, Publisher*. O'Reilly Media, Inc.

Sha, K., Wei, W., Andrew Yang, T., Wang, Z., & Shi, W. (2018). On security challenges and open issues in Internet of Things. *Future Generation Computer Systems*, *83*, 326–337. doi:10.1016/j.future.2018.01.059

Shone, Ngoc, Phai, & Shi. (2018). A Deep Learning Approach to Network Intrusion Detection. *IEEE Transactions on Emerging Topics in Computational Intelligence*, *2*(1), 41-50. doi:10.1109/TETCI.2017.2772792

Wang, M., Cui, Y., Wang, X., Xiao, S., & Jiang, J. (2018). Machine Learning for Networking: Workflow, Advances and Opportunities. *IEEE Network*, *32*(2), 92–99. doi:10.1109/MNET.2017.1700200

Witten & Tibshirani. (2013). *An Introduction to Statistical Learning with Applications in R*. Academic Press.

Xiao, Liang, Wan, Lu, Zhang, & Wu. (2018). *IoT Security Techniques Based on Machine Learning*. CoRR abs/1801.06275

Zumel & Mount. (2014). *Practical data science with R*. Manning Publications.

APPENDIX

Table 2.

Code	Description
# Chunk1 A1<- c(10, 30, 54, 12, 16, 29, 43,4 9, 12, 37) A2<- c(14.4, 25.3, 37.2, 15.2, 18.5, 27.3, 36, 10.4,15.2, 26.1) mean(A 1) sd(A2) cor(A1, A2) plot(A1, A2) q()	A Sample R code Creating two attributes; Compute mean, standard deviation correlation Plot x vs. y Quit the session
# Chunk2 setwd("C:/rdemo/basics") options() options(digits=4) B1 <- runif(25) Summary(B1) hist(B1) savehistory() save.image()	R Workspace managing commands

# Chunk3 	
?plot
help.start()
library("vcd") # or use install.packages()
help(mtcars) # mtcars is an inbuilt data
View(mtcars)
example(mtcars)
	Installing and Working with R packages
	Getting help about R commands

# Chunk4 	
A1 <- seq(-3:3)
b <- c("CSE", "IT", "ICT","PG")
logi<- c(TRUE, TRUE, TRUE, FALSE, TRUE)
# # subscripts usage 	
A1 <- c(1, 2, 5, 3, 6, -2, 4)
A1 [4]
A1 [c(1, 3, 5)]
A1 [2:6]
	Vcd package installation and using their functions
	Getting data Arthritis information
	Creating & accessing vectors

# Chunk5 mat <- matrix(1:20, nrow = 4, ncol = 5) mat Value <- c(11, 16, 4, 6,34,56,45,78,66) rwnames <- c("Rw1", "Rw2","Rw3") conames <- c("Co1", "Co2","Co3") Newmatrix <- matrix(Value, nrow = 3, ncol = 3, byrow = TRUE, dimnames = list(rwnames, conames)) Newmatrix Newmatrix <- matrix(Value, nrow = 3, ncol = 3, byrow = FALSE, dimnames = list(rwnames, conames)) Newmatrix Bmat <- matrix(1:10, nrow = 2) Bmat [2,] Bmat [, 2] Bmat [1, 4] Bmat [1, c(4, 5)]	Creating & accessing Matrices

#Chunk6
D1 <- c("Ar1", "Ar2")
D2 <- c("Bo1", "Bo2", "Bo3")
D3 <- c("Cd1", "Cd2", "Cd3", "Cd4")
Ar <- array(1:24, c(2, 3, 4), dimnames = list(D1, D2, D3))
Ar
#dataframe
staffID <- c(11, 12, 13, 14)
age <- c(26, 33, 29, 56)
worktype <- c("PG", "UG", "UG", "PG")
designation <- c("Prof", "ACP", "SAP", "AP")
socdata <- data.frame(staffID, age, worktype, designation)
socdata
socdata[1:2]
socdata[c("worktype", "designation")]
socdata$age
str(socdata)
summary(socdata)
	Creating & accessing an array, dataframe

continued on following page

Table 2. Continued

Code	Description

#Chunk7
# print current working directory. 	
    print(getwd())
# Set current working directory. 	
    setwd("/NW/security")
# Get and print current working directory. 	
    print(getwd())
	Working directory setting

#Chunk8
#Reading Table
Newdata <- read.table("c:/Newdata.csv", header=TRUE, sep=",", row.names="id")
#Reading from Excel (with single sheet)
library(xlsx)
Newdata <- read.xlsx("c:/Newexcel.xlsx", 1)
# read in the worksheet named *mysheet* (from multiple sheet of excel, read from particular sheet, named datasheet) 	
Newdata <- read.xlsx("c:/Newexcel.xlsx", sheetName = "datasheet")
#Reading from csv file
Newdata <- read.csv("input.csv")
#Browse and select the file
Newdata <- read.csv(file.choose())
	Reading Data

#Chunk9
#Writing into txt file
write.table(Datavalue, "c:/Newdata.txt", sep="\t")
#Writing into excel file
library(xlsx)
write.xlsx(Datavalue, "c:/Newdata.xlsx")
#Writing into csv file
write.csv(Datavalue,"c:/Newdata.csv")
	Writing Data

#Chunk 10
library(tidyverse) # for visualization of data
library(gridExtra) # for plots
NewData <- read.csv("C:/ NewData.CSV")
# extracting all features, except class-label (assuming class-label is 1st column) to apply PCA 	
    NewData=data[,-1]
# variance computation of each feature 	
    apply(NewData, 2, var)
# create new data frame with centered variables 	
    scaleDt <- apply(NewData, 2, scale)
# Compute eigenvalues and eigenvectors 	
NewData.covari <- cov(scaleDt)
NewData.eigen <- eigen(NewData.covari)
str(NewData.eigen)
VariPro <- NewData.eigen$values / sum(NewData.eigen$values)
round(VariPro, 2)
# VariPro plot, example assumption 30 features 	
VariProplot <- qplot(c(1:30), VariPro) +
geom_line() + xlab("Principal Component") +
ylab("Variance Proportion") +
ggtitle("Scree Plot to find the significant
components") + ylim(0, 1)
grid.arrange(VariProplot)
# by using in built function prcomp without plot 	
    pca_outcome <- prcomp(NewData, scale = TRUE)
    (Vari <- pca_outcome$sdev^2)
    pca_vari <- Vari / sum(Vari)
    round(pca_vari, 2)
#Outcome: 30 components since we gave 30 features
[1] 0.44 0.19 0.09 0.07 0.05 0.04 0.02 0.02 0.01 0.01 0.01 0.01 0.01 0.01 0.00
[16] 0.00 0.00 0.00 0.00 0.00 0.00 0.00 0.00 0.00 0.00 0.00 0.00 0.00 0.00 0.00
The values in bold conveys 44+19+9+7+5+4= 88% of variance.
	Principal Component Analysis

#Chunk11
library(infotheo) # for discrete and mutinformation
NewData=iris
# the values should discrete for mutual information calculation 	
NewData=discretize(NewData)
class_pos=ncol(NewData)
#to get the relationship based on the entropy of the empirical probability distribution
EMI=mutinformation(NewData,method= "emp") #MI between features and class
EMI[-class_pos,class_pos] #MI between each feature and class; assuming class label is the last column
#to get the relationship based on the Miller-Madow asmptotic empirical estimator
MMI=mutinformation(NewData,method= "mm")
MMI[-class_pos,class_pos]
#to get the relationship based on the shrinkage estimation of entropy (Dirichlet probability distribution)
DPI=mutinformation(NewData,method= "shrink")
DPI[-class_pos,class_pos]
#to get the relationship based on Schurmann-Grassberger estimate of the entropy (DP)
SGI=mutinformation(NewData,method= "sg")
SGI[-class_pos,class_pos]
	Mutual information (MI):
	Mutual Information measures the mutual dependency between the feature and class label.

continued on following page

Table 2. Continued

Code	Description

#Chunk12
Species=as.numeric(iris[,5])
NewData=cbind(iris[,1:4],Species)
class_pos=ncol(NewData)
correlation1=cor(NewData,method= "pearson") #pearson correlation between features and class
#cor between each feature and class; assuming class label is the last column
pearson=correlation1[-class_pos,class_pos]
correlation2=cor(NewData,method= "kendall") #kendall correlation between features and class
kendall=correlation2[-class_pos,class_pos]
correlation3=cor(NewData,method= "spearman") #spearman correlation between features and class
spearman=correlation3[-class_pos,class_pos]
result=cbind(pearson,kendall,spearman)
result
	Correlation: Correlation measure between the feature and class label can be calculated from the following code.

#Chunk13
# linear regression 	
model<- lm(mpg ~ wt, data = mtcars)
summary(model)
mtcars$mpg
fitted(model)
residuals(model)
# height Vs weight- scatter plot 	
plot(mtcars$hp, mtcars$mpg, main = "mtcars")
# display best fit line 	
abline(model)
#Polynomial regression
Model2 <- lm(mpg ~ wt + I(wt^2), data = mtcars)
summary(Model2)
#Multiple LR
data(mtcars)
View(mtcars)
Model <- lm(mpg ~wt + hp + hp:wt, data = mtcars)
summary(Model)
library(effects)
plot(effect("hp:wt", Model, list(wt = c(2.3, 3.1, 4.1))), multiline = TRUE)
	Regression

#Chunk14
data(breslow.dat, package = "robust")
names(breslow.dat)
summary(breslow.dat[c(6, 7, 8, 10)])
# plot distribution of post-treatment seizure counts 	
opar <- par(no.readonly = TRUE)
par(mfrow = c(1, 2))
attach(breslow.dat)
hist(sumY, breaks = 20, xlab = "Seizure Count", main = "Distribution of Seizures")
boxplot(sumY ~ Trt, xlab = "Treatment", main = "Group Comparisons")
par(opar)
# regression 	
Model <- glm(sumY ~ Base + Age + Trt, data = breslow.dat, family = poisson())
summary(Model)
# interpret model 	
coef(Model)
exp(coef(Model))
# evaluate over dispersion 	
library(qcc)
qcc.overdispersion.test(breslow.dat$sumY, type = "poisson")
# using quasipoisson 	
Model1 <- glm(sumY ~ Base + Age + Trt, data = breslow.dat, family = quasipoisson())
summary(Model1)
	Poisson Regression

continued on following page

Table 2. Continued

Code	Description
``#Chunk15
data(sleep, package = "VIM")
# list the missing values rows
sleep[complete.cases(sleep),]
list one or more missing values rows
sleep[!complete.cases(sleep),]
# number of missing values on Dream
sum(is.na(sleep$Dream))
# percent of cases with missing values on Dream
mean(is.na(sleep$Dream))
# percent of cases with one or missing values
mean(!complete.cases(sleep))
# tabulate missing values
library(mice)
md.pattern(sleep)
# plot missing values patterns
library("VIM")
# close GUI window
aggr(sleep, prop = FALSE, numbers = TRUE)
matrixplot(sleep) # use mouse to sort columns, STOP to move on
marginplot(sleep[c("Gest", "Dream")], pch = c(20), col = c("darkgray", "red", "blue"))
# explore missing values using correlations
A <- as.data.frame(abs(is.na(sleep)))
head(sleep, n=5)
head(A, n=5)
B <- A[which(sd(A) > 0)]
cor(B)
cor(sleep, B, use = "pairwise.complete.obs")
# complete case analysis (listwise deletion)
cor(na.omit(sleep))
Model <- lm(Dream ~ Span + Gest, data = na.omit(sleep))
summary(Model)
# multiple imputation
library(mice)
data(sleep, package = "VIM")
imp <- mice(sleep, seed = 1234)
Model1 <- with(imp, lm(Dream ~ Span + Gest))
pooled <- pool(Model1)
summary(pooled)
imp
dataset3 <- complete(imp, action=3)
dataset3
pairwise deletion
cor(sleep, use="pairwise.complete.obs")```	Imputation

continued on following page

Table 2. Continued

Code	Description
| ```
#Chunk 16
library(cluster)
# prepare matrix of data
# Dataset 1
Values<-c(1.0,1.0,1.5,2.0,3.0,4.0,5.0,7.0,3.5,5.0,4.5,5.0,3.5,4.5)
Values
rwnames<-c("A","B","C","D","E","F","G")
rwnames
conames<-c("X","Y")
conames
mat<-matrix(Values,nrow=7,ncol=2,byrow=TRUE,dimnames= list(rwnames,conames))
mat
# run K-Means
km<- kmeans(x,2,15)
# print components of km
print(km)
# plot clusters
plot(mat,col=(km$cluster+1),main="K means Clustering",pch=20,cex=5)
### method2
# import data in csv format
dt <- read.csv("E:/.../kmeans.csv")
dt
# run K-Means
km<- kmeans(dt,2,15)
# print components of km
print(km)
# plot clusters
plot(dt,col=(km$cluster+1),main="K means Clustering",pch=20,cex=5)
# Agglomerative Nesting (AGNES) - Hierarchical Clustering
library(cluster)
df <- USArrests
df
df <- na.omit(df)
df
df <- scale(df)
df
head(df)
# Dissimilarity matrix
d <- dist(df, method = "euclidean")
# Hierarchical clustering using single method
res.hc <- hclust(d, method = "single")
# Plot the obtained dendrogram
plot(res.hc, cex = 0.6, hang = -1)
# Hierarchical clustering using average method
res.hc <- hclust(d, method = "average")
# Plot the obtained dendrogram
plot(res.hc, cex = 0.6, hang = -1)
# Hierarchical clustering using complete method
res.hc <- hclust(d, method = "complete")
# Plot the obtained dendrogram
plot(res.hc, cex = 0.6, hang = -1)
#Divisive Analysis (DIANA) - Hierarchical Clustering
# Compute diana()
res.diana <- diana(df)
# Plot the tree
pltree(res.diana, cex = 0.6, hang = -1,main = "Dendrogram of diana")
#Agglomerative Nesting (AGNES) - Hierarchical Clustering
# Example 2: mtcars
# prepare hierarchical cluster
mtcars
d <- dist(as.matrix(mtcars)) # find distance matrix
hc = hclust(d)
# very simple dendrogram
plot(hc)
#Example3:Iris Dataset
set.seed(1)
i=iris[-5]
s=sample(1:150,10)
s
da=i[s,]
as=scale(da)
di=dist(das)
hcs=hclust(di,method='single')
plot(hcs)
hcc=hclust(di,method='complete')
plot(hcc)
hca=hclust(di,method='average')
plot(hca)
``` | Clustering |

continued on following page
```

Table 2. Continued

Code	Description

`#Chunk 17`
`set.seed(0)`
`actual = c('a','b','c')[runif(100, 1,4)] # actual labels`
`actual`
`predicted = actual # predicted labels`
`predicted[runif(25,1,100)] = actual[runif(25,1,100)] # introduce incorrect predictions`
`predicted`
`cm = as.matrix(table(Actual = actual, Predicted = predicted)) # create the confusion matrix`
`cm`
`# displaying simulated actual Vs predicted label`
`cb=cbind(actual, predicted)`
`cb`
`###### Basic Varialbles Reqd`
`n = sum(cm) # number of instances`
`nc = nrow(cm) # number of classes`
`diag = diag(cm) # number of correctly classified instances per class`
`rowsums = apply(cm, 1, sum) # number of instances per class`
`colsums = apply(cm, 2, sum) # number of predictions per class`
`p = rowsums / n # distribution of instances over the actual classes`
`q = colsums / n # distribution of instances over the predicted classes`
`###### Accuracy`
`accuracy = sum(diag) / n`
`accuracy`
`###### Precision, Recall, f1 measure`
`precision = diag / colsums`
`recall = diag / rowsums`
`f1 = 2 * precision * recall / (precision + recall)`
`data.frame(precision, recall, f1)`
`# box and whisker plots to compare models`
`scales <- list(x=list(relation="free"), y=list(relation="free"))`
`bwplot(results, scales=scales)`
`# density plots of accuracy`
`scales <- list(x=list(relation="free"), y=list(relation="free"))`
`densityplot(results, scales=scales, pch = "|")`
`# dot plots of accuracy`
`scales <- list(x=list(relation="free"), y=list(relation="free"))`
`dotplot(results, scales=scales)`
`# parallel plots to compare models`
`parallelplot(results)`
`# pair-wise scatterplots of predictions to compare models`
`splom(results)`
`# xyplot plots to compare models`
`xyplot(results, models=c("LDA", "SVM"))`
`# difference in model predictions`
`diffs <- diff(results)`
`# summarize p-values for pair-wise comparisons`
`summary(diffs)`
	Performance Evaluation Metrics in R Confusion Matrix

continued on following page

Chapter 14
Information Retrieval in Conjunction With Deep Learning

Anu Bajaj

iD https://orcid.org/0000-0001-8563-6611

Department of Computer Science and Engineering, Guru Jambheshwar University of Science and Technology, Hisar, India

Tamanna Sharma

Department of Computer Science and Technology, Guru Jambheshwar University of Science and Technology, Hisar, India

Om Prakash Sangwan

Department of Computer Science and Technology, Guru Jambheshwar University of Science and Technology, Hisar, India

ABSTRACT

Information is second level of abstraction after data and before knowledge. Information retrieval helps fill the gap between information and knowledge by storing, organizing, representing, maintaining, and disseminating information. Manual information retrieval leads to underutilization of resources, and it takes a long time to process, while machine learning techniques are implications of statistical models, which are flexible, adaptable, and fast to learn. Deep learning is the extension of machine learning with hierarchical levels of learning that make it suitable for complex tasks. Deep learning can be the best choice for information retrieval as it has numerous resources of information and large datasets for computation. In this chapter, the authors discuss applications of information retrieval with deep learning (e.g., web search by reducing the noise and collecting precise results, trend detection in social media analytics, anomaly detection in music datasets, and image retrieval).

DOI: 10.4018/978-1-5225-9643-1.ch014

Table 1. IR models

IR Models	Description
Boolean Model	In this model, the query is represented by Boolean expression of terms and the terms are connected with Boolean operators.
Vector Space Model	In this model, the word and phrases are known as terms and these terms are represented in form of vectors.
Probabilistic Model	It assesses the probability of significance to the query. The documents are ordered by decreasing probability of their significance known as probability ranking principle.
Inference Network Model	The documents are modeled using the inference process in the inference networks. The documents are ranked according to the term strength.

INTRODUCTION

We come across with huge amount of data day by day, which is mainly because of the social media, web and mobile applications usage, e.g., 15 GB of data is generated by Facebook alone (Kanimozhi & Padmini, 2018). This exponentially growing unstructured data in the form of web logs, data records, and sensor data etc. need to be converted into useful information. The information is what we acquire from the unconstrained data to fill the knowledge gap. For example, we want to buy some product then we need to resort to the customers review about the particular product. On positive response of product we would be likely to purchase the product else not. This is just a small example why information retrieval is important. The archival of the inscribed information may be tracked from 3000 BC where the Sumerians deposited clay tablets with cuneiform inscriptions (Singhal, 2001). For proficient use of information even they also projected special classification for identification of each tablet and its contents. Hence, the information retrieval (IR) is the process of archiving, organizing, maintaining the information collected from a huge database and disseminating the same to fill the user's needs. In other words, IR system reads the user's query and look out for information in the documents (database and knowledge base) for image, text, sound, and sensing data etc. and this retrieved information is responded back to the users (Guan & Zhang, 2008). The retrieved documents are ranked with their estimate of importance of document for a particular query. Intermediate stages are indexing, filtering, searching matching and ranking of the documents. In indexing the documents are indexed using signature files or inverted indices etc. and the filters remove all the stop words white spaces etc., finally the query in searched by using any brute force search, and linear search (Kanimozhi & Padmini, 2018), and the matched documents are ranked based on their similarity with the query. The user is responded back with the top ranked documents. Several models have been proposed for this purpose (Singhal, 2001) as shown in Table 1.

It is different from the Database Management System (DBMS) in the sense that it is probabilistic (unstructured data) in nature while DBMS (structured data in tables) is deterministic. This is because the IR system searches the documents for the keywords provided by the query and in response give all the significant documents containing the required information. On the other hand, DBMS respond to exact match of the query and give the very specific response. It has started its journey from the library management which expands to office automation, knowledge extraction, multimedia management, medical information management, etc. applications. Due to the advent of internet, the data is growing exponentially day by day which needs to be handled efficiently. Hence some sort of automation is re-

Figure 1. Information retrieval architecture

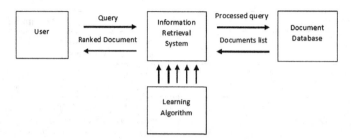

quired to retrieve the information from such a large archive. Researchers started experimenting IR with machine learning techniques which is discussed in the section 3. The next section 4 explains why the deep learning techniques are more prominent than the machine learning techniques. Finally, we have concluded this chapter in the last section 5.

INFORMATION RETRIEVAL WITH MACHINE LEARNING

IR becomes more efficient and effective with the help of machine learning algorithms. Figure 1 show the complete IR process. The machine learning algorithms are classified into two parts: supervised and unsupervised learning (Alzubi, Nayyar, & Kumar, 2018) as shown in Table 2.

IR is used in various domains like digital libraries, medical diagnostics, image retrieval, chemo-informatics, music systems, question answering, social media analytics etc. In this section we are providing the literature work done in the domain of IR using machine learning approaches.

Simple query asked by the user is no longer provide appropriate results. Hence, the query needs to be modified using the similar terms for better results. The authors (Kim, Seo, & Croft, 2011) have proposed a Boolean query expansion method and exploited the decision trees for producing the Boolean queries by learning through pseudo labelled documents and ranking is done on the basis of query quality predictors. A query expansion method (Diaz, Mitra, & Craswell, 2016) was developed on the basis of local trained word embedding that captured the nuances of topic specific language. They suggested to use large topically-unconstrained corpora instead of topically constrained corpora. Support vector machine (Drucker, Shahrary, & Gibbon, 2002) has been used to provide relevant feedback for the queries in which we have less number of retrieved documents to enhance the response.

Medical diagnostic systems have also started using machine learning techniques for decision making in emergency context e.g. for prioritization of requests. The authors (Pollettini, Pessotti, Filho, Ruiz, & Junior, 2015) have used the conceptual IR i.e. the textual processing of the clinical data e.g., diagnosis, chief complaint etc. to discover the similar cases in the databases. The patients' appropriate destination the priority of the request was automatically assigned by using top k cases and voting system. The researchers have found that the use of decision tree with random forest gave good results for the classification. They also found that the semantic approach is better and faster than the text mining approaches. In the study (Song, He, Hu, & He, 2015) two re-ranking method for medical decision support systems was developed. Content based image retrieval (Sinha & Kangarloo, 2002) was proposed with principal

Table 2. Machine learning approaches

Machine Learning	Methods	Description
Supervised Learning	Multiple Regression Analysis	It is a statistical approach that determines relation amongst independent variables and dependent variables.
	k-Nearest Neighbor (kNN)	It classifies the object surrounded by its k (integer) nearest neighbor using the majority rule.
	Naive Bayes	It is a probabilistic method which uses Bayes formula for predicting membership with the assumption that the features are independent.
	Random forest	It is used to classify the objects based on the majority voting rules and ensemble of the multiple decision trees.
	Neural network and deep learning	Neural network (NN) has layers of connected neurons which learns from with input layer, hidden layers (multiple in case of deep learning) and output layers.
	Support vector machine	It is a technique which draws input to high dimensional space by constructing a set of hyperplanes through some non linear mapping.
Unsupervised learning	k-means Clustering	It is a classification approach to classify observations into k clusters by minimizing the total intra-cluster variance.
	Hierarchical Clustering	It generates a hierarchical clusters for classification by agglomerative (merge up smaller clusters) clustering or divisive (split larger clusters) clustering.
	Principal Component Analysis	It is a technique for transformation of a set of interrelated features to principal components by using the orthogonal procedure.
	Independent Component Analysis	It is a statistical technique to separate the multivariable output from statistical independent additive components.

component analysis that reduced the search dimensionality using a set of prototype images. The match is found by producing the projection vector of query image and comparing to that of the database images.

Text retrieval using the Naïve Bayes method have been proposed by (Lewis, 1998) for independent text classification. The authors (Kumar, Ye, & Doermann, 2012) have applied learning techniques on the document images for retrieval and classification. The images have different patch code words which have been used for their retrieval. The labelled images are recursively partitioned into horizontal and vertical partitions and a histogram of patches of each partition is then calculated which gave very high precision and recall when trained with random forest classifier. Image retrieval was done by (Fu & Qui, 2012) using the random forest machine learning technique in which they used visual features to divide the tree nodes and image labels for supervising the division so that the similar semantic images may get located to same tree node. Semantic neighbor set of the querying image is found first and then the ranking is done with the help of semantic similarity measurement amongst the querying image and the image in its semantic neighbor set.

The authors (Maarek, Berry, & Kaiser, 1991) have constructed the software libraries by first aggregating the attributes from the natural language documents using indexing technique and then the hierarchy for browsing was automatically generated by clustering of these documents on the basis of the extracted attributes. Probabilistic model has been used to examine the lexical information for software clustering (Corazza, Di Martino, Maggio, & Scanniello, 2011). Information was retrieved from six different vocabularies, i.e., class, method, comments, and source code statements by applying automatic weight mechanism to check the contribution of each vocabulary. These weights are optimized by using iterative expectation-maximization algorithm. Vector space model has been applied for computing the similarity among classes which is useful in making the software clusters.

The authors (Sathya, Jayanthi, & Basker, 2011) projected intelligent cluster search engine by using k-means clustering because the traditional search engines used ranking algorithm which did not properly classify the web pages, therefore, did not provide the relevant web pages. The IR technique had been improved by comparing co-occurring terms and documents clustering. In the study (Yang & Lee, 2006) have used the machine learning technique for information searching. A navigational map has been established for the World Wide Web by using the proposed learning technique. The web pages mapping was done with self-organization map and their relation with thematic keywords were established by the feature maps. These maps were then used to develop a structure for assisting the users in IR. Learning to rank method have been used for combining translation resources to cross-lingual IR (CLIR). CLIR search information in one language while the query is produced in other language. Monolingual IR features (Azarbonyad, Shakery, & Faili, 2019) have been used to map to the cross lingual IR by using translation information from different translation resources. It is showed that learning to rank techniques have improved the CLIR performance.

Another application of IR is community question answering where some people ask questions and anybody who has knowledge of the subject may answer the query. We have microblog platforms also where one can find answers to some specific event, subject or task. These knowledge bases are becoming larger day by day. For example twitter data is real time and social or geographical impact, therefore, valuable historic information is context rich and up to date also. Hence, there is need for some automation learning mechanism to answer the complex queries. Learning to rank (LTR) mechanism (Herrera, Poblete, & Parra, 2018) has been applied to re-rank the significant answers on the top locations. IR is also used for trend detection in social media analytics. The authors (Hore & Bhattacharaya, 2019) have used machine intelligence for classifying the opinions or suggestions of people in India on the hot topic of "save the girl child" under the slogan of "Beti Bachao Beti Padhao".

Chemo informatics extract, process and extrapolate the meaningful data from chemical structures. Due to huge amount of drug data it is impossible for drug designers to extract specific drug properties for specific drug designing. In the study (Lo, Rensi, Torng, & Altman, 2018) have used the machine learning technique and QSAR analysis for chemical fingerprints and similarity analysis. Several other works based on chemo informatics in combination with machine learning algorithms are there in the literature e.g. regression analysis (Eriksson et al., 2003), naïve base classifiers (Chen, Sheridan, Hornak, & Voigt, 2012), k nearest neighbors (Lo et al., 2015) etc.

Unsupervised learning was applied (Lu, Wu, Lu, & Lerch, 2016) for anomaly detection in music datasets. Music IR is the combination of various fields, i.e., electrical engineering, psychology, musicology and computer science and engineering. They have retrieved the music data by using statistical model and common features were extracted. The appropriate labelling of the anomalous music genre dataset is done by labelling them as corrupted, distorted or mislabeled clips without any requirement of training data. Probability density function has been used (Hansen et al., 2007) for clean the broadcast and CD collections on the basis of segmentation problems, missing and wrong meta-data. They found the relation between the music features and meta-data and also spotted the unlikely music features by training conditional and unconditional densities.

Table 3. Deep learning techniques

Deep Learning Techniques	Description
Deep Neural Networks (DNN)	It comprises of multiple hidden layers with each layer having hundreds of nonlinear processing components. It takes large number of input features and extract features automatically from various hierarchical stages by using neurons of different layers.
Convolution Neural Networks (CNN)	It consists of several convolutional layers (having a set of filters with small receptive fields and learnable parameters) and subsampling layers (reduces the feature map size). The feature maps are joined to get fully connected layers to get a final output.
Recurrent Neural Networks (RNN)	It takes sequential data as input and forms a directed cycle by allowing the connections among neurons in the same hidden layers. It may diminish the vanishing gradient problem by using long short term memory (LSTM).
Autoencoder	It has encoder NN which converts the information from input layer to some hidden layers and then fed to decoder NN which rebuild its own inputs using lesser number of hidden layers. Hence its basic purpose is dimensionality reduction.

Information Retrieval in Conjunction with Deep Learning

As we have discussed in introduction section that the data is growing exponentially and to learn from such a huge database is cumbersome task. Hence, traditional machine learning algorithms are not suitable for big data which have volume (scalable data), velocity (data growth), variety (diverse sources) and veracity (uncertain data). Therefore, deep learning approaches came into practice which vanishes the effects of gradients, so, more suitable to use with raw high-dimensional data (Hinton, Osindero, & The, 2006). Deep learning found its origin from Neural Networks in which feed forward NN combined with many hidden layers i.e. it learns from low features to high level features e.g. it can learn raw pixel input as color information and in the next layer it may go up to edge of the object using the previous layer information. Deep learning automatically select raw, heterogonous, high dimensional data, without manual selection. As a result, machine learning has shifted towards deep learning due to data driven and computational power driven activities. The major deep learning techniques are presented in Table 3. Here, we have reviewed the current status of deep learning techniques used in the IR studies and provide a brief summary of their advantages and future perspectives.

Due to general constraint of available human labelled data for a huge database, the authors (Palangi et al., 2016) developed a model for sentence embedding using RNN with LSTM cells which extracted the information from each word of the sentence and embedded it into semantic vector. They have trained the model in weakly supervised manner i.e. with long term memory the model kept on accumulating the information entered by the user till the last word of the sentence. The hidden layer provided the semantic representation of the whole sentence by automatically discarding unimportant words and keeping the important ones. It showed that the semantic vector evolved over time and took only important data from any new input. Also these detected words automatically activated the cells of RNN-LSTM to activate the cells of the similar topic. These automatic word detection and topic allocation supported LSTM-RNN for document retrieval. The proposed method outperformed the paragraph vector method. Deep learning vectors has been developed (Almasri, Berrut, & Chevallet, 2016) to train high quality vector representations for huge amount of unstructured terms. It also get a big number of term relationships for query expansion technique. The method was empirically analyzed and the results were proved to be better than other expansion models.

Medical researchers have started using deep learning algorithms for diagnostics of disease. For example, deep CNN showed great potential in classification of skin lesions by using input as pixels and disease labels of the images. It has been showed that the deep learning can classify the most common and most deadly skin cancer with the competence level equivalent to dermatologists (Esteva et al., 2016). The authors (Gulshan, Peng, Coram, Stumpe, & Wu, 2016) developed a deep NN for automatic finding of diabetic retinopathy and macular edema and classification using retinal fungus images.

Deep NN for software bug localization (Lam, Nguyen, Nguyen, and Nguyen, 2015) has been proposed to automatically locate the documents containing bug. The major challenge in software bug localization is the lexical mismatch. They have used vector space model for textual similarity and DNN for learning the lexical mismatch in bug reports and source files.

The authors (Zhuang, Liu, Li, Shen, & Reid, 2017) developed a weakly supervised deep learning approach to automatic label the web image information. They have used two strategies random grouping, which piled various images in one training instance to increase the labelling accuracy at group level and attention. It surpassed the noisy signals from the incorrectly labeled images. The authors (Jaderberg, Simonyan, Vedaldi, & Zisserman, 2016) developed end to end text reading pipeline-detecting and recognizing text from natural scene images. CNN was used for recognition and region proposal mechanism for detection purposes. The networks were produced wholly by a synthetic text generation engine without any human labelling. The proposed system worked well for both image retrieval and text spotting comparing to other methods for all standard datasets.

In community question answering the difficulty lies in semantic matching between question answer pairs and modeling of contextual factors. An attentive deep NN was proposed (Xiang, Chen, Wang, & Qin, 2017) to learn the deterministic facts for answering the question. The pros of this method is that it can support various input formats by using CNN, attentive based LSTM ad conditional random fields. The authors (Hoogeveen, Bennett, Li, Verspoor, & Baldwin, 2018) proposed the learning algorithms for detection of the misflagged duplicate questions i.e. the questions which were mistakenly flagged as duplicate from the archived ones but their meanings are actually different. The text features alone cannot model the duplicates, therefore, meta-information of user posting the question and the questions themselves is required. The researchers used various machine learning and deep learning approaches for classification or detection of duplicates and found that random forest worked well than other algorithms.

Deep learning outperformed machine learning techniques in designing chemically valid and synthetically accessible molecules with appropriate characteristics for drug discovery (Blaschke, Olivecrona, Engkvist, Bajorath, & Chen, 2018). In the study (Gómez-Bombarelli et al., 2018) developed a technique to automate molecular design by using auto-encoders. The network was fed with thousands of structures to derive a set of coupled functions. By using vector decoding, perturbing known chemical structures and interpolation among chemical structures, the DNN succeeded to develop new molecules with drug like properties.

In music genre system, the defined music features have been used for retrieving information but Deep Belief Networks (DBN) were used (Lee, Largman, Pham, & Ng, 2009) to scale spectrograms which automatically learned the features and outperformed the traditional audio features in music genre recognition. The learned feature representation from the unlabeled data showed very good performance for multiple music classification tasks. The authors (Hamel & Eck, 2010) have used the DBN on Discrete Fourier Transform (DFT) of audio data for the automatic feature extraction to solve the task of genre

Table 4. Summary of machine learning techniques in association with IR based applications

Authors	Purpose for information retrieval	Machine Learning/Deep Learning Technique Used	IR Model Used
Lam et al., 2015	Addressed the problem of lexical mismatch	Deep Neural Network	Vector Space Model
Herrera et al., 2018	Learning to rank framework was used for aggregation of microblog information and QA task	MART, RankNet, RankBoost, LambdaMart	tf-idf Model
Kumar et al., 2012	Efficient query generation	Decision Trees	-
Kim et al., 2011	Comparison between local and global embedding	Word2Vec, GloVe	Local Latent Semantic Analysis
Diaz et al., 2016	Query expansion using deep learning outperformed the language model based query expansion.	Word2Vec	Dirichlet Model
Almasri et al., 2016	Try to overcome the language barriers.	Learning to Rank	Cross-Language Information Retrieval
Azarbonyad et al., 2019	Used for audio classification	Convolutional Deep Belief Network	-
Lee et al., 2009	Auto tagging of musical data	Radial Basis Model	-
Zhuang et al., 2017	Text recognition task from the images	Convolutional Neural Network	-
Jaderberg et al., 2016	Automated music performance assessment	Deep Neural Networks	-
Xiang et al., 2017	Classifying misflagged questions from community question answering database	Convolutional Neural Network	tf-idf Model

recognition and auto-tagging. Computational models (Pati, Gururani, & Lerch, 2018) has been built for automatically assessing the music performance, i.e., rating the performance on several criteria like musicality, etc. by analyzing the audio recording. The researchers used deep NN for feature learning instead of hand crafted feature. The results showed that supervised feature learning technique better characterize the music performance than the baseline approaches. We have summarized the purpose of IR along with the machine learning techniques in the Table 4.

This table represents machine learning techniques in association with IR. It summarizes potential of the machine learning algorithms at different stages of IR based applications like chemo-informatics, music genre system etc.

CONCLUSION

In this chapter, we discussed about how the IR process can be enhanced by using machine learning approaches. The learning algorithms help in better classification and ranking of the relevant documents. However, due to drastic growth of data, it is difficult to retrieve information from such a huge database. Researchers started using deep learning techniques for handling big data and automatic labelling of raw and heterogeneous data. These learning algorithms shown good performance for various applications of IR e.g. image retrieval, music information systems, chemo-informatics, medical management systems etc. We can conclude that deep learning algorithms have great potential in solving IR problems.

REFERENCES

Almasri, M., Berrut, C., & Chevallet, J. P. (2016). A Comparison of Deep Learning Based Query Expansion with Pseudo relevance Feedback and Mutual Information. *European Conference on Information Retrieval*, 709–715. 10.1007/978-3-319-30671-1_57

Alzubi, J., Nayyar, A., & Kumar, A. (2018). Machine learning from theory to algorithms: an overview. *Journal of Physics: Conference Series, 1142(1)*. doi:10.1088/1742-6596/1142/1/012012

Azarbonyad, H., Shakery, A., & Faili, H. (2019). A Learning to Rank Approach for Cross-Language Information Retrieval Exploiting Multiple Translation Resources. *Natural Language Engineering*, 1–22.

Blaschke, T., Olivecrona, M., Engkvist, O., Bajorath, J., & Chen, H. (2018). Application of Generative Autoencoder in De Novo Molecular Design. *Molecular Informatics, 37*(1-2). doi:10.1002/minf.201700123 PMID:29235269

Chen, B., Sheridan, R. P., Hornak, V., & Voigt, J. H. (2012). Comparison of Random Forest and Pipeline Pilot Naive Bayes in Prospective QSAR Predictions. *Journal of Chemical Information and Modeling, 52*(3), 792–803. doi:10.1021/ci200615h PMID:22360769

Corazza, A., Di Martino, S., Maggio, V., & Scanniello, G. (2011). Combining Machine Learning and Information Retrieval Techniques for Software Clustering. In A. Moschitti & R. Scandariato (Eds.), *Eternal Systems. EternalS, Communications in Computer and Information Science, 255* (pp. 42–60). Berlin, Heidelberg: Springer.

Diaz, F., Mitra, B., & Craswell, N. (2016). *Query expansion with locally-trained word embeddings.* arXiv preprint arXiv:1605.07891

Drucker, H., Shahrary, B., & Gibbon, D. C. (2002). Support Vector Machines: Relevance Feedback and Information Retrieval. *Information Processing & Management, 38*(3), 305–323. doi:10.1016/S0306-4573(01)00037-1

Eriksson, L., Jaworska, J., Worth, A. P., Cronin, M. T., McDowell, R. M., & Gramatica, P. (2003). Methods for Reliability and Uncertainty Assessment and for Applicability Evaluations of Classification and Regression-Based QSARs. *Environmental Health Perspectives, 111*(10), 1361–1375. doi:10.1289/ehp.5758 PMID:12896860

Esteva, A., Kuprel, B., Novoa, R., Ko, J., Swetter, S., Blau, H. M., & Thrun, S. (2016). Dermatologist-Level Classification of Skin Cancer. *Nature*.

Fu, H., & Qiu, G. (2012). Fast Semantic Image Retrieval Based on Random Forest. *Proceedings of the 20th ACM International Conference on Multimedia*, 909-912. 10.1145/2393347.2396344

Gómez-Bombarelli, R., Wei, J.N., Duvenaud, D., Hernández-Lobato, J.M., Sánchez-Lengeling, B., Sheberla, D., … Aspuru-Guzik, A. (2018). Automatic Chemical Design Using a Data-Driven Continuous Representation Of Molecules. *ACS Central Science, 4*(2), 268-276.

Guan, S., & Zhang, X. (2008). *Networked Memex Based on Personal Digital Library. In Encyclopedia of Networked and Virtual Organizations* (pp. 1044–1051). IGI Global. doi:10.4018/978-1-59904-885-7.ch136

Gulshan, V., Peng, L., Coram, M., Stumpe, M. C., Wu, D., Narayanaswamy, A., … Kim, R. (2016). Development and Validation of a Deep Learning Algorithm for Detection of Diabetic Retinopathy in Retinal Fundus Photographs. *Journal of the American Medical Association, 316*(22), 2402–2410. doi:10.1001/jama.2016.17216 PMID:27898976

Hamel, P., & Eck, D. (2010). Learning Features from Music Audio with Deep Belief Networks. *Proceedings of International Society for Music Information Retrieval Conference*, 339–344.

Hansen, L. K., Lehn-Schiøler, T., Petersen, K. B., Arenas-Garcia, J., Larsen, J., & Jensen, S. H. (2007). Learning and Clean-up in a Large Scale Music Database. *2007 15th European Signal Processing Conference*, 946-950.

Herrera, J., Poblete, B., & Parra, D. (2018). Learning to Leverage Microblog Information for QA Retrieval. In *European Conference on Information Retrieval*. Springer. 10.1007/978-3-319-76941-7_38

Hinton, G. E., Osindero, S., & Teh, Y. W. (2006). A Fast Learning Algorithm for Deep Belief Nets. *Neural Computation, 18*(7), 1527–1554. doi:10.1162/neco.2006.18.7.1527 PMID:16764513

Hoogeveen, D., Bennett, A., Li, Y., Verspoor, K. M., & Baldwin, T. (2018). Detecting Misflagged Duplicate Questions in Community Question-Answering Archives. *Twelfth International AAAI Conference on Web and Social Media*.

Hore, S., & Bhattacharya, T. (2019). Analyzing Social Trend Towards Girl Child in India: A Machine Intelligence-Based Approach. In *Recent Developments in Machine Learning and Data Analytics* (pp. 43–50). Singapore: Springer. doi:10.1007/978-981-13-1280-9_4

Jaderberg, M., Simonyan, K., Vedaldi, A., & Zisserman, A. (2016). Reading Text in the Wild with Convolutional Neural Networks. *International Journal of Computer Vision, 116*(1), 1–20. doi:10.100711263-015-0823-z

Kanimozhi, S., & Padmini Devi, B. (2018). A Novel Approach for Deep Learning Techniques Using Information Retrieval from Big Data. *International Journal of Pure and Applied Mathematics, 118*(8), 601–606.

Kim, Y., Seo, J., & Croft, W. B. (2011). Automatic Boolean Query Suggestion for Professional Search. *Proceedings of the 34th International ACM SIGIR Conference on Research and Development in Information Retrieval*, 825–834. 10.1145/2009916.2010026

Kumar, J., Ye, P., & Doermann, D. (2012). Learning Document Structure for Retrieval and Classification. *Proceedings of the 21st International Conference on Pattern Recognition*, 1558-1561.

Lam, A. N., Nguyen, A. T., Nguyen, H. A., & Nguyen, T. N. (2015). Combining Deep Learning with Information Retrieval to Localize Buggy Files for Bug Reports (N). *2015 30th IEEE/ACM International Conference on Automated Software Engineering (ASE)*, 476-481. 10.1109/ASE.2015.73

Lee, H., Largman, Y., Pham, P., & Ng, A. Y. (2009). Unsupervised Feature Learning for Audio Classification Using Convolutional Deep Belief Networks. *Advances in Neural Information Processing Systems*, 1–9.

Lewis, D. D. (1998). Naive (Bayes) at Forty: The Independence Assumption in Information Retrieval. *European conference on machine learning*, 4-15. 10.1007/BFb0026666

Lo, Y. C., Rensi, S. E., Torng, W., & Altman, R. B. (2018). *Machine learning in Chemoinformatics and Drug Discovery. In Drug Discovery Today*. Elsevier.

Lo, Y. C., Senese, S., Li, C. M., Hu, Q., Huang, Y., Damoiseaux, R., & Torres, J. Z. (2015). Large-Scale Chemical Similarity Networks for Target Profiling of Compounds Identified in Cell-Based Chemical Screens. *PLoS Computational Biology*, *11*(3), e1004153. doi:10.1371/journal.pcbi.1004153 PMID:25826798

Lu, Y. C., Wu, C. W., Lu, C. T., & Lerch, A. (2016). An unsupervised approach to anomaly detection in music datasets. *Proceedings of the 39th International ACM SIGIR conference on Research and Development in Information Retrieval*, 749-752. 10.1145/2911451.2914700

Maarek, Y. S., Berry, D. M., & Kaiser, G. E. (1991). An Information Retrieval Approach for Automatically Constructing Software Libraries. *IEEE Transactions on Software Engineering*, *17*(8), 800–813. doi:10.1109/32.83915

Palangi, H., Deng, L., Shen, Y., Gao, J., He, X., Chen, J., ... Ward, R. (2016). Deep Sentence Embedding Using Long Short-Term Memory Networks: Analysis and Application to Information Retrieval. *IEEE/ACM Transactions on Audio, Speech and Language Processing*, *24*(4), 694–707.

Pati, K., Gururani, S., & Lerch, A. (2018). Assessment of Student Music Performances Using Deep Neural Networks. *Applied Sciences*, *8*(4), 507. doi:10.3390/app8040507

Pollettini, J. T., Pessotti, H. C., Filho, A. P., Ruiz, E. E. S., & Junior, M. S. A. (2015). Applying Natural Language Processing, Information Retrieval and Machine Learning to Decision Support in Medical Coordination in an Emergency Medicine Context. *IEEE 28th International Symposium on Computer-Based Medical Systems*, 316-319. 10.1109/CBMS.2015.82

Sathya, M., Jayanthi, J., & Basker, N. (2011). Link based K-Means Clustering Algorithm for Information Retrieval. *International Conference on Recent Trends in Information Technology*, 1111-1115. 10.1109/ICRTIT.2011.5972402

Singhal, A. (2001). Modern Information Retrieval: A Brief Overview. *IEEE Data Eng. Bull*, *24*(4), 35–43.

Sinha, U., & Kangarloo, H. (2002). Principal Component Analysis for Content-Based Image Retrieval. *Radiographics*, *22*(5), 1271–1289. doi:10.1148/radiographics.22.5.g02se021271 PMID:12235353

Song, Y., He, Y., Hu, Q., & He, L. (2015). ECNU At 2015 CDS Track: Two Re-Ranking Methods in Medical Information Retrieval. *Proceedings of the 2015 Text Retrieval Conference.*

Xiang, Y., Chen, Q., Wang, X., & Qin, Y. (2017). Answer Selection in Community Question Answering via Attentive Neural Networks. *IEEE Signal Processing Letters, 24*(4), 505–509. doi:10.1109/LSP.2017.2673123

Yang, H. C., & Lee, C. H. (2006). Mining Unstructured Web Pages to Enhance Web Information Retrieval. *International Conference on Innovative Computing, Information and Control*, 429-432.

Zhuang, B., Liu, L., Li, Y., Shen, C., & Reid, I. (2017). Attend In Groups: A Weakly-Supervised Deep Learning Framework for Learning from Web Data. *Proceedings of the IEEE Conference on Computer Vision and Pattern Recognition*, 1878-1887. 10.1109/CVPR.2017.311

Chapter 15
Interactive Game–Based Motor Rehabilitation Using Hybrid Sensor Architecture

Ahona Ghosh
Maulana Abul Kalam Azad University of Technology, India

Sriparna Saha
Maulana Abul Kalam Azad University of Technology, West Bengal, India

ABSTRACT

Game consoles that use interactive interfaces have drawn users' attention as they reduce the total cost and are user-friendly too. This chapter introduces an interactive game to aid motor rehabilitation applicable to patients belonging to all age groups. In the system, the users receive some audio instructions regarding the action they have to perform next. According to that instruction, the user tries to complete the 'Fruit-to-Basket' game as soon as possible by dropping all the fruits into the basket. Kinect sensor placed in front of the user detects their motions using skeletons containing three-dimensional coordinates of 20 body joints. The speeds of the movements are detected by the accelerometer. After extracting the required features from skeleton and speed, the use of principal component analysis is proved to be effective for feature space reduction. Then support vector machine is used efficiently to recognize the action. The experimental result indicates that the proposed algorithm is best suited in this domain and a very promising one.

INTRODUCTION

Motor rehabilitation (Piscitelli, 2016) is the process to restore someone from physical weakness and disability through some training or therapy. The rapid development in sensor technology (Trankler & Kanoun, 2001) has made action identification presently an interesting research area. The application of video games as a restoration strategy (Bonnechère, Jansen, Omelina, & Van Sint, 2016) has immensely drawn attention of medical persons in the last decade and interactive game motivates one to be physi-

DOI: 10.4018/978-1-5225-9643-1.ch015

cally active without or with very less intervention of a trainer (Russell & Newton, 2008; Warburton et al., 2007).

Numerous works have been done in this domain. In (Schuldt, Laptev, & Caputo, 2004), authors introduced space-time feature to identify complex motion patterns with support vector machine (SVM). But it is limited to only some actions, while our proposed work deals with a larger set of actions. A serious game has been designed by Pedreza *et al.* (Pedraza-Hueso, Martín-Calzón, Díaz-Pernas, & Martínez-Zarzuela, 2015) for improving the physical and as well as cognitive functions of aged people. The first part of the game detects the player's mobility, flexibility, strength and capacity where in the second part, the patient is asked to remember all the elements he/she had to face while playing the game. To overcome the problems of existing balance games like Nintendo Wii Fit, Lange *et al.* have proposed an iterative system to increase postural stability (Lange, Flynn, Proffitt, Chang, & "Skip" Rizzo, 2010) and improve weight shift. The problem definition, discussion and refinement of ideas take place repetitively until the team decides the most appropriate idea. In (Nenonen et al., 2007), Nenonen *et al.* proposed a game, pulse master biathlon for skiing and shooting where the heartbeat of the subject controls the speed of skiing and with the increase of heart rate, the shooting screen gets faded, and so the player has to maintain a controlled heart rate to achieve good score in the game. Su *et al.* used dynamic time warping and fuzzy logic to design a home-based rehabilitation system (Su, 2013) where physicians get the summary report of exercise performed from cloud platform and prescribe medicine and exercise accordingly. Effects of virtual reality (VR) training have been investigated by Askin *et al.* for regaining of upper body functioning in stroke patients (Aşkın, Atar, Koçyiğit, & Tosun, 2018). Further studies having a higher number of patients need to be done to establish its effectiveness in neuro-rehabilitation.

This chapter presents a novel approach to motor rehabilitation by designing a strategy of score calculation while the game is being played by the subjects. The game is designed in such a fashion that the subjects are asked to perform certain tasks by moving their body parts based on specific audio commands. While doing so, the subjects' body movements are measured using two distinct sensors, namely Kinect sensor (Lun & Zhao, 2015) (for action recognition) and Accelerometer (Chen, Liu, Jafari, & Kehtarnavaz, 2014; Tamura, 2014) (for speed calculation of body parts). We have incorporated these audio commands into a simple game of 'Fruit-to-Basket' in animated background. Here, the player has to collect different fruits according to some audio instructions and put them into the basket as fast as possible and also in an efficient manner (without colliding with obstacles). Game scores and performance details are stored in the computer and are analyzed after the completion of the game.

The next section of this chapter focuses on application of machine learning in rehabilitation domain and detailed descriptions of data acquisition devices: the Kinect sensor and the accelerometer are in Section 3. The methodology for action recognition is provided in Section 4. The attainment of the proposed work is evaluated and analyzed with the existing ones in Section 5. The conclusion drawn from the total chapter is stated finally in Section 6.

MACHINE LEARNING IN MOTOR REHABILITATION-BASED HEALTHCARE SERVICES

Machine learning in healthcare has been an emerging subject of study in the last few years. Rehabilitation can improve a person's quality of life and overall health. In (Zhu et al., 2014), the authors proposed a predictive mechanism where they have identified the specific people for whom the rehabilitation will be more beneficial from a group of people. And in the second part of their work, they have incorporated an explanatory task where based on the characteristics of the clients, they have decided who will receive the training. And finally, they have illustrated the use of a machine learning algorithm in both analytical and explanatory tasks to forecast whether a patient needs to undergo a long-term care and identify the risk factors of long-term care placement. Two machine learning techniques, namely Support Vector Machine (SVM) and k-Nearest Neighbor (kNN) (Ahuja et al., 2019) have been compared with already existing rehabilitation assessment measures and shown a better performance. A Fuzzy Inference System (FIS) has been developed in (Oliver et al., 2018), which collects knowledge of a rehabilitative expert and remotely monitors the exercises performed by the patient. Here both physical and cognitive rehabilitation have been considered to overcome the limitations of previous works which dealt with only physical rehabilitation. Depending upon the mental condition and stress measure of the trainee, the structure controls the difficulty level of the exercises, offers help to him/her and sometimes stops the execution whenever needed. After evaluating the performance of machine learning algorithms over conventional protocols in this field, authors in (Zhu et al., 2007) came to a conclusion that machine learning approaches are less illustratable but improved clinical protocols can be developed using it always. (Procházka et al., 2018) analyzed physiological data collected from heartbeat and thermal camera sensors during activities of rehabilitation. The system is capable of predicting the changing pattern of temperature ranges and by applying image processing algorithms, it evaluated the frequency of breathing. The statistical coefficients of a neural network are optimized using machine learning and the experimental results are analyzed after applying it to a real time scenario of cycling expedition using GPS. It can be extended further by applying convolutional neural networks (Pandey and Solanki, 2019) to detect the possible health disorder and improve the remote monitoring of exercises performed by patients. (Snoek et al., 2012) combined feature extraction and classification into a solo model and used Bayesian optimization method to automatically optimize the machine learning hyper-parameters. A user is able to perform upper body related rehabilitative trainings with the help of a robotic arm in this system and the performance is determined by the ability of the system to distinguish between a correctly and incorrectly executed posture and direct the user hence. Machine learning classifiers like multiclass SVM and Hidden Markov Model (HMM) SVM have been used to classify the postures and they have been compared according to the accuracy rates shown. (Lin et al., 2018) used machine learning methods like logistic regression, SVM and random forest to forecast the clinical data of patients suffering from a post-acute care-cerebrovascular disease. Experimental results proved that effectiveness of machine learning algorithms in rehabilitation is more than the current works in healthcare.

DESCRIPTION OF DATA ACQUISITION DEVICE

For collecting the dataset, one Microsoft Kinect sensor in front of the subject and one wearable inertial sensor on the subject's hand is used. Both of these sensors consume less power for the collection of real time data and are widely available in market. We have set the Kinect sensor's frame rate as 10 frames per second and the inertial sensor's rate of sampling is considered as 50Hz here.

Figure 1. Different parts of Kinect sensor.

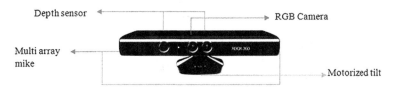

Kinect Sensor

Kinect sensor (Mousavi et al., 2014 and Naeemabadi et al., 2018) tracks position of human body joints situated within a certain range (1.2M-3.5M) from it and creates the corresponding skeleton. Kinect consists of mainly four parts shown in Figure1.The RGB camera is a VGA camera which detects the x and y coordinates of the body joints and depth sensor enables the system to detect the corresponding z coordinates. Multi array mike isolates the voice of the subject from the noise in the room. The motorized tilt enables us to tilt the sensor head up and down up to ±27° according to the need. Twenty body joints captured by Xbox 360 Kinect sensor are shown in Figure 2. Kinect sensor has its application in various fields (Lun et al., 2015; Li et al., 2012; Gaglio et al., 2015) like rehabilitative purpose, gesture recognition, virtual-reality interaction etc. Figure 3 shows the tracking of human skeleton by Kinect sensor.

Accelerometer

The accelerometer used here is the inertial sensor (Tamura et al., 2014) manufactured in ESSP Laboratory of University of Texas at Dallas (Chen et al., 2015). It is made of a MEMS sensor containing 9 axes used to capture x, y, z axis acceleration, angular velocity and magnetic strength, a 16bit microcontroller, a dual mode Bluetooth unit and an interface amid MEMS and the microcontroller. Its acceleration range is within ±8g and is able to rotate in ±1000 degrees/second. It has applications in mostly rehabilitative field where higher accuracy is not necessarily required (Chen et al., 2014; Bayat et al., 2014). Human activity recognition (Twomey et al., 2018) which has applications in various fields like healthcare (Chen et al., 2014), smart environments and homeland security can be achieved by it also. Pictorial view of accelerometer is displayed in Figure 4.

Proposed Methodology

This section describes feature extraction and feature selection method followed by the description of classifier used here.

FEATURE EXTRACTION

Here we have dealt with two types of features; one has been extracted from the Kinect sensor and the second one from Accelerometer (Figure 5).

Figure 2. Skeleton joint locations and names captured by Kinect sensor.

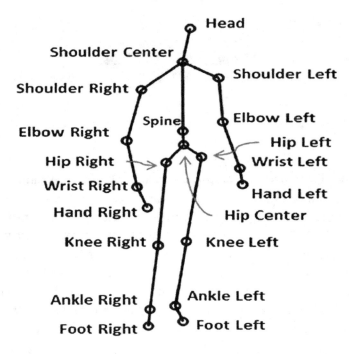

Figure 3. Tracking of human skeleton by Kinect sensor.

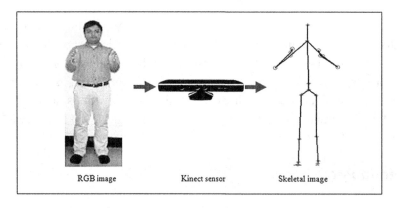

Figure 4. Pictorial view of accelerometer.

Figure 5. Features extracted from Kinect sensor and accelerometer.

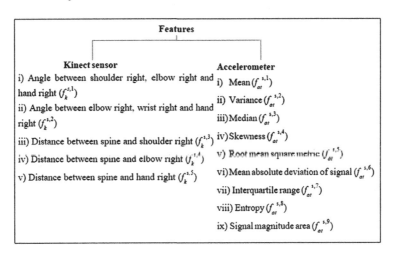

Using Kinect

The features extracted from the Kinect sensor dataset are:

i)   Angle between shoulder right, elbow right and hand right,
ii) Angle between elbow right, wrist right and hand right,
iii) Distance between spine and shoulder right,
iv) Distance between spine and hand right,
v)   Distance between spine and elbow right.

The distance features have been normalized using the distance between the wrist right and spine to overcome the effect of different body structures. The average value of feature values from each frame has been considered here.

Using Accelerometer

From the accelerometer, 9 time domain features have been extracted from each window and every axis x, y and z. Statistical attributes like mean, variance, median, root mean square metric, signal magnitude area, entropy, skewness, interquartile range and mean absolute deviation of signal are involved in each individual feature.

The arithmetic-mean of a set of n numbers x_1, x_2, ..., x_n can be denoted by

$$\bar{x} = \frac{1}{n}\sum_{i=1}^{n} x_i \tag{1}$$

The variance of x when x is a random variable, is measured by the expectation of standard deviation from its mean and can be denoted by

$$Variance(X) = E\left[(X - \bar{x})^2\right] \tag{2}$$

The median is the middle value in a sorted list of numbers and can be denoted by

$$Median = val(\frac{n}{2}) \; if \; n \; is \; odd$$

$$= val(\frac{n+1}{2}) \; if \; n \; is \; even \tag{3}$$

The skewness in statistics is defined by the asymmetry in a probability distribution and denoted by

$$Skewness = \sqrt{\frac{\sum_{i-1}^{n}(x - \bar{x})^3}{(n-1)s^3}} \tag{4}$$

Where x is the observation, $\bar{x}$ is the mean, n is the total number of observations and s is the variance.

After finding the arithmetic mean of the squares of a set of values, the square root of that mean is called root mean square. It is denoted by

$$x_{rms} = \sqrt{\frac{1}{n}\left(x_1^2 + x_2^2 + ... + x_n^2\right)} \tag{5}$$

The mean absolute deviation (MAD) of a signal is defined by the mean of the absolute deviation from a mid-point and denoted by

$$MAD = \frac{1}{n}\sum_{i=1}^{n}\left|x_i - m(X)\right| \tag{6}$$

Figure 6. Linearly and not linearly separable data points.

When we divide data set into some quartiles, the measure of variability is called the interquartile range. It breaks down at 25% that is why it is often chosen over total range. For a dataset divided into two quartiles, the interquartile range is

IQR=Median of upper half-Median of lower half (7)

Entropy is defined as the amount of disorder of a system or the randomness which characterizes an input image. In case of reversible process, the entropy is denoted by

$$Entropy = \frac{Qrev}{T}$$ (8)

Where Q_{rev} is the heat absorbed and T is the temperature.
The mean signal magnitude area (*sma*) of n number. of values can be denoted by

$$sma_x - \sum_{i=1}^{n} x_n$$ (9)

Feature Selection Using PCA

For reducing the feature space dimension, Principal Component Analysis (PCA) has been used (Shlen et al.,2014). If n number of trials are considered having p number of variables, then the amount of principal components (Pal et al., 2014) is min(n-1,p). The feature selection is done in such a way that the feature having maximum possible variance becomes the first principal component and each succeeding component is arranged according to the decreasing order of variance only if it is orthogonal (Oja et al., 1998) to the preceding components.

Classification Using SVM

Presently, Support vector machine (SVM) algorithm finds wide application in classification, regression analysis and pattern recognition problems. The basic support vector machine algorithm works as a non-probabilistic binary linear classifier (Fan et al., 2008) which takes a set of inputs and distributes those into two classes. Data points are divided based on the gap between them. It constructs a model that classifies the given data points into one or the other class. The gap may or may not be clear between

Figure 7. Corresponding geometry for the decision line showing g(y)>0 and g(y)<0.

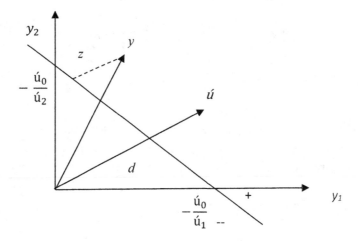

the set of two class data points. The data points can be separable or non-separable based on the gap, as is shown in Figure 6.

Hyper Planes

In Figure 6, the dark line is called hyperplane (Stanley et al., 2004). Generally, the hyperplanes get adopted to classify the training vectors efficaciously. Let's assume that y_i is the feature vector of the training set Y. Here the values of i belong to the set 1, 2, ..., N. It is assumed that these feature vectors belong to either in class $\acute{u}_1$ or in $\acute{u}_2$, where $\acute{u}_1$ and $\acute{u}_2$ are linearly separable. The hyperplane function which classifies all the training vectors is denoted by $g(y)$ in

$$g(y) = \acute{u}^T y + \acute{u}_0 = 0 \tag{8}$$

Here, $\acute{u} = \left[\acute{u}_1, \acute{u}_2, \acute{u}_3 .....\acute{u}_l \right]^T$ is the weight vector and $\acute{u}_0$ is the threshold. Let y_1 and y_2 be two values in the decision hyperplane, then

$$0 = \acute{u}^T y_1 + \acute{u}_0 = \acute{u}^T y_2 + \acute{u}_0 \Rightarrow \acute{u}^T (y_1 - y_2) = 0 \tag{9}$$

Referring to Figure 7,

$$d = \frac{|\acute{u}_0|}{\sqrt{\acute{u}_1^2 + \acute{u}_2^2}} \tag{10}$$

Figure 8. Hyperplanes to separate to two class of data.

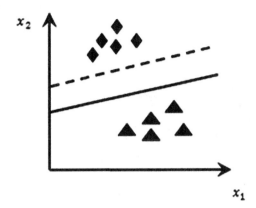

$$z = \frac{|g(y)|}{\sqrt{\acute{u}_1^2 + \acute{u}_2^2}} \tag{11}$$

$|g(y)|$ is considered as the Euclidean distance between the point y and the decision hyperplane. While one side of $|g(y)|$ has negative values, the other side has positive values. The hyperplane passes through the origin when $\acute{u} = 0$.

Separable Classes

This approach basically deals with a different validation for fabricating linear classifiers. Figure 8 also elucidates the classification problem with two possible linear classifiers or hyperplanes. The hyperplanes are quite reliable when the question of handling unknown data comes to the fore. The generalization performance of the classifier brings up a crucial colossal issue while designing a classifier. This is delineated by a succinct definition, which states it as the ability of the classifier, using the trained data, for operating reasonably with data not belonging to the set. Hence, it is construed that a practical selection for the hyperplane classifier is crucial behind leaving the highest difference from both the classes. Hyperplanes should have the ability to leave more space on either side, so that the data points can migrate easily and hence have less chances of causing error.

To quantify the term margin, the example illustrated in Figure 9. The dark lines in the figure represent the hyperplanes. They have two directions viz. direction 1 and direction 2. The margin for the 1st direction is given by $2z_1$ while that for 2nddirection is $2z_2$. The main aim of this illustration is determination of direction with the maximum possible margin. The distance between any point and the hyperplane is expressed by

$$z = \frac{|g(y)|}{\|\acute{u}\|} \tag{12}$$

Figure 9. An illustration of a linearly separable binary class model having two linear classifiers.

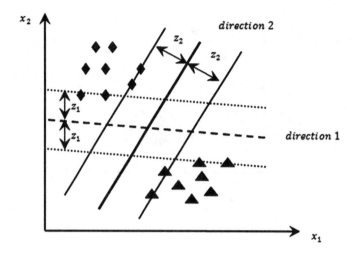

The value of $\acute{u}$ and $\acute{u}_0$ are now be scaled in such a manner where the value of $g(y)$ at the nearest points of $\acute{u}_1$, $\acute{u}_2$ is equal to 1 for $\acute{u}_1$ and -1 for $\acute{u}_2$. This is similar to having a margin of

$$\frac{1}{\|\acute{u}\|} + \frac{1}{\|\acute{u}\|} = \frac{2}{\|\acute{u}\|} \tag{13}$$

This requires

$$\acute{u}^T y + \acute{u}_0 \geq 1 \forall y \in \acute{u}_1 \tag{14}$$

$$\acute{u}^T y + \acute{u}_0 \leq 1 \forall y \in \acute{u}_2$$

The parameters $\acute{u}$ and $\acute{u}_0$ are calculated in order to minimize

$$J(\acute{u}, \acute{u}0) = 0.5\|\acute{u}\|^2 \tag{15}$$

Subject to

$$b_i\left(\acute{u}^T y + \acute{u}0\right) \geq 1; i = 1, 2, \ldots, N \tag{16}$$

From these equations, it is understood that the Lagrangian multipliers (Klein et al.,2004) are either zero or positive. The vector $\acute{u}$ is called the Support Vector and it is represented by

Figure 10. Classification of training feature vectors in non-separable classes.

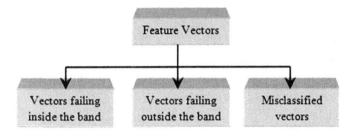

$$\acute{u} = \sum_{i=1}^{Ns} »_i b_i x_i \quad (17)$$

Non-Separable Classes

This approach deals with problems where the classes are not distinguishable and is illustrated in Figure 9. In such cases, the training feature vectors are categorized as vectors failing inside the band, vectors failins outside the band and misclassified vectors. This is depicted in Figure 10.

The vectors falling inside the band satisfy the following inequality

$$0 \le b_i\left(\acute{u}^T y \middle| \acute{u}_0\right) < 1 \quad (18)$$

The vectors that fall outside the band comply with the constraints as is shown in (18). Misclassified vectors, on the other hand, satisfy the following inequality

$$b_i\left(\acute{u}^T y \middle| \acute{u}_0\right) < 0 \quad (19)$$

The cases mentioned above are treated by a single constraint by the introduction of a variable called 'Slack Variable' (Joachims et al., 2006) as is given in the following equation

$$b_i\left(\acute{u}^T y + \acute{u}_0\right) \ge 1 - \xi_i \quad (20)$$

The optimization of the Slack variable can be realized by adopting a minimized cost function as

$$J\left(\acute{u}, \acute{u}_0, \xi\right) = \frac{1}{2}\|\acute{u}\|^2 + C\sum_{i=1}^{N} I\left(\xi_i\right) \quad (21)$$

where, ξ is the vector of the parameter ξ

$$I(\xi_i) = \begin{cases} 1 & \xi_i > 0 \\ 0 & \xi_i = 0 \end{cases} \tag{22}$$

'C' acts as a positive constant which manages the relative effect of the two relative factors. Since the optimization of $I(\ )$ is difficult, a cost function is adopted and optimized and the goal becomes minimize

$$J(\acute{u}, \acute{u}_0, \xi) = \frac{1}{2}\|\acute{u}\|^2 + C\sum_{i=1}^{N} I(\xi_i) \tag{23}$$

subject to

$$b_i(\acute{u}^T y_i + \acute{u}_0) \geq 1 - \xi_i \tag{24}$$

where $i = 1, 2, \ldots . N$ and $\xi_i \geq 0$

The only difference between the separable and non-separable classes is that for the latter one the Lagrangian multipliers should be bounded above by C. The slack variables and the Lagrangian multipliers don't enter the problem directly but their presence is indirectly shown through C.

Multiclass

These problems are also called M-class problems as it deals with classification of more than two classes unlike the earlier two cases. Normally, the 'One against all' (Liu et al., 2005) approach is adopted. However, owing to certain drawbacks like generation of indeterminate regions, where more than one optimal discriminant function is positive and difficulty in handling larger number of classes, an alternative technique is being used. This is called the 'One against one' (Milgram et al., 2006) approach, where a set of binary classifiers are given training and each of them partitions a couple of classes. The conclusion taken is mainly based on the vote of majority. However, this technique also suffers from a disadvantage like the prerequisite of training a large number of binary classifiers. The third methodology is quite fascinating. It uses the principle of the error coding scheme. For an M-class problem, L number of binary classifiers is chosen by the designer. While training for the ith classifier, the desired label y is chosen to be either +1 or -1. Here, the value of I ranges from 1 to L. The desired labels vary for each classifier and this result in the formation of an $M \times L$ matrix. Let us take the example of an $M \times L$ matrix where $M=4$ and $L=4$.

$$\begin{bmatrix} -1 & -1 & +1 & -1 \\ +1 & -1 & -1 & -1 \\ +1 & +1 & -1 & -1 \\ -1 & -1 & +1 & +1 \end{bmatrix}$$

Figure 11. Block diagram of the overall system.

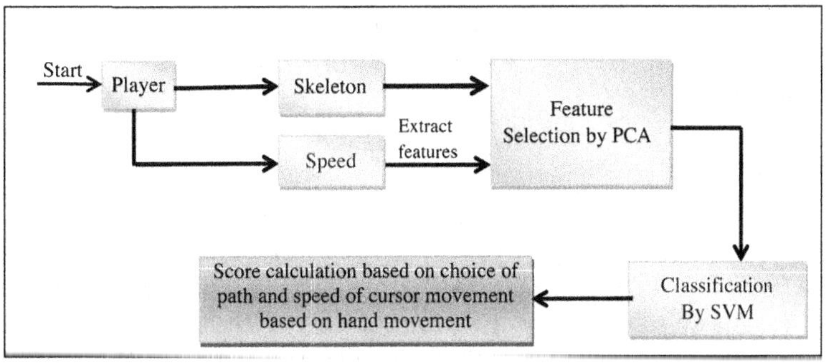

During training, the first classifier is designed in such a manner that it responds (-1 +1 +1 -1) for patterns created from classes $\acute{u}_1$, $\acute{u}_2$, $\acute{u}_3$, $\acute{u}_4$ respectively. Similarly, the second classifier responds (-1 -1 +1 -1) respectively. This process is similar to clustering the classes into L number of pairs and for every couple, a binary classifier is trained. After inputting an unknown pattern, the output from every binary classifier is noted. This gives rise to a code word. Further, the Hamming distance (Norouzi et al., 2012) of this code is calculated with respect to the M code words where the design belongs to the class having minimum distance. This construes the major importance of the algorithm. This is due to the design of code words considered such that if the Hamming distance between them be 'd', then a conclusion is declared as correct even if the results of $\left\lfloor \dfrac{d-1}{2} \right\rfloor$ among the L classifiers are wrong. Here $\lfloor \ \rfloor$ indicates floor operation.

EXPERIMENTAL SETUP AND RESULTS

The section starts with the design of the interactive game for motor rehabilitation, and then the description of the dataset used by the authors has been given. After that, the sample features, actions and instruction set have been given respectively followed by the scenario of the designed game according to audio instructions and performance evaluation of our proposed system.

Design of Interactive Game

The block diagram of our proposed system has been illustrated in Figure 11. After logging into the game, for each action, the player's skeleton is detected by the Kinect sensor and the speed of cursor movement is measured by the accelerometer worn by the player. From the skeleton, 5 features are extracted in terms of distance and angle between certain body joints according to the requirement and from the speed, 9 features have been extracted by MATLAB R2015A simulation (Figure 5). To reduce the large feature space, PCA has been used and after that SVM has been used to classify the set of actions performed by the player. And finally, the game score has been calculated and the effectiveness of proposed algorithm has been contrasted with the existing ones.

Figure 12. Skeletons generated from six actions.

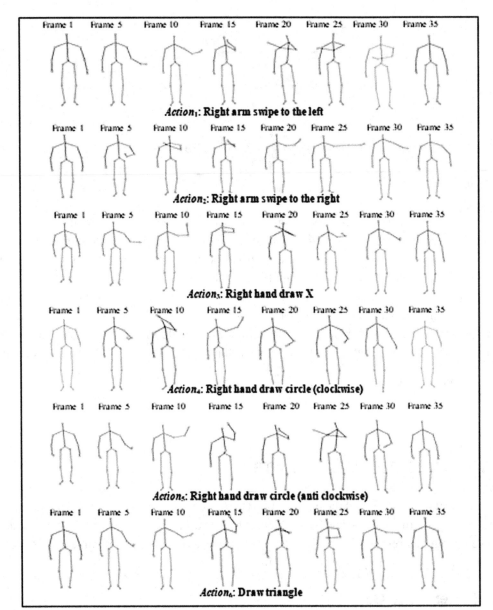

Dataset Preparation

A publicly available dataset called UTD-Multimodal Human Action Dataset (UTD-MHAD), where six actions each performed by eight persons (four male and four female) four times, has been used here (Chen, Jafari, & Kehtarnavaz, 2015). The dataset is able to process large intra-class differences as it deals with the following scenarios

i) The speed of actions vary in different trials performed by the subjects
ii) Subjects were of different heights and body structures.

Three channels were used, where the first one was for capturing the depth video and skeletons by Kinect sensor, the second one was capturing RGB videos and the third one was for capturing the inertial signals (3-axis accelerometer and 3-axis angular velocity).

Sample Actions Set

To achieve the goal of putting the fruits in the basket, one has to follow some actions. To avoid the obstacles, sometimes the player has to deviate from the predefined shortest path and follow some another action. The concerned set of actions (Chen et al., 2015) is

i) Right arm moves to the left ($Action_1$)
ii) Right arm moves to the right ($Action_2$)
iii) Right hand design x ($Action_3$)
iv) Right hand design circle (clockwise) ($Action_4$)
v) Right hand design circle (anti clockwise) ($Action_5$)
vi) Design triangle ($Action_6$)

The performed actions are shown by skeletal images in Figure 12.

Instruction Set

The following set of instructions define one of the probable complete instruction sets used to reach the goal of dropping all the fruits in the basket

i. Select the grape
ii. Drag the fruit and drop it to the basket
iii. Select the orange colored fruit
iv. Drag the fruit and drop it to the basket
v. Select the fruit which is kept opposite to the banana
vi. Drag the fruit and drop it to the basket
vii. Select the fruit which is more than one in number
viii. Drag the fruit and drop it to the basket

Sample Feature Set

Six actions performed by eight subjects each four times create a large feature space. As it is not feasible to show the result of feature extraction of all the 6 actions (refer to Section 4.3) for all the 59 feature values (3 axis acceleration and 3 axis rotation values of 9 accelerometer features + 5 Kinect feature values) and 192 observations (6 actions* 8 persons* 4 trials), one observation from each action randomly chosen has been shown in Table 1. To reduce the dimensionality of feature space, PCA has selected only 10 features (F_1 to F_{10}), given in Table 2.

Table 1. Result of sample data before PCA (refer to Figure 15).

Actions	$f_k^{s,1}$	$f_k^{s,2}$	$f_k^{s,3}$	$f_k^{s,4}$	$f_k^{s,5}$	$f_{at}^{s,1}$	$f_{at}^{s,2}$	$f_{at}^{s,3}$	$f_{at}^{s,4}$	$f_{at}^{s,5}$	$f_{at}^{s,6}$	$f_{at}^{s,7}$	$f_{at}^{s,8}$	$f_{at}^{s,9}$
$Action_1$						-0.556	696.7	-0.951	0.285	0.714	0.416	0.844	1.689	14.85
						-0.091	721.5	-0.105	-0.09	0.467	0.339	0.541	1.062	2.435
	16.596	10.778	0.7612	1.2111	0.72846	-0.550	696.9	-0.161	-0.36	0.624	0.250	0.462	1.132	14.682
						31.58	6841.6	0.091	1.003	66.431	49.94	81.81	1.022	842.13
						0.721	9719.7	15.57	0.177	94.62	62.07	45.08	2.167	19.242
						-26.95	6291.4	-8.335	-0.56	83.77	60.01	56.50	2.002	718.66
$Action_2$						-0.699	11.799	-1.0034	-0.013	0.838	0.433	0.8276	1.821	19.7
						-0.195	8.6487	-0.1765	0.465	0.526	0.381	0.7004	1.235	5.5099
	22.353	2.9443	0.8023	1.1851	0.7854	-0.305	9.2063	0.125	-0.170	0.490	0.318	0.6962	1.075	8.6051
						-2.739	6170	-3.511	0.956	78.409	56.66	70.58	1.934	77.15
						-0.286	3840.1	1.8015	-0.038	61.897	42.69	37.145	1.839	8.061
						2.7044	15422	-1.1298	-0.030	124.22	98.83	236.1	1.832	76.173
$Action_3$						-0.696	506.75	-0.938	0.1788	0.8379	0.403	0.7675	1.791	18.69
						-0.217	528.61	-0.2429	-0.890	0.5886	0.383	0.5036	1.278	5.845
	85.514	36.349	0.3416	1.0476	0.7188	-0.446	518.58	-0.1359	-1.303	0.9547	0.567	0.5941	1.107	11.975
						-6.180	9523.7	-5.8626	-0.946	96.292	74.50	134.99	1.904	165.83
						-23.10	30041	-2.0763	-0.746	174.86	126.1	164	1.889	619.99
						-23.20	15598	-1.1908	-1.330	127.03	86.76	89.282	1.849	622.61
$Action_4$						-0.658	1.238	-0.9733	0.1447	0.8090	0.398	0.644	1.629	23.045
						-0.158	2.527	-0.2292	0.0355	0.5661	0.399	0.548	1.190	5.533
	22.726	8.097	0.7375	1.1458	0.7330	-0.591	1.551	-0.1562	-0.708	0.8634	0.490	0.765	1.078	20.711
						-40.22	8130.4	-6.900	-0.917	90.894	62.109	86.107	1.735	1407.8
						-9.383	18960	-2.839	0.1592	137.8	98.375	116.67	1.679	328.42
						-1.662	13880	-2.809	-0.035	117.82	90.339	147.88	1.692	58.351
$Action_5$						-0.612	31.74	-0.9563	0.31	0.7905	0.424	0.684	1.583	19.599
						-0.431	33.81	-0.2841	-0.949	0.6652	0.367	0.464	1.250	13.823
	22.335	5.803	0.6902	1.138	0.7089	-0.439	33.83	-0.090	-0.776	0.7469	0.429	0.646	1.001	14.061
						24.45	4479.8	-2.229	1.208	64.316	44.70	65.35	1.586	782.48
						-16.45	14134	-7.908	0.099	119.58	91.05	142.5	1.673	526.52
						-6.224	15401	0.2137	0.341	124.26	91.30	142.66	1.150	199.2
$Action_6$						-0.521	0.657	-0.915	0.451	0.7621	0.487	0.979	2.251	15.732
						-0.159	1.2822	-0.291	-0.420	0.6327	0.498	0.791	1.601	4.8125
	0.7207	1.2385	0.7701	9.8321	17.157	-0.502	0.7339	-0.144	-0.451	0.7837	0.476	0.772	1.273	15.151
						8.473	4636.9	-20.916	-0.524	67.947	53.63	77.084	2.18	255.61
						-12.95	25455	-11.145	-0.146	159.63	122.1	186.48	2.094	390.66
						-1.112	17135	0.885	-0.443	130.9	95.70	119.18	2.238	33.547

Figure 13. Game interface of the task todrop the fruits into the basket

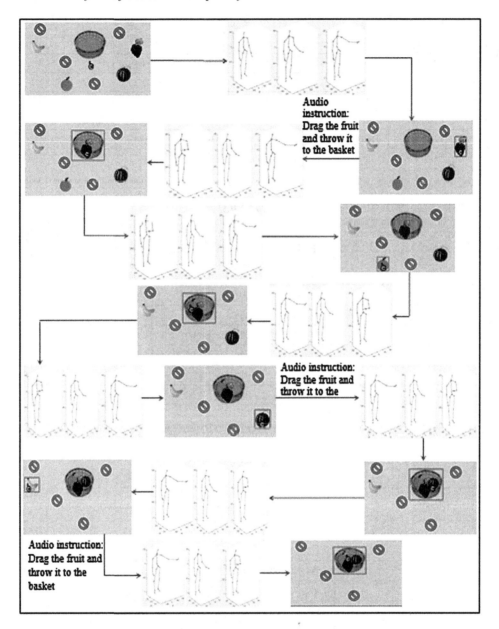

Scenario of the Designed Game Based on Audio Instructions

Figure 13 is showing the game interface for an audio instruction with its corresponding skeletons in action.

Table 2. Result of sample data after PCA.

Actions	F_1	F_2	F_3	F_4	F_5	F_6	F_7	F_8	F_9	F_{10}
$Action_1$	-11218.4	-3524.1	-3045.76	922.6671	-115.436	322.495	-55.217	-16.630	29.8124	-31.842
$Action_2$	-10168.6	5775.79	2530.513	-516.662	-382.5	259.5115	87.14988	-3.7438	-51.367	-20.812
$Action_3$	-9199.4	-5019.2	1259.79	12.22321	249.456	-375.243	36.42255	-8.8239	-13.871	0.424699
$Action_4$	15677.8	-10362	-8222.31	-709.229	40.49254	253.1125	73.65311	1.64474	2.63245	-20.0705
$Action_5$	-11532.9	-631.86	137.792	559.770	23.8678	69.7327	-126.078	-2.6742	0.4932	34.2891
$Action_6$	5626.713	585.9608	-11463.	11.21927	-111.50	-39.71	156.061	-17.33	-2.852	15.9635

Table 3. Detailed values for obtained results for TD-SVM.

Class	TP	FP	Precision	Recall	F-Measure	MCC	ROC Area	PRC Area
$Action_1$	1.00	0.00	1.00	1.00	1.00	1.00	1.00	1.00
$Action_2$	1.00	0.00	1.00	1.00	1.00	1.00	1.00	1.00
$Action_3$	1.00	0.00	1.00	1.00	1.00	1.00	1.00	1.00
$Action_4$	1.00	0.00	1.00	1.00	1.00	1.00	1.00	1.00
$Action_5$	1.00	0.00	1.00	1.00	1.00	1.00	1.00	1.00
$Action_6$	1.00	0.00	1.00	1.00	1.00	1.00	1.00	1.00
Weighted average	1.00	0.00	1.00	1.00	1.00	1.00	1.00	1.00

Table 4. Detailed values for obtained results for VD-SVM.

Class	TP	FP	Precision	Recall	F-Measure	MCC	ROC Area	PRC Area
$Action_1$	0.063	0.000	1.000	0.063	0.118	0.229	0.531	0.219
$Action_2$	0.125	0.094	0.211	0.125	0.157	0.039	0.516	0.172
$Action_3$	0.094	0.000	1.000	0.094	0.171	0.282	0.547	0.245
$Action_4$	0.469	0.463	0.169	0.469	0.248	0.005	0.503	0.168
$Action_5$	0.344	0.300	0.186	0.344	0.242	0.035	0.522	0.173
$Action_6$	0.094	0.106	0.150	0.094	0.115	-0.015	0.494	0.165
Weighted average	0.203	0.159	0.589	0.203	0.179	0.135	0.522	0.202

Performance Evaluation

The comparative results are shown for training (TD) and validation (Cawley et al., 2006) dataset (VD) for support vector machine (SVM) (Abe et al.,2005) and sequential minimal optimization (SMO) (Zeng et al.,2008). The performance parameters (Sokolova et al., 2006) chosen for this particular work is True Positive (TP), False Positive (FP), Precision, Recall, F-Measure, Matthews Correlation Coefficient

Table 5. Detailed values for obtained results for TD-SMO.

Class	TP	FP	Precision	Recall	F-Measure	MCC	ROC Area	PRC Area
$Action_1$	0.688	0.031	0.815	0.688	0.746	0.704	0.937	0.714
$Action_2$	0.688	0.019	0.880	0.668	0.772	0.741	0.960	0.762
$Action_3$	0.938	0.025	0.882	0.938	0.909	0.891	0.984	0.872
$Action_4$	0.906	0.088	0.674	0.906	0.773	0.732	0.936	0.633
$Action_5$	0.750	0.050	0.750	0.750	0.750	0.700	0.919	0.657
$Action_6$	0.719	0.050	0.742	0.719	0.730	0.677	0.911	0.623
Weighted average	0.781	0.044	0.791	0.781	0.780	0.741	0.941	0.710

Table 6. Detailed values for obtained results for VD-SMO.

Class	TP	FP	Precision	Recall	F-Measure	MCC	ROC Area	PRC Area
$Action_1$	1.000	0.013	0.941	1.000	0.970	0.964	0.994	0.941
$Action_2$	0.844	0.000	1.000	0.844	0.915	0.905	0.987	0.930
$Action_3$	1.000	0.000	1.000	1.000	1.000	1.000	1.000	1.000
$Action_4$	1.000	0.031	0.865	1.000	0.928	0.915	0.984	0.865
$Action_5$	0.969	0.013	0.939	0.969	0.954	0.945	0.990	0.925
$Action_6$	0.906	0.000	1.000	0.906	0.951	0.943	0.985	0.948
Weighted average	0.708	0.058	0.710	0.708	0.706	0.650	0.915	0.627

Figure 14. Confusion matrix.

32	0	0	0	0	0
0	32	0	0	0	0
0	0	32	0	0	0
0	0	0	32	0	0
0	0	0	0	32	0
0	0	0	0	0	32

TD-SVM

2	4	0	17	0	9
0	4	0	19	0	9
0	3	4	15	0	10
0	3	0	18	0	11
0	2	0	19	2	9
0	3	0	20	0	9

VD-SVM

22	1	0	0	6	3
0	22	0	7	0	3
0	0	30	1	0	1
1	1	0	29	1	0
2	0	0	5	24	1
2	1	4	1	1	23

TD-SMO

20	2	0	0	7	3
1	21	0	8	0	3
0	0	30	1	0	1
2	2	0	23	3	2
2	1	0	5	24	0
3	3	5	1	2	18

VD-SMO

Figure 15. Comparison of other performance parameters.

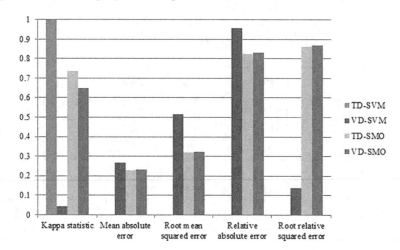

Figure 16. Plotting of features for all the actions performed.

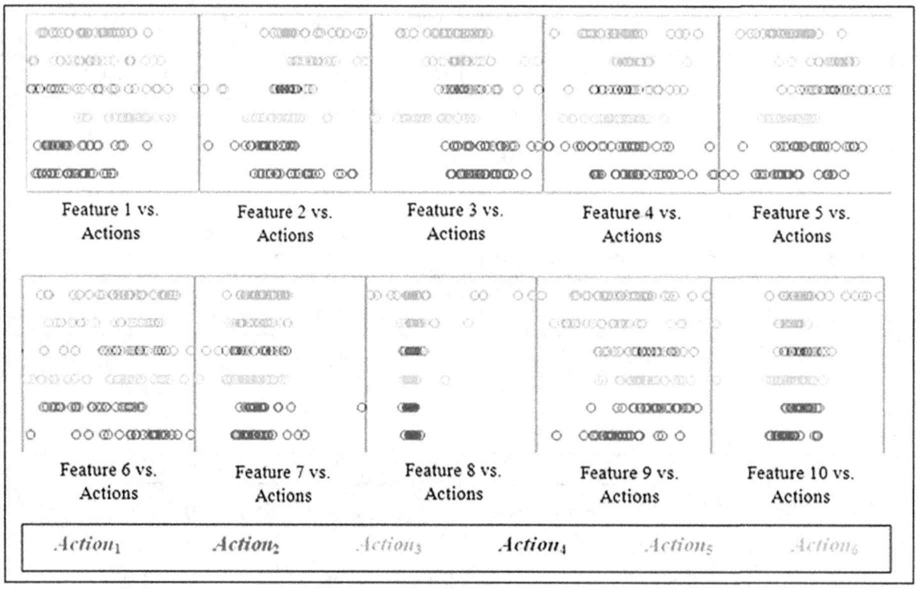

(MCC), Region of Convergence (RCC) and Precision Recall Curve (PRC). The evaluation results for these parameters are shown in Table 3-6 for the already stated six classes. The corresponding confusion matrixes (Deng et al., 2016) are given in Figure 15. Figure 16 represents the measure of other different performance metrics during classification.

Justification About Obtained Performances

For the proposed chapter, we have obtained values for 8 performance parameters. In Table 3, the SVM is taken as the classifier. Here, the data, that is taken from 192 observations (explanation of this is given in Section 5.5), is used for training as well as testing. From these 192 observations, randomly 1 is selected for testing and with the remaining 191 observations, training is done. If that 1 instance is correctly classified then accuracy score becomes 100, otherwise 0. This arbitrary selection of 1 observation is done 500 times, then the average is calculated, which becomes the overall accuracy of TD-SVM. As the features are linearly separable (which can be confirmed from Figure 16), thus 100% accuracy is obtained. This same procedure is again carried out in Table 5, but the classifier chosen here is SMO. As this classifier is weaker than SVM in respect of correctly classifying SVM, so the accuracy decreases to 78.13%.

Next, we have incorporated the concept of 10-fold cross-validation technique. The program randomly divides the 192 observations into two groups. 173 observations are used for training and remaining 19 ($\approx 192/10$) for validation purpose. From these 19 instances, 1 at a time is taken and corresponding accuracy is calculated. The average of these 19 accuracy results is given in Table 4 and 6 for SVM and SMO respectively. As the accuracy values given in Table 4 and 6 are less than those in Table 3 and 5, it could be the scenario that proper division is not possible while segregating the dataset into training and validation, the 19 instances chosen for validation set come from one particular action, thus making a weaker pattern for that action, so wrong classification occurs. This in turn makes the average accuracy lower than the earlier ones. As this division of dataset done automatically by the algorithm, so proper shuffling of observations is not present over there.

DISCUSSION AND FUTURE SCOPE

This paper describes a unique method of motor rehabilitation which uses an interactive game with overall 100% accuracy of classification by SVM. The hybrid sensor architecture of Kinect sensor and accelerometer as data acquisition devices has been executed well, as they are efficient in extracting features and PCA has been effective to reduce the feature dimension to the minimal. The chapter can be summarized by the following points:

1. *Robustness analysis*: Players who are performing the actions during the game can have dissimilar structures of body, weights, heights and gender. Our proposed method is said to be well suited in all of these scenarios after verification on different datasets. In spite of having noise prone datasets, the method provides robustness.
2. *Convenience*: The proposed system requires the least hardware and cost. Kinect sensor has been used which does not need any refreshing time and works 24×7. On the other hand, accelerometer is reliable and can be operated anytime by low cost current sources. Processing of data requires these two hardware only. A single Kinect is adequate to work in a room provided it is kept in a proper position. The proposed system is obviously suitable for applying in other places, like office, educational organizations and even at home where the time flexibility is provided to the user.
3. *Benefits*: The main aim of this system is to provide rehabilitative aid to different age group subjects in the form of physical and mental exercises through games.
4. *Productivity*: After implementation, the system shows100% accuracy to recognize six actions.

5. *Convergence*: The time taken for acquiring the desired outputs is less. The merging of the PCA in feature selection and SVM in classification is quite fast.
6. *Flexibility*: Our proposed system is applied to a huge number of subjects and trials. Body weights, heights and gender vary among subjects and the postures can vary in different trials also. The approach is flexible in all the situations mentioned above.
7. *Feasibility*: Our proposed system has been tested on research scholars of the university and is implemented easily. So, feasibility is not a concern of issue. It is independent of the constraints like background, subjects' dress and circumstance's noise.
8. *Efficiency*: The performance of the given approach has been examined by comparing it with different relative works and explained in the paper. Accuracy of 100% has been achieved for classifying the actions. So the approach is convenient and efficient enough.
9. *Computational time*: The time needed to correctly identify an unknown action is in order of 5s on Intel Core 2 Duo processor @ 1.60GHz and 8GB RAM running WEKA 3.8 software.
10. *Reliability*: Our proposed design is reliable for implementation in the real-world setup. It is created depending on Kinect which identifies the 3D image of an object situated within a finite range. By using its software development kit (SDK) it detects the skeleton and performed actions regardless of the skin shade or the person's dress or the circumstances.

This work can be extended by applying Electroencephalogram (EEG) analysis in it. The use of EEG in finding the ability of the player of following the shortest path and measuring the actual path from the shortest path will eventually help us to detect the exact area and reason of player's fault. If it detects that there is problem in occipital region of the brain, then it will mean that the player is visually weak. If there is problem in any lobe other than the occipital, then it can be depicted that there is problem in audio signal processing. By adding EEG, we will be able to measure mental judgement power and that will contribute in cognitive rehabilitation also.

REFERENCES

Abe, S. (2005). *Support vector machines for pattern classification* (Vol. 2). London: Springer.

Ahuja, R., Nayyar, A., & Solanki, A. (2019). Movie Recommender System Using K-Means Clustering AND K-Nearest Neighbor. In *9th International Conference on Cloud Computing, Data Science & Engineering*. Amity University. DOI: 10.1109/CONFLUENCE.2019.8776969

Allen, H. V., Terry, S. C., & De Bruin, D. W. (1989). Accelerometer systems with self-testable features. *Sensors and Actuators*, *20*(1-2), 153–161. doi:10.1016/0250-6874(89)87113-6

Aşkın, A., Atar, E., Koçyiğit, H., & Tosun, A. (2018). Effects of Kinect-based virtual reality game training on upper extremity motor recovery in chronic stroke. *Somatosensory & Motor Research*, *35*(1), 25–32. doi:10.1080/08990220.2018.1444599 PMID:29529919

Bayat, A., Pomplun, M., & Tran, D. A. (2014). A study on human activity recognition using accelerometer data from smartphones. *Procedia Computer Science*, *34*, 450–457. doi:10.1016/j.procs.2014.07.009

Bonnechère, B., Jansen, B., Omelina, L., & Van Sint, J. (2016). The use of commercial video games in rehabilitation: A systematic review. *International Journal of Rehabilitation Research. Internationale Zeitschrift fur Rehabilitationsforschung. Revue Internationale de Recherches de Readaptation, 39*(4), 277–290. doi:10.1097/MRR.0000000000000190 PMID:27508968

Cawley, G. C. (2006, July). Leave-one-out cross-validation based model selection criteria for weighted LS-SVMs. In *The 2006 IEEE international joint conference on neural network proceedings* (pp. 1661–1668). IEEE.

Chen, C., Jafari, R., & Kehtarnavaz, N. (2015, September). UTD-MHAD: A multimodal dataset for human action recognition utilizing a depth camera and a wearable inertial sensor. In *2015 IEEE International conference on image processing (ICIP)* (pp. 168-172). IEEE. 10.1109/ICIP.2015.7350781

Chen, C., Liu, K., Jafari, R., & Kehtarnavaz, N. (2014, August). Home-based senior fitness test measurement system using collaborative inertial and depth sensors. In *2014 36th Annual International Conference of the IEEE Engineering in Medicine and Biology Society* (pp. 4135-4138). IEEE. 10.1109/EMBC.2014.6944534

Deng, X., Liu, Q., Deng, Y., & Mahadevan, S. (2016). An improved method to construct basic probability assignment based on the confusion matrix for classification problem. *Information Sciences, 340*, 250–261. doi:10.1016/j.ins.2016.01.033

Fan, R. E., Chang, K. W., Hsieh, C. J., Wang, X. R., & Lin, C. J. (2008). LIBLINEAR: A library for large linear classification. *Journal of Machine Learning Research, 9*(Aug), 1871–1874.

Gaglio, S., Re, G. L., & Morana, M. (2015). Human activity recognition process using 3-D posture data. *IEEE Transactions on Human-Machine Systems, 45*(5), 586–597. doi:10.1109/THMS.2014.2377111

Hondori. (2014). A review on technical and clinical impact of Microsoft kinect on physical therapy and rehabilitation. *Journal of Medical Engineering*.

Joachims, T. (2006, August). Training linear SVMs in linear time. In *Proceedings of the 12th ACM SIGKDD international conference on Knowledge discovery and data mining* (pp. 217-226). ACM.

Kean, S., Hall, J., & Perry, P. (2011). *Meet the Kinect: An introduction to programming natural user interfaces*. Apress. doi:10.1007/978-1-4302-3889-8

Klein, D. (2004). Lagrange multipliers without permanent scarring. University of California at Berkeley, Computer Science Division.

Lange, B., Flynn, S., Proffitt, R., & Chang, C. Y., & Rizzo, A. (2010). Development of an interactive game-based rehabilitation tool for dynamic balance training. *Topics in Stroke Rehabilitation, 17*(5), 345–352. doi:10.1310/tsr1705-345 PMID:21131259

Lange, B., Koenig, S., McConnell, E., Chang, C. Y., Juang, R., Suma, E., . . . Rizzo, A. (2012, March). Interactive game-based rehabilitation using the Microsoft Kinect. In 2012 IEEE Virtual Reality Workshops (VRW) (pp. 171-172). IEEE. doi:10.1109/VR.2012.6180935

Laptev, I., & Caputo, B. (2004, August). Recognizing human actions: a local SVM approach. In null (pp. 32-36). IEEE.

Li, Y. (2012, June). Hand gesture recognition using Kinect. In *2012 IEEE International Conference on Computer Science and Automation Engineering* (pp. 196-199). IEEE. 10.1109/ICSESS.2012.6269439

Lin, W. Y., Chen, C. H., Tseng, Y. J., Tsai, Y. T., Chang, C. Y., Wang, H. Y., & Chen, C. K. (2018). Predicting post-stroke activities of daily living through a machine learning-based approach on initiating rehabilitation. *International Journal of Medical Informatics*, *111*, 159–164. doi:10.1016/j.ijmedinf.2018.01.002 PMID:29425627

Liu, Y., & Zheng, Y. F. (2005, July). One-against-all multi-class SVM classification using reliability measures. In *Proceedings. 2005 IEEE International Joint Conference on Neural* Networks, *2005* (Vol. 2, pp. 849-854). IEEE.

Lun, R., & Zhao, W. (2015). A survey of applications and human motion recognition with Microsoft kinect. *International Journal of Pattern Recognition and Artificial Intelligence*, *29*(5). doi:10.1142/S0218001415550083

Milgram, J., Cheriet, M., & Sabourin, R. (2006, October). "One against one" or "one against all": Which one is better for handwriting recognition with SVMs? In *Tenth international workshop on frontiers in handwriting recognition*. Suvisoft.

Naeemabadi, M. R., Dinesen, B., Andersen, O. K., Najafi, S., & Hansen, J. (2018). *Evaluating Accuracy and Usability of Microsoft Kinect Sensors and Wearable Sensor for Tele Knee Rehabilitation after Knee Operation*. BIODEVICES. doi:10.5220/0006578201280135

Nenonen, V., Lindblad, A., Häkkinen, V., Laitinen, T., Jouhtio, M., & Hämäläinen, P. (2007, April). Using heart rate to control an interactive game. In *Proceedings of the SIGCHI conference on Human factors in computing systems* (pp. 853-856). ACM. 10.1145/1240624.1240752

Norouzi, M., Fleet, D. J., & Salakhutdinov, R. R. (2012). Hamming distance metric learning. In Advances in neural information processing systems (pp. 1061-1069). Academic Press.

Oja, E. (1997). The nonlinear PCA learning rule in independent component analysis. *Neurocomputing*, *17*(1), 25–45. doi:10.1016/S0925-2312(97)00045-3

Oliver, M., Teruel, M. A., Molina, J. P., Romero-Ayuso, D., & González, P. (2018). *Ambient intelligence environment for home cognitive telerehabilitation* (p. 18). Sensors.

Pal, M., Saha, S., & Konar, A. (2014). A fuzzy C means clustering approach for gesture recognition in healthcare. *The Knee*, *1*, C7.

Pandey, S., & Solanki, A. (2019). Music Instrument Recognition using Deep Convolutional Neural Networks. International Journal of Information Technology. doi:10.100741870-019-00285-y

Pedraza-Hueso, M., Martín-Calzón, S., Díaz-Pernas, F. J., & Martínez-Zarzuela, M. (2015). Rehabilitation using kinect-based games and virtual reality. *Procedia Computer Science*, *75*, 161–168. doi:10.1016/j.procs.2015.12.233

Piscitelli, D. (2016). Motor rehabilitation should be based on knowledge of motor control. *Archives of Physiotherapy*, *6*(1), 5.

Procházka, A., Charvátová, H., Vaseghi, S., & Vyšata, O. (2018). Machine learning in rehabilitation assessment for thermal and heart rate data processing. *IEEE Transactions on Neural Systems and Rehabilitation Engineering, 26*(6), 1209–1214. doi:10.1109/TNSRE.2018.2831444 PMID:29877845

Russell, W. D., & Newton, M. (2008). Short-term psychological effects of interactive video game technology exercise on mood and attention. *Journal of Educational Technology & Society, 11*(2), 294–308.

Shlens, J. (2014). *A tutorial on principal component analysis.* arXiv preprint arXiv:1404.1100

Snoek, J., Taati, B., & Mihailidis, A. (2012). An Automated Machine Learning Approach Applied To Robotic Stroke Rehabilitation. *2012 AAAI Fall Symp. Ser.*, 38–41.

Sokolova, M., Japkowicz, N., & Szpakowicz, S. (2006, December). Beyond accuracy, F-score and ROC: a family of discriminant measures for performance evaluation. In *Australasian joint conference on artificial intelligence* (pp. 1015-1021). Springer.

Stanley, R. P. (2004). An introduction to hyperplane arrangements. *Geometric Combinatorics, 13*, 389-496.

Su, C. J. (2013). Personal rehabilitation exercise assistant with kinect and dynamic time warping. *International Journal of Information and Education Technology (IJIET), 3*(4), 448–454. doi:10.7763/IJIET.2013.V3.316

Tamura, T. (2014). Wearable inertial sensors and their applications. In *Wearable Sensors* (pp. 85–104). Academic Press. doi:10.1016/B978-0-12-418662-0.00024-6

Trankler, H. R., & Kanoun, O. (2001, May). Recent advances in sensor technology. In *IMTC 2001. Proceedings of the 18th IEEE Instrumentation and Measurement Technology Conference. Rediscovering Measurement in the Age of Informatics (Cat. No. 01CH 37188)* (Vol. 1, pp. 309-316). IEEE. 10.1109/IMTC.2001.928831

Twomey, N., Diethe, T., Fafoutis, X., Elsts, A., McConville, R., Flach, P., & Craddock, I. (2018, June). A comprehensive study of activity recognition using accelerometers. In Informatics (Vol. 5, No. 2, p. 27). Multidisciplinary Digital Publishing Institute. doi:10.3390/informatics5020027

Warburton, D. E., Bredin, S. S., Horita, L. T., Zbogar, D., Scott, J. M., Esch, B. T., & Rhodes, R. E. (2007). The health benefits of interactive video game exercise. *Applied Physiology, Nutrition, and Metabolism, 32*(4), 655–663. doi:10.1139/H07-038 PMID:17622279

Zeng, Z. Q., Yu, H. B., Xu, H. R., Xie, Y. Q., & Gao, J. (2008, November). Fast training support vector machines using parallel sequential minimal optimization. In *2008 3rd international conference on intelligent system and knowledge engineering* (Vol. 1, pp. 997-1001). IEEE.

Zhu, M., Cheng, L., Armstrong, J. J., Poss, J. W., Hirdes, J. P., & Stolee, P. (2014). *Using Machine Learning to Plan Rehabilitation for Home Care Clients: Beyond "Black-Box" Predictions.* Berlin: Springer.

Zhu, M., Zhang, Z., Hirdes, J. P., & Stolee, P. (2007). Using machine learning algorithms to guide rehabilitation planning for home care clients. *BMC Medical Informatics and Decision Making, 7.* PMID:18096079

Chapter 16
Leveraging Natural Language Processing Applications Using Machine Learning:
Text Summarization Employing Deep Learning

Janjanam Prabhudas

https://orcid.org/0000-0001-5381-8699

VIT-AP University, India

C. H. Pradeep Reddy

VIT-AP University, India

ABSTRACT

The enormous increase of information along with the computational abilities of machines created innovative applications in natural language processing by invoking machine learning models. This chapter will project the trends of natural language processing by employing machine learning and its models in the context of text summarization. This chapter is organized to make the researcher understand technical perspectives regarding feature representation and their models to consider before applying on language-oriented tasks. Further, the present chapter revises the details of primary models of deep learning, its applications, and performance in the context of language processing. The primary focus of this chapter is to illustrate the technical research findings and gaps of text summarization based on deep learning along with state-of-the-art deep learning models for TS.

DOI: 10.4018/978-1-5225-9643-1.ch016

INTRODUCTION

The basic unit of information called data which is alarming to the heights of uncertainties over period laid many challenges to researchers. It is well known that the data generated in the past 20 years is been produced in a week. As such data leaps over the gigantic curve, efficient models have evolved to process and analyze information for effective applications. Collaborating abundant information, computational abilities, and outstanding Artificial Intelligence techniques, the internet has upgraded from web 2.0 (dynamic web page interaction, independence to exhibit opinions, social blogging and media) to web 3.0 (leveraging information extraction, semantic web, artificial intelligence) elucidating the significance of processing Natural Language (NLP) by employing Machine Learning.

NLP is termed as an automatic process of analyzing, understanding and generating human language utilizing computational models. It has transformed from the early ages where batch processors are used to processing a single sentence that could consume 7 minutes to an era of search engines that process and analyze hundreds of web pages in not more than second. Today with redefined methods in NLP, few popular real-time applications that outperformed literature results are Machine Translation, Speech Recognition, Text Summarization, Virtual assistant chatbots, Sentiment analysis.

Since the language itself is ambiguous and unstructured, traditional methods and machines can't able to cope up with unstructured data and insufficient in dealing with challenges arises due to lexical and structural ambiguities. Lexical ambiguities include similar words that occur in a sentence tent to behave differently according to its context, structural ambiguities are common in a language where a sentence can have multiple inferences or predictions. Consider the following Sentence, "Due to environmental disasters there was a big hole in the forest; a team of professionals is looking into it". Here, humans can easily understand as "a team is working on the cause of the hole in the forest" but a system can interpret it as "a team is staring into the hole" which is of no meaning. To catch the clear meaning of the sentence the system should understand the language thoroughly and hence Machine Learning changed the perspective of earlier methods in dealing text.

There was a sudden leap of NLP applications in its performance when employing Machine Learning (ML) models. The notable achievements are during the 1990s, core NLP tasks are transformed via learning models from large quantities of available data. Core NLP tasks like tagging words with its grammatical structure using the Hidden Markov model, Named Entity Recognition, Syntax trees, Language modeling (N-Grams) using Markov chain process have achieved great improvements over traditional approaches. With the available Linguistic Data in the form of text and acoustics made available by Linguistic Data Consortium 1992, data was used to train and learn efficient ML models. Effective improvement of parallel processing made the evolution of statistical Natural Language Processing advanced applications like Sentiment analysis (Munjal, Kumar, Kumar, & Banati, 2019), text classification, spam email detection, automatic word correction, sentence recommendations in search engines.

Employing supervised or unsupervised popular and successful ML techniques like SVM, Logistic regression, Bayesian Classifier, Clustering for NLP tasks are based on words which are a statistical method. Though these methods succeeded in building successful applications like Apple Siri, IBM Watson, internally they rely on Bag of words (BOW), language modeling which are statistical approaches that work with individual word co-occurrences and probabilities. To make this informal these systems are like a learned parrot which repeat words without known actual meaning (Cambria & White, 2014)). The limitation with traditional ML models is they only consider statistical facts leaving semantics of

Figure 1. Trends of NLP and its transformation over the decades of time

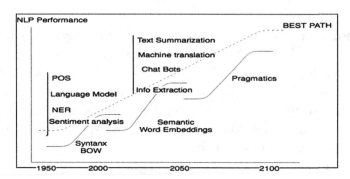

Figure 2. A quick glance of machine learning

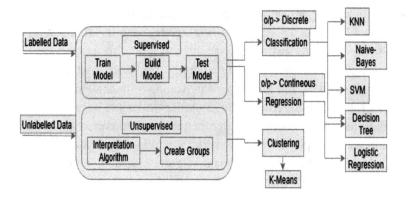

language which can be overcome by engaging distributional semantics. The trends of NLP and the transformation of applications of NLP over the decades are seen in Figure 1.

This chapter will revise the details of Machine Learning and the primary models of Deep Learning, its applications, and performance. The primary focus of this chapter is to illustrate the technical research findings and gaps of Text Summarization based on Deep Learning along with the avant-garde models. Succeeding chapters are categorized as follows. 1st Section details about Machine Learning and then the section tries to elaborate on the process of Text Summarization employing Deep Learning. Section 2 will describe Text features and their representations. Section 3 demonstrates about Deep Learning based TS, its models, and issues. Section 4 deals with future research directions. Section 5 will end the chapter with a conclusion.

GLANCE OF MACHINE LEARNING

ML is an Artificial Intelligence study that provides Machines the capability to learn from its own experiences by itself without being programmed explicitly. Simply it is a programming model that learns and try to adapt from experiences 'Exp' concerning to work on some task 'Tsk' along with a measure of performance 'Per', the performance of the model is proportional to its experiences. It works with data; ML algorithm will learn from annotated training data that works on generalization tasks like classifica-

Figure 3. Performance metrics of machine learning algorithms and deep learning w.r.t training data

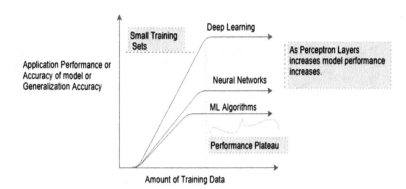

tion, prediction tasks called Supervised Learning or if data was unannotated the algorithm can prepare data into groups called Unsupervised Learning. Learning a model from data is nothing but learning a mapping or approximation function that maps a set of input features to a target feature (Alzubi, J., Nayyar, A., & Kumar, A, 2018). Details of Machine Learning concepts are represented in Figure 2.

ML models for NLP tasks accepts a set of linguistic feature vectors as input and model is trained employing linear models like SVM, Logistic Regression, Naïve Bayes in which the linguistic features are encoded into vectors having high dimensionality. The models accuracy entirely depends on the feature's quality, a standard way of extracting features is done by using a statistical method called Bag of Words. NLP has achieved great peaks from the past decade with the introduction of Neural Networks (sub-branch of ML) in dealing with language processing applications. Neural Networks with multi-layered perceptron called Deep Learning and has become very popular which performed never than before in many language-oriented tasks. The present technologies of NLP are built on the base of Deep Learning, the breakthrough was by employing the Deep Learning model for Machine Translation. However, ML model's performance depends entirely on considering the quantity of data it is being trained. With a huge rise of interest on Big Data and the availability of information along with computational abilities of processing tasks, Deep Learning has achieved performance that is never seen before in ML for NLP applications. The performance metrics are seen in Figure 3.

There are huge improvements in NLP using Deep Learning than ML because Sparse vector representation in ML generally contains huge dimensionality which leads degradation of model performance and they are computationally very complex. However Deep Learning models contain nonlinear transformations of vectors with Dense representation which are low dimensional, and the vector is encapsulated with syntactical and semantical information of the text. Deep Learning structure is organized as Hierarchical representation of data which has huge computational capabilities such that the feature extraction process is done automatically whereas for ML much of the time will be consumed in feature preparation step (Young, Hazarika, Poria, & Cambria, 2017). A model with Neural Network illustrated by (Collobert, et al., 2011) outperformed Successful Machine Learning based core NLP applications like Parts of Speech tagging (POS), Named Entity Recognition (NER), Semantic role labeling, chunking tasks which became a turning point for NLP using Deep Learning. Popular core NLP applications with their accuracies by employing ML and Deep Learning are depicted in Figure 4 based on the results published by (Collobert, et al., 2011).

Figure 4. Accuracy of core NLP applications w.r.t machine learning and deep learning

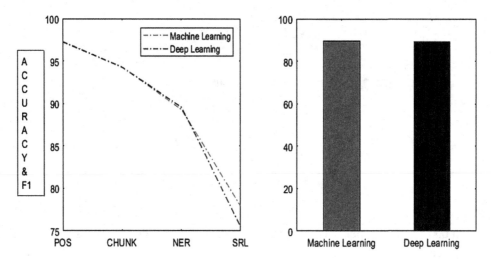

Hence with the promising results of Deep Learning, it has applied to many applications outperforming state of the art results. A recent breakthrough in the field was by (Bahdanau, et.al 2014) who used the sequence to sequence multi-layered neural network model (RecurrentNeural Network model) for Machine Translation task and successfully achieved best results that are never been before. Inspired by (Bahdanau, Cho, & Bengio, 2014) many researchers have marked the best performance of NLP applications using different Deep Learning models. A very recent application which is in early stages of research is Text Summarization (TS) and its performance has recently geared up with the introduction of Deep Learning models. TS is an automatic process of condensing information from multiple sources (forming an abstract of the document), thus providing user understand the content of whole information in a minimum amount of time. Summarizing multiple documents is a solution to information overload problem because single information can be found in many sources which will consume time to go through every page to get the gist of the topic.

Document Summarization indeed used for a variety of applications in NLP like Question Answering systems, information extraction, examples include a virtual assistant chat-bot system that satisfies the user query with a suitable responsive answer. The task of summarization is categorized into Extraction and Abstraction. Extractive summarization is so popular that most of the work was done on extraction employing Deep Learning. It includes creating a set of sentences $\{s1, s4 \ldots Sm\}$ with readability and information from a document or multiple documents $D = \{s1, s2, s3 \ldots, Sn\}$. Machine Learning tasks employed for summarization will identify salient sentences using statistical and linguistic features of text and then map them to target summary from training corpus containing document summary pairs. Based on the features identified, sentences in the document are given with score in which scores are generated by a weighted sum of feature scores such as Score $S = \sum_{w \in s} Vd(w)$. Few salient features are

Cue words, Position of the sentence, Parts of speech indication, Term Frequency-Inverse Document Frequency so on. Final Summary is formed by picking top 'K' most sentences from informative sentences.

Figure 5. Example of summary formed by summarization model

Gold Summary: Redpath has ended his eight-year association with Sale Sharks. Redpath spent five years as a player and three as a coach at sale. He has thanked the owners, coaches and players for their support.	Salience	Content	Novelty	Position	Prob.
Bryan Redpath has left his coaching role at Sale Sharks with immediate effect.	0.1	0.1	0.9	0.1	0.3
The 43 - year - old Scot ends an eight-year association with the Aviva Premiership side, having spent five years with them as a player and three as a coach.	0.9	0.6	0.9	0.9	0.7
Redpath returned to Sale in June 2012 as director of rugby after starting a coaching career at Gloucester and progressing to the top job at Kingsholm .	0.8	0.5	0.5	0.9	0.6
Redpath spent five years with Sale Sharks as a player and a further three as a coach but with Sale Sharks struggling four months into Redpath's tenure, he was removed from the director of rugby role at the Salford-based side and has since been operating as head coach .	0.8	0.9	0.7	0.8	**0.9**
"I would like to thank the owners, coaches, players and staff for all their help and support since I returned to the club in 2012.	0.4	0.1	0.1	0.7	0.2

Figure 6. The Current State of research on Deep Learning based Text Summarization as per recent literature

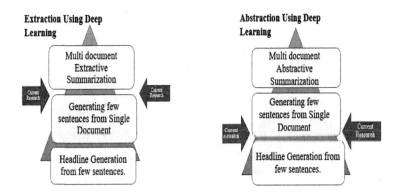

Abstractive summarization resembles human behavior in generating summaries, it does by first understanding the document thoroughly and then generating the summary sentences with words that are not there in vocabulary. Figure 5 demonstrates the summarization model output taken from (Nallapati, et.al 2016) who used Sequence-based Recurrent Neural Network for Extractive Summarization. Popular benchmark datasets available online are DUC datasets (Document Understanding Conference), CNN and Daily Mail news datasets, Gigaword dataset available as training and testing sets. The effectiveness of the summary is measured by means of ROUGE ("Recall-Oriented Understudy for Gisting Evaluation") score, the better the ROUGE score is the better the summary. Researchers in the fields improve performance of summary with a better ROUGE score, the ROUGE software tool is available in python language.

Though the task of TS is challenging, many researchers have published best results on TS by employing Deep Learning framework compared to recent literature methods. The current state of research on Deep Learning based TS as per recent literature are depicted in Figure 6.

There are many challenges and limitations to be considered in doing Deep Learning based TS, this chapter will make the researcher understand technical perspectives regarding Feature representation and their models.

FEATURE REPRESENTATIONS OF TEXT

Textual features denote contextual units of text data such as unique words in the corpus and linguistic features such as the grammatical category of words (POS tagging), Noun or Verb Phrases. NLP applications employing ML models generally work using Bag of words model with expensive hand-crafted features represented over vector space, trained on spare vectors that are of having huge dimensionality denoting curse of dimensionality. ML models that learn on such data can fail to generalize well on unseen data leading to overfitting problem (Kumar, et.al, 2018). Though efficient dimensionality reduction techniques are available in decomposing the matrix to low dimensions, the process is time complex. One-hot encoding is the technique used most widely for many NLP tasks. Consider the following small corpus having two sentences,

"This is the first sentence"

"This is not first sentence but actually second sentence"

There are 9 unique words in the above corpus then the vocabulary has 9 words which denote Bag of words V= {"this", "is", "the", "sentence", "not", "first", "second", "actually", "but"}.

The vectors are formed by converting free form text using one-hot vectors indicating 1 if the word is present and 0 if word not present. Each vector has its own dimension represented in single dimensional space equal to the vocabulary size. For the word "sentence", representation of one-hot is as follows: [0,0,0,1,0,0,0,0,0]. For the sentence "This is the first sentence" the vector is represented as follows: Vector = {1,1,1,1,0,1,0,0,0}. Accordingly, in real-time applications, the corpus size would be millions of words indicating the curse of dimensionality and the models undergo extreme computational complexities. This led to the motivation of distributional semantics by studying statistical patterns of word usage by (Bengio et al., 2003). In distributional semantic, the semantically similar words tend to have similar distribution patterns represented as vectors. Vectors are obtained by statistical analysis of the linguistic context of words. The distribution is represented as vectors denoting different words in multidimensional semantic space. It is built by choosing Target words and Context words from the corpus and the size of a window for context is decided by the number of words surrounded by the target word. It is represented as a distribution matrix with vectors built out of there co-occurrence count. An example regarding distributional semantics is illustrated in Figure 7 and the following example depicts the concept clearly. NLP Applications that rely on the linear representation of data using spare vectors are computationally very complex than applications that cope up with non-linear representations usually done in Deep Learning. A popular type of distributional semantics is word embeddings. Deep Learning covers the expensiveness of task-specific feature extraction by automatic extraction of features from the text in low dimensions, consequently, automatic feature extraction will generalize NLP applications like Machine Translation, Text Summarization, Speech Recognition.

Figure 7. Distribution of vectors in space

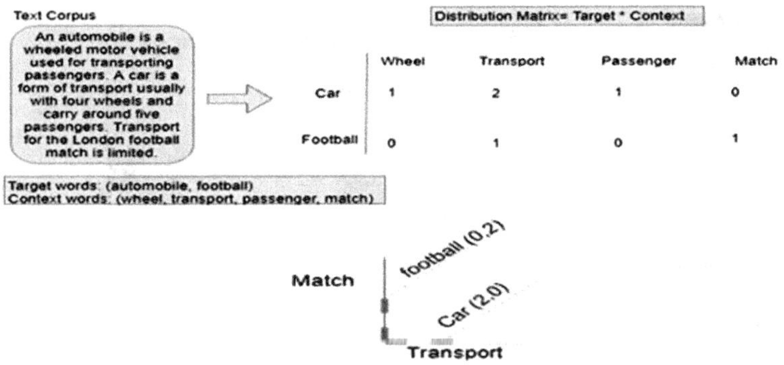

WORD EMBEDDINGS

Word Embeddings represent words in multi-dimensional distributional space along with syntactic and semantic information, it is simply a vector of weights. The intuition is words that occur in similar context are related to each other. While employing Deep Learning for NLP tasks the first layer of the network will be plugged by word embeddings. The pre-trained word embedding model that predict words based on context words from a large corpus of unannotated data are done by using Neural Networks who presented Word2Vec that learned word embeddings. The intuition behind Word2Vec is any word 'W$_i$' in the corpus is given a distributional representation by an embedding, W$_i$=R^d, where 'd' is dimensional vector. Dimension can be of any length, it can be from 50 to 500. Learning word vectors predicts surrounding words of every word instead of capturing co-occurrence counts directly. Word embeddings learning using word2vec is accomplished by using two models: a. Continuous Bag of Words (CBOW) and b. Skip Gram.

CBOW

CBOW model will predict target word considering context words surrounded by it with window size 'k', generally, the size of the window depends on the number of context words in the corpus. In detail, it predicts the center word by considering its previous and next words surrounded by center word. Consider the following example: "--- an efficient method of **Learning** high quality distributed vectors ---", with a window of size 8, 4 previous words and 4 next words: here the focus word is 'Learning' in which CBOW model should predict. The objective of the model is to predict the highest probability of center word using joint probability, typically it is an n-gram language model that finds the probability of a sequence of words in a sentence. If the conditional probability of observing actual words given input context words is not maximizing, the vectors are rearranged, and the weights of the network are updated. This process will continue until it reaches maximum probability for target word given context words. In the above example for the given context words {"an", "efficient", "method", "of", "high", "quality", "distributed", "vectors"} the network should predict the maximum probability of getting "Learning" as output. Figure 8 will elaborate on the details of building CBOW model using a neural network.

Figure 8. Building CBOW model using a neural network

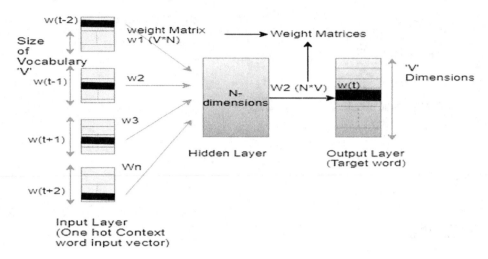

For 8 different input words, 8 different one-hot vectors are formed as an input to Neural Network. The input vector is multiplying with a weight matrix to learn hidden layer and the hidden layer is passed to the output layer with another weight matrix, SoftMax function is used to change the values to probabilities.

Skip Gram Model

Skip Gram is quite dissimilar to CBOW, where the objective of Skip Gram is to find context words surrounded by target word (Predicting Surrounded words in a window of length 'k' of each word). The input to the network is target vector that passes to hidden layer which tries to learn the hidden representation of input and forward the representations to output layer. The network will learn the probabilities of each context word in vocabulary that is nearer to the given input target word. The training objective of Neural Network can be mathematically determined in the following equation: $\sum_{-k \le j \le k} logP(Wt + j|Wt)$,

where $Wt + j$ is context word for given target word Wt. The only limitation with word embeddings is they can only represent single words, it cannot able to capture phrases such as two or more words combined to form a phrase like 'hot cake', 'ice melting', 'no boundaries', so on.

GLoVE

Global vector for word representation is a powerful word embeddings model that represents vectors and its meanings in multi-dimensional vector space with meaning as dimensions, it is based on co-occurrence count modeling whereas word2vec is a predictive model that aims in maximizing predictability of context or target word is given target or context word (considering local contexts) using Neural Networks. Instead of considering Target and context words in a fixed window size by word2vec form the vocabulary available, GLoVE considers the whole word to document or word to word statistical co-occurrences usually concealed in a matrix (considers global statistical counts). The model is trained by considering its global count statistics along with meaning dimensions, the aim is to predict co-occurrence ratios of words among contexts. The comparisons of GLoVE with respect to Word embeddings were drawn by (Pennington, Socher, & Manning, 2014).

Significance of Text Features for TS

As TS is concerned, feature engineering is crucial for ML-based TS treated as a two-class Classification Problem. It requires a set of valuable features based on which an approximation function is learned to map salient sentences to Summary generation. Text Features are essential in indicating significant sentences for the task of TS and will depict the core theme of the document. A simple question that would arise is how to determine the saliency of text, how can a model decide such extracted sentences will present the theme of a summary including readability. The simple answer to the above questions is to identify Text Features using linguistics that analyses and depicts the core sentiment of sentences. Most of the researchers have successfully summarized textual documents using statistical and linguistic features, the very first successful work is by (Luhn, 1958) who used phrase frequency as a feature. A number of features were introduced by many researchers and this chapter will present popular text features. Automatic feature recognition models posed as optimization problem are seen in the article (Kumar, Sharma, Sharma, Sharma, & Bansal, 2018).

Before identifying features for sentence extraction, the free form text in a cluster of documents which is unstructured should be converted to structured raw data which is then transformed into a vector of features. Preprocessing of the document includes Segmenting content of the document from whole text to paragraph, paragraph to individual sentences. Segmented sentences are converted to individual words via tokenization, the resultants are tokens (words or attributes) represented as BOW's. Stop words like conjunctions (and, or, but) and pronouns (she, he, it) which do not show their significance and used quite often in the text are eliminated. The final tokens undergo stemming and lemmatization. Stemming is a process of normalizing words into their base form, prefixes and suffixes are chopped off. Example, if Running is a token then stem is Run. Lemmatization also called Morphological analysis is like stemming that converts to base form considering dictionary, the final word is lemma, an actual base form of the word. The above process can be done using the Java-based Stanford core NLP tool or python NLTK. Authors in (Oliveira, et al., 2016) and (Ferreira et al., 2013) demonstrated popular text features considered for leveraging multi-document summarization. The popular statistical and linguistic features of the text are as follows:

Term Frequency-Inverse Sentence Frequency (TF/ISF)

It is similar to TF/IDF (Inverse Document Frequency) where TF/IDF is applied to the sentence level. The equation is as follows:

$$tf\left(w\right) = {}^{n}/_{N}, idf\left(w\right) = \log(\frac{D_{n}}{D_{w}})s$$

Where n is the count of particular word occurs inside a document, N is the count of total words in the document, Dn refers to total documents count and Dw refers to count of documents containing word. Equation 1 will describe the method.

$$tf \,/\, idf = tf\left(w\right)*idf\left(w\right)$$ (1)

In this method rather than computing term frequency in sentences, it calculates at the document level. This method assumes that if a word occurs frequently in a sentence then it is likely to be included in the summary.

Title Word Matching

The sentences that have title word will be assumed as important and they are included in the summary. The title normally prefers as an essential keyword, the similarity is measured based on the score of sentences with the title word. Computation of Feature is presented in Equation 2.

$$Sim(s_i) = \frac{S_{wi} \bigcap W_t}{|W_t|}$$ (2)

Where S_{wi} is a number of words that a sentence contains S_i, W_t refers to number of particular words in the title and $|W_t|$ is a total number of words in the title.

Position of Sentence

The first sentence of the text is considered most important as it contains the most related content like title words and the importance will get decreased as it goes down. Considering beginning and end sentences can get more score as they cover most context. The ranking scheme is followed as 1 for the first sentence and 1-n/n for the second sentence and so on, where n is a threshold value (number of sentences considered).

Length of Sentence

Sentences that are short or long are considered as trivial and they were excluded from the summary; short sentences do not contain information and long sentences contain unrelated matter. The Score is calculated as in equation 3

$$slen(s_i) = \frac{no\_of\_words\_in\_sentence(s_i)}{Max\_no\_of\_word\_in\_sentence}$$ (3)

Cue-Words

The use of certain words can determine the importance of sentences that start or end with a conclusion, Summary, vital, significance soon has a higher possibility to be included in the summary.

Verb and Noun Phrase

Generally, sentences that contain Nouns, Proper Nouns and verbal phrases cover main entities of context. The sentences are termed as important if they contain Noun and verbal phrases. For example, Person over the bridge jumped into the river after his dog slipped, the piece Person over the bridge is a Noun phrase and Jumped into the river after his dog slipped is a verb phrase.

POS and NER Tagging

Parts of Speech (POS) tag helps in identifying nouns and verb phrases of text. It is accomplished by finding out the grammatical group to which the word belongs to and functions on single tokens, Penn treebank and RDRPOSD (Nguyen, Nguyen, Pham, & Pham, 2014). are popular trained POS tagger that will help in tagging the text with POS. Named Entity Recognition (NER) accepting POS tagging as input is about annotating tokens by identifying Name, location and time present in data. NER helps in categorizing data while overcoming reference resolution, disambiguation. The functionality of this method is shown in Equation 4, the greater number of entities the sentence has the more important it is.

$$NER(S_i) = \frac{No\_of\_entities\_in\_S_i}{total\_entites\_in\_sentence} \tag{4}$$

(Wang, Li, Wang, & Zheng, 2017) illustrated nine heuristic methods for sentence extraction and successfully categorized different domains that used diverse features with best-performed analysis.

Similarity Measures

Multi-document summarization suffers from information overload problem as relevant information can be found in many documents leading to redundant information in summary. However, in a vast quantity of data, it is critical to cover information across documents by avoiding redundancy called diversity. Similarity measures pave an advantage to cover maximum information by minimizing redundancy. The premise features will assign an informative score to each sentence in the document, equation 5 elucidates scoring scheme.

$$Doc(D_i) = \{S_1, S_2 \ldots S_n\}, Score(S_k) = \sum_{j=1}^{n} S(f_j) \tag{5}$$

where for some D_i represents document consists 'n' number of sentences (n>0), Score(S_k) where $S_k \in D_i$ represents scoring scheme of individual sentences in the document with the sum of informative feature scores and $S(f_j)(j>0)$ refers score of the feature.

Since the Document is composed of informative sentence scores, similarity measures are implied to discover how similar the sentences are with each other. The primary part of finding similarity is between words and then sentences and paragraphs. The two types of text similarities are a lexical and semantic similarity. The lexical similarity of text contains a pair of words that have the same sequence of characters in the vocabulary. Semantic similarity of words or sentences is defined as syntactically different yet contextually same. Consider a pair of words Deer-elk, Deer-Mouse, Deer-horse; between the listed pair of words Deer-Elk are semantically similar. The conceptual similarity between pair of words, sentences or documents is the distance between them with respect to their meaning. Though various methods exist in lexical (String-based) and Semantic similarity (Corpus and knowledge-based), this chapter will project methods that are widely used in text summarization.

Modified Cosine Similarity

Cosine similarity is the common way of finding similarity between documents with vector representations. Many researchers have followed using cosine similarity in text summarization to find similarity between sentences that ranges from 0 to 1. Cosine similarity works based on word frequency occurrences in certain text. However, the performance of similarity measure for cosine is comparably less efficient when compared to Modified Cosine Similarity with respect to Importance of words in the text and its length, because word importance may vary from one text to other. For effective similarity, instead of considering word frequency based on occurrences, IDF for word occurrences yields effective similarity measure. The details of the Modified Cosine similarity are shown in equation 6.

$$Modified\_\cos ine(A,B) = \frac{\sum_{w \in a,b} tf_{w,a} * tf_{w,b} * (idf_w)^2}{\sqrt{\sum a_{i \in a} \left(tf_{a_i,a} idf_{a_i}\right)^2} * \sqrt{\sum b_{i \in b} \left(tf_{b_i,b} idf_{b_i}\right)^2}} \qquad (6)$$

where tf_w, a are the frequency of word 'w' (cosine similarity) in sentence A_1. tf_w, b are Term frequency for word 'w' in sentence B_1, and IDF is seen in Equation 1.

Manhattan Distance

Considering two vectors, the similarity is measured as the minimum distance between them. Considering two vectors, the Manhattan or absolute value distance is measured as the addition of the pair absolute differences. If x and y are two vectors and n is a number of terms in vector, then Manhattan distance is calculated as in equation 7.

$$Mdis(x,y) = \sum_{i=1}^{n} |x_i - y_i| \qquad (7)$$

Euclidean Distance

It is the commonly used distance metrics, it is defined as the total path between two vectors connecting. If a and b are two vectors then it is calculated as the squared root of the summation of squared differences for two vectors as shown in equation 8.

$$|a \rightarrow b| = \sqrt{\sum_{i=1}^{n} (a_i - b_i)^2} \tag{8}$$

Jaccard Coefficient

Jaccard coefficient operates on an unordered collection of vector sets, if x and y are two sets then the similarity is measured as the division of intersection of sets x, y by the union of sets x, y. The details are shown in Equation 9.

$$J(X,Y) = \frac{|X \cap Y|}{|X \cup Y|} \tag{9}$$

Normalized Google Distance

Normalized google distance is a corpus-based semantic similarity that works based on the hits Google search engine provides for a combination of words. The google distance is minimum if the words are similar and for diverse words, the distance is far. The distance between search items 'v' and 'u' are formulated as in equation 10.

$$NGD(u, v) = \frac{\max\{\log f(u), \log f(v)\} - \log f(u, v)}{\log N - \min\{\log f(u), \log f(v)\}} \tag{10}$$

Where f(u) and f(v) are search term hits, F (a, b) are the terms that occur in a number of web pages and N specifies overall web pages search by google.

Deep Learning Based Text Summarization

The proliferation of data across diverse domains laid many opportunities for NLP applications employing Deep Learning. Neural Network with multiple perceptron's have been adopted by many researchers in successfully implementing applications like Text Summarization (Yao, Zhang, Luo, & Wu, 2018), Machine Translation (Bahdanau, Cho, & Bengio, 2014), Automatic Question Answering systems (Ma, et al., 2018), Sentiment Classification (Munjal, Narula, Kumar, & Banati, 2018), Speech to Text conversion. The breakthrough of Deep Learning models for NLP Applications was laid by (Bahdanau, Cho, & Bengio, 2014), in which many researchers are inspired by it and lead to the innovation of different Deep Learning based Summarization techniques. Most of the research in TS is based on Extractive because by default the sentences are grammatically correct and summary can be formed by picking out the most important sentences. Abstractive summarization, however, contains many challenges compared to Extraction, recently researchers are gaining interest in dealing with Abstractive based TS due to the promising results of Deep Learning particularly Reinforcement Learning (Yao et al., 2018) and Recur-

Figure 9. Feed-Forward neural network with 2 hidden layers

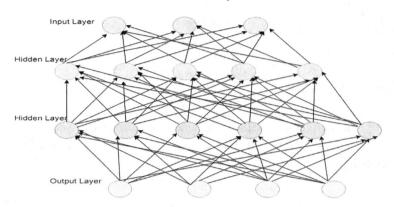

rent Neural Networks (See, Liu, & Manning, 2017) are trending. Deep Learning Architecture models are detailed as follows.

Multi-layered Perceptron Models

Neural Network an accountable successful model of Machine Learning mimics human brain in learning through carefully observed information. It is organized with processing elements called neurons, neurons do the computations in solving a specific problem. Due to its computational ability, Neural Networks with multiple perceptron layers are applied in many applications for Image recognition, language processing. Popular models are Multi-layered perceptron or Deep Learning models as are follows.

Feed-Forward Neural Network

As we know that neuron takes a major role in the human brain, likewise neural-network organized with computational neurons are also imitated by the computational processing of brain having neurons. Each neuron is compacted with a rigorous processing unit that takes weight associated input to process and produce outputs in a scalar representation. The inputs given to the neuron are represented as an addition of product of weights associated with each feature called linear transformation; then, non-linear function is applied to the computed linearity, the resultant is forwarded to the connected output. The above computational processing of a neuron occurs at each and every neuron of the network packed with multiple neurons, where the outputs generated after each computational process of neuron in layer "l-1" is passed as an input to the connected neuron associated with weight in layer "l". For the optimal weights set after learning the network to each and every connected edge of a neuron can merely estimate any complex function. The typical representation of neural network with more than 1 hidden layer is shown in Figure 9;

The circles shown in Figure 9 are neurons, incoming arrows give input from the previous layer and outgoing arrows results in the output of neurons. Neurons are arranged in layers, where the first layer has no incoming data and it is the input to the network. The last layer has no incoming data and is the output to the network, where other layers are considered as "hidden".

Non-Linear Activation Function

Activation functions are significant processing elements for Neural Network. Activation function aims in transforming the input to a higher lever resulting complex data pattern learning. The purpose of activation function is to amplify the network ability in approximating non-linearities of data present in the network, which transfers the "weighted sum" in to a non-linear scale, making a neuron either to fire or activate. The performance of the network toward complex data is enhanced in learning complex patterns inside data through non-linearity. Popular activation functions used by researchers are as follows.

1.   Sigmoid Function

In the sigmoid function, the values are scaled between 0 and 1 by applying a threshold. The equation $f(x) = \dfrac{1}{1+e^{-(x)}}$ represents the sigmoid function. The values are scaled when we change the weighted sum for X.

2.   Tanh function (Hyperbolic Tangent)

The Tanh function rescales the values between -1 and 1 by applying a threshold as a sigmoid function. The values of tanh are '0' centered which helps the next neuron, through propagating. The equation of tanh

$$g(x) = \frac{e^x}{1+e^x}$$

$$\tanh(x) = 2g(2x) - 1 \qquad (11)$$

$$\tanh(x) = \frac{e^x - e^{-x}}{e^x + e^{-x}}$$

When assigned input weighted sum to x in the above equation, the values are rescaled from -1 to 1.

3.   Rectified Linear Unit ("ReLU")

"ReLU", the most recommended function by recent researchers has proven to achieve better results in some tasks when compared to other functions. "ReLU" benefits in sparsity, this allows only positive values to process whereas other than positive values are scaled to zero which bring down the chance of occurrence of a dead neuron. Equation of "ReLU" is represented as $f(x) = (0, max)$. The limitation of "ReLU" leads to "dying relu" where the values is always 0, which doesn't allow negative gradients in backpropagation.

4.   Leaky "ReLU"

The limitation of "ReLU" can come across by using Leaky "ReLU", which indicate a tiny negative value when backpropagating in case of dead "ReLU" drawback, resulting the activation of neuron. Equation of Leaky "ReLU" is stated as $f(a) = 1(a < 0)(\alpha * a) + 1(a \geq 0)(a)$ where α is a small constant.

Convolution Neural Networks (CNN's)

Convolution neural networks are alike of ordinary neural networks which comprise neurons capable of learning optimal weights and biases using backpropagation. Unlike usual Neural Networks, CNN's has the ability to share weights through layers but the weights are associated as kernels. As a result of sharing weights, features are learned automatically and the learned parameters are reused in identifying new features. The features are recognized and weights are learned by a computation as a weighted sum of kernel weights and feature weights followed by a non-linear activation function, usually this process is called convolution (Solanki & Pandey, 2019). The usual Neural Network is organized in a way that each preceding layer of (input) neuron is attached with succeeding layer of (output) neuron. CNN's have the similar functionality but instead of having neuron layers, CNN's are designed to have convolution layers for preceding and succeeding layers of model. The significant feature of CNN is the usage of pooling layers, which are usually applied next to the convolutional layers. TS using CNN is seen in (Bawa & Kumar, 2019). The convenient manner of efficient model is to compute max pooling operation for every outcome of the kernel. Pooling operation outputs a predetermined matrix which is used for classification purpose. As a result of pooling, dimensionality of the output is maintained by not exceeding and it allows in preserving significant information.

Recurrent neural networks (RNN's)

RNN is a DL model meant to process sequential text data or time series information. Apart from usual networks with a single hidden layer, RNNs consider every input is to be independent and are designed to undertake arbitrary size inputs. The word "recurrent" infers, implementing identical task on every occurrence of the sequence so that, input relays on the earlier computations and outcomes. In general, the sequence is represented by a vector (size is fixed) plugging to the recurrent unit token by token. RNNs contain "memory" of earlier computations and make use of that information on existing processing. The template that is used here are naturally suitable for several NLP application like text summarization (Nallapati, et.al., 2016), machine translation (Bahdanau, et.al., 2014), language modelling (Karafi & Cernock, 2010), image captioning, speech recognition (Sutskever, Vinyals, & Le, 2014) etc.

Need for recurrent networks: RNNs have the capability to process long term dependencies across units in a network, where units are in the network can be characters, words, or even sentences. The individual unit in a network could constitute an RNN with GRU or LSTM. In general, RNNs are popular for language modeling tasks, which the model is plugged with a language where each word in the vocabulary is associate with neighboring words based on their context. RNNs are particularly capable of dealing with contextual oriented language since understanding sentences require language modeling techniques by maintaining word sense. This is one of the reasons researchers are turning towards RNN compared to CNN. Due to the computational capabilities of RNNs that deal with textual information in conserving long term dependencies, researchers consider RNN's rather than CNNs for textual processing or text involved applications (Chung, Gulcehre, Cho, & Bengio, 2014).

Several NLP tasks need semantic modeling throughout the sentence, which includes generating a meaning of the sentences in a static dimensional hyperspace. For instance, in Machine translation the variable size input in the form of vectors are mapped to multi-dimensional feature space where the contextual semantic units are captured and linked to produce a target sequence. Sequence labeling tasks like POS tagging, named entity recognition, word sense disambiguation approaches under this domain. Applications include document classification (Chaturvedi, Ong, Tsang, Welsch, & Cambria, 2016), multi-label text categorization, subjective detection (Chaturvedi, Ragusa, Gastaldo, Zunino, & Cambria, 2018) and multimodal sentiment analysis (Poria, et al., 2017). These are some of the significant reasons which motivate researchers to choose RNNs.

CNN's and RNNs both have various objectives while modeling a sentence, where CNN's extract the significant n-grams, and RNNs tries to generate a structure of an arbitrarily long sentence including unbounded context. Even though they justify an efficient method for language modeling tasks (n-gram modeling), it is limited to particular task as it fails in maintaining word ordering and cannot remember longer sentences. The tests that are performed by researchers on multiple NLP tasks which include QA, POS tagging (Chung, Gulcehre, Cho, & Bengio, 2014) and sentiment classification. They have summarized that none of the tasks could process longer sentences with word ordering as the key metric to achieve effective performance lies in maintaining semantic structure of sentence. A network with bunch of layers can be able to produce good performance but it's quite challenging to get desired output, because the model may face vanishing or exploding gradient in learning the data. Different configurations of RNNs are as follows:

Vanilla RNN:

From the NLPs perspective, the RNNs are initially based on a three-layered network call "Elman network". Over time RNNs are transformed to process variable length sequential data. Consider an input ' a_t ' to the network at 't' time instance and the hidden layer associated with the particular time instance 't' is denoted as s_t. The equation for s_t depends on

$$s_t = f\left(Aa_t + Cs_{t-1}\right) \tag{12}$$

Where s_t is produced by computing linear combination followed by non-linearity function of inputs from previous hidden layer and from present input layer at time instance 't'. Here 'f' is denoted as function of nonlinear activation similar to "tanh", "ReLU" and learned weights are shared across time. From the concept of NLP, a_t contains a sparse vector or word embeddings. y_t Defines, the network output which undergoes non-linear transformations among hierarchically organized layers.

The hidden state in the RNN is considered a crucial element as most of the computational part exists in hidden layers. In general, a simple RNN may prone from vanishing or exploding gradients. Vanishing or exploding gradients appears in learning the network through back propagation, as a result the model fails to remember long range dependencies of input sequence. In practice a typical RNN contains bunch of layers, the last layers is more likely to not bother about the earlier layer input. As a result of it parameter tuning is nearly impossible to make the network learn.

In order to control the above-mentioned limitations, computational nodes like gated recurrent units (GPUs), residual networks (ResNet) and long short-term memory (LSTM) were introduced with notable results. GRUs and LSTM are the key variants of RNN and used in trending applications of NLP.

LSTM

Most usable computational unit at hidden layer by researchers is LSTM by (Gers, Schmidhuber, & Cummins, 2000) contains extra "forget" gates across the simple RNN. LSTM has unique functionality in overcoming vanishing gradient and lets the network to remember the sequence using memory units encoded inside LSTM computational unit.

Unlike an unusual RNN, using LSTM the parameters of the models network at each layer are updated by propagating the error back to the earlier layers at every timestep. Each computational unit of LSTM contains 3 steps: "input gate, forget gate and output gate". This allows to compute the network hidden layers at a certain time instance. The computational details are listed in the mathematical equations below:

$$a = \begin{bmatrix} h_{t-one} \\ a_t \end{bmatrix}$$

$$f_t = \sigma \left(C_f . a + b_f \right)$$

$$i_t = \sigma \left(C_i . a + b_i \right)$$

$$y_t = \sigma \left(C_o . a + b_o \right)$$

$$c_t = f_t \odot c_{t-1} + i_t \odot tanh \left(C_c . X + b_c \right) \tag{13}$$

$$h_t = o_t \odot tanh \left(c_t \right)$$

Gated Recurrent Units

In most of the tasks, GRU (Cho, et al., 2014) have lesser complexity when similar performances are compared to LSTM. GRU when compared to LSTM with three gates has two operations inside its computational unit called update gate and reset gate, the data flow inside GRU resembles LSTM unit in remembering long term dependencies. GRU has shown its remarkable results in many applications of NLP like machine translation, text summarization, virtual assistance box etc. The computational complexity of GRU is comparably less than the complexity of LSTM, which is why GRU is termed as an efficient model compared to LSTM. The computational unit of GRU are listed below:

$$z = \sigma \left(U_z \cdot x_t + W_z \cdot h_{t-1} \right)$$

$$r = \sigma \left(U_r \cdot x_t + W_r \cdot h_{t-1} \right)$$

$$s_t = tanh \left(U_z \cdot x_t + W_s \cdot \left(h_{t-1} \odot r \right) \right) \tag{14}$$

$$h_t = \left(1 - z \right) \odot s_t + z \odot h_{t-1}$$

The suitable computational unit for RNN is challenging to decide in advance and researchers face difficulty in selecting which falls as a task to the researchers working in area.

State-of-the-Art of Text Summarization employing Deep Learning

Deep Learning applied to Text Summarization outperformed state-of-the-art results. The breakthrough was by (Bahdanau, Cho, & Bengio, 2014) who used the encoder-decoder model for Machine Translation, inspired by him researchers in (Rush, Chopra, & Weston, 2015) leveraged Text Summarization by employing attention based encoder-decoder model for Abstractive Summarization and outperformed non-deep learning-based approaches. The authors in (yao, et.al., 2018) utilized deep reinforcement learning for extractive document summarization and achieved good results using CNN/Daily mail dataset and Document Understanding Conference 2002, 2004 dataset. In paper (Nallapati, et.al., 2016) authors employed sequence to sequence-based Recurrent Neural Networks and successfully summarized (Extraction) multiple documents using CNN/Daily Mail Corpus with effective results. Abstractive summarization by (Nallapati, zhon et.al., 2016) implemented the encoder-decoder attention-based model to summarize large content of the document and achieved notable results.

Researchers in (Chopra, Auli, & Rush, 2016) invoked the attentive based Recurrent model in performing abstractive summarization using DUC-2004 dataset and achieved forming a summary with good results. Researchers in (See, Liu, & Manning, 2017) performed Abstractive Summarization by invoked hybrid pointer generator networks utilizing CNN/Daily Mail dataset and generated an effective summary by covering different topics.

Issues, Controversies, Problems

The present deep learning models used by researches for abstractive summarization can successfully generate single-line summaries, but the approaches are error prone to long documents.

By default, Extractive summaries are linguistically proper and grammatically correct in forming a summary, but the system can fall behind the redundancy problem. Sentences that are identified as significant can be redundant in a different context and the summary model has more priority in selecting those sentences.

The models may not generalize well if the test data is scalable. Most of the summarizer work based on the informative scores of sentences omitting semantics.

In most existing approaches of ML based feature representation, features are represented as a statistical unit of text which mainly focusses on term co-occurrences.

Though advanced models are there to generate a summary, models cannot handle out of vocabulary words. A summary can be generated from the same vocabulary in which the model is trained.

Summarization training data contains document-summary pairs, those summaries act as ground truths which are human-made abstracts. The dataset containing human abstracts many not provide good summaries for extraction-based summarization.

Most document summarization datasets available for research are DUC, CNN and Daily Mail, Giga-word datasets, mostly from news domains.

FUTURE RESEARCH DIRECTIONS

Models may prone to generalize well if approaches like semi-supervised learning are used in the feature learning process, which may help in effective parameter updating in gradient descent.

Data-driven approaches (automatic feature extraction by the neural network model) achieved effective summaries compared to traditional hand-engineered based features.

Unsupervised methods used in representing vectors in multi-dimensional vector space encapsulates semantics of text and thus providing good summarization results.

CONCLUSION

This chapter is initiated by justifying the importance of Deep Learning and tried depicting the significance Natural Language Processing employing Deep Learning and presented with the current research trend in TS. It is organized to make the researchers understand technical perspectives regarding Feature representation and their models to be considered before applying them. Further, the present chapter revises the details of primary models of Deep Learning, its applications and performance in the context of language processing. By illustrating the technical research findings and gaps of Text Summarization using Deep Learning along with the literature Deep Learning models for TS, researchers can improve the efficiency of TS keeping in mind technical perspectives.

REFERENCES

Alzubi, J., Nayyar, A., & Kumar, A. (2018, November). Machine learning from theory to algorithms: An overview. *Journal of Physics: Conference Series, 1142*(1), 012012. doi:10.1088/1742-6596/1142/1/012012

Bahdanau, D., Cho, K., & Bengio, Y. (2014). *Neural Machine Translation by Jointly Learning to Align and Translate.* arXiv e-prints, arXiv:1409.0473

Bawa, V. S., & Kumar, V. (2019). Linearized sigmoidal activation: A novel activation function with tractable non-linear characteristics to boost representation capability. *Expert Systems with Applications*, *120*, 346–356. doi:10.1016/j.eswa.2018.11.042

Chaturvedi, I., Ong, Y.-S., Tsang, I. W., Welsch, R. E., & Cambria, E. (2016). Learning word dependencies in text by means of a deep recurrent belief network. *Knowledge-Based Systems*, *108*, 144–154. doi:10.1016/j.knosys.2016.07.019

Chaturvedi, I., Ragusa, E., Gastaldo, P., Zunino, R., & Cambria, E. (2018). Bayesian network based extreme learning machine for subjectivity detection. *Journal of the Franklin Institute*, *355*(4), 1780–1797. doi:10.1016/j.jfranklin.2017.06.007

Cho, K., Merrienboer, B., Gulcehre, C., Bahdanau, D., Bougares, F., Schwenk, H., & Bengio, Y. (2014). *Learning Phrase Representations using RNN Encoder-Decoder for Statistical Machine Translation.* arXiv e-prints, arXiv:1406.1078

Chopra, S., Auli, M., & Rush, A. M. (2016, 6). Abstractive Sentence Summarization with Attentive Recurrent Neural Networks. *Proceedings of the 2016 Conference of the North American Chapter of the Association for Computational Linguistics: Human Language Technologies*, 93-98. 10.18653/v1/N16-1012

Chung, J., Gulcehre, C., Cho, K., & Bengio, Y. (2014). *Empirical Evaluation of Gated Recurrent Neural Networks on Sequence Modeling.* arXiv e-prints, arXiv:1412.3555

Collobert, R., Weston, J., Bottou, L., Karlen, M., Kavukcuoglu, K., & Kuksa, P. (2011). *Natural Language Processing (almost) from Scratch.* arXiv e-prints, arXiv:1103.0398

Ferreira, R., De Souza Cabral, L., Lins, R. D., Pereira, E., Silva, G., Freitas, F., ... Favaro, L. (2013). Assessing sentence scoring techniques for extractive text summarization. *Expert Systems with Applications*, *40*(14), 5755–5764. doi:10.1016/j.eswa.2013.04.023

Gers, F. A., Schmidhuber, J., & Cummins, F. (2000). Learning to Forget: Continual Prediction with LSTM. *Neural Computation*, *12*(10), 2451–2471. doi:10.1162/089976600300015015 PMID:11032042

Kumar, S., Sharma, B., Sharma, V. K., & Poonia, R. C. (2018). Automated soil prediction using bag-of-features and chaotic spider monkey optimization algorithm. *Evolutionary Intelligence*.

Kumar, S., Sharma, B., Sharma, V. K., Sharma, H., & Bansal, J. C. (2018). Plant leaf disease identification using exponential spider monkey optimization. *Sustainable Computing: Informatics and Systems*.

Luhn, H. P. (1958). The Automatic Creation of Literature Abstracts. *IBM Journal of Research and Development*, *2*(2), 159–165. doi:10.1147/rd.22.0159

Ma, S., Sun, X., Li, W., Li, S., Li, W., & Ren, X. (2018). *Query and Output: Generating Words by Querying Distributed Word Representations for Paraphrase Generation.* arXiv e-prints, arXiv:1803.01465

Munjal, P., Kumar, L., Kumar, S., & Banati, H. (2019). Evidence of Ostwald Ripening in opinion driven dynamics of mutually competitive social networks. *Physica A*, *522*, 182–194. doi:10.1016/j.physa.2019.01.109

Munjal, P., Narula, M., Kumar, S., & Banati, H. (2018). Twitter sentiments based suggestive framework to predict trends. *Journal of Statistics and Management Systems, 21*(4), 685–693. doi:10.1080/097205 10.2018.1475079

Nallapati, R., Zhai, F., & Zhou, B. (2016). *SummaRuNNer: A Recurrent Neural Network based Sequence Model for Extractive Summarization of Documents.* arXiv e-prints, arXiv:1611.04230

Nallapati, R., Zhou, B., Nogueira dos Santos, C., Gulcehre, C., & Xiang, B. (2016). *Abstractive Text Summarization Using Sequence-to-Sequence RNNs and Beyond.* arXiv e-prints, arXiv:1602.06023

Nguyen, D. Q., Nguyen, D. Q., Pham, D., & Pham, S. B. (2014). *A Robust Transformation-Based Learning Approach Using Ripple Down Rules for Part-of-Speech Tagging.* arXiv e-prints, arXiv:1412.4021

Oliveira, H., Ferreira, R., Lima, R., Lins, R. D., Freitas, F., Riss, M., & Simske, S. J. (2016). Assessing shallow sentence scoring techniques and combinations for single and multi-document summarization. *Expert Systems with Applications, 65*, 68–86. doi:10.1016/j.eswa.2016.08.030

Pennington, J., Socher, R., & Manning, C. (2014, 10). Glove: Global Vectors for Word Representation. *Proceedings of the 2014 Conference on Empirical Methods in Natural Language Processing (EMNLP)*, 1532-1543. 10.3115/v1/D14-1162

Poria, S., Cambria, E., Hazarika, D., Majumder, N., Zadeh, A., & Morency, L.-P. (2017). Context-Dependent Sentiment Analysis in User-Generated Videos. *Proceedings of the 55th Annual Meeting of the Association for Computational Linguistics*, 1, 873-883. 10.18653/v1/P17-1081

Rush, A. M., Chopra, S., & Weston, J. (2015). *A Neural Attention Model for Abstractive Sentence Summarization.* arXiv e-prints, arXiv:1509.00685

See, A., Liu, P. J., & Manning, C. D. (2017). *Get To The Point: Summarization with Pointer-Generator Networks.* arXiv e-prints, arXiv:1704.04368

Solanki, A., & Pandey, S. (2019). Music instrument recognition using deep convolutional neural networks. *International Journal of Information Technology.*

Sutskever, I., Vinyals, O., & Le, Q. V. (2014). *Sequence to Sequence Learning with Neural Networks.* arXiv e-prints, arXiv:1409.3215

Wang, W. M., Li, Z., Wang, J. W., & Zheng, Z. H. (2017). How far we can go with extractive text summarization? Heuristic methods to obtain near upper bounds. *Expert Systems with Applications, 90*, 439–463. doi:10.1016/j.eswa.2017.08.040

Yao, K., Zhang, L., Luo, T., & Wu, Y. (2018). Deep reinforcement learning for extractive document summarization. *Neurocomputing, 284*, 52–62. doi:10.1016/j.neucom.2018.01.020

Young, T., Hazarika, D., Poria, S., & Cambria, E. (2017). *Recent Trends in Deep Learning Based Natural Language Processing.* arXiv e-prints, arXiv:1708.02709

Chapter 17

Machine Learning in 5G Multimedia Communications:
Open Research Challenges and Applications

Dragorad A. Milovanovic
University of Belgrade, Serbia

Zoran S. Bojkovic
University of Belgrade, Serbia

Dragan D. Kukolj
ⓘ https://orcid.org/0000-0003-0711-0168
Faculty of Technical Sciences, University of Novi Sad, Serbia

ABSTRACT

Machine learning (ML) has evolved to the point that this technique enhances communications and enables fifth-generation (5G) wireless networks. ML is great to get insights about complex networks that use large amounts of data, and for predictive and proactive adaptation to dynamic wireless environments. ML has become a crucial technology for mobile broadband communication. Special case goes to deep learning (DL) in immersive media. Through this chapter, the goal is to present open research challenges and applications of ML. An exploration of the potential of ML-based solution approaches in the context of 5G primary eMBB, mMTC, and uHSLLC services is presented, evaluating at the same time open issues for future research, including standardization activities of algorithms and data formats.

INTRODUCTION

5G is a wireless communication system based on a collection of advanced technologies and architectures that can be configured for different purposes. As 5G networks are software-based and programmable, they can be configured to meet virtually any set of requirements. As consequence of various require-

DOI: 10.4018/978-1-5225-9643-1.ch017

ments, and heterogeneity in devices and applications, the 5G network is complex system. In service-driven network, a single infrastructure efficiently and flexibly supports (enhanced) mobile broadband, (ultra-reliable) low-latency communications and (massive) machine type communications (Bojkovic, 2017; Shafi, 2017). Moreover, mobile operators straggle to extend service coverages and increase network capacity. Traditional approach for complex networks planning, control, operation and optimization is centrally-managed and reactive. A novel proactive, adaptive and predictive networking is necessary (Jiang, 2017). The 5G system is self-adaptive and operate autonomously. We explore in this chapter, challenges and open issues for research in ML communications.

Overall, 5G networks are more challenging in evolving service requirements and complicated configuration issues. As 5G standard specifications have been developing quickly and commercially deployed worldwide, mobile operators straggle with network complexity and quality of user experience. Network complexity refers to deployment of densely distributed 5G base stations, configuration of large-scale antenna arrays, and global scheduling of virtualized cloud networks. Networks are maintained and operated in a smarter and more agile manner. 5G is at an advanced stage of technical development and standardization. The first set of technical specifications were completed in 2018 and further standardization is in progress until 2020. The 3G Partnership Project (3GPP) Release 15 includes New Radio (NR) technical specification for non-standalone architecture (NSA) and eMBB services. The standalone (SA) version of the NR standard is formally completed in June 2018. Current Release 16 study on further NR enhancements and transition to the 5G core network until March 2020. Technical specifications enhances massive MIMO technology, introduces the non-orthogonal multiple access (NOMA), and network virtualization and network slicing based on cloud computing (Wang, 2015; Cui, 2018; Awan, 2018; Gui, 2018).

5G communication system jointly optimizes key performance indicators (KPIs), including connection density, latency, reliability, and user experience. Recently, applied machine learning (ML) provides new concepts and possibilities (Fig. 1) for research in academia, industry and standardization organizations (Simeone, 2018; You, 2019; Li, 2017). The partnership project 3GPP eNA (*Enablers for Network Automation*) and focus group ITU ML5G (*Machine Learning for Future Networks*) have proposed research projects on ML communications. 5G supports ultra-reliable, high-speed, low-latency communication, and massive Internet of Things (IoT) services in real-time. Operation in dynamic wireless environment requires quality of service (QoS) guarantees, while ML technology is integrated on network infrastructure and end-user devices (Cayamcela, 2018).

Multi-disciplinary data-driven techniques have been extensively studied and applied to optimize complex networks (Cote, 2018). Rapid developments in computing and data storage technologies regains applied Artificial Intelligence (AI) in communications. AI greatly helps mobile operators to improve network planning, coverage optimization, capacity expansion, smart slicing, smart MIMO, and dynamic cloud resource management.

Machine learning (ML) is undergoing rapid development today, even in low-cost consumer mobile terminals by virtue of massive online data and increase in processing power available to application developers. In the early days of AI, there was significant work on learning from data. The 1990s reinvented machine learning to solve practical problems of pattern recognition using statistics. Recently, ML goals are data-driven models that can make decisions without following pre-defined rules. Proposed machine learning algorithms are categorized by model structure into supervised, unsupervised and reinforcement learning. With *supervised* ML algorithms we use labeled training data set to develop the model which represents the relation between the input, output and system parameters. The goal of *unsupervised* ML

Figure 1. Applied machine learning (ML) in communication areas

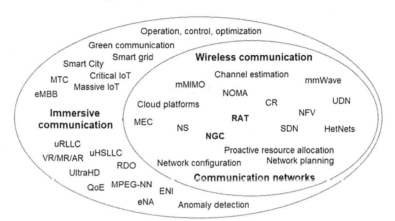

algorithms is to classify the sample sets into clusters based on the similarity between the input samples. In *reinforcement* ML algorithms, the agent interacts with its environment and online learns through the reward/penalty process (Zhang, 2018). An exploration of ML-based approaches in the context of multimedia eMBB, mMTC and uHSLLC services is presented in this chapter. Open issues for future research are evaluated, too.

The chapter is organized as follows. The convergence of machine learning algorithms and communication technology are highlighted in the first part. Intelligence in key 5G functional blocks and services, including immersive media coding is analyzed in the second part. A range of future research ideas on machine learning in 5G and beyond networks are summarized in the third part of the chapter.

CONVERGENCE OF MACHINE LEARNING AND COMMUNICATIONS

Developing an efficient ML algorithms to deal with complex problems in different network scenarios is challenging task. 5G systems generate a huge amount of traffic data, which is used in machine learning methods to improve the design and management of networks (Ibnkahla, 2018; Samek, 2017; Rafique, 2018). Wireless network is complex interacting system consists of core transport and access network, wireless edge and mobile connectivity (Fig.2).

Terminals (UE) at the edges of the network, radio access network (RAN) and core network (Core)

Core network consists of switches and subscriber-information management equipment. Mobile terminals (UE) communicate with the core network via radio access network (RAN). The 3GPP 5G Core supports the different throughput, latency and mobility requirements with the introduction of Services Based Architecture (SBA) and Control and User Plane Separation (CUPS). The 3GPP SA (Service and System Aspects) group formulates specifications in relation to service requirements, architecture, security, coding and network management (service-based architecture, enhanced support for virtualization, network slices, mobile management and session control procedures).

Figure 2. A generic network architecture: erminals (UE) at the edges of the network, radio access network (RAN) and core network (Core).

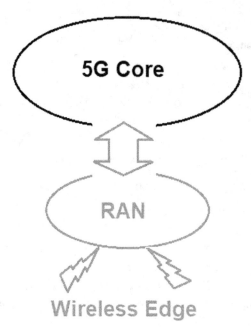

Table 1. The evolution of ML in 5G systems

	4G	**5G**	**ML**	**Modules**
Services	MBB	eMBB, mMTC, uRLLC	service-aware	
Radio resource management	granted	• granted or grant-free • flexible bandwidth • flexible symbol length	UE-specific on-demand	sensing, mining, reasoning
Mobility management	unified	• on-demand	location tracking/awareness	sensing, prediction, reasoning
Management and orchestration	simple	• operator-tailored	enhanced self-organization and trouble-shooting capability	sensing, mining, prediction, reasoning
Service provisioning management	unified	• end-to-end network slicing	network slice auto-instantiation	mining, prediction, reasoning

Machine learning techniques have been used in the network field for a long time for prediction and classification (Ge, 2018). ML is highly suitable for complex system modeling (Wang, 2018; Alsheikh, 2018). The evolution of sensing, mining, prediction and reasoning modules in mobile networks is shown in Table 1. The 5G services are improved in terms of throughput, latency, peak data rate as well as spectral and energy efficiency (Jiang, 2017).

Ml Algorithms In 5g Networks

Machine learning has great potential to improve communication systems. A ML based solution does not require a rigidly defined network model and could be end-to-end optimized for real communication systems. Traditional model is based on chain of well-defined independent processing blocks. The signal processing algorithms are optimized for mathematically convenient models (linear, stationary with Gaussian distribution), but not for real systems with many imperfections and nonlinearities (O'Shea, 2018; O'Shea, 2017). The performance of each module could be improved or optimized criteria of reliability, latency, and energy efficiency. However, individually optimization of processing blocks could not achieved the best possible end-to-end performance. It is necessary to jointly optimize end-to-end metrics over all modules (Table 2).

ML workflow in 5G systems is similar to the classical machine learning.

Problem formulation (classification, clustering, decision making): A given problem is classified into one of the ML categories. An improper problem formulation results in model with unsuitable structure and unsatisfactory performance.

Data collection (traffic traces, performance logs): In this step, huge quantity of data is measured and aggregated. According to the application needs, tie data are recorded in two phases from different network layers. In the offline phase, filtered representative data are used for model training. In the online, real-time network parameters and performance indicators are used as feedback inputs. The run-time data are used in model adaption.

Data analysis (preprocessing, feature extraction): Networks are affected by many factors, but usually only several characteristics have the significant impact on performance metric. The goal of this stage is to find the most influencing features for model training.

Model construction (training and tuning): Model selection and training according to the size of the dataset and the problem category are crucial. The tuning process is based on exhaustive search in a large parameter space.

Model validation (error analysis): Offline validation evaluates the learning algorithm. Cross validation tests the overall accuracy of the model against overfitting or under-fitting. The results are guidance for optimization of the model, reducing model complexity as well as increasing the data volume.

Deployment and inference (tradeoffs): The tradeoff between accuracy and the computational complexity is significant for the system performance under limited computation or energy resources. Machine learning often does not provide any performance guarantee because it works in a best-effort mode.

Model life cycle: In the maintenance of ML model is important to identify the model update cycle duration considering the computational and validation complexity of updated ML model.

ML tasks could be classified as supervised, unsupervised and reinforcement learning (Rafique, 2018; Alzubi, 2018)

Supervised learning: In this approach a ML model is created in an iterative process of model parameters updating. In this process, the set of input variables is transformed to their corresponding output characteristics. ML model generalization capabilities and estimation of ML model unknown parameters is based on a sufficient train dataset. Depending on application purpose, ML tasks could be further categorized into classification and regression. KNN (*K-Nearest Neighbors*) is non-parametric

Table 2. ML algorithms categories for 5G technology and applications

Category	Learning techniques	Key characteristics	Application
Supervised machine learning	*Regression models*	Learn the relationship between variables in the dataset: • estimate the variables' relationships • linear and logistics regression	• massive MIMO estimation/detection • mobile users' locations and behaviors • dynamic frequency and bandwidth allocation
	K-Nearest Neighbor	• majority vote of neighbors	• user location/behavior classification
	Support Vector Machines	Classify data into given set of categories: • non-linear mapping to high dimension • separate hyperplane classification	• path loss prediction model for urban environments • energy learning
	Bayesian learning	Bayes rule to infer model parameters: • *a posteriori* distribution calculation • GM, EM, and HMM	• massive MIMO estimation/detection • CR spectrum sensing/detection • cooperative wideband spectrum sensing
	Decision tree	Iteration the input data through a tree-like graph/model to learn decision rules	• service classification • resource allocation
Unsupervised machine learning	*K-means clustering* *SOM*	Group similar data points into a cluster: • iterative updating algorithm	• users' behavior-classification • access point association • heterogeneous base station clustering • cooperative spectrum sensing
	PCA (Principal Component Analysis)	Transformation of set of observations into a set of linearly uncorrelated variables	• anomaly/fault/intrusion detection • smart grid user classification • CR scenarios
	ICA (Independent Component Analysis)	Finds additively separable components: • reveal hidden independent factors	• signal dimension reduction • CR spectrum sensing
Reinforcement learning	*MDP (Markov decision process)* *POMDP (Partially observable Markov decision process)*	A system must learn the expected output on its own in sequential decision problems and use evaluative feedback as a performance measure: • system's state space • action space • reward function	• decision making in unknown conditions • inferring mobil users' decision making under unknown network conditions • channel access under unknown channel availability conditions in spectrum sharing • distributed resource allocation under unknown resource quality conditions in femto/small-cell networks • modeling in energy harvesting
	Q-learning	• learn a policy with stochastic transitions and rewards	• resource competition in femto/small cells
	Multi-armed bandit	• exploration-exploitation tradeoff dilemma	• proactive resource allocation • D2D spectrum sharing (user is modeled as a player of the MAB game)

algorithm based on dissimilarity between the samples. ANN (*Artificial Neural Network*) are multi-layer perceptron, convolutional neural network, recurrent neural network (Pandey, 2019). Challenges in ANNs are selection of number of hidden layers or neurons, ANN training computational complexity, and multidimensional parameters optimization (Kumar, 2018; Munjal, 2018; Munjal, 2019). SVM (*Support Vector Machine*) is a primary classification method. The input feature space is separated by maximizing margins between the classes.

Unsupervised Learning: Labeled data are not easily accessible or plentifully available in practice. An unsupervised algorithms are capable to re-organize an input data set without given associated labels by identifying internal characteristics of considered input data. Algorithms are *clustering* of data into groups of similar samples, or discovering *association rules* by identifying relationships among features. K-means algorithm separates all of the samples into *k* groups based on dissimilarity metrics. PCA (*Principal Component Analysis*) reduces problem dimension by transforming the original variable set into linearly uncorrelated variables using the singular value decomposition procedure. SOM (*Self-Organizing Maps*) reduces problem dimension, where an SOM is trained using unsupervised learning to re-organize samples positions in a high dimensional space.

Reinforcement Learning: algorithms create and adapt a model using an agent's direct interaction with its own environment, without an explicit training phase. The relationship between input–output features is learned using the initial model and test data. Here is a tradeoff between the model exploitation and data exploration. Reinforcement learning is iterative decision-making process characterized with dynamically adaptation and gradually refinement. The objective function called reward function, parameterized policy and strategy is necessary to specify (Luong, 2018). The goal of Q-leaning is to define agent's actions considering circumstances determined by the value function $Q(s, a)$. K- or N-armed (*multi-armed bandit*) algorithm allocated fixed limited set of resources between available alternative resources maximizing their expected gain. POMDP (*Partially observable Markov decision process*) estimates a set of possible states and its probability distribution. The penalty function minimizes the expected cost of the optimal action policy. The optimal policy of the agent is sequence of optimal actions in its environment.

5G Technology and ML

There is no doubt that the complexity of 5G network systems could be managed with ML applications. Machine learning provides solutions for many wireless networks technology components such as software defined network (SDN) and network function virtualization (NFV), network slicing, mobile edge computing (MEC), massive multiple-input multiple-output (mMIMO), new radio access technology (RAT), mmWave access, and green communications (Wu, 2018; Perez, 2015; Tran, 2018). ML techniques for efficient operation, control and optimization are necessary in a fully operative and efficient 5G network (Table 3, Table 4).

Smart mMIMO: The beamforming for mMIMO channels matches cell user distribution and minimize the interference from neighboring cells. The critical factor that affects the beamforming effect is weight setting for mMIMO base station. The adjustment is based on actual needs and an expert experience. However, many adjustments are necessary to get close to the optimal value. ML technologies improve the system by identifying the rule of change in user distribution and forecast the distribution. The smart system automatically identify a different scenarios and make adaptive optimization of the weights to obtain best user coverage (Di Huang, 2018; Klautau, 2018; Ramesh, 2017; Yang, 2018; Magdalinos, 2017; Pérez-Romero, 2015; Moysen, 2018).

Table 3. 5G Functional challenges in different ML-based solutions

Solutions	ML algorithm	Data model	Challenges
mMIMO	*Regression analysis* *KNN* *SVM* *Bayesian learning*	• regression function • majority vote • non-linear mapping • Gaussians mixture model, expectation maximization, hidden Markov models	• channel estimation and data detection • designing pilot patterns • estimating or predicting radio parameters • optimal handover solutions • interfering links of the adjacent cells • user location/behavior learning/classification
mmWave	*Multi-armed bandit* *DL (Deep learning)*	• online learning	• beam selection with environment-awareness • model of propagation channel • clustering and power allocation • spectral white state estimation, prediction and handoff decisions in CR networks
Cognitive Radio	*KNN* *SVM*	• majority vote • non-linear mapping	• spectrum sensing and white space detection • cognitive spectrum sensing/detection • cooperative wideband spectrum sensing • resource management
HetNets	*K-means clustering* *Q-learning* *Multi-armed bandit*	• mixed integer programming • model-free reinforcement • model resource allocation problem • multi-parametric modeling	• cell clustering in cooperative ultra-dense small-cell networks • clustering to avoid interference • network selection/association problems • self-configuration/optimization femtocells • cell outage management and compensation • allocation problems in wireless scenarios • load-balancing • user association (cell selection) mechanisms
NOMA	*K-means clustering*	• online adaptive learning detection • deep learning	• tradeoff between the cluster size and the incurred interference error • detection sharply changing channel conditions • clustering

NOMA: Non-Orthogonal Multiple Access is an improvement of multiple access techniques based on assignment of users with different power levels according the channel quality. User clustering is a critical in NOMA transmission. There is system's tradeoff of capacity (energy conservation) and guaranteeing fairness among the multiplexed users. The classical *max-min* fairness criterion (maximizing the minimum user rate) is formulated in MIMO NOMA systems and classical suboptimal

Table 4. 5G Non-functional challenges in different ML-based solutions

Solution	ML algorithm	Data model	Challenges
Energy modeling	Regression analysis POMDP	• regression function • generalization of Markov decision	• energy demand prediction • recover simultaneous wireless transmissions • transmission power control in energy harvesting • base station association under the unknown energy status
Anomaly/fault/intrusion detection	PCA/ICA DL NN	• linear mixtures of variables	• detector act as classifiers • recover statistically independent source • signals from their linear mixtures • analysis of network flows
Users' behavior-classification	Unsupervised ML	• clustering and decision tree classification	• context extraction and profiling
Network planning	Supervised ML	• classification and prediction	• network capacity planning and operation
Network deployment, maintenance/optimization, management	Depp Learning	• self-organizing network	• adaptive and autonomous functions • monitoring network slicing • network configuration, optimization, healing

solution is proposed (Timotheou, 2015; Liu, 2016). An ML-based user clustering, beamforming and power allocation algorithm in mmWave-NOMA transmission scenario are developed (Cui, 2018). The impact of the number of clusters on the system performance has investigated in system simulation. The performance of the K-means based clustering method depends on the chosen k number of clusters. Computational complexity K-means optimal solution is also NP-hard (non-deterministic polynomial acceptable problems).

Cognitive Radio: A cognitive radio (CR) is programmed and configured for dynamic management of available channels in a given spectrum band at one location. According to changes of transmission or reception parameters, the cognitive engine configures system enabling optimum wireless communications channel (Zhang, 2019). A 5G network demands more capacity and spectrums, as well as improvement in energy efficiency, which results in integration with CR. A 5G mobile terminal supports multiple Radio Access Technologies (RATs) based on software defined radio (SDR) technology. A classic user association problem based on the max-SINR (signal to interference plus noise ratio) criterion is converted into a complex decision process. Addition more criteria in RAT selection leads to multi-parametric optimization. However, the computational complexity of multi-parametric approaches are high as well as practical modeling has not been completely solved. In order to obtain a decision policy for user RAT association problem given the state of the terminal, reinforcement Q-learning is proposed (Perez, 2017). The set of actions is defined to be the set of available network attachment points. The user/network state model is formulated based on unsupervised K-nearest neighbors (KNN) algorithm. The effective user association policy based on reinforcement algorithm has low computational complexity and high flexibility in comparison to supervised machine learning techniques.

Smart Life-Cycle of Slices: 5G network slicing enables end-to-end virtual networks. The key is to ensure a good quality of experience (QoE) for users in a vertical application domains. It is primarily necessary to collect information in real time about slice users, subscription, QoS, performance, events and logs for multidimensional analysis. ML algorithms are used to analyze, forecast and guarantee an optimal slicing. For modeling user portraits and guaranteeing an efficient operation of slices, experience of different vertical applications are evaluated, analyzed and optimized. ML are also used to generate the slicing strategy and resolve slice faults, and optimize the performance automatically, in order to achieve smart scheduling of slice resources and give optimal configuration.

ML-based anomaly detection: 5G network works as traffic classifiers in supervised, semi-supervised and unsupervised mode. In supervised mode, a labeled dataset is used to find a boundary between normal and anomalous traffic. The main challenge is how to properly label anomalous traffic. In semi-supervised mode, the training dataset contains only normal traffic. The main challenge is how to estimate probability distribution and define tight boundary where a data is classified as normal traffic. In unsupervised mode, the main challenge is to cluster similar examples within the data, or density estimation within input data space, or reduces problem dimension by transforming the original variable data (Maimo, 2017, 2018).

MULTISERVICES NETWORK

5G mobile networks support wide range of scenarios, including enhanced mobile broadband, low-latency communications, and machine type services. In the near future, users will use a new class of smart devices which require high performance computing capability. And with implementation of machine learning algorithms, users' devices may become smart objects capable of learning and acting. However, these scenario involves a number of open research challenges (Demestichas, 2015).

The use case of multimedia content requires special considerations for the reason that the data is typically of very high dimension. Mobile video is the most significant service in 5G networks. It is estimated that video services will be 80 percent of Internet traffic in 2019. A particular challenge is quality improvement of video in a transmission system. Quality of service (QoS) optimization involves efficient video compression and network resource allocation (Said, 2018). Also, it is important to evaluate quality of experience (QoE) in the interactions between users and services. The new measurement approach for multimedia services are based on definition influencing factors, assessment methods, models, and control methods (Wang, 2017). 5G networks support three generic category of services: enhanced mobile broadband (eMBB), ultra-reliable/high-speed and low-latency (uR/uHS LLC) services and machine-type (mMTC) communications. Multimedia applications challenge new performance criteria for peak throughput, latency, reliability, system spectral/energy efficiency, connection and capacity density.

Intelligence in Enhanced Mobile Broadband

Enhanced mobile video creates challenges for new immersive formats in real-time multimedia applications with Quality of experience (QoE) guarantees. The multimedia broadcast eMBMS (Multimedia Broadcast Multicast Service) supports high-quality live video streaming with significantly lower end-to-end latencies and higher connection reliability (Milovanovic, 2019b). The challenges in fast and reliable service deployment of mobile multimedia delivery platform are exploding traffic volumes and diverse mobility/radio conditions, as well as higher monetization of service and the cost efficiency. The trend is that 5G network becoming more cloud platform based on SDN and NFV. The importance of advanced ML-based management intelligence is also pointed out.

Intelligence in Lot-Based Networks

5G networking supports new scalable, connected and location independent infrastructure for massive and critical Internet of Things (IoT). Constrained nature of IoT networking presents more challenging issues. Massive application has specific requirements on extended coverage area and high scalability, low-cost user equipment and low-energy consumption. Examples of critical IoT application include Smart Grids, traffic and industrial control (Tsai, 2014; Werbos, 2011). Smart City ultra-urban concept involves an emerging Multimedia IoT (MIoT) with camera sensors and distribution of multimedia content. However, requirements of integrated image processing, computer vision and networking are high in capacity and computer capabilities. There are numerous initiatives focused on the analysis of process conception, implementation methods, and outcomes. A joint initiative of the EU and the ICT industry 5G PPP (Infrastructure Public Private Partnership) defines the following groups of uses: densely populated urban areas, broadband access at any location, connected autonomous vehicles, smart office of the future, Tactile Internet/Automation. For each individual case, key KPIs (Key Performance Indicators) are defined corresponding to performance requirements (in terms of user service experience) supported by the 5G network. 5G PPP classifies the basic functionality on the following parameters: density of the device in a given space, mobility, infrastructure topology, type of traffic, user data flow, latency, reliability, availability, category 5G communication. The solutions are intelligent perception of sensitive environment, smart video analysis for compression of visual data, software-defined video for generating elastic visual streams, flexible control of optimal adaptation, and efficient transmission for resource utilization enhancement (Ji, 2019; Wang, 2017).

Major requirements in 5G IoT networks are coexistence of different network technologies and efficient use of spectrum. There is a need for interoperability and standard development. 3GPP specification Release 13 introduces Narrowband-IoT (NB-IoT) and eMTC. Specification Release 14 introduces further improvements. Specification Release 16 is going to support new types of service/devices, new implementation models and new spectrum sharing types. The large number of devices generate massive data (Table 5), so it is necessary to incorporate ML technology in IIoT (Intelligent IoT) to make efficient decisions (Javaid, 2018).

ML for Immersive Media

The new 3D immersive applications of virtual reality (VR), mixed reality (MR) and augmented reality (AR) are computing intensive and demands high throughput up to 5 Gbps, low latency and high reliability. An efficient resource distribution, quality of experience (QoE) guarantees, and interaction between multiple users are also required. The challenges are user experience modeling, tracking accuracy, and efficient video compression (Milovanovic, 2019a). The key enabling service is ultra-high speed low latency (uHSLLC) on mmWave connections and Multi-access Edge Computing (MEC) cloud at the edge of mobile network (Tran, 2018; Asadi, 2018). Machine learning address the critical requirements of emerging use cases of VR. ML predict the users' locations and orientations, data rate requirements

Table 5. The ML opportunities for IoT in 5G networks

Opportunities	Smart Health, traffic control, business analytics, agriculture, education	Internet of cars, Smart City, ultra wireless connectivity	Hyper connected environments, horizontal platform	Long network lifetime, high data rates, high bandwidth	Intelligent horizontal platform, energy efficient routing, smart security
Solution	mMIMO, mWave, HetNets, RANs, RATs, NR	D2D, NS, CR, mMIMO, uRLLC, mMTC	Cloud&Fog nodes, Smart Phones, mobile edge	NB-IoT, RATs, RANs, NS, CR	Cloud and Fog computing, CR, NB-IoT, SDN
Challenges	heterogeneity, latency, spectrum management	reactive/proactive spectrum&energy management	energy constraints, IoT connectivity, latency, bandwidth	energy management, mobility, heterogeneity	security, latency, data rate, mobility, interoperability

first and, then, optimize the allocation of resources. The format and quality of images are adaptively optimized and adjusted to the 5G network environment (Elbamby, 2018; Nayyar, 2018).

Machine learning has been producing significant impact on immersive media coding and transport. ML algorithms are extending and developing in order to improve media compression and bandwidth reduction. The techniques theoretically yield compression gains, but it is challenging to extend beyond simple cases, optimize and implement. Digital media compression are developing based on explicit mathematical models, which are then used to develop practical methods. The ML optimization of compression tools is based on combination of models, training data and some quality criteria, plus considerations about computational complexity. Adaptive encoders search for the best coding tools on each media segment. Operational parameters is chosen in iterative encoding of training media segments. The set of rate-distortion results are base for min-max optimization under constraints of maximal available bit-rate or allowable media distortion. The optimization is complex as it involves a number of computations in hierarchical media segmentation and selecting the partition with the least cost. Machine learning SVM classifiers has been proposed as solution for computation of rate-distortion weights and construction decision-trees for adaptive media segmentation without exhaustive search all possible modes. The decision trees *if-then* statements reduce complexity significantly (Said, 2018; Das, 2016; Topiwala, 2018).

Optimal Deployment of Network Slices

The concept of infrastructure network slicing (NS) is based on multiple dedicated logical wireless networks. Network slices are the chains of virtualized network functions (VNF). Researches focus is on service description, resource virtualization, and service mapping. NS models allows telecom operators to define slice requests and map them to the limited network resources to suit a particular 5G use case (Li, 2018). The main challenge is fast end-to-end deployment based on policies for typical slices. The objectives of typical slices are to efficiently take advantage of network resources. Usage of eMBB in high user density area requires very high traffic capacity, low mobility and higher user data rate. Usage of mMTC covers a huge number of connected devices which transmit relatively low volume of non-delay sensitive data. Usage of uRLLC has strict requirements in throughput, latency and availability. The collected network slice requests are possible to classify and implement by different mapping algorithms for VNF placement and the selection of link paths. The network slice request could be deployed as static (permanent) or dynamic (recycled). Extensive system simulations are necessary to validate the performance of NS deployment (Guan, 2018).

FUTURE TOPICS

At the present stage 2018-2019, ML algorithms are embedded into certain network elements and maintenance tools, in order to perform offline training and model-based reasoning. The local quick application is relatively low complex, but upgrade is time-consuming and has limited strategic coordination in the network. At the next stage 2019-2020, ML platforms are embedded in the operations system for centralized deployment and online training. The advantages are in covering cross-domain and large-scale data, using specialized ML hardware for faster computation, and online training. However, this deployment mode cannot achieve the reasoning in real time. At the stage after 2020 in 5G large-scale deployment, lightweight ML platforms could be used at the Multi access Edge Computing (MEC). The advantage is training and reasoning close to the edges of network for low-latency services in smart scenarios (Zhang, 2018).

We summarizes some topics of research on machine learning in 5G systems (Table 2):

- Supervised learning techniques are based on known models and labels in estimation of unknown system parameters. The possible application are CR spectrum detection, cooperative wideband spectrum sensing, antenna selection, massive MIMO estimation/detection, energy learning and adaptive signal processing.
- Unsupervised learning are based on heuristics in the input data. The possible utilization are users' behavior classification, anomaly detection, cooperative cell clustering, heterogeneous base station clustering, access point association and load-balancing.
- Reinforcement learning are based on a dynamic iterative learning and decision making in unknown conditions. The possible applications are inferring the mobile users' decision making, channel access in spectrum sharing, distributed resource allocation, and base station association in unknown energy status.
- Deep learning (DL) has recently become particularly popular. The possible utilization are network configuration with the aid of ML techniques, as well as spectral estimation and handoff decisions in CR (Zhang, 2018; Mao, 2018; Fadlullah, 2017).

    Low Complexity Models: State-of-the-art ML models are complex with difficult implementation in systems with limited computational and energy resources. Recently, complexity of deep neural networks is reduced, and efficient compression techniques are used to store and transmit models. Further research should reduce complexity of models for implementation with limited computational resources at minimal performance loss.

    Transparency and Privacy Mechanisms: ML models are often applied as black-box systems. Lack of transparency is disadvantage because prevents the comprehensive reasoning and validate predictions. Mechanisms which increase reliability could be implemented as an integral part of the model or communication protocol, or as separate inspection process. Further research results could improve interpretability and security.

Radio Resource And Network Management: Management of resources at system level strongly influences end-to-end performance of 5G networks. The objective is to utilize the infrastructure as efficiently as possible. Further research of ML models and data-driven management are necessary under inherent uncertainties and the lack of complete network state information (Huang, 2017).

Green Networks: Existing networks are dimensioned for the worst case scenario in which huge amounts of power is wasted. Energy efficiency is key concept in 5G networking where solutions are based on dynamic adjustment on instant needs. ML algorithms estimate instant traffic conditions and determine to switch the base stations. Also, ML could learn individual user position patterns and reserve resources in advance, reducing the energy consumption (Xu, 2017).

Networks Beyond 5G: Future-generation wireless networks will support emerging media and service types. New requirements will grow up to 1Tbps bandwidth for 20G pixel count in 3D video services which involve all human senses with sub-ms latency. Immersive video formats 4K/8K require data rate 35-140Mbps and latency 15-35ms, while VR/AR systems are based on 2Mbps – 5Gbps throughput and 5-7ms latency. New user experience in teleport (5-sense hologram, industrial avatar) requires 4-10Tbps and super ultra-low latency (<1ms) communications. High-precision services, such as remote surgery and industrial Internet require on-time delivery. Guaranteed services such as AR/VR, autonomous driving and ITS (Intelligent Transportation System) require absolute (in-time) delivery. Such huge increase in service types and the network performance needs new network architectures based on convergence of terrestrial and space federated networks, decentralized infrastructure, and trustable infrastructure. The networks become increasingly decentralized, dense, heterogeneous, and ad-hoc in nature and they include numerous and diverse network entities. Moreover, conventional approaches for innovative service management that require complete and perfect knowledge of the systems are inefficient or even inapplicable in networks beyond 5G. We consider that the future development of complex networks must be driven by real-time machine learning technology (Wang, 2019).

FUTURE NETWORKS

Telecommunication union study group 13 established the focus group on *Machine learning for future networks including 5G* (ITU-T, 2019). The technical reports and specifications include network architectures, protocols, interfaces, algorithms and data formats. The objective is identification of ML relevant gaps and issues in standardization activities as well as technical aspects such as use cases, possible requirements, and architectures. The group also is open platform for ML research in future networks (Bogale, 2018).

The objectives of focus group include:

- ML communication use cases, data formats, algorithms, protocols, interfaces, system architecture, interoperability, performance, security and protection of personal information
- survey, review and study of existing ML technologies, platforms, guidelines and standards
- review and study ML algorithms in training, adaptation, compression and interaction with each other

- highlight and recognize the ML perspectives for networking and computing systems
- identify ML requirements in network functionality, interfaces and capabilities
- promote the development of new ML methods for variety of fixed and mobile communication systems
- identify ML challenges in the standardization activities
- identify the relevant scope of ITU-T recommendations on ML topics and develop a roadmap
- establish liaisons and relationships with other organizations
- enable safe and trusted use of ML frameworks.

Standardization Activities

The standardization in ML communication increases the interoperability and modularity of a systems. Current activities of telecommunications standards institute (ETSI) is in industry specification group for automating network configuration and monitoring. The partnership project (3GPP) study enablers for network automation (eNA) based on 5G data analytics (Kibria, 2018). Experts group ISO/IEC MPEG-NN standardize interoperable format for digital compression of trained neural networks.

ETSI ENI

The experimental network intelligence (ENI) group specifies an architecture of cognitive network management based on ML techniques and context-aware policies. The objective is to configure services depending on user needs and environmental conditions (ETSI, 2019). Metrics for the optimization and adjustment are specified based on *monitor-analyze-plan-execute* control model. The closed-loop ML policies enable actionable decisions. The group ENI has derived requirements for *observe-orient-decide-act* control loop in following technical reports and specifications:

- Technical report GR001 describes set of use cases and defines the expected benefits for telecom operators in infrastructure management, network operations, service orchestration, and assurance.
- Specification GS002 describes requirements how ML improve operators' experience in different scenarios of service provision and network operation. ML enables dynamic autonomous behavior and adaptive policy driven operation in a changing context.
- Technical report GR003 analyses work in various SDOs and open source consortia on policy management.
- Specification GS006 is a framework for Proof of Concepts (PoC) in technical feasibility of ENI within the industry.

3GPP eNA

The IMT-2020 key performance indicators (KPI) enforce great challenge on manual and semi-automated network management. 3GPP Release 8 has introduced the concept of self-organized network to enable self-configuration, -healing and -optimization (Klaine, 2017; Jiang, 2017). The main benefits are the reduction of operating expenses (OPEX) and the improvement performance. Additionally, network data analytics (NWDA) function can be used in QoS guarantees, traffic steering, dimensioning, and security

(3GPP, 2018). Analytics function has been introduced in Release 15 mainly for network slice level data analytics. Further study in Release 16 kicked off in 3GPP SA2 (Service and System Aspects - Architecture).

ISO/IEC MPEG-NN

Standardized formats are necessary in ML communications applications for training, compressing and exchanging models (MPEG, 2019). Furthermore, multiple ML models interact with each other and should fulfills certain security or privacy requirements. MPEG-NN digital representation of neural network specifies compressed, interpretable and interoperable representation for trained neural networks:

- represent different artificial neural network types
- enable scalability, trading off compression rate vs. performance of the neural network
- enable efficient incremental updates of compressed representations of neural networks
- allow inference without performing full reconstruction of the original network, in order to enable faster inference than with the original network
- enable use under resource limitations (computation, memory, power, and bandwidth).

Experts group MPEG has identified a set of relevant use cases and related requirements, including applications of neural networks in multimedia communications, analysis and processing, media coding, and data analytics. While the underlying technology has been known for decades, the recent success is based on two main factors. The first is the ability to process much larger and complex deep neural networks than in the past; and the second, the availability and capacity of large-scale training data sets. These two aspects not only make trained networks powerful, but also mean that they resulting in quite large sizes of the trained neural networks (several hundred MBs). The scope of technology *Call for Proposals* (CfP) is to reduce the size of trained neural networks, providing a complete representation of the parameters/weights of the neural network. The description of the network structure/topology itself is not in the scope of the call, but such a description may be provided along the compressed information. The proposed representation shall enable integration into existing neural network exchange formats (NNEF, ONNX). The size reduction impacts the size of the serialized/stored network and/or the memory footprint of the reconstructed network used for inference. The complexity of compression and particularly of decompression needed for inference is taken into account, as well as the impact of the applied compression technology on the complexity of inference.

CONCLUDING REMARKS

One of the main objective in this chapter is to point out that the performance of each module in communication systems could be improved or optimized using machine learning. The recent improvements in ML methodology support new optimization methods in end-to-end communications. Classification and prediction are important in selection and performance prediction. Machine learning provides new possibilities to construct the generalized model applicable in various networking scenarios. We pointed out that the availability of reliable, scalable and cost-efficient machine learning technology is of a huge significance in complex 5G wireless environments.

Following recent research activities, we have demonstrated that ML has great potential to break the bottleneck of complex multimedia communication frameworks. Indeed, motivation and objectives for ML is not only to enhance, but also to enable future mobile networking technology. Our focus is on high-speed, ultra-reliable, low-latency immersive media communication and management of a massive number of devices in real-time within a dynamic wireless networking. We review the fundamental trad-eoffs in terms of complexity and performances of 5G networks. The process of managing poses challenges in ML for efficient operation, control and optimization 5G complex systems confront with many challenges including managing, maintenance and traffic optimization. Globally accepted specifications and standards are prerequisite for future 5G development. Complex networks beyond 5G will support innovative media and immersive service types must be driven by real-time machine learning technology because classical optimization algorithms are inefficient or even inapplicable. The standardization of ML algorithms and data formats increases the interoperability and modularity of a system.

Developing efficient ML algorithms to deal with different networking scenarios is a challenging task. Starting from the collected requirements and identified challenges, we will continue to further refine the emerging 5G technology.

ACKNOWLEDGMENT

This work was partially supported by the Ministry of Education, Science and Technology Development of the Republic of Serbia under the Grant TR32034.

REFERENCES

Alsheikh, M.A., Lin, S., Niyato, D., & Tan, H.-P. (2018). Machine Learning in wireless sensor networks: Algorithms, strategies, and applications. *IEEE Communications Surveys & Tutorials*, *16*(4), 1996-2018.

Alzubi, J., Nayyar, A., & Kumar, A. (2018). Machine learning from theory to algorithms: An overview. *Journal of Physics: Conference Series*, *1142*(1), 012012. doi:10.1088/1742-6596/1142/1/012012

Asadi, A. (2018). FML: Fast machine learning for 5G mmWave vehicular communications. *IEEE Int. Conf. on Computer Communications (INFOCOM)*, 1-9.

Awan, D. A. (2018). Detection for 5G-NOMA: An online adaptive machine learning approach. *IEEE Int. Conf. on Communications (ICC)*, 1-6.

Bogale, T. E. (2018). *Machine intelligence techniques for next-generation context-aware wireless net-works. ITU Journal*, 1–11.

Bojkovic, Z., & Milovanovic, D. (2017). A technology vision of the Fifth Generation (5G) wireless mobile networks. *Lecture Notes in Electrical Engineering*, *416*, 25–43.

Cayamcela, M. E. M., & Lim, W. (2018). Artificial intelligence in 5G technology: A survey. *Proc. Int. Conf. on Information and Communication Technology Convergence (ICTC)*.

Cote, D. (2018). Using Machine Learning in communication networks. *Journal of Optical Communications and Networking, 10*(10), D100–D109. doi:10.1364/JOCN.10.00D100

Cui, J. (2018). The application of machine learning in mmWave-NOMA systems. *IEEE Vehicular Technology Conference*, 1-6. 10.1109/VTCSpring.2018.8417523

Das, S., & Pawar, C. S. (2016). Machine learning based algorithm for high efficiency video coding. Int. *Journal of Advances in Electronics and Computer Science, 3*(7), 92–95.

Demestichas, P., Georgakopoulos, A., Tsagkaris, K., & Kotrotsos, S. (2015). Intelligent 5G networks: Managing 5G wireless/mobile broadband. *IEEE Vehicular Technology Magazine, 10*(3), 41–50. doi:10.1109/MVT.2015.2446419

Di Huang, Y. (2018). A Machine learning approach to MIMO communications. *IEEE Int. Conf. on Communications (ICC),* 1-6. 10.1109/ICC.2018.8422211

Elbamby, M. S., Perfecto, C., Bennis, M., & Doppler, K. (2018). Toward low-latency and ultra-reliable Virtual Reality. *IEEE Network, 32*(2), 78–84. doi:10.1109/MNET.2018.1700268

ETSI ENI ISG (2019). *Experiential Networked Intelligence Industry Specification Group.* Author.

Fadlullah, Z. M., Tang, F., Mao, B., Kato, N., Akashi, O., Inoue, T., & Mizutani, K. (2017). State-of-the-art Deep Learning: Evolving machine intelligence toward tomorrow's intelligent network traffic control systems. *IEEE Communications Surveys and Tutorials, 19*(4), 2432–2455. doi:10.1109/COMST.2017.2707140

Ge, X. (2018). Distinguished capabilities of Artificial Intelligence wireless communication systems. *Computing Research Repository.* (preprint)

Guan, W., Wen, X., Wang, L., Lu, Z., & Shen, Y. (2018). A service-oriented deployment policy of end-to-end network slicing based on complex network theory. *IEEE Access: Practical Innovations, Open Solutions, 6*, 19691–19701. doi:10.1109/ACCESS.2018.2822398

Gui, G., Huang, H., Song, Y., & Sari, H. (2018). Deep learning for an effective Non-Orthogonal Multiple Access scheme. *IEEE Transactions on Vehicular Technology, 67*(9), 8440–8450. doi:10.1109/TVT.2018.2848294

Huang, J. (2017). A big data enabled channel model for 5G wireless communication systems. *IEEE Communications Magazine, 55*(9), 150–157.

Ibnkahla, M. (2018). Applications of neural networks to digital communications – A survey. *Signal Processing, 80*(7), 1185–1215. doi:10.1016/S0165-1684(00)00030-X

ITU-T Focus Group. (2019). *Machine Learning for Future Networks including 5G.* no Author.

Javaid, N., Sher, A., Nasir, H., & Guizani, N. (2018). Intelligence in IoT-based 5G networks: Opportunities and challenges. *IEEE Communications Magazine, 56*(10), 94–100. doi:10.1109/MCOM.2018.1800036

Ji, W., Xu, J., Qiao, H., Zhou, M., & Liang, B. (2019). Visual IoT: Enabling Internet of Things visualization in Smart Cities. *IEEE Network, 33*(2), 102–110. doi:10.1109/MNET.2019.1800258

Jiang, C., Yhang, H., Ren, Y., Han, Z., Chen, K.-C., & Hanzo, L. (2017). Machine Learning paradigms for next-generation wireless networks. *IEEE Wireless Communications*, *24*(2), 98–105. doi:10.1109/MWC.2016.1500356WC

Jiang, W., Strufe, M., & Schotten, H. D. (2017). SON decision-making framework for intelligent management in 5G mobile networks. *IEEE Int. Conf. on Computer and Communications (ICCC)*, 1-5.

Kibria, M. G., Nguyen, K., Villardi, G. P., Zhao, O., Ishizu, K., & Kojima, F. (2018). Big data analytics, machine learning and artificial intelligence in next-generation wireless networks. *IEEE Access: Practical Innovations, Open Solutions*, *6*, 32328–32338. doi:10.1109/ACCESS.2018.2837692

Klainc, P. V., Imran, M. A., Onircti, O., & Souza, R. D. (2017). A survey of machine learning techniques applied to self-organizing cellular networks. *IEEE Communications Surveys and Tutorials*, *19*(4), 2392–2431. doi:10.1109/COMST.2017.2727878

Klautau, A. (2018). 5G MIMO data for machine learning: Application to beam-selection using deep learning. Proc. Information Theory and Applications Workshop (ITA), 1-9.

Kumar, S., Sharma, B., Sharma, V. K., & Poonia, R. C. (2018). *Automated soil prediction using bag-of-features and chaotic spider monkey optimization algorithm. In Evolutionary intelligence* (pp. 1–12). Springer.

Latah, M., & Toker, L. (2018). *Artificial intelligence enabled Software Defined Networking: A comprehensive overview*. IET Networks.

Li, R., Zhao, Z., Sun, Q. I., C-Lin, Q., Yang, C., Chen, X., Zhao, M., & Zhang, H. (2018). Deep reinforcement learning for network slicing. Academic Press.

Li, R., Zhao, Z., Zhou, X., Ding, G., Chen, Y., Wang, Z., & Zhang, H. (2017). Intelligent 5G: When cellular networks meet artificial intelligence. *IEEE Wireless Communications*, *24*(5), 175–183. doi:10.1109/MWC.2017.1600304WC

Liu, Y. (2016). Fairness of user clustering in MIMO non-orthogonal multiple access systems. *IEEE Communications Letters*, *20*(7), 1465–1468.

Luong, N. C. (2018). Applications of deep reinforcement learning in communications and networking. *Survey (London, England)*, 1–37.

Magdalinos, P., Barmpounakis, S., Spapis, P., Kaloxylos, A., Kyprianidis, G., Kousaridas, A., ... Zhou, C. (2017). A context extraction and profiling engine for 5G network resource mapping. Journal. *Computer Communications*, *109*, 184–201. doi:10.1016/j.comcom.2017.06.003

Maimo, L. F. (2017). On the performance of a deep learning-based anomaly detection system for 5G networks. *IEEE SmartWorld*, *2017*, 1–9.

Maimo, L. F. (2018). A self-adaptive deep learning-based system for anomaly detection in 5G networks. *IEEE Access: Practical Innovations, Open Solutions*, *6*, 7700–7712. doi:10.1109/ACCESS.2018.2803446

Mao, Q., Hu, F., & Hao, Q. (2018). Deep Learning for intelligent wireless networks: A comprehensive survey. *IEEE Communications Surveys and Tutorials*, *20*(4), 2595–2621. doi:10.1109/COMST.2018.2846401

Milovanovic, D., & Bojkovic, Z. (2019a). 5G Ultra reliable and low-latency communication: Fundamental aspects and key enabling technologies. *LNEE Series, 561*, 372–379.

Milovanovic, D., Bojkovic, Z., & Pantovic, V. (2019b). Evolution of 5G mobile broadband technology and multimedia services framework. *LNEE Series, 561*, 351–361.

Moysen, J., & Giupponi, L. (2018). From 4G to 5G: Self-organized network management meets machine learning. Journal. *Computer Communications, 129*, 248–268. doi:10.1016/j.comcom.2018.07.015

MPEG. (2019). *Digital representation of neural networks*. MPEG.

Munjal, P., Kumar, L., Kumar, S., & Banati, H. (2019). Evidence of Ostwald Ripening in opinion driven dynamics of mutually competitive social networks. *Physica A, 522*, 182–194. doi:10.1016/j.physa.2019.01.109

Munjal, P., Narula, M., Kumar, S., & Banati, H. (2018). Twitter sentiments based suggestive framework to predict trends. *Journal of Statistics and Management Systems, 2*(4), 685-693.

Nayyar, A., Mahapatra, B., Le, D., & Suseendran, G. (2018). Virtual Reality (VR) & Augmented Reality (AR) technologies for tourism and hospitality industry. *International Journal of Engineering & Technology, 7*(2.21), 156-160.

O'Shea, T., & Hoydis, J. (2017). *An introduction to machine learning communications systems*. Computing Research Repository.

O'Shea, T., Hoydis, J. (2018). An introduction to Deep Learning for the Physical Layer. *IEEE Transactions on Cognitive Communications and Networking, 3*(4), 563-575.

Pandey, S., & Solanki, A. (2019). *Music instrument recognition using Deep Convolutional Neural Networks. International Journal of Information Technology*, 1–10.

Perez, J. S. (2017). Machine learning aided cognitive RAT selection for 5G heterogeneous networks. *IEEE Int. Black Sea Conference on Communications and Networking (BlackSeaCom2017)*, 1-5.

Pérez-Romero, J., Sallent, O., Ferrús, R., & Agustí, R. (2015). Artificial intelligence-based 5G network capacity planning and operation. *Int. Symposium on Wireless Communication Systems (ISWCS)*.

Rafique, D., & Velasco, L. (2018). Machine Learning for network automation: Overview, architecture, and applications. *Journal of Optical Communications and Networking, 10*(10), D126–D143. doi:10.1364/JOCN.10.00D126

Ramesh, M. (2017). Design of efficient massive MIMO for 5G systems - Present and past: A review. *Int. Conf. on Intelligent Computing and Control (I2C2)*, 1-4.

3. rd Generation Partnership Project; Technical Specification Group Services and System Aspects; Release 15 Description; 3GPP TR 21.915 V15.0.0 (2019-09)

3. rd Generation Partnership Project; Technical Specification Group Services and System Aspects; Study of Enablers for Network Automation for 5G (Release 16) 3GPP TR 23.791 V16.0.0 (2018-12).

Said, A. (2018). *Machine learning for media compression: Challenges and opportunities. APSIPA Trans. on* Signal and Information Processing.

Samek, W., Stanczak, S., & Wiegand, T. (2017). The convergence of machine learning and communications. ITU Journal, 1-8.

Shafi, M. (2017). 5G: A tutorial overview of standards, trials, challenges, deployment, and practice. *IEEE J. Sel. Areas Commun., 35*(6), 1201-1221.

Simeone, O. (2018). A very brief introduction to machine learning with applications to communication systems. *IEEE Trans. on Cognitive Communications and Networking, 4*(4), 648–664. doi:10.1109/TCCN.2018.2881442

Timotheou, S., & Krikidis, I. (2015). Fairness for non-orthogonal multiple access in 5G systems. *IEEE Signal Processing Letters, 22*(10), 1647–1651. doi:10.1109/LSP.2015.2417119

Topiwala, P., Krishnan, M., & Dai, W. (2018). Deep learning techniques in video coding and quality analysis. *Int. Conf. SPIE Applications of Digital Image Processing.* 10.1117/12.2322025

Tran, D. D., Ha, D. B., & Nayyar, A. (2018). Wireless power transfer under secure communication with multiple antennas and eavesdroppers. *Proc. Int. conference on Industrial Networks and Intelligent Systems, Springer LNICST*, 208-220.

Tran, G. K. (2018). Architecture of mmWave Edge cloud in 5G-MiEdge. *IEEE Int. Conf. Communications Workshops*, 1-6.

Tsai, C.-W., Lai, C.-F., Chiang, M.-C., & Yang, L. T. (2014). Data mining for Internet of Things: A survey. *IEEE Communications Surveys and Tutorials, 16*(1), 77–97. doi:10.1109/SURV.2013.103013.00206

Wang, M., Cui, Y., Wang, X., Xiao, S., & Jiang, J. (2018). Machine learning for networking: Workflow, advances and opportunities. *IEEE Network, 32*(2), 1–8. doi:10.1109/MNET.2017.1700200

Wang, Q. (2017). Multimedia IoT systems and applications. *Global Internet of Things Summit (GIoTS).*

Wang, T. (2019). Machine learning for 5G and beyond: From model-based to data-driven mobile wireless networks. *Journal. China Communications, 16*(1), 165–175.

Wang, X., Li, X. M., & Leung, V. C. (2015). Artificial intelligence-based techniques for emerging heterogeneous network: State of the arts, opportunities, and challenges. *IEEE Access: Practical Innovations, Open Solutions, 3*, 1379–1391. doi:10.1109/ACCESS.2015.2467174

Wang, Y., Li, P., Jiao, L., Su, Z., Cheng, N., Shen, X. S., & Zhang, P. (2017). A data-driven architecture for personalized QoE management in 5G Wireless Networks. *IEEE Wireless Communications, 24*(1), 1–9. doi:10.1109/MWC.2016.1500184WC

Werbos, P. J. (2011). Computational intelligence for the smart grid: History, challenges, and opportunities. *IEEE Computational Intelligence Magazine, 6*(3), 14–21. doi:10.1109/MCI.2011.941587

Wu, X., Jiang, M., & Zhao, C. (2018). Decoding optimization for 5G LDPC codes by machine learning. *IEEE Access: Practical Innovations, Open Solutions, 6*, 50179–50186. doi:10.1109/ACCESS.2018.2869374

Xu, Z., Wang, Y., Tang, J., Wang, J., & Gursoy, M. C. (2017). A deep reinforcement learning based framework for power-efficient resource allocation in cloud RANs. *IEEE Int. Conf. on Communications (ICC)*, 1-6. 10.1109/ICC.2017.7997286

Yang, Y., Li, Y., Li, K., Zhao, S., Chen, R., Wang, J., & Ci, S. (2018). DECCO: Deep-learning enabled coverage and capacity optimization for massive MIMO systems. *IEEE Access: Practical Innovations, Open Solutions, 6,* 23361–23371. doi:10.1109/ACCESS.2018.2828859

You, X., Zhang, C., Tan, X., Jin, S., & Wu, H. (2019). AI for 5G: Research directions and paradigms. *Science China. Information Sciences, 62*(2), 1–13. doi:10.100711432-018-9596-5

Zhang, C., Patras, P., & Haddadi, H. (2018). Deep Learning in mobile and wireless networking: A survey. *IEEE Communications Surveys and Tutorials,* 1–67.

Zhang, J., & Wang, F. (2019). Signal identification in cognitive radios using machine learning. In Applications of Machine learning in wireless communications, IET Telecommunications series, (pp. 159-96). Academic Press.

Chapter 18
Machine Learning in Text Analysis

Neha Garg
ⓘ https://orcid.org/0000-0003-3806-6964
Manav Rachna International Institute of Research and Studies, India

Kamlesh Sharma
ⓘ https://orcid.org/0000-0002-6000-5933
Manav Rachna International Institute of Research and Studies, India

ABSTRACT

This chapter provides a basic understanding of processes and models needed to investigate the data posted by users on social networking sites like Facebook, Twitter, Instagram, etc. Often the databases of social networking sites are large and can't be handled using traditional methodology for analysis. Moreover, the data is posted in such a random manner that can't be used directly for the analysis purpose; therefore, a considerable preprocessing is needed to use that data and generate important results that can help in decision making for various areas like sentiment analysis, customer feedback, customer reviews for brand and product, prevention management, risk management, etc. Therefore, this chapter is discussing various aspects of text and its structure, various machine learning algorithms and their types, why machine learning is better for text analysis, the process of text analysis with the help of examples, issues associated with text analysis, and major application areas of text analysis.

INTRODUCTION

Machine learning in the context of text analysis is a set of statistical techniques that are used for identifying a part of speech, entities, sentiments of users etc. Today, we live in a competitive world. This competition is a key to innovation and discovery. Due to this competition, customer is getting desired item at reasonable price and good quality. With increasing competition, to sustain and to progress, it is inevitable for any organization to provide the product to the market before competitors do. Customer feedback plays very important role in this which enables one to establish demand. With decision making

DOI: 10.4018/978-1-5225-9643-1.ch018

analysis based on customer feedback, one can be able to predict the future demand of the market and new product can be introduced accordingly. The accuracy of decision making analysis is what makes any organization be at pole position or doom (Tripathy, Agrawal, & Rath, 2015). As the time has progressed, customer feedback is not the only source of customers' opinion. The use of social media (SM) such as Facebook, Twitter and Instagram etc. by an individual is another mode where personal choices and interests are expressed (James, April 23, 2014). This social media data can be extracted and put to use to decision making(Analytics, 2018). With the increasing usage of social media (SM) by various kinds of users in an unpredictable manner, data is generated at a very rapid pace (Laney, 2001),(Gandomi & Haider, 2015),(Beyer, 2012). Using social media networks, users express their views about the event and occasions in all forms of data(Sagiroglu & Sinanc, 2013). By using this huge amount of information, available on social sites, one can enhance the worth of decision making by improving the outcomes, extracted from databases (Lesser et al., 2000). Hence the various methods to handle all form of data has been introduced, out of them text analysis is still a challenge for machine learning.

BACKGROUND

Machine learning in Text analysis is a process of extracting information from the textual data, based on the historical data. Text analysis process constitutes a series of sub-processes which has mainly unstructured and semi-structured data in nature and each step perform operation to identify the patterns, so that decision making can be done based on these patterns automatically.

In order to deal with unstructured data a process called data preprocessing is performed, to remove unwanted words from the text, which is preceded by a number of process to extract features from the text and based on the problem statement choosing a machine learning model and improvise decision making.

WHAT IS TEXT?

The very first question which arises in mind is what is classified as a text? According to literature "anything that can be read" is called text. It can be an article in newspaper, a sentence in a book, a blog on a social networking site or a tweet etc. it can consist of alphanumeric values, symbols, emoticons etc.

STRUCTURE OF TEXT

According to the situation and usage the text can have any kind of organization (format) like the chapter in a book, article in a newspaper, a blog, tweet etc. everywhere text is organized in an inherited way. Moreover with the advancement of World Wide Web (WWW) many users are getting associated with social media,(Manyika et al., 2011) reading e-newspapers, e-books, shop online, filling e-forms and posting their views, feelings, emotions, thinking and expression in the languages they are familiar most probably their mother tongue, English, Hindi, Telgu, Kannad, Spanish, German etc. further they may use multiple languages in a single sentence to make the sentence more impactful which give rises to code switching. The properties of these categories are summarized in a Table 1 below:

Table 1. Various data types

Sr. No.	Data Types	Source	Format
1	Structured Data(Jha, Dave, & Supriya Madan, 2016),(Gandomi & Haider, 2015),(Beyer, 2012)	Business Applications Like financial, student information, employees management system etc.	RDBMS, OLAP, Data Warehouse(Reddy, 2010)
2	Semi Structured Data(Gandomi & Haider, 2015; Jha et al., 2016), (Beyer, 2012)	Web Applications like emails, e-newspapers	XML, HTML
3	Unstructured Data (Jha et al., 2016),(Gandomi & Haider, 2015),(Beyer, 2012)	Social media data like reviews, comments, blogs etc, sensors data like weather data, maps, traffic jam	Any type of Image, Audio, Video

Figure 1. Example of structured data

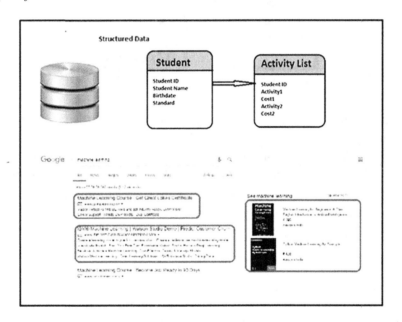

1. **Structured Data-** In structured form data is organized properly into a formatted repository. For representation in structural form certain relational tables are used, having some rows and columns. The data must have some relational keys and can be mapped into fields. (Jha et al., 2016)The structural data are the simplest form to be processed and managed. Structured data is generally stored in SQL, Oracle, MS-Access etc. in structured form the analysis can be done in powerful way, the data can be valuable like various organizations are having customers details in large spreadsheets and maintained in real time scenario but can't visualize this data(Analytics, 2018). While in case of big data the data can also visualize. Some examples of structured data are shown in figure 1.

Figure 2. Example of semi structured data

Semistructured Data

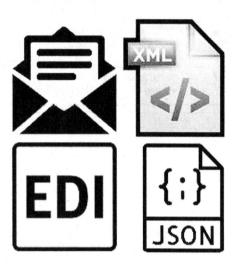

2. **Semi-Structured Data-** Semi Structured Data is not referred to the tabular format but any data that have some organizational property,(Beyer, 2012) and find some relationship between its entities based on their organization for example by using heading tag in html,(Jha et al., 2016)can easily find out that this tag is related to the heading of content. It can be easily converted to the structured form for analysis and can be analyzed in their actual form too. E.G. XML data, emails, Jason database, EDI database and NoSQL databases. Some examples of semi structured data are shown in figure 2.

3. **Unstructured Data-** Unstructured data is different from structured data as its structure can't be predicted. The examples of unstructured data are blogs, tweets, posts on social sites, videos, images. (Jha et al., 2016) It also includes some data generated by machine and sensors also. This form is not organized into a pre-defined manner and is not good for relational algebra. Hence the unstructured data can't be handled by traditional database systems, so we use alternative methods like Hadoop, Business Intelligence software, data integration tools, document management systems etc.. Some examples of unstructured data are shown in figure 3.

The text generally posted is unstructured and semi-structured in nature. The unstructured text may also be identified as a loosely structured data where data source may include a data structure but all data in dataset may not follow the same rule or the data in dataset have no strong relationship. The resources of information includes World Wide Web(WWW),(James, April 23, 2014) government electronically available repositories, blogs, tweets, reviews, feedback, articles, chats, spreadsheets which comes in

Figure 3. Example of unstructured data

Unstructured Data

category of structured and unstructured data(data generally has no internal relationship e.g- remarks, feedbacks, title of topics) etc. therefore a proper classification is needed to extract a proper knowledge.

TEXT ANALYSIS

Text analysis is used to parse the unstructured data into machine readable form (structured data). The process can be thought of a slicing; dicing heap of unstructured data into easily managed and interpreted data. (Ilinska, Ivanova, & Senko, 2016)This structured data can be further used to identify and analyze the polarity of sentences (whether it is in favor or not), find patterns/insights/trends based on which make decisions and do a future forecasting.

The major challenge in text analysis is ambiguity of data which may lead to misinterpretation of patterns, and situation and failed in accurate decision making. However, proper domain knowledge requires providing an appropriate result.

MACHINE LEARNING

Machine learning is branch of data science which has concern with the design and development of algorithm to develop a system that can learn from data, identify the complex patterns and provide intelligent, reliable, repeatable decisions and results with minimal human interaction based on the provided input.(Mujeeb, 2015)It's a branch of artificial intelligence which uses a set of statistical techniques for problem solving. Machine learning is field of study that provides computing abilities to the system without being explicitly programmed. (Gandomi & Haider, 2015)The focus is to develop systems that are too difficult and too expensive to be developed manually. The system must automatically adopt and

Figure 4. NLP & ML& deep learning

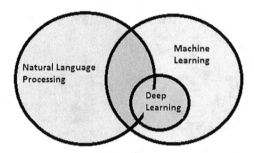

customize themselves according to the requirement of individual users like customized newspapers, emails and chat-boxes etc.

WHY WE NEED MACHINE LEARNING FOR TEXT ANALYSIS?

Machine learning is a most common approach used for text analysis. As it requires some basic patterns based on which the system enhance its learning and provide the reliable decisions and results. However, the other techniques are also available for text analysis, so a comparative analysis is provided to find where and when one can use machine learning algorithms for text analysis.

- **Machine Learning (ML) &Natural Language Processing (NLP)** - Natural language processing(Solanki and Kumar, 2018) is the ability of computer program to understand human language as it is spoken or handwritten. NLP is used when an accurate knowledge of linguistic structure is available as natural language processing uses contextual knowledge, semantic knowledge and syntactical knowledge for understanding the morphology of sentence and develops a model accordingly. (Young, Hazarika, Poria, & Cambria, 2018)

Drawbacks of NLP-

- However, the communication of human is sometimes is vague that its morphology can't be understood.
- Sometimes the ambiguous words are more often used that one can't understand the context of sentence.

So, when a proper structure of statements is missing like in blogs, reviews, feedback of social media, usual chat among some friend etc. then NLP should be combined with machine learning.

- **Machine Learning & Deep Learning-** Deep learning is an extension of machine learning approach, which uses neural network. (Young et al., 2018) Deep learning is basically used for vision-based classifications like distinguishing a boy from a cow.(PAT RESEARCH) But can be used for text analysis purpose also when a more layer of analysis is required.

So, in Figure: 4, one can see that deep learning is a part of machine learning techniques and NLP and ML are overlapping. This figure can be concluded as in NLP the proper linguistic knowledge is required, which can't be achieved without human intervention. Once proficiency in linguistic knowledge and human reasoning is achieved an automated model can be developed based on this input data to streamline the processes.

The major roles of machine learning are observed in the following areas-

1. When no human expert exists for the desired system. For example, if you are having a new machine and it is showing certain failures, so to check those failures system can take previous failure data from sensors and generate a proper analysis report.
2. Machine learning algorithms help in mapping the input to the expected outcomes like handwriting matching.
3. Machine learning algorithms help in decision making in real time scenario where frequent changes occur and one must take decision accordingly like share market.
4. Machine learning algorithms help in developing applications that need to be customized according to the need of individual users or group of peoples like spam message filtering, appropriate advertisement etc.

TYPES OF MACHINE LEARNING ALGORITHMS

Based on the working of model Machine Learning Techniques are defined as follows.

1. **Supervised Machine Learning Algorithms-** Supervised algorithms mean that a system is developed or modeled on predetermined set of sample data, which helps in finding an approximate output when new data is supplied in place of predetermined dataset (Bringmann, Berlingerio, Bonchi, & Gionis, 2010).

Drawbacks of Supervised Learning

- Most of the time one can't make the proper prediction for the problem, which may lead to the incorrect decision making.
- Secondly these systems are totally dependent on the assumptions of input and their behaviour made by human, which may be biasedat certain points.

Various types of supervised algorithms are tabulated in Table 2.

Table 2. Categories of supervised algorithm

S. No.	Algorithm Type	Description	Input values	Example
1.	Regression Algorithms(Doan & Kalita, 2015),(Ray, 2014)	• These algorithms formed a model to estimate the relationship between dependent and independent variables. • With the help of multiple such examples, a model/function is developed which help in decision making.	Dependent and independent variables	• Ordinary Least Squares Regression (OLSR), • Linear Regression, • Logistic Regression, • Stepwise Regression
2.	Instance based Algorithms (Beringer J., 2007)	• In this algorithm already available example-data is examined to model the relationship with current targeted value. • So, it's using a measure to find similarity, to get optimal match and make prediction. • For example, speller correction, search ranking, etc. can be solved under this algorithm.	Predefined data set	• k-Nearest Neighbor (kNN), • Learning Vector Quantization (LVQ), • Self-Organizing Map (SOM)
3.	Regularization Algorithms (Bauer, Pereverzev, & Rosasco, 2007)	• If the prediction performance is not so good, then the issue is called as over fitting problem. This can be removed by Regularization algorithms.	Finite set of variables	• Ridge Regression, • Least Absolute Shrinkage and Selection Operator (LASSO), • Elastic Net, Least-Angle Regression (LARS).
4.	Decision Tree Algorithms(PAT RESEARCH)	• Decision tree is a binary form for a set of attributes to be tested in order to predict the output. • The nodes of the tree split the data to find a classifying variable. • This algorithm handles the problem logically and does step-wise execution to get good results.	Set of attributes either having continuous values or binary values.	• Classification and Regression Tree (CART), • Iterative Dichotomies 3 (ID3), • C4.5 and C5.0 (different versions of a powerful approach), • Conditional Decision Trees.
5.	Bayesian Algorithms (Domingos & Pazzani, 1998)	• Those algorithms that incorporate Bayes Theorem. • Bayesian method means the one which believes on subjective probability and results in some future reference.	Expected probability	• Naive Bayes, • Gaussian Naive Bayes, • Multinomial Naive Bayes.
6.	Artificial Neural Network Algorithms (PAT RESEARCH)	• The aim of neural network is to solve the problem as solved by human brain with intelligence. • Hence it is used in ML. • The area is much related to pattern matching problems.	Single neuron with arbitrary number of inputs.	• Preceptor, • Back-Propagation, • Hopfield Network.
7.	Deep Learning Algorithms(PAT RESEARCH; Young et al., 2018)	• Deep learning algorithms are one of the special cases of Artificial Neural Networks. • They help in building more complex neural networks and work for voluminous datasets.	• Use a cascade of multilayer of non-linear processing units. • Each layer takes output of previous layers as the input.	• Deep Boltzmann Machine (DBM), • Deep Belief Networks (DBN), • Convolution Neural Network (CNN)

Table 3. Categories of unsupervised algorithms

S. No.	Algorithm	Description	Example
a.	Clustering Algorithms(Francesco Musumeci, 2018)	Clustering algorithms helps in creating cluster/group of similar elements/ data/ problems.	• k-Means, • k-Medians, • Expectation Maximization (EM), • Hierarchical Clustering.
b.	Dimensionality Reduction Algorithms(Cortés, Benitez, García, Alvarez, & Ibáñez, 2016)	In dimensionality reduction, the number of dimensions of internal structure of data is reduced without harming the actual data content.	• Principal Component Analysis (PCA), • Principal Component Regression (PCR), • Partial Least Squares Regression (PLSR)
c.	Association Rule Algorithms(Francesco Musumeci, 2018)	Finds the relationship between dataset and data	• Apriori algorithm, • Éclat algorithm

Figure 5. Reinforcement learning

2. **Unsupervised Machine Learning Algorithms-**Unsupervised algorithms mean that a program is provided with some collection of data, with no predetermined dataset being available, and patterns or relations among those data values are developed. (Neha Garg, 2018). The data given to unsupervised algorithms are not labeled, which means the input variables are given with no specified output variables. In this type of algorithms, the pattern is discovered according to problem definition. Following are different types of Unsupervised algorithms in Table 3.

3. **Semi Supervised Machine Learning Algorithms-** In the above-mentioned categories either the model is developed in such a way that either there are labels exist for all kind of observations or there is no label exist. (Guimarães Pedronette, Calumby, & S. Torres, 2015)Semi supervised algorithm somehow lies between these two. Here based on few labeled data, the labels of other unlabeled data are built. In this method however the group membership of unlabeled data is unknown, but this model can generate useful information for group parameters.

Figure 6. Phases of text analysis

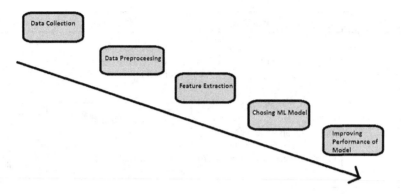

4. **Reinforcement Machine Learning Algorithm-**This model gathered information based on the interaction of system with the environment to take actions that would maximize the rewards and in turn minimizes the risk. In reinforcement learning agent continuously learns from the experience, it has during its interaction with the environment in an iterative manner until it explores all possible states.(Whitehead & Ballard, 1991).

PROCESS FOR TEXT ANALYSIS

The process of text analysis is an iterative process and can be modify according to the basic structure of the organization but for the ease of understanding we are discussing here it as a linear approach (like waterfall model of SDLC, where succeeding phase can start only after the completion of preceding phase) having multiple phases-

1. **Data Collection-** Data can be collected from various heterogeneous sources like social networking sites, within the organization, some government sites, survey data, feedback data etc. and once it is collected we need to find a proper method for data management and storage.(Philip Chen & Zhang, 2014)
2. **Data Pre-Processing-** There are multiple steps for data extraction, cleansing, annotation, integration(Philip Chen & Zhang, 2014) as follows-
   a. *Data Cleansing-* Cleansing of data consists of several parts-
      I. *Removing Punctuation-* Punctuation can provide a better understanding for context. But for vectorization of data, which counts the number of words not the context, the punctuations and special characters will add no value.(Nabi, 2018)***E.G. - Oh! It's raining again. →Oh It's raining again.***
      II. *Tokenization-* Tokenization converts a text into small units such as converts a sentence into word.(Nabi, 2018)For tokenization supervised machine learning with multiple NLP tasks can be perform, i.e. from NLP an understanding for the context of sentences can developed which in turn can help to identify words from the sentence. For example – in English language we may say that whitespaces are used as a separator between words.

      III. *Removing Stop Words-* Stop words are the most frequent words that appear in our text more often but add no value in data.(Nabi, 2018)For example, if, the, or, in, is, etc.

  b. ***Annotations-*** Annotation means labeling of data which can be used to train the machine learning model.

      I. *Part of Speech (POS)* -Part of speech is used to identify the theme of sentence or to identify the entity set which can be further used to identify the sentiments towards the given entity set.("Words, Parts of Speech, and Morphology," 2006) It is simply understanding as identifying noun, verb, adjective etc. in a sentence.

  c. ***Name Entity Recognition-*** In machine learning we use a lot of training data so that a model can easily identifies the people, place; things etc. name entity recognition is needed part of speech as an input, so it is rely on the tagging of POS.

  d. ***Normalization-*** Normalization refers to the translation of terms in the scheme(García, Ramírez-Gallego, Luengo, Benítez, & Herrera, 2016) and linguistic reduction through stemming and lemmatization.

      IV. *Stemming-* In stemming words are converted to a stem by removing unnecessary inflammation like cries, crying can be converted to a single stem "cry".(Nabi, 2018)So that related words can be treated in the same way. It generally reduces the suffix of words like ing, es, er etc. It reduces the corpus of words, but sometimes actual words are neglected.

      V. *Lemmatization-* Lemmatization is another way for removing inflammation by using part of speech. (Nabi, 2018)It works on the canonical form (lemma) of the word or we may say the root of words. It is better than stemming as it works on morphological analysis of word. For example – ***Better → good***

Stemming is a fast approach as it is simply cut off the suffix of word and attaches it with the related words but sometimes the context of the word is neglected. Lemmatization is slow but when the context of a word matters a lot, it is very useful.

  e. ***Noises Removal-*** As this process is not linear in nature, noise removal can be a subtask of previously define stages.(Philip Chen & Zhang, 2014) Noise removal means removing the unwanted terms form the text so that it can be easily processed. (García et al., 2016)Such as

- Removing hash tag from the tweets
- Removing HTML, XML markup tags
- Removing emoticons

Only thing which should be understand that noises are tasks specific, what is categorized as noise for one task can be a meaningful data for other task. So, noises can't be generalized.

3. **Feature Extraction**- In data processing stage, words of the text represent discrete features. Based on these features, one need to choose a model to smoothen down the features and mapped them to a vector model.(Nabi, 2018) This whole process is called feature extraction. Various techniques for feature extraction are as follows-

Figure 7. Example of text corpus

Document 1		Document 2		Document 3	
this	2	this	3	this	1
day	2	day	0	day	1
nice	3	nice	2	nice	2
tea	1	tea	2	tea	0
have	0	have	1	have	0
good	1	good	0	good	2
song	0	song	2	song	3

a. **Vectorization-** In vectorization process each word is assigned a unique numeric value. If the data is storing in the array, based on which feature vector is created in such a way that machine learning algorithm can understand the inputted data and process it in the required manner. There are various methods for numericizing the data-

b. **Bag of words (BOW) -**In this approach, a fixed length vector is used to make entry in this vector corresponds to a word of predefined dictionary. The size of vector is equal to the size of dictionary.(Nabi, 2018) The entry in the vector represents the occurrence of a word in a text. If the word is present in the text, then it counts 1 otherwise it will count 0.For example- In a dictionary contains, {this, is, great, news, to, have, not, weather}and the text need to be vectorized is {this, is, great, news}, then the BOW for this text will be {1,1,1,1,0,0,0,0}.

c. **Term Frequency Inverse Document Frequency (TF/IDF) -**The most commonly used technique is term frequency and inverse document frequency (TF/ IDF), it computes the frequency of a word appears in a document to the frequency of its occurrence in all documents. (Nabi, 2018) It is useful to identify the high frequency word throughout the data. Here term frequency is the first phase and IDF is the second phase it can be used for stop-word filtering too.

In first phase, it calculates the total number of occurrences of a word in a specific document.
$$TF = \frac{Number\ of\ times\ term\ t\ appears\ in\ doc}{Total\ number\ of\ terms\ in\ doc}$$ .In second phase, it measures how important a term is? The occurrences of words like the, is, are, of etc. will be high but in contextual view these words are least important. Thus, in this phase the TF/IDF need to scale up the terms according to their importance, here weigh down the most frequent terms and scaling up the rare ones.

$$IDF(t) = \log\_e\left(\frac{Total\ number\ of\ document}{Number\ of\ document\ with\ term\ t\ in\ it}\right)$$ .Let's take an example to calculate TF/ IDF for a document.

TF ('nice', Document 1) =3/9;
IDF ('nice') =log_e(3/3);

d. **N-gram-**A group of words in a sequence is called n-gram.(Šilić, Chauchat, Dalbelo Bašić, & Morin, 2007) There are many variations of this technique exists for n = 1, 2, ------- values.

Figure 8. Example for gender corpus

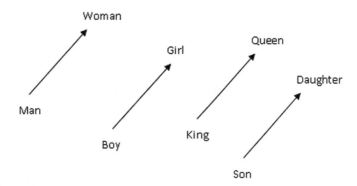

When n = 1 means a single word is taken under consideration, it is called unigram. For example- good, better etc.

Similarly, n=2, means combination of two words is taken, it is called bigram and so on. For example- great news, nice tea etc.

I. *Word Embedment-* This is the most powerful technique for capturing the context of words in a document. In this approach the synonyms or in other words semantically and syntactically similar words have similar representation.(Nabi, 2018)In other words, in this technique words are represented in a coordinate system where related words, having some relationship in text corpus are placed together.(Grant et al., 2018)In mathematical terms the cosine of angles between these two vectors should be 1, i.e. the angle ' , ' .ust be zero.

⇨ Similarity between two text A and B is given by

$$sim(A,B) = \cos(\theta) = \frac{A.B}{\|A\|\|B\|}$$

The techniques for word embedment are-

i. **Word2Vec-** The Word2Vec has a large corpus of text as input and generate a vector space (Grant et al., 2018)such that each unique word is being assigned a relative vector in the vector space in such a manner that similar words having similar context are placed together in vector space.(Nabi, 2018) The Word2Vec are performed by using two techniques-

a) Continuous Bag Of Words (CBOW) - This method takes the word as an input and predicts the next word in the sentence corresponding to the context. Suppose for a sentence containing word "have a nice day!", after inputting a word "great" in the system, the prediction for the targeted word in sequence is to be made.

Here input word is called one hot encoded vector of size V as all the words are independent from each other, in process of finding targeted word, the vector representation for the targeted word is needed.

For example- boy is to girl then what will be the answer of son is to? Words *son* and *girl* while subtracting *boy* is equal to the vector associated with *Daughter*.

b) Skip-Gram- Skip-gram is used to create a sentence from an inputted word, or in other words in this model multiple layers of CBOW is used to provide the output of skip-gram. The working of skip-gram is inverse of that of word2Vec, because here based on target word; prediction of context words is done. In this approach the model is learning from the statistics of number of times a pair is occurring. For example, the model is going to get more pair of {'nice', 'tea'} than of {'nice', 'day'}. So, when the training is completed after inputting the word 'nice', the probability of getting 'tea' as output is high than that of 'day'.

ii. GloVe – GloVe is the abbreviation of Global Vector. GloVe is the extension of word2Vec method for efficiently learning the relationship between input and the target words.(Pennington, Socher, & Manning, 2014)

4. **Choosing Machine Learning Model-** For predicting the behavior of human against one's organization, machine learning algorithms are very useful. Supervised algorithm utilizes a named dataset where each record of training set is named with suitable sentiment. Though, unsupervised learning incorporates unlabeled dataset where content is not labeled with proper sentiments(Yogesh, Bhatia, & Omprakash, 2007),(Tripathy et al., 2015),(Bringmann et al., 2010). Based on the problem statement and data availability, there are various machine learning models for text-based applications. Here Classical machine learning models like Naïve-bayes and support vector machine (Tripathy et al., 2015)are generally used for a task having some predefined rules, for example for spam filtering etc. Similarly, Deep learning model are used for natural language processing. (Bringmann et al., 2010). So based on the problem statement, the machine learning model is chosen.

5. **Improvising Performa nce of Text Analysis Using Machine Learning-**As the environment is changing; the needs of users are changing very often. And to evolve the business according to the market demands, the changes should also be inculcating in the business environment. To meet all these requirements, once a model is developed for text analysis according to the business needs, its performance should be improvised. To adopt all the environment changes the machine learning model should be flexible and scalable enough otherwise the model will be obsolete. And the development for the new model needed to be started from scratch, and all the stages of text analysis process will start from the first phase. This will result in wastage or misuse of manpower, resources, money, infrastructure etc. The model should be flexible enough that can be evolve based on customer's need and market requirements.

ISSUES

1. **Domain Specific Features in Corpus:** For classification and clustering it is very important to classify the corpus carefully.(Nabi, 2018)For example- the text related to news should be categorized into a news related corpus.
2. **Exhaustive list of Stop-words:** Stop words are used to define the structure of text not the context, (Nabi, 2018)treating these words as feature words will result into the poor performance of classifier.
3. **Language Translation:** To translate a sentence from source language into target language.(Mahesh, Sinha, & Thakur, 2005)
4. **Sentiment Analysis:** To analyze the polarity of sentiment for an event is positive or negative or neutral.(Pang, Lee, & Vaithyanathan, 2002; Tripathy et al., 2015)
5. **Feature Extraction** is a challenge to decide on which the algorithm need to pay attention. (Nabi, 2018)
6. **Spam Filtering** is to detect unwanted email/ messages should vary according to the usage and profile of users, this should not be generalized in nature.
7. **Part of Speech (POS):** The meaning and context of a sentence may vary from user to user, hence finding POS should be done very carefully.("Words, Parts of Speech, and Morphology," 2006)
8. **Code-Mixing (CM)** can be done by embedding phrases, words, and morphemes of one language into an expression of another language, which is commonly observed in multilingual communities(McClure, 1995; Poplack & Walker, 2003). To converting embedding phrases, words, and morphemes of one language into an expression of another language is very difficult at multiple levels like POS, Feature extraction, Ambiguity handling etc.
9. **Ambiguous Words:** The words can be mis-interpretive in translating from one language to another; because of ambiguous words usage like "bus" has different meaning in English as well as in Hindi (Mahesh et al., 2005).
10. **Inconsistent Spelling Usage:** Although there are standard for transliterations are available, but people can use inconsistent spelling for the same word as the most common hindi word "मैं" should be written as 'mai' but some may write it as 'mei' or 'mein'. (Jhamtani, Suleep Kumar, & Raychoudhury, 2014).
11. **Some other issues are** developing a bag of words (Nabi, 2018)to provide a proper path of relationships among the words.

FUTURE TRENDS

The application area of text analysis is very vast. Following are some area of applications-

1. **Sentiment Analysis-** This is the current area of research where many researchers are working. This is the process to identify the attitude of user towards an entity e.g.- movie review, customer sentiments towards a product or brand etc.(Pang et al., 2002)
2. **Predictive Analysis-** Predictive analysis is generally used to forecast the decision based on the historical data e.g.- weather forecasting, identifying global warming, situation of flood and drought, risk management etc.(Yogesh et al., 2007)

3. **Sequential Analysis-** Sequential analysis means to identify what will be the next event in the sequence. E.g.- Identifying on the pattern of orders on online shopping site, what is the next product the customer going to order or identifying what will be next change or new requirement in the market.(Lewis & Gale, 1994)

4. **Political Analysis-** Political analysis is done to identify whether the work of the government in the area or region is satisfactory or not.(Grimmer & M. Stewart, 2013)

5. **Prediction And Prevention From Crime –** By using text analysis the crime branches and identify beforehand where and when the crime may take place and take precautionary actions for prevention.(Grover, Adderley, & Bramer, 2007)

6. **Knowledge Management-** In many industries like healthcare, education, banks etc. the data is growing rapidly. The manual management of this data in such a way that the information can be access at the point of need, is very tedious task. The text analysis systems are very helpful in these fields and providing a relevant information as and when needed.(Philip Chen & Zhang, 2014)

7. **Customer Care Services-** The text analysis and natural language processing is being used by customer care of sectors like healthcare, financial services in terms of chat or video call. Here chatbot is mimicking a human and storing and managing the complete information of their customers and providing a justified solution to their problems.(Shum, He, & Li, 2018)

8. **Personalized Advertisements-** On social networking sites like Facebook and on online shopping sites, the advertisement is viewed by users according to the data they posted or the searches they generally perform. This all process is done by analyzing their search history.

9. Other application areas are Spam filtering, Content enrichment, inventory analysis etc.

CONCLUSION

As an explanatory study, the results of text analysis using machine learning models are promising. This chapter provides the insight of classification of structures of text, different kinds of machine learning models, the process and sub-processes of text analysis. In addition to discussing the application of basic measures of specific task, generic measures are also present. Instead of listing hundreds of sub-process, their measures and applications, the key sub-processes, their working and applications are discussed and further references for the literature is also provided. The chapter provides a current state of art in machine learning for text analysis. These are probably going to remain legitimate sources for the latest improvements in the continually developing field of text analysis.

REFERENCES

Analytics, B. D. (2018). *Big Data Analytics | IBM Analytics*. Retrieved from https://www.ibm.com/analytics/hadoop/big-data-analytics

Bauer, F., Pereverzev, S., & Rosasco, L. (2007). On regularization algorithms in learning theory. *Journal of Complexity, 23*(1), 52–72. doi:10.1016/j.jco.2006.07.001

Beringer, J. H. E. (2007). An Efficient Algorithm for Instance-Based Learning on Data Streams. Advances in Data Mining. Theoretical Aspects and Applications, 4597. doi:10.1007/978-3-540-73435-2_4

Beyer, M. A. L. D. (2012). The Importance Of 'Big Data': A Definition. Stamford, CT: Gartner.

Bringmann, B., Berlingerio, M., Bonchi, F., & Gionis, A. (2010). *Learning and Predicting the Evolution of Social Networks* (Vol. 25). Academic Press.

Cortés, G., Benitez, C., García, L., Alvarez, I., & Ibáñez, J. (2016). *A Comparative Study of Dimensionality Reduction Algorithms Applied to Volcano-Seismic Signals*. Academic Press.

Doan, T., & Kalita, J. (2015). *Selecting Machine Learning Algorithms Using Regression Models*. Academic Press.

Domingos, P., & Pazzani, M. (1998). *On the Optimality of the Simple Bayesian Classifier Under Zero-One Loss* (Vol. 29). Academic Press.

Gandomi, A., & Haider, M. (2015). Beyond the hype: Big data concepts, methods, and analytics. *International Journal of Information Management, 35*(2), 137-144. doi:10.1016/j.ijinfomgt.2014.10.007

García, S., Ramírez-Gallego, S., Luengo, J., Benítez, J. M., & Herrera, F. (2016). Big data preprocessing: Methods and prospects. *Big Data Analytics, 1*(1), 9. doi:10.118641044-016-0014-0

Grant, R. N., Kucher, D., León, A. M., Gemmell, J. F., Raicu, D. S., & Fodeh, S. J. (2018). Automatic extraction of informal topics from online suicidal ideation. *BMC Bioinformatics, 19*(8), 211. doi:10.118612859-018-2197-z PMID:29897319

Grimmer, J., & M. Stewart, B. (2013). *Text as Data: The Promise and Pitfalls of Automatic Content Analysis Methods for Political Texts* (Vol. 21). Academic Press.

Grover, V., Adderley, R., & Bramer, M. (2007). *Review of Current Crime Prediction Techniques*. Paper presented at the Applications and Innovations in Intelligent Systems XIV, London, UK.

Guimarães Pedronette, D. C., Calumby, R. T., & Torres, S. (2015). A semi-supervised learning algorithm for relevance feedback and collaborative image retrieval. *EURASIP Journal on Image and Video Processing, 27*(1). doi:10.118613640-015-0081-6

Ilinska, L., Ivanova, O., & Senko, Z. (2016). Teaching Textual Analysis of Contemporary Popular Scientific Texts. *Procedia: Social and Behavioral Sciences, 236*, 248–253. doi:10.1016/j.sbspro.2016.12.020

James, J. (2014). *Data Never Sleeps 2.0*. Retrieved from https://www.domo.com/blog/data-never-sleeps-2-0/

Jha, A., Dave, M., & Supriya Madan, D. (2016). *A Review on the Study and Analysis of Big Data using Data Mining Techniques* (Vol. 6). Academic Press.

Jhamtani, H., Suleep Kumar, B., & Raychoudhury, V. (2014). *Word-level Language Identification in Bi-lingual Code-switched Texts*. Academic Press.

Laney, D. (2001). *3-D Data Management: Controlling Data Volume* (Vol. 6). Velocity, and Variety.

Lesser, V., Horling, B., Klassner, F., Raja, A., Wagner, T., & Zhang, S. X. Q. (2000). BIG: An agent for resource-bounded information gathering and decision making. *Artificial Intelligence, 118*(1), 197–244. doi:10.1016/S0004-3702(00)00005-9

Lewis, D. D., & Gale, W. A. (1994). *A Sequential Algorithm for Training Text Classifiers.* Paper presented at the SIGIR '94, London, UK.

Mahesh, R., Sinha, K., & Thakur, A. (2005). *Machine translation of bi-lingual Hindi-English (Hinglish) text.* Academic Press.

Manyika, J., Chui, M., Brown, B., Bughin, J., Dobbs, R., Roxburgh, C., & Hung Byers, A. (2011). *Big data: The next frontier for innovation, competition, and productivity.* Academic Press.

McClure, E. (1995). Duelling languages: Grammatical structure in codeswitching. In *Carol Myers-Scotton* (Vol. 17). Academic Press.

Mujeeb, S. a. (2015). A Relative Study on Big Data Applications And Techniques. *Int. J. Eng. Innov. Technol, 4*(10), 133–138.

Musumeci, Nag, Macaluso, Zibar, Ruffini, & Tornatore. (2018). *An Overview on Application of Machine Learning Techniques in Optical Networks.* Academic Press.

Nabi, J. (2018). *Machine Learning—Text Processing.* Retrieved from https://towardsdatascience.com/machine-learning-text-processing-1d5a2d638958

Neha Garg, D. K. S. (2018). *The Journey of BIG Data Analysis.* Paper presented at the NDIACom-2018, Bhartiya Vidyapth, Delhi, India.

Pang, B., Lee, L., & Vaithyanathan, S. (2002). Thumbs up? Sentiment classification using machine learning techniques. *Proceedings of the ACL-02 conference on Empirical methods in natural language processing,* 10. 10.3115/1118693.1118704

Pennington, J., Socher, R., & Manning, C. (2014). *Glove: Global Vectors for Word Representation* (Vol. 14). Academic Press.

Philip Chen, C. L., & Zhang, C.-Y. (2014). Data-intensive applications, challenges, techniques and technologies: A survey on Big Data. *Information Sciences, 275,* 314–347. doi:10.1016/j.ins.2014.01.015

Poplack, S., & Walker, J. (2003). Pieter Muysken, Bilingual speech: a typology of code-mixing. Cambridge, UK: Cambridge University Press.

Predictive Analytics Today. (2018). *What is Predictive Analytics?* Retrieved from https://www.predictiveanalyticstoday.com/what-is-predictive-analytics

Ray, S. (2014). *7 Types of Regression Techniques You Should Know!* Retrieved from https://www.analyticsvidhya.com/blog/2015/08/comprehensive-guide-regression/

Sagiroglu, S., & Sinanc, D. (2013). Big data. *RE:view.*

Shum, H.-y., He, X.-d., & Li, D. (2018). From Eliza to XiaoIce: challenges and opportunities with social chatbots. *Frontiers of Information Technology & Electronic Engineering, 19*(1), 10-26. doi:10.1631/FITEE.1700826

Šilić, A., Chauchat, J.-H., Dalbelo Bašić, B., & Morin, A. (2007). *N-Grams and Morphological Normalization in Text Classification: A Comparison on a Croatian-English Parallel Corpus.* Paper presented at the Progress in Artificial Intelligence, Berlin, Germany.

Solanki, A., & Kumar, A. (2018). *A system to transform natural language queries into SQL queries.* International Journal of Information Technology, 1–10. doi:10.100741870-018-0095-2

Tripathy, A., Agrawal, A., & Rath, S. K. (2015). Classification of Sentimental Reviews Using Machine Learning Techniques. *Procedia Computer Science, 57*, 821–829. doi:10.1016/j.procs.2015.07.523

Whitehead, S. D., & Ballard, D. H. (1991). Learning to perceive and act by trial and error. Machine Learning, 7(1), 45-83. Retrieved from doi:10.1007/BF00058926

(2006). Words, Parts of Speech, and Morphology. InNugues, P. M. (Ed.), *An Introduction to Language Processing with Perl and Prolog: An Outline of Theories, Implementation, and Application with Special Consideration of English, French, and German* (pp. 113–145). Berlin: Springer Berlin Heidelberg. doi:10.1007/3-540-34336-9_5

Yogesh, S., Bhatia, P., & Omprakash, S. (2007). *A review of studies on machine learning techniques* (Vol. 1). Academic Press.

Young, T., Hazarika, D., Poria, S., & Cambria, E. (2018). *Recent Trends in Deep Learning Based Natural Language Processing* (Vol. 13). Academic Press.

KEY TERMS AND DEFINITIONS

Bag of Word (BOW): To map the words into a fixed length vector according to the predefined dictionary.

Business Intelligence: A technological driven process for analyzing data and presenting information, in such a way that user can take immediate actions and unable decision making.

Continuous Bag of Words: A process of taking words as a input and predict the next word in the sequence.

Data Cleaning: A sub-process in data preprocessing, where we remove punctuation, stop words, etc. from the text.

Data Collection: A process of storing and managing data.

Data Preprocessing: A process for making data ready for analysis purpose by eliminating unwanted things from data.

Deep Learning: An extension of machine learning approach, which uses neural network.

Facebook: An online social networking site.

Feature Extraction: A process of finding features of words and map them to vector space.

GloVe: The extension of word2Vec method for efficiently learning the relationship between input and the target words.

Hadoop: A framework that allow for the distributed processing for large datasets.

Instagram: A video and photo sharing social site owned by Facebook.

Lemmatization: A process to reduce words into its root, generally by reducing second form and third form of verb to first form, etc.

Machine Learning: Machine learning is branch of data science which has concern with the design and development of algorithm to develop a system that can learn from data, identify the complex patterns and provide intelligent, reliable, repeatable decisions and results with minimal human interaction based on the provided input.

N-Gram: Making group of 'n' words from a sequence to convey some meaningful things.

Natural Language Processing (NLP): Natural language processing is the ability of computer program to understand human language as it is spoken or handwritten.

Part of Speech: Used to identify the theme of sentence.

Predictive Analysis: To predict the future based on historical data.

Reinforcement Machine Learning Algorithm: This model gathered information based on the interaction of system with the environment to take actions that would maximize the rewards and in turn minimizes the risk.

Semi-Structured Data: Data that have some organizational property, but not having some row and column relationship.

Semi-Supervised Machine Learning Algorithms: In this category either the model is developed in such a way that either there are labels exist for all kind of observations or there is no label exist.

Sequential Analysis: Based on the pattern of historical data, to identify what will be the next pattern in the sequence.

Skip-Gram: Inverse process of Word2Vec, here based on targeted words, prediction of context word is done.

Social Media (SM): The interactive computer-based technologies that facilitate the creation and sharing of information, ideas, feelings, etc.

Stemming: Stemming is the process of reducing word to stem. By removing unnecessary inflammation this is done by removing suffix.

Structured Data: Data is organized properly into a formatted repository.

Supervised Machine Learning Algorithms: Supervised algorithms mean that a system is developed or modeled on predetermined set of sample data.

Term Frequency/Inverse Document Frequency (TF/IDF): To identify the occurrence of a word in document and finding the most probable word in the text.

Text Analysis: Text analysis is used to parse the unstructured data into machine readable form.

Tokenization: A process of converting a sentence into small identifiable units.

Twitter: An online news and social networking service on which user can share message called tweets.

Unstructured Data: Data structure or organization can't be predicted.

Unsupervised Machine Learning Algorithms: Unsupervised algorithms mean that a program is provided with some collection of data, with no predetermined dataset being available.

Vectorization: A process to assign a numeric value to the features of words.

Word2Vec: One method of word embedment is word2Vec where similar words have same vector representation.

Word Embedment: A process to find context of words, here similar words have same representation.

Chapter 19
Machine Learning in the Medical Industry

Utsha Sinha
Netaji Subhas University of Technology, India

Abhinav Singh
Netaji Subhas University of Technology, India

Deepak Kumar Sharma
 https://orcid.org/0000-0001-6117-3464
Netaji Subhas University of Technology, India

ABSTRACT

Currently, machine learning and artificial intelligence technology is one of the fastest growing trends all over the world, especially in the medical industry. The rise in the machine learning applications in the healthcare domain is giving substantial hope to the human race for achieving greater abilities to diagnose and treat illness. Machine learning is not only used in the diagnosis of the disease but also its prognosis. From discovering a compound as a drug to the marketing as well as monitoring of the potential drug, machine learning plays a vital role in each stage. Nearly, all the major companies in the medical space are moving towards machine learning and its potential applications in the medical industry. This chapter explains the concept of machine learning and its working as well as the applications in the medical industry. While it describes the basic concepts of machine learning in the medical industry, it also proposes future challenges for the aforementioned subject.

INTRODUCTION

The medical industry uses predictability at various stages and realms of its operation. Traditional and ongoing processes use the present level of prevalent technology to optimize these operations. The same processes can be further efficiently carried out by incorporating machine learning utilizing the existing medical data. Machine learning algorithms can be used to optimize the predictions from the stage of

DOI: 10.4018/978-1-5225-9643-1.ch019

discovery of a compound to its effective monitoring in the market and analyzing the safety atrocities. Machine learning is also operational in the process of medical data collection and analysis. Big corporates like Mckinsey, Frost and Sullivan has shown in their researches that machine learning and big data has the potential to generate 100 billion dollars annually and artificial intelligence has the capability to generate 6.7 billion in revenue by 2021. Through advancements in these technologies, the healthcare sector is on its way to generate huge revenues and provide better care (Rai, 2018).

This chapter covers the various present and possible applications of machine learning in medical industry processes. It goes over the traditional methods and their shortcomings as well as demonstrates the corresponding advancements on incorporating machine learning. This chapter also presents some past and present works involving machine learning, deep learning and artificial intelligence in healthcare.

BACKGROUND

With the advent of machine learning, realms affecting lifestyles to industries have undergone major changes. A technology where computers are taught to imitate human decision-making skills according to Dhunay (2019) has also made its way it the healthcare industry. Over the years, machine learning has taken over businesses and visibly resulted in higher revenue generations and profits. Charts and statistics show how significantly businesses incorporating machine learning have taken over their respective industries. (Murphy, 2019).

Among the various other applications of machine learning, one such is the healthcare industry. The medical industry lays a huge scope and opportunities for machine learning to fulfill. This industry is very vital for a country's growth and prosperity and plays an important role in the economy and GDP. Machine learning is continuously being incorporated by companies in studying and analyzing genetic data and making insightful interpretations (Gabutt, 2015). Machine learning is used in the very first stage of treatment, disease diagnosis, where the symptoms are used to classify the disease. Various systems and tool are developed and are used by doctors to cross-check their prediction as well as by patients and companies manufacturing wearables. Following diagnosis comes the drug for its treatment. Drug discovery and development involves various stages and spans over 13-15 years until a drug is ready to be marketed. The various stages involve some degree of predictability which is efficiently performed in silico reducing cost and time compared to in vitro. Machine learning is used in various stages of drug discovery using the –omics data (e.g. Chemogenomics) in lead discovery, virtual screening, target fishing, chemogenomics and determining the safety measures. The huge repositories generated from the various hospitals and institutions are mined upon and analyzed using data mining and machine learning techniques to extract insightful information. There still lies huge scope and future opportunities for machine learning in this industry to provide better patient care at reduced costs.

MACHINE LEARNING

When a man comes to question how do one start to learn, the answer goes back to his infant stage. An infant is taught by his mother the various body parts. His mother when then asks him to point to his head, he points, if he is wrong he is corrected by his mother and if he is right, the mother rewards him, consequently, he learns gradually. So as he grows up, he keeps learning, he is being taught in different ways. He might be wrong many numbers of times but eventually, he learns and memorizes each time he is corrected. Then when asked a question he tries to recall from his memory and past experiences. Thus established that learning begins from infantry. The mouldable mind is taught the basics things and stores the information throughout. The concept behind machine learning or per se deep learning is inspired by an infant's brain though there are many kinds of learning methods and rules wherein some might not even require a teacher to teach, some might have a critic but the fundamental idea is inspired by the working of the human nervous system. An infant's brain is like a sponge; it is mold-able depending upon what is taught to it. In a similar fashion, the computer can be trained to gain human-like decision-making capabilities (Dhunay, 2019).

The brain learns in a way that it stores what it is being taught and later when asked it tries to recall from its memory. Based on past experiences the brain solves various kinds of problems by making important decisions, the one thing that computers cannot be simply programmed to do. Now, the human brain has the amazing ability to make decisions. A person looks up at the sky and looking at the clouds, sensing the wind speed and the humidity in the air, he comments "it might just rain today", such decision making or predicting skills is what inspires the idea behind machine learning, before the advent of machine learning a computer could not be simply programmed to do so on its own. Basically, it is the working of the human nervous system that inspires the idea of deep learning, a super-set of machine learning or alternatively, it can be stated as the driving force behind machine learning. The human nervous system can be seen as one processing system consisting of a network of elementary processing units or the so-called neurons which inspires the artificial neural networks. These neurons store information by adjusting the synaptic gap between them. The information is stored in these connecting links. New data entered is stacked by changing the synaptic gaps. Fundamentally, the brain tries to figure out answers from past experiences and lessons. It uses past familiarity to predict the result.

With generations passing by, mankind tries to lessen the burden of work off its shoulders. Man-made machines to elaborate his work, to get the work done by the machine rather manually. A man's decisions are based on his personal opinion on the subject, which in turn is formed with time and experiences, whereas a machine would take decisions based on the logic that is fed into it. Machines don't make mistakes, the humans who operate them do. Hence machine making a decision would be accurate, reliable and completely unbiased. With the evolution of machines and computers doing faster computations for humans, why not make them take the decisions for mankind now? Man is continuously advancing machines to copy human behavior and make things easier for himself. Making machines reason like a human brain. This is where the core concept of machine learning lies. In simple words, it is teaching the machine function just like the brain does. The very working of neurons in the brain has inspired the working and structure of artificial neural networks. With machine learning, we are automating processes in almost all the industries. With the advent and progress in machine learning, besides the doctor's predictions, there is a machine confirming the diagnosis results based upon the test results. Based upon the ups and downs of the market, using machine learning future stock prices are predicted. Every enterprise and industry is progressing towards automating their methods and is trying to incorporate the fundamentals of machine learning in its functioning to a possible extent.

Molding towards machine to imitate but rather say inspire from human ways of thinking and logic solving. The concept of machine learning involves schooling the computer of the data and its output to help us find the solution when we bring in new data. That is, it is programming the computer, the machine to learn itself. Contrary to traditional programming methods, the input is data and the output of the data in machine learning to get the program or model as the output. It can be described as the process of "automating the process of automation" (Brownlee, 2015). Machine Learning is a particular method of data analytic that automates model building, as it relates to the development of models. With machines learning to utilize certain algorithms, they can find hidden insights from data; it is important to note that in machine learning, we are not telling the machines where to look. The iterative nature of machine learning allows the machine to adapt its methods and outputs as it is exposed to new situations and data. Bill Gates, the former Microsoft chairman said, "A breakthrough in machine learning would be worth ten Microsoft", which extensively cites the importance of machine learning in every industry today. A top fifteen global brands ranking by Interbrand from the year 2000 to present made one point very clear about the various top brands and industries, that the ones with machine learning as its core technology or even the ones using machine learning techniques in its business development improved its income the most over the years and topped the chart, making huge margin with its followers. Around the start of the year 2000, lifestyle and food manufacturers were in the top positions. With companies like Apple nowhere around the top 16. With time passing by tech companies like Microsoft, Google and IBM started rising towards the top leaving other industries behind. With the advent of machine learning techniques, some of these companies incorporated artificial intelligence and machine learning into their products as well as businesses, leaving all other brands to value much less. Towards the year 2016, the chart occupied the majority of tech companies highlighting the importance of machine learning (Murphy, 2019). Machine learning is used in industries in decision making, natural language processing, text recognition, voice recognition, virtual agents, biometrics, image and video analysis, semantics as well as in artificial intelligence optimized hardware (Press, 2017). Just as the emergence of the assembly line in mass production changed the whole manufacturing industry and methods of manufacturing, as quoted by Google's chief economist Hal Varian, machine learning or automation will change the businesses and processes in a similar manner. "Machine learning is here to stay" (Priyadharshini, 2019).

Artificial Neuron Vs Biological Neuron

Computers are automated to take decisions like the human brain but keeping this fact besides, there are a lot of categories where a computer can outperform the brain.

A comparison can be made between the biological decision maker and the artificial decision maker as per the following: -

- **Speed:** As computers are faster in processing, thus owing to this fact, artificial neural networks take around nanoseconds whereas the biological neuron takes milliseconds to execute. The former being faster than later.
- **Processing:** Though biological neurons can do massive parallel processing, the artificial neuron process faster than the brain.
- **Size and Complexity**: The total number of neurons in the brain is about 10^{11} and the total interconnections are 10^{15}. Processing in biological neuron takes place in the cell body, axon, synapse, etc and thus the biological neural network is much larger and complex than the artificial neural network which depends upon the application and is designed accordingly.
- **Storage:** In computers, data is stored in contiguous memory locations. Sometimes memory may overload and as a result older addresses may be overwritten. But in case of the brain, data is stored in the form of synaptic adjustments and thus any amount of data can be stored without any overwriting or loss of old data but it might hinder the recollection of stored information. Whereas, in

Figure 1. Biological neuron

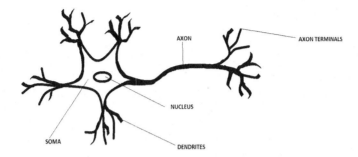

artificial neural networks, data once stored can be retrieved from the associated memory location. Thus, artificial neural networks are more adaptive.

- **Tolerance:** Biological neurons are tolerant to fault owing to their distributed nature. Even if there is some degree of disconnection in their interconnections, they will function. Even if some cell die human nervous system appears to perform with the same efficiency, whereas, artificial neural networks are intolerant to a fault. If information gets corrupted, the interconnections are disconnected.
- **Control Mechanism**: The control unit in the central processing unit controls the processing whereas there is no such control unit in the brain. The chemical reaction determines the strength of a neuron in a brain. Thus the control mechanism in the brain is complex compared to artificial neurons.

The representation of the artificial neuron & the biological neuron is depicted in the figure 2 and figure 1 respectively. Figure 1 shows the biological neuron and its various parts, the dendrites receive messages from other cells, the cell body is the power house of the cell, the axon passes the message to the terminals to form junction with other cells. The message is in the form of chemical signals. In figure 2 x1, x2 and x3 are inputs to our network, and y is the output to the network. There is a net function which is calculated and activation is applied to get the desired output. There are no chemical reactions rather electrical signals are passed and processed.

Applications of Machine Learning

Besides the numerous applications of Machine learning in medicine and healthcare, it also has a variety of applications in the following fields according to Sivanandam and Deepa (2011): -

- **Social Media Platforms:** Machine learning is used in social media platforms to personalize it for their users. For example, the people you may know feature on Facebook, suggests friends based upon the people the user frequently visits, might be on the users saved contacts or based upon common friends. Another example used heavily across social media platforms is facial recognition.
- **Spam Filters**: A very extensive application of machine learning in classifying emails as spam or not.

Figure 2. Artificial neuron

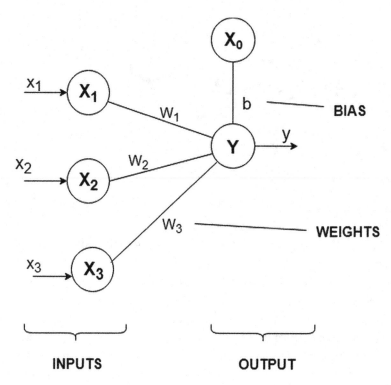

- **Search Engines:** The search engines operate based upon user response to the search results. It refines the result for every next search depending upon which search result the user chose and if it was found beneficial.
- **E-Commerce**: Machine Learning is used to suggest products to buyers similar to what they've recently bought. For example, if a user buys a phone, it'll prompt the user to buy a cover for that phone.
- **Finance:** Machine learning algorithms are used to identify financial frauds, money laundering, and other illegal activities in financial firms. Stock trading companies use machine learning to predict future stock prices.
- **Detecting Identity Thefts and Frauds:** Machine learning is used in an automated transaction machine, surveillance cameras, banks in order to detect robbery and theft which when detected gets immediately reported to the concerned authorities.
- **Handwriting and Typewriting Recognition:** Also known as optical character recognition, used to detect manually written piece upon scanning.
- **Staff Scheduling:** Machine learning algorithms are used to optimize staff scheduling in order to attain efficiency in the workplace.
- **Weather Prediction:** It is possible to gather analog data as input to predict the output as the weather in certain areas.
- **Traffic Flow Control:** Using machine learning signal timing could be optimized. The neural network could recognize rush hours and fewer traffic flows and optimize the lights accordingly.

- **Inventory Management:** Inventories could be managed by predicting future demand based on past patterns of inflow and outflow.

These are some applications of machine learning but besides these machine learning is used almost in every possible compass. Businesses, industries are propelling towards automation. Machine learning is one such step. As businesses receive large amounts of data, traditional programs are not able to handle and process that amount of data, sometimes it is so complex that it might be incomprehensible and unintelligible, thus machine learning is used increasingly nowadays with massive amounts of data in businesses and industries in order to make sense out of that data and take necessary actions.

CATEGORIES OF LEARNING

There might be variations on how to define types the various types of machine learning but mostly they can be defined into the following categories: -

1. **Supervised Learning:** here the computer is fed with training data, that is labeled data and the machine is made to learn the pattern or the mapping between the feature values and the class, the relationship between the input data and its output. It can be thought of as function approximation, where the machine tries to find out the best way to map the inputs with its outputs. This is then used to predict the output of new data set which is not known to us using the relation or function obtained from training the machine. It includes regression (with continuous data set) and classification (with discrete data set). supervised learning can be thought of learning under a teacher. When the machine makes some error, the teacher is there to correct it and thus making it learn from its mistakes. It is analogous to a teacher teaching a baby. The teacher trains and models the child and supervises his study. If the child makes a mistake the teacher corrects it. In the supervised learning method, the target, output or label values are known (Sivanandam & Deepa, 2011). The figure 3 illustrates the working of supervised learning.

2. **Unsupervised Learning:** this is used when the developer isn't sure what to look for in a data or when we don't have the labels along with their features and want the machine to look for patterns in the unlabeled data. Groups of data points with similar features, which are supposed to fall under the same labels are divided into clusters. This learning is thus performed without any supervision or teacher as in supervised learning. The input data is classified into one of the clusters without any prior knowledge of how the clusters look like. During the training, the machine recognizes the distinguishing pattern in the underlying data and forms clusters of data with similar features. When test data arrives, the machine classifies it into one of the existing clusters matching its features. If the class for the new data is not found, it generates a different class for the data. The network organizes itself in the process of finding similarities, dissimilarities among the data objects. The mechanism of unsupervised learning is described in the figure 4.

Figure 3. Supervised learning

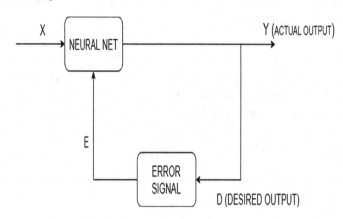

Figure 4. Unsupervised learning

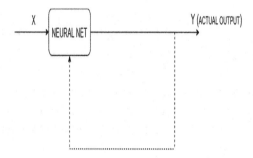

3. **Semi-Supervised Learning:** this falls between supervised and unsupervised learning. Here the data consists of labeled and unlabeled data. Labeling data comes with a cost. The cost here is time and expertise. It takes skills of the domain experts to label the data in the repositories. For example, in a set of labeled data classifying breast cancer as benign and malignant, we need sample test results, the knowledge of medicine and the required skills to classify them as benign and malignant. For speech recognition and web page classification semi-supervised learning is a good use. Here first the algorithm uses the labeled data and finds out specific labels of data then it works on the unlabeled data to find out other groups that might haven't been labeled or classify the data whose labels are already present.

4. **Reinforcement Learning:** here in reinforcement learning the goal is to maximize the reward. This learning is similar to supervised learning in the sense that the labels are known to us and it is similar to unsupervised learning in the sense that there is no error correction. There is an agent, who performs a task, goes through certain states and reaches the destination. The agent is either penalized or rewarded for each of his actions. The path or set of actions with maximum reward is chosen as the solution. Thus here the machine learns how to behave through punishments and rewards. Unlike supervised learning, there is no teacher supervising the learning process but there is a critic. The critic tells the machine if it is wrong or right but does not correct it. Thus it only gives the evaluative information. Q Learning, temporal difference are some common algorithms.

Figure 5. Reinforcement learning

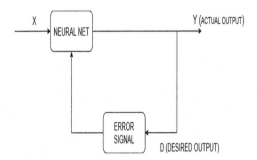

5. **Ensemble Learning**: this type of learning involves combining multiple models in order to obtain a better predictive model in terms of performance. Also known as multiple classifier systems, this is used in order to avoid the risk of poor classification choosing any one classifier, so instead of choosing one, multiple models are combined according to some numerical algorithm or rule to give better accuracy than individual performances. Though there is no guarantee that in every case a combination of classifiers will give better performance than individual classifiers but they do reduce the risk involved in choosing one. These are particularly helpful in case of too much or too fewer data (Polikar, 2009).

HEALTHCARE INDUSTRY

Healthcare is one of the most important and most focused sectors in a country. It plays an important role in the economy and gross domestic product (GDP) of a country. Doctors, nurses, administrative and other staff, hospitals, medical services, medical equipment and infrastructure, pharmacies, vets, dentists, medical devices, telemedicine, medical tourism comprises of the health care industry. It has been proven via various economic statistics and reports that healthy people lead to higher life expectancy, greater income and self-sufficiency, and thus better economy. It also reduces infertility, childbirths and accidental deaths leading to better life span in a country. Not only owing to the health of the people but the healthcare industry also generates massive employment. Statistics tell that in the year 2004, 13.5 million jobs were given alone by the healthcare industry in the US. This sector is booming at a great rate and the medical industry in India is expected to reach 372 billion dollars by 2022 giving rise to higher incomes, better health, and lifestyle to its people. The healthcare sector has given way for 476 medical colleges until the financial year 2018 according to the health report by IBEF. The number of certified medical professionals have increased to 841,104 in 2017. The medical infrastructure has thus grown evidently in the last two decades (Aggarwal, 2019). The Indian healthcare industry comprises of the private and the public sector. The public sector consists of the government-run medical facilities providing basic health services reaching every remote location. The government-run primary health centers (PHCs) vows to provide basic healthcare facilities for free or negligible cost. Though times are improving most of the primary health care centers only provide basic services and lack any specialized infrastructure. They fail to deliver optimum results at some places due to lack of doctors, hospital beds,

Figure 6. Ensemble learning

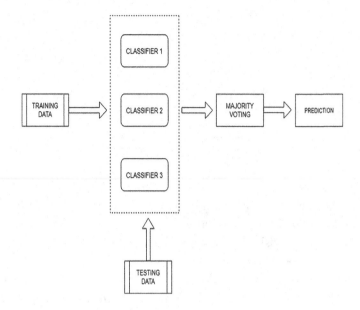

medicines or equipment. The government allocates an adequate amount of funds every year towards the development and maintenance of these health centers. The private sector consists of mid-tier and top tier hospitals providing specialized and top-class facilities at a cost. Private hospitals can be multiple specialty or super-specialty hospitals focusing on specializing in certain areas. Sometimes the private hospitals charge huge fees rendering it impossible for a certain class of people to access their services. According to Kavitha (2012), the treatment of patients in a hospital goes through six stages. It starts from admitting the patient, diagnosing the disease followed by its treatment, then inspection or monitoring followed by control and lastly discharge of the patient from the hospital. Telemedicine has emerged over the time in the healthcare industry. It involves treatment over telecommunication. The patient need not visit the doctor rather through video conferencing accessing the healthcare facilities is referred to as telemedicine. The patient can get medical consultation, assessment over his health without having to visit the clinic (Rouse, 2018). the 'tele' in telemedicine refers to 'distance' in Greek. The healthcare sector in India is slowing pacing towards using telemedicine. The change is slow because evidently, not even basic healthcare facilities have reached all the location in the country. The Apollo group of hospitals were the first ones to start using the telemedicine technology in India using simple web cameras to provide necessary medical services in a village. Telemedicine program is actively supported by many organizations and institutions in India including ISRO, DIT, state governments, etc. The telemedicine network is expanding and connecting institution and hospitals together providing consultations and services through the web. Though there is a lot to be done with time crossing the many obstacles presently faced by the telemedicine technology (Dasgupta & Deb, 2008).

Machine Learning in Health Industry

Machine learning has just so progressed in healthcare and bio-informatics that businesses like Deep Genomics are interpreting DNA by studying the variations in genes through deep learning. This technology is predicting diseases by analyzing gene mutations. 23AndMeand Rthm are similar companies working on genetic data (Gabutt, 2015). Advances in the field of technology and the introduction of machine learning and artificial intelligence have also quickened the process of drug discovery. Machine learning or any technology needs vast amounts of data in order to operate and give the desired results. Without this data, there is no operation of such technologies. Machine learning uses healthcare data for its application in the medical field. This data comes in various forms and structures. There are various levels of data from the physical level to the logical and conceptual level. The data used in applications is in the form of text, graphics, audio, video, and multimedia. Data generated at the hospitals include data from a lot of different sources which might not be patient oriented. This data may be structured or unstructured and includes patient information, lab tests and results, scanned images from ultrasound imaging, X-ray etc., physiological data, recorded signals from ECG, EEG, etc., treatment plans, notes, etc. Owing to advances in machine learning and artificial intelligence, it is much easier now to extract important information from his data through pattern recognition, natural language processing, and image processing. Various software is used by health professionals to extract vital information from the data. If not through the help of technology this would have taken up a lot of time and labor to complete yet with uncertain accuracy and efficiency (Mohammad & Gupta, 2017). Gathering data from the healthcare sector has been time-consuming and expensive over the years. But nowadays, big giants like Apple are using their technology in the healthcare sector to extract data, which can later be processed to get valuable insights. Machine Learning is a particular method of data analytic thatautomates model building, as it relates to the development ofmodels. Machine learning utilizes certain algorithms to find hidden insights from the data, which can later be utilized to take necessary actions and measures. In machine learning, we are not telling the machine where to look. The model adapts itself and outputs results when encounters with new data (Murphy, 2018). Before application of data in machine learning, it needs to be preprocessed. Preprocessing involves removing useless data to increase efficiency. Preprocessing is an integral step in machine learning because it is very rare that the developer gets a completely perfect data set which matches the specifications required for the data to be processed. Thus the developer preprocesses the raw data and prepares it to be fed into the algorithm. Preprocessing is necessary because most of the times the data received has incomplete value, missing values, and noise in the data. This data is then fed into the algorithm and the machine recognizes the hidden patterns in the data to draw insightful conclusions.

Machine Learning in Disease Diagnosis

The term diagnosis has Greek origin meaning "discrimination between two possibilities". But in the medical field, it refers to the determination of a disease via various procedures and tools. The first stage in treatment is its diagnosis. It is referred to as Dx or Ds. Diagnosis is based upon pattern recognition wherein the pattern can be extracted from scanned images, digital reports, using techniques of image processing, natural language processing, text classification. The user can also manually input the details to the model. Based on past medical data and information available, the computer based upon the patterns derived classifies the disease categories and generates the required results (Razia, Prathyusha,

Krishna, & Sumana, 2017).Diagnosis is an important and sensitive stage in the treatment process. Bad results, inefficient information or in cases wrong detection hinders the treatment process and incurs a cost. If not correctly and fully diagnosed the treatment may further sequel complications. On the other hand, an accurate and complete diagnosis of a disease at an early stage will help the professional in classifying the sickness precisely and ease him in further treatment meticulously.There might be many signs and symptoms behind the disease but all of them might not be relevant. Choosing the relevant information for the model for correct recognition of a pattern in the data in an important aspect behind disease diagnosing systems and models.

In 2006 a literature review on CDSS (clinical decision support systems) as an important tool to work aside professionals in the field and aid their job. In the past few decades, we have observed the evolving methods of improvement of data storage, representation, transfer, and processing. The emphasis on information standardization, formal means of communications and exchange of medical data and globalization of terminologies. It has also observed the advent of electronic health records (EHR) and the use of CDSS as a tool to reduce the gap between actual practices and best practices currently performed. Being human, the professionals might make mistakes thus the use of decision systems will aid them in gathering relevant data, determining the disease, finding efficient methods, trace the process and advancements, documentation and so reduce the chances of error in the process. the paper talks about the need for such systems, the current level of understanding in their design and implementation, the task of modeling and integrating them with external environment and tools (Brigle, 2006).Parvathi & Rautaray (2014) presented the survey of various techniques of data mining used in disease diagnosis. The paper emphasized the process of data mining in the process of knowledge discovery in databases. The process compromises of selection of data, then the selected data is pre-processed, cleaned, and necessary transmutations are applied, data mining techniques are then applied to derive the required knowledge or interpretation from the data. The success of data mining process also depends highly upon the availability of clean medical data, which is not easily gathered. The useful insights drawn from this process is used in disease classification in diagnosis and prognosis as well. The paper highlights that out of all the techniques used in data mining, classification is the most used technique, either alone or coupled with other necessary techniques and algorithms forming a hybrid model to derive the necessary knowledge. The paper also speaks of classification of the dataset in the healthcare sector on the basis of specialty. it uses WEKA as a tool and draws a comparison between WEKA and XLMiner. It states the advantage of data mining by presenting its various advantages like in extracting predictive knowledge, analyze the data faster, ease of working with large datasets and consequently increases efficiency and reduces cost. Parthiban and Srivatsa (2012) presented a paper on disease classification using Naive Bayes and support vector machine, opens by stating how in many ways diabetes can be called a silent killer and one of the major reasons behind cardio diseases. The author showed the result of diagnosing the chance of a diabetic patient having heart disease. It collected 500 patient data having diabetes. Out of which 142 had a highly likely chance of getting heart disease and the rest 358 were less likely to get affected by any cardiovascular diseases. The classification was done using an open source platform WEKA. Ten-fold cross-validation was used along with naive Bayes, thus increasing the efficiency. The accuracy turned out to be 74%, precision 71% on average, recall 74% on average measure 71.2% on average. A total of nine attributes were used with classification using naive Bayes and not all directly contributed to the classification process. For the classification performed with support vector machine, eleven attributes were used. The kernel parameters were varied and the model was trained for all the variations. The overall accuracy achieved was higher than using naive Bayes, being 94.6%, precision for the positive class was

97.52%, recall for this class 83.10%. in case of negative class, the precision and recall were respectively 93.67% and 99.10%. the authors conclude the paper with the importance of data mining techniques and how useful hidden relations between different data attributes can be extracted from data mining, some of which at first sight are not direct indicators of vulnerability. Sunny et al., 2018 proposed a system for diagnosing diseases which accepts symptoms as input by the doctors and the patients and the result can then be used by them for validation and cross-checking. The paper attempts to figure out the best-suited algorithm for the dataset. The dataset was prepared by New York Presbyterian hospital from patients admitted during the year 2014. the system can be used by doctors to cross-check their prediction and analysis in order to eradicate any possibility of human error. This system can also be used by patients to find the disease based upon their symptoms and consult a specialist accordingly. Supervised learning algorithm was used on text-based data for classification. The following algorithms were used, K nearest neighbor, decision tree, naive Bayes and apriori. Put of which the first two gave a very poor result. On pre-processing the data and using a manual implementation of naive Bayes, good results were obtained but the best result was obtained using apriori algorithm which also gave the probability of occurrence of the disease and possibility of multiple diseases.

DRUG DISCOVERY AND DEVELOPMENT

Drug discovery refers to the process of transforming the idea of a drug from the minds of the scientist or researcher into a tangible product which can be consumed by the human or animal. It can be also called as the process of developing or inventing a drug or medication for a certain disease pertaining to a specific target. Drugs are developed in order to improve the quality of life, longevity, treat disease and relieve suffering. Drug discovery is a very complex process which goes through many stages. It is very time-consuming as it takes around 13-15 years on an average to deliver a drug successfully to market. Drug discovery not only needs the knowledge f chemists, biologists, biochemists but rather it requires multidisciplinary expertise and involves considering many domains until its delivery to the consumers and further successful marketing and monitoring. The traditional drug discovery methods were either based on modifying traditional remedies or serendipity but modern methods involve innovative approaches. Drug discovery is a very costly affair and consumes a lot of resources compared to the successes of the drugs being developed. It takes 3.5-4 billion USD on an average to bring a drug to the market which consists of all the costs involved on failed compounds and tests. It can be seen as one drug being approved and brought to market which further awaits consumer validation and checks out of the 25000 compounds the development process initially started with. Drugs are aimed to prevent, treat, mitigate and relieve pain from human beings (Kapetanovic, 2011).The drug discovery and development consists of the following three phases: -

1. Pre-Discovery
2. Drug Discovery
3. Drug Development

Prediscovery phase can be broken down into: -

- Understanding the Disease
- Target Identification
- Target Validation

In this phase, the various kinetic, chemical and biological reactions due to the disease are studied. It requires detailed knowledge of the physiological, biochemical and pathological mechanisms of disease. Understanding how the cause enters and body and effects the system is very necessary to detect the target and develop the counter mechanism in order to fight it. Then this phase comes to target identification. Component of the disease chosen as target assuming a modification of the target will modify the disease. An effective target is chosen out of the many in the disease and is then verified in the step called target validation. It is validated that the target does the necessary job as when modified. Out of the many possible targets, the one chosen is validated to modify the disease pathology.

The next stage is **drug discovery** which can be further broken down into the following stages:

- Lead generation
- Lead optimization
- Pre-Clinical trials

Lead generation refers to the generation of a lead compound, a compound which acts on the target and has the potential to become a new drug. Thus lead generation refers to identifying the potential compound as a drug. A researcher can find out lead compounds in the following ways: -

- General Screening: A library of compounds is selected and each one is tested for activity on the target
- Molecular Modification: Slight modification in existing compounds results into production of new lead compounds
- Clinical observation: Observations in the clinic sometimes lead to the discovery of new drugs
- Serendipity: Chance or accidental discovery of lead compounds. Traditionally this method was used for drug discovery.

All the leads compounds chosen undergo early safety tests, where they are tested for various aspects and functionality and prioritized accordingly. Some lead compounds might not contain all the characteristics and qualities required to be transformed into a drug, lead optimization refers to the addition of these characteristics into the leads in order for them to have all the required characteristics and function effectively. Thus molecular modification is carried out that affects the properties of the molecules and this is how molecules are optimized for conversion into drugs. The next stage consists of the testing of chosen lead compounds in clinics in order to check their fitness for testing in human beings. They are tested on human and animal cells, tissues and models. The tests determine pharmacokinetics, systemic toxicity studies, and various others such studies (Williams, 2015).On successful passing of all previous phases, comes the drug development phase. This phase includes (1) Clinical trails (2) Regulatory Approvals.On successful passing of pre-clinical tests, investigational new drug (IND) application is filed. This application is for seeking permission for testing of the drug on humans. This Investigational new drug (IND) application includes details of manufacturing information, details on origin and formulation of the drug, preclinical results, the action of the drug and the mechanism of its working, possible side effects, details of target and details of clinical trial on whom, when and how it is to be tested. After receiving permission for clinical trials, trials begin. The trials take place in the following stages: -

- Clinical Trial Phase 1
- Clinical Trial Phase 2
- Clinical Trial Phase 3
- Regulatory Authority Approval of Marketing Application
- Phase 4 Clinical Trial & Post Marketing Monitoring

The phase 1 clinical trial consists of tests which mainly determines the safety and side effects. Its non-therapeutic trial. In this phase, we determine the necessary doses and the side effects of the same. This test is conducted on a small number of people of both the genders. Successful conduction of phase 1 tests, drives to phase 2 clinical tests. The patient pool widens and this time may include some people affected by the disease. This stage determines the therapeutic effects of the drug and the effective dose range. This study is limited to 3-4 centers. Safety is highlighted upon and short term side effects are monitored. Successful conduction of phase 2 tests, drives to phase 3 where safety still remains the concern but the patient pool further widens. The test is conducted in multiple centers. The ability of the drug to produce the desired effects or meet the expectations it majorly tested. Successful conduction of phase 3 tests indicates moving on to marketing approval. If the drug meets its requirements, fulfills its duties, has no critical side effects and is safe, it is then ready to be marketed. Successful conduction of the tests, NDA in filed and FDA reviews and approves the application if it passes the necessary criteria. The regulatory authorities weigh the benefits and risks of the drug. If approved the drug is labeled and marketed. It is then under long term surveillance, as being used by the consumers and is evaluated for any new indications and feedback.

All these processes of drug discovery and development take around 13-15 years, but recently computational methods are increasingly used to innovate the processes and generate efficient results prone to less failure compared to using traditional methods. Machine learning is increasingly used in stages of drug discovery and development as they involve a huge degree of prediction, machine learning models are used for such purposes and help in reduction of failure rates by using computational models to screen the compounds, predict their structure, activities, likely targets, drug likeliness, perform safety tests and also used in fields like chemical genetics and many other such applications (Wale, 2011). Figure 8 illustrates the drug discovery and development timeline.

According to Rifaioglu et al., 2018 machine learning is increasingly used in virtual screening of molecules, which involves the prediction of compounds for drug likeliness. The experimental screening process is tiresome, labor-intensive and costly and nevertheless, have higher chances of failure than in silico methods. Virtual screening is essentially computational methods to derive significant and unknown target compound interaction using the previous and validated biological information of the compound and the protein along with their known chemical and physico structure and function information. Since this involves a degree of the predictive outcome, machine learning techniques are increasingly used to get a better prediction on the available data. Computational models are used to analyze the compounds for their structure and activity and rank them in order of their drug likeliness. Compounds crossing a certain threshold are then called to be preferable or active. For a novel compound, the output class is

Figure 7. Drug discovery & development timeline

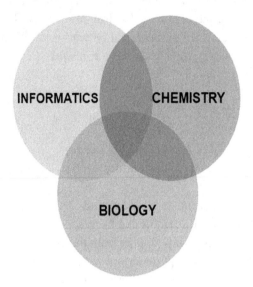

predicted using computational models called structure activity relationship (SAR) or structure property relationship (SPR). some reference compounds are also added in order to aid the computer to learn the models better and filter out compounds unlikely to be drugs. Learning methods such as artificial neural networks, support vector machines, naive Bayes classification methods, decision trees, as well as others like random forest techniques are used. Application of these methods also requires effective cleaning and preparation of data for the corresponding machine learning model. Virtual screening is analogous to high throughput screening (HTS). it refers to the filtering or classifying of compounds based upon their activity or property in silico. High throughput screening stands with many chances of failure and error due to a large amount of data whereas using machine learning and computational models in virtual screening, a small subset from the database is used and the compounds are ranked accordingly and thus using these ranks a threshold value is utilized in order to ultimately classify them. But recent developments are also aiming at mirroring High throughput screening and ranking compounds in large datasets (Melville, Burke, & Hirst, 2009). Application of simple to complex rules like QSAR, Lipinsky are also employed. Out of all the supervised learning methods used, support vector machines turned out to outperform all others. Ning & Karypis (2011) highlights the use of support vector machines in drug discovery. In this paper support vector machine and artificial neural network was tested for different datasets and SVMs projected better results than ANN, also highly depending upon the description of the compounds. It projected the resultant higher accuracy using support vector machines compared to artificial neural networks. A reason why support vector machines outperformed others is that they have many parameters that can be tuned according to the dataset in order to get the optimum results. Artificial neural networks were used in computational models but owing to their setbacks like their "black box" nature, which hinders one from interpreting the actual model, the risk of ANNs modeling the dataset too closely and learning the noise in the data, is some reason SVMs outperformed them. They are in the least as much as powerful as ANNs.

Figure 8. Chemogenomics

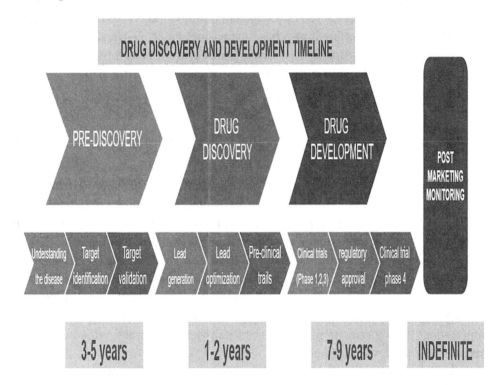

Machine learning is also being increasingly used in chemogenomics where machine learning is used to learn more about the target and the target families which in turn leads to better drug discovery. Chemogenomics is the interaction of the three fields of chemistry, informatics, and biology as shown in figure 7. It involves studying the data available for understanding the targets and focuses on ligands, targets or both in the field of drug discovery. Machine learning in chemogenomics involves learning the biological and structural relationship between the target proteins and compounds. It involves two things: (1) The representation of biological and chemical data and their interaction & (2) The learning methods in order to study their relationship for structure activity relationship model, using which the predictability of new targets from the same is calculated (Ning & Karypis, 2011). Among other applications of machine learning in drug discovery and development, target fishing has huge potential to advance the process of drug discovery using computational models and tools. In silico target, fishing is the interaction of bioinformatics, cheminformatics and machine learning with the sole aim of target identification. Target fishing refers to identifying all possible targets for a drug. A large amount of data generated via various other processes are used in computational methods to generate all likely targets. Based upon models these targets are ranked, and the one most suitable is selected as the drug target owing to their chemical structure, activity and safety attrition. Based on the previously learned target ligand pairs as training data, the machine learning model predicts the target likeliness for a novel compound. Target fishing is performed either on the basis of chemical similarity, similar structure prediction based upon the biological activity or panel docking. In silico target fishing methods are used as a complementary consensus to experimental methods in case they generate multiple targets to reach a common decision (Wang & Xie, 2014). Machine learning is also been increasingly used in detecting the safety of drugs. Many drugs are pulled off from the market, the development process halts for some drugs and incurs a lot of costs. Machine learning models can determine the toxicity and safety measures.

MEDICAL DATA ANALYSIS

Data collected is of no use if insights are not drawn from them and actions taken.

Medical data is a broad aspect. It comprises of various kinds of clinical data. Medical data is complex and takes a long time to gather. One might visit a hospital for a regular check-up of his heart rate but even this data holds very crucial significance and potential. Medical data comprises of clinical data that is patient records which in turn comprises of patient information like gender, age, name, and their visit-related information like the diagnosed disease, prescription, tests, heart rate, blood pressure, body temperature, and various other factors. It also comprises of the test results which can be either in the form of scanned images like X- rays, Citi - scans or in the form of text like written reports. The information comprises of vital signs in the form of numeric representation, diagnosis-related data and finally the treatment information. It comprises of various omics data (chemogenomics, proteomics, etc), medical and health records data (Ristevski & Chen, 2018).

Electronic health records are one of the most convenient forms of data storage of clinical data. It is a computerized representation of a patient's health data and information comprising of all related data to the patient in digital form. Apart from patient data, medical data also comprises administrative information about the clinic, the health surveys, patient registry, and readmission information, information about the staff and doctors, clinical research data. Medical data can be unstructured, discrete and in complex forms.

What is the potential of this data?

Healthcare providers have the task to provide the best medical facilities and services to its patients, reduce the costs associated, manage the staff and infrastructure, check if all the government norms and safety requirements are meant and thus maintain a balance between the various dynamics involved. This data has the potential to make the working better by systemic analysis and interpretation gathered from this data. Useful analytic gathered from this data can be used to improve the internal working of the medical institution. Such analytics is also used by businesses to develop gadgets and applications for users to track their personal well-being at their ends. Such analytic also help in studying the spread of diseases and thus enabling appropriate research for their treatment. Also such insights help in bridging the gap between the cost and the services as well as mishandling of patients and mishappening in treatments. "Actionable insights" must be drawn from the data in order to bridge the gap between costs and services and for better business and service outcomes. Data is just raw facts and figures without any revelation that drives change and innovation coming from them. Furthermore, the data shall not only be used to get valuable information but also as an answer to questions (Dykes, 2016). Application of machine learning, big data analysis requires pre-processing a cleaning of this large data set. This is necessary as this data involves missing values, bigger dimension, and other technical issues. Pre-processing is done on the data before gathering any analytics by filling the missing values with any calculated numerical value like the mean or with zeroes. It also involves preserving the privacy of the patient by making necessary changes. Relevant features are then selected to perform the necessary analysis of the data. Data analysis can be done using supervised, unsupervised or ensemble learning. Supervised learning involves training the machine with labeled data and correcting if the wrong prediction is made on receiving the test data. Thus it involves a teacher teaching the machine and correcting it every time it makes a mistake. Supervised learning is used in medical image analysis. The scanned image of a brain can be fed into a system to recognize pattern using supervised learning in order to detect brain tumors. In unsupervised learning, there is no error correction or teacher involved, the model learns the patterns in the underlying data itself and forms a cluster of data having a similar pattern. An example can be the classification of thyroid patients into three clusters using unsupervised learning (Albayrak, 2003). Ensemble learning refers to a combination of multiple learning models in order to generate better predictive models. It is been observed that ensemble classifiers do give better accuracy in medical data diagnosis in some cases but in some other cases, it is better if not proposed (Srimani & Koti, 2013). Girija & Shashidhara (2012) uses data mining techniques on the medical data on women uterine fibroids. This condition involves risk in women uterus. The paper uses the WEKA 3.7.5 tool to implement classification into three categories using decision tree J48 algorithm. Meaningful insights were drawn as a result of this research and it was concluded that women are not aware of the risks involved. Machine learning and deep learning techniques can be applied to a huge amount of administrative data from hospitals in order to optimize staff allocation. Efficient staff allocation will ensure greater care and better services to the patients. Allocating and managing hospital staff is an important aspect of hospital management as less staff may cause risks in patient care and treatment and overstaffing may results in higher costs. Using data analytics and big data techniques previous databases can be used to derive predict the daily inflow of patients. This method has been used in four hospitals in Paris using the data from 10 years. Daily prediction of the model resulted in an 80 - 90 percent accuracy. Time series forecasting methods were used to detect patterns in the collected data on the inflow of patients. Once a technique is identified, machine learning models can be used to make necessary future predictions on the inflows and readmission. Accordingly, staffing can be managed and necessary services and doctors can be allocated at times needed. Using technology as data analytics gives businesses a competitive edge over others. The presently big four product based companies use data analytics in every aspect of their business in order to increase customer engagement and satisfaction. Such use of analytics in healthcare is just as important for the sector to advance and provide better and optimized services to its customers. Technologies like big data, data mining and machine learning are used in order for the data in these industries including healthcare to make sense. Those using these data and deriving necessary analysis and taking appropriate actions are the ones providing better, efficient and customer curated services (Reddy & Mathew, 2018).

CONCLUSION & FUTURE SCOPE

With the advent of machine learning, it has affected almost all the industries. The medical industry is no such exception. Machine learning tools and techniques are used in almost all possible application in the healthcare industry, optimizing processes and methods and thus giving efficient and consumer-oriented results. All across the world, these technologies are affecting the way the medical industry affects our daily lives. Starting from the first stage of treatment, that is diagnosing to analyzing the data gathered from the patients, machine learning, and artificial intelligence has affected these processes to generate efficient outcomes, and valuable insights, thus exhibiting conductive actions to be taken. The future is being shaped by wearable gadgets. These gadgets are personalized according to one's needs and they employ certain technology to track the user's health and well-being. This data is too collected by the medical industry to analyze and develop better devices as well as assist professionals in the field using the data. Evidently, to utilize these technologies to their full potential, necessary data must be available. Gathering data is one of the most challenging and crucial tasks in the medical industry. It is associated with aspects like patient privacy, data security and most importantly the consent of a patient. There is thus a need to develop an efficient and conducive method to collect data from the health centers. Given the data, the next challenge that befalls the way is having a structured universal framework or format for this data. Medical data comes from a variety of sources and forms like text, scanned images, signals, etc. This data can be structured or unstructured in form. It is sometimes either continuous or discrete. There is no formal method to organize this data and no global format to structure it. So it hinders in the process of sharing the data among concerned bodies. It also affects their storage. There is an immediate need in this industry to have a global framework like a digital health record system to gather and structure the data in order to help bodies effectively share and communicate among themselves using this data also making its effective utilization and analysis. A universal framework or tool will make the information available to all and further help in research and sharing in the domain also taking into account the privacy and safety concerns. One opportunity that lies ahead is the prescribed use of wearables under the watch of a professional. It is the idea of a professional suggesting a personalized gadget to the patient to track his well-being, this idea can be furthered by tracking the data generated by these devices and using professional opinion upon it. There are incidents reported where doctors have made wrong predictions during diagnosis or prognosis, using a system utilizing past data using machine learning models to predict based upon the symptoms can help the doctors cross-check their prediction and avoid any miscalculation. Telemedicine holds a lot of future potentials. This technology is very important in terms of how the medical profession and the patient communicate. If effectively implemented it can help in providing health services at remote areas and at the patient's convenience. Without having to physically visit the health center for treatment can be a great step forward for this industry. This can compensate for the expensive expansion of hospitals at places to meet the basic health and consultation needs.

Thus the medical industry is utilizing the potential of machine learning but there is yet a lot to bring into active operation. This industry awaits the aforementioned future prospects in order to take a step forward to provide better facilities and reduce the cost and risks involved.

REFERENCES

Aggarwal, V. (2019). *Indian Healthcare Industry Analysis*. Retrieved from https://www.ibef.org/industry/healthcare-presentation

Ahuja, R., & Solanki, A. (2019). Movie Recommender System Using K-Means Clustering AND K-Nearest Neighbor. In *9th International Conference on Cloud Computing, Data Science & Engineering*. Amity University. DOI: 10.1109/CONFLUENCE.2019.8776969

Albayrak, S. V. (2003). Unsupervised Clustering Methods for Medical Data: An Application to Thyroid Gland Data. In *Proceedings of Joint International Conference of ICANN/ICONIP*. Istanbul, Turkey: ICANN. 10.1007/3-540-44989-2_83

Brigl, B. (2006). Decision support, knowledge representation and management: A broad methodological spectrum. Findings from the Decision Support, Knowledge Representation and Management. *Yearbook of Medical Informatics*, *45*(01), 81–83. PMID:17051299

Brownlee, J. (2015). *Basic Concepts in Machine Learning*. Retrieved from https://bit.ly/2HT3qTC

Dasgupta, A., & Deb, S. (2008). Telemedicine: a new horizon in public health in India. *Indian Journal of Community Medicine*, *33*(1), 3–8.

Dhunay, N. (n.d.). *Deep Learning and the human brain: Inspiration, not Limitation*. Retrieved from https://www.imaginea.com/sites/deep-learning-human-brain-inspiration-not-imitation/

Dykes, B. (2016). *Actionable Insights: The Missing Link Between Data And Business Value*. Retrieved from https://bit.ly/2WFek2z

Gabutt, A. C. (2015). *Using deep learning to analyze genetic mutations: an interview with Brendan Frey*. Retrieved from https://bit.ly/2Uolrz4

Girija, D. K., & Shashidhara, M. S. (2012). Classification of Women Health Disease (Fibroid) Using Decision Tree algorithm. *International Journal of Computer Applications in Engineering Sciences*, *2*(03), 205–209.

Kapetanovic, I. M. (2011). *Drug Discovery and Development: Present and Future*. Rijeka, Croatia: InTech. doi:10.5772/1179

Kavitha, R. (2012). Healthcare Industry in India. *International Journal of Scientific and Research Publication*, *2*(8), 1–4.

Melville, J. L., Burke, E. K., & Hirst, J. D. (2009). Machine Learning in Virtual Screening. *Combinatorial Chemistry & High Throughput Screening*, *12*(4), 332–343. doi:10.2174/138620709788167980 PMID:19442063

Mohammad, Q., & Gupta, M. (2017). *Advances in AI and ML are reshaping healthcare*. Retrieved from https://techcrunch.com/2017/03/16/advances-in-ai-and-ml-are-reshaping-healthcare/

Murphy, J. (2019). *Best Global Brand 2018 Rankings*. Retrieved from https://bit.ly/2O0XCuG

Ning, X., & Karypis, G. (2011). In Silico Structure-Activity-Relationship (SAR) Models From Machine Learning: A Review. Drug Development Research, 138-146.

Pandey & Solanki. (2019). Music Instrument Recognition using Deep Convolutional Neural Networks. International Journal of Information Technology. doi:10.100741870-019-00285-y

Parthiban, G., & Srivatsa, S. K. (2012). Applying Machine Learning Methods in Diagnosing Heart Disease for Diabetic Patients. *International Journal of Applied Information Systems*, *3*(07), 25–30. doi:10.5120/ijais12-450593

Parvathi, I., & Rautaray, S. (2014). Survey on Data Mining Techniques for the Diagnosis of Diseases in Medical Domain. *International Journal of Computer Science and Information Technologies*, *5*(1), 838–846.

Polikar, R. (2009). Ensemble Learning. *Scholarpedia.*, *4*(1), 2776. doi:10.4249cholarpedia.2776

Press, G. (2017). *Top 10 Hot Artificial Intelligence Technologies.* Retrieved from https://bit.ly/2YM2x4H

Priyadharshini, K. (2019). *Machine Learning: What is it and Why it Matters.* Retrieved from https://bit.ly/2ezVTs8

Rai, A. (2018). *These 6 Machine Learning Techniques Are Improving Healthcare.* Retrieved from https://bit.ly/2YJsu4y

Razia, S., Prathyusha, P. S., Krishna, N. V., & Sumana, N. S. (2017). A Review on Disease Diagnosis Using Machine Learning Techniques. *International Journal of Pure and Applied Mathematics*, *117*(16), 79–85.

Reddy, D., & Mathew, S. (2018). *Revolutionizing healthcare analytics through artificial intelligence and machine learning.* Retrieved from https://bit.ly/2JZbc07

Rifaioglu, A. S., Atas, H., Martin, M. J., Atalay, R. C., Atalay, V., & Dogan, T. (2018). Recent applications of deep learning and machine intelligence on in silico drug discovery: Methods, tools and databases. *Briefings in Bioinformatics*, 1–36. PMID:30084866

Ristevski, B., & Chen, M. (2018). Big Data Analytics in Medicine and Healthcare. *Journal of Integrative Bioinformatics*, 1–5. PMID:29746254

RouseM. (2018). *Telemedicine.* Retrieved from https://bit.ly/2Ah4hs1

Sivanandam, S. N., & Deepa, S. N. (2011). *Principles of Soft Computing.* New Delhi, India: Wiley.

Srimani, P. K., & Koti, M. S. (2013). Medical Diagnosis Using Ensemble Classifiers - A Novel Machine-Learning Approach. *Journal of Advanced Computing*, *1*, 9–27.

Sunny, A.D., Kulshreshtha, S., & Singh, S., Srinabh, B. M., & Sarojadevi, H. (2018). Disease Diagnosis System By Exploring Machine Learning Algorithms. *International Journal of Innovations in Engineering and Technology*, *10*(2), 14–21.

Wale, N. (2011). *Machine Learning in Drug Discovery and Development.* Wiley. doi:10.1002/ddr.20407

Wang, L., & Xie, X. Q. (2014). Computational Target Fishing: What Should Chemogenomics Researchers Expect For the Future of in Silico Drug Design and Discovery? *Editorial Special Focus: Computational Chemistry*, *6*(3), 247–249. PMID:24575960

Williams, S. (2015). *The Drug Development Process: 9 Steps From the Laboratory to Your Medicine Cabinet.* Retrieved from https://bit.ly/2Ebgfrr

Chapter 20
Machine Learning in Video Games

Jayakumar Kaliappan

https://orcid.org/0000-0002-6044-6667

Vellore Institute of Technology, Vellore, India

Karpagam Sundararajan

Spectrum Info Tech, India

ABSTRACT

Machine learning is a part of artificial intelligence in which the learning was done using the data available in the environment. Machine learning algorithms are mainly used in game development to change from presripted games to adaptive play games. The main theme or plot of the game, game levels, maps in route, and racing games are considered as content. Context refers to the game screenplay, sound effects, and visual effects. In any type of game, maintaining the fun mode of the player is very important. Predictable moves by non-players in the game and same type of visual effects will reduce the player's interest in the game. The machine learning algorithms works in automatic content generation and non-payer character behaviours in gameplay. In pathfinding games, puzzle games, strategy games adding intelligence to enemy and opponents makes the game more interesting. The enjoyment and fun differs from game to game. For example, in horror games, fun is experienced when safe point is reached.

MACHINE LEARNING

Machine learning is a subset of AI, it doesn't need any human intervention. It learns by themselves from the set of data in the working environment. It can flexibly change the algorithms as they learn more about the information they are processing. Machine learning is now used in most of the equipment to improve their performance. It is used in medical diagnosis, speech processing, image processing, statistical arbitrage, learning associations, classification, prediction, extraction, and financial services.

DOI: 10.4018/978-1-5225-9643-1.ch020

NEED FOR MACHINE LEARNING IN GAME DEVELOPMENT

Algorithms Playing As Nonplayer Characters

When playing with pre-scripted Non-Playable-Characters (NPC), there won't be any surprises and it makes the game boring, but a machine learning-based NPC gives you a challenging playground with unpredictable foes. In the machine learning algorithm, Non-Player Characters (NPC) behavior are used to optimize the dynamic difficulty adjustment feature. Avoiding the hard coding of Non-Player characters would reduce the development cycle time from days to hours. NPC's will become smarter and smarter when more about data the player's behavior on the particular NPC is gathered.

Modelling Complex Systems

The machine-learning algorithm has a high ability to model complex systems which make games to be more impressive and realistic. To bring in the realistic environment, the players' emotions and the audience reactions were learned from the real games and it will get applied in our game at required points. Machine learning algorithms are able to predict the downstream effects of player actions. The FIFA game is the most successful game in modeling the complex system. In this, a team's chemistry is calculated based on the number of players go along with each other.

Making Games More Beautiful

The game scenes have to be designed attractive according to human vision the objects in the distance will not be clearer, but when it is brought into the nearer focus the clarity of the object increases. Computer vision algorithm powered with machine learning is in development so that the real-time, dynamic rendering of images with high clarity is viewed.

More Realistic Interactions

The real environment will be created, when the player is able to communicate with the NPC's in a natural way. It will improve the fun level and the involvement of the player also. In video games, the techniques used by the player to interact with his speech or the body movements, which mimic the same task used in the real world are called Natural interaction techniques. With the help of natural language processing, voice-based interaction with the NPC's can be done. In some games, the story is designed to get some secrets from the friendly NPCs after crossing the levels. This interaction will be script formatted, but to make it very real the voice-based communication can be used. Like Alexa and Google Assistant more friendly atmosphere is created. When there is a use of a sword in a game, when swinging of the sword is done in a natural way with hand movements it will be interesting rather than searching for a button click.

Universe Creation on the Fly

The most loved video games, nowadays are the games where the player enjoy exploring the massive landscape. Machine learning algorithms operate in this open-world designs to solve the struggles in finding the path and in improvising world creation mechanisms. Machine learning algorithms could help with pathfinding and world creation. Endless games are created in real-time. The new environment creation is based on player profiles and values. So the contents are created which fits in to the respective user's profiles. Hence every player will get attracted into the game and also enjoy the game.

More Engaging Mobile Games

As the power of the hardware in mobile phones continues to improve, making mobile gaming more realistic, interactive, and immersive with machine learning will be an easier job. Reducing the game space is very important and this is possible with machine learning. The machine learning algorithms are able to produce novel contents, unlike the pre-scripted games which will depict only the contents that are previously loaded into the game memory.

MACHINE LEARNING GAMES VS PRESCRIPT GAMES

In a predefined script, the personalized game settings cannot be done and the nature of the game is predictable. Adaptive gameplay is designed to overcome the above-mentioned pitfalls and makes the game more challenging, appealing and hence maintains the player's attention. The game designers get input for the player's preference profiles and tried to create content based on this to improve the game fun (Sehrawat, & Raj, 2018). But this was not much success because this couldn't be implemented for a large population.

Dynamic difficulty adjustment is possible in games using machine learning techniques. When the difficulty levels of the contents are created and implemented at runtime. Based on the player's playing capability, it is called dynamic difficulty adjustment. In this, a heuristic function or a challenging function is constructed and its value gives you the difficulty level of your game. The challenge function value is based on their current game status, the number of successful hits, the number of life points, the number of badges collected, etc.

The production cost, developer's efforts and development time all are very high in content generation for video games. The content generation is divided into functional content generation and cosmetic content generation. In a functional content generation, the contents like game level maps, storyline decoration, the card's behavior etc. are done. In a cosmetic content generation, the visual and sound effects for the non-player characters are done. In the future, this will be of greater importance because of its reduced development time and development are done online with machine learning reduces the storage space also.

SERIOUS GAME VS COMMERCIAL GAME

Serious games refer to educational games and their design involves the adaptation of content and context. They concentrate on the knowledge transfer to the players so they have to balance between the learning, anxiety, boredom, and fun. In the case of commercialization, the complete focus is on creating more fun for the players.

Section 2: Explains about the terminologies used in game development, coding stages and machine learning techniques used in coding.

The next section moves towards the implementation concepts of machine learning in game development. The basic terminologies used in game development like NPC, different types of agents are explained. The pros and cons of inclusion of machine learning in the design stage and running stage are discussed.

TERMINOLOGIES USED IN GAME DEVELOPMENT

The machine learning process can be included in the game at two different stages. One is learning at design-time or offline period, where the results of learning are applied before publishing the game; the other is learning at runtime or online period, fitted to a particular player or game session.

Examples Of Learning At Design-Time:

The game City Conquest uses ML to guide the design and to balance the game units.

Examples Of Learning At Runtime:

- Black and White video game developed by Lion studios follows learning at runtime. The player takes the role of god and they teach the other creature NPC in the game. The player teaches how to eat, attack and defend. Whenever the player's pet creature learns correctly, it is rewarded and punishments are given for its mistake. The creatures' learning and their decision-making processes are done using the Belief–desire–intention model.
- The story plot of the game creature's series is to raise the alien's creatures. The other name for the alien creature is Norns. The Norn don't know any skills, they are just like a newborn baby. The player has to teach them how to survive and defend against the other dangerous species, how to breed, etc. The players help them in exploring the world. The above activities are done by the neural network learning and a hormonal system that controlled the entity. Since the learning is based on biological and neurological behavior, it gives many unexpected results. Emotional bonding between the player and the creature gets developed as the game progress. And this emotional bonding development is also one of the success requirement of the game.
- Forza Motorsports is a simulation racing video game. In this game, the simulation of driving is done i.e. a drivatar is created by training. Now, this drivatar can imitate the player's play. It plays the player's match as a proxy and gets ranked.

Automatic ML application to games is yet another growing field. In automatic data collection and analysis, the design perceptive such as combined with manual operation, human interpretation and application were deeply studied, for example:

- Level heatmaps, used by action games such as Halo. Such a strong opponent on the battlefield is created using behavior trees.
- Zynga free-to-play game makers collect data from gameplay to model the game player.

Figure 1. Learning environment model by Unity

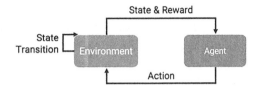

LEARNING ENVIRONMENT

Through machine learning, the autonomous agents were made intelligent through interactions in the training environment. Previously it was coded by hand. The core idea is to tightly couple the learning agent and the training environment. Based on the actions of the agent the environment is changed and the rewards are given based on this. Unity had given the model of the autonomous agent.

A typical learning environment model given by Unity is given in Fig 1.

In the beginning, the environment is specifically available in a specific state s that executes an action a in order to change the state into s'. To explore this exact action effectively, the instant reward is calculated r. Future rewards denote the rewards obtained from the environment for the same action a. The Q-function termed as $Q(s,a)$ will give you the total of immediate and future awards that can be collected by you in state s with action a'.

$$Q(s,a) = r + \gamma * Q(s',a') s \qquad (1)$$

Where:

s – state

a – action in state s

γ – the discount factor for uncertainty in predicting the future.

The three main parts of a machine learning environment are agent, brain, and academy.

Agent – Character acting on the environment.

Brain - controls the actions of the agents

Academy - Only one per environment, it controls all settings in the environment.

Definition of Agent

The agentis the characters that act on the environment. An agent studies its environment through sensors and acts on it through effectors. All the agents are given the freedom of actions with some constraints on what the agent is to produce. The agent should be autonomous, proactive and reactive. The brain of the agent decides its action.

Definition of Brain

The brain is responsible for each and every action executed by its linked agent. The brain is designed to have two components, a specific state definition, and action space reservation. The brain can be operated in four different modes. In mode one, the action decisions are made by the Machine learning algorithm of your choice, hence it is termed as an external mode. The second one is an internal mode or experimental mode. In this, a trained model embedded in the project is used to provide action-based decisions. The third mode is player mode, where action decisions are made using player input. The fourth mode is heuristic that uses hand-coded behavior to complete the action-based decisions.

Academy

For each environment, there is one academy. The work of the academy is to define the environment scope based on the factors like engine configuration, frame skips, and episode length. The academy object for each scene holds all brain within the environment as children.

- The engine configuration object deals with the speed and rendering quality of the game engine in both training and inference modes.
- Frame skip object deals with a number of engine steps that can be made by an agent before it is resetting itself.
- Global episode length deals with the time period the episode will last when all the agents are set to be done.

FACTORS TO CONSIDER WHEN CREATING A LEARNING AGENT

Adaptable games performance depends on the learning agent that has been raised. A learning agent comprises the element of learning, the performance component, an element which piques curiosity, and a critic to examine the performance.

The Learning Element

Learning element is concerned with modifying the behavior of the system. Basically, if there is a new skill to be learned, this element ensures that such an advance is acquired by the agent.

The Performance Element

The performance element is able to generate input or receive information from the system. It then takes decisions based on the input received. For example, in a game is if there is an obstacle when moving from point A to point B, then the performance element is concerned with the obstacles and how the agent will make the appropriate movement.

The Problem Generator

The problem generator element is the element that generates curiosity or problems for the agent to navigate.

The Critic

The critic is also known as the performance analyzer, it concentrates on measuring the performance of the strategies of the system. It measures how well the system achieves the stipulated objectives. This is mostly measured with respect to a given threshold and after analysis, the performance analyzer has to determine if there are improvements that can be made in the future.

PROCEDURAL CONTENT GENERATION (PCG)

Game development is a very complex process because it involves the development of a lot of artifacts. The various artifacts in development are game environments, the plot, the features of each character and many more. The process is labor-intensive and incurs a heavy cost. The gaming industry works on many new machine learning techniques to reduce production costs and to speed up game development.

Procedural content generation (PCG) is a major work area in game development. Procedural content generation refers to the automatic creation of levels, maps, weapons, stories, dialogues and decorative aspects like background scenery like terrain, vegetation, and music for computer games (Adam Summerville, Sam Snodgrass, &Matthew Guzdial, 2017). To create a very good, competent content, intelligent generative methods with high-quality design knowledge is used. In most of the cases, the design knowledge is provided in the form of hand-coded heuristics or evaluation functions. The drawback of the Hand-coded heuristics and evaluation functions is procedural content generation is that it has some belief or hard rules on what makes a particular type of content good. But this will be get biased to the beliefs of the particular system designer. Instead of that, it is better to extract the design knowledge from the game itself. For example, when the system parses through the game level files, it can extract level design patterns. Procedural content generation with machine learning means the content generation with machine learning models that does the learning from the existing content.

The three main reasons for the application of PCG with machine learning to the game development and maintenance of the games are:

1. The first reason is to reduce the total space of the game, memory space reduction is an important constraint in many platforms. Mainly in mobile platforms, space reduction plays a major role. So there is a need for a technique to produce content that was not part of the deployed game software. The PCG generated by applying compression or programmatic approaches can save an important amount of space.
2. The second reason is the high complexity involved in manually producing the game contents. The need for writing complex codes and the search for the new design templates can be replaced by the use of automatic support and design tools. To produce a game environment like levels, maps, scenery, non-player character position and movements. These tools reduce the production time involved in the development of massive open worlds which will need to setup large sets of this kind of content in their scenarios.

3. The third reason to apply PCG to game development is the possibility of creating completely new game content, even in real-time, where it is possible to create endless games. The design parameters are characterized by certain values that are tracked by the particular player's play style creation.

These techniques applied to the automatic creation of game content is referred to as Procedural Content Generation. The contents developed ranges from non-player characters (NPC) to scenarios. The scenario set includes aspects such as terrain, maps, levels, stories, dialogues, quests, characters, rule-sets, dynamics, and game items. The potential benefits obtained from this is potentially infinite content was getting without having to design it by hand. Since the content generation is done at run time it can also help reduce storage space demands.

There are many AI-based procedural content generation methods like solver-based, search-based, and grammar-based methods. But the main usage of Machine learning techniques is in an autonomous generation, cocreation/mixed-initiative design, and data compression. PCGML get rid of the complicated steps done by experts in coding their design knowledge and intentions

Rogue-like games demands for the online or runtime content generation, so there is a need for the automatic content generation In search based PCG the developer has to design the algorithm for generating the content and then a fitness function to evaluate the newly developed artifact. It follows the generate and test framework. But with Machine learning usage in PCG, a different approach is used. The developer creates a sample of artifacts and feeds this as input to the machine learning algorithm. Then the generator will produce new artifacts based on the above samples.

The co-creation/mixed-initiative design is in its infancy stage of development. In this human and machine works in a closed-loop to create content. Both suggest, creates, evaluates, modifies and then reevaluate. So with a lot of iterations, the problem space is fully explored. In machine learning algorithms the user communicates with the machine in its own language, without the burden of writing programs. So the frustration is minimized, user error is reduced

The repair operation is operated by PCGML to make the game interesting. When there is an unreachable level or a rule which is very hard to follow it can be repaired through PCGML. From its library of existing representative content, PCGML algorithm was able to identify the hurdles in the game. hurdles represent the areas that have too strict rules or maybe a meaningless rule, so the player cannot play in that level. PCML was able to fix it.

The recognition, critique, and analysis of other game content can be done. From the training model of existing game content, it was able to analyze other game content. The previous AI approach uses supervised learning for these, but PCGML does this with unsupervised learning methods.

Nowadays, most of the video games are occupying large storage space and hence this is a major problem to be solved. Most of the game running platforms demands for minimum storage usage. The machine learning can be applied to compress larger game data into smaller data and the game running platforms get efficient game content storage space. The machine learning algorithm make use of the constancy in a large number of content instances for compression and then the distinctive features are stored. Unsupervised learning methods such as autoencoders, PAQ8 can be used in this compression work.

MACHINE LEARNING ALGORITHMS USED IN-GAME TRAINING

In order to maintain the fun and re-playability of computer games the role of a good AI agent is a must. Developing competent AI agents by hand-coding is a difficult and time-consuming task.

The application of AI has been done successfully many games, but that is not a true AI since there is the use of predefined scripts to simulate artificial intelligence. So now the developers are moving to the machine learning algorithm.

Machine learning algorithms under categories like supervised learning, unsupervised learning, and evolutionary computing are used in game development. From the supervised learning category, there are classification algorithms like Hidden Markov Models, Bayesian Network, Markov Logic Networks, Input-Output Hidden Markov Model, Decision Tree, Support Vector Machine, Neural Network, Recursive Neural networks, Long Short-Term Memory Network, Deep learning, K-Nearest Neighbor. And the regression algorithms like linear regression, Regression trees, Additive regression, Logistic regression.

The unsupervised learning algorithms that can be used for clustering are k-means, CURE (Clustering Using Representatives), SOM (Self-Organizing Map), Spectral clustering, LDA (Linear Discriminant Analysis). And evolutionary algorithms like genetic algorithm and particle swarm optimization is used.

MACHINE LEARNING ALGORITHMS IN ONLINE TRAINING

rtNEAT

Real-time Neuro-Evolution of Augmenting Topologies (rtNEAT) is the Neuro evolutionary algorithm which evolves online or real-time. Neuro Evolution of Augmenting Topologies (rtNEAT) method for artificial neural networks with increasing complexity evolved over online or real-time Hence it is used in online game design. The rtNEAT method gives rights to the agents to change and improve during the game. In fact, the player with rtNEAT executes a series of customized training exercises. Teaches a team of agents in a video game. It has originally been created for NERO (Neuro Evolving Robotic Operatives game) where two teams of agents have to be trained for a battle. The better-trained team wins the battle. A team of robots is trained by the player for combat. In NEAT entire population get replaced at every generation. But in rNEAT single individual is replaced with the child of the parent in the best population (Kenneth Stanley, Bobby Bryant, & Risto Miikkulainen, 2005).

Q-Learning

Q-Learning is the reinforcement learning algorithm based on Temporal Difference Learning (Nenad Bojkovski, & Ana Madevska Bogdanova, 2012). The agent learning process is done here. From the learning process the agent was able to deploy an action in the working environment for the given state. Q- Learning problem is modelled with three parameters (Agent involved, set of states, action taken in each state) (Dobrovsky, Borghoff, &Hofmann, 2019). So a Function Q is needed which calculates the quality of state-action combination - Q(s, a) s - state and a - action performed. In traditional algorithms, the input and a target or class label is given and importance was not given to the action taken at each state. But in QLearning, a new system of rewarding was introduced. For each and every action taken at

Figure 2. Multiagent reinforcement learning

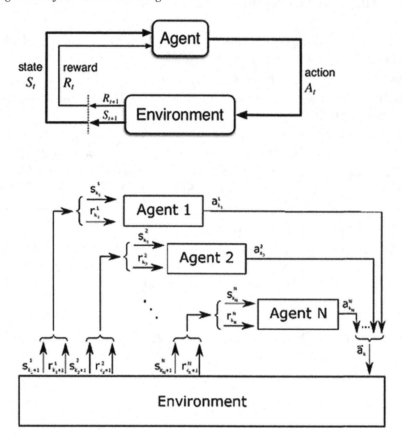

a particular state a reward was assigned. The reward indicates whether the action performed is good or bad. From the rewards the agent learns what to do. It is also used in NERO games.

Multiagent Reinforcement Learning

Most of the video gameplay rules are not based on a single agent, usually, a multiagent is involved in it. There is a need for models that include multiple agents that learn by dynamically interacting with their environment. Multiagent Reinforcement Learning (MARL) is designed to serve the purpose. MARL environment as a tuple {X1-A1, X2-A2…. Xn-A}, where Xm is any given agent and Am, is any given action, then the new state of the environment is the result of the set of joint actions defined by A1xA2x…. An. In other words, the complexity of MARL scenarios increases with the number of agents in the environment.

Hamlet

Playing video games becomes boring, when the game is very easy to play and it becomes more frustrating when it is hard to play. Video games have the option for selection of difficult levels like easy, medium, hard, etc., but since it is a static one the well versed players easily learn the game environment and succeed in the game. The well versed players need surprises and dynamic changes in the game. To construct dynamic difficulties in a game, Hamlet is used (Nenad Bojkovski, & Ana Madevska Bogdanova, 2012). Hamlet is embedded as a set of libraries in the Half Life game engine. The special statistical metrics are used to evaluate the incoming game data. The library function does the work of monitoring game data and comparing it with the predefined metrics. There are functions to define and execute the adjustment policies. Certain functions helps in control system settings. The aim of the system is to adjust game difficulty on-line to keep the player in the engaged mode. The adjustment actions and adjustment policies are framed. For e.g. FPS game the author (Robin Hunicke, & Vernell Chapman, 2012) had designed adjustment actions as reactive and proactive. For reactive actions the entities that are in game like strength of weapon, life of player are adjusted. In proactive actions the off stage entities that are The adjustment policies are framed as comfort Zone policy and discomfort zone policy. For example in FPS game the comfort zone policy will maintains the average healthline as 50% and occasionally dip it to 25%.In discomfort zone policy the average the health line is maintained around 15%,so the player will be in the edge of the seat.

Particle Swarm Optimization (PSO)

The nature inspired algorithms are very much successful in finding out the optimal solutions for many of the computer science problems. Particle Swarm Optimization (PSO) is built on the social intelligence expressed by bird flocking. PSO is a population-based stochastic optimization technique. There are many similarities between PSO and evolutionary computation techniques such as Genetic Algorithms (Nenad Bojkovski, & Ana Madevska Bogdanova, 2012). Evolutionary algorithms have lot of parameters to adjust, but PSO can be easily implemented. The system is initialized with a population of random solutions and searches for optima in every generations. Izitok Fister in his work had used PSO algorithm to create graphic characters (Iztok Fister, Matjaz˘ Perc, Karin Ljubic, Salahuddin Kamal, &Andres Iglesias, 2015). In his work he had taken a snow man image as a base and then with PSO created many different snow man graphic charater. Joho Antonio (Duro, & de Oliveira, 2008) in his work had developed a chess player agent and compared it with the agent developed using simulated annealing.

Hybrid Learning Approaches

Hybrid approaches, as the name indicates it is the approach of combining two or more machine learning approaches. In most of the video game development, it combines deep learning methods with other machine learning approaches. A famous game developed with the hybrid method is the board game "AlphaGo" that relied on deep neural networks and tree search methods. It was able to defeat the world champion in Go, and that applies planning on top of a predictive model.

Section 3: Describes the famous games developed using machine learning algorithms.

DEEP REINFORCEMENT LEARNING IN FIFA GAME

Deep Reinforcement Learning works by combining Reinforcement learning and neural networks. Neural networks act as function approximators (Dobrovsky, Borghoff, & Hofmann, 2019). In FIFA, with the help of a bunch of codes the NPC's, are made to play like human beings, but the goal is not fully reached.

Figure 3. Deep reinforcement learning in Fifa game

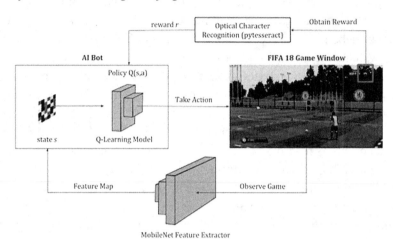

The AI code is not able to match up with a human player. The solution for this is allowing the NPC's to learn from the natural game. There is no need to access the game's internal code. The learning agent will learn it just from the screenshots of the game. A simple screenshot having the visual information is fed into the game engine. The game engine processes the visual information and outputs the moves to be taken at each step.

The development of game intelligence is done as a two-step process.

Step1: The Convolution Neural Network is used to learn the screenshot image. The detection accuracy of CNN (Pandey and Solanki, 2019) is well known. For fast processing in real-time, mobile nets are used. Mobile nets are used for mobile and embedded vision applications.

Step2: Deep Reinforcement Learning (DRL) is used to learn the game and to take the next move at each step of the game. It is an unsupervised learning technique. In Reinforcement Learning (RL), an agent learns a mapping of situations to actions by interaction with and getting a reward from an environment. The Q function discussed in the previous section gives the expected final rewards count due to an action. In DRL this Q function is learned by Deep Neural Network.

For the FIFA game, the author (Chintan Trivedi, 2018) had tried to train the system for free kicks.

States: Screenshot images of the game processed through a MobileNet CNN giving 128-dimensional flattened feature map.

Actions: Four possible actions to take shoot_low, shoot_high, move_left, move_right.

Reward: If upon pressing shoot, in-game score increases by more than 200, we scored a goal so r=+1. If we missed the goal, the score remains the same so r=-1. Finally, r=0 for actions related to moving left or right.

Policy: Two-layered Dense Network that takes the feature map as input and predicts total final reward for all 4 actions.

The average goal-scoring rate grows from 30% to 50% on an average after training for 1000 epochs. This means the current bot scores about half of the free kicks it attempts (for reference, a human would average around 75–80%). Do consider that FIFA tends to behave non-deterministically which makes learning very difficult.

REINFORCEMENT LEARNING IN SUPER MARIO GAME

The primary objective of the Mario game is to cross the levels without dying. The secondary objectives are to collect the coins and kill the enemies. Mario game environment contains a lot of stationary NPCs and moving NPCs. The agents are made to learn about the progress of each and every NPC's at every frame of the gameplay. The stationary NPCs are bricks, borders, hills, flower pots or pipes, cannons or towers. The moving NPC is the enemies. Bricks can release coins or power-ups if hit by large Mario. Borders are the blockage for Mario movements. Mario has to jump up through a hill to cross it, it cannot pass down. Enemy flowers appear periodically from pipes, Mario dies when it is get caught in it. Cannons periodically shoot out flying bullets. There are a lot of enemies with a variety of forms like Goombas, koopas, and their winged and spiky appearance.

Yanzhu (Yanzhu Du, Shisheng Cui, &Stephen Guo 2009) in his work had captured 24 frames in a second. The window size is of 22 X 22.In this 484 squares, the agent has to search for the stationary and moving NPC's mentioned above. The state-space of this problem is 10^{484} complete search is computationally intractable. The mathematical models are used by MDPs for modeling decision-making. It is done in situations where the outcome depends partly on the random change in the outcomes and partly under the control of a decision-maker. The algorithm needs to minimize its search space and design its reward function. Reducing state space improves training efficiency, but it has to be done without losing more information. So Mario's observation window is decomposed to get the following features:

- Status of Mario is found from the movements possible like standing in the ground, jumping, throwing a fireball, etc.
- Tracking two cells that are present directly ahead and behind of Mario
- Tracing out whether there are gaps in front of Mario?
- Finding out the distance of enemies in front of Mario.
- Cell types are classified into four categories as:1) Passable cell 2) Obstacles (bricks, borders, flower pots, cannons) 3) Half-borders 4) Enemies Now the total feature space size is 3*219.

Actions

Mario's actions are restricted to always move to the right. Mario's action space contains these four actions: 1) Right, 2) Right Fast, 3) Right Jump, 4) Right Fast Jump.

Reward Function

A reward function of the form R(S, a) is designed. In this, the low penalty is levied whenever there is random jumping and low reward is given for staying away from enemies and gaps. A high penalty is given for touching the enemy.

Transition Probability Function

This game is mostly deterministic, because of limited visibility of 22x22 window and feature mapping. But the feature space state transition is not deterministic. Therefore, there is a need to learn about empirical transition probabilities to estimate.

Value Function

In the training process, the author formed a form of asynchronous value iteration in order to converge towards the optimal value function of the Bellman equation. The update equation used during training is given below:

$$V(s) := \min_a \left(R(s,a) + \gamma \sum_{s'} P_{sa}(S')V(s') \right) \qquad (2)$$

The game states now considered by the author are the feature states/vectors in feature space, not the original game states. The value function is trained by making the MDP agent get executed on many randomly generated levels and collect statistics about P_{sa}, while updating. Once the training is completed, the MDP agent uses the computed value function V to define a policy π. During gameplay, when the agent is presented with a game state, the state is mapped into a feature vector, which is then given to the policy to determine the next action to be taken.

HYBRID APPROACH USED IN FPS

The 3D environments in first-person shooter games are very difficult to play since it involves partially observable states. A new hybrid approach is designed for learning. A divide and conquer strategy is followed. Lample (Guillaume Lample, &Devendra Singh Chaplot, 2017) in his approach divides the problem into two phases: the navigation phase and an action phase. In the navigation phase, the map is explored to gather objects and detect enemies. In the action phase, the task is to observe the fight happening with the enemies. As per the divide and conquer technique, two networks are used to work out with the action phase and navigation phase. The action network makes use of DRQN augmented with game features. A simple DQN is used in the navigation network. The author had proved that the DQRN loaded with game features, gives a drastic improvement, especially in the games like deathmatch.

During the training phase, with Deep reinforcement learning methods, in order to have natural language communication, only the visual inputs are taken for training. The phase-separated training induces modularity, hence the work is done easily and quickly. In this, the author had presented a method to augment these models. Augmentation of game features represents the details about the visible entities added into the frame. The visibility of entities in a frame is given as a Boolean value, which is added to the frame. The entities can be an enemy, a Weapon, a health pack, ammo, etc. The speciality of this model is, two process are simultaneously done here (i.e.) learning of the features and minimizing a Q-learning objective. This model had shown dramatic improvement in the training speed and performance of the agent.

The author trained two different networks for the agent. Adding game features to DQRN is easier, but with DQN it is a little bit difficult. DRQN with augmented game feature information is designed to detect the enemies accurately in Deathmatch tasks. Whenever the network receives a frame at training time, it receives a boolean value of each entity also. With this boolean value, the author decides whether the entity appears in the frame or not. The action phase is called at each step, when the frame confirms that there are no enemies and no more ammos are left, the navigation phase is invoked.

In the initial model, the score for action is predicted based on its current frame and the hidden state, for this, output of the convolutional neural network (CNN) is passed to an LSTM. Now the design is modified to have two fully-connected layers of size 512 and k get connected to the output of the CNN. k – represents the number of game features to be detected. Here only one feature i.e. enemy alone is needed.

In training, the reward function was shaped to avoid sparse table and late reward problems. When the reward is calculated with the formula of, number of the kills minus number of suicides, the replay table will be extremely sparse. The agent finds difficulty in learning about the favourable actions. The rewards are assigned only when the agent finds an enemy and accurately aims and shoot. Rewards are not assigned for a specific action.

The reward function is shaped to give importance to each and every action and a positive and negative type reward is also added. The positive reward is given, when the player picksup a health, weapon or ammo. The negative reward is given for losing health, unnecessary shooting or for losing ammo. Frameskip is done to accelerate the training phase. Frameskip of $(k+1)$ indicates that it receives a screen input every $(k+1)$ frames. A frameskip of 4 is found to be good so that with good acceleration not a single information is missed out. In the evaluation phase, the action network is invoked at each step. If it was notable to detect any enemies in the current frame, or if the agent is not left out with any ammos, the navigation network is called to decide the next action.

In the next step, DRQN updates are done. A different approach is followed in updation.The updates with history alone ae updated.

PROCEDURE CONTENT GENERATION IN MARIO GAME

Mathew (Matthew Guzdial, &Mark Riedl, 2015) had done three phases of work. In the first phase, getting knowledge about the game level design from the game play videos is done. In the second phase, the probabilistic model for level set up was framed. In third phase, creating new level designs from the acquired knowledge is done.

In the first phase work, the videos of the Mario game are given as input to the OpenCV for processing. Whenever there is a death of Mario, the screen turns to black and it is also considered as level endpoints. So only the video of expert game play where Mario is taken through all levels without dying is taken. The openCV separates it in to frames and learns about the position of sprites and enemies for certain time period. The openCV finds out the players interaction level from the frames in the records having a minimum movements and a maximum movements. The frames with maximum movements are the areas with higher interaction level. A graph of a video's level sections vs intensity values is plotted. Next the categorization is done to identify level sections. Only the high interaction level area are clustered using Kmean ++. With Euclidean measure, sprite and its respective count is noted For e.g. brick is a sprite and the number of bricks in a scene is noted. In underground screen set up, there will be more number

Figure 4. Tree structure

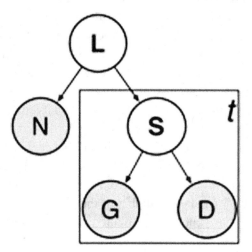

of bricks. The author was able to get the eleven full playthroughs of Super Mario Bros and from this 21 clusters of frames was collected.

From the first phase, design knowledge was gathered. In second phase this design knowledge, is represented using probabilistic model. Kalogerakis's probabilistic model was followed which can generate 3D model from a sample data. The author had used Kalogerakis's model as a baseline and had made some changes in the way of learning and constructing new level designs.

A tree-like structure given in Figure 4 with five major components(Level(L), shape(S), count(N), geometric information(G) and Relational information(D)) is used. The model uses three types of nodes, (G, D, N), to collect observable data from an initial data set, each of which collects unique information. The two latent or hidden nodes are S and L, that are derived from the observed information. The G Node position is shown in the Figure 5 left portion. From the G Node the distance of the sprites from others is shown in Figure 5 right portion.

In the third phase, the probabilistic models of the second level is used to generate new game level sections. The generation algorithm starts with a empty level and after that recursively the (G,D) pairs are created. Two control parameters P_E and P_C are used. P_E controls the level of similarity between older level and the newer level created. The P_C controls the playability of the level. The algorithm stops generating (G,D) pairs when two condition are met. First one is when the sprite count comes equal or closer to N.

The evaluation of this method is done with 20 generated level sections. The content generated is as expected, showing a strong correlation between the values of the variable and generated level playability (Pearson's r coefficient value is obtained as 0.8778).

OBSTACLES IN APPLYING MACHINE LEARNING TO GAME DEVELOPMENT

The first obstacle is query on whether the player will enjoy a strong competitor. When the player plays the game, the computer opponent is made to learn about the moves of the player. This learning process development may be a difficult task, but whether it is ok to do so is a great query. When the computer

Figure 5. Procedure content generation in Mario game

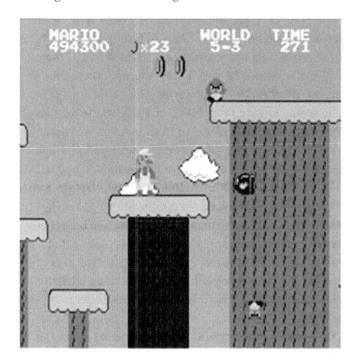

had learnt very well about the player strategies, it will surely give a very tough competition to the player. Some group of players may enjoy it, but some others may don't like this.

The second obstacle is the data unavailability for new games. In game development the machine is made to learn the game from an expert in that game. For example if a tennis game is created, the data for learning can be obtained from Roger Federer or Serena Williams. But when a novel game is created, one cannot get the learning for development.

The third obstacle is in deciding the level at which the training has to be given. A bot that had gained knowledge from the less difficult level of play, might not be able to complete or even compete in difficult levels. The computer always tries to generalize the solution for a problem, so whenever computer gets into new levels new specific learning method is needed by the computer.

The fourth obstacle is that the ML algorithms, need long time and vast data for training. A meaningful target function as learning objective must be defined. But the developers are more often left out with restricted time and limited resources to develop game AI.

CASE STUDY ON THE POKÉMON GO GAME

Pokemon go game is an augmented reality game played using mobile phones. The game was launched with around 150 species of Pokémon, then it was increased over 460 by 2019. The game download has crossed 1 billion downloads worldwide in February 2019.

Creating a bot to play Mario game is an easy task. Because the objective of the Mario is only one (i.e.) to reach the destination point crossing all the levels. The branching factor of Mario is to move left, right or to jump. But Pokemon has many objective like, to beat the Elite 4, to catch all the Pokemon, to train the strongest team. Pokemon is an open world game, which means there is a lot of choices at any given time. The branching factor cannot be simply moving up, down, left, or right. This movements alone isn't a useful measure to calculate the branching factor. Instead, look at the next meaningful action. Is that next action going to battle, talking to an NPC, or going to the next local area on the left, right, up or down? The number of possible choices range from large to very large as you progress through the game. So it can be viewed as a Multiple Objective Optimization problem. The short term goals in the immediate geographic area is considered as local optimization. The long term goals in the distant geographical area is considered as global optimization. Protective Optimization Technologies (POTs), Genetic algorithms or A* algorithm can be used for optimization.

For predicting the Pokémon a decision tree approach can be used. Decision Trees comes under the category of non-parametric supervised learning method which is used for classification and regression. From the data features and decision rules the tree model is constructed to predict the value of any target variable. The nodes in the tree structure represent the decision of an attribute, there may be split in the branches indicating the different decisions possible. The leaf nodes gives the final resultant state of following different decision combinations.

A dataset describing the features like hit point, defense, Special attack, special defense, speed, legendry for 800 species was created.

SUMMARY

To make the video game playing more interesting, the game has to be developed according to the playstyle of the player. The strong and efficient players expect more risks in the game, so the game content has to be modified dynamically online to match with the player expectation. The medium level player expects more success and this success will keep him in the game. This dynamic game development needs machine learning. The application of machine learning techniques in video game development was discussed in this chapter.

The chapter is divided into five sections. In the first section the cons of prescripted games were given. In the second section, the basics of game development terminologies and learning agent was given. The third section gives an overview of the machine learning techniques applied in video game development. In Section 4, various works of eminent authors were discussed. The player agent for FPS game developed by Lample is discussed in Section 4. The explanation of the work of content generation for a Mario game by Mathew is done. Finally, in the last section the case study on Pokemon go was discussed.

REFERENCES

Bojkovski, N., & Madevska-Bogdanova, A. (2012). *Machine Learning Algorithms for Player Satisfaction Optimization*. Retrieved from http://ciit.finki.ukim.mk/data/papers/9CiiT/9CiiT-30.pdf

Dobrovsky, A., Borghoff, U. M., & Hofmann, M. (2019). Improving Adaptive Gameplay in Serious Games Through Interactive Deep Reinforcement Learning. In *Cognitive Infocommunications, Theory and Applications* (pp. 411–432). Cham: Springer. doi:10.1007/978-3-319-95996-2_19

Du, Y., Cui, S., & Guo, S. (2009). *Applying Machine Learning in Game AI Design*. Retrieved from http://cs229.stanford.edu/proj2009/DuCuiGuo.pdf

Duro, J. A., & de Oliveira, J. V. (2008, June). Particle swarm optimization applied to the chess game. In 2008 IEEE Congress on Evolutionary Computation (IEEE World Congress on Computational Intelligence) (pp. 3702-3709). IEEE.

Fister, I. Jr, Perc, M., Ljubič, K., Kamal, S. M., Iglesias, A., & Fister, I. (2015). Particle swarm optimization for automatic creation of complex graphic characters. *Chaos, Solitons, and Fractals*, *73*, 29–35. doi:10.1016/j.chaos.2014.12.019

Guzdial, M., & Riedl, M. (2016). *Toward game level generation from gameplay videos*. arXiv preprint arXiv:1602.07721

Hunicke, R., & Chapman, V. (2004). *AI for Dynamic Difficulty Adjustment in Games*. Retrieved from https://users.cs.northwestern.edu/~hunicke/pubs/Hamlet.pdf

Lample, G., & Chaplot, D. S. (2017, February). Playing FPS games with deep reinforcement learning. In *Thirty-First AAAI Conference on Artificial Intelligence*. AAAI.

Sehrawat, A., & Raj, G. (2018, June). Intelligent PC Games: Comparison of Neural Network Based AI against Pre-Scripted AI. In *2018 International Conference on Advances in Computing and Communication Engineering (ICACCE)* (pp. 378-383). IEEE. 10.1109/ICACCE.2018.8441745

Solanki, A., & Pandey, S. (2019). Music instrument recognition using deep convolutional neural networks. International Journal of Information Technology, 1-10.

Stanley, K. O., Bryant, B. D., & Miikkulainen, R. (2005). Evolving neural network agents in the NERO video game. *Proceedings of the IEEE*, 182-189.

Summerville, A., Snodgrass, S., Guzdial, M., Holmgård, C., Hoover, A. K., Isaksen, A., ... Togelius, J. (2018). Procedural content generation via machine learning (PCGML). *IEEE Transactions on Games*, *10*(3), 257–270. doi:10.1109/TG.2018.2846639

Trivedi, C. (2018). *Building a Deep Neural Network to play FIFA 18*. Available Online at: https://towardsdatascience.com/building-a-deep-neural-network-to-play-fifa-18-dce54d45e675

Chapter 21
Multi–Layer Hybrid Credit Scoring Model Based on Feature Selection, Ensemble Learning, and Ensemble Classifier

Diwakar Tripathi
SRM University, Amaravati, India

Alok Kumar Shukla
G.L. Bajaj Institute of Technology and Management, Greater Noida, India

Ramchandra Reddy B.
SRM University, Amaravati, India

Ghanshyam S. Bopche
SRM University, Amaravati, India

ABSTRACT

Credit scoring is a process to calculate the risk associated with a credit product, and it directly affects the profitability of that industry. Periodically, financial institutions apply credit scoring in various steps. The main focus of this study is to improve the predictive performance of the credit scoring model. To improve the predictive performance of the model, this study proposes a multi-layer hybrid credit scoring model. The first stage concerns pre-processing, which includes treatment for missing values, data-transformation, and reduction of irrelevant and noisy features because they may affect predictive performance of model. The second stage applies various ensemble learning approaches such as Bagging, Adaboost, etc. At the last layer, it applies ensemble classifiers approach, which combines three heterogeneous classifiers, namely: random forest (RF), logistic regression (LR), and sequential minimal optimization (SMO) approaches for classification. Further, the proposed multi-layer model is validated on various real-world credit scoring datasets.

DOI: 10.4018/978-1-5225-9643-1.ch021

INTRODUCTION

Credit scoring is a way to determine the risk united with credit products by applying statistical or machine learning techniques on applicants' historical data (Mester,1997). It is indicated by (Thomas, Edelman, & Crook, 2002) "Credit scoring is a set of decision models and their underlying techniques that aid credit lenders in the grantingof credit (Louzada, Ara, & Fernandes, 2016). It attempts to separate the effect of different candidates' characteristics dependent on criminal conduct and defaults. The primary focal point of credit scoring is to pick whether a credit candidate has a place with reliable or non-financially sound group. Credit represents to the amount that is borrowed by a customer from a financial institution. Credit limit to a customer is decided by system on the basis of customer's credentials like annual income, property and etc. Various advantages of credit scoring for credit businesses incorporate ascertaining and diminishing credit risk and cash flow improvement (Paleologo, Elisseeff, &Antonini, 2010) and its performance is accountable for the effectiveness of credit industries. It is not a single step process, periodically; financial institutions carry out it in various steps(Paleologo, Elisseeff, &Antonini, 2010),(Edla, Tripathi, Cheruku, &Kuppili, 2018) as follows:

- **Application Scoring:** It is utilized for evaluating the authenticity and suspiciousness of new candidates. That assessment is done based on social, monetary, and other information gathered while submitting the application.
- **Behavioral Scoring:** It is comparative as previous case; however it is for the current clients to investigate their personal conduct standards and to help dynamic portfolio administration processes.
- **Collection Scoring:** It categorizes customers into various groups. According to their group belongingness, banking system pays attention on those groups such as more, moderate, no etc.
- **Fraud Detection:** Fraud scoring models rank the candidates agreeing to the relative likelihood that a candidate might be unscrupulous.

Along with credit cards and home loans various credit products such as education loan, personal loan, car loan, mortgage finance, mini & micro finance etc. are also offered by financial organizations. Due to large number of new applicants and existing customers, credit scoring is not possible to do manually or it requires huge number of experts with domain knowledge and behaviors of customer. Currently, credit scoring is not limited to banking or credit industries only, various other domains such as telecommunication, real estate etc. are also applying credit score prediction models for analysis of customers' behavior. Therefore, artificial intelligence may overcome the problem of manual credit scoring. Improving the predictive performance of model especially applicants with non-creditworthy group will have great impact for financial institution (Wang, Ma, Huang, & Xu, 2012),(Tripathi, Edla, &Cheruku,2018). This study focuses to enhance the classification performance of model by reducing the irrelevant and noisy features.

Reminder of the study is structured as follows: Section 2 describes a concise literature review, Section 3 presents proposed credit scoring model, and Section 4 exhibits the test results investigation of proposed approach along with the comparative analysis on credit scoring datasets followed by the concluding remarks based on obtained experimental results.

LITERATURE SURVEY

The greater part of the scientists have considered to acknowledge risk assessment as a twofold class order issue and observed it to be dependable to investigate shrouded designs in the credit scoring information. These frameworks help experts to improve their insight for credit risk assessment. In this unique circumstance, an assortment of Machine Learning (ML) strategies is used to put on view the risk assessment frameworks.Family of classifiers such as "Artificial Neural Network (ANN)" and "Support Vector Machine (SVM)" with various kernel approaches and many more classifiers have contributed significantly to improve credit risk prediction.

SVM (Vapnik, 2013) because of its "superior features of generalization performance and global optimum" many researchers have utilized it as classification tool in various applications. Li et al. (Li, Shiue, & Huang, 2006) have proposed a credit assessment model using SVM with data pre-processing to recognize potential candidates for consumer loans. Gestel et al. (Gestel, Baesens, Suykens, Van den Poel, Baestaens, &Willekens, 2006) have utilized "Least Squares Support Vector Machine (LSSVM)" to analyze the creditworthiness of potential corporate clients. Xiao and Fei (Xiao, & Fei, 2006) have presented an approach based on SVM with optimal parameters' values. Zhou et al. (Zhou, Lai, & Yen, 2009) have applied weighted SVM for credit scoring model etc. West (West, 2000) has applied various classification approaches and evaluated the performance of classifiers in terms of classification accuracy. A hybrid system is a dynamic system that combines the steps of various approaches towards the improvement of a particular outcome. As in credit scoring dataset, dataset has heterogeneous attributes (categorical, numerical with small range and numerical with large range) and there may be some redundant or irreverent feature which can degrade the model's performance. So, various researchers have applied various data-preprocessing steps such as feature selection, outlier detection etc. and detailed descriptions about these approaches are as follows.

Hybrid credit scoring models with SVM and feature selection approaches based on "Multivariate Adaptive Regression Splines (MARS)" and F-score are proposed (Chen, Ma, & Ma, 2009). "Stepwise Regression (SR)" and ANN are combined for credit scoring (Wongchinsri, &Kuratach, 2017). Lee and Chen (Lee, & Chen, 2005) have applied MARS based feature selection with ANN as classification tool. Oreski and Oreski(Oreski, &Oreski, 2014) have applied "Genetic Algorithm (GA)" for selecting the valuable features.Further, datasets with selected features are applied for classification. Wang et al. have applied "Rough Set and Tabu search" for feature selection (Wang, Guo, & Wang, 2010). Huang and Dun have applied "Binary Particle Swarm Optimization (BPSO)" for feature selection along with SVM as classification tool (Huang, & Dun, 2008). Various authors have applied ensemble classification approaches for improving the predictive performance of credit scoring model with various feature selection approaches(Tripathi, Edla, &Cheruku, 2018), (Tripathi, Edla, Kuppili, Bablani, &Dharavath, 2018), (Tripathi, Cheruku, &Bablani, 2018), (Tripathi, Edla, Cheruku, &Kuppili, 2019) and (Edla, Tripathi, Cheruku, &Kuppili,2018).

From the literature survey it is observed that, most of researchers have applied feature selection approaches for the reduction of irrelevant and noisy features. And, by applying the ensemble classifiers, model's performance can be improved and prediction will be more robust. Ensemble techniques utilize various learning calculations to acquire preferable prescient execution over could be acquired from any of the constituent learning calculations alone. So, by considering all the advantages of various approaches towards to improvement of predictive performance of credit scoring model, this study proposes a hybrid model for credit score prediction.

Figure 1. Proposed multi-layer hybrid credit scoring model

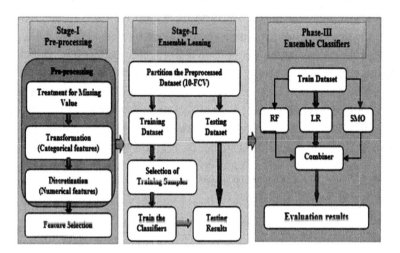

PROPOSED MODEL FOR CREDIT SCORING

In this study, we have applied multi-layer hybrid frame work for credit scoring for credit risk analysis which consists of pre-processing, ensemble learning and ensemble classifier as revealed in Figure 1. All stages are briefly described in following sub-sections.

Pre-Processing

Data pre-processing is a significantfootstep in the modelingprocess. The point of this progression is to expand the viability of the classification procedure by utilizing steady dataset and is explained as follows.

- *Data Cleaning:*In this progression, the entire dataset is considered and checked for missing values, and samples with missing values are disposed of.
- *Data Transformation:* As in credit scoring datasets havenumerical and categorical features. But some classification approaches such as SVM and NNs are applicable with numerical data only. Data transformation is required "To translate categorical features to numerical features, a unique integer number is assigned to each unique categorical value in each feature set".
- *Data Discretization:* As in preceding step categorical feature values are replaced by numerical values and it has a small range of numerical values, but the numerical features have a wide range of numerical values. So, for converting the numerical feature values into a balanced range, discretization is utilized. In order to discretize the numerical features, "Boolean Reasoning algorithm (Nguyen, 1997), (Ong, Huang, & Tzeng, 2005)" and it considers optimized hyper-plane to separate the feature values is utilized.
- *Feature Selection:* Feature selection is an important step and it plays a vital role for improving the classification performance and reducing the computational costs. The main aim of "feature selection is to determine, from the original set of features in a given dataset, a subset of features that is ideally necessary and sufficient to describe the target concept". In this step we have considered Feature Ranking with Correlation Coefficients (CFS) for feature selection which considers the fea-

ture on the basis of how the features are associated with class label. CFS, this approach evaluates subsets of features on the basis of the hypothesis: "Good feature subsets contain features highly correlated with the classification, yet uncorrelated to each other"(Hall, 1999), (Senliol, Gulgezen, Yu, &Cataltepe, 2008). For assessment of each feature, it considers how well an individual feature contributes to the separation capability and it is utilized for feature ranking. The correlation coefficients defined as in Equation 1 (Guyon, Weston, Barnhill, &Vapnik, 2002).Where, μ_i and σ_i denote the mean and standard deviation of ith feature, (+) and (-) associated with μ_i and σ_i denote same with positive and negative class respectively "Positive w_i values shows strong correlation with (+) class whereas negative w_i values shows strong correlation with (-) class".

$$W_i = \frac{\mu_i^+ - \mu_i^-}{\sigma_i^+ - \sigma_i^-}.$$

(1)

Ensemble Learning

In machine learning, ensemble techniques utilize various learning calculations to acquire preferable prescient execution over could be acquired from any of the constituent learning calculations alone (Opitz, & Maclin, 1999), (Polikar, 2006),(Senliol, Gulgezen, Yu, &Cataltepe, 2008). Supervised learning (classification) approaches are most regularly depicted as playing out the errand of looking through a theory space to locate an appropriate speculation that will make great expectations with a specific issue. Regardless of whether the theory space contains speculations that are very appropriate for a specific issue, it might be hard to locate a decent one. Groups consolidate different theories to shape an (ideally) better theory. The term ensemble is normally saved for strategies that produce various speculations by utilizing a similar base learner. The more extensive term of different classifier frameworks additionally covers hybridization of assumptions that are not actuated by a similar base learner.

Assessing the prediction of an ensemble normally requires more calculation than assessing the prediction of a solitary model, so ensembles might be thought of as an approach to make up for poor learning calculations by playing out a great deal of additional calculation. A group is itself a directed learning calculation, since it tends to be prepared and after that used to make prediction. The prepared ensemble, in this manner, speaks to a solitary theory. This theory, be that as it may, isn't really contained inside the speculation space of the models from which it is fabricated. In this way, outfits can be appeared to have greater adaptability in the capacities they can speak to. This adaptability can, in principle, empower them to over-fit the preparation information in excess of a solitary model would, but in practice, some ensemble procedures (particularly sacking) will in general decrease issues identified with over-fitting of the preparation information.

Bagging

Bootstrap AGGregatING (Bagging) is an ensemble learning technique (Breiman, 1996). In this approach, $n' = (1 - 1/e)$ (approximately 63.2%) actual training samples are considered and rest (n-n') are duplicated samples are considered (Bauer, &Kohavi, 1999) where n denotes the number of training samples. Further, it creates various training samples sets form actual training samples, let it as M, and models are trained with various training set. Finally, the outputs predicted by various models are combined by averaging the output and voting in case of regression and classification respectively.

Adaptive *Boosting*

Adaptive Boosting (Freund, &Schapire, 1996) also requires bootstrapping. Unlike bagging, boosting weights each sample of data, means some samples will be used more often than others. In addition, the boosting algorithm has access to the weak learning algorithm, which is denoted generically as WeakLearn. It fits an advancement of weak learners on dissimilar weighted training data. It starts by anticipating unique dataset and gives measure up to weight to every perception. In the event that forecast is off base utilizing the primary learner, at that point it gives higher load to perception which has been anticipated erroneously. This is an iterative methodology; it continues including learner(s) until a limit is come to in the amount of models or accuracy.

Decorate

"Diverse Ensemble Creation by Oppositional Relabeling of Artificial Training Examples (Decorator)" is an approach for producing ensemblesthat directly creates diverse hypotheses using additional artificially-generated training samples (Melville, & Mooney, 2003). In this method, the classifiers are trained with actual training samples along with artificial data samples. In each iteration, synthetic training samples are generated from the data distribution, and the number of artificial data samples depends on size of actual training samples. For generating the artificial training data, random data points by applying the approximation on training data distribution. Such as, in case of numerical features mean and standard deviation and Gaussian distribution are utilized to produce new set from training dataset. In case of nominal attributes, likelihood of occurrence of everydistinctive value with Laplace smoothing, and labels for these generated training samples are preferred so as to contrast maximally from the present outfit's forecasts.

Random Subspace

Similar to bagging, in Random Subspace technique (Ho, 1995), the features are arbitrarily sampled, with substitution, for each learner. Casually, this causes individual learners to not over-focus on features that emerge highly analytical or expressive in the training set, but fail to be as projecting for points outside that set. Let, there is n number of samples in training dataset with D number of features and L individual models which are considered for ensemble. For every individual model l, pick $n_l(n_l < n)$ features for l. For every l, make a preparation set by picking dl features from D with substitution and train the model. Further, it consolidates the outputs of the L models by "majority voting" or by combining the "posterior probabilities".

Rotation Forest

To produce the training data for a base classifier, the list of capabilities is discretionary isolate into "K subsets (K is a parameter of the algorithm)" and "Principal Component Analysis (PCA)" is associated with each subset (Rodriguez, Kuncheva, & Alonso, 2006). All chief segments are occupied with request to preserve the conflicting data in the information. Thu-sly, K subsets pivots occur to shape the new highlights for a base classifier. The motivation behind the pivot approach is to give certainty simultaneously singular exactness and assorted variety inside the group. Respectable variety is progressed through the constituentwithdrawal for each base classifier.

Dagging

Similar to bagging, Dagging refers to combine the multiple trained models to derive a single model with difference that bagging uses bootstrapping approach but it uses the disjoint set of samples (Ting, & Witten, 1997).

MultiBoost

MultiBoosting is an expansion to the very effective AdaBoost strategy for framing decision committees. It is a hybrid approach by consolidating AdaBoost with Wagging (Webb, 2000), "Wagging (Bauer, &Kohavi, 1999) is alternative of bagging, which requires a base learning calculation that can use preparing cases with differing weights", "As the mechanisms differ, their combination may out-perform either in isolation". The motivation behind using those approaches is as follows "baggingmainly reduces variance, while AdaBoost reduces both bias and variance" and "there is evidence that bagging is more effective than AdaBoost at reducing variance".

Ensemble Classifier

Broad research has been directed on data classification. Be that as it may, there is no particular method to foresee which classifier will deliver the best outcomes on a particular dataset. "A particular classifier might be superior to others for a particular dataset, yet another classifier could perform superior to that on other dataset and ensemble of classifiers has the capability to produce the near to optimal results on each dataset". The main motivationin the wake of multi-layer ensemble classifier framework is thatwhen classifiers settle on a choice, one ought not be subject to just a solitary classifier's choice, yet, rather, expect classifiers to take part in the basic leadership process by conglomerating their individual expectations and it outflanks their base classifiers. There are two most common approaches to aggregate the outputs predicted by the classifiers, which are Majority Voting (MV), Average Probability (AP) and Maximum Probability (MP) and all are briefly explained in following subsections. It is appeared in(Tsai, Lin, Yen, & Chen, 2011) that there is no huge distinction among homogeneous and heterogeneous ensemble system with larger part casting a ballot yet homogeneous classifier gathering with lion's share casting a ballot expectation ability is great towards the fitting class mark. In this way, in this examination we have considered three heterogeneous classifiers to be specific RF, LR and SMO and are accumulated by MV, AP and MP.

Random Forest

Random forest (RF) (Breiman, 2001) is an approach for classification and regression problem in association with ensemble learning. In case of RF, randomness is introduced by recognizing the best split feature instead of a random selection of a subset of available features in data. Further, ensemble classifier combines the individual predictions of various trees to combine them into a final prediction and it utilizes a majority voting approach to combine the individual predictions of tree. Random decision forest is better way for decision trees' in case of over-fitting problem with training set (Friedman, Hastie, &Tibshirani, 2001).

Linear Regression

LR (Le Cessie, & Van Houwelingen, 1992) can be considered as an extraordinary case of linear regression models. Be that as it may, with binary class classification, "it violates normality assumptions of general regression models. LR demonstrates that an appropriate capacity of the fitted probability of the occasion is a straight capacity of the watched estimations of the accessible illustrative factors". The significant preferred standpoint of this methodology is that it can create a straightforward probabilistic recipe of characterization. The shortcomings are that LR can't appropriatelymanage the issues of non- linear and intelligent impacts of informative factors. Discriminant function analysis is fundamentally the same as LR, and both can be used to answer the same research questions (Hansen, 2005). LR does not have as many assumptions and restrictions as DA. However, when discriminant analysis assumptions are met, it is more dominant than LR (Hastie, Tibshirani, Friedman, & Franklin, 2005). In contrast to LR, DA can be utilized with little sample sizes. It has been demonstrated that when test sizes are equivalent, and homogeneity of fluctuation/covariance holds, DA is progressively precise. With such a lot of being considered, calculated relapse has turned into the basic decision, since the presumptions of DA are once in a while met. It has been demonstrated that when test sizes are equivalent, and homogeneity of fluctuation/co-variance holds, discriminant analysis is increasingly precise. With such an excess of being considered, logistic regression has turned into the basic decision, since the presumptions of DA are once in a while met.

Sequential Minimal Optimization

Sequential Minimal Optimization (SMO) SVM has better generalized classification performance but it has slower, complex and subtle training (Platt, 1999) "As SVM training is much more complex and it requires expensive third-party quadratic programming (QP) solvers (Rifkin, 2002)". In view of aforementioned problems with SVM, SMO is an approach to solve QP problem that arises during the training of SVM (Platt, 1999). SMO solves the SVM's QP problem by decomposing the overall problem into various subproblems. Unlike SVM, it uses smallest possible optimization approach at each step with two Lagrange multipliers to find the optimal values. For binary class classification problem with a dataset $\{x_1, x_2, ..., x_n\}$ and $\{y_1, ..., y_n\}$, where xi denotes an input vector and y_i denotes class labels of corresponding input vector. "A soft-margin SVM is trained by solving a QP problem", which is articulated in the twofold form as displayed in Equation 2.

$$\max_{\propto} \sum_{j=1}^{n} \propto_i - \frac{1}{2} \sum_{i=1}^{n} \sum_{j=1}^{n} y_i y_j K\left(x_i, x_j\right) \propto_i, \propto_j, \qquad (2)$$

Subject to: $0 \leq \propto_i \leq C$, for i = 1, 2, ..., n.

Where, C presents SVM hyper parameter and $K(x_i, x_j)$ is the kernel function, and these are calculated by Lagrange multipliers.

Majority Voting

In majority voting approach, the output is the class which has the uppermost votes. This is somewhat obfuscating a very simplemethod "for class j, the sumPT t=1 presents the numeral of votes for j". Plurality chooses the class j which maximizes the sum. Along these lines, their notation should be something like as in Equation 4 (Brown, 2010).

$$\sum_{t=1}^{T} d_{tj} = {}_{j=1}^{C} Max \sum_{t=1}^{T} d_{tj}. \tag{4}$$

Max Probability

It combines the results obtained by the base classifiers by consideration of approximating the sum of the maximum of the posterior probabilities and is as follows in Equation 5 (Kittler, Hater, &Duin, 1996).

$$_{j=1}^{C} MaxP(W_j \mid X_i) = {}_{k=1}^{M} Max\ {}_{j=1}^{C} Max \sum_{t=1}^{T} P(W_j \mid X_i). \tag{5}$$

Average Probability

It combines the results obtained by the base classifiers by consideration of approximating the average posteriori probability for each class over all the classifier outputs and is as follows in Equation 6 (Kittler, Hater, &Duin, 1996).

$$_{j=1}^{C} MedP\left(W_j \mid X_i\right) = {}_{k=1}^{M} Med\ {}_{j=1}^{C} Max \sum_{t=1}^{T} P\left(W_j \mid X_i\right). \tag{6}$$

EXPERIMENTAL RESULT ANALYSIS

This section presents the description about datasets along with performance measures used to validate the proposed approach and detailed result analysis on these credit scoring datasets.

Table 1. Description of credit scoring datasets

S. No	Dataset	Samples	Class1/Class2	Features
1	Australian	690	307/383	14
2	Japanese	690	307/383	15
3	German-categorical	1000	700/300	20
4	German-numerical	1000	700/300	24

Experimental Datasets and Performance Measures

The proposed Multi-layer credit scoring model has been tested on four credit scoring datasets namely "Australian credit scoring", "Japanese credit screening", "German-categorical and German-numerical (GND) loan approval". All datasets are obtained from the "UCI Machine Learning Repository Asuncion, & Newman, 2007)". All datasets used in this article are twofold class datasets where positive class represents approved and negative class represents not approved applications. Detailed descriptions about all aforementioned credit scoring datasets are tabulated in table 2.

As discussed above about the datasets, all are having twofold class and anticipated model focuses to classification problem. In this paper, we have considered the accuracy as performance measure. Accuracy (as in equation 7) displays the predictive performance of classifier.

$$Accuracy = \frac{TP + TN}{TP + TN + FP + FN} \tag{7}$$

Where, TP, FP, TN and FN indicate "True Positive", "False Positive", "True Negative" and "False Negative" respectively.

RESULTS AND ANALYSIS

As per the proposed model first pre-processing is applied which consist of three steps. First treatment for missing values "in this steps samples with missing values are eliminated", Second step, data transformation "in this step categorical values are replaced by numerical values, a unique integer number is assigned to each unique categorical value in each feature set". Third step is data discretization "In order to discretize the numerical features, Boolean reasoning algorithm which separates the feature values in an optimal set of the hyper-plane, is used". At last step is feature selection and for feature selection we have considered the CFS. Further, the pre-processed dataset with selected features is fed to model for training. As in this work, we have applied ensemble learning and ensemble classifiers for credit score prediction model. So, here for comparative analysis, various ensemble learning approaches namely Bagging, AdaBoost, Decorator, Rotation forest, Random subspace, Dagging, MultiBoosting, with various aggregation approaches for ensemble classifier namely Majority Voting (MV), Average Probability and Maximum Probability with Random Forest, Linear Regression and Sequential Minimal Optimization as base classifiers with CFS based feature selection and with all features are compared.

Table 2. Performances comparison of ensemble classification with ensemble learning approaches on Australian dataset

	RF	LR	SMO	MV	AP	MP
All-features	86.36	87.53	86.36	88.40	87.37	87.07
CFS	86.87	87.69	86.57	88.70	87.39	87.18
Bagging	87.39	87.24	86.51	88.55	88.10	87.66
Bagging+CFS	87.47	87.95	87.36	89.25	88.81	87.81
AdaBoost	86.80	87.53	84.90	87.66	86.18	85.00
AdaBoost +CFS	87.14	87.93	85.19	88.10	87.51	86.77
Decorator	88.27	86.51	86.36	88.40	88.25	88.70
Decorator +CFS	88.75	88.68	88.96	88.89	88.51	89.40
RSubspace	86.51	87.39	86.07	87.81	88.10	88.55
RSubspace+CFS	87.22	87.19	87.53	87.95	88.44	89.29
ROForest	88.70	87.53	86.36	88.40	87.51	87.22
ROForest+CFS	88.76	87.89	86.73	88.75	87.77	87.83
Dagging	87.24	87.24	86.80	88.25	87.96	88.70
Dagging+CFS	87.53	87.53	86.91	88.36	87.95	88.81
Multiboost	86.80	87.68	87.24	87.66	87.51	88.40
Multiboost+CFS	87.43	87.93	88.22	88.91	88.09	88.57

For comparative result analysis, we have considered 10-Fold-Cross-Validation approach with 50-Iteration and mean of the results are considered. Starting from the results on Australian dataset with all features LR has the best performance as compared to RF and SMO and by applying ensemble approaches on RF, LR and SMO it improves the classification performance approximately by 2% and MV has better performance as compare to AP and MP. In association with CFS based feature selection with all aforementioned approaches it slightly improves the classification performance of all mentioned approaches. From the experimental results as in Table 2 it is observed that LR has the best classification accuracy as compared to other two classifiers such as SMO and RF and with features selected by CFS, it makes significant improvement with all three classifiers. By applying aggregation function namely MV, AP and MP, MV has the best classification accuracy and it improves the classification accuracy as compared to its base classifiers. As in this study we have applied various ensemble learning approaches namely Bagging, AdaBoost, Decorator, Rotation forest, Random subspace, Dagging, MultiBoosting, from the results it is observed that these all approaches improve the classification accuracy of all approaches RF,SMO, LR, MV, MP, AP most of the cases. With all aforementioned approaches, CFS improves the classification accuracy. Overall, CFS based feature selection with Bagging and MV has the best classification accuracy.

Similar to Australian dataset all approaches are applied Japanese dataset (as in Table 3), German-categorical dataset (as in Table 4) and German-numerical dataset (as in Table 5) and these tables store the mean of 10-fold-cross-validation, 50-iteration. From the results, it is observed that various ensemble learning approaches are the strong approaches towards to improvement the classification approaches and MV with Decorator and CFS based feature selection has the best classification accuracy. In case of German-categorical dataset, CFS based feature selection with ROForest and MV has the best classifi-

Table 3. Performances comparison of ensemble classification with ensemble learning approaches on Japanese dataset

	RF	LR	SMO	MV	AP	MP
All-features	86.55	87.39	87.72	88.59	88.76	88.59
CFS	86.85	87.51	87.89	88.72	88.91	88.82
Bagging	88.06	87.39	87.72	89.10	88.76	88.59
Bagging+CFS	88.03	88.56	87.97	89.59	89.37	88.86
AdaBoost	86.72	87.39	87.56	87.91	88.25	88.50
AdaBoost+CFS	87.03	88.48	87.87	88.83	88.42	88.67
Decorator	87.05	86.72	87.72	88.42	88.59	88.27
Decorator+CFS	87.69	86.88	88.67	89.91	89.72	89.10
RSubspace	87.22	87.56	85.31	87.70	87.40	87.23
RSubspace+CFS	87.88	87.55	85.71	88.56	88.08	88.32
ROForest	87.89	87.39	87.72	88.71	88.59	88.58
ROForest+CFS	88.13	87.99	87.98	89.06	88.98	88.70
Dagging	89.07	87.05	87.72	89.59	89.25	89.31
Dagging+CFS	89.89	87.56	87.86	89.83	89.48	89.59
Multiboost	88.73	87.22	87.72	89.09	88.91	88.88
Multiboost+CFS	88.97	87.99	87.92	89.55	89.42	89.02

cation accuracy. In case of German-numerical dataset, CFS based feature selection with Decorator and MV has the best classification accuracy. Over in case of credit scoring datasets, all CFS based feature selection approach improves the classification performance of RF, SMO and LR along with various ensemble learning approaches ensemble classifiers frameworks.

CONCLUSION

In this chapter, we have presented a Multi-layer hybrid model for credit score prediction. First stage concerns about Pre-processing, which includes "treatment for missing values", "data-transformation" and "reduction of irrelevant and noisy features" because they may affect predictive performance of model. Second stage applies various ensemble learning approaches such as Bagging, Adaboost, Decorator, Random Subspace, Rotation Forest and Dagging. At last layer, it applies Ensemble classifiers approach which combines three heterogeneous classifiers namely: Random Forest (RF), Logistic Regression (LR) and Sequential Minimal Optimization (SMO) approaches for classification. At last layer, RF, SMO and LR are aggregated by Majority Voting, Average Probability and Maximum Probability. Further the proposed multi-layer model is validated on various real-world credit scoring datasets namely: "Australian credit scoring dataset", "Japanese credit screening dataset", "German categorical and numerical loan approval datasets". Further, experimental outcomesare compared in terms of classification accuracy.

From the experimental outcomes, it is visible that CFS base feature selection approach makes a significant improvement with all three classifiers and ensemble framework. As, we have applied vari-

Table 4. Performances comparison of ensemble classification with ensemble learning approaches on German-categorical datasets

	RF	LR	SMO	MV	AP	MP
All-features	74.84	76.26	75.35	76.85	76.35	76.43
CFS	75.42	76.45	75.42	77.14	76.87	76.82
Bagging	75.85	76.05	75.65	76.05	76.56	76.15
Bagging+CFS	76.11	77.04	76.22	76.54	76.73	76.23
AdaBoost	75.25	76.26	75.35	76.91	76.54	76.31
AdaBoost+CFS	75.82	76.35	75.52	77.33	76.53	76.44
Decorator	76.46	75.55	75.14	76.83	76.55	76.79
Decorator+CFS	76.82	76.15	75.34	77.44	76.86	76.94
RSubspace	75.35	73.53	71.91	75.71	75.53	75.62
RSubspace+CFS	75.52	74.52	72.20	76.12	75.91	75.93
ROForest	77.16	76.26	75.65	77.85	77.45	77.61
ROForest+CFS	77.42	76.25	75.42	78.04	77.91	77.82
Dagging	75.65	75.45	75.14	76.75	76.55	76.95
Dagging+CFS	75.84	75.95	76.11	77.23	76.83	77.07
Multiboost	75.45	75.85	75.35	76.74	76.35	76.21
Multiboost+CFS	76.10	76.25	76.83	76.94	76.54	76.43

Table 5. Performances comparison of ensemble classification with ensemble learning approaches on German-numerical datasets

	RF	LR	SMO	MV	AP	MP
All-features	74.13	77.57	77.37	78.34	78.35	78.13
CFS	74.22	78.26	77.55	79.01	78.89	78.78
Bagging	76.26	77.97	77.77	78.85	78.13	78.23
Bagging+CFS	77.01	78.36	77.94	79.27	78.97	78.77
AdaBoost	74.24	77.57	77.37	77.83	77.50	77.89
AdaBoost+CFS	75.10	77.66	78.01	78.95	78.87	78.36
Decorator	77.57	77.27	77.67	79.92	78.64	79.15
Decorator+CFS	77.81	77.85	77.75	80.26	79.36	79.49
RSubspace	74.84	75.65	70.90	75.84	75.74	75.85
RSubspace+CFS	75.12	75.93	71.70	75.93	75.91	75.97
ROForest	78.88	77.57	77.67	79.54	79.34	79.23
ROForest+CFS	79.71	78.26	77.93	79.69	79.58	79.47
Dagging	75.25	78.58	75.14	79.40	79.22	79.31
Dagging+CFS	75.53	78.46	75.33	79.66	79.21	79.46
Multiboost	76.66	77.47	77.87	78.54	78.32	78.51
Multiboost+CFS	77.31	78.36	78.25	78.93	78.69	78.70

ous ensemble learning approaches with three classifiers and ensemble classifier framework. From the experimental results, it is visible that all approaches made a significant improvement toward to classification accuracy. And Bagging and Decorator with SMO, RF and LR based ensemble framework aggregated by Majority Voting has the best Classification accuracy with most of the cases. Finally, it is concluded that feature selection with ensemble learning and ensemble classifier framework is the best way to improve the classification performance.

REFERENCES

Alzubi, J., Nayyar, A., & Kumar, A. (2018, November). Machine learning from theory to algorithms: An overview. *Journal of Physics: Conference Series*, *1142*(1), 012012. doi:10.1088/1742-6596/1142/1/012012

Aslam, J. A., Popa, R. A., & Rivest, R. L. (2007). On Estimating the Size and Confidence of a Statistical Audit. *EVT*, *7*, 8.

Asuncion, A., & Newman, D. (2007). *UCI machine learning repository*. Retrieved from https://archive.ics.uci.edu/ml/index.php

Bauer, E., & Kohavi, R. (1999). An empirical comparison of voting classification algorithms: Bagging, boosting, and variants. *Machine Learning*, *36*(1-2), 105–139. doi:10.1023/A:1007515423169

Breiman, L. (1996). Bagging predictors. *Machine Learning*, *24*(2), 123–140. doi:10.1007/BF00058655

Breiman, L. (2001). Random forests. *Machine Learning*, *45*(1), 5–32. doi:10.1023/A:1010933404324

Brown, G. (2010). Ensemble learning. *Encyclopedia of Machine Learning*, 312-320.

Chen, W., Ma, C., & Ma, L. (2009). Mining the customer credit using hybrid support vector machine technique. *Expert Systems with Applications*, *36*(4), 7611–7616. doi:10.1016/j.eswa.2008.09.054

Edla, D. R., Tripathi, D., Cheruku, R., & Kuppili, V. (2018). An efficient multi-layer ensemble framework with BPSOGSA-based feature selection for credit scoring data analysis. *Arabian Journal for Science and Engineering*, *43*(12), 6909–6928. doi:10.100713369-017-2905-4

Freund, Y., & Schapire, R. E. (1996, July). Experiments with a new boosting algorithm. In ICML (Vol. 96, pp. 148-156). Academic Press.

Friedman, J., Hastie, T., &Tibshirani, R. (2001). *The elements of statistical learning* (Vol. 1, No. 10). New York: Springer Series in Statistics.

Guyon, I., Weston, J., Barnhill, S., & Vapnik, V. (2002). Gene selection for cancer classification using support vector machines. *Machine Learning*, *46*(1-3), 389–422. doi:10.1023/A:1012487302797

Hall, M. A. (1999). *Correlation-based feature selection for machine learning*. Academic Press.

Hansen, J. (2005). *Using SPSS for windows and macintosh: analyzing and understanding data*. Academic Press.

Hastie, T., Tibshirani, R., Friedman, J., & Franklin, J. (2005). The elements of statistical learning: Data mining, inference and prediction. *The Mathematical Intelligencer*, *27*(2), 83–85. doi:10.1007/BF02985802

Ho, T. K. (1995, August). Random decision forests. In *Proceedings of 3rd international conference on document analysis and recognition* (Vol. 1, pp. 278-282). IEEE. 10.1109/ICDAR.1995.598994

Huang, C. L., & Dun, J. F. (2008). A distributed PSO–SVM hybrid system with feature selection and parameter optimization. *Applied Soft Computing*, *8*(4), 1381–1391. doi:10.1016/j.asoc.2007.10.007

Kittler, J., Hater, M., & Duin, R. P. (1996, August). Combining classifiers. In *Proceedings of 13th international conference on pattern recognition* (Vol. 2, pp. 897-901). IEEE. 10.1109/ICPR.1996.547205

Le Cessie, S., & Van Houwelingen, J. C. (1992). Ridge estimators in logistic regression. *Journal of the Royal Statistical Society. Series C, Applied Statistics*, *41*(1), 191–201.

Lee, T. S., & Chen, I. F. (2005). A two-stage hybrid credit scoring model using artificial neural networks and multivariate adaptive regression splines. *Expert Systems with Applications*, *28*(4), 743–752. doi:10.1016/j.eswa.2004.12.031

Li, S. T., Shiue, W., & Huang, M. H. (2006). The evaluation of consumer loans using support vector machines. *Expert Systems with Applications*, *30*(4), 772–782. doi:10.1016/j.eswa.2005.07.041

Louzada, F., Ara, A., & Fernandes, G. B. (2016). Classification methods applied to credit scoring: Systematic review and overall comparison. *Surveys in Operations Research and Management Science*, *21*(2), 117–134. doi:10.1016/j.sorms.2016.10.001

Melville, P., & Mooney, R. J. (2003, August). Constructing diverse classifier ensembles using artificial training examples. *IJCAI (United States)*, *3*, 505–510.

Mester, L. J. (1997). What's the point of credit scoring? *Business Review (Federal Reserve Bank of Philadelphia)*, *3*(Sep/Oct), 3–16.

Nguyen, H. S. (1997). *Discretization of real value attributes, boolean reasoning approach*. PhD Thesis.

Ong, C. S., Huang, J. J., & Tzeng, G. H. (2005). Building credit scoring models using genetic programming. *Expert Systems with Applications*, *29*(1), 41–47. doi:10.1016/j.eswa.2005.01.003

Opitz, D., & Maclin, R. (1999). Popular ensemble methods: An empirical study. *Journal of Artificial Intelligence Research*, *11*, 169–198. doi:10.1613/jair.614

Oreski, S., & Oreski, G. (2014). Genetic algorithm-based heuristic for feature selection in credit risk assessment. *Expert Systems with Applications*, *41*(4), 2052–2064. doi:10.1016/j.eswa.2013.09.004

Paleologo, G., Elisseeff, A., & Antonini, G. (2010). Subagging for credit scoring models. *European Journal of Operational Research*, *201*(2), 490–499. doi:10.1016/j.ejor.2009.03.008

Platt, J. (1999). Fast training of support vector machines using sequential minimal optimization. In Advances in Kernel Methods—Support Vector Learning (pp. 185–208). MIT Press.

Polikar, R. (2006). Ensemble based systems in decision making. *IEEE Circuits and Systems Magazine*, *6*(3), 21–45. doi:10.1109/MCAS.2006.1688199

Rifkin, R. M. (2002). *Everything old is new again: a fresh look at historical approaches in machine learning* (Doctoral dissertation). Massachusetts Institute of Technology.

Rodriguez, J. J., Kuncheva, L. I., & Alonso, C. J. (2006). Rotation forest: A new classifier ensemble method. *IEEE Transactions on Pattern Analysis and Machine Intelligence, 28*(10), 1619–1630. doi:10.1109/TPAMI.2006.211 PMID:16986543

Senliol, B., Gulgezen, G., Yu, L., & Cataltepe, Z. (2008, October). Fast Correlation Based Filter (FCBF) with a different search strategy. In *2008 23rd international symposium on computer and information sciences* (pp. 1-4). IEEE.

Senliol, B., Gulgezen, G., Yu, L., & Cataltepe, Z. (2008, October). Fast Correlation Based Filter (FCBF) with a different search strategy. In *2008 23rd international symposium on computer and information sciences* (pp. 1-4). IEEE.

Thomas, L. C., Edelman, D. B., & Crook, J. N. (2002). *Credit scoring and its applications.* Society for industrial and Applied Mathematics.

Ting, K. M., & Witten, I. H. (1997). *Stacking bagged and dagged models.* Academic Press.

Tripathi, D., Cheruku, R., & Bablani, A. (2018). Relative Performance Evaluation of Ensemble Classification with Feature Reduction in Credit Scoring Datasets. In *Advances in Machine Learning and Data Science* (pp. 293–304). Singapore: Springer. doi:10.1007/978-981-10-8569-7_30

Tripathi, D., Edla, D. R., & Cheruku, R. (2018). Hybrid credit scoring model using neighborhood rough set and multi-layer ensemble classification. *Journal of Intelligent & Fuzzy Systems, 34*(3), 1543–1549. doi:10.3233/JIFS-169449

Tripathi, D., Edla, D. R., Cheruku, R., & Kuppili, V. (2019). A novel hybrid credit scoring model based on ensemble feature selection and multilayer ensemble classification. *Computational Intelligence, 35*(2), 371–394. doi:10.1111/coin.12200

Tripathi, D., Edla, D. R., Kuppili, V., Bablani, A., & Dharavath, R. (2018). Credit Scoring Model based on Weighted Voting and Cluster based Feature Selection. *Procedia Computer Science, 132*, 22–31. doi:10.1016/j.procs.2018.05.055

Tsai, C. F., Lin, Y. C., Yen, D. C., & Chen, Y. M. (2011). Predicting stock returns by classifier ensembles. *Applied Soft Computing, 11*(2), 2452–2459. doi:10.1016/j.asoc.2010.10.001

Van Gestel, T., Baesens, B., Suykens, J. A., Van den Poel, D., Baestaens, D. E., & Willekens, M. (2006). Bayesian kernel based classification for financial distress detection. *European Journal of Operational Research, 172*(3), 979–1003. doi:10.1016/j.ejor.2004.11.009

Vapnik, V. (2013). *The nature of statistical learning theory.* Springer science & business media.

Wang, G., Ma, J., Huang, L., & Xu, K. (2012). Two credit scoring models based on dual strategy ensemble trees. *Knowledge-Based Systems, 26*, 61–68. doi:10.1016/j.knosys.2011.06.020

Wang, J., Guo, K., & Wang, S. (2010). Rough set and Tabu search based feature selection for credit scoring. *Procedia Computer Science, 1*(1), 2425–2432. doi:10.1016/j.procs.2010.04.273

Webb, G. I. (2000). Multiboosting: A technique for combining boosting and wagging. *Machine Learning*, *40*(2), 159–196. doi:10.1023/A:1007659514849

West, D. (2000). Neural network credit scoring models. *Computers & Operations Research*, *27*(11-12), 1131–1152. doi:10.1016/S0305-0548(99)00149-5

Wongchinsri, P., & Kuratach, W. (2017, June). SR-based binary classification in credit scoring. In *2017 14th International Conference on Electrical Engineering/Electronics, Computer, Telecommunications and Information Technology (ECTI-CON)* (pp. 385-388). IEEE.

Xiao, W. B., & Fei, Q. (2006). A study of personal credit scoring models on support vector machine with optimal choice of kernel function parameters. *Systems Engineering-Theory & Practice, 10.*

Zhou, L., Lai, K. K., & Yen, J. (2009). Credit scoring models with AUC maximization based on weighted SVM. *International Journal of Information Technology & Decision Making*, *8*(4), 677–696. doi:10.1142/S0219622009003582

Chapter 22
Overview of Machine Learners in Classifying of Speech Signals

Hemanta Kumar Palo

Siksha 'O' Anusandhan (Deemed), India

Lokanath Sarangi

College of Engineering, Biju Patnaik University of Technology, India

ABSTRACT

Machine learning (ML) remains a buzzword during the last few decades due to the requirement of a huge amount of data for adequate processing, the continuously surfacing of better innovative and efficient algorithms, and the advent of powerful computers with enormous computation power. The ML algorithms are mostly based on data mining, clustering, classification, and regression approaches for efficient utilization. Many vivid application domains in the field of speech and image signal processing, market forecast, biomedical signal processing, robotics, trend analysis of data, banking and finance sectors, etc. benefits from such techniques. Among these modules, the classification of speech and speaker identification has been a predominant area of research as it has been alone medium of communication via phone. This has made the author to provide an overview of a few state-of-art ML algorithms, their advantages and limitations, including the advancement to enhance the application domain in this field.

INTRODUCTION

Use of data-driven approach in ML makes it more reliable than man-made rules. It is more dependable in a situation where a human being remains inefficient to cope with. It follows an automated method to find the desired hypotheses that explain the data without any human experts. The ML algorithms can be applied to almost any learning tasks with flexibility and economically. A few applications of the ML algorithm are shown in Figure 1.

Advancement in classification algorithms involving speech signal can create a suitable platform for resource allocation, gender and age detection, language identification, digit and word recognition, emotion identification, security and criminal investigation, robotics and computer games, on-line tutoring,

DOI: 10.4018/978-1-5225-9643-1.ch022

Figure 1. Applications of machine learning algorithms

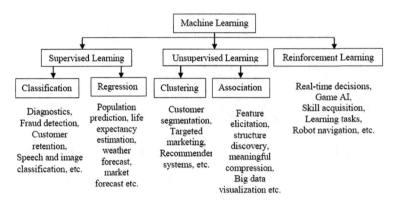

counseling and psychological assistance to children and affected person and many similar fields (Sinha & Shahnawazuddin 2018; Palo & Mohanty 2018A; Palo, Chandra & Mohanty, 2017A; Geiger, Leykauf, Rehrl, Wallhoff, & Rigoll, 2014;Franke&Srihari 2008; Litman& Forbes 2003). The recognition system allows a machine to emphasize on phrases or words in a spoken conversation. Similarly, speech to text conversion helps the user to verbally communicate with the machine rather than typing the text chosen. Thus, the ML algorithm must be trained with numerous amounts of words, vocabularies, terminologies (medical, industrial, technical, legal, etc.), phrases, and languages to make it user-adaptive. A few of the other real-world applications are listed below

- Dialogue management: The human-machine-interface must include dialogues to enable either the machine or the user to initiate or choose different responses to genuine queries. However, sufficient progress in this field is yet to be made to provide such mixed-initiative recognition systems.
- Telecommunications: Credit card recognition, third party billing, operator-assisted calling, rejection or acceptance of billing charges identifying the selected speaker, voice dialing (call the workplace, school or home, etc.) call-center application, voice calling, customer care, command and control of resource allocation, etc.
- Desktop/office management: Internet voice browsing, voice dialer, desktop voice navigation, dictation, etc.
- Legal/ medical: The creation of medical and legal reports using speech to text conversation.
- Aids to handicapped/ Games/ robotics: Manipulation of wheelchair carrying patients, climate control, control of selective parameters of games using speech signal, human-robot interaction, etc.
- In-car application: Audio prompting the driver by identifying the known passenger, vehicular maneuvering, initiate phone calls, tuning the radio stations or activating music systems, etc.
- Military applications: Setting up the radio-frequencies, steer-point, autopilot commanding, coordinate and control of weapon release features, control of flight display system, etc.
- Education system: Language learning (choice of proper pronunciation, enhancing speech fluency and speaking style or skills), voice activation system and information dissemination to a blind person, relieving a paralyzed person from writing, typing, browsing of the internet or use of computers using their recognized voice samples, etc.

Figure 2. Classification of machine learning algorithms

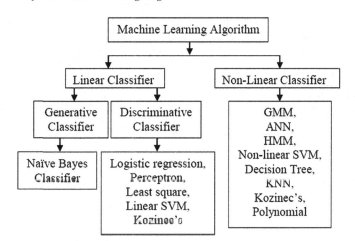

There are many ML algorithms efficiently employed in the field of pattern recognition with their advantages and limitations. Nevertheless, to set a comparable platform among these classifiers is very difficult as the recognition accuracy is largely data-driven and task-dependent. Further, the reliability of features describing the patterns and data size remains pivotal in deciding the classification performance (Palo &Mohanty, 2018B; Alzubi, Nayyar, & Kumar, 2018). This has made the linear classifiers such as the Fisher's linear discriminant, Logistic regression, etc. more versatile for linearly separable classes in comparison to other nonlinear sophisticated classifiers (Gromski et al., 2015). Similarly, there has been a wide variation in the literature on the classification accuracy, using the same classifier due to the choice of data set, feature extraction techniques involved, the classification algorithm employed and the number of classes chosen for identification.

The ML algorithms for classification used in the field of pattern recognition are broadly segmented into two categories (Kaur& Jain 2015; Zhou, Hansen, & Kaiser, 1998). It has been briefed below and is categorically shown in Figure 2.

1. Linear classifiers
2. Non-linear classifiers.

The linear classifiers are either generative type or discriminative type. While logistic regression, perceptron classifiers, linear Support Vector Machines (SVM), least-square methods and kozinec's algorithm are considered to be in the discriminative category, the NB classifier is generative. Among widely discussed non-linear classifiers, the Gaussian Mixture Model (GMM), Decision Trees (DT), Hidden Markov Model (HMM), non-linear or smooth SVM, KNN, Discriminant Analyzers, Artificial Neural Network (ANN), and polynomial classifiers have been used for pattern recognition such as Speech Recognition. ML learning algorithms are categorized broadly into the followings (HaCohen-Kerner, Gross, &Masa, 2005).

1. *Supervised or discrimination learning*: The method requires a set of labeled data (each data sample must have a correct label) for achieving the desired level of classification. The major objective is to approximate the mapping function suitably to accurately predict the desired output (Y) when the network is presented with a new set of input (X). Classification and regression analysis comes in this category. The important advantage of the technique is that it helps in the formation of rules automatically and is less cumbersome. One of the limitations of this method is that the rules formed automatically may not be accurate or specific always. Further, the method suffers from data over-fitting in case the algorithm is versatile enough to memorize special cases although not fitting to the more general principles.

2. *Unsupervised or clustered Learning*: In this, the network is usually presented with uncategorized, unstructured or unlabeled data and no prior training is provided to the system. The network output is decided based on some sort of coding algorithms. Clustering and association or dimensionality reductions come in this category. The parametric unsupervised learning produces very precise and accurate results with more statistical power. However, due to the use of many assumptions than non-parametric methods, the method may mislead in case the assumptions are incorrect. The parametric method is simple and faster to compute, although it is not robust. On the contrary, the non-parametric method makes less stringent demands for the data. The method is suitable to obtain a quick solution with fewer computations and does not take any statistical assumptions of the observed data. However, as the name implies, quantitative statements are very difficult to make due to non-involvement of any parameters. In this method, much of the information is discarded hence are robust under specific conditions.

3. *Reinforcement Learning*: The algorithm interacts with its environment without human intervention. It is based on dynamic programming to train the algorithms. It optimizes the rewards with correct identification and minimizes the punishment by eliminating wrong judgments based on the knowledge it acquires from the environment.

Classification comes under supervisory ML category. Broadly, there are two types of machine learners used in classification tasks (Grimaldi & Kokaram, 2006). These are:

1. The lazy learners: It stores the input training set and waits for the testing data to the surface. It compares the test data with the training data for the classification purpose. Due to this, the prediction time is usually large, although the learners take less time for training as compared to the eager learners. Case-based reasoning, K-Nearest Neighbor (KNN), etc. comes in this category.

2. The eager learners: In this case, it is not necessary for the ML waiting for the testing data to develop the desired training classification model. However, the learner should be able to hypothesize the desired model representing the designated feature space of concern. Thus, such algorithms take a large time to train the network, although the prediction time remains less. Machine learners such as the (ANN), the Naïve Bayes (NB), and the DT, etc. come in this category.

This paper reviews the use of machine learners in the classification of speech signals. The area remains a challenge due to the followings:

- Natural speech is continuous, so it is difficult to determine word boundaries
- Natural speech contains disfluencies (speakers change their mind in mid-sentences, hesitations, filled pauses, false starts)
- Speech rate locally and globally differs, so same pronunciation may have different spectrum depending on speakers
- A large vocabulary is often confusable. There are also issues of out of vocabulary words.
- Recorded speech is variable over room acoustics, channel characteristics, microphone characteristics and background noise (tilting a microphone at a different angle will change the frequency response).
- Desire to develop human-machine interfaces that are more adaptive and responsive to a user's behavior.
- There is an increasing need to know not only what information a user conveys but also how it is being conveyed.

The objective is to provide the principles, advantages, and limitation of these models for accurate predictions of a class or a pattern by learning from past observations. Such application has benefited many industries relying on artificial intelligence by providing intelligent insights as explained earlier. The field creates interest among the research community as speech remains a sole medium of communication via phone. The area remains a challenging domain of research since an accurate characterization and classification of the voice samples rely on the speech production mechanism, authentic database acquisition, suitable classification algorithms, and the extraction of discriminative speech parameters (Palo, Kumar, &Mohanty, 2017B; Palo, Mohanty, & Chandra, 2015). In the speech production point of view, the speech signal is considered to be a combined effect of the vocal tract and excitation source transfer functions. Due regard to both these components remains vital for accurate characterization and extraction of reliable features of a voice sample. A speech corpus with an adequate number of samples and a sufficient number of speakers is an essential aspect need to be considered in speech analysis. Further, the corpus should be balanced with gender to represent speech characteristics to suit the ML algorithms which are dimensional dependent. The recorded signal passes through the pre-processing, normalization and, the mean subtraction stages to contain the speaker and environmental variability at the lowest level. Since the speech signal is non-periodic or non-stationary in nature, it needs to be analyzed in frame-level for better accuracy. A frame size of 20ms to 30ms with 50% overlapping among adjacent frames of the signal is generally used to obtain the segmented speech signal. To extract the windowed signal, the popular Hamming window is mostly preferred. The window gets rid of the edge effects resulted due to sharp discontinuities at the frame boundary. Similarly, a few researchers have extracted the desired features of the speech signal at the utterance-level without using the framing/ windowing approach for characterization and classification of the signal. Nevertheless, the effectiveness of the frame-level or the utterance-level feature extraction technique depends on the size of the database and the chosen classification algorithm thus, is task-dependent.

Figure 3. The classification model concept

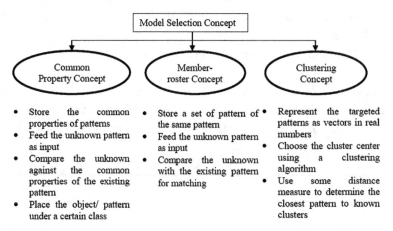

Figure 4. Classifier design approaches

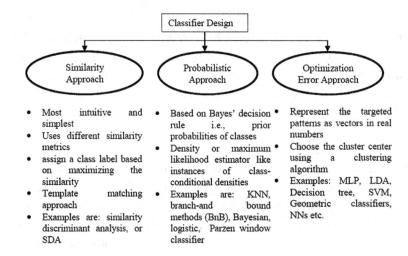

The Speech Classification Concept

The classification models of the desired pattern are obtained based on a few important attributes of the chosen feature/ sample sets. Figure3 below provides the classification model concept in the field of speech recognition application (Devijver & Kittler, 2012; Anusuya & Katti, 2011). Each concept has its characteristics and should be applied to the specific task concerned.

There are roughly three classifier design approaches that are extended in the field of speech and emotional speech recognition (Palo, Mohanty,& Chandra, 2016A; Jain, Duin, & Mao,2000).These are based on (a) concept of similarity(b) probabilistic approach(c) Decision boundary approach based on error optimization. These approaches along with their features are shown in Figure 4.

Figure 5. The classification taxonomy for speech processing

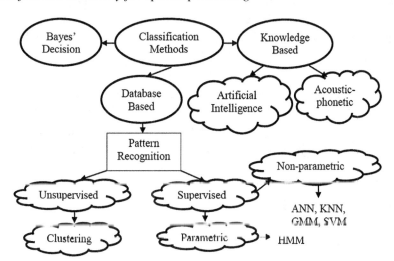

Figure 6. Acoustic-phonetic approach

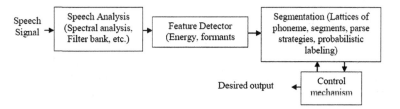

Similarly, Figure 5 provides the taxonomy of classifiers explored in the field of speech signal analysis based on the density functions and the classification techniques. These fields include speech, speaker, language, age, isolated word, emotions, etc. recognition and identification (Palo &Mohanty 2016B). Two approaches that use the explicit rules of human knowledge in the knowledge-based classification scheme are (Bourlard& Morgan 2012; Nandhakumar & Aggarwal 1985; Bahl, Jelinek, & Mercer, 1983).

- Acoustic Phonetic Approach (AP)
- Artificial Intelligence Approach (AI)

The AP approach describes the words of a lexicon, the syntax of knowledge, etc. based on the phonetic and linguistic principles. It relies on the AP theory which postulates that each spoken language comprises of many distinctive, finite phonetic units characterized by a set of parameters in a signal or its spectrum. The parameters of phonetic units differ among speakers and also between adjacent phonemes. Thus, the analysis of speech signals using this approach involves segmentation and labeling. The main advantage of the AP approach is that it is not essential to use all the APs for every decision. Further, the physical interpretation of APs is very strong. Thus, the source of error can be emphasized easily to determine a failed pattern matcher. However, the phonemes chosen are liable to have many choices such as second

(B and AX) or third (L) choices. Henceforth, it is not obvious to match a phonetic sequence with a word or a group of words. Figure 6 shows the steps of Acoustic-phonetic Approach.

The AI approach uses different knowledge sources to compile and incorporate the desired knowledge for a possible classification problem. For example, it uses the knowledge of phonemic, lexical, syntactic, semantic and pragmatic to find the solution to the segmentation and labeling. The benefits of this scheme are that it can limit the sub-symbolic problem-solving. The approach can deal with incomplete or uncertain data using the probability concept. It gives high priority to algorithms with better efficient problem-solving ability. However, the approach needs vast resources for computation of complex tasks. Further, it requires more memory and time for computation when the data size is large.

CLASSIFICATION ALGORITHMS

There are several classification algorithms that have been effectively employed for speech, speaker, language, and emotional speech recognition. Among these, the NN classifier model the decision function that discriminates the desired states within a given set (Haykin, Haykin, Haykin, Elektroingenieur, & Haykin, 2009). Thus, a smaller number of parameters are sufficient for NN based modeling as compared to individual modeling approaches followed by other classifiers. These classifiers have better processing quality, simpler model and ability to discriminate speech signals adequately. The models can capture the complex relationship between the input and the target more accurately (Bishop 1995). The NN classifiers are suitable for non-linear mapping and outperform the GMM/HMM for low dimensional feature sets (El Ayadi, Kamel, & Karray, 2011). Due to parallel distributed structure, NNs do not require any assumption for its input distribution and are flexible in merging multiple inputs. These classifiers outperformed stochastic classifiers like GMM and HMM in describing speech signals with the reduced feature set. However, a major disadvantage of NN modeling is that the network needs to be retrained completely in case the system is added to a new state.

Among NNs, the Radial Basis Function Network (RBFN) requires only one hidden layer, unlike Multilayer Perceptron (MLP). This model is more input noise-tolerant than MLP and is suitable for highly correlated training or testing data. Hence it is applicable for speech signal analysis over a small segment (Palo, &Mohanty 2018C). Further, the network is parallel and statistical that suits it for speech processing as speech frequencies appear in parallel. The design of RBFN is a combination of a nonlinear mapping between the input and the hidden layer and a linear mapping between the hidden and the output layer. In the case of MLP, these layers are non-linear. The MLP is designed using stochastic/ recursive approximation whereas the RBFN applies curve fitting approximation to map high dimensional space. The possibility to use a table look-up interpolation scheme in RBFN makes it better for the reduced feature sets (Haykin, Haykin, Haykin, Elektroingenieur, & Haykin, 2009). The RBFN does not use any back-propagating algorithm, unlike MLP and hence it is faster with higher recognition accuracy than the MLP. Similarly, the Probabilistic Neural Network (PNN) utilizes an activation function which is a statistically derived rather than the non-linear sigmoidal function, unlike MLP. Hence, the network asymptotically approaches the Bay's optimal solution and is faster by 200,000 to 1 with better accuracy (Mao 2000; Specht1990). Further, the weights in PNN can be all set to one, while these need to be adjusted in RBFN, hence the former shines better for a small set of features without over-fitting of data. As compared to these NNs, the Deep Neural Network (DNN) emerges as a state-of-art classifier in recent years in the field of speech recognition (Hinton et al., 2012). It is a feed-forward NN (FFNN) with many hidden layers (h) having many neurons in each hidden layer. Thus, the network can handle very large data sets that pass through the non-linear functions. Further, the use of large feature sets has preserved the model power and reduces data over-fitting. Nevertheless, there is an increase in computational complexity and slower response as a tradeoff. However, NN based classifiers have a slower response time, particularly when the feature size is large or the network is to be retrained for better performance. The range of accuracy from 47% to 90% was reported by different researchers for recognition of speech emotion using NN based classifiers (Sinha & Shahnawazuddin, 2018; Palo, Mohanty, & Chandra, 2016C).

Probabilistic models such as GMM and HMM can model speech signals influenced by noise and channel degradation adequately. HMM can take into account the temporal sequencing, which found to be suitable in a text-dependent platform (Stan, Yamagishi, King, & Aylett, 2011). However, for text-independent cases, the sound sequences present in the training data is not necessarily reflected in the test data. Further, HMM's impose a Markovian constraint between the sound states of a designated class during modeling, which is absent in GMM classifiers (Noman et al., 2018; Williams & Katsaggelos 2002). These probabilistic classifiers provide a separate model for each state. HMMs can handle complex tasks and can scale well as each HMM utilizes only positive data, although it requires maximizing the observed probabilities. On the contrary, the HMMs are good when teaching is good which is not always true. The classifier is most suitable for spectral features extracted at a frame-level and used in combination with prosodic speech features for better recognition accuracy (Bitouk, Verma, & Nenkova, 2010). The technique makes many assumptions which make the accuracy suffer. Further, the use of the Markovian assumption leads to a subtle effect in which both the transition and the emission probabilities are based on the current state. In such a case, the state of probability in remaining in a designated state drops off exponentially. For continuous-density HMM, the assumption of Gaussian Mixture is very large and it is not always advisable to have a normal distribution of the chosen values (Woodland, 2001). It requires much parameter adjustment for the efficient use of the algorithm. The HMM classifier suits better for large feature dimension and fails in case of small feature sets. The reason is that in the HMM, the Viterbi algorithm used allocates frames to the states and there is every likelihood of the frames associated with a state to change resulting in susceptibility to the parameters.

Ease of implementation, well-defined input, and output relationship, ability to handle a large amount of data with fast learning are few positive attributes of a Decision tree classifier. Due to its simplicity and easy rule formation, modeling of speech signals can be efficiently made using this classifier (Lee, Mower, Busso, Lee, & Narayanan, 2011; Akamine & Ajmera, 2012). However, the classifier is sensitive to outliers or noise and produces anomalies due to over-fitting of the data in its many branches. The performance remains poor in the presence of unseen data, thus it is found to be used with known input. The issue can be resolved by the early halting of undue tree construction using pre-pruning or eliminating grown tree using post-pruning. Further, there is a chance of over-complex tree formation that may not generalize adequately besides the formation of new trees on account of small input variation (Wang, Wu, Deng, & Yan, 2008; Lavner & Ruinskiy 2009).

As compared to this, the SVM classifier can handle large characteristic spaces that are multifaceted and can regulate over-fitting using a delicate edge approach. Use of a simple convex optimized algorithm makes it converge to an individual global solution with a better-generalized ability. It is a powerful model for UL (utterance level) features whereas classifiers like GMM or HMM are more suitable for FL (frame-level) features (Schuller, Rigoll, & Lang, 2004; Campbell, Campbell, Reynolds, Jones, & Leek, 2004). Nevertheless, it is noise sensitive and the performance is degraded even with a small number of mislabeled examples.

Compared to this, the Bayesian network can accommodate incomplete details. The NB is a generative learning model, simple to implement and is based on Bayes' theorem. Over-fitting of details and need for pre-processing is not desired by this network. It assumes data independence even in case of features that are related which helps to contribute to the probability distribution in the feature space (Pearl 2014). It does not use iterative approximation during training and the use of linear approximation makes it more scalable to the large feature set. However, the classifier suffers from zero probability problems. Due to this, it is unable to provide a valid prediction for a particular attribute in case the conditional probability is zero (Wu & Cai, 2014; Bjaili, Daqrouq, & Al-Hmouz, 2014). Similarly, it is difficult to specify the network a priori that makes it often cumbersome. Similarly, for high dimensional data inputs having features obeying normal distributions, NB classifier found to be computationally efficient. It can solve real-world problems despite naïve assuming class independence. A few examples on the related work in this field have been briefed below.

The benefits of time-frequency wavelet analysis have been explored in comparing the recognition accuracy of speech signal using three classifiers such as the SVM, ANN, and the Naive Bayes (Suuny, Peter, & Jacob, 2013). The highest recognition accuracy of 89% has been reported by the authors as compared to 86.6% and 83.5% with SVM and NB respectively. Nevertheless, the SVM classifier has shown to outperform the K-nearest Neighbor (KNN) when simulated using prosodic and spectral features such as the Zero Crossing Rate (ZCR), short-time energy, spectral flux, and spectral centroid in classifying the audio signal (Mahana & Singh, 2015). Among spectral features, the Mel-frequency Cepstral Coefficient (MFCC) has been quite effective in speaker accent recognition. The feature has been tested for classification accuracy using many classifiers such as LDA, QDA, SVM, and KNN in literature. Among these classifiers, the KNN is found to be faster computationally with better accuracy (Ma & Fokoué 2015). Recently, the DNN has been applied in the field of pattern recognition such as music instrument classification, emotional speech identification, speech and speaker recognition with efficient results (Solanki & Pandey 2019; Zhang, Zhang, Huang, & Gao, 2017; Graves, Jaitly, & Mohamed, 2013; Hinton et al., 2012). However, the classifiers require a large feature dimension, many hidden layers with many neurons in each hidden layers and large computation time in recognizing the desired pattern.

The recognition of emotions from human voices has been an area of research involving many ML algorithms actively. The authors have compared the effectiveness of a few important prosodic parameters in describing the speech emotion using the NN based Multilayer Perceptron with excellent results (Palo, et al., 2016). Among NNs, the PNN has shown to outperform both the RBFN and MLP for low feature dimension while the GMM has provided improved accuracy for large feature dimension as compared to NNs (Palo, et al., 2018; Palo, et al., Palo et al., 2017). From the survey of pieces of literature, it can be concluded that the choice of the ML algorithm is purely task-dependent and rely on the feature robustness and its dimension. Hence, a judicious selection of the classification algorithm needs to be considered while dealing with different patterns related to a speaker, his/ her voice, and emotional states.

This work aims to overview the generalized principles of classification using different ML architectures. A few of the important and most prominent classification algorithms used in the fields of speech, emotional speech, language, gender and age identification, and detection have been briefed in this section.

Neural Networks

The neural network or the connectionist model is a parallel distributed processing (PDP) model and is suitable for speech analysis as the speech frequencies occur in parallel. It consists of broadly three layers as input, hidden and output with a dense interconnection of nonlinear elements by weights and biases (Bishop, 1995, Haykin, et al., 2009). The sigmoid nonlinearities or activation functions are preferred as these are continuous and differentiable. The sigmoid activation function $f(x)$ is given by

$$f(x) = tanh(\beta x), \quad \beta > 0 \tag{1}$$

Three popular topologies of NNs used for pattern recognition. These are (a) single or multilayer perceptron (b) Recurrent or Hopfield networks (c) Self-organizing or Kohonen networks. In single or multilayer perceptron a connection of the output of one layer is made to the input of the other with suitable weights and biases. Only one hidden layer is kept in a single layer, whereas the multilayer perceptron has many hidden layers. In the recurrent or the Hopfield network each computational element has the inputs and the outputs. The self-organizing or Kohonen network uses the clustering algorithm in the input space to generate a codebook of stable patterns.

Multilayer Perceptron (MLP)

In MLP, the features are fed in as input to this classifier. Updating of weight takes place as the features propagate from the input to the output layer via the hidden layer during the forward pass. The calculation of error takes place during the backward pass of the training and testing features using the back-propagation algorithm (Bishop, 1995). A generalized MLP structure is shown in Figure 7.

Let's indicate the input training vector $s = \{s_1, s_2, \ldots, s_p, \ldots, s_n\}$, the hidden vector as $z = \{z_1, z_2, \ldots, z_q, \ldots, z_m\}$ the output vector as $y = \{y_1, y_2, \ldots, y_r, \ldots, y_o\}$ and learning parameter as $\propto$. For a hidden unit q given by z_q, the net input without activation function 'f' is given by

$$z_{inq} = v_{0q} + \sum_p s_p v_{pq} \tag{2}$$

With an activation function, the hidden layer has the output as given by

$$z_q = f(z_{pq}) \tag{3}$$

Where the qth hidden unit bias vector and input weight vectors are denoted by v_{0q} and v_{pq} respectively. Similarly, for the rth output unit given by y_r, the net input from the hidden unit is given by

$$y_{inr} = w_{or} + \sum_q z_q w_{qr} \tag{4}$$

Figure 7. A basic MLP structure

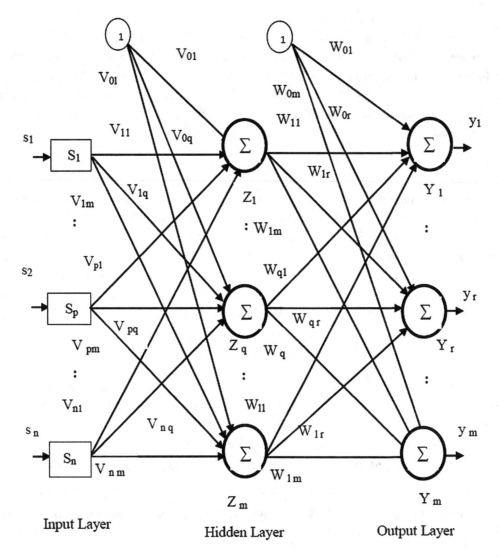

where w_{or} is the bias on the rth output unit. For an activation function indicated as 'f' the final output can be expressed as

$$y_r = f\left(w_{or} + \sum_q z_q w_{qr}\right) \tag{5}$$

Figure 8. a simplified structure of rbf network with 'h' number of rbf units and a single output unit

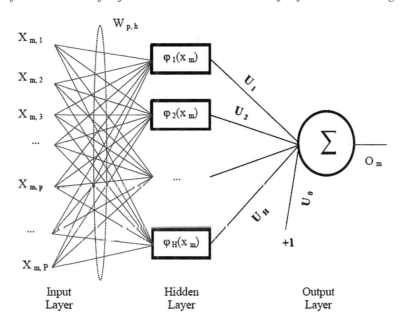

Radial Basis Function Network (RBFN)

As shown in Figure 8, the RBFN network comprises of P inputs, H RBF units, and one output. To classify multiple outputs several similar units are used. Features of the speech signals are fed as inputs and can be represented as $S_M = \left\{ S_{m,1}, S_{m,2}, \ldots, S_{m,p}, \ldots, S_{m,P} \right\}$, $1 \le m \le M$. The operation of RBFN is explained as below (Palo, Mohanty, & Chandra, 2016C).

Let $W_{p,h}$ represent the weights between the pth input and the h RBF units. Each input $S_{m,p}$ is scaled by the RBF index gives the scaled inputs $q_{m,h} = \left\{ q_{m,h,1}, q_{m,h,2}, \ldots, q_{m,h,p}, \ldots, q_{m,h,P} \right\}$, $1 \le h \le H$, $1 \le p \le P$ and is represented as

$$q_{m,h,p} = S_{m,p} W_{p,h} \tag{6}$$

The activation function $\varphi_h \left(\cdot \right)$ used in this network is given by

$$\varphi_h \left(\cdot \right) = \sum_{h=1}^{H} \varphi_h q_{m,h} - \mu_h \tag{7}$$

where $\varphi_h q_{m,h} - \mu_h$ denotes the hidden layer RBF units and $\lVert \cdot \rVert$ represents the Euclidean distance norm. The Gaussian activation function $\varphi_h \left(\cdot \right)$ with RBF unit h, width σ_h and center μ_h used in RBFN gives an output

Figure 9. A generalized PNN Structure

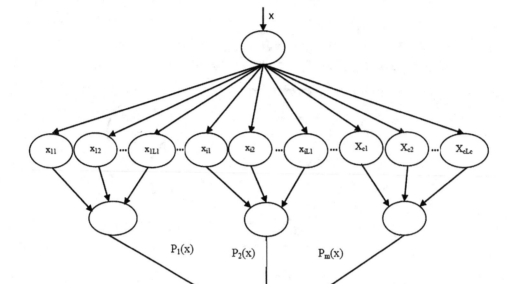

$$\varphi_h\left(S_m\right) = exp\left(\frac{q_{m,h} - \mu_h^{\ 2}}{\sigma_h}\right) \tag{8}$$

Let the weights between RBF unit h, and the network output is denoted as U_h with bias U_0. With the input pattern S_m, the output of RBFN is computed as

$$O_m = \sum_{h=1}^{H} \varphi_h\left(S_m\right)U_h + U_0 \tag{9}$$

Probabilistic Neural Network (PNN)

The PNN is a non-parametric classifier and outperforms the MLP in terms of accuracy, shorter training time and discriminating ability. Further, the network requires single processing during training. Using only a single parameter adjustment, it can tolerate erroneous samples and can accommodate training with sparse input data. These features make PNN a potential candidate for real-time classification and pattern diagnosis problems.

A basic PNN structure is shown in Figure 9. It has four stages as the input, pattern, summation and the decision layer. On the arrival of input pattern x having z-dimension, the pattern layer neuron $x_{i,h}$ provides an output as given by (Palo, Chandra, &Mohanty, 2018D; Mao, Tan, &Ser, 2000).

Figure 10. A generalized DNN structure

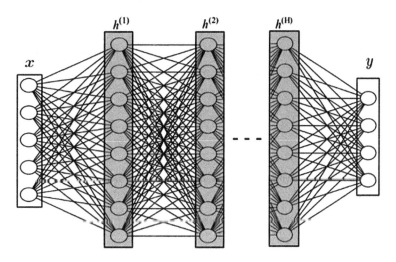

$$\varphi_{i,h}(x) = \frac{1}{(2\pi)^{\frac{z}{2}} \mu^z} exp\left[-\frac{(x-x_{i,h})^T (x-x_{i,h})}{2\mu^2} \right] \tag{10}$$

Here, the terms z, μ, and $x_{i,h}$ are the pattern vector dimension, smoothing parameter, and the neuron vector respectively. A maximum likelihood of x is computed by the summation layer which summarizes and computes the average of all the neuron outputs corresponding to a particular class E_i for classification of the pattern as belonging to that class.

$$p_i(x) = \frac{1}{(2\pi)^{\frac{z}{2}} \mu^z} \frac{1}{L_i} \sum_{h=1}^{L_i} exp\left[-\frac{(x-x_{i,h})^T (x-x_{i,h})}{2\mu^2} \right] \tag{11}$$

where the number of features of a class O_i is denoted as L_i. Assuming equal *a priori* probability for all the chosen classes, the decision layer classifies the desired class based on the summation layer neuron's output. The layer follows the Bayes' rule to classify the pattern x. Letting the loss incurred in taking a wrong decision to be the same for all the chosen states, the targeted class $O(x)$ of the pattern x is given by

$$O(x) = \arg\max\{p_i(x)\}, i = 1, 2, \ldots, c \tag{12}$$

where 'c' is the number of classes in the training features.

Deep Neural Network

A generalized DNN structure is shown in Figure10.

Let the input feature vector x_n is of n-dimensional which is mapped into the first hidden layer of m_1 units. The hidden vector can be represented as (Hinton, et al., 2012).

$$h^{(1)}(x) = f\left(\left(w^{(1)}\right)' x + b^{(1)}\right) = f(a) \tag{13}$$

where f is the non-linear activation function, typically a logistic function with growth rate or steepness of k and is given by

$$f\left(a^{(1)}\right) = \frac{1}{1 + e^{-ka^{(1)}}} \tag{14}$$

The weights $w^{(1)}$ and bias $b^{(1)}$ matrix have the dimension of $n \times m_1$ and m_1 respectively. Similarly, the activation of the succeeding layers can be obtained based on the previous activation vector $h^{(j-1)}$ and is given by

$$h^{(j)}(x) = f\left(\left(w^{(j)}\right)' h^{(j-1)} + b^{(j)}\right) = f\left(a^{(j-1)}\right) \tag{15}$$

where the terms $w^{(j)}$ and $b^{(j)}$ are the weights and biases vectors involving the jth hidden layer with the dimension of $m_{j-1} \times m_j$ and m_j respectively, where m_j denotes the number of neurons in j^{th} hidden layer.

The output layer uses a soft-max function as given by

$$y_l = \frac{e^{\left(\left(w_l^{(o)}\right)' h^{(H)} + b_l^{(o)}\right)}}{\sum_c^{m_o} e^{\left(\left(w_c^{(o)}\right)' h^{(H)} + b_c^{(o)}\right)}} \tag{16}$$

where m_o is the number of units in the output layer and y_l is the output layer for l^{th} output unit. The activation function corresponding to the last hidden layer is denoted by $h^{(H)}$ and the term 'c' indicates the index of all classes.

The Bayesian Network

The Bayesian network can accommodate incomplete details more efficiently in analyzing the speech signals (Bjaili, Daqrouq, & Al-Hmouz, 2014). The Naïve Bayes' (NB) is a generative learning model, simple to implement and is based on Bayes' theorem. Over-fitting of details and need for pre-processing is not desired by this network. It assumes data independence even in case of features that are related which helps the probability distribution in a chosen feature space. It does not use iterative approximation during training and the use of linear approximation makes it more scalable to the large feature set. However, the classifier suffers from zero probability problems. Due to this, it is unable to provide a valid prediction for a particular attribute in case the conditional probability is zero. Similarly, it is difficult to specify the network a priori that makes it often cumbersome. Similarly, for high dimensional data inputs having features obeying normal distributions, NB classifier found to be computationally efficient. It can solve real-world problems despite naïve assuming class independence.

Consider the speaker class as c_j, $j = 1, 2, \ldots, C$ and b denotes the feature values that provide information on speaker identity, then

$$P\left(c_j | b\right) = \frac{P\left(b | c_j\right) P\left(c_j\right)}{\sum_j P\left(b | c_j\right) P\left(c_j\right)} \tag{17}$$

where $P\left(b | c_j\right)$ is the likelihood function. For each speaker, there exists a probability score. Thus, indicating a feature in the feature vector as b_k, the probability can be found as

$$P\left(c_j | b_k\right) = \frac{P\left(b_k | c_j\right) P\left(c_j\right)}{\sum_j P\left(b_k | c_j\right) P\left(c_j\right)} \tag{18}$$

and

$$P\left(c_j | b_1, b_2, \ldots, b_K\right) = \frac{P\left(b_1, b_2, \ldots, b_K | c_j\right) P\left(c_j\right)}{\sum_j P\left(b_1, b_2, \ldots, b_K | c_j\right) P\left(c_j\right)} \tag{19}$$

where K describes the total number of features. The Maximum A Posteriori Probability (MAP) of speaker class c_j can be used to find the class of the speaker which maximizes the term $P\left(c_j | b_1, b_2, \ldots, b_K\right)$, i.e.

$$Argmax_j = P\left(c_j | b_1, b_2, \ldots, b_K\right) \tag{20}$$

Hidden Markov Model (HMM)

The HMM hasa first-order Markov chain with hidden states from an observer. This means the observer cannot directly examine the internal behavior of the model while the data's temporal structure is recorded by these states (Noman, et al., 2018; Williams, & Katsaggelos 2002). To express this in mathematical terms, for modeling a sequence of observable data vectors, $s_1, \cdots, s_T$ by an HMM, it is essential to assume the existence of a hidden Markov chain which generates the observable data sequence. Let π_j represents the number of states, where $j = 1, \cdots, J$ deontes the initial state probabilities of the hidden Markov chain. The term a_{jk}, $j = 1, \cdots, J$, $k = 1, \cdots, J$ represents the transition probability between the state k and the state j. Let's represent a true state sequence $x_1, \cdots, x_T$, then the likelihood of the observable data can be expressed as

$$p\left(s_1, x_1, \cdots, s_T, x_T\right) = \pi_{x_1} \, bx_1\left(s_1\right) a_{x_1, x_2} \, bx_2\left(s_2\right) \ldots a_{x_{T-1}x_T} \, bx_T\left(s_T\right) p\left(s_1, x_1, \cdots, s_T, x_T\right)$$

$$= \pi_{x_1} \, bx_1\left(s_1\right) \prod_{t=2}^{T} a_{x_{t-1}x_t} \, bx_t\left(s_t\right) \tag{21}$$

The HMM is also a sequential generating probabilistic model, which means that the classifier acts on the assumption that neighboring frames are closely related. While this is valid for speech signal frames, there are better alternatives due to its assumption and algorithm complexity.

The Support Vector Machine (SVM)

The SVM is a discriminative classifier with linear and nonlinear separating hyper-planes to classify data. The classifier uses the maximum-margin fitting functions for regularization and better generalization. For classification purposes, the classifier constructs an N-dimensional hyper plane for optimal separation of clusters of vectors into two categories. The vectors that positions close to the hyper-plane are known as support vectors (Schuller, Rigoll, & Lang, 2004). Although the SVM is binary it can be extended to multiclass pattern recognition.

In a two-class SVM problem, a boundary is defined between the classes based on maximal separation of the closest features.

Consider a linear separable feature set $F = \left\{\left(A_i, B_i\right), A_i \in \mathbb{R}^p, B_i \in \{-1, 1\}\right\}_{i=1}^n$. Fig. 9 provides the objective of the SVM classifier in maximizing the margin (the shortest perpendicular distance between the observed feature values and the hyper-plane) (Campbell, Campbell, Reynolds, Jones, & Leek, 2004). The margin refers to the width or the distance in the blank space as shown in Figure11. The equation of any hyper-plane can be expressed as

$$w.a - p = 0 \tag{22}$$

Figure 11. The concept of support vector machine

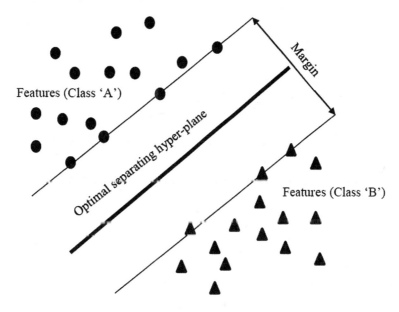

where w denotes the coefficient vector while p is a constant. For a linearly separable data set, we can expect two hyper-planes for complete separation of the dataset while no feature values appear in between. These two hyper-planes in Figure11are indicated as

$$w.a - p = -1$$

and

$$w.a - p = +1$$

The goal of the SVM is to optimize the margin by minimizing w. To achieve the desired classification, the following relationship can be used.

$$class\left(a_i\right) = \begin{cases} 1 & w.a_i - b > 0 \\ -1 & w.a_i - b \leq 0 \end{cases}$$

For non-linearly separable data, different kernel functions are considered to linearize the data. To achieve this, the kernel function transforms the non-linearly separable feature sets into an inner product space. The Radial Basis Function (RBF) kernel has been mostly used due to its similarity to the simple Euclidean distance measure with a norm $\|\cdot\|$ and is given by

$$K\left(a,b\right) = exp\left(-\frac{a-b^2}{2\sigma^2}\right) \tag{23}$$

Figure 12. The GMM model with M component densities

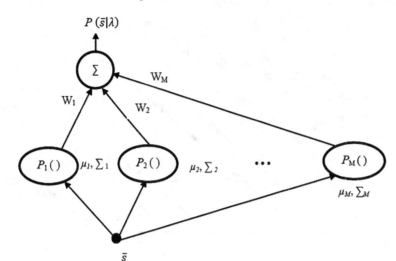

where σ denotes the spread constant as explained earlier. Similarly, the polynomial kernel has been also popularly used in the linearization of non-linearly separable feature sets in SVM. The advantage of using this kernel is that it not only helps to find the similarity in a given feature set but also in a combination of feature sets. The polynomial kernel can be expressed as

$$K\left(a,b\right)=\left(a^{T}b+c\right)^{d} \tag{24}$$

where $c \geq 0$, helps to trade-off the influence of higher andthe lower-order terms in the polynomial. For $c = 0$, the kernel becomes homogeneous (Shashua, 2009).

Gaussian Mixture Model (GMM)

Broad classes of signal models in pattern recognition are the established statistical models that rely on the statistical parameters of a signal. The basic assumption in these models considersthe analyzing signal as a parametric random process. The stochastic process parameters are estimated in a well-defined manner with precision. Poisson processes, Gaussian processes, Markov or hidden Markov processes fall in these categories. This section emphasizes on the GMM based stochastic signal model that represents some broad acoustic emotional classes. The model requires a judicious selection of model order and the initialization of model parameters for its practical and successful implementation.

The GMM is a probability density model having several Gaussian function components (Reynolds & Rose 1995). A weighted sum of *M* component densities is used to estimate the Gaussian mixture densities as shown in Figure12. In the process, a multimodal density has resulted in a combination of these component functions. A GMM can be represented as

$$P(S) = \sum_{m=1}^{M} w_m p_m(\vec{s}) = \sum_{m=1}^{M} w_m \mathcal{N}(\vec{s}; \mu_m, \Sigma_m) \tag{25}$$

where $\mathcal{N}(\vec{s}; \mu_m, \Sigma_m)$ denotes the normal distribution and M represents the number of mixtures whereas μ_m, Σ_m and w_m are the mean vector, covariance matrix, and the mixture weights respectively that characterize the distribution. These vectors from all component densities are essentially parameterized the complete Gaussian mixture density denoted by

$$\lambda = (\mu_m, \Sigma_m, w_m) \, m = 1, 2, \ldots \ldots M$$

To recognize human speech emotion, each class is described by a GMM model λ.

To guarantee a valid probability model of a pattern the condition to be satisfied is given by $\sum_{m=1}^{M} w_m$ $=1$ since each mixture component is indeed Gaussian. For any feature space of d dimension, the Gaussian distribution can be described as:-

$$\mathcal{N}(s; \mu_m, \Sigma_m) = \left(2\pi^{-\frac{d}{2}} \right) |\Sigma_m|^{-\frac{1}{2}} \exp \left\{ -\frac{1}{2}(\vec{s} - \vec{\mu}_m)^T \vec{\Sigma}_m^{-1} (\vec{s} - \vec{\mu}_m) \right\} \tag{26}$$

Among several GMM parameter estimation methods, the maximum likelihood (ML) is quite popular in finding the best matches of the training pattern distribution. It maximizes the GMM likelihood of a training data sequence that can guarantee the estimation of the local maximum. Consider a speech training data sequence represented by T training vectors, i.e. $S = \{s_1, s_2 \ldots s_T\}$. The following relation will provide the GMM likelihood:-

$$P(S|\lambda) = \prod_{t=1}^{T} P(\vec{s}_t \mid \lambda) \tag{27}$$

Unfortunately, it is difficult to obtain direct maximization as the expression given in the above equation which tends to be a nonlinear function of λ. To alleviate the problem, an iterative algorithm of ML parameter estimation is instead found more useful. The algorithm is a special case of ML estimation and is known as the expectation-maximization (EM) algorithm. In this case, the new model $\bar{\lambda}$ is estimated from an initial model λ by satisfying the condition $P(S \mid \lambda) \geq P(S \mid \bar{\lambda})$. The next new model is based on the previous new model and so on. The process continues until some convergence threshold is achieved. The iterative algorithm uses the re-estimation formula as given in equations below to guarantee a monotonic growth in the desired model's likelihood value.

Means

$$\vec{\mu}_m = \frac{\sum_{t=1}^{T} P_m\left(m\mid\vec{s}_t\right)\vec{s}_t}{\sum_{t=1}^{T} P_m\left(m\mid\vec{s}_t\right)} \tag{28}$$

Variances

$$\vec{\Sigma}_m = \frac{\sum_{t=1}^{T} P_m\left(m\mid\vec{s}_t\right)\left(\vec{s}_t-\vec{\mu}_m\right)^{\mathrm{T}}\left(\vec{s}_t-\vec{\mu}_m\right)}{\sum_{t=1}^{T} P_m\left(m\mid\vec{s}_t\right)} \tag{29}$$

Mixture Weights

$$\vec{w}_m = \frac{\sum_{t=1}^{T} P_m\left(m\mid\vec{s}_t\right)}{\sum_{t=1}^{T}\sum_{m=1}^{M} P_m\left(m\mid\vec{s}_t\right)} \tag{30}$$

For an emotional class 'm', a posteriori probability is estimated as:-

$$P\left(m\mid s_t,\lambda\right) = \frac{w_m p_m\left(\vec{s}_t\right)}{\sum_{k=1}^{M} w_k p_k\left(\vec{s}_t\right)} \tag{31}$$

Compared to HMMs, GMM is superior in training and testing due to their efficiency in modeling multi-modal distributions as a whole. GMMs are used in SER when global features are the main focus. But due to this feature, GMMs are not suited when the user would like to model the temporal structure.

OTHER CLASSIFIERS

A few other classifiers used in analyzing the speech signal have been briefed in this section. The KNN classifier postulates that for each class if the costs of error are equal, then the estimated class corresponding to an unknown sample should be the class most commonly described in the set of its k-nearest neighbors (Kacur, Vargic, & Mulinka, 2011). Thus, the classification scheme is based on the closest features in the sample space. The KNN is a lazy learner or instance-based learner in which the approximation of the function is accomplished locally and the calculations are deferred until classification. In this, an object is classified based on a majority vote concerning its neighbors. The object will be assigned to a class which is more familiar amongst its k nearest neighbors, where k is a small positive integer. For $k = 1$, the object is assigned to the class of its nearest neighbor. For smoother and low locally sensitive function, a higher value of k is used.

The decision tree is another similar classifier often discussed in this area. It is a tree-structured network and utilizes a mutually exclusive and exhaustive if-then rule set for classification. To learn the rules, the training data are used sequentially one at a time. On learning a particular rule, the tuples associated with that rule are eliminated and the training process continues until a termination condition is reached. The tree follows a top-down recursive divide-and-conquer manner using either the categorical or discretized attributes. The concept of information gain is used to identify the attributes positioned in the top of the tree as these are most influential in pattern classification.

The literature on classification model used in speech processing is vast and growing. Arguably, a research can't focus all the works on the classification of a speech signal. There are many empirical and theoretical issues yet to be identified and suitably addressed in the current scenario. Further, each classification model has its limitations and advantages. The choice of a classifier is based on many factors such as the feature extraction techniques used, type and size of the dataset and most importantly the task in hand. To take into account the benefits of prominent classifiers, many researchers have adopted the combination, fusion, and hybridization of different classification algorithms (Tulyakov, Jaeger, Govindaraju, &Doermann, 2008). The relative strengths of both SVM and HMM have been explored to develop a hybrid SVM/HMM model for speech recognition application with better results (Ganapathiraju, Hamaker, &Picone, 2000). The combination of Deep Bidirectional LSTM (DBLSTM) and HMM has shown to outperform both GMM and DNN with less word error rate (Graves, Jaitly, & Mohamed, 2013).

A summary of different classification algorithms with their advantages and limitation is shown in Table 1.

A comparison of some of the state-of-art classification algorithm explored in the field of speech signal identification has been tabulated in Table-2

CONCLUSION

Recognition of speech signal remains a complex task due to the involvement of acoustic cues that relate a speaker voice to its mood, age, gender, demographic profile, and environment. These factors control the classification accuracy drastically and have been focused by the speech community based on suitable research inputs. Among these factors, this work provides a detailed survey of the classification schemes employed in the domain of speech recognition. The relative advantages and the limitations of these classifiers are also briefed for their applicability to a specific task. Among the discussed classifiers, the NNs found to outperform the conventional GMM/HMM/SVM for smaller samples. However, the DNN with many hidden layers and with many neurons in each hidden layer remains suitable for the data mining task. The performance of the classifier degrades for smaller feature sets. On the contrary, the classifiers like the GMM or SVM found to model the desired speech signal well when the number of samples under consideration is high or for large dimensional feature sets. The classification models are many and it is hard to reach a consensus for the optimum classifier. An extensive survey of the literature shows, the choice of classifier largely depends on the task in hand, the type, and size of the database, feature extraction techniques involved, etc. The fusion of different classification algorithm and their

Table 1. Summary of classifiers used in speech recognition with their advantages and limitations

Classifier	Advantage	Disadvantages
HMM	(1) Text-independent. (2) Bigger HMM possible by combinations of HMMs.	(1) Significant increase in computational complexity. (2) The requirement of a suitable model parameter initialization procedure before training. (3) Comparatively more times require to train the classifier.
GMM	(1) Probabilistic framework (robust). (2) Computationally efficient. (3) Use of the expectation-maximization in this network makes faster modeling of the patterns involving large data set. (4) Easy to implement. (5) Text independent. (6) Suited for extracting global features.	(1) Require to gather all the model parameters for comparison. (2) Cannot exclude exponential functions. (3) The network performance is poorer in the presence of fewer data. (4) It is not possible to assume the data to be Gaussian distributed randomly for the network to perform better. (5) With insufficient features per mixture, it is difficult to compute the covariance matrices and the algorithm diverges. In this case, the network finds boundless likelihood results and requires artificial regularization of the covariance matrix.
ANN	(1) Fewer parameters (2) Better accuracy potential with more hidden layers (3) Data-driven and self-adaptive-learning (4) Can accomplish tasks not possible by a linear programming technique. (5) It learns and needs to be reprogrammed. (6) When any element fails, it continues to function since parallel structured. (7) No assumption for data distribution unlike in statistical modeling. (8) Suitable for multivariate non-linear tasks. Can model real-world complex tasks. (9) Can approximate any function with arbitrary accuracy since they are universal functional approximators. (10) Noise tolerant. (11) Suitable for continuous valued inputs and outputs.	(1) Requires training for operation. (2) Large processing time for large network size. (3) Slow if the data size is large. (4) Requires complex computational effort to minimize over-fitting of data. (5) It's a black box approach without analytical basis since a relationship between the individual output and input variables are not made. (6) May fall in local minima or does not converge to a stable version unlike SVM.
SVM	(1) Use linear discriminants to learn. (2) Use Risk Minimization (RM) or Empirical RM to reduce misclassification in a sample set. (3) It has a guaranteed convergence to the minimum of associated cost function due to a unique solution. (4) Can handle large dimensional data due to use of kernel matrix for minimization and as its generalization error is unrelated to the input feature dimension but related to the margin that separated the features. (5) In a high dimensional space, it is possible to train generalizable, nonlinear classifiers with a small training set.	(1) It has a space complexity problem since the algorithm computes and stores the entire kernel matrix of the input samples in the memory. (2) Thus, not suitable for very large dataset. (3) Optimality is kernel dependent and it is not sure which kernel suits a particular task. (4) Can classify fixed-length data vectors only and not suitable to variable-length data classification.
KNN	(1) A powerful and simple clustering algorithm. (2) A common method to estimate the bandwidth or adaptive mean shift.	(1) Susceptible to noise due to high local sensitivity, lack of robustness. (2) Memory intensive. (3) Estimation, detection, and classification are slow for large size data. (4) Decision boundary depends on the computation complexity hence on the boundary complexity. (5) Inefficient in presence of redundant or noisy data. (6) The prediction accuracy degrades if the number of attributes increases.
MLP	(1) Class separation using hyper-planes. (2) Distributed learning.	(1) More hidden layers. (2) Slower to train.
RBFN	(1) Class separation using hyper-spheres. (2) Faster to train and higher learning rate.as no back-propagation is required. (3) Universal approximation and good generalization capability.	(1) More hidden layers. (4) Localized training. (5) Multi-parameter adjustment.
PNN	(1) Faster and accurate than MLP. (2) Can approach A Bayes' optimal solution. (3) Robust to noise. (4) Guaranteed to converge with an increase in training features. (5) Easy to train (instantaneous training) (6) Insensitive to outliers. (7) Weights are not assigned rather than trained. (8) Single parameter adjustment.	(1) Slower than MLP to classify new cases. (2) Larger memory. (3) Required a representative training feature set.
DNN	(1) Best-in-class performance in multiple domains. (2) Suitable for data-mining and large feature sets. (3) Reduce the need for feature engineering, selection, and optimization which consume much time. (4) Can adapt to new problems easily.	(1) Not suitable for small feature sets needs thousands of samples to perform satisfactorily. (2) Computationally expensive to train (requires GPU in most cases due to its requirement of large data handling). (3) No strong theory or properly defined mathematical model to guide for determination of DNN topology, training method, favor, hyper-parameters. Learning is spread over the hidden layers and hence is a black-box approach. (4) It is not possible to comprehend what is being learned.

Table 2. Comparison of classifiers based on the size of data, features, and results in recognizing speech signals

Literatures	Features	Size of Data	Classifier	Results/ Comments
Alexandre-Cortizo, Rosa-Zurera, & Lopez-Ferreras, 2005	Prosodic and spectral	13 coefficients per frame	KNN LDA	a probability error of 4.09% and 4.910% respectively achieved using MFCC
Han, Chan, Choy, & Pun,2006	Modified MFCC	23 coefficients per frame	HMM	94.43%
Hossan, Memon, & Gregory,2010	Distributed DCT based MFCC	-	GMM-EM	96.72%
Bhattacharjee, &Sarmah 2013	MFCC+prosodic	12 MFCCs+deltas+double deltas.	GMM	8.70% equal error rate (EER) in Hindi language identification
Kumar, Prabhakar, &Sahu,2014	MFCC, LPC, and PLP	-	ANN, HMM, VQ	Accuracy of MFCC is higher. VQ (96.5%), ANN (51.2%), HMM (86.67%)
Suuny, Peter, & Jacob, 2013	Wavelet features	-	ANN, SVM, NB	ANN (89%), SVM (86.6%), NB (83.5%)
Kumar,Biswas, Mishra, & Chandra, 2010	Revised PLP	13 coefficients per frame	GMM	88.75% using
Bjaili,Daqrouq, & Al-Hmouz,2014	Wavelet Packet (WP) LPC + Wavelet_LPC	-	NB	93.55%

subsequent modification have provided better results in classifying speech signal than the conventional algorithms. However, ensemble or fusion of classification methods remains complex and cumbersome, thus, are task-dependent. Finally, recognition of speech signal

REFERENCES

Akamine, M., & Ajmera, J. (2012). Decision tree-based acoustic models for speech recognition. *EURASIP Journal on Audio, Speech, and Music Processing*, *2012*(1), 10. doi:10.1186/1687-4722-2012-10

Alexandre-Cortizo, E., Rosa-Zurera, M., & Lopez-Ferreras, F. (2005, November). Application of fisher linear discriminant analysis to speech/music classification. In *EUROCON 2005-The International Conference on Computer as a Tool* (Vol. 2, pp. 1666-1669). IEEE.

Alzubi, J., Nayyar, A., & Kumar, A. (2018, November). Machine learning from theory to algorithms: An overview. *Journal of Physics: Conference Series*, *1142*(1), 012012. doi:10.1088/1742-6596/1142/1/012012

Anusuya, M. A., & Katti, S. K. (2011). Classification Techniques used in Speech Recognition Applications: A Review. *Int. J. Comp. Tech. Appl*, *2*(4), 910–954.

Bahl, L. R., Jelinek, F., & Mercer, R. L. (1983). A maximum likelihood approach to continuous speech recognition. *IEEE Transactions on Pattern Analysis and Machine Intelligence, PAMI-5*(2), 179–190. doi:10.1109/TPAMI.1983.4767370 PMID:21869099

Bhattacharjee, U., & Sarmah, K. (2013, March). Language identification system using MFCC and prosodic features. In *2013 International Conference on Intelligent Systems and Signal Processing (ISSP)*, (pp. 194-197). IEEE. 10.1109/ISSP.2013.6526901

Bishop, C. M. (1995). *Neural networks for pattern recognition*. Oxford University Press.

Bitouk, D., Verma, R., & Nenkova, A. (2010). Class-level spectral features for emotion recognition. *Speech Communication, 52*(7-8), 613–625. doi:10.1016/j.specom.2010.02.010 PMID:23794771

Bjaili, H., Daqrouq, K., & Al-Hmouz, R. (2014). Speaker Identification Using Bayesian Algorithm. *Trends in Applied Sciences Research, 9*(8), 472–479. doi:10.3923/tasr.2014.472.479

Bourlard, H. A., & Morgan, N. (2012). *Connectionist speech recognition: a hybrid approach* (Vol. 247). Springer Science & Business Media.

Campbell, W. M., Campbell, J. P., Reynolds, D. A., Jones, D. A., & Leek, T. R. (2004). Phonetic speaker recognition with support vector machines. In Advances in neural information processing systems (pp. 1377-1384). Academic Press.

Devijver, P. A., & Kittler, J. (Eds.). (2012). *Pattern recognition theory and applications* (Vol. 30). Springer Science & Business Media.

El Ayadi, M., Kamel, M. S., & Karray, F. (2011). Survey on speech emotion recognition: Features, classification schemes, and databases. *Pattern Recognition, 44*(3), 572–587. doi:10.1016/j.patcog.2010.09.020

Franke, K., & Srihari, S. N. (2008, August). Computational forensics: An overview. In *International Workshop on Computational Forensics* (pp. 1-10). Springer.

Ganapathiraju, A., Hamaker, J., & Picone, J. (2000). Hybrid SVM/HMM architectures for speech recognition. *Sixth international conference on spoken language processing*.

Geiger, J., Leykauf, T., Rehrl, T., Wallhoff, F., & Rigoll, G. (2014). The robot ALIAS as a gaming platform for elderly persons. In *Ambient Assisted Living* (pp. 327–340). Berlin: Springer. doi:10.1007/978-3-642-37988-8_21

Graves, A., Jaitly, N., & Mohamed, A. R. (2013, December). *Hybrid speech recognition with deep bidirectional LSTM. In 2013 IEEE workshop on automatic speech recognition and understanding* (pp. 273–278). IEEE. doi:10.1109/ASRU.2013.6707742

Grimaldi, M., & Kokaram, A. (2006). Discrete wavelet packet transform and ensembles of lazy and eager learners for music genre classification. *Multimedia Systems, 11*(5), 422–437. doi:10.100700530-006-0027-z

Gromski, P. S., Muhamadali, H., Ellis, D. I., Xu, Y., Correa, E., Turner, M. L., & Goodacre, R. (2015). A tutorial review: Metabolomics and partial least squares-discriminant analysis–a marriage of convenience or a shotgun wedding. *Analytica Chimica Acta, 879*, 10–23. doi:10.1016/j.aca.2015.02.012 PMID:26002472

HaCohen-Kerner, Y., Gross, Z., & Masa, A. (2005, February). Automatic extraction and learning of keyphrases from scientific articles. In *International Conference on Intelligent Text Processing and Computational Linguistics* (pp. 657-669). Springer.

Han, W., Chan, C. F., Choy, C. S., & Pun, K. P. (2006, May). An efficient MFCC extraction method in speech recognition. In 2006 IEEE international symposium on circuits and systems (pp. 4-pp). IEEE.

Haykin, S. S., Haykin, S. S., Haykin, S. S., Elektroingenieur, K., & Haykin, S. S. (2009). *Neural networks and learning machines* (Vol. 3). Upper Saddle River, NJ: Pearson.

Hinton, G., Deng, L., Yu, D., Dahl, G., Mohamed, A. R., Jaitly, N., ... Sainath, T. (2012). Deep neural networks for acoustic modeling in speech recognition. *IEEE Signal Processing Magazine, 29*.

Hossan, M. A., Memon, S., & Gregory, M. A. (2010, December). A novel approach for MFCC feature extraction. In *2010 4th International Conference on Signal Processing and Communication Systems* (pp. 1-5). IEEE. 10.1109/ICSPCS.2010.5709752

Jain, A. K., Duin, R. P. W., & Mao, J. (2000). Statistical pattern recognition: A review. *IEEE Transactions on Pattern Analysis and Machine Intelligence, 22*(1), 4–37. doi:10.1109/34.824819

Kacur, J., Vargic, R., & Mulinka, P. (2011, June). Speaker identification by K-nearest neighbors: Application of PCA and LDA prior to KNN. In *2011 18th International Conference on Systems, Signals and Image Processing* (pp. 1-4). IEEE.

Kaur, K., & Jain, N. (2015). Feature Extraction and Classification for Automatic Speaker Recognition System-A Review. *International Journal of Advanced Research in Computer Science and Software Engineering, 5*.

Kumar, J., Prabhakar, O. P., & Sahu, N. K. (2014). Comparative Analysis of Different Feature Extraction and Classifier Techniques for Speaker Identification Systems: A Review. *International Journal of Innovative Research in Computer and Communication Engineering, 2*(1), 2760–2269.

Kumar, P., Biswas, A., Mishra, A. N., & Chandra, M. (2010). *Spoken language identification using hybrid feature extraction methods.* arXiv preprint arXiv:1003.5623

Lavner, Y., & Ruinskiy, D. (2009). A decision-tree-based algorithm for speech/music classification and segmentation. *EURASIP Journal on Audio, Speech, and Music Processing*, (1).

Lee, C. C., Mower, E., Busso, C., Lee, S., & Narayanan, S. (2011). Emotion recognition using a hierarchical binary decision tree approach. *Speech Communication, 53*(9-10), 1162–1171. doi:10.1016/j.specom.2011.06.004

Litman, D., & Forbes, K. (2003). Recognizing emotions from student speech in tutoring dialogues. In *2003 IEEE Workshop on Automatic Speech Recognition and Understanding (IEEE Cat. No. 03EX721)* (pp. 25-30). IEEE. 10.1109/ASRU.2003.1318398

Ma, Z., & Fokoué, E. (2015). *A comparison of classifiers in performing speaker accent recognition using MFCCs.* arXiv preprint arXiv:1501.07866

Mahana, P., & Singh, G. (2015). Comparative analysis of machine learning algorithms for audio signals classification. *International Journal of Computer Science and Network Security*, *15*(6), 49.

Mao, K. Z., Tan, K. C., & Ser, W. (2000). Probabilistic neural-network structure determination for pattern classification. *IEEE Transactions on Neural Networks*, *11*(4), 1009–1016. doi:10.1109/72.857781 PMID:18249828

Nandhakumar, N., & Aggarwal, J. K. (1985). The artificial intelligence approach to pattern recognition—a perspective and an overview. *Pattern Recognition*, *18*(6), 383–389. doi:10.1016/0031-3203(85)90009-3

Noman, F., Salleh, S. H., Ting, C. M., Samdin, S. B., Ombao, H., & Hussain, H. (2018). A *Markov-Switching Model Approach to Heart Sound Segmentation and Classification*. arXiv preprint arXiv:1809.03395

Palo, H. K., Chandra, M., & Mohanty, M. N. (2017A). Emotion recognition using MLP and GMM for Oriya language. *International Journal of Computational Vision and Robotics*, *7*(4), 426–442. doi:10.1504/IJCVR.2017.084987

Palo, H. K., Chandra, M., & Mohanty, M. N. (2018D). Recognition of Human Speech Emotion Using Variants of Mel-Frequency Cepstral Coefficients. In *Advances in Systems, Control and Automation* (pp. 491–498). Singapore: Springer. doi:10.1007/978-981-10-4762-6_47

Palo, H. K., Kumar, P., & Mohanty, M. N. (2017B). Emotional Speech Recognition using Optimized Features. *International Journal of Research in Electronics and Computer Engineering*, *5*(4), 4–9.

Palo, H. K., Mohanty, J., Mohanty, M. N., & Chandra, M. (2016A). Recognition of Anger, Irritation and Disgust Emotional States based on Similarity Measures. *Indian Journal of Science and Technology*, *9*, 38.

Palo, H. K., & Mohanty, M. N. (2016). Performance analysis of emotion recognition from speech using combined prosodic features. *Advanced Science Letters*, *22*(2), 288–293. doi:10.1166/asl.2016.6855

Palo, H. K., & Mohanty, M. N. (2016B). Modified-VQ Features for Speech Emotion Recognition. *Journal of Applied Sciences (Faisalabad)*, *16*(9), 406–418. doi:10.3923/jas.2016.406.418

Palo, H. K., &Mohanty, M. N. (2018B). Comparative Analysis of Neural Networks for Speech Emotion Recognition. *International Journal of Engineering & Technology*, *7*(4.39), 112-116.

Palo, H. K., & Mohanty, M. N. (2018C). Wavelet based feature combination for recognition of emotions. *Ain Shams Engineering Journal*, *9*(4), 1799–1806. doi:10.1016/j.asej.2016.11.001

Palo, H. K., Mohanty, M. N., & Chandra, M. (2015). Use of different features for emotion recognition using MLP network. In *Computational Vision and Robotics* (pp. 7–15). New Delhi: Springer. doi:10.1007/978-81-322-2196-8_2

Palo, H. K., Mohanty, M. N., & Chandra, M. (2016C). Efficient feature combination techniques for emotional speech classification. *International Journal of Speech Technology*, *19*(1), 135–150. doi:10.100710772-016-9333-9

Palo, H. K., Mohanty, M. N., & Chandra, M. (2018A). Speech Emotion Analysis of Different Age Groups Using Clustering Techniques. *International Journal of Information Retrieval Research*, *8*(1), 69–85. doi:10.4018/IJIRR.2018010105

Pearl, J. (2014). *Probabilistic reasoning in intelligent systems: networks of plausible inference*. Elsevier.

Reynolds, D. A., & Rose, R. C. (1995). Robust text-independent speaker identification using Gaussian mixture speaker models. *IEEE Transactions on Speech and Audio Processing, 3*(1), 72–83. doi:10.1109/89.365379

Schuller, B., Rigoll, G., & Lang, M. (2004, May). Speech emotion recognition combining acoustic features and linguistic information in a hybrid support vector machine-belief network architecture. In *2004 IEEE International Conference on Acoustics, Speech, and Signal Processing* (Vol. 1). IEEE. 10.1109/ICASSP.2004.1326051

Shashua, A. (2009). *Introduction to machine learning: Class notes 67577*. arXiv preprint arXiv:0904.3664

Sinha, R., & Shahnawazuddin, S. (2018). Assessment of pitch-adaptive front-end signal processing for children's speech recognition. *Computer Speech & Language, 48*, 103–121. doi:10.1016/j.csl.2017.10.007

Solanki, A., &Pandey, S. (2019). Music instrument recognition using deep convolutional neural networks. *International Journal of Information Technology*, 1-10.

Specht, D. F. (1990). Probabilistic neural networks. *Neural Networks, 3*(1), 109–118. doi:10.1016/0893-6080(90)90049-Q PMID:18282828

Stan, A., Yamagishi, J., King, S., & Aylett, M. (2011). The Romanian speech synthesis (RSS) corpus: Building a high quality HMM-based speech synthesis system using a high sampling rate. *Speech Communication, 53*(3), 442–450. doi:10.1016/j.specom.2010.12.002

Suuny, S., Peter, S. D., & Jacob, K. P. (2013). Performance of different classifiers in speech recognition. *Int. J. Res. Eng. Technol, 2*(4), 590–597. doi:10.15623/ijret.2013.0204032

Tulyakov, S., Jaeger, S., Govindaraju, V., & Doermann, D. (2008). Review of classifier combination methods. In *Machine learning in document analysis and recognition* (pp. 361–386). Berlin: Springer. doi:10.1007/978-3-540-76280-5_14

Wang, J., Wu, Q., Deng, H., & Yan, Q. (2008, March). Real-time speech/music classification with a hierarchical oblique decision tree. In *2008 IEEE International Conference on Acoustics, Speech and Signal Processing* (pp. 2033-2036). IEEE. 10.1109/ICASSP.2008.4518039

Williams, J. J., & Katsaggelos, A. K. (2002). An HMM-based speech-to-video synthesizer. *IEEE Transactions on Neural Networks, 13*(4), 900–915. doi:10.1109/TNN.2002.1021891 PMID:18244486

Woodland, P. C. (2001). Speaker adaptation for continuous density HMMs: A review. *ISCA Tutorial and Research Workshop (ITRW) on Adaptation Methods for Speech Recognition*.

Wu, J., & Cai, Z. (2014). A naive Bayes probability estimation model based on self-adaptive differential evolution. *Journal of Intelligent Information Systems, 42*(3), 671–694. doi:10.100710844-013-0279-y

Zhang, S., Zhang, S., Huang, T., & Gao, W. (2017). Speech emotion recognition using deep convolutional neural network and discriminant temporal pyramid matching. *IEEE Transactions on Multimedia, 20*(6), 1576–1590. doi:10.1109/TMM.2017.2766843

Zhou, G., Hansen, J. H., & Kaiser, J. F. (1998). Linear and nonlinear speech feature analysis for stress classification. *Fifth International Conference on Spoken Language Processing*.

Chapter 23
Self–Driving Cars:
Role of Machine Learning

Pooja Jha
Amity University, Jharkhand, India

K. Sridhar Patnaik
https://orcid.org/0000-0002-4994-4489
Birla Institute of Technology, Mesra, India

ABSTRACT

Human errors are the main cause of vehicle crashes. Self-driving cars bear the promise to significantly reduce accidents by taking the human factor out of the equation, while in parallel monitor the surroundings, detect and react immediately to potentially dangerous situations and driving behaviors. Artificial intelligence tool trains the computers to do things like detect lane lines and identify cyclists by showing them millions of examples of the subject at hand. The chapter in this book discusses the technological advancement in transportation. It also covers the autonomy used according to The National Highway Traffic Safety Administration (NHTSA). The functional architecture of self-driving cars is further discussed. The chapter also talks about two algorithms for detection of lanes as well as detection of vehicles on the road for self-driving cars. Next, the ethical discussions surrounding the autonomous vehicle involving stakeholders, technologies, social environments, and costs vs. quality have been discussed.

INTRODUCTION

The transportation sector has developed with a sequence of in-depth transformation from various levels like operations and maintenance besides services to passengers. This has further influenced automobile and road transport sectors also.

When we talk about technology side of the term "autonomous", it refers to a computer controlled system that is capable of taking their own actions with or without little human intervention [Clough, 2002]. An important point to be noted about an autonomous system is that it is able to make decisions about almost all the activities with or without human interference. Generally the term "self-driving,"

DOI: 10.4018/978-1-5225-9643-1.ch023

"driverless," and "autonomous" mean "fully autonomous" automobile.The term means that it is competent of moving from one place to another itself without any involvement of instructor or driver. A fully automated vehicle is capable of making all crucial driving assessments like navigation, braking, velocity, spacebetween vehicles, path selection choice, obeying traffic signs, direction-finding, evading hindrances. The responsibility of the human is restricted generally in selecting destination.While in partially autonomous vehicles, involvement of both thecomputer system(For example, urgent situation braking) and human (e.g., ordinary braking, navigation, velocity) control is observed (Kalra, Anderson & Wachs 2009).

Over one million miles have been driven by these cars on public roads (Robson 2014). In self driving cars, the humans are the passengers and in fact all the operations like navigation the car, speed, applying brakes and traffic obeying are handled by the computers. The system has sensors to catch the information about road and nearby surroundings that helps in their automated decisions. These decisions are about where and when to stop.

Technology, now-a-days is almost on the way to reform the transportation to higher level. Vehicles are these daysmore automated and coupled. For this severalplans are considered for progress towardsassociated, automated and autonomous vehicles. Acommon example that can be citedis the Google and Tesla driver-less cars (Wavestone, 2017).

Automation started several decades ago with automation of functionalities such as anti-lock braking systems (ABS)(Wavestone, 2017). Apart from these, the vehicles are becoming more associatedwiththe outside world. The merger of pioneering technologies is therefore steadilyoverlaying the way for the autonomous vehicle.Society of Automotive Engineers (SAE), classifies various stages of autonomy for developing several development models.

There have been numerouspaybacks of self driving cars over traditional vehicles. There is prediction that self driving cars offerssecurerides than human as drivers. Most of the accidents, about ninety percent is due to human errors which may involve factors such asuse of alcohol, lack of concentration, lethargy, or tremendous speeding (Schoettle, Sivak 2015). This is not amatter for autonomous cars. It is anticipated that the overall accidents shoulddecline between thirty and eighty percent(Hyken, 2008) One moreadvantage of autonomouscars can be thought of isexpediency offered to human drivers as they too become passengers and can enjoy reading or working. Also, the self driving cars offer improved movement to those who cannot drive themselves, such as elderly or disabled personshighway traffic safety admin., (Nat'l highway motor vehicle crash causation survey, 2014). Some other advantages that are offered are reduction in level of car ownership, low-cost sharing of vehicle etc. (Kresge, 2015, Bertoncello & Wee2015).

There are many opportunities for autonomous vehicle. The number of private vehicles will be reduced. Occupation rates of cars which isthe ratio of rental cars rented versus the total number in the city, could be a constraint that is considered in mobility facilities and even a regulatory commitment for transportation. Another aspect can be well managed traffic system. The problem of adjusting routes by private vehicles due to traffic congestion can be eased by automated vehicles. This will help in managing the count of vehicles on circulation. Apart from managing traffic, the fuel consumption can also be minimized by grouping and thereby plummetingeffluence(Wavestone 2017).

Besides the benefits and opportunities associated with the introduction of self driving cars, there are certain challenges that cannot be ignored. Debates have been always going around challenges like accountability of damage, privacy loss, cyber security etc. Implementing the concept of self driving cars is actually not so easy task. The car manufacturers have been working on this concept for years. They

Table 1. Challenges and issues in self driving cars

Challenges and Issues	Self-Driving Cars	Traditional Vehicles
Safety and Crashes	Most experts predict that self-driving cars will be saferdrivers than people. Some expect overall accidents to decrease between thirty and eighty percent	Over 90% of car accidents today are attributed to human error caused by factors such as intoxication, inattention, sleepiness, or extreme speeding
Convenience	Mobility for reading or working while driving	Not possible in case of human is driving
Congestion	Traffic can get worsen as self driving vehicles which are empty keep waiting for the next rider.	Traditional cars tend to cause frequent blockages on roads as they look for parking spots within urban centers
Regulations	The issue of ownership is of concern. The current legal assumption says that AVs will be purchased and owned by customers. But what is more likely is that AVs will simply accelerate the shift to transportation-as-a-service. The fact is giving license to minors.	Rules and regulations are standarised for human driving

are optimistic about their take over the car market in future. Supporters assert that soon the driver less cars will enhance the road safety.The issues are presented briefly in Table 1below:

Next, an insight is presented about the demerits of automated cars. These de-merits are actually the problems that need to be resolved. Automated cars are based on instructions from computers, which rely on the information that are loaded into these computers. If any information about the road changes, then exact location cannot be traced. It is impossible for automated cars to deal with unexpected changes that may occur. An incident to quote is a case where human "safety driver" tried to apply brake when automated car came to a crosswalk and slowed down to allow someone on foot to cross the street.Although, no casualty occurred but the automated car was hit by another car(Martin, Lardy, and Laumon2011)

LITERATURE REVIEW

The chapter begins with a brief literature study. The first part of this section deals with the general applications and research done in the area of machine learning.

Authors (Balakrishnan,2009) have discussed ontology of a theory of learning and also have developed a learner framework that aimed to improve their skills of learning. Machine learning is a valuable technique, with the aim to distinguish unidentified sample in the course of learning from identified samples. A new method using machine double-layer was constructed (Chen, Hou, 2007)with the objectives to train samples and starting outer constraints, to test the samples by fitness functions using Genetic Algorithm and finally implementing outer layer to get the outer constraints of the framework.

There has been opinion poll going on to determine whether the machine has capability to beat the intelligence of man or not (Xue, Zhu, 2009) People favours that the machine are developed and controlled by human and this is the main reason the machine can never beat the humans. But the ability of machine to learn cannot be surpassed by any reason. Also, the capability of machine increases in application. A hybrid system was developed by authors (Khan, Doucette, Cohen and Lizotte, 2012) Integrating that offered better performance when compared with machine learning systems and purely knowledge-based systems. They were successfully able to show error-free solution to DSS (Decision Support System) and were utilized in medical areas.

Research (Raufi, Xhaferri, 2018) has been successfully able to demonstrate amalgamation of machine learning algorithms and mobile based algorithms in identifying hate speech and offensive language detection which can later be prevented. A method, C-ELM construction approach (Lee, Su,, Lin, Lee, 2017), added hidden neurons by increments the output weights were obtained without re-calibrating. A self-training semi-supervised SVM algorithm (Li, Guan, Chin, 2007)was proposed by comparing in several real-world datasets, the efficiency and fast convergence were highlighted.

Next part in the literature review, we included papers related to Self driving cars.

A new method for learning neural networks for real world self driving was developed (Kim, Lim, Kim, 2009)to be relevant to virtual game. Authors (Aziz, Hindersah, Prihatmanto 2017) have discussed the outcomes of execution of lane detection algorithm on toll road and the result demonstrated some methods need to be altered so that the parameters can change during day and night adaptively.

Three specific challenges (Rao, Frtunikj 2018) related to functional safety during the development of deep learning approaches for self-driving cars were included as validating completeness of training and testing dataset, tracing safety requirements to the source code level, and including transfer learning for different areas. Simulation results (Okuyama, Gonsalves, Upadhay 2018) of an autonomous car learning to move in a basic environment containing only lane markings and static obstacles were presented where learning was based on the Deep Q Network. A method of semantic ego lane estimation (Kim, Park, 2017) to train a deep network had recognized left and right ego lanes without postprocessing directly and independently. This involved a two transfer learning steps, where the first step alters the network's demonstration realm from a general scene to a road scene and the second step minimizes the target from road objects in general, to left and right ego lanes.

A visual-based end to end lane following architecture (Ou, Bedawi, Koesdwiady, Karray, 2018),was proposed which fuses temporal and spatial visual information to predict current and future control variables. The results showed that the neural network can approximate human driving behaviours with high accuary. It has been shown that hardware neural networks (Kang, Yin, and Berger, 2019),can have considerable gains in performance and energy. The study also demonstrates the significance of conquering the die memory capacity and memory bandwidth limitations.

The implementation of an end to-end learning approach (Simmons, Adwan, Pham, Alhuthaifi, and Wolek, 2019) that enables a small, low-cost, remote control car to lane-follow in a simple indoor environment was discussed where a deep neural network (DNN) and a convolutional neural network (CNN) were trained to record unrefined images from a forward-looking camera to steering and speed commands.

EXPEDITION IN TECHNOLOGY

The early days of 1930s, when computer did not exist, no one ever imagined about autonomous cars. The emergence of digital computers gave rise to a once so thought fictitious self-driving cars. Till 1960s, self-driving vehicles were thought to navigate common streets. Pioneering in 1980s by Ernst Dickmanns. He used Mercedes van to travel miles of distances independently on main roads. It had an incredible feature particularly with the calculating power in terms of time.In the middle of 2000s, the DARPA (Defense Advanced Research Projects Agency) sorted out the Grand Challenges,in which the groups accumulated to assert with self-driving vehicles somewhere. It was in 2009, Google started the self-driving car endeavorthat created a history in the innovation. By 2012, Google tested the automated cars with several sensors, radars, lasers, GPS (Global Positioning System). Comprehensive maps and many morethings were profoundly used to drive carefully and move on its own without any interference.These cars were capable to park itself on its own. The inbuilt camerasdetect things which were processed by its computers.Google in May 2014, came out with a new perceptionof their autonomous car that neitherhad a navigation wheel nor pedals. Anarchetype was tested in 2015. In 2015 itself, Google initiated and tested some more characteristics with a detachable navigation wheel, pedals for accelerator and brake,which helped to take charge of driving as and when required (Memon, Qudsia et al.,2016)

Automation of vehicles has been categorised into five different levels by National Highway and Traffic Safety Administration (NHTSA)(U.S. Department of Transportation, Automated Driving Systems - A Vision for Safety. September, 2017). The levels/stages are briefly explained as below:

i) *Level 0 i.e. No automation:* The computer has no role at this level. All the driving functions are handled by human.

ii) *Level 1 i.e. Driver Assistance:* At this level the car assists the driver in some functions like steering or braking. It is noted that both functions are not provided to the driver simultaneously. Some examples are path keeping, cruise control or assisted breaking

iii) *Level 2 i.e. Partial automation:* At this level, car is able to perform both the functions of steering and accelerating/decelerating. The remaining functions are still performed by human driver. One such example is Tesla Autopilot (Motors, 2017)

iv) *Level 3 i.e. Conditional automation:*Here, the human driver is expected intervene in the driving system only required. The driving system takes complete control over the entire driving job under special conditions. An example is Waymo (Google) self-driving car (LLC,W.Waymo, 2017)

v) *Level 4 i.e. High automation:* The complete control is taken by machine under special circumstances. The human driver need not has to consider or interfere in those circumstances. If a change of situations arises, the car needs to be able to stop and park securely in case the person driving the car does not retake control. Waymo announced in 2017 that they are testing level 4 driving (Waymo, 2017)

vi) *Level 5 i.e. Full automation:* The driving system takes complete control over the entire driving task under all conditions. The person driving the carneed not be inside the car. An example is JohnyCab from Total Recall.

WORKING PRINCIPLE

The GPS component of software is responsible for recording signs and directions for traveling. All new signs are detected are registered by the moving vehicle; this will assist other users by the modification in degree of confidence and degree of recognition. Besides the GPS component, software helps in recognizing the demarcation lines between lanes.This component makes use of three cameras of different types to approximate the location of car on the road, to locate sides of roads as well as suggest original direction even when there is no traffic signs. This component also utilizes Artificial Intelligence from webcam images(Saquib, Ashraf and Malik, 2017)

Implementing an autonomous vehicle is not an easy task. It involves a wide range of technicalities. The control of autonomous vehicles is important and is segregated into lateral control and longitudinal control. The former is involved in controlling of the navigation, whereas the longitudinal gets involved incontrolling the speed.Here, lateral control keeps the vehicle on the chosen path. Fewexpertises to provide assistance in the lateral control are LDWS(Lane Departure Warning Systems), and LKA(Lane Keeping Assist Systems) and Parallel Parking Assist. A brief about these technologies is discussed below.

i) ***LDWS(Lane Departure Warning System):*** This technology helps inpreventing go-off the road and crashes due to sideswipe(Saquib, Ashraf and Malik, 2017). For this it is important that the vehicle should sense the lane on which it is positioned and about the road boundaries. To achieve this,several methods are explored by researchers in the form of entrenched magnetic markers which are in the paths, extremelys GPS and digital maps, as well as image processing. The entrenched magnetic markers are the most appropriate method to locate a lane. The vehicles have sensors which detects the magnetic field emitted by these markers. This provides a path for vehicle to stay in. It is only possible if all the current as well as the future roads are embedded with magnets. Another approach can be to utilizeprecise digital plotting of the roadway paths with positioning precision(Saquib, Ashraf and Malik, 2017). For this, detailed digital map needs to be combined with accurate GPS to identify the location of vehicles inside path.

The above methodhas beenassessed in Minneapolis, MN for transportationvia buses. This narrow-pathmakes the peopleto be vigilant and drive slowly during the travel.

Both these methods, that is, magnetic marker methods and accurate GPS and digital maps methods are likely in tiny and controlled environments, yet difficult to be considered as the best choice among the methods. The best method is image processing. The camera creates a virtual path. If the monochrome video camera is used for image processing, this would take out the lane and boundary markings on the road more clearly.

A problem related to thismethod is that it makes complicated to see properly the lane markings by the camera,especially when the road markings are covered by snow, worn down. A solution to such problems is the special detection algorithm that can spot the wear-out lanes in the snow. Another solution can be done by implementing infrared sensors on the underneath the vehicle. The sensors record any alterationin the reflectivity of uncoveredroadway and markings on the path.Avariety of vigilance from perceptible beeps asthe physical response to the person driving the caris delivered to warn them that they are moving away in the lane(Saquib, Ashraf and Malik, 2017).

ii) ***LKA(Lane Keeping Assist System):*** A driver on a highway most of the times has to make small alterations to the steer wheel, so that he stays on the path.This system provides the driver some amount of actuation to steering. Also, the torque required to turn the wheel is quite less, therefore it is quitesimple for the person to override the support offered by the system. Some more sensors like radar, LIDAR (laser radar), ultrasonic range finders, and image processing with video cameras exist in the car to examine various factors like crosswinds, road surface geometry, detection of the current lane and curves. One problem that may occur with the system is that the driver has to be attentive when the car is adjusting the navigation wheel. Hence, the developers thought of including the input from the driver input over time or the make the system respond by alarm beep(Saquib, Ashraf and Malik, 2017).

iii) *Parallel Parking Assist:* This system is currently available for community. Toyota, in 2003 was introduced first time for the community. The system has rear camera that assists in parallel parking. The driver opts for the spot where he wishes to park, take on reverse, and then employ the dashboard screen thatexhibitsthe image from the rearview camera. Then the driver identifies a box like symbol over the markwhere they want to park.The person driving the car has to manage the brake and speed, andmanaging of steeris done by the vehicle, back into the spot effectively(Saquib, Ashraf and Malik, 2017). Then the driveragain has to gear to pull frontward and park parallel.

The frontward and backwardroutes of the automated vehicle are managed by the longitudinal control system. The system comprises of applications that manage the momentum of the vehicle aas well as help the driver to move in frontward or take reverse. Next, the types of applications for longitudinal control are briefly discussed.

i) *Rear Parking Assist:* The rear bumper of the car has embedded ultrasonic range finders that help the driver by making a changing audible sound as the distance reduces. There are many types of systems that help the driver while parking. The embedded devices have the drawbackas they candetect distanceonly within short area, within a few meters. Thevideo cameras at the rearof the vehicle assistswhen the driver moves in back direction(Saquib, Ashraf and Malik, 2017).

ii) *Adaptive Cruise Control (ACC):*Itassists the driver by managing the velocity at which the caris movingwith respect to the other carsahead of it. Arange of ACC systems like high-speed ACC, low speed ACC, and full ACCexists that help in assisting the driver. A variety of sensors help in providing an ACC system. The radar based ACC,which is most commonly used sensor,estimates the distanceof the vehicle moving ahead of the car. Also, the instance at which the vehicle in front is reaching or going away is computed. Thus, information helps inregulating the vehicle speed so that distance is sufficient from thevehicle moving in front is maintained.In case, another vehicle comes inside the samepath, the deviceregulates the velocity to revisit to the distance already set. Thelaser technology in LIDAR based systems locates the distance between vehicles. The distinguishable feature among three variations of ACC is discussed next. The control of the brakes is managed by the high speed ACC and attempts to compete the speed of the vehicle moving in frontwhen it comes nearer. Once it gets the laneclear, the software system comes back to cruishing speed. The low speed ACC is more appropriate for those areas where there is congestion because of the traffic. In such cases, the driver is warned about the approaching object and thereafter, the driver is accountable to halt the car as well as to resume driving after it has been stopped.A full ACC combines features of both the previous ACC where the system adjustsfor high velocity highway driving and low velocity traffic or city driving(Saquib, Ashraf and Malik, 2017).

iii) *Pre crash brake assist:*The system utilizes ACC to identifyprobablecrashes by computing the speed when a driver comes closer to an approaching object. In case, the rate is quite high, a pre-alarmis sent by the device to the brakes. Hence, braking occurs at the best level.It will help to decreasethe halt distance as well as impact velocity, if any crashoccurs(Saquib, Ashraf and Malik, 2017).

Figure 1. Modules in prototype

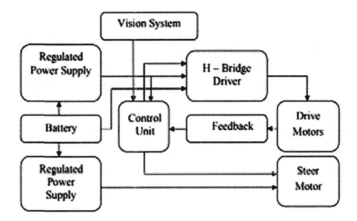

A PROTOTYPE OF SELF DRIVING VEHICLE

A simple prototype is considered while explaining the architecture of self-driving cars. The automobile prototype has to be balancing to aidindependentperformance of the vehicle. The prototype must have collection of sensors for image, mechanism to control the steering wheel for lateral control and drive mechanism for longitudinal control, communication components for vehicle and control unit for controlling the autonomous nature of the vehicle. Figure 1 depictsvarious modules helpful in the proposed modelof the vehicle.A brief description of these parts is discussed hereafter(Luu, and Chirita 2019).

a)   *Vision System:*A competent track sensing method is highly demanded for achieving the autonomous behavior of the vehicle. The extent of independent vehicle relies on the quantity of information that is gathered from the track as well as from the surroundings. This in turn depends on the sensor capabilities of the vehicle.

b)   *Steering Mechanism:* For an effective autonomous vehicle, the steer needs to beentirely automated. The user is required to have either no or limited control over the steering. Thus, it requires anaccurate steer capability and increased reliability.

c)   *Drive Mechanism:* Vehicle intrinsically demands portability. Therefore, asuitable driving method is required. In this prototype, DC motors with a properlesser gear collection is used for longitudinal drive mechanism.

d)   *Control Unit:*It is the hub of all gathered information. It also serves as the execution hub for data gathered from the sensors as well as is the sourceof the control signals of the actuators.

DECISION MAKING PROCESS IN SELF-DRIVING CARS

A driver who performs all complex tasks of driving will become obsolete with the popularity of autonomous cars. A common reason isthe role is now played by computer system. A comparison is shown in figure 2. The difference can be seen in the feedback loop. People constantly discover from their faults,

Figure 2. Comparative view of human and computer sense

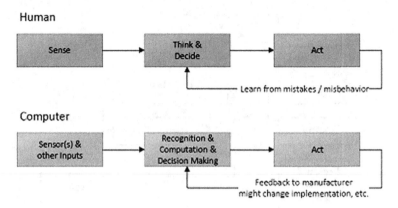

Figure 3. Composition of autonomous vehicles in decision making

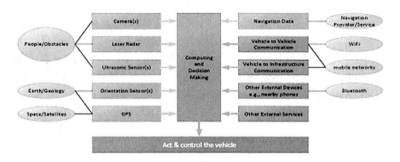

it takes software to show slow updates. The self-adaptive software, like the machine learning can learn and respond instantaneously. The aim is to overcome such constraint.

Many times, unpredicted situations like attacks are not correctly understood by a self-driving car, when they are evaluated in comparison with humans. Here, behavior and excellence of information differ depending on the knowledge and sensors used. The software (Broy, Kruger,. Pretschner, and Salzmann, 2007), of the autonomous vehicle decides most of the functions. The software which is the base of the self-driving cars depends on various disciplines like computer vision, machine learning, and parallel computing. The process of calculating a decision is not a simple process as it requires testing all possible conditions that exist in real world (Waldrop, 2015). These are only abstraction which is the approximate depiction of real life situation and aids for decision making in the world.It might be that availability of more information, which is required for better decision making may lead to more time engaged in interpretation and filtration of data. The representation is shown in figure 3.

Figure 4. Flowchart for the algorithm I

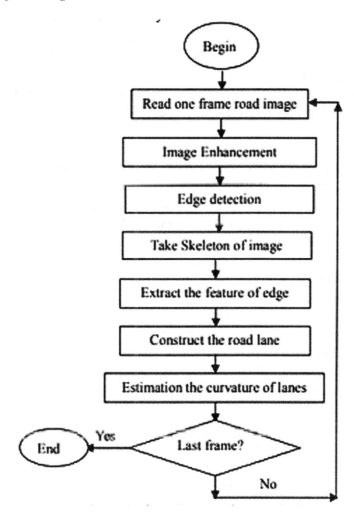

ALGORITHMS USED IN SELF-DRIVING CARS

Detection of lanes is important as it related to lateral control which is based on the vision. At the same time it is crucial inproviding advise the driver about lane departure. There are three categories of vision based lane detection methods; region-based, feature-based and model-based methods.

The problems with lane detectionincludes of feature extraction, feature de-correlation and reduction, and clustering and segmentation (Liu, Zheng, Cheng, Xing, 2003)(Jeong, Kim, Lee, Ha, Lee, Lee, Hashimoto, (2001). Inthe first algorithm (Algorithm I), the significant arrangement of the road (that is, paths or markings on the path) iscreated which rely on some characteristics extracted from frame image. Generally, many models exist for vision-based methods for lane detection. Thesemodels utilize a geometric framework to distinguish the lane whichmaps the examined images with a assumedframework of the road. The methoduses the postulation that the outlineof the lane can be characterized by straight lines, parabolic curves, or snack-like curves (Jeong, Kim, Lee, Ha, Lee, Lee, Hashimoto, (2001), (Asif,

Arshad, Wilson, 2005)(Boumediene, Ouamri, and Dahnoun, 2007). This chapter discusses one of the algorithms in a simplified way.

Firstly, image processing techniques is used to enhance the road image.Next, parallel thinning algorithm (Lu, Wang, 1986, Hastings, 2004)is utilized forframing map to get the image.Then the detected lane marking pixels wereemployed to select control points for Non-uniform B-Spline (NUBS) interpolation to form left and right road paths. Finally, aneasy mathematical framework to approximate left path and correct curvature for self-driven car vehicle system is introduced. This is shown in figure 4.

A brief about the techniques involved in above algorithm is stated next. The captured image isimproved using Gaussian and Median filter to decrease the noise in the image followed by histogramprocessing technique which isapplied to improve brightness and contrast of captured image. Canny edge detection algorithm was applied to obtain rough edge map from enhanced image.

An important component which is generally overlooked in many societal relevant robotic systems is the object recognition (Levinson, Askeland, Becker, Dolson, Held, Kammel, Kolter, Langer, Pink, Pratt, Sokolsky, Stanek, Stavens, Teichman, Werling, and Thrun., 2011)Besides that such vehicles have the probability to decrease the number of car mishaps, it can save the time that is wasted while commuting and hence increasing the overall productivity. Also, the fuel efficiency can be increased and thereby reducing the carbon-dioxide emission.Google (Urmson 2011),had shown the new innovation of autonomous cars towards the long-term vision. Deep learning based object detection method is commonly taken into consideration these days. Another algorithm(Hinton, Osindero, and Teh, 2006) based on CNN (Convolutional Neural Network) is briefly explained which explores the use of object detection using CNN.

1. Using tracking and classification for detecting moving object: The unlabeled data which is obtained from the camera is classified as below:
    a) The space from the object is calibrated and the inaccuracy is estimated by the sensor data.
    b) The object size is determined from the sensor based on the information about the particular class.
2. Sensor Fusion: The various steps included are:
    a) The collected sensor data which is obtained from earlier step is utilized to estimate or decide the attributes of the object.
    b) Using various probabilistic methods on the collected sample of data, a complex depiction of hypotheses is determined.
    c) The momentary changes in accordance with the object description is managed by the dynamic fusion strategy.
3. Continuously tracking using deep learning technique helps to learn data.
    a) The information gathered from different levels of previous output are used in the deep learning method. It involves a machine vision methodsforpreparing the data from various layers. The detection model can betrained offline, but is executed in real-time by the real-life camera data mounted on carcontrol panel. The various steps involvedare:
        (i)   Training a deep-layered Convolutional Neural Network (CNN) toidentify the objects from data collected from image
        (ii)   Evaluatingperformance of real-life detection of the framework that has been trained using camera data
        (iii) Detecting distance of barriersby the RADAR
        (iv)   Detecting short range objects by the ultrasonic transducer

Figure 5. The flow of algorirthm II

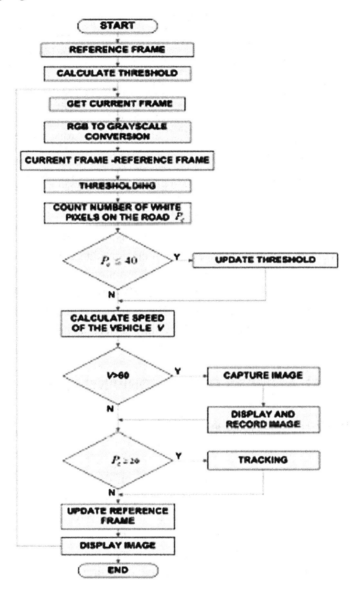

(v) Performing a lower level sensor synthesis with facts from mm wave radar ultrasonic distance sensor so as to createamalgamated data capturing short and long range object data with varying level of horizon;

(vi) Feeding the complexspace data in real-time to CNN model to enhance the object detection performance.

Another algorithm discussed is Vehicle detection algorithm (Algorithm II). The algorithm (Department of Motor Vehicles, 2017) is based on three frames. The detection of motion requires two frames and the third frame requires ensuring that the motion of the object is consistent over time. The detection based on three frames allows for accurate results. The algorithm is explained as below in figure 5:

Table 2. Algorithms at a glance

Algorithm Discussed	Technology Used	Performance Enhancement
Algorithm I	Canny edge detection algorithm, Thinning algorithm . Process involved in reducing an object in a digital image to the minimum size which was required for machine recognition of that object.	The lane –detection algorithm was able to identify the lane marking line well even in the cases of severe noises.
Algorithm II	Video pre-processing techniques were used, The interframe difference was compared with the background removal method in vehicle speed measurement. Image processing techniques including RGB to grayscale conversion, image subtraction and thresholding.	The systems were real time and the vehicle speed measurement performances of the proposed systems were 97.41% and 97.17% for the interframe difference and background removal techniques respectively.

The flowchart in Figure 5shows the descriptions about the algorithm. Once the binary image is obtained, the quantity of white pixels shows the level of alterationthat occurred due to moving objects. If the white pixel count, P_c, is less than a threshold, then the amount of change is not adequate to specify the presence of a moving vehicle. This threshold value (i.e. 40) was heuristically determined. When there isnot adequate change in the current frame, then the threshold is updated for the next frame.

Next in a tabular form, thesealgorithms are briefly summarized as below:

ETHICAL AND SOCIAL ASPECTS OF SELF-DRIVING CARS

The moral discussions about the autonomous vehicle are around stakeholders, technologies, social environments, costs and the excellence. Some of the issues that are considered are given below:

i) **Safety:**Safety has been the most basicprerequisite of self-directed cars. The vitalqueryremainsfor testing of a self-driving car.Also, someguiding principles should be satisfied to make certain that it is safe to use. ISO 26262 is such standard that identifies the security standard for road vehicles. For automated car, standards based on experiencesare framed. Google Car has been tested for one million kilometers safely, but whether this dataconfirmworking of its software is the question to answer.Only for this ground, it cannot be considered as assurance for safety.

The source code of such cars isnormally commercial and inaccessible for community. Such complex arrangement can be better understood by the developers of the car manufacturer or supplier.Today, testing these automatedvehicles should reveal the complianceof their performance with legislative norms (Department of Motor Vehicles, (2017)(Dixit, Chand, and Nair, 2016). The cost of laser radars compared to cameras or ultra-sonic sensors are another issue to discuss as they are very costly, but conveygoodclass data in variousclimate conditions.When we talk about ultra-sonic sensors or cameras, they havelow precision and are receptive under adverse weather conditions like rain. The ethical issue from manufacturer point of view is that whether he should compromise aninexpensive over an expensive sensor for likelihood of inaccuracy or mistakes or mishaps. In sophisticated driving support systems, the person driving the car takescharge, if a vitalconditionis difficult to be handled by the system. But in autonomous cars, ther is a difference. It makes us think whether the car is just going to discontinue and stay until the rain is over or are the passengers competent and permitted to interfere and if yes, then under which conditions. Also, does it require having a driving certificate for a self-driving carand what will happenif a car behaves inefficiently or even hazardously?It is quite possible that an automated driving car would lead to a wrong decision with use of low-cost equipment. The wrong verdict can lead to failure of lives or assets. Hence, cheap equipment will be ethically unwelcome.

ii)   ***Security***: Security is of chief significance and of elementary requirement. UK's Department for Transport, provided "Key principles of vehicle cyber security for automated vehicles" in a form of document(Department for Transport and Centre for the Protection of National Infrastructure (CPNI), 2017). The document established right basic principles:

   (a)   Safety of the organization is personal, directed, and encouraged at board level;
   (b)   Safety risks are evaluated and supervised suitably and proportionately, including those explicit to the supply chain;
   (c)   Organizations require aftercare and eventreaction to guarantee systems are protectedin their lifetime;
   (d)   All organizations, which also includes sub-contractors, suppliers, and probablethird parties, work together to enhance the security of the system;
   (e)   Systems are framed using a defence-in-depth method;
   (f)   Safety of the software is supervisedfor lifetime;
   (g)   The storage and communication of data areprotected and can be restricted;
   (h)   The system is fabricated to be flexible to attacks and act in responsesuitably when its defences or sensors fail.

The question comes up here in regard to the security issues and software updates The researchers think that whether a self-driving car be permitted to drive, even if,there isa failurein the latest software version. Also, how the bugs in the updated software kept at check.It would be unethical not to installinstantly new software/new version of the software on the car. Especially, if there is confirmation that the new update will renovatesignificanttroubles that might endanger human lives.

iii)   ***Privacy:***Privacy depends upon the amount of information required in decision making as the interference with data is increased.For example, a sensor that identifiesbarrier, such as humanbeings in front of the car depends on visual information. Even the employing of a distinct sensor could invade privacy, if the data is recorded or reported and/or dispersed without the permission of the involved people.

Privacy gets affected by the amount of data collected for decision making. This also includes accessibility of data, demolishing of data, devices that emits active signals to detect obstacles and involvement of the community who do not bearsuch devices.

iv)   ***Trust:*** Trust for autonomous cars exists from the time in manufacturing, to prerequisite for both hardware as well as software partsand to its usage. The self-driving car mayby nowhave allocated data like the target position to a number of external services, such as traffic information or navigation data, which are used in the computation of the route however, there is a dilemma about trust to data sources like GPS, map data, external devices, other vehicles.

In regard of the used sensors and hardware, the question exists about the trust to implement, when various systems are involved.

v) *Transparency:* Transparency is an important factor as it is needed for analysis of data. It is defined as the ethical involvement inthe development of autonomous cars(McBride, 2016). The question that arises about transparency is that how much information has to be disclosed and to whom.

Apart from this, another question is whether transparency is linked with entire ecosystem or not. Another issue to think about is about the management of intellectual property rights. The outcome that can be understood from transparency is that it ensures respecting subjects involving copyright, corporate secrets, security concerns and many other related topics.

vi) *Reliability:*Reliability means testing the system under absurd conditions like the behavior of autonomous cars when there is no mobile network, or when the sensors fail. The question arises about the threshold value that makes the system reliable.

There are some more issues like responsibility and accountability, quality assurance which is also of prime concern but not covered in this chapter.

CONCLUSION

Autonomous vehicles could offer remarkable benefits not only to the users, but also to the society. There are many prospects for improving social welfare, saving lives and reduction in money during crashes that can be done at its early stages of development. Self-driving cars can lead to reducing of congestion. Fully automated vehicles could also boostthe mobility in transportation. It can help to access the populations who are not benefited, also at pricesbelow those of accessible services. Incoherentstate laws mayadd to prices and hamperutilization of this technologyin a way that harms social interests for smallnoticeableincrease.

The lane-detection algorithm discussed above is able to distinguish the lane marking line quite better even when there are severe noises.In the same manner, the object tracking and detection algorithm were able to track the lane and objects as well as there was remarkable increase in the performance by about 97%.

It will be beneficial if the state lawmakers continueto be attentive and approve legislative solutions. Further efforts to expand a framework statuteto endorse uniformity in requirements may be fruitful. Authorizing the inclusion of autonomous vehicle technologies may beinappropriate till the following circumstances are fulfilled. First of all, the technology needs to be intelligentas par so that manufacturers are convinced in their functionas well as are convinced that they will not be responsible if they do not function perfectly. Second, the effects on securityneed to be well stated. It will include accepting the behavior of different technologies in varioussituations and with a set of various users. Third, the costs and benefits has to be correctlyconsidered.

In the coming years, millions of automated cars are likely to wander the roads and take instantaneousassessment in significantcircumstancesinvolving humans. Such machine-driven decision-making process has an ethical dimension, which is not sufficiently examined with respect to its effect on the self-driving car acceptance.

REFERENCES

Asif, M., Arshad, M.R., & Wilson, P.A. (2005). AGV Guidance System: An Application of Simple Active Contour for Visual Tracking. *Proceeding World Academy of Science, Engineering and Technology, 6,* 74–77.

Aziz, M. V. G., Hindersah, H., & Prihatmanto, A. S. (2017). Implementation of vehicle detection algorithm for self-driving car on toll road cipularang using Python language. *2017 4th International Conference on Electric Vehicular Technology (ICEVT),* 149-153. 10.1109/ICEVT.2017.8323551

Balakrishnan, A. (2009). Development of an ontology of learning strategies and its application to generate open learner models. *IEEE Proceedings of the 8th International Conference on Machine Learning and Applications.* 10.1109/ICMLA.2009.58

Bertoncello & Wee. (2015). *Ten Ways Autonomous Driving Could Redefine the Automotive World.* Retrieved from http://www.mckinsey.com/insights/ automotive_and_assembly/ten_ways_autonomous_driving_could_redefine_the_automotive_world

Boumediene, M., Ouamri, A., & Dahnoun, N. (2007). Lane Boundary Detection and Tracking using NNF and HMM Approaches. *Proceeding 2007 IEEE Intelligent Vehicles Symposium,* 1107–1111. 10.1109/IVS.2007.4290265

Broy, M., Kruger, I. H., Pretschner, A., & Salzmann, C. (2007). Engineering Automotive Software. *Proceedings of the IEEE, 95*(2), 356–373. doi:10.1109/JPROC.2006.888386

Bryce, S., Pasham, A., Huong, P., Yazeed, A., & Artur, W. (2019). Training a Remote-Control Car to Autonomously Lane-Follow using End-to-End Neural Networks. *53rd Annual Conference on Information Sciences and Systems (CISS).*

Chen, G., & Hou, R. (2007). A New Machine Double-Layer Learning Method and Its Application in non-Linear Time Series Forecasting. *Proceedings of the 2010 International Conference on Mechatronics and Automation (ICMA).* 10.1109/ICMA.2007.4303646

Chris. (2011). The google self-driving car project. *Talk at Robotics: Science and Systems.*

Clough Bruce T. Metrics. (2002), Schmetrics! How The Heck Do You Determine a UAV's Autonomy Anyway? *Air Force Res. Libr.* Retrieved from http://www.dtic.mil/dtic/tr/fulltext/u2/ a515926.pdf

David, R. (2014). Truth About Driverless Vehicles. *BBC.* Retrieved from http:// www.bbc.com/future/story/20141013-convoys-of-huge-zombie-trucks

Department for Transport (DfT) and Centre for the Protection of National Infrastructure (CPNI). (2017). *The key principles of cyber security for connected and automated vehicles.* Technical report.

Department of Motor Vehicles (State of California). (2017). *Testing of Autonomous Vehicles*. Retrieved from https://www.dmv.ca.gov/portal/dmv/detail/vr/autonomous/testing

Dixit, V. V., Chand, S., & Nair, D. J. (2016). Autonomous vehicles: Disengagements, accidents and reaction times. *PLoS One*, *11*(12), 1–14. doi:10.1371/journal.pone.0168054 PMID:27997566

Erin, H. (2004). *A Survey of Thinning Methodologies*. College of Engineering and Computer Science, University of Central Florida.

Hinton, G. E., Osindero, S., & Teh, Y.-W. (2006). A fast learning algorithm for deep belief nets. *Neural Computation*, *18*(7), 1527–1554.

Hyken, S. (2008). Four Ways Self-Driving Cars Will Improve Customer Service. *Forbes*.

Jean-Louis, M., Audrey, L., & Bernard, L. (2011). Pedestrian Injury Patterns According to Car and Casualty Characteristics in France. Academic Press.

Jesse, L., Jake, A., Jan, B., Jennifer, D., David, H., & Soeren, K. (2011). Towards Fully Autonomous Driving. *Systems and Algorithms. In Intelligent Vehicles Symposium*.

Jiman, K., & Chanjong, P. (2017). End-to-End Ego Lane Estimation based on Sequential Transfer Learning for Self-Driving Cars. *IEEE Conference on Computer Vision and Pattern Recognition Workshops*.

Kalra, Anderson, & Wachs. (2009). *Liability and regulation of autonomous vehicle technologies*. Rand Corp.

Khan, A., Doucette, J. A., Cohen, R., & Lizotte, D. J. (2012). Integrating Machine Learning Into a Medical Decision Support System to Address the Problem of Missing Patient Data. *Machine Learning and Applications (ICMLA), 2012 11th International Conference on, 1*, 454-457. 10.1109/ICMLA.2012.82

Kresge, N. (2015). *Smart Self-Driving Cars Still Need to Factor in Human Error*. Bloomberg.

Lee, C. H., Su, Y. Y., Lin, Y. C., & Lee, S. J. (2017). Machine learning based network intrusion detection. *Proceedings of the 2017 2nd IEEE International Conference on Computational Intelligence and Applications (ICCIA)*, 79–83. 10.1109/CIAPP.2017.8167184

Li, Y., Li, H., Guan, C., & Chin, Z. (2007). A Self-Training Semi-Supervised Support Vector Machine Algorithm and Its Applications in Brain Computer Interface. *Proceedings of the IEEE International Conference on Acoustics, Speech, and Signal Processing*.

Lu, H. E., & Wang, P. S. P. (1986). A Comment on A Fast Parallel Algorithm for Thinning Digital Patterns. *Communications of the ACM*, *29*(3), 239–242. doi:10.1145/5666.5670

Luu, D. L., Lupu, C., & Chirita, D. (2019). Design and Development of Smart Cars Model for Autonomous Vehicles in a Platooning. *2019 15th International Conference on Engineering of Modern Electric Systems (EMES)*, 21-24. 10.1109/EMES.2019.8795199

McBride, N. (2016). The ethics of driverless cars. *SIGCAS Comput. Soc.*, *45*(3), 179–184. doi:10.1145/2874239.2874265

Memon, Q. (2016). Self-driving and driver relaxing vehicle. *2016 2nd International* Conference on Robotics and Artificial Intelligence *(ICRAI)*, 170-174. 10.1109/ICRAI.2016.7791248

National Highway Traffic Safety Administration. (2014). *Traffic safety facts: Alcohol impaired driving.* Author.

Ou, Bedawi, Koesdwiady, & Karray. (2018). Predicting Steering Actions for Self-Driving Cars Through Deep Learning. *IEEE 88th Vehicular Technology Conference (VTC-Fall).*

Qing, R. (2018). Deep Learning for Self-Driving Cars: Chances and Challenges. *ACM/IEEE 1st International Workshop on Software Engineering for AI in Autonomous Systems.*

Raufi, B., & Xhaferri, I. (2018). Application of Machine Learning Techniques for Hate Speech Detection in Mobile Applications. *International Conference on Information Technologies (InfoTech-2018).*

Saquib, Ashraf, & Malik. (2017). Self Driving Car System Using (AI) Artificial Intelligence. *Asian Journal of Applied Science and Technology, 1*(7), 92-94.

Schoettle, B., & Sivak, M. (2015). *Potential impact of self-driving vehicles on household vehicle demand and usage.* Academic Press.

Takafumi, Tad, & Jaychand. (2018). *Autonomous Driving System based on Deep Q Learnig.* Academic Press.

Tesla Motors. (2017). *Tesla Autopilot.* Retrieved from https://www.tesla.com/autopilot

Tie, L., Zheng, N., Hong, C., & Xing, Z. (2003). *A Novel Approach of Road Recognition Based on Deformable Template and Genetic Algorithm.* IEEE.

U.S. Department of Transportation. (2017). *Automated Driving Systems - A Vision for Safety.* Retrieved from: https://www.nhtsa.gov/sites/nhtsa.dot.gov/files/documents/13069a-ads2.0_090617_v9a_tag.pdf

Waldrop, M. M. (2015). Autonomous vehicles: No drivers required. *Nature, 20*(3). PMID:25652978

Wavestone. (2017) Rectrieved from https://www.wavestone.com/en/insight/driverless-car-reality-making/

Waymo, L. L. C. W. (2017). *Self-Driving Car Project.* Retrieved from:https://waymo.com

Waymo. (2017). *Waymo's fully self-driving vehicles are here.* Retrieved from: https://medium.com/waymo/with-waymo-in-the-drivers-seat-fully-self-driving-vehicles-can-transform-the-way-we-getaround-75e9622e829a

Xue, M., & Zhu, C. (2009). A Study and Application on Machine Learning of Artificial Intellligence. *International Joint Conference on Artificial Intelligence*, 272-274. 10.1109/JCAI.2009.55

Yue, Hang, & Christian. (2019). Test Your Self-Driving Algorithm: An Overview of Publicly Available Driving Datasets and Virtual Testing Environments. *IEEE Transactions on Intelligent Vehicles, 4*(2).

Chapter 24
Sentiment Analysis on Social Media:
Recent Trends in Machine Learning

Ramesh S. Wadawadagi

https://orcid.org/0000-0002-6669-7344

Basaveshwar Engineering College, Bagalkot, India

Veerappa B. Pagi

Basaveshwar Engineering College, Bagalkot, India

ABSTRACT

Due to the advent of Web 2.0, the size of social media content (SMC) is growing rapidly and likely to increase faster in the near future. Social media applications such as Instagram, Twitter, Facebook, etc. have become an integral part of our lives, as they prompt the people to give their opinions and share information around the world. Identifying emotions in SMC is important for many aspects of sentiment analysis (SA) and is a top-level agenda of many firms today. SA on social media (SASM) extends an organization's ability to capture and study public sentiments toward social events and activities in real time. This chapter studies recent advances in machine learning (ML) used for SMC analysis and its applications. The framework of SASM consists of several phases, such as data collection, pre-processing, feature representation, model building, and evaluation. This survey presents the basic elements of SASM and its utility. Furthermore, the study reports that ML has a significant contribution to SMC mining. Finally, the research highlights certain issues related to ML used for SMC.

OVERVIEW

In recent days, social media applications have emerged as leading mass media, as they allow users to work collaboratively and publish their content (Wadawadagi & Pagi, in press; Anami et al. 2014). Accordingly, large volumetric semantically rich information is being generated and accumulated every day in the form of tweets, posts, blogs, news, comments, reviews, etc. Investigating hidden but potentially useful patterns

DOI: 10.4018/978-1-5225-9643-1.ch024

from a huge collection of SMC is a critical task, due to users struggle with overloaded information (Yang & Rim, 2014). SASM is a practice of collecting data from social networks and automatically identifying whether a phrase comprehends sentiment or opinionative content, and further determines the opinion polarity (Jianqiang & Xiaolin, 2017). However, detecting sentiment in SMC faces several challenges, as they are composed of incomplete, chaotic and unstructured sentences, erratic phrases, ungrammatical expressions, and non-lexical words. Moreover, it is hard to detect correlations among opinion sentences due to the broad range of linguistic issues and drives the SA still more challenging (Choi & Park, 2019). To cope with these challenges a real-time SA system needs to be developed to process a large volume of sentiment data in very little time. Furthermore, knowing the public emotions is very useful in many fields, including marketing, politics, online shopping, and many more (Jianqiang & Xiaolin, 2017). To increase productivity, many business firms encourage their customers to participate in virtual discussions, asking for their feedback, opinions, and suggestions.

SASM is generally operated at different levels-of-granularity varying from coarse-grained to fine-grained levels. The coarse-grained analysis deals with determining the sentiment of a whole phrase, while fine-grained analysis is related to attribute level SA. However, employing the right methodology to any key business will drive SASM as a powerful tool for steering organizations and their individual business units as successful outcomes. After several years of constant development, the methodology of SASM is slowly emerging from a disparate set of tools and technologies to a unified framework. The general framework of SASM is depicted in Figure 1. The framework consists of a series of sub-tasks, in which the first task is data acquisition that acquires sentiment data from different sources and stores using different formats. Soon after data acquisition, the data can either be directly streamed to memory for rapid evaluation of unstructured data (in-memory processing) or can be archived to disk (in-database processing) as messages, files, or any machine-generated content. It is being the case that SMC is generally messed up with inconsistent, incomplete and non-dictionary terms, it needs pre-processing before feature vectors are generated. During pre-processing, a series of techniques (e.g., tokenization, stopwords removal, URL pre-treatment, stemming, replacing emoticons) are employed to decrease the amount of irregularity in the data. Additionally, to facilitate the process of identifying document relevancy, the data need to be transformed from a full-text version to a document vector representation that describes the content of the opinion sentences. Two types of representations are extensively used in the literature, namely feature-based representation and relational representation. Perhaps, the most prevalent feature-based representation technique is a vector space model (VSM) (Salton & Yang, 1975). Deduced from basic VSM, some other representation techniques have been used such as n-gram, key-phrase, and hypernym representations. Recently, an alternative document representation based on distributed representation known as semantic word spaces or word-embeddings has shown great success in capturing fine-grained semantic regularities (Mikolov et al., 2013). These vectors consist of low-dimensional real-valued scores that model syntactic and semantic information of individual words. Eventually, these vectors are used as pre-trained features for many sentiment classification tasks. It is evident from the current research, that the earlier SMA systems were designed to facilitate analysts in writing decision rules, while later systems introduce ML for automatic rule generalization. ML algorithms use an example training set of input data to construct a model to make predictions expressed as outputs. Finally, the business analysts or researchers can make critical decisions based on this rich and high-quality data patterns discovered. The key objective of this chapter is to give a comprehensive survey on recent advances in ML techniques used for SASM and its applications. Investigation and analysis of SMC are potentially useful for many

Figure 1. A general framework of SASM system

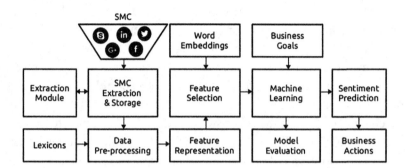

ongoing topics of interest such as identification of topics from social interaction among the folks and grouping members based on their ideologies.

The rest of the chapter is arranged according to the following sections. In Section 2, the methodologies required for information extraction (IE) from social media applications are discussed. However, Section 3 covers the important pre-processing techniques applied for SMC. The different ML techniques employed for sentiment classification are presented in Section 4. Numerous applications based on SASM are elucidated in Section 5. Lastly, Section 6 cites many promising and open issues concerned with SMC analysis research.

INFORMATION EXTRACTION FROM SMC

The main goal of IE systems is to extract structured data (e.g. events, entities and relationships) from unstructured text present over the social media sites. However, textual content on social media poses several challenges that potentially hinder the task of IE. The use of informal languages in social media posts formed by misspellings, unconventional abbreviations, and grammatically incorrect statements makes IE more difficult. Especially, lack of punctuation and syntax in short sentences place further challenges to disambiguate specified entities and also to resolve co-references among sentences. A typical IE system involves a series of sub-tasks including named-entity extraction (NEE), factual data extraction (FDE), named-entity disambiguation (NED), etc. that need to be applied to the input text. However, rapid developments are seen in more complex tasks such as the extraction of online reviews, opinions, and sentiments.

Web IE and noise removal have been studied in many earlier techniques. In the early systems, programmers are encouraged to write extraction rules; in contrast, contemporary systems adopt ML techniques for automated rule generalization. Taking account of this, Web IE systems can be classified into rule-based extraction; NLP based approaches and based on ML techniques. The rule-based systems depend on knowledge engineering that uses a handcrafted rule set for each work. These systems consider input text as a sequence of characters, and extraction rules are generated using regular expressions over lexical features. For example, ontology-based IE (OBIE) systems have grabbed more attention from the Web mining research community recently. In consequence, an ontology-based IE (OBIE) system to recognize and extract semantic disambiguation of named entities from Twitter data is proposed (Nebhi, 2012). The OBIE systems exhibit different traits by determining the type of entity retrieved and relate them to a semantic description in the formal ontology. This model subsequently combines the problem of named-entity recognition (NER) and a disambiguation component. The empirical study reveals that the OBIE systems exhibit good performance when tested with connected data as free-base and syntactical context for disambiguation. Furthermore, techniques based on NLP are also been addressed by many researchers. These models receive natural language text as input and based on certain criteria they produce structured information relevant to a given application (Singh, 2018). In particular, an open-source NLP pipeline for a micro-blog message extraction model called TwitIE (Bontcheva et al., 2013) is designed. TwitIE is an extended version of open-source software called GATE-ANNIE pipeline (Cunningham et al., 2013) used for news text mining. It consists of two modules, namely, importing Twitter-specific data and handling metadata. The pipeline describes each phase of the TwitIE in the extraction process. The GATE is an open-source IE framework consisting of ANNIE a general-purpose IE pipeline. This further includes essential components of IE such as tokenizer, sentence extractor, POST (Parts-of-Speech tagging) module, lexicon, finite state transducer, orthomatcher, and coreference resolver. The literature study shows that the new open-source TwitIE offers a researcher the best way of dealing with micro-blog extraction challenges. The key benefits of rule-based models include readability, ease of maintenance and ability to transfer the domain knowledge directly into rules. However, the drawbacks of rule-based system are the amount of expertise involved in writing the rules and interoperability of rule languages (Waltl et al., 2018). A paradigm shift in automating IE has unfolded from knowledge-based systems to learning-based extractors. Consequently, a diverse set of ML algorithms have been successfully applied for the task of IE. In the following paragraph, many contemporary ML techniques suggested in the literature for extracting relevant information from social media data are discussed.

Benson et al., (2011) addressed how to extract canonical records of events from Twitter data using conditional random fields (CRF). The CRF is a discriminative model used for predicting sequences in streaming data. The model utilizes a CRF subsystem for extracting aspect values such as event location and performer's name from individual tweets and segregates them according to events with a canonical value assigned for all individual event property. To maintain the internal regularity of each event cluster, the local decisions formed by CRF are regularized according to canonical record values. A factor-graph technique is employed for discovering the relationships between each of these decisions. These variational Bayesian methods appear to be efficient in making predictions on a huge collection of text messages. The extraction of key-phrases from Twitter data for analysis and summarization of tweets is discussed by Zhao et al., (2011). The model employs a three-stage process, namely, keyword ranking, generating cadidate key-phrases, and key-phrase ranking. For keyword ranking, a context-sensitive topical PageRank algorithm is proposed. However, for key-phrase ranking, a probabilistic ranking function that models both relevance and interestingness of key-phrases is used. Furthermore, the model is evaluated over a huge collection of Twitter data, and the experimental results reveal that these methods are very effective in extracting topical key-phrases. The work also studies that the proposed ranking technique can incorporate a user's interests by modeling retweeting behavior. Furthermore, an open-source event extraction and classification model named TwiCal for Twitter data is presented by Ritter et al., (2011). TwiCal is designed to extract a four-tuple signature of events identified as a named-entity, event phrase, event date, and event type respectively. The format chosen resembles the actual event information present on many tweet messages. The model proceeds in three stages. Firstly, the tweet messages collected from streaming are tagged with part-of-speech. Then, the named entities with their associated event phrases and dates involved in significant events are extracted. Further, the temporal expressions involved in events extracted are categorized into different classes. Finally, the proximity of association between each named-entity and date value on which the number of tweets co-occurs is measured to determine whether an event is significant or not.

On the other hand, micro-blogging sites play a critical role in disseminating information among the communities during natural calamities. The size and the speed at which messages are transmitted during crises tend to be very high and needs a real-time extractor. Hence, Meier et al., (2013) presents a system to extract disaster related information from micro-blogs using ML techniques. The model proceeds in two stages, classification of tweets and extraction of tweets. A Naïve Bayesian (NB) classifier is employed to perform fine-grained classification of tweets and later, to extract short messages for analysis. The efficiency is measured on a real-life disaster-related dataset containing a huge collection of micro-blog messages. However, the dataset for training the model is prepared through crowd-sourcing. Empirical results show that ML techniques are well suited for structured data extraction from unstructured short messages. In recent days, user profile extraction on social media has grabbed more attention from the research community. For instance, to extract user profiles from Twitter using a weakly-supervised learning method is illustrated by Li et al., (2014). Interestingly, user profiles from other social networks like Facebook and GooglePlus are utilized as a remote source of supervision. In addition to linguistic features, the model takes into account the network information as a unique feature offered by social media. The proposed model is tested on three user attributes including education, profession, and marital status. The experimental results reveal that the model yields accurate predictions for extracting user attributes on tweets data. Yet another important task of IE from social media is to extract arguments from discussions. Goudas et al., (2014) discussed a two-stage process for argument text extraction from a corpus of social media discussions on a topic of "renewable energy sources". During the first step, k^{th} nearest neighbor (kNN) is employed for the classification of sentences into sentences containing arguments and sentences containing no arguments. In the second step, the model identifies fragments of sentences containing arguments using CRF. The results are quite promising and the model outperforms several baselines. The task of IE is not restricted to those techniques discussed above; however, researchers are trying to develop new IE systems that are more accurate and scalable. Nevertheless, web documents are often incorporated with extra information such as emblems, advertisements, redundant pages, feeds, copyrights, etc., which are irrelevant to the true content and are considered as noise. A framework to remove noise and extract subjective content from online reviews based on the document object model tree (DOM-tree), SMOG readability and linguist tree kernels is addressed by Wadawadagi & Pagi (2019). Firstly, the content of each DOM-tree node is analyzed to predict the perplexity of vocabulary and syntax using SMOG readability test. Then, the semantic tree kernels (STK) embedded with word vectors are employed for the classification of nodes into subjective or objective content. Finally, the nodes carrying subjective content are extracted from the DOM-tree. Table 1 depicts the summary of various IE techniques based on ML and their merits.

PRE-PROCESSING TECHNIQUES

SMC itself is noisy and hence needs pre-processing before ML algorithms are applied productively. Many scholarly approaches have been reported in the literature, and the survey reveals that the most widely accepted techniques for pre-processing SMC include, lexicon-based approaches and techniques based on computational linguistics.

Lexicon-based approaches exploit the features of dictionaries that prepare the data suitable for learning algorithms. For instance, the most commonly used pre-processing technique for sentence-level cleaning is the removal of stopwords (Zhang et al., 2009). Stopwords consist of inferential terms, pronouns, and other lexical terms that do not carry much semantic information alone. The basic idea of removing stopwords is to eliminate terms that carry less or no content information, such as articles, prepositions and conjunctions. Stopwords removal helps in retrieval engines to focus on searching documents that contain relevant keywords. Similarly, morphological and deflective endings from words in English can be removed using a simple pre-processing technique called stemming. Stemming reconstruct the words to its base form, e.g., eliminating 's' from plural nouns, the 'ing' from verbs, or any other affixes. A stem is a natural group of words with identical meanings. Hence, after stemming, each word is delinated by its base word. Porter (2006), originally proposed a set of production rules that perform iterative transforms over English words into their stems called Porter stemmer. In (Pappas et al., 2012), a process called lemmatization is used to extract term scores from SentiWordNet (Baccianella et al., 2010) that converts each token to its dictionary equivalent. Lemmatization maps each verb form to several tenses and nouns to a singular form. Both, stopwords removal and lemmatization will enhance the recall by automatically truncating word endings to their base words, which also help in indexing and searching. Key-phrase extraction algorithms have a critical role in the automatic extraction of topical words and phrases from opinion content (Zhao et al., 2011; Turney, 2000). They provide a concise description of a document's content and are useful in many SASM tasks.

Furthermore, pre-processing techniques based on computational linguistics are utilized to characterize the data, which increases the learning capabilities of ML algorithms. The following are some approaches used frequently with SMC. Word sense disambiguation (WSD) is one among those techniques extensively used in SASM, to address the issue of choosing the most suitable meaning for a term concerning the given context (Tsatsaronis et al., 2010). WSD employs semantic models to recognize the context of a word used in a sentence when the occurrence of a word has multiple meanings. This is essential in several applications such as discourse analysis, anaphora resolution, and improves the relevance of search engines (Wadawadagi & Pagi, in press). Another important pre-processing technique termed, named-entity recognition (NER) (Nadeau & Sekine, 2007) can be applied as a pre-processing technique to locate and classify the information units from given text content into predefined categories. NER task labels sequence of words in a sentence that are the names of things, such as person and company names, or city and country. Additionally, techniques from NLP such as POST and word-net semantic categories are used as augmented features. Given each word in a sentence, POST assigns the proper part-of-speech tags, like noun, verb, adverb, adjective, etc. (Charniak, 1997). This helps to disambiguate homonyms and assigns linguistic information to sub-sentential units. Nevertheless, the above list is not exhaustive, but also includes many other techniques such as negation phrase identification (NPI), bi-term extraction, URL pre-treatment, removal of replicated characters from fancy words, replacement of emoticons, substitute abbreviations by their full names and many more. The comparative study of different IE tasks and pre-processing techniques, and their applicability to various SMC analysis tasks is presented in Table 1.

Table 1. Comparative study of IE tasks and pre-processing techniques

Task domain	Applicability	Process domain	Utility
Arguments extraction	IE task	Identifies and extracts the conflict statements from social media feeds.	Beneficial in fine-grained analysis of sentiments in social media posts.
Bi-term extraction	Pre-processing	Generates the word co-occurrence patterns and learns the topics directly from social media posts.	Improves topic learning by modelling word co-occurrence patterns.
Canonical and event records extraction	IE task	Learns the hidden set of records and record-message alignment.	Useful for converting unstructured text to structured format.
Key-phrases extraction	IE task & Pre-processing	Identifies a set of words and phrases that indicates the topical relevance of a social media post.	It provides a concise description of text content and quantifies semantic similarity between them.
Negation phrases detection	IE task & Pre-processing	Identifies and extracts the negative phrases in the SMC for a given context.	Often useful in polarity detection of and content filtering.
User profiles extraction	IE task	Extracts users's profile information in social networking websites.	Frequently used in grouping of users based on their profile.
Subjective content extraction	IE task	Identifies and extracts the subjective information from social media posts.	Beneficial in subjective content analysis and summerization.
Named-entity extraction	IE task & Pre-processing	Labels each word in a social media post to denote the name of a person, place, object, organization and some times numerical expressions such as date, time and currency.	Useful in finding and categorizing expressions of special meaning in blog posts.
Part-of-speech tagging	Pre-processing	Labels each word in a sequence of text content as mapping to a specific part-of-speech based on definition and context.	It helps to disambiguate homonyms and assigns linguistic information to sub-sentential units and also useful in authorship detection.
Replacement of emoticons	Pre-processing	Removes non-letter symbols and punctuation from feeds, and replacing emoticons with single words and abbreviations by its corresponding full form text.	It improves content representation and makes it suitable for learning algorithms.
Stemming and lemmatization	Pre-processing	Reduces deflective and morphological endings of a word to a common base form.	Helps in indexing and searching and other sentiment classification tasks.
Stopwords removal	Pre-processing	Removes the words that are commonly used in a given language.	Helps retrieval engines to actually focus on searching pages that contain the important words.
URL pre-treatment	Pre-processing	Models navigational and behaviour patterns of users by extracting relevant information from a link and URL.	Useful in web personalization, web log analysis, content filtering and objectionable content detection.
Word sense disambiguation	Pre-processing	Identifies the context for a given word used in a sentence when the occurrence of a word has multiple meanings.	Useful in discourse analysis, improves relevance of search engines and anaphora resolution.

MACHINE LEARNING TECHNIQUES

In this section, several contemporary ML techniques applied for SASM are discussed and evaluated from the perspective of the underlying concepts used. There are different ways that an ML algorithm can model a problem based on its interaction with the input data. Following this trend, we can classify

ML techniques into three main categories: (1) Supervised learning, (2) Unsupervised learning, and (3) Semi-supervised learning.

Supervised Learning

In ML paradigm, supervised learning is being referred as classification or inductive learning. This kind of learning is similar to human learning from past evidences to obtain new knowledge, and to improve our ability to solve real-life problems. Thus, in supervised learning techniques, all classes obtained are meaningful to humans, and can easily be applied to discriminative pattern classification. There has been a significant amount of contribution to supervised learning available in the literature to address the challenges of SASM.

In the first place, the naive Bayes classifier (NBC) is the simplest probabilistic classifier derived from Baye's theorem with strong (naive) independence assumptions between the features is utilized (Russell & Norvig, 2003). In connection to sentiment classification, NBC estimates the posterior probability of a class based on the distribution of lexical terms present in the opinion sentence (Medhat et al., 2014). The NBC is consistent with bag-of-words (BOW) feature representation that does not include positions of the words in the sentence. Furthermore, NBC could be employed for both coarse-grained (binary) and fine-grained (multi-class) sentiment classification tasks. For instance, fast and efficient methods of monitoring public sentiments over social media are discussed in (Anjaria & Gudetti, 2014; Alkhodair et al., in press; Chen, et al., 2014). Here, the models have utilized unigram, bigram, and hybrid (unigram and bigram) word vectors as features for NBC. A specific type of NBC known as a multinomial naive Bayes classifier (MNBC) is also used effectively in SASM (da Silva et al., 2014; Vermeer et al., in press). Unlike NBC, MNBC follows multinomial distribution across the feature values instead of features to be conditionally independent of each other. The distribution is estimated through the generative NB principle with the assumption that features are distributed multinomially for computing the probability of the sentence for each class. Classifiers based on NB are known to be computationally efficient in terms of computational time and memory. In addition to NBC, a probabilistic classifier that refers to a group of exponential models known as maximum-entropy (MaxEnt) classifiers are also utilized. The MaxEnt classifiers in no case consider the features to be conditionally independent; however, it is based on the principle of maximum-entropy (Li et al., 2014). The MaxEnt principle asserts that the probability distribution of available information represented in an optimal manner leads to distribution with highest information entropy. In the context of sentiment classification, MaxEnt transforms labelled feature sets to vectors using encoding schemes (Anjaria & Gudetti, 2014; Alkhodair et al., in press). These encoded vectors are utilized to compute the weights for each feature, and are further combined to obtain the most likely label for that feature set. In contrast to MaxEnt, Bayesian network (BN) or probabilistic directed acyclic graph (PDAG) is a probabilistic graph model that represents a set of random variables and their conditional dependencies through a directed graph (Russell & Norvig, 2003; Medhat et al., 2014; Arbelaitz et al., 2013). In such a graph, each vertex corresponds to a random variable $p(x)$, and the edge between the vertices $p(y|x)$ represents the conditional dependency between the variables. The vertices and edges define the structure of the BN, while the conditional probabilities are the parameters for this graph. Inference and structure learning are two main learning tasks for BN. In the simplest case, network structure can be specified manually instead of learning it from data. Once the structure is obtained, classification can be conducted through inference. Similarly, conditional random fields (CRF) are a genre of the discriminative models often used for sentence structure prediction (Pang et al., 2002). CRF utilizes contextual information from previous labels to enhance the amount of information required for making optimal predictions. They find numerous applications in SA including shallow parsing, key-phrase identification, and named-entity recognition.

An alternative to probabilistic classifiers, yet another group of classifiers named as linear classifiers are extensively used in sentiment classification. Linear classifiers carry out classification based on the values of a linear combination of the feature vectors (Medhat et al., 2014; Li et al., 2009). In the case of binary classification task, a linear classifier can be visualized as a hyperplane that separates a high-dimensional input space into two partitions: all points on the one side are classified as *'true'*, and the other side as *'false'*. Linear classifiers are more suitable for specific problems in pattern recognition such as document classification and importantly for data objects comprising more features, reaching high accuracy levels comparable to non-linear classifiers while consuming less time for training. Two of the most important linear classifiers used in SASM are support vector machines (SVM) (Cortes & Vapnik, 1995) and artificial neural networks (ANN) (Wasserman, 1993). The SVM classifier generates an optimal hyper-plane form a given set of labelled training samples, and further categorizes new samples based on the hyper-plane obtained, making it a non-probabilistic binary linear classifier. The hyper-plane is a reference line obtained to best separate the data points in the input space through their class labels into *'true'* or *'false'*. Furthermore, SVM constructs a non-linear decision surface in the original feature space by mapping the data objects non-linearly to an inner product space, where the class labels can be separated linearly with a hyper-plane (Aizerman et al., 1964). The SVM classifier is ideally suitable for handling user-generated content present on the web, this is due to the sparse behavior of textual content in which certain features are not relevant, but they often tend to be correlated with each another. Consequently, SVM is efficiently used in several sentiment classification tasks (Anjaria & Gudetti, 2014; Alkhodair et al., in press; da Silva et al., 2014; Vermeer et al., in press), as this is highly reliable for traditional text classification. A variation of SVM, called passive-aggressive model (PAM) is also used for solving numerous SA related problems (Vermeer et al., in press). PAM models are similar to SVM, but they use margin to update the parameter values of a classifier. In simple words, if the prediction is correct then it will be passive, otherwise, when the prediction goes wrong then weights are updated for correct classification.

On the contrary, ANN is composed of artificial neurons that imitate the biological neurons of the human brain (Medhat et al., 2014; Ruiz & Srinivasan, 1999; Schultz & Reitmann, 2018). These neurons are connected by links and are capable of interacting with each other. The inputs of neurons are represented by the feature vector X_i which denotes the term frequencies of the ith document. Each edge of the network is associated with certain weights for computing the input function. The output of each neuron is then transferred to other neurons in a sequence. The output at each node is referred to as its activation or a node value. They are capable of learning through updating the weight values of each link. Furthermore, multi-layer neural networks which are also called as deep neural networks (DNN) solve the classification problem for non-linear sets by employing hidden layers, to induce multiple piecewise linear boundaries, that are used to approximate enclosed regions belonging to a particular class (Pandey & Solanki, 2019). Accordingly, the output of neurons in the previous layers is fed into the neurons of next layers. The additional hidden layers can be interpreted geometrically as extra hyper-planes, which improve the separation capability of the network. The training process of DNN is more complex because the errors need to be back-propagated over different layers.

Random forest (RF) is one of the other ML techniques that is frequently used in sentiment classification (Alkhodair et al., in press; da Silva et al., 2014; Vermeer et al., in press). It is an ensemble learning method that constructs a multitude of decision trees while training and returns the class with the mode of the classes or mean prediction of the individual trees (Wan & Gao, 2015). The strength of RF classifier is that, it creates a huge number of random classification trees. That is, it randomly resamples the data to train a new classifier for each subsample with a random subsample of available variables. Furthermore, it exhibits robustness against overfitting, and is easy to use, as it needs only two arguments, the number of variables for building the individual trees and the number of trees.

Unsupervised Learning

In several cases, the class labels are unknown to the classification algorithms. However, the analyst wants to investigate the data for mining some interesting patterns underlying the dataset. Unsupervised learning techniques are advantageous to address the issues of identifying hidden patterns in unlabelled data. Many researchers have been tried to explore this phenomenon to provide the solution for sentiment classification problems. For instance, a framework based on unsupervised TRI-clustering is proposed for analyzing both user-level and tweet-level sentiments (Zhu, 2014). The TRI-clustering mechanism exploits the property of duality for both sentiment clustering and tripartite graph co-clustering. However, co-clustering is an unsupervised learning technique and it does not require labelled data. But, the model uses high quality labelled data for experimentation in view of achieving improved performance. Finally, a non-negative matrix co-factorization technique is used to compute the best co-cluster of a tripartite graph. Further, the model uses emotion consistency regularization to generate the clusters of features that are relevant to the feature lexicon, and closer to the sentiment classes. Similarly, an unsupervised and distributed model for twitter data that uses different domain-independent sentiment lexicons, namely, SentiWordNet, SenticNet, and SentiSlangNet is proposed (Pandarachalil et al., 2015). In this technique, a sentiment score for each tweet in a corpus is determined using the SENT_SCORE algorithm. The n-grams of tweet messages are obtained through pre-processing and are input to the algorithm. The results prove that SenticNet yields better polarity scores for several n-grams which are frequently used in tweets and hence, improves the performance of the model. In (Lim et al., 2017), an unsupervised learning technique to discover the real-world latent infectious diseases from social media data is discussed. The model investigates the public's expressions about symptoms, body parts, and location information present in SMC. The emotion detection algorithm called SentiStrength (Thelwall et al., 2010) is efficiently employed to perform the unsupervised SA task. The SentiStrength algorithm receives social media text as input and generates a sentiment score that ranges between -5 to 5. Subsequently, a weight vector of symptoms and a period of individual sentiments can be recorded. Finally, the weight vectors obtained are used to discover the latent infectious disease-related information. In addition to this, a novel approach for predicting sentiments in Twitter messages using unsupervised dependency parsing-based text classification that jointly works with NLP techniques and sentiment lexicons is presented (Fernández-Gavilanes et al., 2016). The sentiment lexicons are created through a semi-automatic polarity expansion algorithm, enabling them for domain-specific applications. Further, NLP techniques are applied to capture the linguistic peculiarities from the tweets that improve detection performance. The list mentioned above is however not exhaustive, but suggestive of a wide range of ML techniques used for SASM.

Semi-Supervised Learning

Recently, semi-supervised learning techniques have been extensively used to address the problem of insufficient labelled data readily available for training. Hence, semi-supervised learning techniques use limited amount of labelled data with a huge amount of unlabelled data to train an accurate model. For example, in (Khan et al., 2017), a semi-supervised model that combines a lexicon-based (SentiWordNet) approach with a SVM to perform sentiment classification is proposed. The model utilizes two statistical techniques namely, information gain (IG) and cosine similarity to update the sentiment scores defined in SentiWordNet, and further they are termed as Senti-IG and Senti-Cosine respectively. The subjective features are then extracted using Senti-IG and Senti-Cosine for processing. Interestingly, nouns are treated as semantic words when combination with adjectives, verbs and adverbs. Finally, a context-specific hybrid learning model coupled with SVM is developed to achieve desirable performance. Furthermore, a model based on non-negative matrix factorization (NMF) termed as constrained-NMF (CNMF) that imposes labelled information constrain and sparseness constrain for social media spam detection is presented (Yu et al., 2017). The learned representation presents highly distinguishable features through the data provided by a few labelled samples and a large amount of unlabelled samples. The performance of the model is estimated through the iterative update rules (IUR) and optimization of the CNMF-based social media spammer detection. In addition to this, an emerging semi-supervised learning technique for the task of emotion recognition in social media posts using multi-dimensional scaling (MDS) through random projections and biased-SVM (bSVM) is presented (Hussain & Cambria, 2018). The above model uses biased regularization that provides an easy way to implement an inductive bias in kernel machines. This aspect carries great importance in ML theory and characterizes the generalization capability of a learning system.

Gupta et al., (2018) presents a new approach based on semi-supervised and transfer learning for the task of sentiment classification. This model is designed based on the principle of coherent implementation of several technologies will yield good results. Hence, this model uses dense feature representations, pre-training, and manifold regularization. In the first stage, the model learns dense representations for opinion sentences with *doc2vec* word-embeddings, and later performs classification with pre-training and manifold regularization. The research records significant improvements in results for supervised learning techniques when a good amount of data is available. Similarly, an ensemble semi-supervised learning technique that blends label propagation and transductive-SVM (TSVM) with Dempster–Shafer theory is presented for accurate prediction of social lending in unlabelled data (Kim & Cho, 2019). Label propagation is a technique used to assign class labels to previously collected unlabelled data so that data with similar features are mapped to the same class. The TSVM classifier is responsible for discriminating data with different features, and Dempster–Shafer fusion method measures whether unlabelled data can be classified on the basis of results obtained for semi-supervised learning methods. The effectiveness of the proposed model is illustrated with the experiment being conducted over the social loan data comprising two-third unlabelled data.

Table 2. Different learning models and their merits

Learning model	Methodology	Merits
Artificial neural networks	Based on biological neural networks that learns to accomplish tasks through instances without being explicitly programmed with any task-specific rules.	A robust data-driven, flexible and self-adaptive learning model resilient to capture non-linear and complex underlying characteristics with a high degree of accuracy.
Naive Bayes	A probabilistic model originated from Bayes theorem with strong independence assumptions among the features.	Highly scalable and fast model construction with linear predictors and row scoring scales. Effectively used for both binary and multi-class problems.
Support vector machines	A classifier learns from labelled data and generates optimal hyper-planes that categorize new examples.	Merits includes kernel based model, absence of local minima, sparseness of the solution, and capacity to control the margin by optimization.
Maximum entropy	The probability distribution that best represents the current knowledge will be the one with the largest entropy subjected to precisely stated prior data.	The facts used to model the data are linguistically very simple, but yet succeed in approximating complex linguistic relationships.
Bayesian networks	A probabilistic graphical model that characterizes a set of random variables and their conditional dependencies through a directed acyclic graph.	Readily handles incomplete data, and facilitates use of prior knowledge. Also provides an efficient method for preventing the over-fitting of data.
Random forests	Constructs a forest of decision trees during training and results a class with mode of the classes or mean prediction of the individual trees.	Highly accurate classifier for scalable dataset and also useful in estimating prime attributes in the classification process.
Passive aggressive models	This model is streaming ML technique used for classification and regression.	A fast classification model for big streaming data and easy to implement, but does not guarantee global parameters observed in SVM.
TRI-clustering	It uses an automatic boundary searching algorithm based on a divide-and-conquer technique capable of identifying statistically significant REV values that correspond to a 3D region in the whole data space.	Provides an explicit representation of the regulatory effects in the dataset and identifies transitions in the network from condition-to-condition implicit in the boundaries of the identified TRI-clusters.
Non-negative matrix factorization	Factorizes a iven matrix into two matrices based on non-negative constraints, which allow learning parts from objects.	Efficiently extracts features from the text contents, and generates feature-document matrix that describes clusters of related documents.

CHALLENGES OF APPLYING ML TECHNIQUES TO SMC

The application of ML techniques to SMC exhibits several intellectual challenges. In the following paragraph, many issues and challenges of applying ML techniques to social media data are presented. In the first place, the unique qualities of SMC, which is being formed by short text messages, pose a major challenge (Sapountzi & Psannis, 2018). It is seen that short messages carry sparse data and often depends on the context in which they are stated. Accordingly, they differ substantially from other sentiment data such as online reviews. Hence, the feature vectors obtained on a specific corpus of SMC may not yield sufficient productivity for document similarity. Furthermore, social media platforms support informal writing, where people use idiomatic and creative phrases in their posts. This causes ML algorithms hard for them to build automated models for large-scale SA. Additionally, short messages streaming over the social media in large quantities, leads to labelling problems when used for supervised training.

Finding adequate techniques for real-time analysis of streaming data is a potential problem (Ji et al., 2015). However, unsupervised training does not require labelled data and hence, clustering has become a promising ML approach for real-time analysis of social media data.

Secondly, SMC is inherently noisy, consisting of unconventional words, misspells, grammatical errors, acronyms, spammers, and even slang. A considerable amount of pre-processing is required before applying ML techniques to social media data (Goswami & Kumar, 2017). Formulating business strategies with inaccurate and noisy data leads to distortion in the results of analytics. However, pre-processing is still a time-consuming process. Moreover, processing and analysis of privacy-preserved data is another critical challenge in SASM (Bello-Orgaz et al., 2016). Many social media data providers vend their data to various third party customers such as companies and analysts. To prevent data from privacy breaching and attacks, it is often protected with privacy-preserving techniques. It is hard to evaluate and test privacy-preserved data using traditional ML techniques. Therefore, it would be interesting to design and develop specialized techniques and benchmark datasets to address this issue. Finally, each research problem in SASM adopts a different ML technique; many researchers are concerned about how some ML techniques can hardly be validated (Wadawadagi & Pagi, in press). Although most researchers use popular validation techniques such as confusion matrix, precision and recall, area under curve (AUC), etc. for their models, some researchers do not use any measurements. Hence, much of the debate on validating techniques for automated SASM is misguiding. Further, automated SASM methods are incorrect models of languages. This means that the performance of any technique on a new dataset cannot be guaranteed, and therefore validation is important when applying these methods.

APPLICATIONS

Investigation and analysis of SMC have potential advantages over several ongoing topics of interest such as investigating how topics evolve along with the underlying social interactions between participants, and to distinguish vital members who have a great influence on various topics of discussion. Based on the study of current literature, the following paragraphs present several application areas of SASM.

Brand Sentiment Analysis

Social media messages are extensively used to investigate consumer's sentiment towards a brand. They offer a unique repository of customer reviews in the world of brand sentiment. Popular brands and celebrities receive opinions and comments directly from consumers or members in real-time through a public forum. Both the targeted and competing brands have the opportunity to interpret the opinions for bringing transformation in consumer sentiments towards their brand (Ghiassi et al., 2013). For example, TripAdvisor is America's biggest tourist web portal providing reviews of travelers about their experiences in flights, hotels, and restaurants. These customer opinions may have a positive or negative influence on brand perception, loyalty, and promotion. Thus, SA on large-scale user opinions will help enterprises to tap into customer's insight for improving their quality of product, services, or even anticipate new business opportunities and other activities accordingly.

Political Ideology Detection

The identification of political ideology from micro-blog contents is extremely useful in analyzing one's affinity towards a political movement. This brings an ideal environment for advertising political thoughts during the heat of election campaigns (Chen et al., 2017). Though political ideologies follow diverse and complex phenomenon, yet they can be approximated through the utilization of NLP and ML techniques. The basic concept of discovering ideologies is to understand the difference of opinions toward certain topics. Then, based on the distribution of opinions quoted different ideologies can be grouped (Gu et al., 2016). Most of the research work on ideology detection has been discussed as a binary classification problem, i.e. grouping people into liberal or a conservative. However, this ignores the fact that people's ideology always lies in a broad spectrum (Larsen, 2015). Every individual carries different ideology which differs his stand on political matters. Hence, it is important to infer ideologies not only based on opinions but also the target entities or topics on which the sentiment is expressed. Further, this may also help in exploring and tracking electoral preferences (political trends) of citizens in the country.

Emotion Detection

Emotion detection in SMC is beneficial for several applications such as recommendation systems, personalized advertising, developing automated counseling systems, emergency response systems, etc. It deals with the investigation of emotional state of individuals or communities who are participating in online campaigns. Emotion detection systems are instrumental in disaster management, where people use social media to report emergency service agencies (Ceron et al., 2015). These messages often carry not only sentiments related to disaster management, but also contain status information. Hence, specialized models need to be designed to address sentiment prediction infused with other emotion-related traits. In addition to this, social media offers an opportunity to acquire insights through which the emotional pulse of the nation can be determined, and hence, to discover web communities (Bügel & Zielinski, 2013; Kanavos et al., 2017). Web communities are created through the identification of associated clusters based on similar emotional behaviors.

Implicit Sentiment In Financial News

The exploitation of sentiments in financial news enables business analysts to study the impact of news on the company's growth (Kauter et al., 2015). However, the term sentiment in financial domain is used in a different perspective as "the expectations of stakeholders relative to some standards". Essentially, this kind of analysis helps in predicting the effect of financial news on stock markets. In practice, business analysts carry out manual predictions of the stock exchange based on comments and reports in the news articles. Through advanced language models and machine intelligence, the activity of stock market prediction can be performed with better accuracy over a huge collection of text content. Recently, the formulation of domain-specific ontology enabled automatic processing of information through knowledge representation. There is a growing demand for the construction of precise and powerful ontology in the financial domain.

Monitoring Public Health

Surveillance of communicable diseases (epidemics) caused by viruses or bacteria, which spreads among the people can be a challenging problem (Ji et al., 2015). Keeping records of infectious diseases in the interest of public health and identifying its causes are therefore important. On the other hand, monitoring emotional changes of the public after being affected by diseases is also a prime concern of the public health department. In view of this, SASM offers a better tool for public health inspectors and concerned authorities to take the measure of concern expressed by the public. For instance, Twitter as a micro-blog service alone generates 400 million tweets every day, directly received from the public. Tweets expressing concerns about certain diseases may not have a direct emotional impact of that disease on the public. However, messages that are re-tweeted with emotional expressions might be directly affected.

Sarcasm Detection

The term sarcasm refers to a kind of irony broadly used in social media and micro-blogging posts. It is sophisticated form of opinon statement used to express implicit information of a person such as criticism or mockery (Bouazizi & Otsuki, 2016). However, identification of sarcasm is difficult even for human beings. Hence, recognition of sarcastic phrases could be beneficial in improving the automated SA of data collected from micro-blogging or social media posts. The use of aggressive, violent or offensive language, hateful comments, targeting a specific group of people sharing common property, whether this property is their gender (i.e., sexism), their ethnic group or race (i.e., racism) or their believes and religion are considered as hate messages. However, most of the online social networks and micro-blogging websites forbid the use of hate content. The size of these networks and websites makes it almost impossible to control all of their content.

CONCLUSION

This chapter focused on numerous state-of-the-art ML techniques used in the domain of sentiment analysis on social media (SASM) and its applications. The research sheds light on several techniques used for extracting relevant information from social media content (SMC). Further, the work studied important pre-processing techniques employed to filter out the noise from SMC. Subsequently, many issues and challenges of applying ML techniques to SMC are also presented. Finally, the chapter discussed several application areas that assert the importance of ML techniques in SASM. Despite, the continuous evolution of SASM techniques, still there are ample opportunities and challenges for researchers. Interest in SMC for regional languages other than English is growing as there is still a lack of tools and technologies concerning these languages. Lexicons similar to WordNet which supports many regional languages other than English need to be developed. In many cases, opinions are very much dependent on the context. Hence, it is beneficial to study the context of the opinion and research needs to be focused on context-based SASM systems.

REFERENCES

Aizerman, M., Braverman, E., & Rozonoer, L. (1964). Theoretical foundations of the potential function method in pattern recognition learning. *Autom. Rem. Cont.,* 821–837.

Alkhodair, S. A., Ding, S. H. H., Fung, B. C. M., & Liu, J. (in press). Detecting breaking news rumors of emerging topics in social media. *Information Processing & Management.* doi:10.1016/j.ipm.2019.02.016

Anami, B. S., Wadawadagi, R. S., & Pagi, V. B. (2014). Machine learning techniques in web content mining: A comparative analysis. *Journal of Information & Knowledge Management, 13*(1), 1–14. doi:10.1142/S0219649214500051

Anjaria, M., & Gudetti, R. M. R. (2014). A novel sentiment analysis of social networks using supervised learning. *Social Network Analysis and Mining, 4*(3), 181–193. doi:10.100713278-014-0181-9

Arbelaitz, O., Gurrutxaga, I., Lojo, A., Muguerza, J., Maria, J., & Perona, P. I. (2013). Web usage and content mining to extract knowledge for modeling the users of the Bidasoa Turismo website and to adapt it. *Expert Systems with Applications, 40*(18), 7478–7491. doi:10.1016/j.eswa.2013.07.040

Baccianella, S., Esuli, A., & Sebastiani, F. (2010). Sentiwordnet 3.0: an enhanced lexical resource for sentiment analysis and opinion mining. *Proc. of the Annual Conference on Language Resources and Evaluation,* 2200–2204.

Bello-Orgaz, G., Jung, J. J., & Camacho, D. (2016). Social big data: Recent achievements and new challenges. *Information Fusion, 28,* 45–59. doi:10.1016/j.inffus.2015.08.005

Benson, E., & Haghighi Barzilay, R. (2011). Event discovery in social media feeds. *Proc. of the 49th Annual Meeting of the Association for Computational Linguistics: Human Language technologies, 1,* 389-398.

Bontcheva, K., Derczynski, L., Funk, A., Greenwood, M. A., Maynard, D., & Aswani, N. (2013). TwitIE: a fully-featured information extraction pipeline for microblog text. *Proc. of the International Conference On Recent Advances In Natural Language Processing,* 83-90. *doi:*10.6084/m9.figshare.1003767.v2

Bouazizi, M., & Otsuki, T. (2016). A pattern-based approach for sarcasm detection on twitter. *IEEE Access: Practical Innovations, Open Solutions, 4,* 5477–5488. doi:10.1109/ACCESS.2016.2594194

Bügel, U., & Zielinski, A. (2013). Multilingual analysis of twitter news in support of mass emergency events. *International Journal of Information Systems for Crisis Response and Management, 5*(1), 77–85. doi:10.4018/jiscrm.2013010105

Ceron, A., Curini, L., & Iacus, S. M. (2015). Using sentiment analysis to monitor electoral campaigns: Method matters-evidence from the United States and Italy. *Social Science Computer Review, 33*(1), 3–20. doi:10.1177/0894439314521983

Charniak, E. (1997). Statistical techniques for natural language parsing. *AI Magazine, 18*(4), 33–44.

Chen, W., Zhang, X., Wang, T., Yang, B., & Li, Y. (2017). Opinion-aware knowledge graph for political ideology detection. *Proceedings of the Twenty-Sixth International Joint Conference on Artificial Intelligence (IJCAI-17),* 3647-3653. 10.24963/ijcai.2017/510

Chen, X., Vorvoreanu, M., & Madhavan, K. (2014). Mining social media data for understanding students learning experiences. *IEEE Transactions on Learning Technologies*, *7*(3), 246–259. doi:10.1109/TLT.2013.2296520

Choi, H. J., & Park, C. H. (2019). Emerging topic detection in Twitter stream based on high utility pattern mining. *Expert Systems with Applications*, *115*, 27–36. doi:10.1016/j.eswa.2018.07.051

Cortes, C., & Vapnik, V. N. (1995). Support-vector networks. *Machine Learning, 20*(3), 273–297. doi:10.1007/BF00994018

Cunningham, H., Tablan, V., Roberts, A., & Bontcheva, K. (2013). Getting more out of biomedical documents with gate's full lifecycle open source text analytics. *PLoS Computational Biology*, *9*(2), e1002854. doi:10.1371/journal.pcbi.1002854 PMID:23408875

da Silva, N. F. F., Hruschka, E. R., & Hruschka, E. R. Jr. (2014). Tweet sentiment analysis with classifier ensembles. *Decision Support Systems*, *66*, 170–179. doi:10.1016/j.dss.2014.07.003

Fernández-Gavilanes, M., Álvarez-López, T., Juncal-Martínez, J., Costa-Montenegro, E., & González-Castaño, F. (2016). Unsupervised method for sentiment analysis in online texts. *Expert Systems with Applications*, *58*, 57–75. doi:10.1016/j.eswa.2016.03.031

Ghiassi, M., Skinner, J., & Zimbra, D. (2013). Twitter brand sentiment analysis: A hybrid system using n-gram analysis and dynamic artificial neural network. *Expert Systems with Applications*, *40*(16), 6266–6282. doi:10.1016/j.eswa.2013.05.057

Goswami, A., & Kumar, A. (2017). Challenges in the Analysis of Online Social Networks: A Data Collection Tool Perspective. *Wireless Personal Communications*, *97*(3), 4015–4061. doi:10.100711277-017-4712-3

Goudas, T., Louizos, C., Petasis, G., & Karkaletsis, V. (2014). Argument extraction from news, blogs, and social media. In A. Likas, K. Blekas, & D. Kalles (Eds.), Lecture Notes in Computer Science: Vol. 8445. *Artificial Intelligence: Methods and Applications. SETN 2014*. Cham: Springer.

Gu, Y., Chen, T., Sun, Y., & Wang, B. (2016). *Ideology detection for twitter users with heterogeneous types of links*. ArXiv:1612.08207

Gupta, R., Sahu, S., Espy-Wilson, C., & Narayanan, S. (2018). *Semi-supervised and transfer learning approaches for low resource sentiment classification*. arXiv:1806.02863

Hussain, A., & Cambria, E. (2018). Semi-supervised learning for big social data analysis. *Neurocomputing*, *275*(31), 1662–1673. doi:10.1016/j.neucom.2017.10.010

Ji, X., Chun, S. A., Wei, Z., & Geller, J. (2015). Twitter sentiment classification for measuring public health concerns. *Social Network Analysis and Mining*, *5*(13).

Jianqiang, Z., & Xiaolin, G. (2017). Comparison research on text pre-processing methods on Twitter sentiment analysis. *IEEE Access: Practical Innovations, Open Solutions*, *5*, 2870–2879. doi:10.1109/ACCESS.2017.2672677

Kanavos, A., Perikos, I., Hatzilygeroudis, I., & Tsakalidis, A. (2017). Emotional community detection in social networks. *Computers & Electrical Engineering, 65*, 449–460. doi:10.1016/j.compeleceng.2017.09.011

Kauter, M. V., Breesch, D., & Hoste, V. (2015). Fine-grained analysis of explicit and implicit sentiment in financial news articles. *Expert Systems with Applications, 42*(11), 4999–5010. doi:10.1016/j.eswa.2015.02.007

Khan, F. H., Qamar, U., & Bashir, S. (2017). A semi-supervised approach to sentiment analysis using revised sentiment strength based on SentiWordNet. *Knowledge and Information Systems, 51*(3), 851–872. doi:10.100710115-016-0993-1

Kim, A., & Cho, S. (2019). An ensemble semi supervised learning method for predicting defaults in social lending. *Engineering Applications of Artificial Intelligence, 81*, 193–199. doi:10.1016/j.engappai.2019.02.014

Larsen, M. E., Boonstra, T. W., Batterham, P. J., O'Dea, B., Paris, C., & Christensen, H. (2015). We feel: Mapping emotion on Twitter. *IEEE Journal of Biomedical and Health Informatics, 19*(4), 1246–1252. doi:10.1109/JBHI.2015.2403839 PMID:25700477

Li, J., Ritter, A., & Hovy, H. E. (2014). Weakly supervised user profile extraction from twitter. *Proceedings of the 52nd Annual Meeting of the Association for Computational Linguistics,* 165–174.

Li, X., Nsofor, G. C., & Song, L. (2009). A comparative analysis of predictive data mining techniques. *International Journal of Rapid Manufacturing, 1*(2), 50–172. doi:10.1504/IJRAPIDM.2009.029380

Lim, S., Tucker, C. S., & Kumara, S. (2017). An unsupervised machine learning model for discovering latent infectious diseases using social media data. *Jouranl of Biomedical Information, 66*, 82 94. doi:10.1016/j.jbi.2016.12.007 PMID:28034788

Medhat, W., Hassan, A., & Korashy, H. (2014). Sentiment analysis algorithms and applications: A survey. *Ain Shams Engineering Journal, 5*(4), 1093–1113. doi:10.1016/j.asej.2014.04.011

Meier, P., Castillo, C., Imran, M., Elbassuoni, S. M., & Diaz, F. (2013). Extracting information nuggets from disaster-related messages in social media. *10th International Conference on Information Systems for Crisis Response and Management,* 1-10.

Mikolov, T., Sutskever, I., Chen, K., Corrado, G., & Dean, J. (2013). *Distributed representations of words and phrases and their compositionality.* Arxiv:1310.4546

Nadeau, D., & Sekine, S. (2007). A survey of named entity recognition and classification. *Lingvisticae Investigationes,* 3–26.

Nebhi. (2012). Ontology-based information extraction from Twitter. *Proc. of the Workshop On Information Extraction And Entity Analytics On Social Media Data,* 17–22.

Pandarachalil, R., Sendhilkumar, S., & Mahalakshmi, G. S. (2015). Twitter sentiment analysis for large-scale data: An unsupervised approach. *Cognitive Computation, 7*(2), 254–262. doi:10.100712559-014-9310-z

Pandey, S., & Solanki, A. (2019). Music Instrument Recognition using Deep Convolutional Neural Networks. *International. Journal of Information Technology.* doi:10.100741870-019-00285-y

Pang, B., Lee, L., & Vaithyanathan, S. (2002). Thumbs up? Sentiment classification using machine learning techniques. *Proc. of the Conference On Empirical Methods in Natural Language Processing (emnlp), Philadelphia, July 2002, Association for Computational Linguistics*, 79-86.

Pappas, N., Katsimpras, G., & Stamatatos, E. (2012). Extracting informative textual parts from web pages containing user-generated content. *Proc. of 12th International Conference on Knowledge Management and Knowledge Technologies, 4,* 1–8. 10.1145/2362456.2362462

Porter, M. F. (2006). An algorithm for suffix stripping. *Electronic Library and Electronic Systems, 40,* 211–218.

Ritter, A., Clark, S., & Etzioni, O. (2011). Named entity recognition in tweets: An experimental study. *Proc. of the Conference on Empirical Methods in Natural Language Processing (EMNLP 2011),* 1524–1534.

Ruiz, M., & Srinivasan, P. (1999). Hierarchical neural networks for text categorization. *ACM SIGIR Conference, Proc. of the 22nd Annual International ACM SIGIR Conference on Research and Development in Information Retrieval,* 281–282. 10.1145/312624.312700

Russell, S., & Norvig, P. (2003). *Artificial intelligence: a modern approach* (2nd ed.). Prentice Hall.

Salton, G., & Yang, C. S. (1975). A vector space model for automatic indexing. *Communications of the ACM, 18*(11), 613–620. doi:10.1145/361219.361220

Sapountzi, A., & Psannis, K. (2018). Social networking data analysis tools & challenges. *Future Generation Computer Systems, 86,* 893–913. doi:10.1016/j.future.2016.10.019

Schultz, M., & Reitmann, S. (2018). Machine learning approach to predict aircraft boarding. *Transportation Research Part C, Emerging Technologies, 98,* 391–408. doi:10.1016/j.trc.2018.09.007

Singh, S. (2018). *Natural Language Processing for Information Extraction.* CoRR abs/1807.02383

Thelwall, M., Buckley, K., Paltoglou, G., Cai, D., & Kappas, A. (2010). Sentiment strength detection in short informal text. *Journal of the American Society for Information Science and Technology, 61*(12), 2544–2558. doi:10.1002/asi.21416

Tsatsaronis, G., Varlamis, I., & Nørvg, K. (2010). An experimental study on unsupervised graph based word sense disambiguation. *Computational Linguistics and Intelligent Text Processing, LNCS, 6008,* 184–198. doi:10.1007/978-3-642-12116-6_16

Turney, P. (2000). Learning algorithms for keyphrase extraction. *Information Retrieval, 2*(4), 303–336. doi:10.1023/A:1009976227802

Vermeer, S. A. M., Araujo, T., Bernritter, S. F., & Noort, G. (in press). Seeing the wood for the trees: How machine learning can help firms in identifying relevant electronic word-of-mouth in social media. *International Journal of Research in Marketing.* doi:10.1016/j.ijresmar.2019.01.010

Wadawadagi, R. S. & Pagi, V. B. (in press). An enterprise perspective of web content analysis research: *A strategic road-map. International Journal of Knowledge and Web Intelligence.* doi:10.1504/IJKWI.2017.10010794

Wadawadagi, R. S., & Veerappa, B. (2019). A multi-layer approach to opinion polarity classification using augmented semantic tree kernels. *Journal of Experimental & Theoretical Artificial Intelligence, 31*(3), 349–367. doi:10.1080/0952813X.2018.1549108

Waltl, B., Bonczek, G., & Matthes, F. (2018). Rule-based information extraction: advantages, limitations, and perspectives. *Jusletter IT, 22*.

Wan, Y., & Gao, Q. (2015). An ensemble sentiment classification system of twitter data for airline services analysis. *IEEE International Conference on Data Mining Workshop (ICDMW)*, 1318–1325. 10.1109/ICDMW.2015.7

Wasserman, P. D. (1993). *Advanced Methods in Neural Computing.* New York: John Wiley & Sons, Inc.

Yang, M. C., & Rim, H. C. (2014). Identifying interesting Twitter contents using topical analysis. *Expert Systems with Applications, 41*(9), 4330–4336. doi:10.1016/j.eswa.2013.12.051

Yu, D. N., Chen, F. J., Fu, B., & Qin, A. (2017). Constrained NMF-based semi-supervised learning for social media spammer detection. *J. Knowledge-Based Systems, 125*, 64–73. doi:10.1016/j.knosys.2017.03.025

Zhang, X., Xu, C., Cheng, J., Lu, H., & Ma, S. (2009). Effective annotation and search for video blogs with integration of context and content analysis. *IEEE Transactions on Multimedia, 11*(2), 272-285.

Zhao, X., Jiang, J., He, J., Song, Y., Achanauparp, P., Lim, E., & Li, X. (2011). Topical keyphrase extraction from Twitter. *Proc. of the 49th Annual Meeting of the Association for Computational Linguistics: Human Language Technologies*, 379–388.

Zhu, L. (2014). Tripartite graph clustering for dynamic sentiment analysis on social media. *Proc. ACM SIGMOD International Conference on Management of Data (SIGMOD 14)*, 1531 1542. 10.1145/2588555.2593682

Chapter 25
Social Big Data Mining:
A Survey Focused on Sentiment Analysis

Anisha P. Rodrigues

(iD) https://orcid.org/0000-0002-3050-4555

NMAM Institute of Technology, Nitte, India

Niranjan N. Chiplunkar

NMAM Institute of Technology, Nitte, India

Roshan Fernandes

NMAM Institute of Technology, Nitte, India

ABSTRACT

Social media is used to share the data or information among the large group of people. Numerous forums, blogs, social networks, news reports, e-commerce websites, and many more online media play a role in sharing individual opinions. The data generated from these sources is huge and in unstructured format. Big data is a term used for data sets that are large or complex and that cannot be processed by traditional processing system. Sentimental analysis is one of the major data analytics applied on big data. It is a task of natural language processing to determine whether a text contains subjective information and what information it expresses. It helps in achieving various goals like the measurement of customer satisfaction, observing public mood on political movement, movie sales prediction, market intelligence, and many more. In this chapter, the authors present various techniques used for sentimental analysis and related work using these techniques. The chapter also presents open issues and challenges in sentimental analysis landscape.

INTRODUCTION

These days use of smart devices and the high speed Internet has led to lots of people to engage in social media sites like Twitter, Facebook, and Instagram. Due to the high social interaction, the data produced by these sites increases drastically. The number of active social media users keeps growing. According

DOI: 10.4018/978-1-5225-9643-1.ch025

Figure 1. 5vs of big data (Pouyanfar, S., Yang, Y., Chen, S. C., Shyu, M. L., &Iyengar, S. S.,2018)

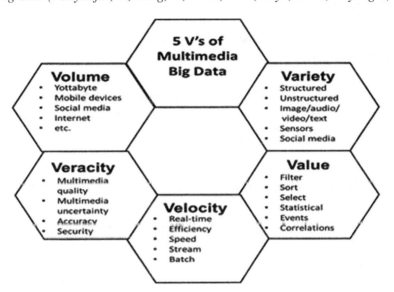

to the Global WebIndex statistics the number of people using mobile phones has reached 3.7 billion (Chaffey, D., 2016). According to Facebook, the number of active users has reached 1.59 billion (Tan, W., Blake, M. B., Saleh, I., & Dustdar, S., 2013). A large amount of data is produced by many Internet users while using online social networking media. The term big data is defined as a data with huge volume, complex in nature and inundates business on a day-to-day basis. Big Data is a term that describes data with "3V"s. They are Volume, Variety and Velocity. Volume signifies huge amount of data. Variety signifies various forms of data that is structured, semi-structured and unstructured generated from various sources. Velocity represents the speed at which the data generated. These characteristics were first identified by Doug Laney (Laney, D., 2001). More recently, two additional V's are added to the description of bigdata, namely, Veracity and Value. Hence big data is a data with "5V"s. Figure 1 shows 5vs of big data. Due to these characteristics of data, traditional processing system is unable to process it.

Big Data mining or analytics is the task of analyzing data of 5V's to extract the hidden interesting patterns, market trends, and unknown relations-associations, analyze customer behavior, their preferences and other useful business intelligence information. People share their views on various topics using social media platform. Earlier, before the invention of the Internet or Web, the companies used the techniques like surveys, polls to collect opinions of the people. Now, due to increase in the use of the Web, people openly discuss their ideas on social media and the companies can easily collect people's opinion using the Web. In today's world, there exists a huge competition among the organizations. Within a competitive market, sentiment analysis helps to understand the customer needs. Bigger organizations makes use of social media for promoting their business and marketing purpose. Mining the data generated by social media is called Social Big data mining. Due to the abundance of social media sentiments and emotions, analyzing these sentiments has become challenging. Sentiment analysis attempts to derive the sentiment expressed by an author against an entity. This chapter highlights various techniques used to mine these sentiments.

Outline of the Chapter

In this chapter, we described basic introductory concepts of a sentiment analysis. We focused on different levels of sentiment analysis in Section 3.1 and also explained each techniques used for sentiment analysis, with their applications in section4. Applications of sentiment analysis are outlined in Section 7.Open challenges related to sentiment analysis are discussed in Section 8, which guides interested researchers in their future work. This chapter guides the researchers about the best classifier model in terms of performance for sentiment analysis.

LEVELS OF SENTIMENT ANALYSIS

Sentiment analysis or opinion mining is the learning of people's opinions, attitudes and feelings expressed in the text. Analyzing sentiments and studying the product reviews helps a lot in the growth of the e-commerce as e-commerce mainly depends on the customer reviews. Sentiment analysis helps various retailors to analyze which products are most liked and reviewed by the customers and those details can be used to improve the business and to provide best quality service to the user. Analyzing all the customer opinions expressed on review sites is tedious. So, it is essential to have automatic sentiment analysis and summarization systems. The three important elements of opinions are: (i) opinion target, a target object that the opinion has been expressed upon, (ii) opinion holder, is the person who has expressed the opinion, and (iii) sentiment value about the entity. Liu (Qiu,2010) proposed an opinion quintuple model that includes opinion expressed time and entity feature along with above mentioned three elements.

In *quintuple* $(e_j, a_{jk}, so_{ijkl}, h_i, t_l)$ model,

e_j is the target entity

a_{jk} is the aspect of the entity *ej*

so_{ijkl} is the sentiment value of the opinion which is positive, negative, neutral or a more coarse-grained/fine-grained rating.

h_i is the opinion holder

t_l is the time when the opinion expressed.

Given an opinionated text, the main objective of sentiment analysis is to find all *quintuple*$(e_j, a_{jk}, so_{ijkl}, h_i, t_l)$ or solve the simpler forms of the problem that is sentiment classification by Document level, Sentence level or Aspect level. Figure 2 shows Levels of sentiment classification.

Document Level Sentiment Analysis

In the document level text classification, entire document will be analyzed to detect the emotions expressed (polarity)in the document and whole document is taken as one unit of information. It is assumed that whole document is having opinionated text on one target entity that is on film, book, hotel, and so on. Positive documents will have majority of positive words/sentences (ex. good), which expresses positive sentiments towards the entity. Negative documents will have negative words/sentences (ex. bad), which expresses negative sentiments towards the entity. The entire document will be scanned and polarity of the entire document will be determined and it will be classified as positive or negative.

Figure 2. Levels of sentiment classification

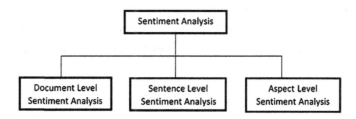

For example, we consider a customer review on iPhone, "I brought an iPhone a few days back. Although the size is large, it is a nice phone. The voice quality is very clear. The touch screen is cool. I simply love it!". In document level sentiment analysis, this entire review is taken as one document and classified it into positive.

In the document level sentiment analysis, analysis is done by considering entire document contains opinion about on one target entity. Hence, this level of analysis is not suitable, if the document contains opinions on different target entities.

Sentence Level Sentiment Analysis

Sentence level analysis is similar to document level but the opinion summarization is carried out at the sentence level because it assumes that every single sentence in the review document contain the details of one entity. Sentence level analysis emphases on determining the sentiment value of each sentence. There view document will be broken in to a set of sentences and each sentence will be analyzed to determine polarity towards target entity. The sentence polarity is determined by the polarity of word present in the sentence. The word is classified based on whether it is expressing a positive or negative opinion. Some of the opinion words are - amazing, great, excellent, worst, bad, and horrible.

For example, in the sentence "The touch screen is good" the sentence is classified as positive because of positive opinion word "good" present in the sentence.

Aspect Level Sentiment Analysis

Sometimes the users express their opinions on particular feature of the product. Such reviews can also be studied to understand the best and worst features of the product. This kind of analysis names as Aspect/Feature level sentiment analysis. Aspect level sentiment analysis assumes that the review text comprises opinion on different entities and their respective features. So, the sentence will be analyzed to determine the opinion of the user towards the particular feature of the product. For example, in the review sentence, "The iPhone's battery life is short but voice quality is good", the customer review on iPhone is particularly talking on voice quality and battery of iPhone. In aspect level sentiment analysis, battery life and voice quality are extracted as aspects. After the analysis, the former phrase is classified as positive and latter phrase is classified as negative sentence. Aspect level analysis gives fine grained information of various aspects of a service or product. Some features of product or services are explicitly mentioned in the text like "The battery of this phone is good". In this text, the product aspect – battery, is explicitly mentioned and sentiment on battery is expressed. However, this is not always the case. In the sentence: "The phone lasts all day", we can infer that review is about the product feature-battery even though the word "battery" is not mentioned in the text. These types of aspects are named as implicit aspects and detecting implicit aspects are not easy and open challenges for researchers.

As a summary in the review document: "I feel the latest laptop from Mac is really good overall. It has amazing resolution. The computer is really very sleek and can slide into bags easily. However, I feel the weight is a letdown. The price is a bit expensive given the configurations. I expect an SSD storage. However, the processor seems really good."

At document level text classification, entire review is taken as one entity and it is having many positive sentences compared with negative so classified as positive.

At a sentence level text classification, analysis is done sentence level where document is broke into six sentences. Each sentence is analyzed for subjectivity and classified into positive, negative or class.

At aspect level, sentiment classification is done towards the aspects price, storage, and weight so on.

SENTIMENT ANALYSIS TECHNIQUES

Sentiment analysis techniques can be classified into two major groups namely, the machine learning approach and the lexicon based approach. The machine learning technique makes use of different learning methods for sentiment analysis. The machine learning technique are of two types: supervised learning, which learns from labelled training dataset and predicts the future class and unsupervised learning, identifies hidden pattern from the input data. Different Supervised learning approaches for sentiment classification are shown in Figure 5.Follwing sections briefs sentiment analysis techniques.

Lexicon Based Approach

A Lexicon is means a dictionary which consists of list of words which has a pre-defined polarity. The effectiveness of the Lexical approach strongly depends on Lexical resource that is lexicon dictionary or sentiment corpus. In Lexicon based approach, the dictionaries can be created manually (Tong, 2001) or automatically by means of seed word formation (Turney,2002). Adjectives are taken as indicator for semantic orientation of text in much of lexicon based Research (Hatzivassiloglou, V, McKeown& K. R,1997), (Hu, M., & Liu, B.,2004), (Taboada, M., Brooke, J., Tofiloski, M., Voll, K., & Stede, M., 2011). At the first step, a dictionary formed from an adjective words and their respective sentiment values (polarity). Then, all adjectives are extracted from the given input text and semantic orientation value is obtained from dictionary. These semantic orientation values are aggregated to produce single score for the text. The open lexicon resources such as Sentiwordnet (Baccianella, 2010), (Esuli & Sebastiani, 2006), WordNet-Affect (Valitutti,2004), Q-wordnet (Garcia, 2010) are developed for supporting sentiment analysis. Figure 3 shows the Lexicon based approach. Lexicon based methods does not rely on labelled dataset. So, the sentiment analysis is done without the training dataset. Limitation of lexicon based approach is that, it lags in identifying context specific and domain oriented opinions since it uses sentiment lexicons. This approach requires more manual work on document.

Figure 3. Lexicon based approach

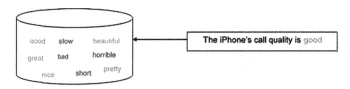

Figure 4. Machine learning approach

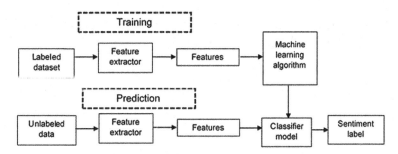

Figure 5. Machine learning techniques to build the classifier

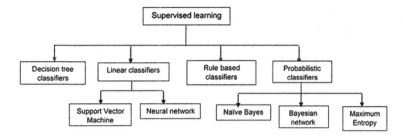

Machine Learning (ML) Approach

In addition to Lexicon based approaches, most research studies on sentiment analysis use supervised machine learning techniques. Dependency on labelled data is major disadvantage of machine learning models. Let the training records be $D = \{X_1, X_2, ..., X_n\}$. Here $X_1, X_2...X_n$ are different features of training record and class label associated with each training record. The classifier is learned from these training records. This classifier is used for the prediction of target value of new observations. There are different algorithms are used to build the classifier. Figure 4 shows the flow of training and prediction phases of supervised machine learning approach.

Figure 5 shows different machine learning approaches used to build the classifier for sentiment classification. The following sections briefs about most frequently used supervised classifiers for sentiment analysis.

Probabilistic Classifiers

Probabilistic classifier model predicts probability distribution of classes of sample input instead of predicting the most likely class that sample belong to. Let $D = \{f_1, f_2, ..., f_n\}$ refers to training document and f_i refers to i^{th} features/attributes of the training document D. The following section discusses three famous probabilistic classifiers.

Naive Bayesian classifier(NBC)

Using Bayes Theorem, Naïve Bayesian classifier predicts the target class of a random feature set. Equation 1 gives the probability of class c given the features f.

$$P(c \mid f) = \frac{P(f|c) * P(c)}{P(f)} \tag{1}$$

$P(c)$ is the prior probability of a class label from the training dataset.
$P(f)$ is the prior probability of a feature set.
$P(f \mid c)$ is the likelihood of feature belong to class.

NBC works on class independence assumption means that for a given class, the features are conditionally independent to each other. Given the features, the equation for posterior probability of class label, $P(c \mid f)$ could be rewritten as:

$$P(c \mid f) = \frac{P(f_1|c) * P(f_2|c) * ... * P(f_n|c) * P(c)}{P(f)} \tag{2}$$

The probability of new *feature f* with a *class c* is calculated using equation 2. As per the Bayes rule, the *class c* that achieves highest posterior probability is the outcome. When comparing with other approaches, NBC does sentiment classification with less computing power. So they are frequently used in sentiment classification but feature independent assumptions during the calculation of likelihood will provide inaccurate results. Variants of NBC are include:

1) Multinomial Naïve Bayes –This is used when multiple occurrence of feature matters a lot in sentiment classification. This technique better suits for the topic classification.
2) Binarized Multinomial Naïve Bayes –This technique is used when the frequency of features is not essential in classification. This technique is best suited for the sentiment analysis regardless of how frequently the word 'bad' or 'good' occurs; rather only the fact matters.
3) Bernoulli Naïve Bayes - This is used when the nonexistence of a particular word matters. Bernoulli Naïve Bayes technique is commonly used in Adult Content Detection or Spam and gives good results.

According to (Ye, Q., Zhang, Z., & Law, R., 2009), NBC gives better result for the problems that can be linearly separated but may not work so well for the non-linearly separable problems. The accuracy he achieved by the NBC is 79%.(Pak, A., & Paroubek, P.,2010), builds n-gram sentiment classifier using multinomial Naive Bayes classifier and constructs feature vector using Parts of Speech tagged dataset. N-gram is a combination of adjacent n-words present in the sample text. N-gram of size 1 is denoted as uni-gram, size 2 is denoted as bi-gram, and size 3 as tri-gram. They have tested the classifier on a set of real Twitter posts. They have experimented the effect of orderings of n-grams on the classifier's performance and concluded that bigrams provides good stability between an analysis (unigrams) and has a capacity to capture correct sentiment patterns (trigrams).(Dave, K., Lawrence, S., &Pennock, D. M.,2003), have performed sentiment analysis using NBC method on n-gram patterns and reported that bi-gram and tri-gramgive better result for product reviews.

Bayesian Network

Bayesian Network is the model of variables and their relationships and constructed with the assumption that variables are fully dependent on each other. In sentiment analysis the variables represent feature sets and edges represent dependency between feature sets. Bayesian Network classifier learns structure from training datasets with Conditional Probability Tables (CPT). CPT provides the Condition probability values between the variables of Bayesian Network. Bayesian Network is constructed according to two-step process called search-score model. The first step is carried out to search an element on a search space associated with Bayesian networks and second one to find score function that assesses degree of fitness between each element in a typical search space. Much of the research on Bayesian Network focus on development of scoring function for Bayesian Network classifier (Campos, L. M. D., 2006).In order to extract sentiments from movie reviews, (Airoldi, F., Bai, X , & Padman, R., 2004) and (Bai, X., 2011) proposed Bayesian Network classifier in association with Two-stage Markov Blanket Classifier. It studies Conditional dependencies among an elements in a network and discovers the network part that falls within the range of Markov Blanket. For high cross validated accuracy, (Glover, F., & Laguna, M., 1998) used Tabu Search algorithm to prune the resulting Markov Blanket network. To solve in Bayesian network classifiers (Friedman, N., Geiger, D., & Goldszmidt, M., 1997), Markov Blanket is proved as effective method. But in Markov Blanket Classifier, sentiment dependencies are learned from the existence of words in their original sentiment class only.

Maximum Entropy Classifier

The Maximum Entropy Classifier belongs to a class of exponential model. Unlike the Naive Bayesian, it does not assumes features conditionally independent to each other. Probability distribution function $P(features|class)$ is eliminated, instead feature function $f(features|class)$ is taken as constraint for classification.λ_i is the weight parameter of the feature function.

Figure 6. SVM in a classification

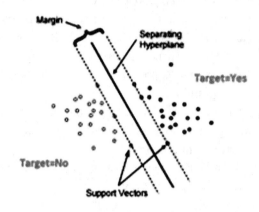

$$P(class \mid features\lambda) = \frac{\exp\left(\sum_i \lambda_i f_i(features \mid class)\right)}{\sum_c \exp\left(\sum_i \lambda_i f_i(features \mid class)\right)} \tag{3}$$

To classify tweets, (Parikh, R., &Movassate, M., 2009), used a Maximum Entropy model, Naive Bayes unigram models for unigram and bigram feature sets. Bernoulli and multinomial naïve Bayes are used for the study.To select correct feature sets and to maximize the log-likelihood of tweet test data, theyhave used preprocessing that smoothens maximum entropy classifier. According to studies, author concluded that multinomial Naive Bayes classifier gave better accuracy compared to Maximum Entropy classifier. (Wang, Y. Y., &Acero, A., 2007), propose that the Maximum Entropy model can obtain global optimization due to the properties of the convex objective function.

Linear Classifier

With the normalized text word frequency $X = \{x_1, x_2,...,x_n\}$, vector of coefficients $A = \{a_1, a_2,..., a_n\}$, and scalar variable b, the linear predictor that is a separator for different classes is defined as $p = AX + b$. This. Among the various linear classifiers, Support Vector Machines is a classifier that gives a better separation between the classes.

Support Vector Machine(SVM) Classifier

The SVM classifiers acts as a best linear separator for the various classes of a given data space. The data points used for classification are termed as support vector. Hyper plane separates different classes of target variable and margin is the width between the hyper plane and support vector. The hyper plane which has maximum margin is selected for classification. Figure 6 shows the set of data points labeled with two classes Yes or No. Where target equals to Yes taken as positive class and target equal to No is taken as negative class.

In SVM, hyper plane are found by minute subset of the trained datasets named as support vectors. Due to the correlation nature of the text features, SVM is well suited for text classification. (Pang, B., & Lee, L., 2008), used ML techniques like NBC and SVM. The author has analyzed the movie reviews. For the experiment the author collected the data from the IMDb.com. The author used the unigram feature selection method along with the classifiers. The author successfully got the accuracy of 82.9%. (Dang, Y., Zhang, Y., & Chen, H., 2009),proposed the SVM classifier for sentiment analysis. Along with SVM other famous feature selection methods were also used. The author considered the 305 positive reviews and 307 negative reviews of the camera. Author (Blitzer, J., Dredze, M., & Pereira, F., 2007), performed the experiment using the kitchen appliance reviews. The author used the SVM. The SVM was trained using the domain dependent, domain free, and sentiment features. The author obtained the accuracy of around 84.15%. (Chen, C. C., & Tseng, Y. D., 2011), have used multiclass classifications. People's sentiment towards the digital cameras and MP3 player reviews were studied by them. They have used the Information Quality framework. According to author the SVM works best for analyzing the reviews. It outperforms all other methods. SVMs was also used by (Li, Y. M., &Li, T. Y., 2013) and they focused on more than binary classification problem. Author says that opinions subjectivity also plays an important role in analyzing the reviews. Author used Twitter data for the analysis. The accuracy achieved by the SVM is 88.353%.

Back Propagation Neural Network

Neural Networks (NN) are used in text classification to perform the task such as, sentence modeling, word representation estimation, text generation, vector representation, feature presentation and sentence classification. The neurons are the basic building block of NN which imitates the structure and function of human brain. The neural network is defined by the function:

$$p_i = W^* X_i \tag{3}$$

Where W represents weights of neurons and X_i represents the word frequency. In the multilayer neural network, the output of the earlier layer neurons is fed as input to the next layer neurons. The errors in this model are back propagated in the training process and hence the computation cost becomes heavy. Figure 7shows the structure of neural network.

Neural network has three layers:

1. Input layer: This layer consists of units called as neurons which passes input data X to first hidden layer. This data is then multiplied with hidden layer's weights.
2. Hidden layer: Neurons of this layer will get data from the preceding input layer. This layer is hidden between input and output layer and perform computation on weighted input and produces net output through activation function and passes to the next hidden layer. The more number of hidden layers will increase the complexity.
3. Output layer: Neurons of this layer will get the data from the preceding hidden layer and produces the required output and this is the last layer of neural network.

Figure 7. Structure of neural network

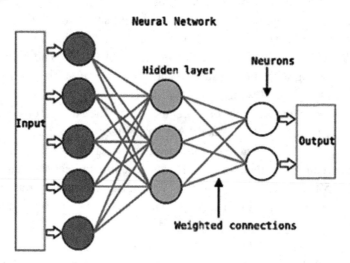

Much of the research [1990] on sentiment analysis using Backpropagation Neural Network used with one or two layers and reported that, as the hidden layer increases, the NN structure becomes more complicated and computationally expensive. Recently from the past 10 years due to the accessibility of computing power and huge set of training data, training "deep" (neural networks with more layers) Neural Networks popularly used for sentiment analysis. Deep learning has networks such as Convolutional Neural Network (CNN), Recurrent Neural Network (RNN), Recursive Neural Network and Deep Belief Networks (DBN).Using Amazon and TripAdviser datasets, (Bespalov, D., Bai, B., Qi, Y., & Shoko-ufandeh, A., 2011) Built neural network classifier with error rate 7.12 and 7.37.Using this classifier, he experimented effect higher order n-gram features in sentiment analysis. Deep learning researchers (Goller, C., & Kuchler, A., 1996) have proposed folding architecture to train recurrent neural networks and got better results compared to simple Recurrent Neural network. Furthermore, to produce more promising result on sentiment analysis task, (Socher, R., Perelygin, A., Wu, J., Chuang, J., Manning, C. D., Ng, A., & Potts, C., 2013) has proposed complex models such as Recursive Neural Tensor Networks and Matrix-Vector RNN.

Rule-Based Classifier

In this technique, set of rules are defined to train the data space. The typical rule is given in the form A→B, where A and B are sentiment patterns. The right hand side of the rule represents the target class label. The left hand side of the rule specifies the condition on the data set which may be given in the disjunctive normal form. The important criteria used in defining these rules are support and confidence. Support is a percentage of transactions containing both A and B. Confidence is the percentage of trans-action D containing A that also contain B. Based on these two parameters the rules are constructed in the training phase. These two parameters judge how closely the data sets are related to each other. These classifiers then tries to predict class label of sample data.(Yang, C. S., & Shih, H. P., 2012),proposed Rule based sentiment analysis and reported that Rule based technique achieves comparable performance with supervised approach in which preparation of training dataset is critical.(Qiu, G., He, X., Zhang,

Table 1. Popular research articles and sentiment analysis techniques on sentiment analysis

Sentiment analysis Techniques		Data scope	Author
Machine Learning Approach	Naive Bayesian Classifier	Twitter data	(Ye, Zhang, & Law, 2009)
		Product reviews	(Dave, Lawrence, &Pennock, 2003)
	Naive Bayes classifier and Maximum Entropy classifier.	Twitter data	(Parikh & Movassate, 2009)
	Maximum Entropy classifier	Air Travel Information System dataset and Product review	(Wang & Acero, 2007)
	Support vector machine	Twitter posts (blogs)	(Li & Li, 2013)
		Product reviews	(Dang, Zhang, & Chen, 2009), (Blitzer, Dredze, & Pereira, 2007), (Chen & Tseng, 2011)
	Support Vector Machine, Naive Bayesian classifier	Restaurant reviews	(Kang, Yoo, & Han, 2012)
		Movie reviews	(Pang & Lee, 2008)
	Bayesian Networks	Twitter data	(Airoldi, Bai, & Padman, 2004), (Bai, 2011)
	Rule based	Web forums	(Yang & Shih, 2012), (Qiu, He, Zhang, Shi, Bu, & Chen, 2010)
	Neural networks	Amazon and TripAdvisor datasets	(Goller & Kuchler, 1996)
		Movie reviews	Socher, Perelygin, Wu, Chuang, Manning, Ng, & Potts, 2013), (Kim, 2014)
Lexicon-based Approach	Annotated Dictionary and sentiment corpus	Product reviews	(Tong, 2001), (Turney, 2002), (Hatzivassiloglou & McKeown, 1997), (Hu & Liu, 2004), (Taboada, Brooke, Tofiloski, Voll, & Stede, 2011)

F., Shi, Y., Bu, J., & Chen, C., 2010),proposed pre-set rule sentiment classification method for targeted advertising to handle consumers' attitude identification and topic word extraction. Experiments show that, for advertising keyword extraction, proposed method beats the term-frequency inverse document frequency method.

Decision Tree Classifier

Decision tree is a hierarchical tree structure for representing training records in which each non-leaf node is split based on attribute condition value. In Decision Tree classifier, each interior node represented by an attribute or features, branches that are leaving the interior node represents test on feature of the dataset and children nodes are the outcome of the test. The leaves of Decision tree are class labels. The training data space is divided recursively till the leaf node ends with the minimum records. The variants of decision tree for text classification are mainly subjected to feature measures used for splitting node such as ID3 and C4. (Li, Y. H., & Jain, A. K., 1998), have used the C5 algorithm for sentiment analysis which is a SuccessorofC4.5 algorithm. The main advantages of decision tree classifier are, it is easier to understand and does not require statistical knowledge to interpret them. Decision tree classifier form complicated trees if poor feature measure methods incorporated in constructing tree and such trees cannot generalized easily.

Some of the popular research articles and sentiment analysis techniques on sentiment analysis are listed in Table1.

Twitter attracts more and more users and analysis of tweets gives useful information for data analytics to make important decisions. Twitter is considered as popular and very rich opinion source and provides user views on various topics. Twitter data can be collected using Twitter API from Twitter source using hashtags as keywords. Twitter analysis offers an entirely different challenge, which is use of nonstandard and short notations used by Twitter users. Preprocessing of dataset has significant impact on the accuracy of an analysis. Many researchers analyzed Twitter data using machine learning techniques because tweet text contain 140 characters and due to the availability of corpus for analysis. Out of different machine learning techniques, Artificial NN, NBC and SVM are popularly used. Artificial NN outperformed in terms of accuracy compared to other sentiment classification techniques but it takes more time for learning phase. So, by considering both execution time and accuracy, SVM and NBC are popularly used for sentiment analysis. In n-gram feature analysis, bigram feature set gives better results. Sarcasm tweets detection and multilingual tweets analysis are highlighted as challenges.

Even the retailer sites provide the user views on different services and products. These reviews are in the document form which can be analyzed using document level, sentence level and aspect level. Product review analysis has its challenges like rating inconsistency, sparse data, skewed data distribution, ambivalence and comparative sentences make sentiment analysis difficult.

PRELIMINARY STEPS OF SENTIMENT ANALYSIS

Information provided by the user may not be in structured format. Sentiment analysis faces various challenges due to this. Data can be of any format, namely, audio, video, or text. To ease the processing of large amount of data many techniques are developed which automates the process of sentiment analysis. Some part of the input dataset may have a structure where as some part may not have any structure. The unstructured data cannot be used as it is as it contains a large amount of unwanted (or unnecessary) information which will slow down the processing. Data acquisition and data pre-processing are the two important steps which helps to reduce the noise in the data.

Data Acquisition

The process of extracting the data from various sources is called Data collection. With an increase in the use of the Internet and other online activities, enormous information is available on the web. The data will be collected from various sources which will then be subjected to various mining techniques. Various microblogs provides the API's to collect public data from their sites. Various APIs are available for collecting and searching the tweets. To search and extract tweets, Twitter provides the search/tweets API. For the search API, keywords are passed as the queries. More than one query can be clubbed together and used together as a comma separated list. Information like user profile information and the user tweets can be extracted from the Twitter source by using Twitter REST API.(Kumar, S., Morstatter, F., & Liu, H.,2014),work discusses about collecting and analyzing the Twitter data and past tweets can be searched using this API. Twitter4J is popularly used for tweet extraction. (Khan, F. H., Bashir, S., & Qamar, U., 2014), worked on Twitter datasets and used the Twitter4J library for data acquisition process.

Pre-Processing Steps

During pre-processing phase, the data will be subjected to cleaning, noise removal and the data will be prepared for the classification process. The data accessed from online is unformatted and contains noise and unwanted information such as tags, advertisements which must be removed for better result. In some cases the words used in a given sentence may not convey any meaning. Many pre-processing techniques are available for removing the stop words and the nouns, adjectives etc. which are present in the sentence. Tokenization is the method which divides the task into words and sentences by removing the punctuation marks. Some example of stop word are the, at, which etc. These parts of speech words present in the text can be removed by using the POS tagging. Some examples of parts of speech are nouns, pronouns, adjectives, adverbs etc. In a sentence large amount of sentiment is described by the adjectives and adverbs.

COMPARATIVE ANALYSIS OF SEVERALTECHNIQUES USED FORSENTIMENT ANALYSIS

(Hailong, Z., Wenyan, G., & Bo, J., 2014), has done survey and comparative study on Lexicon based approaches, Machine learning, cross lingual and cross domain sentiment classification. Author has concluded in his research article, that Machine learning approaches like SVM and NBC gives higher precision results compared to Lexicon based approaches. Even the lexicon based approaches are equally competitive but they require more human efforts and less sensitive to training dataset. Accuracy, Precision, Recall and F-measure are the four performance measurement metrics used of sentiment classification. Accuracy is the number of correct prediction out of the total observation. Precision says out of those predicted positive, how many of them are actual positive. Recall gives the true positive rate that is, what portion of actual positive was identified correctly. F-measure will give the harmonic mean of precision and recall. The calculation are obtained confusion matrix which has True Positive (TP), True Negative (TN), False Positive (FP) and False Negative (FN) instances. Table 2displays the confusion matrix and Equation (4), (5), (6) and (7) shows the formula to calculate performance matrices.

$$Accuracy = \frac{TP + TN}{TP + TN + FP + FN} \tag{4}$$

$$Precision = \frac{TP}{TP + FP} \tag{5}$$

$$Recall = \frac{TP}{TP + FN} \tag{6}$$

Table 2. Confusion matrix

	Predicted Positive	Predicted Negative
Actual Positive	TP	FN
Actual Negative	FP	TN

Table 3. Comparison of different sentiment classification techniques

	Data set	Method	Accuracy	Author
Machine Learning Approach	Movie reviews	SVM	86.40%	(Pang & Lee, 2008)
	Twitter	Co-Training SVM	82.52%	(Qiu, He, Zhang, Shi, Bu, & Chen, 2010)
	Standard sentiment Treebank	Deep learning	80.70%	(Socher, Perelygin, Wu, Chuang, Manning, Ng, & Potts,)
Lexicon Approach	Product Reviews	Corpus	74.00%	(Turney, 2002)
	Amazon	Dictionary	---	(Taboada, Brooke, Tofiloski, Voll, & Stede, 2011)
Cross-lingual	Amazon	Ensemble	81.00%	(Wan, 2012)
	Amazon, IT168	Co-Train	81.30%	(Wan, 2009)
	IMDb movie review	EWGA (entropy weighted genetic algorithm)	>90%	(Abbasi, Chen, & Salem, 2008)
	MPQA, NTCIR, ISI	CLMM (Cross lingual Mixture Model)	83.02%	(Meng, Wei, Liu, Zhou, Xu, & Wang, 2012)
Cross-domain	Book, DVD, Electronics, Kitchen	Active learning	80% (average)	(Li & Chen, 2009)
		Thesaurus		(Bollegala, Weir, & Carroll, 2012)
		SFA (spectral feature alignment)		(Pan, Ni, Sun, Yang, & Chen, 2010)

$$F1 = \frac{2 * Precision * Recall}{Precision + Recall} \quad\ldots\ldots\ldots\ldots\ldots\ldots\ldots\ldots\ldots \quad (7)$$

According to these matrices, many researchers have provided comparative study on sentiment analysis using machine and lexicon approaches. Lexicon sentiment classification techniques rely on tagged Lexicons and sentiment dictionary. But the sentiment resources availability for different languages are uneven. For an instance, English sentiment corpus is freely available in Web but lack of Chinese sentiment corpus availability restricts the progress on sentiment analysis of Chinese text. Domain specific sentiment analysis adds more challenges in sentiment analysis task. Contextual information or topic specific information should be considered while analyzing the sentiments. For cross domain sentiment

Table 4. Accuracy comparison of machine learning methods with senti-wordnet

	TP	FP	FN	TN	Accuracy
Senti-WordNet	148	91	52	109	64.25%
NB	156	81	44	119	68.75%
SVM	135	51	65	149	71.00%

analysis, dataset will come from different domains and violates the basic assumption of traditional sentiment analysis. This will directly affect the accuracy of sentiment analysis. So, Author has considered research articles on cross-lingual and cross domain sentiment analysis. Table 3 shows the Performance comparison of sentiment classification technique including cross-lingual and cross-domain.

Further author has performed simple lexicon based sentiment analysis using Senti-WordNet lexical resource and evaluated with SVM and NBC. The dataset is taken for sentiment analysis is SFU review Corpus which is shown in Table4.This shows that one of the popular machine learning approach- SVM gives higher degree of accuracy compared to NBC and Senti-WordNet approach.

APPLICATION OF SENTIMENT ANALYSIS

Stock Market Prediction

Stock market prediction is the act of defining the future value of a company's stock. The successful stock market forecasting helps to gain more profit in the business. The sentiment of the people can be studied to make the stock market prediction. (Liu, B., Hu, M., & Cheng, J., 2005), have proposed a technique called SmeDA-SA, which can be used to analyze and understand the customer opinion. (Hagenau, M., Liebmann, M., & Neumann, D., 2013), has experimented on text data to identify whether the customer opinion affects the stock market.

Prediction Market Box Office Prediction

With the help of the Internet and the Web, people can easily know what is trending in the market. When people express their opinion in the social media it helps other users to know the best quality as well as worst quality of the product. Many people get influenced by the opinion expressed by other people. (Rui, H., Liu, Y., & Whinston, A., 2013), explained how chatter matters in marketing and the influence of tweets on movie sales. The chatting done in the Twitter does matters as it helps the customer to know whether to watch the movie or not. The chatting also provides the kind of advertisement for the movies. (Du, J., Xu, H., & Huang, X., 2014), used a micro blog to predict the box office collection.

Prediction Recommendation System

Recommendation system provides recommendation for the user (Massa, P., &Bhattacharjee, B., 2004). These days, recommendation system shave gained a lot of popularity. With a large amount of information available online the customers have to face the problem of analyzing and selecting only required information. When a customer wants to buy a product with reasonable cost, he has to spend more time in searching various brand products on information search engine to come to a decision. Many approaches were introduced to overcome this problem recommender system is one such case. Usually recommendation system can be classified into two types such as content based system and collaborative system (Massa, P., &Bhattacharjee, B., 2004), (Albadvi, A., & Shahbazi, M., 2009), (Sharma, R., Nigam, S., & Jain, R., 2014), (Li, Y. M., & Chen, C. W., 2009). In content-based system the user is given recommendation depending upon what he has liked in the past (Yang, W. S., & Dia, J. B., 2008). In collaborative system user with same tastes are identified and recommendation is provided based on their taste. The content based recommendation approach has one drawback that is since the items are displayed based on the past likes of the user, the experiments with SVM e-recommendation will be just based on the past likes which restricts the user from seeing other items. The disadvantage of the collaborative system approach is that, when a user whose tastes are not similar to any other user, it leads to poorer recommendations and also when a new item appears without enough information related to rating or user likes, it cannot be recommended to another user. (Balabanović, M., & Shoham, Y., 1997) proposed a hybrid approach which combines both the approaches for more accurate result. They have discussed the various features of the Fab system.

Online Advertising

The online advertising is also similar to recommender system, it can be seen as application of recommender systems. Recommendation is a very powerful way using which the companies can attract the users. Recommender system assists in understanding the taste of the user and provide the offers only based on the user taste. When a customer decides to buy the item his decision is likely to get affected by the experience shared by other users (Pang, B., & Lee, L., 2008). The purchasing decisions usually gets affected by the other people opinion. Before buying any item customers will go through the reviews or the ratings to do a purchase decision. E-commerce companies allows the user to review the products they purchase. Customer can even chat with other people. Customers can also rate the products. The reviewing and rating helps the other user to decide whether or not to purchase the product.

CHALLENGES AND OPEN ISSUES

Fast growth of Internet and related applications made sentiment analysis as exciting and popular research area among Natural Language Processing. Many researchers have implemented various techniques for automated sentiment analysis but still there is a need of automated sentiment analysis that correctly interpreters the context of text. Some of the challenges in sentiment analysis are: Opinions are written by the user who belong to different culture or zone. So, there is a possibility that opinions have abbreviations, poor spelling and grammar, written in a mixed language. Opinion sentences will have emoticons and short informal text words.

The challenges in the analysis of product reviews are (i) Analysis model constructed on one product or product aspect may not suitable for another product. (ii) Opinion words have positive orientation in one situation might show negative orientation in another situation (Qiu, G., He, X., Zhang, F., Shi, Y., Bu, J., & Chen, C., 2010).For example, the sentence "laptop's battery life was long" is a positive sentence but if the sentence "laptop's start up time was long" then it is a negative sentence. (iii) Sentences expresses sentiments on more than one feature e.g., "The battery life of this phone is short but the voice quality is good" (iv) Comparative opinions will relate similarities and differences between two or more entities. In such cases, finding proper sentiment polarity of one entity is really difficult.

The challenges for analysis of tweets are (i) The volume of data generated by Twitter source very large and needs high processing device for storage and analysis (ii) Retrieving datasets: usage of hashtags or keywords may not retrieve all topic oriented data (iii) Twitter users will post tweets on a particular topic. So, we retrieve text on variety of disciplines(iv)Relevancy of collected data (v) A word, which is subjective in one topic, will be objective in another topic (vi) Occurrence of sarcasm sentences (vii) Analysis of non-English sentences (viii) Fake or spam opinions.

According to many articles sentiment classification are done on direct sentiments. Authors have ignored the opinion sentence expressed in sarcastic way due to its complexity. Sarcastic sentiment detection is very challenging. Sarcasms are very common in movie reviews and political discussions. Some examples of sarcastic opinion are -"I love being ignored". The study of sarcastic sentence still need to be enhanced. They appear with and without sentiment word and express conflicting semantic meaning of what is exactly written.

CONCLUSION

With the increase in the use of Internet the information available on the internet will be more valuable and useful for various business organizations. Sentiment analysis used in many practical applications, more importantly, market prognostication and political polarization. In this chapter, we discussed on social big data mining and about the sentiment analysis and how it evolved. For analyzing the user sentiments several machine learning and lexical approaches are used. But, an abundance of work still remains to be done in the area of sentiment classification and it is a fertile area. This is a survey chapter where we have referred to several research articles to analyze and understand the state-of-art in the area of the sentiment analysis over the past years. This chapter discusses how the sentiment can be analyzed and performance can be made better if it is done at the different levels such as word level, document level, and sentence level. Along with this, various techniques used for sentiment analysis are also studied. Presently there are several techniques available in the field of the sentiment analysis, such as SVM, Lexicon based methods Machine learning, Subjectivity classification, Polarity classification etc. All these techniques try to ease the work of the human by analyzing the sizably voluminous data set. User opinions for sentiment analysis are usually obtained from the micro blogs such as Twitter or e-commerce sites. The information accumulated from the web will be too large and too noisy. Some automatic system must be built to remove the unwanted data from the dataset. Noisy data is one important problem of the Sentiment analysis. Care must take to make sure that data used will be noise free as much as possible to get the best result. While analyzing the popularity of the item the product feature must also be considered for better analysis. Sentiment analysis model for analyzing customer opinion in language other than English (cross-lingual) must also need to be developed.

REFERENCES

Abbasi, A., Chen, H., & Salem, A. (2008). Sentiment analysis in multiple languages: Feature selection for opinion classification in web forums. *ACM Transactions on Information Systems*, *26*(3), 12. doi:10.1145/1361684.1361685

Airoldi, E., Bai, X., & Padman, R. (2004, August). Markov blankets and meta-heuristics search: Sentiment extraction from unstructured texts. In *International Workshop on Knowledge Discovery on the Web* (pp. 167-187). Springer.

Albadvi, A., & Shahbazi, M. (2009). A hybrid recommendation technique based on product category attributes. *Expert Systems with Applications*, *36*(9), 11480–11488. doi:10.1016/j.eswa.2009.03.046

Bai, X. (2011). Predicting consumer sentiments from online text. *Decision Support Systems*, *50*(4), 732–742. doi:10.1016/j.dss.2010.08.024

Balabanović, M., & Shoham, Y. (1997). Fab: Content-based, collaborative recommendation. *Communications of the ACM*, *40*(3), 66–72. doi:10.1145/245108.245124

Bespalov, D., Bai, B., Qi, Y., & Shokoufandeh, A. (2011, October). Sentiment classification based on supervised latent n-gram analysis. In *Proceedings of the 20th ACM international conference on Information and knowledge management* (pp. 375-382). ACM. 10.1145/2063576.2063635

Blitzer, J., Dredze, M., & Pereira, F. (2007, June). Biographies, bollywood, boom-boxes and blenders: Domain adaptation for sentiment classification. In *Proceedings of the 45th annual meeting of the association of computational linguistics* (pp. 440-447). Academic Press.

Bollegala, D., Weir, D., & Carroll, J. (2012). Cross-domain sentiment classification using a sentiment sensitive thesaurus. *IEEE Transactions on Knowledge and Data Engineering*, *25*(8), 1719–1731. doi:10.1109/TKDE.2012.103

Campos, L. M. D. (2006). A scoring function for learning Bayesian networks based on mutual information and conditional independence tests. *Journal of Machine Learning Research*, *7*(Oct), 2149–2187.

Chaffey, D. (2016). *Global social media research summary 2016*. Smart Insights: Social Media Marketing.

Chen, C. C., & Tseng, Y. D. (2011). Quality evaluation of product reviews using an information quality framework. *Decision Support Systems*, *50*(4), 755–768. doi:10.1016/j.dss.2010.08.023

Dang, Y., Zhang, Y., & Chen, H. (2009). A lexicon-enhanced method for sentiment classification: An experiment on online product reviews. *IEEE Intelligent Systems*, *25*(4), 46–53. doi:10.1109/MIS.2009.105

Dave, K., Lawrence, S., & Pennock, D. M. (2003, May). Mining the peanut gallery: Opinion extraction and semantic classification of product reviews. In *Proceedings of the 12th international conference on World Wide Web* (pp. 519-528). ACM. 10.1145/775152.775226

Du, J., Xu, H., & Huang, X. (2014). Box office prediction based on microblog. *Expert Systems with Applications*, *41*(4), 1680–1689. doi:10.1016/j.eswa.2013.08.065

Friedman, N., Geiger, D., & Goldszmidt, M. (1997). Bayesian network classifiers. *Machine Learning*, *29*(2-3), 131–163. doi:10.1023/A:1007465528199

Glover, F., & Laguna, M. (1998). Tabu search. In *Handbook of combinatorial optimization* (pp. 2093–2229). Boston, MA: Springer. doi:10.1007/978-1-4613-0303-9_33

Goller, C., & Kuchler, A. (1996, June). Learning task-dependent distributed representations by backpropagation through structure. In *Proceedings of International Conference on Neural Networks (ICNN'96)* (Vol. 1, pp. 347-352). IEEE. 10.1109/ICNN.1996.548916

Hagenau, M., Liebmann, M., & Neumann, D. (2013). Automated news reading: Stock price prediction based on financial news using context-capturing features. *Decision Support Systems*, *55*(3), 685 697. doi:10.1016/j.dss.2013.02.006

Hailong, Z., Wenyan, G., & Bo, J. (2014, September). Machine learning and lexicon based methods for sentiment classification: A survey. In *2014 11th Web Information System and Application Conference* (pp. 262-265). IEEE. 10.1109/WISA.2014.55

Hatzivassiloglou, V., & McKeown, K. R. (1997, July). Predicting the semantic orientation of adjectives. In *Proceedings of the 35th annual meeting of the association for computational linguistics and eighth conference of the european chapter of the association for computational linguistics* (pp. 174-181). Association for Computational Linguistics.

Hu, M., & Liu, B. (2004, August). Mining and summarizing customer reviews. In *Proceedings of the tenth ACM SIGKDD international conference on Knowledge discovery and data mining* (pp. 168-177). ACM.

Kang, H., Yoo, S. J., & Han, D. (2012). Senti-lexicon and improved Naïve Bayes algorithms for sentiment analysis of restaurant reviews. *Expert Systems with Applications*, *39*(5), 6000–6010. doi:10.1016/j.eswa.2011.11.107

Khan, F. H., Bashir, S., & Qamar, U. (2014). TOM: Twitter opinion mining framework using hybrid classification scheme. *Decision Support Systems*, *57*, 245–257. doi:10.1016/j.dss.2013.09.004

Kim, Y. (2014). *Convolutional neural networks for sentence classification*. arXiv preprint arXiv:1408.5882

Kumar, S., Morstatter, F., & Liu, H. (2014). *Twitter data analytics*. New York: Springer. doi:10.1007/978-1-4614-9372-3

Laney, D. (2001). 3D data management: Controlling data volume, velocity and variety. *META Group Research Note*, *6*(70), 1.

Li, Y. H., & Jain, A. K. (1998). Classification of text documents. *The Computer Journal*, *41*(8), 537–546. doi:10.1093/comjnl/41.8.537

Li, Y. M., & Chen, C. W. (2009). A synthetical approach for blog recommendation: Combining trust, social relation, and semantic analysis. *Expert Systems with Applications*, *36*(3), 6536–6547. doi:10.1016/j.eswa.2008.07.077

Li, Y. M., & Li, T. Y. (2013). Deriving market intelligence from microblogs. *Decision Support Systems*, *55*(1), 206–217. doi:10.1016/j.dss.2013.01.023

Liu, B., Hu, M., & Cheng, J. (2005, May). Opinion observer: analyzing and comparing opinions on the web. In *Proceedings of the 14th international conference on World Wide Web* (pp. 342-351). ACM. 10.1145/1060745.1060797

Massa, P., & Bhattacharjee, B. (2004, March). Using trust in recommender systems: an experimental analysis. In *International conference on trust management* (pp. 221-235). Springer. 10.1007/978-3-540-24747-0_17

Meng, X., Wei, F., Liu, X., Zhou, M., Xu, G., & Wang, H. (2012, July). Cross-lingual mixture model for sentiment classification. In *Proceedings of the 50th Annual Meeting of the Association for Computational Linguistics: Long Papers-Volume 1* (pp. 572-581). Association for Computational Linguistics.

Pak, A., & Paroubek, P. (2010, May). Twitter as a corpus for sentiment analysis and opinion mining. In LREc (Vol. 10, No. 2010, pp. 1320-1326). Academic Press.

Pan, S. J., Ni, X., Sun, J. T., Yang, Q., & Chen, Z. (2010, April). Cross-domain sentiment classification via spectral feature alignment. In *Proceedings of the 19th international conference on World wide web* (pp. 751-760). ACM. 10.1145/1772690.1772767

Pang, B., & Lee, L. (2008). Opinion mining and sentiment analysis. *Foundations and Trends® in Information Retrieval, 2*(1–2), 1-135.

Parikh, R., & Movassate, M. (2009). *Sentiment analysis of user-generated twitter updates using various classification techniques*. CS224N Final Report, 118.

Pouyanfar, S., Yang, Y., Chen, S. C., Shyu, M. L., & Iyengar, S. S. (2018). Multimedia big data analytics: A survey. *ACM Computing Surveys, 51*(1), 10. doi:10.1145/3150226

Qiu, G., He, X., Zhang, F., Shi, Y., Bu, J., & Chen, C. (2010). DASA: Dissatisfaction-oriented advertising based on sentiment analysis. *Expert Systems with Applications, 37*(9), 6182–6191. doi:10.1016/j.eswa.2010.02.109

Rui, H., Liu, Y., & Whinston, A. (2013). Whose and what chatter matters? The effect of tweets on movie sales. *Decision Support Systems, 55*(4), 863–870. doi:10.1016/j.dss.2012.12.022

Sharma, R., Nigam, S., & Jain, R. (2014). *Opinion mining of movie reviews at document level*. arXiv preprint arXiv:1408.3829

Socher, R., Perelygin, A., Wu, J., Chuang, J., Manning, C. D., Ng, A., & Potts, C. (2013, October). Recursive deep models for semantic compositionality over a sentiment treebank. In *Proceedings of the 2013 conference on empirical methods in natural language processing* (pp. 1631-1642). Academic Press.

Solanki, A., & Pandey, S. (2019). Music instrument recognition using deep convolutional neural networks. *International Journal of Information Technology*, 1-10.

Taboada, M., Brooke, J., Tofiloski, M., Voll, K., & Stede, M. (2011). Lexicon-based methods for sentiment analysis. *Computational Linguistics, 37*(2), 267–307. doi:10.1162/COLI_a_00049

Tan, W., Blake, M. B., Saleh, I., & Dustdar, S. (2013). Social-network-sourced big data analytics. *IEEE Internet Computing, 17*(5), 62–69. doi:10.1109/MIC.2013.100

Tong, R. M. (2001, September). An operational system for detecting and tracking opinions in on-line discussion. In *Working Notes of the ACM SIGIR 2001 Workshop on Operational Text Classification* (*Vol. 1*, No. 6). Academic Press.

Turney, P. D. (2002, July). Thumbs up or thumbs down?: semantic orientation applied to unsupervised classification of reviews. In *Proceedings of the 40th annual meeting on association for computational linguistics* (pp. 417-424). Association for Computational Linguistics.

Wan, X. (2009, August). Co-training for cross-lingual sentiment classification. In *Proceedings of the Joint Conference of the 47th Annual Meeting of the ACL and the 4th International Joint Conference on Natural Language Processing of the AFNLP* (pp. 235-243). Association for Computational Linguistics.

Wan, X. (2012, December). A comparative study of cross-lingual sentiment classification. In *Proceedings of the 2012 IEEE/WIC/ACM International Joint Conferences on Web Intelligence and Intelligent Agent Technology-Volume 01* (pp. 24-31). IEEE Computer Society. 10.1109/WI-IAT.2012.54

Wang, Y. Y., & Acero, A. (2007, December). Maximum entropy model parameterization with TF* IDF weighted vector space model. In *2007 IEEE Workshop on Automatic Speech Recognition & Understanding (ASRU)* (pp. 213-218). IEEE. 10.1109/ASRU.2007.4430111

Yang, C. S., & Shih, H. P. (2012). A Rule-Based Approach For Effective Sentiment Analysis. In PACIS (p. 181). Academic Press.

Yang, W. S., & Dia, J. B. (2008). Discovering cohesive subgroups from social networks for targeted advertising. *Expert Systems with Applications, 34*(3), 2029–2038. doi:10.1016/j.eswa.2007.02.028

Ye, Q., Zhang, Z., & Law, R. (2009). Sentiment classification of online reviews to travel destinations by supervised machine learning approaches. *Expert Systems with Applications, 36*(3), 6527–6535. doi:10.1016/j.eswa.2008.07.035

Chapter 26
Tool Condition Monitoring Using Artificial Neural Network Models

Srinivasa P. Pai

(iD) https://orcid.org/0000-0002-3858-6014
NMAM Institute of Technology, India

Nagabhushana T. N.
S. J. College of Engineering, India

ABSTRACT

Tool wear is a major factor that affects the productivity of any machining operation and needs to be controlled for achieving automation. It affects the surface finish, tolerances, dimensions of the workpiece, increases machine down time, and sometimes performance of machine tool and personnel are affected. This chapter deals with the application of artificial neural network (ANN) models for tool condition monitoring (TCM) in milling operations. The data required for training and testing the models studied and developed are from live experiments conducted in a machine shop on a widely used steel, medium carbon steel (En 8) using uncoated carbide inserts. Acoustic emission data and surface roughness data has been used in model development. The goal is for developing an optimal ANN model, in terms of compact architecture, least training time, and its ability to generalize well on unseen (test) data. Growing cell structures (GCS) network has been found to achieve these requirements.

INTRODUCTION

Manufacturing industries have seen lot of changes in the last few years. The focus is on reducing cost, improving productivity, by reducing downtime, losses and waste. Machining is an important process used by manufacturing industries. It can be classified as traditional and non-traditional. In traditional machining, turning, planning, shaping etc., uses a single point cutting tool and milling, drilling, grinding etc., are multi-point cutting tool operations. They can be used to machine metals or nonmetals, including

DOI: 10.4018/978-1-5225-9643-1.ch026

composites. Cutting tool is an important part of the machining process. It contributes significantly to the total machining costs. Further the goal in manufacturing is towards automation. In this effort, there is a need to continuously monitor the condition of the cutting tool, so that machine tool and cutting tool are not affected. Cutting tool condition monitoring can include detection of the tool condition in terms of tool wear and fracture or breakage (Chelladurai et al., 2008). Tool breakage is a major reason for unscheduled stopping of operations in a machining centre (Rehorn et al., 2005). Traditional methods of monitoring the condition of the cutting tool has been more dependent on the operator. Hence, he or she was not able to detect the condition of the tool, when it was subjected to sudden failure or more wear. As a result, cutting tools were either underutilized or overutilized. To avoid this problem there is a need to use various types of sensing techniques, which can assist the operator in taking proper decisions. Traditionally tool condition monitoring methods are grouped as 'direct' or 'indirect'. Direct methods involve assessing material removal from cutting tool in terms of mass or volume and tend to be offline in nature, as the tool has to be removed from the machining process for measurement. Hence it takes lot of timetool failure development is not clearly visible. Indirect methods can be implemented online, as it involves measurement of 'signals' generated during machining, which have a direct relation with tool condition and includes cutting force, temperature, vibration, acoustic emission etc. (Pai, 2004).

The focus these days is on automated TCM systems, which will recognize the status of the tool, without the interruption of the machining process, under minimum human supervision. Thus, the goal is to achieve 'unattended' machining systems, which can improve the utilization of the capital equipment and substantially reduce the machining costs. For this, there is a need for an "Intelligent sensor system", as described by Dornfeld (1986) as follows, "an integrated system consisting of sensing elements, signal conditioning devices, signal processing algorithms and signal interpretation and decision-making procedures". "Finally, the effort is towards developing an Automated / Intelligent monitoring system, which should have the capabilities of sensing, analyzing, knowledge learning and error correction".

According to Elbestawi et al. (2006), to replicate human intervention, a typical TCM system should have the following components:

(i)   Sensing technique – use of different sensing signals like cutting forces, vibrations, acoustic emission. There is a need to combine data from different sensors and locations, to maximize yield of useful information.
(ii) Feature extraction – there is a need to extract information from the signals to differentiate different process and tool conditions and also to remove noise from the signals.
(iii) Decision making – strategies, which use the extracted features and map it to a tool condition.
(iv) Knowledge learning – in order to make correct decisions, learning algorithms have to be used.

"The automated TCM systems, have to learn from past information and also learn from the new information generated from the machining process" (Elbestawi, & Dumitrescu, 2006) (Elbestawi & Ng, 2006).

Monitoring systems which are based in laboratories, are multisensory based are require the need for complex Artificial Intelligence (AI) based systems, which can integrate information, extract features and make reliable decisions about the status of the tool (Balazinski et al., 2002). Multi sensor fusion has some benefits for TCM and include – since the signals get distorted by noise during measurement, using multiple signals can maximize the amount of information available for decision making process and since more signals are considered, the certainty of the estimated parameter value improves (Pai, 2004). "Artificial Neural Networks (ANN) and neuro-fuzzy techniques have been extensively studied from the AI domain" (Balazinski et al., 2002). According to Elbestawi et al. (2006), there are two types of monitoring methods: (i) Model-based methods – "this involves finding a model that fits the process and monitors specific parameters in the model to detect changes". They can be considered as failure detection methods. (ii) Feature-based monitoring methods – relates the tool status to the signal features and includes techniques like ANN, expert systems, fuzzy logic etc. These methods have two phases – learning and classification (Elbestawi, & Dumitrescu, 2006) (Elbestawi & Ng, 2006). Proper selection of features is very important for any application and depending upon the application, the process can become complicated and there is a need for sophisticated feature selection techniques, which can improve the performance of the classifier or modeling technique. For e.g. Kumar et al. (2018) propose the use of exponential spider monkey optimization to select best possible features from a high dimensional feature set for automated plant disease detection system. Standard methods like SPAM have been used to generate the high dimensional features and the features selected by the optimization has been fed to support vector machine (SVM) for classifying the plants into diseased and non-diseased (Kumar et al., 2018a). In another study, the authors develop an automated system for grouping soil data sets using images, which can help in taking decisions regarding crops. A Bag-of-words and chaotic spider monkey optimization methods have been used. The optimization algorithm shows good convergence and improved global search over other methods. It has been further used to cluster the key points in Bag-of-words method for soil prediction. The proposed system gave 79% accuracy and the optimization algorithms perform better than other meta-heuristic methods (Kumar et al., 2018b)

Artificial Neural Networks (ANN) has been preferred for fusion of information from multiple sensors in TCM. Conventional methods are not effective enough to provide the desired level of accuracy. In spite of using sensor fusion, where various signals provide different sensitivity to tool condition, the changes in the signals with changes in tool condition or tool wear are non-linear and non-monotonic. Some features of the signals will be correlated with certain levels of tool wear, but not others. Further, the signals are distorted due to noise, which is common in a shop floor environment. Due to this inherent complexity and variability, the underlying distributions in the signal data are either unknown or not clearly understood. In such scenarios, ANN works well. They are not dependent on the distribution governing the data or any other assumptions to model or predict the responses and their relationship with the inputs. They have the capability to understand and develop relationships between the inputs and outputs in the data. "They estimate the functional relationship between the sensed signals and its features and the levels of tool wear / tool condition adaptively using training data via a learning algorithm. This extracted knowledge is stored in the massively parallel interconnected architecture and is generalized for interpretation of novel sensor signals in terms of tool wear / condition" (Pai, 2004). The recent developments in ANN in terms of using deep learning networks for sophisticated applications make this field very interesting and useful. These networks work well, when the data available for training / modeling is very large. For e.g. Solanki & Pandey (2019) used deep convolutional neural network model for musical instrument recognition. The eight layered network was able to achieve an accuracy of 92.8% (Solanki & Pandey, 2019).

This chapter is focused towards development of a best possible ANN based model for predicting tool wear in face milling using indirect and direct signal features, which is compact, has good generalization capability and takes least time for training.

Figure 1.

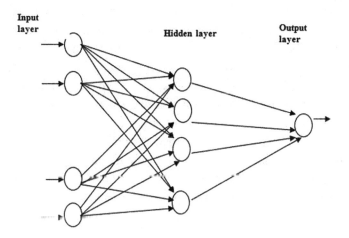

BACKGROUND

"ANN are computing systems that are made up of a number of simple, highly interconnected processing elements, called neurons, that provide the system the capability of self-learning" (Elbestawi, & Dumitrescu, 2006). "It generally has three layers, an input layer, which receives information from the external world, a hidden layer that processes the information and an output layer, which presents the information back to the external world". Fig. 1 shows a general ANN architecture.

"There are two classifications- (i) Supervised learning networks – In these types of networks, both input and the corresponding output data are given to the network during training. E.g. Multilayer perceptron (MLP) trained using Back Propagation (BP) algorithm" (Haykin, 1998).

(ii) Unsupervised learning networks – This involves presentation of only the input patterns. The network learns the similarity in the input data through any learning algorithm. E.g. Kohonen's Self-organizing map (Haykin, 1998).

CURRENT STATUS

Multilayer Perceptron (MLP), a frequently used feed forward model generally has three layers – input, hidden and output. It has been widely used in TCM applications. Different aspects of MLP in terms of error prediction level, convergence, difference in architecture etc. has been studied. Dimla et al. (1997) did a focused evaluation of use of ANN for TCM and MLP was widely used. Sick, B. (2002) presented another critical study of 138 publications dealing with online and indirect tool wear monitoring in turning using ANN. Some other researchers who have used MLP for TCM include: Panda, S.S., et al. (2008) monitored drill flank wear using MLP and RBFNN. They used thrust force, torque and vibration signals as inputs. The inclusion of vibration signals improved the prediction accuracy of the wear. MLP was better than RBFNN. But RBFNN is faster in learning and works well for on-line tool wear monitoring. Chelladurai et al. (2008) monitored tool wear using vibration and strain signals in coated carbide inserts, while turning EN-8 steel. The ANN model was built using the data. The model was developed using MATLAB tool box and trainrp algorithm was found to be robust, along with the use of logsig and tansig activation functions for modeling and predicting flank wear. Chen & Chen (2005) developed an ANN-based in-process tool wear prediction (ANN-ITWP) system to predict tool wear. The inputs included feed rate, depth of cut and average peak force in the y direction. The average peak force in y direction was a significant input, the minimum error made was ± 0.037 mm and there were some limitations to be overcome. Cho et al. (2010) studied the development of an effective multisensory based TCM, while machining 4340 steel using coated carbide end mill cutter. The signals used include force, vibration, acoustic emission and spindle power in time and frequency domain. The MLP and RBF neural network models along with support vector machine (SVM) were used along with feature level and decision level fusion. SVM outperformed MLP and RBFNN as it is based on structural risk minimization. Further use of correlation-based feature selection (CFS) improved the accuracy and robustness of classification.

MAIN FOCUS OF THE CHAPTER

This chapter deals with application of ANN models for tool wear estimation (flank wear) for TCM in milling applications on En-8 (medium carbon steel) using uncoated carbide inserts. Acoustic emission is measured online, whereas tool wear and surface roughness are measured offline during the experiments conducted for different cutting speed, feed and depth of cut. Different ANN models starting with MLP, followed by RBFNN, Resource Allocation Network and Growing Cell structures are investigated to propose an optimal model for tool wear estimation, which is robust, compact, takes least training time and generalizes well on unseen (test) data.

Experimental Details

Face milling operations were performed on a Bharat Fritz Werner (BFW) make vertical milling machine under three different cutting speeds (low – 71 m/min, medium – 112 m/min and high – 176 m/min), a wide range of feed / tooth (0.04 mm, which is the lowest and 0.4 mm, which is the highest) and a fixed depth of cut of 0.8 mm (equal to the tool tip radius of the insert). En-8 steel was used for experiments (medium carbon steel, 0.4711% C and 115 RHB hardness). The face milling cutter used was WIDAX M650 High shear milling cutter using uncoated carbide inserts (SEKN 12 03 AFN TTMS grade, ISO grade P15-P30carbide grades). Fig.2 shows the experimental setup used (Pai, 2004).

Signals Measured For TCM

(a) *Acoustic emission (AE)* – "AE are stress waves generated by dynamic processes in materials". "The emissions occur as a release of a series of short impulsive energy packets". "This energy traverses as a spherical wavefront, which can be picked up from the surface of a structure using a highly sensitive transducer (piezoelectric), which converts mechanical signal into electrical signal. This signal can be processed to understand and reveal useful information about the source" (Pai, 2004).

According to Dornfeld (1989), "the typical sources of AE in metal cutting include plastic deformation of the workpiece, plastic deformation in the chip, friction between tool flank and workpiece resulting in flank wear, friction between the tool rake face and chip resulting in crater wear, collisions between the chip and tool, chip breakage and tool fracture". AE signal sources from machining can be classified as continuous and transient, which have distinctly different characteristics. "Continuous signals are associated with shearing in the primary zone, whereas transient signals can be from tool wear, tool fracture or chip breakage" (Xiaoli, 2002).

The AE signals are non-stationary in nature and can be evaluated by extracting features from the signal, which are of interest and can be correlated with tool condition. These can be analyzed either in time or frequency domain. Some of the features of interest are: ring down count, event, rise time, event duration, peak amplitude, RMS voltage, energy etc. (Xiaoli, 2002) (Pai, 2004).

"Since milling is discontinuous in nature, there are some additional sources of AE like tool entry into and exit from the workpiece, chip thickness variation, chip congestion and multi-teeth cutting configuration" (Pai et al., 2002).

In the current work, the AE signals were captured online during machining using the Babcock & Wilcox AET 5500 system. It is a computer based, multi-channel data acquisition and analysis system. It consists of a sensor (piezoelectric transducer with a resonant frequency of 750 kHz), preamplifier (160 B model, with a gain of 60 dB, with a wide band filter (30 kHz- 2 MHz)), cables and AET mainframe, which performs all the signal processing, with the necessary hardware and software (Pai, 2004).

The AE signal parameters considered in this study for modeling using ANN include –ring down count, rise time, RMS voltage, energy, event duration and mean rise time(Pai, 2004).

(b) *Surface roughness*–In a typical machining operation, surface quality is an important parameter and surface roughness is widely used as its indicator. It is a result of process parameters namely tool geometry and cutting conditions (Ozel & Karpat, 2005). The condition of the cutting tool has a significant influence on the surface roughness and thus it can be used as an indicator of the tool condition. Among the numerous parameters that influence surface roughness, some are controllable and include cutting conditions, cutting tool geometry, machine tool setup etc., whereas uncontrollable include cutting tool, workpiece, machine vibrations, tool wear and tool and workpiece material variability (Pai, 2004). The surface topography of the machined workpiece provides relevant information about the machining process. Thus, by monitoring the same and using necessary information, the machining and tool condition can be monitored (Zeng et al., 2009).

In milling operation, the most notable surface defect, in the absence of BUE are the feed marks. The surface roughness has both large and small wavelengths. The large wavelengths are related to macrophenomenon like cutting conditions, tool vibration etc. The small wavelengths are related to microscopic effects like lamellar formation and shear fronts, depending on the material being cut. The final surface profile may be due to the cumulative effects of factors like BUE, side flow, tearing, tool wear and tool vibrations (Pai, 2004). The surface parameters can be classified as amplitude, spacing, hybrid and other parameters (Zeng et al., 2009). Among these amplitude parameters are most common and include R_a, R_q or R_t, R_z and R_{max}. And these parameters have been used in the current work for modeling purposes.

(i) R_a – arithmetic mean deviation from the mean line of the profile.

(ii) R_q or R_t - root mean square value.

(iii) R_z – ten point heights of irregularities.

(iv) R_{max} - maximum height of irregularity (Jain, 2009).

The surface roughness measurement was done using a M4Pi Perthometer. It is a compact, mains-independent roughness measuring instrument. It can be used for mobile purposes in shop floor applications. The measurements are taken using a stylus. After every two cutting cycles, the surface roughness is measured on the workpiece. The sampling length / tracing length has been selected looking at R_a value.

(c) *Flank wear* - It is commonly occurring wear phenomenon in cutting tools, due to the friction between the tool flank and workpiece. "It is gradual or progressive tool wear phenomenon and involves wear on the nose and primary cutting edge with the accompanying notch". It is a regular wear, as it is always present in a machining operation and have regular cutting time related growth characteristics. The wear on the insert is measured as VB_{max} (maximum flank wear) using a tool maker's microscope (LABO make). The measurement is made for two decimal accuracy, as the least count of the micrometers used for measurement is 0.01 mm. The wear is recorded after each machining pass and the wear value for replacement is taken as 0.4 mm based on the tool manufacturer specification (Pai, 2004).

ANN Model Development

In this work, different ANN models have been investigated and include multilayer perceptron, RBFNN, RAN and GCS, with a goal towards developing a network with compact architecture, faster training time and good generalization ability for TCM application in face milling operation (Pai, 2004).

Multilayer Perceptron

A three-layer MLP model has been developed with input layer, one hidden layer and output layer. The input layer consists of 12 neurons, corresponding to 12 features namely 6 AE features (ring down count, rise time, RMS voltage, energy, event duration and mean rise time), 4 surface roughness features (R_a, R_q or R_t, R_z and R_{max}) and 2 cutting conditions (cutting speed and feed per tooth). The output layer has one neuron corresponding to flank wear (VB_{max}). The training set consisted of 69 patterns and test set 15 patterns.

The data has been suitably normalized, since the input and output parameters are of differing magnitude. To avoid problems like giving preference to a few variables and facilitate proper functioning of different activation functions, normalization is necessary. "The normalization method adopted is very simple: normalized variable $x_{i,norm} = x_i / x_{i,max}$, where x_i is the value of the variable and $x_{i,max}$ is the maximum value of the variable and i represents each pattern".

Table 1. Sample input-output data

Pattern No.	RDC	Rise Time	Rms voltage	Energy	Event duration	Mean Rise Time	R_a	R_t or R_q	R_z	R_{max}	Cutting speed	Feed
1	0.2114	0.2260	0.9778	0.2379	0.2166	0.8731	0.4603	0.5292	0.6504	0.6772	0.3977	0.10
2	0.1430	0.2747	1.0000	0.2199	0.1499	0.9836	0.4226	0.4927	0.5735	0.6724	0.3977	0.10
3	1.0000	1.0000	0.0504	1.0000	1.0000	1.0000	0.7406	0.7299	0.6231	0.5969	0.3977	0.10
4	0.2172	0.0384	0.0805	0.2728	0.2035	0.0142	0.4433	0.4928	0.7760	0.6787	0.6364	0.09
5	0.4468	0.5745	0.1237	0.5590	0.5314	0.1055	0.2874	0.3207	0.4487	0.4249	0.6364	0.09
Test												
1	0.6546	0.7468	0.3547	0.7647	0.7114	0.7336	0.3399	0.2598	0.3761	0.3930	0.6364	0.25
2	0.6359	0.7605	0.3903	0.8122	0.7208	0.9990	0.3077	0.2126	0.4779	0.3805	0.6364	0.25
3	0.5769	0.6913	0.3157	0.7992	0.6855	0.6796	0.2805	0.1859	0.5735	0.4276	0.6364	0.25
4	0.2802	0.0413	0.0201	0.3304	0.2739	0.1967	0.4279	0.4499	0.6269	0.6215	0.3977	0.14
5	0.4020	0.2253	1.0000	0.5151	0.4180	0.7110	0.5673	0.5746	0.6667	0.8224	0.3977	0.14

Training and Testing Results

The focus in use of MLP in TCM applications and in this work, is to study the influence of the nature of the machining data generated from live experiments on the network performance. Accordingly, the data has been formulated in three different formats and the network has been trained as per the requirement.

(i) Type 1 data: both input and output data has been normalized as described before.
(ii) Type 2 data: Input data, that has been normalized has been encoded as binary bits and thus 12 features have been converted into 36 input dimensions, representing each feature using 3 bits.
(iii) Type 3 data: Input data remains in the normalized format and the output, ie., flank wear on the tool has been encoded using 3 bits, representing three classification states of the tool - '0 0 1' - flank wear ($< = 0.2$ mm), the tool condition is called 'initial', '0 1 0' – flank wear between 0.2 and 0.4 mm, the tool condition is called 'normal' and '0 1 1' – flank wear (> 0.4 mm), the tool condition is called 'abnormal'.

Table 1 shows the sample normalized input data and output data

The MLP network has been trained by changing the number of neurons in the hidden layer and it has been done on a trial and error basis. A single hidden layer has been used in the current work. The performance of the network is dependent on the activation function used in the hidden and output neuron, the rate of learning and momentum term. The backpropagation algorithm provides an approximation to the error trajectory in the weight space computed using the method of gradient descent. There is a need to select the learning rate parameter carefully, to prevent too slow or too fast learning. An efficient method to change the rate of learning, without causing any instability is to use the momentum term (Haykin, 1998). The selection of these two parameters have been done in this work on trial and error basis to minimize the mean squared error

$$E^\mu = 1 / 2 \sum_\mu (\zeta^\mu_i - O^\mu_k)^2.$$

Table 2.Results of Training

No. of Hidden neurons	10	20	24	30
No. of Epochs	160237	129830	122692	119234

i) For η=0.85 α=0.05 Error = 0.01

Figure 2.

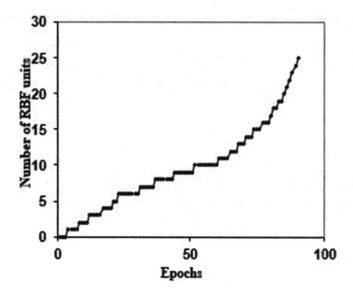

Where μ = 1,2,....n are the number of patterns, k = 1, number of output neuron, ζ^{μ}_{k}, target output, O^{μ}_{k} = 1/ (1 + $e^{-(\Sigma^{w}_{kj} {}^{v}_{j})}$), is the network output (Nagabhushana, 1996).

The training results are as given in Table 2 for different values of hidden neurons, learning rate parameter and momentum term for Type 1 data.

The mean squared error required for convergence is 0.01. The target for the maximum number of epochs is 175000 (considering old Pentium machine and using Borland C compiler for running the MLP codes). After several trial and error, the learning rate parameter (η) has been fixed as 0.85 and the momentum term (α) as 0.05. In the first part of the table, it is clear that as the number of hidden neurons increase, the number of training epochs decrease. Further in the second part of the table, as the ηvalue increases, the number of training epochs decrease, becomes minimum for 0.85 and then increases. Similarly, in the last part of the table, as the αvalue increases, the error increases, with no change in the number of training epochs. Thus, the final simulation parameters selected for Type 1 data is: Network architecture 12-24-1, no. of training epochs 122692, η0.85 and α 0.05. Fig. 2 shows the changes in error with epochs. The error drops quickly in the first 50000 epochs from more than 0.35 to less than 0.05 and then gradually decreases to 0.01 in the 122692 epochs.

Figure 3.

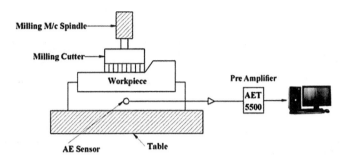

The network output for Type 1 data is considering two classes based on the tool flank wear value. Flank wear is less than or equal to 0.4 mm – if (network output is less than or equal to 0.4) - 'Normal'

Flank wear greater than 0.4 mm – if (network output is greater than 0.4) - 'Abnormal'.

Based on this interpretation of the network output, the classification accuracy on training data is 100% on training data and 87% on test data. Figure 3 shows the changes in actual and network output for test data. There is close correlation between the two, though there is some deviation for a few test data.

For type 2 data, where the input normalized data has been converted into binary strings. Accordingly, the input dimension of the MLP network is 36. The number of hidden neurons and the learning rate parameter and the momentum term has been varied to decide the optimal value in terms of performance. The optimal values are: No. of hidden neurons -10, $\eta = 0.85$ and $\alpha = 0.05$. The network reached the error of 0.14 in 175000 epochs. Thus, it did not converge to the target error of 0.01. The network gave an accuracy of 91% on training data, whereas on test data it was 60%. This is poor, which can be attributed to the format of the data fed as input to the MLP.

For type 3 data, only the output data was coded into binary bits and the interpretation is as described above. The optimal simulation parameters are $\eta = 0.85$ and $\alpha = 0.05$ and the number of hidden neurons is 12 and the number of epochs taken is 36389. This data format gave the best possible performance in terms of a having a compact network with only 12 hidden neurons, taking least training time and the model gave a result comparable to type 1 data namely 100% on training data and 87% on test data. The binary representation of output leads to better results, as it increased the number of output neurons to three. Also, the representation in the binary format is very useful as it is similar to the real-world interpretation of the tool condition. The tool can be in any one of the three states at any point in time and it's belonging to one state will be more compared to the other states (Pai et al., 2002). Table 3 presents the testing results for sample training and test data.

The MLP network architecture developed for three data formats have resulted in good performance, with type 3 format giving the best possible performance in terms of classification accuracy of 100% on training data and 87% on test data. A compact network was generated with only 12 hidden neurons.

Radial Basis Function Network

"A typical RBFNN consists of three layers, an input layer, a hidden layer and an output layer. The neurons in the hidden layer has a Gaussian activation function with a center and width". There is a need to initialize the centers, width and the number of hidden neurons. The width of the centers can be fixed

Table 3. Testing results for type 3 data

Pattern No.	Desired output	Network output	Classification error
		Training data	
1	0 0 1	0.000274 0.00246 0.990788	4.549072 X10⁻⁵
2	0 0 1	5.840795X10⁻⁵ 0.0001520.999986	1.336634 X10⁻⁸
3	0 1 0	0.000122 0.999951 0.001304	8.589129 X10⁻⁷
4	0 1 1	9.118312 X10⁻⁵ 0.981859 0.996363	0.000171
5	0 1 1	0.000129 0.999954 0.986036	9.750266 X10⁻⁵
6	0 1 1	0.000139 0.999963 0.99998	1.055429 X10⁻⁸
7	0 1 1	0.000134 0.999414 0.999978	1.809107 X10⁻⁷
8	0 1 1	0.000142 0.999978 0.99897	5.418951 X10⁻⁷
9	0 0 1	6.581895 X10⁻⁵ 0.018284 0.99881	0.000168
10	0 1 1	0.000109 0.994654 0.999201	1.461647 X10⁻⁵
Test data			
1	0 1 0	6.0325234 X10⁻⁵ 4.899139 X10⁻⁵ 0.999987	0.999938
2	0 1 0	7.348684 X10⁻⁵ 0.000143 0.966013	0.966448
3	0 1 0	9.057237 X10⁻⁵ 0.967371 0.352656	0.062715
4	0 1 0	0.000103 0.995516 0.017462	0.000163
5	0 1 0	9.264296 X10⁻⁵ 0.931347 0.004932	0.002369

Table 4. Change of error with number of RBF units

No. of RBF units	30	60	66	69
Error	0.387277	0.268209	0.2507	0.253681

using a heuristic like P-nearest neighbor or it can be fixed randomly, where the width values are kept constant for all the hidden neurons (Haykin, 1998) (Pai, 2004).

"The learning process taking place in an RBFNN can be understood as – the weights in the output layer vary on a different 'time scale' compared to the nonlinear activation functions in the hidden neurons. These evolve slowly according to some non-linear optimization strategy, whereas the weights in the output layer evolve rapidly through a linear optimization strategy" (Haykin, 1998).

"Three different learning strategies have been chosen for fixing the number of hidden neurons namely fixed centers selected at random, self-organized selection of centers using Batch Fuzzy C means algorithm and initialization of centers using Gradient descent approach" (Haykin, 1998).

Table 5. Change of error with different width values for 66 RBF units

Width value	0.5	0.9	1.5	3.0
Error	0.020268	0.144388	0.429346	0.775172

Table 6. Performance of RBFNN for different number of hidden neurons

No. of RBF units	30	60	66	69
Accuracy on training data	94%	96%	97%	97%
Accuracy on test data	80%	93%	93%	93%

Table 7. Performance of RBFNN with 66 hidden units for different widths

Width value	0.5	0.9	1.5	3.0
Accuracy on training data	100%	99%	97%	90%
Accuracy on test data	87%	93%	93%	80%

Model development: Results and Discussion

(i)   Fixed centers selected at random

The simulation parameters used for weights change in the output layer are fixed as $\eta = 0.85$ and $\alpha = 0.05$ and is maintained constant for all studies. The upper limit on the number of training epochs is 175000. The widths determined using P-nearest neighbor heuristic (with different width value for each RBF unit) has been used. Table 4 shows the corresponding results.

As the number of RBF units increase, the error decreased, reached a minimum for 66 and then started to increase. The drop-in error with number of epochs is very gradual and the target error set is 0.01.

Further to understand the effect of keeping the widths constant for all the RBF units, different values are studied and the outcomes are given in Table 5.

The error increased with width and the optimum value of width is 0.5 for the lowest error value of 0.020268.

The testing results for different number of RBF units is as shown in Table 6. Further results for different width values is given in Table 9 for 66 hidden neurons.

As the number of RBF units increases, the accuracy improves for both training and test data and for number of centers equal to number of input training data, there is no change in the classification accuracies. The best performance on training and test data is for 0.9 width. Hence the optimal RBFNN architecture is 12-66-1.

Table 8. Performance of RBFNN with centers selected using Batch fuzzy-c means

No. of RBF units	20	30	50	60
Accuracy on training data	96%	94%	97%	97%
Accuracy on test data	87%	93%	93%	93%

Table 9. Comparison of RBFNN models for TCM

RBFNN model	Network architecture	Accuracy on Training data	Accuracy on Test data	No. of Epochs
Fixed centers selected at random	12-66-1	97%	93%	175000
Batch fuzzy-c means algorithm	12-50-1	97%	93%	175000
Use of Gradient descent approach	12-60-1	91%	87%	175000

(ii)   Self-organized selection of centers – use of batch fuzzy-c means algorithm

Batch fuzzy-c means algorithm has been used to initialize the centers of the hidden units. "Bezdek developed this algorithm based on fuzzy extensions of the least square criterion" (Pai et al., 2003). The number of units have been initialized randomly. For training this algorithm, the mean squared error has been fixed as 0.001. The number of centers and its location after being established by this algorithm has been used in training and testing the RBFNN. To facilitate learning in the network, the number of training epochs is limited to 175000 and the simulation parameters have been fixed as before. In batch fuzzy-c means algorithm, it is found that as the number of RBF units increases, the error decreases and it is found to be minimum for 50 RBF units, beyond which is starts to increase. The maximum squared error reached is 0.313969 and the drop in the error is gradual (Pai, 2004).

Table 8 gives the details of the results of testing the developed RBFNN for the considered number of RBF units.

The improvement in test performance with changes in number of RBF units is till 50, beyond which there is no much improvement.

(iii)   Center selection using Gradient descent approach

In this strategy, all the free parameters of the network have been modified using gradient descent approach to build the neural network model. Karayiannis (1999) proposed a supervised learning procedure for training reformulated RBF networks. "These networks were generated using linear and exponential generator functions". It was found that use of gradient descent resulted in RBFNN models, which performed better than conventional RBFNN.

In the implementation of this model, the widths of all the hidden units were fixed at 0.9 initially. The RBF units were changed after every 5000 epochs and the widths were calculated using P-nearest neighbor heuristic, which resulted in different width values for different units. The error decreased with increase in the number of RBF units and reached a minimum for 60, and thereafter there was no change.

Table 10. Sample testing results for use of Batch fuzzy-c means algorithm

Pattern No.	Desired output (mm)	Network output (mm)	Classification error
Training data			
1	0.09	0.110032	0.000201
2	0.20	0.181281	0.000175
3	0.30	0.355636	0.001548
4	0.41	0.43981	0.000444
5	0.50	0.504449	9.897484×10^{-6}
6	0.57	0.690509	0.007261
7	0.65	0.58248	0.002279
8	0.73	0.656774	0.002681
9	0.18	0.279994	0.004999
10	0.59	0.429393	0.012897
Test data			
1	0.22	0.235852	0.000126
2	0.25	0.241403	3.695146×10^{-5}
3	0.28	0.315637	0.000635
4	0.31	0.318367	3.500285×10^{-5}
5	0.34	0.353487	9.094973×10^{-5}

The developed RBFNN was tested for different number of centers and for 60 centers, the accuracy on training data was 91% and on test data was 87%. Further increase in centers showed no variation and afterwards there was a drop in the accuracy.

Thus, this research work focused mainly on use of RBFNN for tool condition monitoring application. Different learning strategies were investigated for selecting the number and location of centers and the widths of the Gaussian RBF units in the hidden layer. This was a focused work related to use of RBFNN for a specific application. Table 9 shows a comparison of different learning strategies.

Random selection of centers requires several trials to fix the right number of centers. Batch fuzzy-c means is a robust and effective method to establish the optimal location and number of centers. It uses membership functions to finalize the centers and it will prevent the degradation of the modeling results of the RBFNN, particularly when the data is noisy, as in a shop floor environment. The use of gradient approach has resulted in simultaneous updation of all free parameters of the network, its possibility to be stuck in local minimum is more. Among the three learning strategies, the use of batch fuzzy-c means algorithm has resulted in a compact architecture with 50 centers and has achieved high classification accuracy of 97% and 93% on training and test data for the same training time. Thus, RBFNN are potential neural network models, which can be effectively used in TCM applications (Pai et al., 2002). Table 10 gives sample testing results for RBFNN using batch fuzzy-c means algorithm.

Table 11. Simulation parameters

e_{min}	0.00005
δ_{max}	0.1
δ_{min}	0.01
$\underset{\sim}{K}$	0.2
τ	700
α	0.1
No. of Epochs	16
No. of RBF units	69

Resource Allocation Network (RAN)

"It is a sequential learning, Gaussian Radial basis function network". While developing a basic RBFNN model,the basis functions are usually chosen as Gaussian and its number is fixed, based on the properties of the input data. The weights of the hidden layer are adjusted using some approach like LMS algorithm. The limitation"with this approach is that it is not suitable for sequential learning and also results in too many hidden units"(Yingwei et al., 1998). To overcome these limitations, Platt (1991) "developed an algorithm that adds hidden units to the network based on the 'novelty' of the input data". Further according to him "learning with a fixed size network is a NP-complete problem and by allocating new resources, learning could be achieved in polynomial time". The architecture of RAN is similar to that of RBFNN. Each hidden unit has two parameters, a center x_j and width σ_j. The output of each hidden unit is multiplied by the connecting weights w_{kj} between hidden and output layer and summed to generate the model output, which is given by $O_k = \Sigma_j w_{kj} V_j$, $j = 1....n$, are the hidden units and

V_j where V_j is the response of the jth hidden unit. "The learning phase of RAN involves adding of new hidden units and modification of the free parameters. Initially the network has no hidden neurons and generates the same as it receives the input-output data". "The decision whether to add a new hidden unit or not depends on the novelty of the data, based on the two conditions:

(i) $d = x_j - \xi_i > \delta$ and (ii) $e = \zeta_k - O_k > e_{min}, \delta$ and e_{min} are thresholds to be fixed based upon the data".

"The initial condition is $\delta = \delta_{max}$, where δ_{max} is chosen as the maximum domain of interest in the input space. The distance δ is decayed exponentially as $\delta = max(\delta_{max} e^{-\frac{t}{\tau}}, \delta_{min})$. This reduction of the distance leads to fewer units with large widths initially and as the number of data increases, more basis functions with smaller widths are added to better the final result. The parameters corresponding to the new hidden units are: $w_{kj}^{new} = e$, $x_j^{new} = x_j$ and $\sigma_j^{new} = \underset{\sim}{K} x_j - \xi_i$, where $\underset{\sim}{K}$ is an overlap factor that determines the quantum of overlay of the responses of the hidden units in the input space. As $\underset{\sim}{K}$ grows

Figure 4.

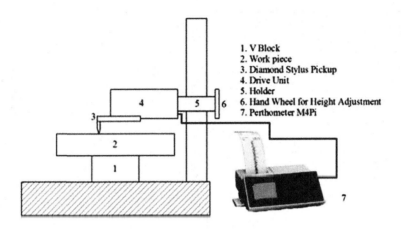

1. V Block
2. Work piece
3. Diamond Stylus Pickup
4. Drive Unit
5. Holder
6. Hand Wheel for Height Adjustment
7. Perthometer M4Pi

Figure 5.

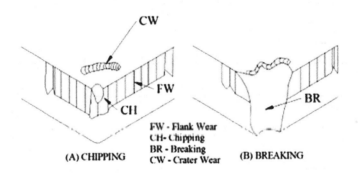

FW - Flank Wear
CH- Chipping
BR - Breaking
CW - Crater Wear

(A) CHIPPING   (B) BREAKING

larger, there is more overlay of responses". When a data pair (ξ_i, ζ_k) does not qualify the novelty criteria, a hidden unit is not added, but the network parameters are modified to adapt to the data(Platt, 1991) (Yingwei et al., 1998). The detailed RAN algorithm is available in (Nagabhushana, 1996)

Model Development: Results and Discussion

Several trials were carried out to fix the optimal values for the simulation parameters namely δ_{max}, $\underset{\sim}{K}$ and learning rate α. It was found that δ_{max} has the maximum influence on the behavior of the model, particularly the learning time and this was followed by overlap factor and learning rate. Variation of decay constant had no much influence on the results of the network. The optimal value of the simulation parameters is as given in Table 11.

Fig. 4 depicts the behavior of error as learning proceeds. The error reduces quickly initially and then the reduction is gradual. Fig. 5 shows the addition of RBF units as the network learns in sequence from the data. In the very first epoch, the model adds 65 hidden units and then the remaining 4 units are added in another two epochs and then it remains constant at 69 till 15 epochs are reached. Further to

Table 12. Performance of RAN network for different simulation parameters

e_{min}	0.00005	0.00005	0.00005	0.00005	0.00005
δ_{max}	0.8	0.6	0.4	0.2	0.1
δ_{min}	0.01	0.01	0.01	0.01	0.01
κ	0.6	0.6	0.6	0.6	0.6
τ	700	700	700	700	700
α	0.1	0.1	0.1	0.1	0.1
No. of Epochs	222	120	85	54	49
Accuracy on Training data	100%	100%	100%	100%	100%
Accuracy on Test data	93%	93%	80%	80%	73%
e_{min}	0.00005	0.00005	0.00005	0.00005	0.00005
δ_{max}	0.1	0.1	0.1	0.1	0.1
δ_{min}	0.01	0.01	0.01	0.01	0.01
κ	0.6	0.5	0.2	0.1	0.05
τ	700	700	700	700	700
α	0.1	0.1	0.1	0.1	0.1
No. of Epochs	49	54	16	18	18
Accuracy on Training data	100%	100%	100%	100%	100%
Accuracy on Test data	73%	80%	80%	80%	80%
e_{min}	0.00005	0.00005	0.00005	0.00005	
δ_{max}	0.1	0.1	0.1	0.1	
δ_{min}	0.01	0.01	0.01	0.01	
κ	0.2	0.2	0.2	0.2	
τ	700	700	700	700	
α	0.01	0.05	0.1	0.5	
No.of Epochs	6	16	16	11	
Accuracy on Training data	100%	100%	100%	100%	
Accuracy on Test data	13%	47%	80%	80%	

clearly understand the importance of different simulation parameters namely δ_{max}, K and α, trials have been conducted. The results of testing on the training and test data set is as shown in Table 12.

The training process begins with $\delta(t) = \delta_{max}$, which is the largest length scale of interest. It is generally the size of the complete input space of non-zero probability density. This distance then starts to decrease, until it reaches δ_{min}, which is the smallest length of scale [23]. From the table it is evident that δ_{max} and α have significant influence on the model behavior, especially on the test data. As δ_{max}

Figure 6.

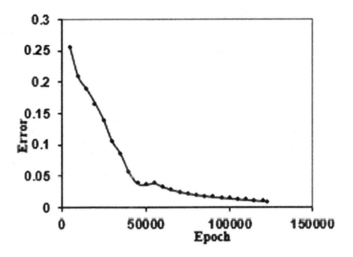

decreases, the performance of the network deteriorates. As α increased, the performance improved till 0.1, beyond which there was no improvement, except for a decrease in the number of training epochs. The increase in κ caused an improvement in performance on the test data till 0.2, beyond which there was no improvement in performance, but the number of training epochs increased. As κ grows larger, there was more overlap among the responses of the hidden units (Platt, 1991). Fig. 6 shows the network output vs desired output for sample training and test data. The network is able to identify 100% of the training data and 80% of the test data.

The RAN was also used to model data in type 3 format, which is the use of binary format for the output. The classification accuracy has been found to be 67% on the test data and required 80 training epochs. Thus, it is clear that the network not only performed poorly on the binary format of the data, but also required five time more training time compared to type 1 data requiring only 16 epochs.

Growing Cell Structures

This chapter discusses about the use of various neural network models for TCM applications. Each neural network type has its own advantages and disadvantages. With regard to MLP, there is a need to specify the optimal number of hidden neurons, it takes longer training time due to the possibility of the training getting stuck in local minima and its poor generalization ability. RBFNN also requires specifying of the number of RBF units again by trial and error, whichever may be the leaning strategy selected. This can be very time consuming and at times frustrating. RAN overcomes the limitation of both MLP and RBFNN in terms of specifying the number of hidden neurons and adds neurons based on the 'novelty' in presented input pattern. But it adds too many neurons, sometimes equal to the number of input patterns, resulting in a large network and memorizes the input patterns. This can affect its generalization performance.

To overcome all these limitations, Growing Cell Structures (GCS) was investigated in many of the real time problems and good results were obtained (Nagabhushana, 1996). In this work, results of applying GCS network to TCM applications has been presented to overcome the limitations of the networks

Table 13. Performance of GCS network for different simulation parameters

α	0.999	0.999	0.999	0.999	0.999	0.999	**0.999**
Amax	11	22	33	44	55	66	**77**
β	10	10	10	10	10	10	**10**
E_{min}	0.3	0.3	0.3	0.3	0.3	0.3	**0.3**
E_{tot}	0.2	0.2	0.2	0.2	0.2	0.2	**0.2**
η	0.05	0.05	0.05	0.05	0.05	0.05	**0.05**
Eps1	0.13	0.12	0.13	0.12	0.13	0.11	**0.12**
Eps2	0.000286	0.000207	0.000286	0.000207	0.000286	0.000146	**0.000207**
No. of Epochs	132	92	88	91	101	89	**90**
No. of RBF units	46	43	43	44	50	43	**25**

i) Varying the value of Amax

already studied and interesting results have been obtained. The authors feel this is the first effort in using this network type for this kind of application.

GCS is an incremental neural network model, where the neurons in the hidden layer are added based on the input data and may vary locally. The architecture starts with two hidden units and adds a unit if certain conditions are violated and determines neurons that fail to perform desirably and removes them to fine tune the performance. It has several advantages over the other neural network models:

(i)   "The incremental nature of the model does not require to prespecify a network size.
(ii) The growth process continues until a user-defined performance criterion or network size is met.
(iii) The network structure is automatically determined from the domain data to form the topology of the network.
(iv) Its ability to insert and delete cells allows the accurate estimation of probability densities of input signals.
(v)   All parameters are constant over time in contrast to other models, which rely on decaying parameters" (Fritzke, 1994) (Azuaje et al., 2000).

A distinct GCS network has three layerssimilar to an RBF neural network. The hidden neurons have Gaussian activation functions with center xj and width σ_j. "The width is defined as the mean length of all edges emanating from the best matching unit. The hidden neurons are fully linked to the output layer nodes through weighted connections, w_{kj}, where k =1 and j =1, 2, ...c".

GCS is a learning algorithm based on radial basis functions, that adds resources, but uses a different approach to generate the network architecture. It combines both unsupervised and supervised stages of conventional learning algorithm, so that center adaptation and weight updation are performed for every presented pattern. The algorithm builds the network based on accumulated error information. The details of the algorithm are available in (Nagabhushana, 1996).

Table 14. Varying the value of β

α	0.999	0.999	0.999	0.999	0.999
Amax	77	77	77	77	77
β	10	20	30	40	50
E_{min}	0.3	0.3	0.3	0.3	0.3
E_{tot}	0.2	0.2	0.2	0.2	0.2
η	0.05	0.05	0.05	0.05	0.05
Eps1	0.12	0.11	0.12	0.13	0.13
Eps2	0.000207	0.000146	0.000207	0.000286	0.000286
No. of Epochs	90	95	121	122	280
No. of RBF units	25	45	46	46	84

Table 15. Varying the value of η

α	0.999	0.999	0.999	0.999	0.999
Amax	77	77	77	77	77
β	10	10	10	10	10
E_{min}	0.3	0.3	0.3	0.3	0.3
E_{tot}	0.2	0.2	0.2	0.2	0.2
η	0.01	0.05	0.1	0.2	0.3
Eps1	0.11	0.12	0.12	0.13	0.11
Eps2	0.000146	0.000207	0.000207	0.000286	0.000146
No. of Epochs	127	90	107	376	127
No. of RBF units	63	25	46	105	63

Model Development: Results And Discussion

The network architecture initially has two RBF units drawn from the input space and adds RBF units during the learning phase. Simulation parameters like α, A_{max}, β, η and the error for convergence need to be set. The behavior of the network has been analyzed by varying the simulation parameters. The objective is to develop a model with optimal number of hidden neurons, takes least training time and gives good prediction performance. Table 13 shows the performance of GCS network for different simulation parameters.

The increase in A_{max} increases decreases the training time. With the increase in the value of β, more number of RBF units are added and the number of epochs required for convergence is also found to increase. Similarly increase of learning rate η causes an increase in training time and the number of RBF units and varies between 25 to 105. The network uses constant adaptation parameters Eps 1 and Eps 2 for determining the optimal cluster centers, which are nothing but RBF centers. "For each input pattern presented, find the nearest localizing unit and call it the 'best matching unit' (BMU) and move the BMU

Figure 7.

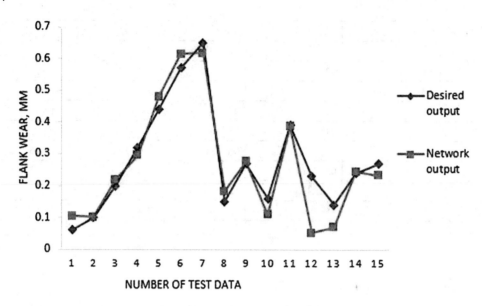

Figure 8.

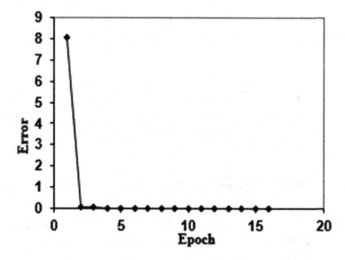

Eps 1 times the current distance towards the input pattern and move all immediate neighbours of BMU, Eps 2 times the current distance towards the input pattern. This process is called 'center adaptation'. The values for Eps1 and Eps 2 have been determined by trial and error". Fig. 7 and 8 shows the behavior of error with epochs and addition of RBF units with epochs.

The error shows a gradual decrease, with some variations in between. The number of RBF units added is almost in a step like manner, till 25 units are added. Table 16 gives the testing results of the developed GCS network for sample training and test data.

Table 16. Sample Testing results for GCS network

Pattern No.	Actual output in mm	Model output in mm	Classification error
Training data			
1	0.09	0.1574	0.004549
2	0.20	0.1959	0.000017
3	0.30	0.3988	0.009770
4	0.41	0.4879	0.006071
5	0.50	0.4862	0.000191
6	0.57	0.4908	0.006274
7	0.65	0.6313	0.000350
8	0.73	0.6765	0.002860
9	0.18	0.3324	0.023217
10	0.59	0.5141	0.005762
Test data			
1	0.22	0.1850	0.001226
2	0.25	0.2411	0.000079
3	0.28	0.2870	0.000048
4	0.31	0.3408	0.000947
5	0.34	0.2875	0.002758

The developed GCS network has been able to provide a prediction accuracy of 96% on the training data and 93% on the test data. The network has a compact architecture with only 25 hidden neurons, as they get added automatically through a growth process, which can be stopped as soon as the network starts giving good prediction results. "Also, the positioning of the RBF units and the supervised training of the connection weights between the hidden and output layer happen in parallel, the current classification error can be used to determine the location of new RBF units.Also, the network generalizes well, as evident from the accuracies"(Fritzke, 1994b).

CONCLUSION

"Monitoring is an important requirement in manufacturing process control and management". Monitoring systems have seen lot of changes in the last several years, which are becoming intelligent (Oborski, 2014). Machining is an important component of any manufacturing process. The automation and optimization of the machining processes is influenced by the condition of the cutting tool. The tool condition influences product quality, increases downtime, increases costs and sometimes affects the machine tool and personnel. Tool Condition Monitoring (TCM) helps in detecting all the major problems related to the cutting tool during machining and helps to improve accuracy in machining and also the availability of machines. The developments in the field of TCM is due to developments in the field of methods, sensors, monitoring and supervision systems, acquisition of data, analysis and decision-making systems. The acquisition of data is related to direct and indirect measurement of signals, which can be either acquired offline after machining or online during machining. "This includes cutting forces, load drives, current, acoustic emission, sound, noise, vibration, vision etc". The data obtained needs to be analyzed using methods like ANN, fuzzy logic etc. The reliability and robustness of a monitoring system can be increased, if data based on several measurement signals are used (Oborski, 2014). This can lead to 'sensor fusion' or 'sensor integration'. This work basically focusses on using acoustic emission, which is an online monitored signal and surface roughness, which has been measured offline along with the cutting conditions to predict the tool wear, particularly flank wear in face milling operations carried out on En 8 steel using uncoated carbide inserts. Accordingly use of AE, surface roughness and cutting conditions has facilitated achieving sensor fusion.

Tool wear monitoring is a complex task and hence signals from two domain have been integrated using artificial neural networks. ANN can interpolate very effectively, even when the data is sparse and noisy. It can effectively model the input output relationships, without knowing the underlying distributions. The focus of this work is to suggest an ANN type, which can generate a compact and optimal architecture, which has good generalization ability, which is the ability to estimate tool wear and accordingly monitor the condition of the tool.

Some of the specific conclusions drawn from the study are as follows (Pai, 2004):

(i)   MLP is a widely used ANN type in tool condition monitoring applications. It performs well when the data is continuous in nature for both input and output. Though it is robust and accurate in estimating tool wear values, it requires longer training time, has problem of local minima and there is a need for several trials to establish the optimum number of hidden neurons.

(ii)   RBF neural networks another class of feed forward network has been explored in terms of learning strategies fixing the location of centers and the width of the hidden neurons. RBFNN using batch fuzzy c means algorithm performs well with good generalization ability. These networks do not get stuck in local minima as in case of MLPNN. But they suffer limitations in terms of fixing the number and location of centers and the widths of the RBF units. Also, the network architecture is not compact as in case of MLPNN.

(iii)   RAN is a variant of RBF neural network, which uses a dynamic learning algorithm that builds the network architecture during training. It learns very fast when compared to other neural network models. Since it adds large number of hidden units, sometimes almost equal to the number of input patterns, it memorizes the data and hence generalizes poorly.

(iv)   GCS is a powerful learning algorithm based on RBF, that builds an optimal architecture. It is an incremental neural network model, wherein it adds and removes hidden units based on certain criteria. GCS network generates very compact network architecture. It trains faster and exhibits good generalization ability.

In this work, a compact ANN model of architecture 12-25-1 has been generated in least time (90 epochs) with good generalization performance in terms of 93% accuracy on tests data.

Thus, this chapter focusses on a systematic and detailed investigation in developing a compact and optimal neural network architecture, which can perform tool wear estimation effectively for TCM and can be easily applied offline in a practical shop floor environment.

ACKNOWLEDGMENT

This research received no specific grant from any funding agency in the public, commercial, or not-for-profit sectors.

Thanks are due to Dr. P.K. Ramakrishna Rao, Former Professor, Dept. of Mechanical Engg., SJCE, Mysuru for allowing the use of research facilities obtained from DST, New Delhi sponsored research project. The support of Dr. S.K. Padma, Professor, Dept. of Computer Science &Engg., SJCE, Mysuru, with regard to help in coding the algorithms used in this work is acknowledged.

REFERENCES

Azuaje, F., Dubitzky, W., Black, N., & Adamson, K. (2000). Discovering relevance knowledge in data: A Growing cell Structures approach. *IEEE Transactions on Systems, Man, and Cybernetics. Part B, Cybernetics*, *30*(3), 448–460. doi:10.1109/3477.846233 PMID:18252376

Balazinski, M., Czogala, E., Jemielniak, K., & Leski, J. (2002). Tool condition monitoring using artificial intelligence methods. *Engineering Applications of Artificial Intelligence*, *15*(1), 73–80. doi:10.1016/S0952-1976(02)00004-0

Chelladurai, H., Jain, V. K., & Vyas, N. S. (2008). Development of a cutting tool condition monitoring system for high speed turning operation by vibration and strain analysis. *International Journal of Advanced Manufacturing Technology*, *37*(5-6), 471–485. doi:10.100700170-007-0986-z

Chen, J. C., & Chen, J. C. (2005). An artificial-neural-networks-based in-process tool wear prediction system in milling operations. *International Journal of Advanced Manufacturing Technology*, *25*(5-6), 427–434. doi:10.100700170-003-1848-y

Cho, S., Binsaeid, S., & Asfour, S. (2010). Design of multisensor fusion-based tool condition monitoring system in end milling. *International Journal of Advanced Manufacturing Technology*, *46*(5-8), 681–694. doi:10.100700170-009-2110-z

Dimla, D. E. Jr, Lister, P. M., & Leighton, N. J. (1997). Neural Network solutions to the Tool Condition Monitoring Problem in Metal cutting – A critical review of methods. *International Journal of Machine Tools & Manufacture*, *37*(9), 1291–1241. doi:10.1016/S0890-6955(97)00020-5

Dornfeld, D. A. (1986). Acoustic Emission Monitoring for Untended Manufacturing. *Proceedings of Japan / USA Symposium on Flexible Automation.*

Elbestawi, M. A., & Dumitrescu, M. (2006). Tool Condition Monitoring in Machining – Neural Networks. In IFIP International Federation for Information Processing, Volume 220, Information Technology for Balanced manufacturing Systems(pp. 5-16). Boston: Springer.

Elbestawi, M. A., Dumitrescu, M., & Ng, E.-G. (2006). Tool Condition Monitoring in Machining. In Condition Monitoring and Control for Intelligent Manufacturing (pp 55-82). Springer-Verlag London Limited. doi:10.1007/1-84628-269-1_3

Fritzke, B. (1994). A Growing Neural Gas Network Learns Topologies. *Advances in Neural Information Processing Systems*, *6*, 625–632.

Fritzke, B. (1994). Growing Cell Structures – A Self organizing network for Unsupervised and Supervised learning. *Neural Networks*, *7*(9), 1441–1460. doi:10.1016/0893-6080(94)90091-4

Haykin, S. (1998). *Neural Networks – A Comprehensive Foundation*. New York: Macmillan College Publishing Company.

Jain, R. K. (2009). *Engineering Metrology*. New Delhi: Khanna Publishers.

Karayiannis, N. B. (1999). Reformulated Radial basis neural networks trained by Gradient descent. *IEEE Transactions on Neural Networks*, *10*(3), 657–671. doi:10.1109/72.761725 PMID:18252566

Kumar, S., Sharma, B., Sharma, V. K., & Poonia, R. C. (2018). Automated Soil prediction using bag-of-features and chaotic spider monkey optimization algorithm. *Evolutionary Intelligence*. doi:10.100712065-018-0186-9

Liang, S., & Dornfeld, D. A. (1989). Tool wear detection using time series analysis of acoustic emission. *ASME J. Eng. Ind. Trans.*, *111*(3), 199–205. doi:10.1115/1.3188750

Nagabhushana, T. N. (1996). *Fault diagnosis of AC and AC-DC systems using Constructive Learning RBF Neural Networks* (PhD Thesis). Dept. of High Voltage Engineering, IISc, Bangalore, India.

Oborski, P. (2014). Developments in integration of advanced monitoring systems. *International Journal of Advanced Manufacturing Technology*, *75*(9-12), 1613–1632. doi:10.100700170-014-6123-x

Ozel, T., & Karpat, Y. (2005). Predictive modeling of surface roughness and tool wear in hard turning using regression and neural networks. *International Journal of Machine Tools & Manufacture*, *45*(4-5), 467–479. doi:10.1016/j.ijmachtools.2004.09.007

Pai, P. S., Nagabhushana, T. N., & Rao, P. K. R. (2002). Flank wear estimation in Face milling based on Radial Basis Function Neural Networks. *International Journal of Advanced Manufacturing Technology*, *20*(4), 241–247. doi:10.1007001700200148

Pai, S. (2004). *Acoustic emission based Tool wear monitoring using Some Improved neural network methodologies* (PhD Thesis). Mysore University, Mysore, India.

Pai, S., Nagabhushana, T. N., & Rao, P. K. R. (2003) Tool wear monitoring in face milling using Fuzzy c means clustering techniques. In *Proceedings of National Conference on Advances in Manufacturing Technology, AMT 2003*. NSS Engineering College.

Panda, S. S., Chakraborty, D., & Pal, S. K. (2008). Flank wear prediction in Drilling using Back propagation neural network and Radial basis function network. *Applied Soft Computing*, *8*(2), 858–871. doi:10.1016/j.asoc.2007.07.003

Pandey, S., & Solanki, A. (2019). *Music Instrument Recognition using Deep Convolutional Neural Networks*. International Journal of Information Technology. doi:10.100741870-019-00285-y

Platt, J. (1991). A resource allocating network for function interpolation. *Neural Computation*, *3*(2), 213–225. doi:10.1162/neco.1991.3.2.213 PMID:31167310

Rehorn, A. G., Jinag, J., & Orban, P. E. (2005). State-of-the-art methods and results in tool condition monitoring- A review. *International Journal of Advanced Manufacturing Technology*, 26(7-8), 693–710. doi:10.100700170-004-2038-2

Sharma, S., Sharma, B., Sharma, V.K., Sharma, H., & Bansal, J.C. (2018). Plant leaf disease identification using exponential spider monkey optimization. Sustainable Computing: Informatics and Systems. doi:10.1016/j.suscom.2018.10.004

Sick, B. (2002). On-line and Indirect tool wear monitoring in turning with artificial neural networks: A review of more than a decade of research. *Mechanical Systems and Signal Processing*, 16(4), 487–546. doi:10.1006/mssp.2001.1460

Xiaoli, L. (2002). A brief review: Acoustic emission method for tool wear monitoring during turning. *International Journal of Machine Tools & Manufacture*, 42(2), 157–165. doi:10.1016/S0890-6955(01)00108-0

Yingwei, L., Sundararajan, N., & Saratchandran, P. (1998). Performance evaluation of a Sequential Minimal Radial Basis Function (RBF) Neural network learning algorithm. *IEEE Transactions on Neural Networks*, 9(2), 308–318. doi:10.1109/72.661125 PMID:18252454

Zeng, W., Jiang, X., & Blunt, L. (2009). Surface characterization-based tool wear monitoring in peripheral milling. *International Journal of Advanced Manufacturing Technology*, 40(3-4), 226–233. doi:10.100700170-007-1352-x

ADDITIONAL READING

Zhou, Y., & Xue, W. (2018). Review of tool condition monitoring methods in milling processes. *International Journal of Advanced Manufacturing Technology*, 96(5-8), 2509–2523. doi:10.100700170-018-1768-5

KEY TERMS AND DEFINITIONS

ANN Architecture: The arrangement of neurons in different layers of a artificial neural network model for a given problem and after fixing the number of neurons in the hidden layer(s) based on the optimization strategy adopted.

ANN Model Development: It is a process of developing a model using artificial neural network type, which can represent the input-output relationships for a given problem.

Automation: It is a technology an activity can be performed with minimum human intervention.

Cutting Tool Failure: It is the inability of a cutting tool to perform its intended role in any machining operation and can occur in terms of wear, fracture or breakage.

Face Milling: It is a machining process, where in the surfaces are produced in a direction perpendicular to the axis of the cutter. It generally produces flat surfaces.

Incremental Neural Network: It is a method of developing an artificial neural network model, where the neurons in the hidden layer are added or removed based on certain criteria and the availability of the training data.

Sensor Fusion: It is a process of combining data from different sensors/sources such that uncertainty in information from one sensor is offset by that from other sensors and more information is available.

Chapter 27

Computer Vision–Based Assistive Technology for Helping Visually Impaired and Blind People Using Deep Learning Framework

Mohamamd Farukh Hashmi
National Institute of Technology, Warangal, India

Vishal Gupta
National Institute of Technology, Warangal, India

Dheeravath Vijay
National Institute of Technology, Warangal, India

Vinaybhai Rathwa
National Institute of Technology, Warangal, India

ABSTRACT

Millions of people in this world can't understand environment because they are blind or visually impaired. They also have navigation difficulties which leads to social awkwardness. They can use some other way to deal with their life and daily routines. It is very difficult for them to find something in unknown environment. Blind and visually impaired people face many difficulties in conversation because they can't decide whether the person is talking to them or someone else. Computer vision-based technologies have increased so much in this domain. Deep convolutional neural network has developed very fast in recent years. It is very helpful to use computer vision-based techniques to help the visually impaired. In this chapter, hearing is used to understand the world. Both sight sense and hearing have the same similarity: both visual object and audio can be localized. Many people don't realise that we are capable of identifying location of the source of sound by just hearing it.

DOI: 10.4018/978-1-5225-9643-1.ch027

INTRODUCTION

Concurring factual investigation of WHO (World Health Organization) (Global Data on Visual Impairments, 2010), roughly 285 million individuals of the globe are visually impaired and 246 million have genuine vision issues. Outwardly debilitated individuals generally face challenges in development just as distinguishing individuals and staying away from obstructions in their everyday exercises. The regular answers for these circumstances are frequently observed to be use of guide sticks to recognize snags before them or hand-off on vocal speculating for distinguishing proof of people. As a result, outwardly disabled individuals can't foresee the careful condition includes about what kinds of items lies before them or whom they are confronting nearness.

Not just for the helping of outwardly disabled individuals, this idea is in usage in numerous areas, for example, security and modern assembling. The productivity and exactness contrasts by the calculation and handling capacities. Distinctive programming framework models are planned all things considered that it initially takes the info pictures of the database and actualize the profound learning procedure to group and afterward explicitly distinguish the required outcome, for example, objects, facial character or appearance, fabrication and so forth for the constant peripheries, the caught information pictures contain a few elements and needs increasingly productive program to extricate and determine the predefined classification and some of the time for continuous investigation, numerous recognition are recognized and it is a test to recognize effectively.

For the growing competitive world around, it is quite difficult for a visually impaired person to move around independently and identify surrounding objectives correctly with ease. With the advancement of technology, there are several solutions but most of them have demerits such as low acceptance, high cost, difficult to usage etc. (Gori, M., Cappagli, G., Tonelli, A., Baud-Bovy, G., & Finocchietti, S., 2016). Based on the demand, devises supporting the visually impaired people has been introduced for a time now. Again, keeping with pace, the more advanced algorithms and processing devises are introduced and progressing to higher accuracy and efficiency. This has inspired us to combine the concepts of implementing a processing devise for serving the blind individuals with a higher efficient methodology.

Literature Review

In various timeframe adaptable a methodology has been being used for recognize questions or distinguish individuals and bolster outwardly disabled people. This sector is highly involving image processing technology as visual activity is involved There exists various instruments to utilize computer vision technology to help daze individuals. The versatile application TapTapSee (Li, K. A., Baudisch, P., & Hinckley, K., 2008) utilizes computer vision and publicly supporting to portray an image caught by visually impaired clients in around 10 seconds. The Blind sight offers a portable application Text Detective including optical character recognition (OCR) innovation to identify and peruse content from pictures caught from the camera. Facebook is developing image captioning technology to help daze clients taking part in discussions with different clients about pictures. Baidu as of late discharged a demo video of a DuLight project.

In 2014, a theory named Smart Vision objected to support blind users with the features of movement within unacquainted surrounding (Henriques, F., Fernandes1a, H., Paredes, H., Martins, P., & Barroso, J, 2014) Another postulation (Bhambare, R. R., Koul, A., Bilal, S., & Pandey, S., 2014) utilized diverse individual gadget partitions for indoor and open-air developments just as consolidated GPS to follow the directions of the position spot of the client. The software implementation was done dependent on MAT-LAB. Likewise, there are cell phone based controlling frameworks with hindrance distinguishing proof and different modes for helpful client interfacing modes (Lin, B. S., Lee, C. C., & Chiang, P. Y. (2017).

With the progression in field of information science and computer vision different implementations in above have come around that give constant usage of such high featured task even on low computation power with promising outcomes and productivity. The algorithm for this proposal is 'YOLO' - (You Only Look Once) (Redmon, J., & Farhadi, A. 2018) which is effective for proficient for ongoing vigorous advancements.

There is a great work in article recognition utilizing customary computer vision techniques (sliding windows, deformable part models). Be that as it may, they do not have the exactness of deep learning-based methods. Among the deep learning-based strategies, two expansive class of techniques are common:

1) Two stage detection which are RCNN, Fast RCNN, Faster RCNN
2) Unified discovery (Yolo, SSD).

The sliding window algorithm slides over the object with a fixed size (es) of window(s) and decides if the object is available or not. In the event that object nearness is discovered, at that point the classifier is utilized to decide the class to which the distinguished article has a place with. This work is computationally pricey and time costly. Better approach to go around is to take a gander at certain areas where the objects can be available i.e. fix the proposed segment to go to the system and run the algorithm on those regions, this lessens the time just as algorithm computation complexity. Maybe a couple of these are to be examined in this segment:

Region-Based Convolution Neural Network (R-CNN)

R-CNN (Jiang, H., & Learned-Miller, E., 2017) use selective search to separate only 2000 region from the object which is called as locale proposition. Presently, rather than endeavouring to group a colossal many regions, we can simply work with 2000 region. These 2000 locale proposition are created utilizing the particular hunt algorithm which is composed underneath.

Particular Search:

1. Produce introductory sub-segmentation, we create numerous applicant areas.
2. Utilize eager algorithm to recursively consolidate comparable region into bigger ones.
3. Use the generated regions to produce the final candidate region proposals.

These 2000 candidate region proposals are twisted into a square and bolstered into a convolutional neural system that delivers a 4096-dimensional element vector as yield. R-CNN can't be actualized constant because to test each image it takes 47 seconds. The specific inquiry algorithm is well defined fixed algorithm. In this way, learning will not happen at that arrange. So bad region proposals will be generated.

Fast RCNN

The methodology is like the R-CNN algorithm.

The "Quick R-CNN" (Girshick, R. 2015) is quicker than R-CNN is on the grounds that we don't need to nourish 2000 regions proposition to the convolutional neural system inevitably. Rather, the convolution activity is done just once per object and an element map is created from it.

This is the manner by which Fast RCNN settle two noteworthy issues of Recursive convolution neural network, i.e., passing 1 rather than 2,000 regions for each object to the ConvNet, and utilizing 1 rather than 3 distinct model for removing highlights, arrangement and creating bouncing boxes. Yet, even Fast RCNN has certain issue zones. It likewise utilizes particular inquiry as a proposition strategy to discover the ROI, which is a moderate and tedious procedure. It takes around 2 seconds for every object to recognize object, where vastly improved contrasted with RCNN. Be that as it may, when we consider extensive genuine datasets, at that point Fast Recursive convolution neural network doesn't look so quick any longer.

Faster RCNN

Faster RCNN is the adjusted adaptation of Fast RCNN. The real distinction among them is that Fast RCNN utilizes particular look for producing Region of Interest, while Faster RCNN utilizes "Region Proposal Network".

The beneath steps are used in Faster RCNN:

1) We accept a image as info and pass it to the ConvNet which restores the component map for that image.
2) Region proposition arrange is connected on these feature maps. This return the object proposition alongside their objectness score.
3) A RoI pooling layer is connected on these propositions to cut down every one of the recommendations to a similar size.

Most of the object recognition algorithm we have talked about so far use locales to recognize the objects. The system does not take a gander at the total image in one go yet centres around parts of the picture successively. This makes two inconveniences:

1. The algorithm requires numerous goes from a single image to remove every one of the objects.
2. As there are distinctive frameworks working consistently, the execution of the frameworks further ahead relies upon how the past frameworks performed.

Our goal is to implement the task as object detection with voice input utilizing YOLO v3 (Redmon, J., & Farhadi, A., 2018) for object detection and afterward we send the word reference content portrayal to Google Text-to-Speech API utilizing the gTTs package (Rodríguez-Fuentes, L. J., Peñagarikano, M., Varona, A., & Bordel, G., 2018). Object detection is a field of now a deep learning combined with computer vision that recognizes occurrences of semantic objects in images/videos (by making bouncing boxes around them for our situation). We can then convert the annotated text into voice responses and give the basic positions of the objects in the person/camera's view.

Figure 1. High – level Function flow of the architecture

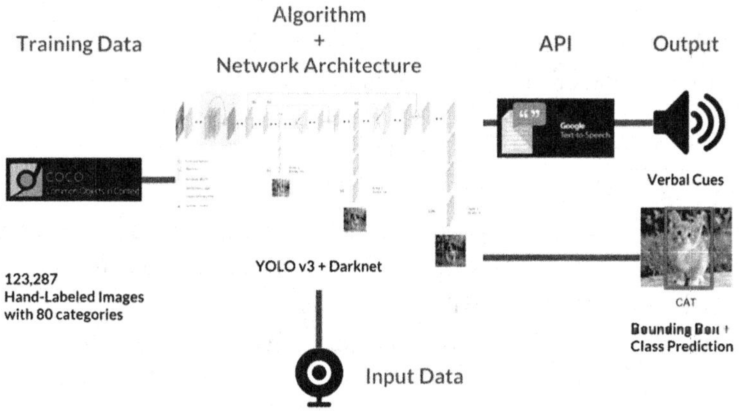

PROPOSED METHODOLOGY

High dimension function process

Prior to recognizing any object or facial personality from information images or constant information, it is first basic to detect and extract the target region from the original image frames There are a few removing algorithms for these divisions of image processing. Additionally, the accumulation of dataset needs a pre-handling to standardize the measurements for better preparing a short time later that outcome in improved accuracy. The dataset utilized for training the proposed model are the COCO dataset (Lin, T. Y., Maire, M., Belongie, S., Hays, J., Perona, P., Ramanan, D., ... & Zitnick, C. L., 2014) (containing 80 classes) and Pascal VOC dataset (Everingham, M., Van Gool, L., Williams, C. K., Winn, J., & Zisserman, A., 2010) (containing 20 classes). After item recognition and distinguishing proof the further task is to give the voice criticism to the client, it is finished utilizing the Google Text-to-Speech API (Google Text to speech API documentation) utilizing the gTTS bundle. Here is the abnormal state outline of our adaptation of usage:

Training Data

The model is prepared with Common Objects in Context (COCO) dataset and Pascal VOC dataset; the images are annotated on utilizing Image Annotation Tools (Image-annotation-services Annotation services API documention).

Model

The model here is the You Only Look Once (YOLO) algorithm that goes through a variety of an amazingly intricate Convolutional Neural Network engineering called the Darknet (Huang, (R., Pedoeem, J., & Chen, C., 2018). Our rendition of execution utilizes 'TensorFlow' deep learning structure (Abadi, M., Barham, P., Chen, J., Chen, Z., Davis, A., Dean, J., ... & Kudlur, M., 2016).

Input Information

We will utilize our webcam to nourish images at 30 outlines for each second to this trained model and we can set it to just process each other edge to speed things up.

API

The class expectation of the objects recognized in each casing will be a JSON word reference for example "feline". We will likewise acquire the directions of the objects in the image and attach the position "top"/"mid"/"base" and "left"/"focus"/"ideal" to the class expectation "feline". We would then be able to send the content portrayal to the Google Text-to-Speech API utilizing the gTTS bundle.

Output

We will also obtain the coordinates of the bouncing box of each object detected in our frames, overlay the crates on the object identified and return the stream of frames as a video playback. We will likewise timetable to get a voice input on the first frame of each second (rather than 30 fps) for example "base left cat"—meaning a feline was detected on the base left of my camera see.

Object Detection and Identification Methodology

Beforehand, classification-based models were utilized to detect objects utilizing limitation, district-based grouping or things, for example, the sliding window. Just high scoring areas of the image are considered as a location and they could be very tedious. The algorithm utilized for item recognition and recognizable able proof for better constant execution is the 'YOLO represents you just look once. It's a mutually prepared technique for item identification and grouping for continuous video. YOLO is relapse based. So the expectations are educated by the worldwide setting in the image. We reframe the item location as a solitary relapse issue, from pixelization to box formations facilitating class probabilities and anchor box detections. YOLO v3 performs at standard with other condition of function Manship finders like RetinaNet, while being significantly quicker, at COCO mAP 50 benchmark. It is additionally superior to SSD and it's variations. Here's an examination of exhibitions directly from the original paper. YOLO vs RetinaNet performance on COCO 50 Benchmark is depicted in fig 1.

System Approach

Basic idea behind YOLO algorithm:

The possibility of this indicator is that you run the image on a CNN show and get the recognition on a solitary pass. First the image is resized to 448x448, at that point nourished to the network lastly the output is separated by a Non-max concealment algorithm. The basic algorithm is depicted as shown down in figure 3.

Figure 2. YOLO vs RetinaNet performance

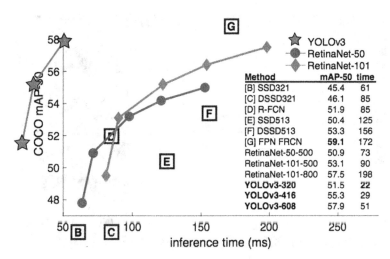

Figure 3. YOLO basic working algorithm

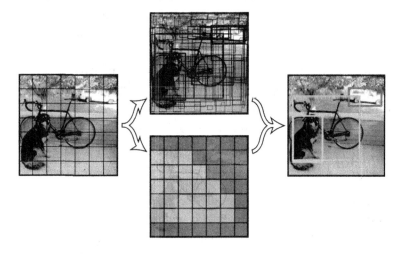

Figure 4. Function flow of YOLO Model with thresholding and NMS

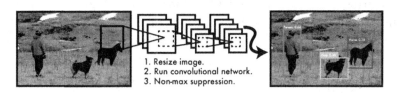

Figure 5. Bounding boxes derivation

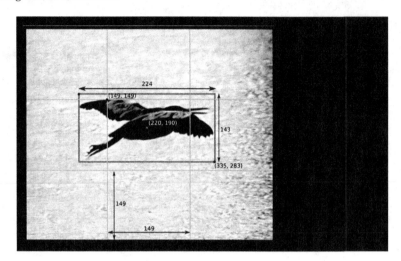

Detailed Function Process of Algorithm

YOLO (You Only Look Once), is a deep learning based convolutional neural network for object detection. The task of object detection comprises of locating the area on the image where specific object classes instances are available, just as ordering those object instances. Past techniques for this, similar to R-CNN and its varieties, utilized a pipeline to play out this errand in different advances. This can be moderate to execute and furthermore difficult to develop upon as network parameters are not flexible and dependent upon each other's, claiming every individual part should be prepared independently. YOLO, does everything with a solitary neural network. So, to put it straightforward, image is accepted as information, go through a neural network.

The Prediction Vector

The initial step to comprehension of YOLO is the means by which the output is encoded. The info image is partitioned into an S x S matrix of cells. For required object instance that is available on the image, the enclosed network cell is said to be "capable" for antedating it. That is where the focal point of the object instance falls into. B bounding boxes and C class probabilities for mentioned classes in the dataset is predicted by network cell. The bouncing box forecast has 5 parts: (x, y, h, w, certainty). The [x, y] facilitates to the focal point of the container, in respect to the network cell area. These directions are standardized to fall somewhere in the range of 0 and 1. The (w, h) box measurements are likewise normalised to [0, 1], in respect to the object instance estimate. Case of how to ascertain enclose arranges a 448x448 pixel matrix image with grid lines partitioning of 3. Note how the (x, y) arranges are determined in respect to the middle matrix cell. The following is depicted in figure down below. There is yet more segments in the bouncing box forecast, which is the confidence score. From the paper: Formally we characterize certainty as Pr (Object) * IOU (pred, truth). On the off chance that no item exists in that cell, the confidence score is necessarily zero.

Figure 6. Prediction vector for an image

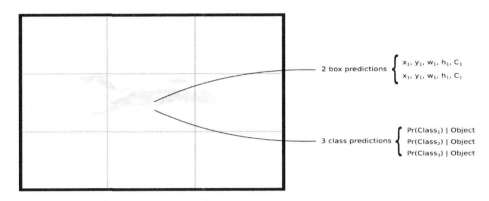

(i)   Prediction vector details:

The confidence value in the output vector dictates the nearness or nonappearance of an object instance of any class. From above there are 5 segments of box expectation, every frame function cell makes B bounding boxes, so there are many outputs identified with the bouncing box forecasts. Again, we determine and antedate probabilities as, Pr (Class (i) | Object). The above representation is the likelihood that one matrix cell contains one object.

On the off chance that no item is available on the lattice cell, the loss capacity won't put out it as a wrong class expectation, the network just predicts one lot of class probabilities per cell, paying little respect to the quantity of B boxes.

. To assess PASCAL VOC, YOLO utilizes 7×7 networks (S×S), 2 limit boxes (B) and 20 classes (C). In this way, this algorithm forecast has a state of [S, S, B×5 + C] = [7, 7, 2×5 + 20] = [7, 7, 30].

The substantial idea of algorithm is to construct neural network to antedate a [7, 7, 30] tensor. It plays out a direct relapse utilizing different completely associated layer to predict 7×7×2 limit box forecasts.

(ii)   The confidence score registered:

Class confidence score = box confidence score x restrictive class likelihood. It quantifies the certainty on both the characterization and the restriction (where an object is found). Mathematically,

Box confidence score $\equiv Pr object.\ IoU$

Conditional class probability $\equiv Pr class_i | object$

Class confidence score $\equiv Pr class_i.\ IoU$

= box confidence scores × conditional class probability

Here

$P_r(object)$ is the probability the box having an object.

IoU is the IOU (intersection over union) because of ground truth and predicted box,

$P_r(class_i \mid object)$ is the probability the object is from *class_i* if an object is present.

$P_r(class_i)$ is the probability that the object is from *class_i*.

Figure 7. YOLO v3 Network Architecture

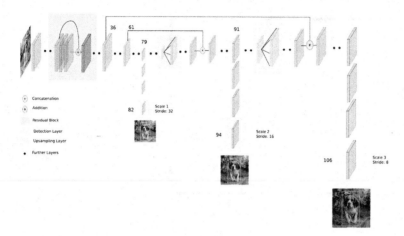

The more current design is based upon the lingering skip associations using the resnet connections, and up sampling.

Class Prediction

YOLOv3 utilizes multi-name order. For instance, the output marks might be "person on foot" and "tyke" which are select type. YOLOv3 replaces the Soft Maxoutput function classifier with autonomous strategic classification ut6ilities to ascertain the likeliness of the info has a place with a particular mark. Rather than using mean square method as a algorithm for computing the order loss, YOLOv3 utilizes twice fold cross-entropy loss for each name. This likewise decreases the algorithm multifaceted nature by staying away from the SoftMax function.

Darknet53: The Network

The frame function cells are passed to YOLO v3 arrange pipeline to be prepared. The system subtleties as pursues:

In YOLO v3 paper, the creators present new, more profound design of highlight extractor called Darknet-53 (Du, P., Qu, X., Wei, T., Peng, C., Zhong, X., & Chen, C., 2018). As its name proposes, it contains of 53 convolutional layers, each pursued by bunch standardization layer and Leaky ReLU actuation. Down sampling is finished by conv layers with stride=2. Initially, YOLO v3 utilizes a variation of the Darknet, which initially has around 53-layer system prepared on ImageNet.

A few remarks about the design:

- The design example for implementation in the Pascal VOC dataset, where the execution utilized S=7, B=2 and C=20. This explains why the last component maps are 7x7, and furthermore explains the span of the total output (7x7x (2*5+20)). Utilization of the above system with an alternate matrix measure or distinctive number of classes may require tuning of the layer measurements.
- The successions of 1x1 tensor vectors decrease layer and 3*3 convolutional layer were enlivened by Inception Net (Google) display
- The last layer utilizes a direct actuation sigmoid function. Every single other layer utilizes a cracked RELU activation function.

Figure 8. Dark net Convolution Model

	Type	Filters	Size	Output
	Convolutional	32	3 × 3	256 × 256
	Convolutional	64	3 × 3 / 2	128 × 128
1×	Convolutional	32	1 × 1	
	Convolutional	64	3 × 3	
	Residual			128 × 128
	Convolutional	128	3 × 3 / 2	64 × 64
2×	Convolutional	64	1 × 1	
	Convolutional	128	3 × 3	
	Residual			64 × 64
	Convolutional	256	3 × 3 / 2	32 × 32
8×	Convolutional	128	1 × 1	
	Convolutional	256	3 × 3	
	Residual			32 × 32
	Convolutional	512	3 × 3 / 2	16 × 16
8×	Convolutional	256	1 × 1	
	Convolutional	512	3 × 3	
	Residual			16 × 16
	Convolutional	1024	3 × 3 / 2	8 × 8
4×	Convolutional	512	1 × 1	
	Convolutional	1024	3 × 3	
	Residual			8 × 8
	Avgpool		Global	
	Connected		1000	
	Softmax			

Loss Function

The above neural network predicts different bouncing boxes per matrix cell. To register the loss for the genuine positive, we just need oversee the item. So we first-class the one with the highest value of IoU calculated with respect to the ground truth. This technique prompts specialization among the jumping box forecasts. Every forecast improves at anticipating certain sizes and viewpoint proportions.

Loss function uses the following:

The grouping loss.

- The confinement loss
- The confidence loss
    - i) Classification loss:

The losses occurred during classification can be recovered.it calculates probabilities of each class in the dataset.

$i=0s21iobjc \in classespi(c-pi'(c))2$ (1)

Where

$1_i^{obj} = 1$ if an object is in cell i, if not then 0.

$pi'c$ represents conditional probability for class c in cell i.

ii)   Localization loss:

It compu*tes* the errors in the boundary box sizes and locations. We only count the box accountable for detected the object.

$\lambda coordi=0s2j=0B1ijobjxi-xi'2+yi-yi'2+\lambda coordi=0s2j=0B1ijobjwi-wi'2+hi-hi'2$ (2)

Where

$1_{ij}^{obj} = 1$ If cell i is capable for detecting the object, if not then 0.

λ_{coord} increase the weigh*t* for the loss in the boundary box coordinates.

We would prefer not to weight blunders boxes of different sizes similarly. YOLO forecasts the square groundwork of the width and tallness rather than the stature and width. Likewise, to gain accentuation on the limit box precision, we duplicate the loss occurring by λ cord.

iii)   Confidence loss:

After the detection of object instance in the image as given by bounding box predictions, the confidence loss is given as:

$i=0s2j=0B1ijobjCi-Ci'2$ (3)

Where

C_i' is the confidence score of the box j in the cell i.

$1ijobj=1$ if the cell i is able to detect object, if not then 0.

In case th*e* object is not able to detected as any of classes, then

$i=0s2j=0B1ijobjCi-Ci'2$ (4)

Where

C_i' is the confidence score of the box j in cell i.

$1ijobj=1$ if cell i is able to detect the object, if not then 0.

The final loss include*s* limitation, certainty a*nd* classification losses together. In YOLO v3 the losses have been supplanted by cross-entropy mistake terms. At the end of the day, object certainty and class expectations in YOLO v3 are presently anticipated through strategic relapse.

Batch Normalization

Including bunch standardization (Ioffe, S., & Szegedy, C., 2015) evacuates the need of dropouts and drives mAP up by 2%. YOLO v3 standardizes the contribution to be in range 0.1. The greater part of the layers in the identifier do group standardization directly after the convolution, don't have inclina-

Figure 9. Different layers of YOLO algorithm

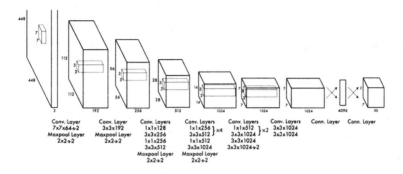

Figure 10. Refined YOLO Architecture

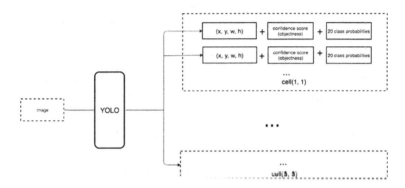

tions and utilize Leaky ReLU actuation. It is helpful to characterize thin arg extension to deal with these cases for use. In the layers which don't utilize BN and LReLU we should verifiably characterize that. NMS algorithm (Neubeck, A., & Van Gool, L., 2006):

There are really B copy location for the **network cell** that is the just a single used to foresee the article (dim green box). NMS stifles location with low box confidence scores: BC, so we don't finish up foreseeing numerous articles when there is just barely one. The execution of NMS proposed is:

Start with the jumping box that has the most astounding BC.

- Remove any remaining bouncing boxes that cover it more than the given limit sum = 0.2
- Proposed changes made to the system:

1. Removal of the completely associated layers in charge of anticipating the limit box. To produce forecasts of the state of 7×7 ($\times 125$), we succeed the last convolution layer with three 3×3 convolutional layers each channelling 1024 outputs. At the end we use 1×1 convolutional layer to change over the $7 \times 7 \times 1024$ tensor vector into $7 \times 7 \times 125$.

Presently we move to the class from the cell level to the box level. By and by, each desire fuses 4 constraints for the farthest point box, 1 box certainty score (objectness) and 20 class probabilities. For instance, 5 limit boxes with 25 constraints: 125 constraints for each system cell. Same as YOLO, the objectness desire still predicts the IOU (Rahman, M. A., & Wang, Y. 2016) of the ground truth and the proposed box.

2. Modify the information pixel matrix estimate from 448x 448 to 416x416. It makes an odd no. spatial measurement (7x7 vs. 8x8 framework matrix). Focal point of an image is frequently involved by an expansive article. With an odd number framework matrix, it is increasingly sure on wherever the object has a place.

Stay boxes decline mAP marginally from 69.5 to 69.2 however the review progresses from 81% to 88%. For example, indeed, the precision is marginally diminished, yet it expands the odds of recognizing all the actual classes.

i)   The Training:
   ●First, pretrain the initial 20 convolutional layers utilizing the proposed datasets, utilizing information of 224x224 sizes.
   ●Afterwards, increment the information goals to 448x448
   ●Utilizing a bunch size of 64, energy of 0.9 and rot of 0.0005, train the system for around 135 ages.
   ●Training rate plan: first ages, the taking in rate was gradually increased from 0.001 to 0.01. Learning around 75 ages, afterward begin diminishing it.
   ●Utilizing information growth with irregular scale level and interpretations, arbitrarily altering introduction and immersion.

Result Filtering

YOLO outputs the top classes and their likelihood for each edge. We accept any likelihood above 20% as a sure recognition result.

Among each of the 20 classes of the current YOLO show, we pick the accompanying classes as major to illuminate the client: "bottle", "seat", "diningtable", "individual", "pottedplant", "couch", "tvmonitor". The output of the procedure is json word reference that is nourished to Google Text-to-Speech API utilizing the gTTS bundle for content to discourse transformation.

gTTs (Google Text-to-Speech), a Python library and CLI instrument to interface with Google Translate's content to-discourse API. Composes spoken mp3 information to a record, a document like item (bytestring) for further sound control, or stdout.

(i)   Highlights of gTTs:
   1 Customizable speech-specific sentence tokenizer that allows for unlimited lengths of text to be read, all while keeping proper intonation, abbreviations, decimals and more;
   2 Customizable text pre-processors which can, for example, provide pronunciation corrections
   3 Automatic retrieval of supported languages.

RESULTS AND DISCUSSION

Experimental Results

YoloV3 has 53 layers and it's neat. Remaining system alongside skip associations have accuracy & efficiency. Rather than maxpooling layers they have utilized strided convolutional layers which are effective. More deep layers increment open fields. Predictions are made on 3 features map where they've utilized FPN (Zhao, X., Zhao, C., Zhu, Y., Tang, M., & Wang, J., 2018,) style up-sampling to make couple of features map. It helps in perceiving objects of various scale. On a coco dataset it demonstrates a major bounce in MAP score and rivals RetinaNet and outperforms SSD show. Darknet 53 demonstrates comparative outcomes to Resnet 101 on ImageNet dataset however computational quicker. Gives better exactness on PASCAL VOC dataset and a 10x and 100x speed improvement over the past cutting edge. Test Set Evaluation

Present day object recognition challenges depend on a measurement called mean average precision (mAP). We register the average precision (AP) independently for each class by arranging the location by their confidences and going down the arranged rundown, and afterward therefore normal over the average precision for each class to process mAP. An detection is viewed as a genuine positive on the off chance that it has IoU with actual box more prominent than some limit (typically 0.5) (mAP @0.5) We at that point join all location from all test pictures to draw an exactness/Recall bend for each class; Average precision is the zone under the bend, processed by means of the Riemann sum:

$$AvgPrecision = k = 1 \, Npk.recall(k) \tag{5}$$

where $p(k)$ is the exactness at each conceivable edge esteem, $\Delta r(k)$ is the adjustment in recall, and k values on each conceivable. To process mAP, we use:

$$MAP = \frac{\Sigma \, AvgPrecision(q)}{Q} \tag{6}$$

For PASCAL VOC, Q = 20 $Avg \, Precision = \Sigma P(k)\_. \, recall(k)$
Exactness catches how precise the reports are given by the algorithm:

$$Precision = \Sigma \frac{Mii}{Mji} \tag{7}$$

Recall estimates what number of ground certainties can be found by the algorithm:

$$Recall = TPTP + FN \tag{8}$$

In PASCAL VOC 2012, a jumping box announced by a process is viewed as right if its territory crossing point over association with actual bouncing box is past half. Formally, detections are viewed as obvious or false positives dependent on the territory of cover with ground truth jumping boxes. To be viewed as a correct detection, the area of overlap between the anticipated bouncing box Bp and ground truth jumping box but must surpass half by the equation

Figure 11a. Graphical Representation of Performance Parameters Calculation

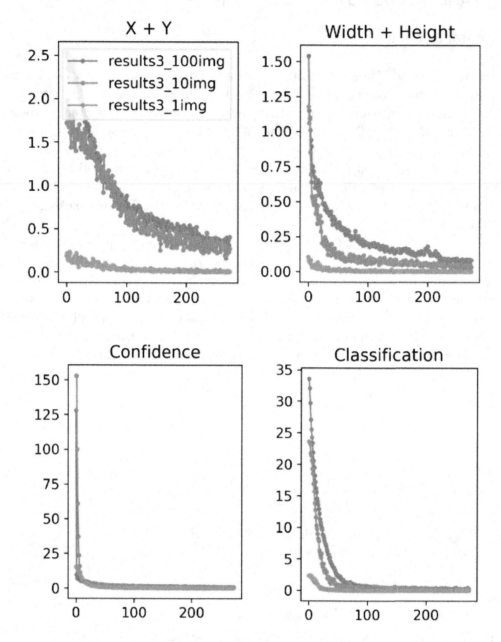

a=*areaBp BgtareaBp Bgt* (9)

We utilize the later estimation of AP that don't assess territory under the accuracy Recall bend at 11 ∈ {0, 0.1, ..., 0.9, 1} but instead at all information focuses. The exactness esteem precision (k) is the extent of tests with parallel than k—1 they are sure (where positions are doled out by diminishing scores). Recall (k) is rather the level of +ve examples that have rank littler or break even with than k − 1. For instance, if the initial two examples are one +ve and one -ve, precision (3) is 1 2. On the off chance

Figure 11b.

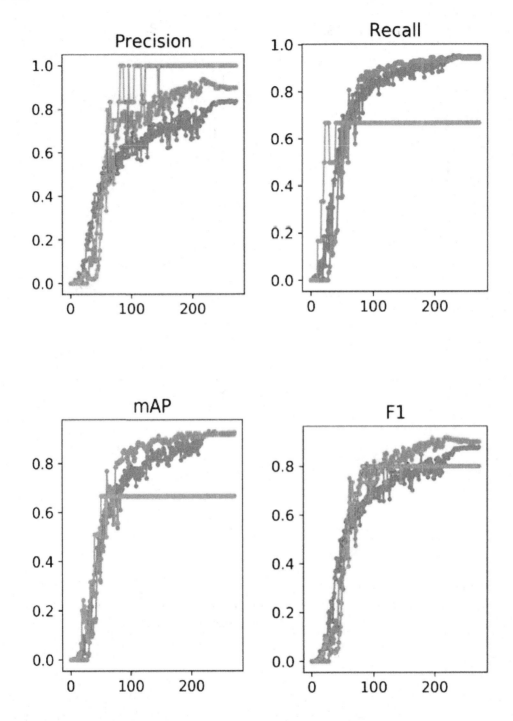

Figure 11c.

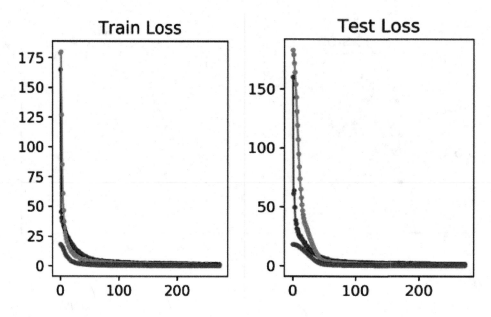

Table 1. Image Augmentation

Augmentation	Description
Translation	+/- 15% (vertical and horizontal)
Rotation	+/- 10 degrees
Shear	+/- 4 degrees (vertical and horizontal)
Scale	+/- 12%
Reflection	50% probability (horizontal-only)
HSV Saturation	+/- 70%
HSV Intensity	+/- 60%

that there are in all out 5 positive examples, at that point recall (3) is 1 5. Looking from rank k to rank k + 1, on the off chance that the example of rank k+1 is sure, at that point both exactness and Recall increment; generally, accuracy diminishes, and Recall remains consistent.

Training

We begin training by downloading the pretrained weights and the required dataset (PASCAL VOC 2012 containing 20 classes), then the training is resumed from the latest checkpoint. Each epoch trains on 2000 images on train and validate from the PASCAL set and tests on 500 images with a training speed of 1.26 s/batch on Google Collaboratory. Here we see the training results from voc_1img.data, voc_10img.data, voc_100img.data that train on 1, 10, 100 images respectively of PASCAL VOC 2012 dataset.

Table 2. Mean AP values

Class	Average Precision
Motorbike	0.768
Bottle	0.472
Bird	0.685
Cat	0.919
Aero plane	0.672
Chair	0.760
Person	0.842
Dining table	0.538
Boat	0.444
Train	0.928
Sofa	0.910
Bicycle	0.682
Bus	0.728
Horse	0.758
Tv monitor	0.634
Cow	0.532
Pottedplant	0.559
Car	0.684
Dog	0.829
sheep	0.533

That predicts the PR bend a trademark saw-shape. For a perfect classifier this positions all the +ve examples first the PR bend is one that portrays opposite sides of the unit square.

Image Augmentation

Image augmentation to increase the dataset using random OpenCV augmentation is used in accordance with following specifications given below in the table 2. The bounding boxes automatically detected and updated with the images.

Quantitative Analysis

The model is executed on VOC data set, using a learning rate of $\alpha = 1 \bullet 10^{-2}$, alongside instatements of weight drawn from an arbitrary ordinary appropriation N (μ, $\sigma = 0.35$) promptly outputted Nans for loss esteems, proposing uniqueness. Assuming that the standard of the weight was excessively vast amid introduction, we utilized Xavier instatement. This arrangement settled the issue until the greatness of the training rate α was low (for example $\alpha = 1 \bullet 10^{-5}$). We subjectively confirmed that mAP was high among anticipated and actual bouncing boxes.

Figure 12. Ground truth comparison

The detections allocated to actual objects and made a decision of valid/false positive by estimating jumping box cover. To view as a right detection, zone of cover among the anticipated bouncing box and ground truth jumping box must surpass an edge. The output of the detections allocated to actual objects fulfilling the cover standard were positioned arranged by (diminishing) con dense output. Different detections of a similar article in a picture were viewed as false location, for example 5 recognitions of a solitary object considered 1 genuine positive and 4 false positives. On the off chance that no forecast is made for an image. The normal accuracy for all the object classes are accounted for in the table beneath the mean average precision for the PASCAL VOC dataset was observed as 0.678. The present best in class best mAP esteem is accounted as 0.73.

Qualitative Analysis

Test results from PASCAL VOC dataset are shown in figure 10.

Among each of the 20 classes of the current YOLO show, we pick the accompanying classes as major to illuminate the client: "bottle", "seat", "diningtable", "individual", "pottedplant", "couch", "tvmonitor". As these are the classes that we deemed relevant for the application to be used on. Again, the accuracy and speed achieved is satisfactory and can be put for real time processing of video frame images running on 25 to 28 fps, as the achieved fps is around 30 to 35 giving a result of around 0.65 mean precision. The above results are conclusion for the assistive help of visually impaired and blind people.

CONCLUSION AND FUTURE WORK

Reimplementation of YOLO as a quick, accurate object detector algorithm in Tensor Flow. Has been discussed in this paper It exhibit the capacity to repeat identifications similar with the first usage. We gain proficiency with the constraints of the system, look at mAP figured from the pre-trained system constraints as an extension of transfer learning. Moreover, we planned a post-training plan to achieve real-time object detection in live video feeds. Pretrained module to port features of YOLO from Dark net to Tensor Flow is used. YOLO can acquire prompt outcomes from our execution to actualize a loss function and back propagation to alter the loads. We stretch out YOLO to follow protests inside a video in Real-time. YOLO is intended to track objects within in grouping; in this way, it has no understanding of fleeting or spatial progression between consecutive casings in a video. A post-handling stage where after element extraction the tensor yield is bolstered to k-means clustering algorithm to distinguish object between the frames has presented. It has been subjectively confirmed that mean normal accuracy was high among anticipated and ground truth bouncing boxes. Present day object discovery challenges are measured on a measurement called mAP. The mean average precision (AP) independently registered for each different classes by arranging the recognitions by their confidences and going down the arranged rundown, and afterward in this manner normal over the average precision(s) for each class to process mean average precision. The current usage is restricted for the situations it can effectively identify; image fidelity and frame rate to be very high, and object can't move at high speed more than the implementation of model. If picture isn't clear, and items moves at fast our execution indicates variable yield. So, improvised work is expected to improve the strength of the picture bunching for above mentioned featured video(s). For the improvisations suggested, to determine the ambiguities over the model loss function by reaching the original authors of and report the mAP over all informational collection parts of our self-prepared model has been planned.

REFERENCES

Abadi, M., Barham, P., Chen, J., Chen, Z., Davis, A., Dean, J., . . . Kudlur, M. (2016). Tensorflow: A system for large-scale machine learning. In 12th {USENIX} Symposium on Operating Systems Design and Implementation ({OSDI} 16) (pp. *265-283). Academic Press.*

Bhambare, R. R., Koul, A., Bilal, S., & Pandey, S. (2014). Smart vision system for blind. International Journal of Engineering and Computer Science, 3(5), 5790–5795.

Du, *P., Qu, X., Wei, T., Peng, C., Zhong, X., & Chen, C. (2018).* Research on Small Size Object Detection in Complex Background. In 2018 Chinese Automation Congress (CAC) (pp. 4216-4220). IEEE. 10.1109/CAC.2018.*8623078*

Everingham, M., Van Gool, L., Williams, C. K., Winn, J., & Zisserman, A. (2010). The pascal visual object classes (voc) challenge. International Journal of Computer Vision, 88(2), 303–338. doi:10.100711263-*009-0275-4*

*Girshick, R. (2015). Fast r-*cnn. In Proceedings of the IEEE international conference on computer vision (pp. 1*440-1448). IEEE.*

*Global Data on Visual Impairments. (2010). Avai*lable online: http://www.who.int/blindness/

Gori, M., Cappagli, G., Tonelli, A., Baud-Bovy, G., & Finocchietti, S. (2016). Devices for visually impaired people: High technological devices with low user acceptance and no adaptability for children. Neuroscience and Biobehavioral Reviews, 69, 79–88. doi:10.1016/j.neu*biorev.2016.06.043 PMID:27484870*

*Hu*ang, R., Pedoeem, J., & Chen, C. (2018, December). YOLO-LITE: A Real-Time Object Detection Algorithm Optimized for Non-GPU Computers. In 2018 IEEE International Conference on Big Data (Big Data) (pp. 2*503-2510). IEEE. 10.1109/BigData.2018.8621865*

Ioffe, S., & Szegedy, C. (2015). Batch normalization: Accelerating deep network training by red*ucing internal covariate shift. arXiv preprint arXiv:1502.03167*

*Jiang, H., & Learned-Mille*r, E. (2017, May). Face detection with the faster R-CNN. In 2017 12th IEEE International Conference on Automatic Face & *Gesture Recognition (FG 2017) (pp. 650-657). IEEE. 10.1109/FG.2017.82*

*Li, K. A., Baud*isch, P., & Hinckley, K. (2008, April). Blindsight: eyes-free access to mobile phones. In Proceedings of the SIGCHI Conference on Human Factors in *Computing Systems (pp. 1389-1398). ACM.*

*Lin, B. S., Lee, C. C., & Chia*ng, P. Y. (2017). Simple smartphone-based guiding system for visually impaired people. Sensors (Basel), 17(6), 1371. doi:10.339017061371 PMI*D:28608811*

Lin, T. Y., Maire, M., Belongie, S., Hays, J., Perona, P., Ramanan, D., ... Zitnick, C. L. (2014, September). Microsoft coco: Common objects in context. In European conference on computer vision (pp. 740-755*). Springer.*

*Neubeck, A., & Van Goo*l, L. (2006, August). Efficient non-maximum suppression. In 18th International Conference on Pattern Recogn*ition (ICPR'06) (Vol. 3, pp. 850-855). IEEE. 10.1109/ICPR.2006.*479

Rahman, M. A., & Wang, Y. (2016, December). Optimizing intersection-over-union in deep neural networks for image segmentation. In International symposium on visual computing *(pp. 234-244). Springer. 10.1007/978-3-319-*50835-1_22

Redmon, J., & Farhadi, A. (2018). Yolov3: An incremental improvement. arXiv *preprint arXiv:1804.02767*

Ren, S., He, K., Girshick, R., & Sun, J. (2015). Faster r-cnn: Towards real-time object detection with region proposal networks. In Advances in neural information processing systems (pp. 91-99). Academic Press.

Rodríguez-Fuentes, L. J., Peñagarikano, M., Varona, A., & Bordel, G. (2018). GTTS-EHU Systems for the Albayzin 2018 Search on Speech Evaluation. In IberSPEECH (pp. 249-253). Academic Press.

Zhao, X., Zhao, C., Zhu, Y., Tang, M., & Wang, J. (2018, September). Improved Single Shot Object Detector Using Enhanced Features and Predicting Heads. In 2018 IEEE Fourth International *Conference on Multimedia Big Data (BigMM) (pp. 1-5). IEEE. 10.1109/BigMM.*2018.8499089

Compilation of References

(2006). Words, Parts of Speech, and Morphology. InNugues, P. M. (Ed.), *An Introduction to Language Processing with Perl and Prolog: An Outline of Theories, Implementation, and Application with Special Consideration of English, French, and German* (pp. 113–145). Berlin: Springer Berlin Heidelberg. doi:10.1007/3-540-34336-9_5

3. rd Generation Partnership Project; Technical Specification Group Services and System Aspects; Release 15 Description; 3GPP TR 21.915 V15.0.0 (2019-09)

3. rd Generation Partnership Project; Technical Specification Group Services and System Aspects; Study of Enablers for Network Automation for 5G (Release 16) 3GPP TR 23.791 V16.0.0 (2018-12).

A Complete Guide to k-Nearest Neighbors with applications in Python and R. (2017). Retrieved from http://www.kevinzakka.github.io/2016/07/13/k-nearest-neighbor/

Abadi, M., Barham, P., Chen, J., Chen, Z., Davis, A., Dean, J., . . . Kudlur, M. (2016). Tensorflow: A system for large-scale machine learning. In *12th {USENIX} Symposium on Operating Systems Design and Implementation ({OSDI} 16)* (pp. 265-283). Academic Press.

Abbasi, A., Chen, H., & Salem, A. (2008). Sentiment analysis in multiple languages: Feature selection for opinion classification in web forums. *ACM Transactions on Information Systems, 26*(3), 12. doi:10.1145/1361684.1361685

Abe, S. (2005). *Support vector machines for pattern classification* (Vol. 2). London: Springer.

Adeborna, E., & Siau, K. (2014, July). *An Approach to Sentiment Analysis-the Case of Airline Quality Rating*. PACIS.

Aggarwal, M., & Madhukar, M. (2017). IBM's Watson Analytics for Health Care: A Miracle Made True. In Cloud Computing Systems and Applications in Healthcare (pp. 117-134). IGI Global. doi:10.4018/978-1-5225-1002-4.ch007

Aggarwal, V. (2019). *Indian Healthcare Industry Analysis*. Retrieved from https://www.ibef.org/industry/healthcare-presentation

Aggarwal, C. C. (2011). An introduction to social network data analytics. In *Social network data analytics* (pp. 1–15). Boston, MA: Springer. doi:10.1007/978-1-4419-8462-3_1

Aguado, B. A., Grim, J. C., Rosales, A. M., Watson-Capps, J. J., & Anseth, K. S. (2018). Engineering precision biomaterials for personalized medicine. *Science Translational Medicine, 10*(424).

Ahlgren, B., Hidell, M., & Ngai, E. C.-H. (2016, November-December). Internet of Things for Smart Cities: Interoperability and Open Data. *IEEE Internet Computing, 20*(6), 52–56. doi:10.1109/MIC.2016.124

Ahuja & Solanki. (2019). Movie Recommender System Using K-Means Clustering AND K-Nearest Neighbor. In *9th International Conference on Cloud Computing, Data Science & Engineering*. Amity University.

Ahuja, R., Nayyar, A., & Solanki, A. (2019). Movie Recommender System Using K-Means Clustering AND K-Nearest Neighbor. In *Confluence-2019: 9th International Conference on Cloud Computing, Data Science & Engineering*. Amity University. DOI: 10.1109/CONFLUENCE.2019.8776969

Airoldi, E., Bai, X., & Padman, R. (2004, August). Markov blankets and meta-heuristics search: Sentiment extraction from unstructured texts. In *International Workshop on Knowledge Discovery on the Web* (pp. 167-187). Springer.

Aizerman, M., Braverman, E., & Rozonoer, L. (1964). Theoretical foundations of the potential function method in pattern recognition learning. *Autom. Rem. Cont.*, 821–837.

Akamine, M., & Ajmera, J. (2012). Decision tree-based acoustic models for speech recognition. *EURASIP Journal on Audio, Speech, and Music Processing*, *2012*(1), 10. doi:10.1186/1687-4722-2012-10

Albadvi, A., & Shahbazi, M. (2009). A hybrid recommendation technique based on product category attributes. *Expert Systems with Applications*, *36*(9), 11480–11488. doi:10.1016/j.eswa.2009.03.046

Albayrak, S. V. (2003). Unsupervised Clustering Methods for Medical Data: An Application to Thyroid Gland Data. In *Proceedings of Joint International Conference of ICANN/ICONIP*. Istanbul, Turkey: ICANN. 10.1007/3-540-44989-2_83

Alemzadeh, H., & Devarakonda, M. (2017, February). An NLP-based cognitive system for disease status identification in electronic health records. In *2017 IEEE EMBS International Conference on Biomedical & Health Informatics (BHI)* (pp. 89-92). IEEE. 10.1109/BHI.2017.7897212

Alexandre-Cortizo, E., Rosa-Zurera, M., & Lopez-Ferreras, F. (2005, November). Application of fisher linear discriminant analysis to speech/music classification. In *EUROCON 2005-The International Conference on Computer as a Tool* (Vol. 2, pp. 1666-1669). IEEE.

Al-Garadi, Ali, Mohamed, Al-Ali, Du, & Guizani. (2018). *A Survey of Machine and Deep Learning Methods for Internet of Things (IoT) Security*. CoRR abs/1807.11023

Alkhodair, S. A., Ding, S. H. H., Fung, B. C. M., & Liu, J. (in press). Detecting breaking news rumors of emerging topics in social media. *Information Processing & Management*. doi:10.1016/j.ipm.2019.02.016

Allen, H. V., Terry, S. C., & De Bruin, D. W. (1989). Accelerometer systems with self-testable features. *Sensors and Actuators*, *20*(1-2), 153–161. doi:10.1016/0250-6874(89)87113-6

Almasri, M., Berrut, C., & Chevallet, J. P. (2016). A Comparison of Deep Learning Based Query Expansion with Pseudo relevance Feedback and Mutual Information. *European Conference on Information Retrieval*, 709–715. 10.1007/978-3-319-30671-1_57

Almayan, H., & Al Mayyan, W. (2016, October). Improving accuracy of students' final grade prediction model using PSO. In *2016 6th International Conference on Information Communication and Management (ICICM)* (pp. 35-39). IEEE.

Alpaydin, E. (2009). *Introduction to Machine Learning* (2nd ed.). Cambridge, MA: MIT Press.

Alpaydin, E. (2009). *Introduction to machine learning*. MIT Press.

Alsheikh, M.A., Lin, S., Niyato, D., & Tan, H.-P. (2018). Machine Learning in wireless sensor networks: Algorithms, strategies, and applications. *IEEE Communications Surveys & Tutorials*, *16*(4), 1996-2018.

Alzubi, J., Nayyar, A., & Kumar, A. (2018). Machine learning from theory to algorithms: an overview. *Journal of Physics: Conference*. Retrieved from iopscience.iop.org

Alzubi, J., Nayyar, A., & Kumar, A. (2018). Machine learning from theory to algorithms: An overview. *Journal of Physics: Conference Series*, *1142*, 12012. doi:10.1088/1742-6596/1142/1/012012

Amati, G., & Rijsbergen, C. J. V. (2002). Probabilistic models of information retrieval based on measuring the divergence from randomness. *ACM Transactions on Information Systems*, *20*(4), 357–389. doi:10.1145/582415.582416

Amplayo, R. K., & Song, M. (2017). An adaptable fine-grained sentiment analysis for summarization of multiple short online reviews. *Data & Knowledge Engineering*, *110*, 54–67. doi:10.1016/j.datak.2017.03.009

Analytics (ANAL). (n.d.). Retrieved from http://pages.cs.wisc.edu/~jerryzhu/cs540/handouts/dt.pdf

Analytics process (AP). (n.d.). Retrieved from https://www.iss.nus.edu.sg/community/newsroom/news-detail/2016/06/24/the-7-step-business-analytics-process

Analytics, B. D. (2018). *Big Data Analytics | IBM Analytics*. Retrieved from https://www.ibm.com/analytics/hadoop/big-data-analytics

Anami, B. S., Wadawadagi, R. S., & Pagi, V. B. (2014). Machine learning techniques in web content mining: A comparative analysis. *Journal of Information & Knowledge Management*, *13*(1), 1–14. doi:10.1142/S0219649214500051

Anand Kumar, M., Singh, S., Kavirajan, B., & Soman, K. P. (2018). Shared Task on Detecting Paraphrases in Indian Languages (DPIL): An Overview. Lecture Notes in Computer Science, 10478, 128-140.

Anand Kumar, M., Singh, S., Kavirajan, B., & Soman, K. P. (1737). DPIL@ FIRE 2016: Overview of Shared Task on Detecting Paraphrases in Indian Languages (DPIL). *CEUR Workshop Proceedings*, 233–238.

Angeline, D. M. D. (2013). Association rule generation for student performance analysis using apriori algorithm. *The SIJ Transactions on Computer Science Engineering & its Applications (CSEA)*, *1*(1), 12-16.

Anjaria, M., & Gudetti, R. M. R. (2014). A novel sentiment analysis of social networks using supervised learning. *Social Network Analysis and Mining*, *4*(3), 181–193. doi:10.100713278-014-0181-9

Anusuya, M. A., & Katti, S. K. (2011). Classification Techniques used in Speech Recognition Applications: A Review. *Int. J. Comp. Tech. Appl*, *2*(4), 910–954.

Anvik, J., Hiew, L., & Murphy, G. C. (2006). Who should fix this bug? *Proceedings of the 28th international conference on Software engineering*.

Appel, O., Chiclana, F., Carter, J., & Fujita, H. (2016). A hybrid approach to the sentiment analysis problem at the sentence level. *Knowledge-Based Systems*, *108*, 110–124. doi:10.1016/j.knosys.2016.05.040

Araque, O., Corcuera-Platas, I., Sanchez-Rada, J. F., & Iglesias, C. A. (2017). Enhancing deep learning sentiment analysis with ensemble techniques in social applications. *Expert Systems with Applications*, *77*, 236–246. doi:10.1016/j.eswa.2017.02.002

Arbelaitz, O., Gurrutxaga, I., Lojo, A., Muguerza, J., Maria, J., & Perona, P. I. (2013). Web usage and content mining to extract knowledge for modeling the users of the Bidasoa Turismo website and to adapt it. *Expert Systems with Applications*, *40*(18), 7478–7491. doi:10.1016/j.eswa.2013.07.040

Ari, S. (2019). An overview of the research work on multispectral imaging, hand gesture recognition, EEG and ECG signal processing. *CSI Transactions on ICT*, 1–5.

Arora, Y., Singhal, A., & Bansal, A. (2014). Prediction & warning: A method to improve student's performance. *Software Engineering Notes*, *39*(1), 1–5. doi:10.1145/2557833.2557842

Arras, L., Montavon, G., Müller, K.R., & Samek, W. (2017). *Explaining recurrent neural network predictions in sentiment analysis*. Academic Press.

Asadi, A. (2018). FML: Fast machine learning for 5G mmWave vehicular communications. *IEEE Int. Conf. on Computer Communications (INFOCOM)*, 1-9.

Asif, M., Arshad, M.R., & Wilson, P.A. (2005). AGV Guidance System: An Application of Simple Active Contour for Visual Tracking. *Proceeding World Academy of Science, Engineering and Technology, 6*, 74–77.

Aşkın, A., Atar, E., Koçyiğit, H., & Tosun, A. (2018). Effects of Kinect-based virtual reality game training on upper extremity motor recovery in chronic stroke. *Somatosensory & Motor Research, 35*(1), 25–32. doi:10.1080/08990220.2018.1444599 PMID:29529919

Aslam, J. A., Popa, R. A., & Rivest, R. L. (2007). On Estimating the Size and Confidence of a Statistical Audit. *EVT, 7*, 8.

Association (ASSO). (n.d.). Retrieved from https://searchbusinessanalytics.techtarget.com/definition/association-rules-in-data-mining

Asuncion, A., & Newman, D. (2007). *UCI machine learning repository*. Retrieved from https://archive.ics.uci.edu/ml/index.php

Atan, O., Jordon, J., & van der Schaar, M. (2018, April). Deep-treat: Learning optimal personalized treatments from observational data using neural networks. *Thirty-Second AAAI Conference on Artificial Intelligence.*

Athitsos, V., & Sclaroff, S. (2005). Boosting nearest neighbor classifiers for multiclass recognition. In *Computer Vision and Pattern Recognition-Workshops, 2005. CVPR Workshops. IEEE Computer Society Conference on* (p. 45). IEEE.

Augarten, S. (1983). *State of the Art: A Photographic History of the Integrated Circuit*. New Haven, CT: Ticknor & Fields.

Awan, D. A. (2018). Detection for 5G-NOMA: An online adaptive machine learning approach. *IEEE Int. Conf. on Communications (ICC)*, 1-6.

Awwalu, J., Garba, A. G., Ghazvini, A., & Atuah, R. (2015). Artificial intelligence in personalized medicine application of AI algorithms in solving personalized medicine problems. *International Journal of Computer Theory and Engineering, 7*(6), 439–443. doi:10.7763/IJCTE.2015.V7.999

Ayer, T., & Chen, Q. (2018). Personalized medicine. Handbook of Healthcare Analytics: Theoretical Minimum for Conducting 21st Century Research on Healthcare Operations, 109-135.

Ayoubi. (2018). Machine Learning for Cognitive Network Management. IEEE Communications Magazine, 56(1), 158-165. doi:10.1109/MCOM.2018.1700560

Azarbonyad, H., Shakery, A., & Faili, H. (2019). A Learning to Rank Approach for Cross-Language Information Retrieval Exploiting Multiple Translation Resources. *Natural Language Engineering*, 1–22.

Aziz, M. V. G., Hindersah, H., & Prihatmanto, A. S. (2017). Implementation of vehicle detection algorithm for self-driving car on toll road cipularang using Python language. *2017 4th International Conference on Electric Vehicular Technology (ICEVT)*, 149-153. 10.1109/ICEVT.2017.8323551

Azuaje, F., Dubitzky, W., Black, N., & Adamson, K. (2000). Discovering relevance knowledge in data: A Growing cell Structures approach. *IEEE Transactions on Systems, Man, and Cybernetics. Part B, Cybernetics, 30*(3), 448–460. doi:10.1109/3477.846233 PMID:18252376

Baccianella, S., Esuli, A., & Sebastiani, F. (2010, May). Sentiwordnet 3.0: an enhanced lexical resource for sentiment analysis and opinion mining. In Lrec (Vol. 10, No. 2010, pp. 2200-2204). Academic Press.

Baccianella, S., Esuli, A., & Sebastiani, F. (2010). Sentiwordnet 3.0: an enhanced lexical resource for sentiment analysis and opinion mining. *Proc. of the Annual Conference on Language Resources and Evaluation*, 2200–2204.

Badjatiya, P., Gupta, S., Gupta, M., & Varma, V. (2017). Deep learning for hate speech detection in tweets. *Proceedings of the 26th International Conference on World Wide Web Companion*, 759-760. 10.1145/3041021.3054223

Bahdanau, D., Cho, K., & Bengio, Y. (2014). *Neural Machine Translation by Jointly Learning to Align and Translate.* arXiv e-prints, arXiv:1409.0473

Bahl, L. R., Jelinek, F., & Mercer, R. L. (1983). A maximum likelihood approach to continuous speech recognition. *IEEE Transactions on Pattern Analysis and Machine Intelligence*, PAMI-5(2), 179–190. doi:10.1109/TPAMI.1983.4767370 PMID:21869099

Bai, X. (2011). Predicting consumer sentiments from online text. *Decision Support Systems*, 50(4), 732–742. doi:10.1016/j.dss.2010.08.024

Balabanović, M., & Shoham, Y. (1997). Fab: Content-based, collaborative recommendation. *Communications of the ACM*, 40(3), 66–72. doi:10.1145/245108.245124

Balaji, S. N., Paul, P. V., & Saravanan, R. (2017, April). Survey on sentiment analysis based stock prediction using big data analytics. In *2017 Innovations in Power and Advanced Computing Technologies (i-PACT)* (pp. 1-5). IEEE.

Balakrishnan, A. (2009). Development of an ontology of learning strategies and its application to generate open learner models. *IEEE Proceedings of the 8th International Conference on Machine Learning and Applications*. 10.1109/ICMLA.2009.58

Balazinski, M., Czogala, E., Jemielniak, K., & Leski, J. (2002). Tool condition monitoring using artificial intelligence methods. *Engineering Applications of Artificial Intelligence*, 15(1), 73–80. doi:10.1016/S0952-1976(02)00004-0

Banerjee, S., Cukic, B., & Adjeroh, D. (2012). *Automated duplicate bug report classification using subsequence matching.* Paper presented at the 2012 IEEE 14th International Symposium on High-Assurance Systems Engineering. 10.1109/HASE.2012.38

Banerjee, S., Majumder, S., & Varma, A. (2017). A Placement Optimization Technique for 3D IC. *2017 7th International Symposium on Embedded Computing and System Design (ISED)*. 10.1109/ISED.2017.8303930

Banfield, R. E., Hall, L. O., Bowyer, K. W., & Kegelmeyer, W. P. (2007). A comparison of decision tree ensemble creation techniques. *IEEE Transactions on Pattern Analysis and Machine Intelligence*, 29(1), 173–180. doi:10.1109/TPAMI.2007.250609 PMID:17108393

Barreiro, A. (2009). *Make it simple with paraphrases: Automated paraphrasing for authoring aids and machine translation* (Doctoral dissertation). Universidade do Porto.

Barrón-Cedeño, A., Vila, M., Martí, M. A., & Rosso, P. (2013). Plagiarism meets paraphrasing: Insights for the next generation in automatic plagiarism detection. *Computational Linguistics*, 39(4), 917–947. doi:10.1162/COLI_a_00153

Bauer, E., & Kohavi, R. (1999). An empirical comparison of voting classification algorithms: Bagging, boosting, and variants. *Machine Learning*, 36(1-2), 105–139. doi:10.1023/A:1007515423169

Bauer, F., Pereverzev, S., & Rosasco, L. (2007). On regularization algorithms in learning theory. *Journal of Complexity*, 23(1), 52–72. doi:10.1016/j.jco.2006.07.001

Bawa, V. S., & Kumar, V. (2019). Linearized sigmoidal activation: A novel activation function with tractable nonlinear characteristics to boost representation capability. *Expert Systems with Applications*, 120, 346–356. doi:10.1016/j.eswa.2018.11.042

Bayat, A., Pomplun, M., & Tran, D. A. (2014). A study on human activity recognition using accelerometer data from smartphones. *Procedia Computer Science*, *34*, 450–457. doi:10.1016/j.procs.2014.07.009

Bello-Orgaz, G., Jung, J. J., & Camacho, D. (2016). Social big data: Recent achievements and new challenges. *Information Fusion*, *28*, 45–59. doi:10.1016/j.inffus.2015.08.005

Benson, E., & Haghighi Barzilay, R. (2011). Event discovery in social media feeds. *Proc. of the 49th Annual Meeting of the Association for Computational Linguistics: Human Language technologies*, *1*, 389-398.

Beringer, J. H. E. (2007). An Efficient Algorithm for Instance-Based Learning on Data Streams. Advances in Data Mining. Theoretical Aspects and Applications, 4597. doi:10.1007/978-3-540-73435-2_4

Bernhard, D., & Gurevych, I. (2008, June). Answering learners' questions by retrieving question paraphrases from social Q&A sites. In *Proceedings of the third workshop on innovative use of NLP for building educational applications* (pp. 44-52). Association for Computational Linguistics. 10.3115/1631836.1631842

Bertoncello & Wee. (2015). *Ten Ways Autonomous Driving Could Redefine the Automotive World.* Retrieved from http://www.mckinsey.com/insights/ automotive_and_assembly/ten_ways_autonomous_driving_could_redefine_the_automotive_world

Bespalov, D., Bai, B., Qi, Y., & Shokoufandeh, A. (2011, October). Sentiment classification based on supervised latent n-gram analysis. In *Proceedings of the 20th ACM international conference on Information and knowledge management* (pp. 375-382). ACM. 10.1145/2063576.2063635

Bettenburg, N., Just, S., Schröter, A., Weiss, C., Premraj, R., & Zimmermann, T. (2008). What makes a good bug report? *Proceedings of the 16th ACM SIGSOFT International Symposium on Foundations of software engineering.* 10.1145/1453101.1453146

Beyer, M. A. L. D. (2012). The Importance Of 'Big Data': A Definition. Stamford, CT: Gartner.

Bhagat, R., & Hovy, E. (2013). What is a paraphrase? *Computational Linguistics*, *39*(3), 463–472. doi:10.1162/COLI_a_00166

Bhambare, R. R., Koul, A., Bilal, S., & Pandey, S. (2014). Smart vision system for blind. *International Journal of Engineering and Computer Science*, *3*(5), 5790–5795.

Bhargava, R., Sharma, G., & Sharma, Y. (2017, July). Deep Paraphrase Detection in Indian Languages. In *Proceedings of the 2017 IEEE/ACM International Conference on Advances in Social Networks Analysis and Mining 2017* (pp. 1152-1159). ACM. 10.1145/3110025.3122119

Bhattacharjee, U., & Sarmah, K. (2013, March). Language identification system using MFCC and prosodic features. In *2013 International Conference on Intelligent Systems and Signal Processing (ISSP)*, (pp. 194-197). IEEE. 10.1109/ISSP.2013.6526901

Bhattacharyya, S., Konar, A., Tibarewala, D. N., Khasnobish, A., & Janarthanan, R. (2014). Performance analysis of ensemble methods for multi-class classification of motor imagery EEG signal. In *Control, Instrumentation, Energy and Communication (CIEC), 2014 International Conference on* (pp. 712–716). IEEE. 10.1109/CIEC.2014.6959183

Biao, M. A., Wensheng, X. U., & Songlin, W. (2013). A robot control system based on gesture recognition using Kinect. *Indonesian Journal of Electrical Engineering and Computer Science*, *11*(5), 2605–2611.

Big data (BD). (n.d.). Retrieved from https://journalofbigdata.springeropen.com/articles /10.1186/s40537-015-0030-3

Big data (BD2). (n.d.). Retrieved from https://klantenffabriek.nl/wp-cgontent/upload/2017/06/bigdata_literature_review.pdf

Bishop, C. M. (1995). *Neural networks for pattern recognition.* Oxford University Press.

Bitouk, D., Verma, R., & Nenkova, A. (2010). Class-level spectral features for emotion recognition. *Speech Communication, 52*(7-8), 613–625. doi:10.1016/j.specom.2010.02.010 PMID:23794771

Bjaili, H., Daqrouq, K., & Al-Hmouz, R. (2014). Speaker Identification Using Bayesian Algorithm. *Trends in Applied Sciences Research, 9*(8), 472–479. doi:10.3923/tasr.2014.472.479

Blaschke, T., Olivecrona, M., Engkvist, O., Bajorath, J., & Chen, H. (2018). Application of Generative Autoencoder in De Novo Molecular Design. *Molecular Informatics, 37*(1-2). doi:10.1002/minf.201700123 PMID:29235269

Blitzer, J., Dredze, M., & Pereira, F. (2007, June). Biographies, bollywood, boom-boxes and blenders: Domain adaptation for sentiment classification. In *Proceedings of the 45th annual meeting of the association of computational linguistics* (pp. 440-447). Academic Press.

Bogale, T. E. (2018). *Machine intelligence techniques for next-generation context-aware wireless networks. ITU Journal,* 1–11.

Bogani, G., Ditto, A., Martinelli, F., Signorelli, M., Chiappa, V., Leone Roberti Maggiore, U., ... Lorusso, D. (2019). Artificial intelligence estimates the impact of human papillomavirus types in influencing the risk of cervical dysplasia recurrence: Progress toward a more personalized approach. *European Journal of Cancer Prevention, 28*(2), 81–86. doi:10.1097/CEJ.0000000000000432 PMID:29360648

Bojkovic, Z., & Milovanovic, D. (2017). A technology vision of the Fifth Generation (5G) wireless mobile networks. *Lecture Notes in Electrical Engineering, 416*, 25–43.

Bojkovski, N., & Madevska-Bogdanova, A. (2012). *Machine Learning Algorithms for Player Satisfaction Optimization.* Retrieved from http://ciit.finki.ukim.mk/data/papers/9CiiT/9CiiT-30.pdf

Bollegala, D., Weir, D., & Carroll, J. (2012). Cross-domain sentiment classification using a sentiment sensitive thesaurus. *IEEE Transactions on Knowledge and Data Engineering, 25*(8), 1719–1731. doi:10.1109/TKDE.2012.103

Bonnechère, B., Jansen, B., Omelina, L., & Van Sint, J. (2016). The use of commercial video games in rehabilitation: A systematic review. *International Journal of Rehabilitation Research. Internationale Zeitschrift fur Rehabilitationsforschung. Revue Internationale de Recherches de Readaptation, 39*(4), 277–290. doi:10.1097/MRR.0000000000000190 PMID:27508968

Bontcheva, K., Derczynski, L., Funk, A., Greenwood, M. A., Maynard, D., & Aswani, N. (2013). TwitIE: a fully-featured information extraction pipeline for microblog text. *Proc. of the International Conference On Recent Advances In Natural Language Processing,* 83-90. *doi:*10.6084/m9.figshare.1003767.v2

Bouazizi, M., & Otsuki, T. (2016). A pattern-based approach for sarcasm detection on twitter. *IEEE Access: Practical Innovations, Open Solutions, 4*, 5477–5488. doi:10.1109/ACCESS.2016.2594194

Boumediene, M., Ouamri, A., & Dahnoun, N. (2007). Lane Boundary Detection and Tracking using NNF and HMM Approaches. *Proceeding 2007 IEEE Intelligent Vehicles Symposium,* 1107–1111. 10.1109/IVS.2007.4290265

Bourlard, H. A., & Morgan, N. (2012). *Connectionist speech recognition: a hybrid approach* (Vol. 247). Springer Science & Business Media.

Bowring, J. F., Rehg, J. M., & Harrold, M. J. (2004). *Active learning for automatic classification of software behavior.* Paper presented at the ACM SIGSOFT Software Engineering Notes. 10.1145/1007512.1007539

Breiman, L. (1996). Bagging predictors. *Machine Learning, 24*(2), 123–140. doi:10.1007/BF00058655

Breiman, L. (2001). Random forests. *Machine Learning, 45*(1), 5–32. doi:10.1023/A:1010933404324

Brigl, B. (2006). Decision support, knowledge representation and management: A broad methodological spectrum. Findings from the Decision Support, Knowledge Representation and Management. *Yearbook of Medical Informatics, 45*(01), 81–83. PMID:17051299

Bringmann, B., Berlingerio, M., Bonchi, F., & Gionis, A. (2010). *Learning and Predicting the Evolution of Social Networks* (Vol. 25). Academic Press.

Brown, G. (2010). Ensemble learning. Encyclopedia of Machine Learning, 312-320.

Brownlee, J. (2015). *Basic Concepts in Machine Learning.* Retrieved from https://bit.ly/2HT3qTC

Broy, M., Kruger, I. H., Pretschner, A., & Salzmann, C. (2007). Engineering Automotive Software. *Proceedings of the IEEE, 95*(2), 356–373. doi:10.1109/JPROC.2006.888386

Bryce, S., Pasham, A., Huong, P., Yazeed, A., & Artur, W. (2019). Training a Remote-Control Car to Autonomously Lane-Follow using End-to-End Neural Networks. *53rd Annual Conference on Information Sciences and Systems (CISS).*

Bügel, U., & Zielinski, A. (2013). Multilingual analysis of twitter news in support of mass emergency events. *International Journal of Information Systems for Crisis Response and Management, 5*(1), 77–85. doi:10.4018/jiscrm.2013010105

Burdea, G. C., & Coiffet, P. (2003). *Virtual reality technology.* John Wiley & Sons. doi:10.1162/105474603322955950

Callison-Burch, C., Koehn, P., & Osborne, M. (2006, June). Improved statistical machine translation using paraphrases. In *Proceedings of the main conference on Human Language Technology Conference of the North American Chapter of the Association of Computational Linguistics* (pp. 17-24). Association for Computational Linguistics.

Cambria, E. (2016). Affective computing and sentiment analysis. *IEEE Intelligent Systems, 31*(2), 102–107. doi:10.1109/MIS.2016.31

Campbell, W. M., Campbell, J. P., Reynolds, D. A., Jones, D. A., & Leek, T. R. (2004). Phonetic speaker recognition with support vector machines. In Advances in neural information processing systems (pp. 1377-1384). Academic Press.

Campos, L. M. D. (2006). A scoring function for learning Bayesian networks based on mutual information and conditional independence tests. *Journal of Machine Learning Research, 7*(Oct), 2149–2187.

Cárdenas, P., Theodoropoulos, G., Obara, B., & Kureshi, I. (2018). A Conceptual Framework for Social Movements Analytics for National Security. Lecture Notes in Computer Science, 10860. doi:10.1007/978-3-319-93698-7_23

Castellano, G., Kessous, L., & Caridakis, G. (2008). Emotion recognition through multiple modalities: face, body gesture, speech. In *Affect and emotion in human-computer interaction* (pp. 92–103). Springer. doi:10.1007/978-3-540-85099-1_8

Catuhe, D. (2012). *Programming with the Kinect for Windows software development kit.* Pearson Education.

Cawley, G. C. (2006, July). Leave-one-out cross-validation based model selection criteria for weighted LS-SVMs. In *The 2006 IEEE international joint conference on neural network proceedings* (pp. 1661–1668). IEEE.

Cayamcela, M. E. M., & Lim, W. (2018). Artificial intelligence in 5G technology: A survey. *Proc. Int. Conf. on Information and Communication Technology Convergence (ICTC).*

Ceron, A., Curini, L., & Iacus, S. M. (2015). Using sentiment analysis to monitor electoral campaigns: Method matters-evidence from the United States and Italy. *Social Science Computer Review, 33*(1), 3–20. doi:10.1177/0894439314521983

Chaffey, D. (2016). *Global social media research summary 2016.* Smart Insights: Social Media Marketing.

Chalothom, T., & Ellman, J. (2015). Simple approaches of sentiment analysis via ensemble learning. In Information science and applications. Springer. doi:10.1007/978-3-662-46578-3_74

Chang, Y. C., Chang, Y. W., Wu, G. M., & Wu, S. W. (2000). B*tree: a new representations for non slicing floorplans. *Proc. ACM/IEEE Design Automation Conf.*, 458–463.

Charette, R. N. (1989). *Software engineering risk analysis and management.* McGraw-Hill.

Charniak, E. (1997). Statistical techniques for natural language parsing. *AI Magazine, 18*(4), 33–44.

Cha, S., Abusharekh, A., & Abidi, S. S. (2015, March). Towards a'Big'Health Data Analytics Platform. In *2015 IEEE First International Conference on Big Data Computing Service and Applications* (pp. 233-241). IEEE. 10.1109/BigDataService.2015.13

Chaturvedi, K., & Singh, V. (2012a). *Determining bug severity using machine learning techniques.* Paper presented at the 2012 CSI Sixth International Conference on Software Engineering (CONSEG). 10.1109/CONSEG.2012.6349519

Chaturvedi, I., Ong, Y.-S., Tsang, I. W., Welsch, R. E., & Cambria, E. (2016). Learning word dependencies in text by means of a deep recurrent belief network. *Knowledge-Based Systems, 108*, 144–154. doi:10.1016/j.knosys.2016.07.019

Chaturvedi, I., Ragusa, E., Gastaldo, P., Zunino, R., & Cambria, E. (2018). Bayesian network based extreme learning machine for subjectivity detection. *Journal of the Franklin Institute, 355*(4), 1780–1797. doi:10.1016/j.jfranklin.2017.06.007

Chaturvedi, K., & Singh, V. (2012b). An empirical comparison of machine learning techniques in predicting the bug severity of open and closed source projects. *International Journal of Open Source Software and Processes, 4*(2), 32–59. doi:10.4018/jossp.2012040103

Chelladurai, H., Jain, V. K., & Vyas, N. S. (2008). Development of a cutting tool condition monitoring system for high speed turning operation by vibration and strain analysis. *International Journal of Advanced Manufacturing Technology, 37*(5-6), 471–485. doi:10.100700170-007-0986-z

Chen, C., Liu, K., Jafari, R., & Kehtarnavaz, N. (2014, August). Home-based senior fitness test measurement system using collaborative inertial and depth sensors. In *2014 36th Annual International Conference of the IEEE Engineering in Medicine and Biology Society* (pp. 4135-4138). IEEE. 10.1109/EMBC.2014.6944534

Chen, J., & Chen, J. (2010). A hybrid evolution algorithm for VLSI floorplanning. IEEE Design Automation Conference in Computational Intelligence and Software Engineering (CISE), 1–4. doi:10.1109/CISE.2010.5676951

Chen, Liu, Zhu, & Zhu. (2017). An adaptive hybrid memetic algorithm for thermal-aware non-slicing VLSI floor planning. *Integration, 58*, 245–252.

Chen, B., Sheridan, R. P., Hornak, V., & Voigt, J. H. (2012). Comparison of Random Forest and Pipeline Pilot Naive Bayes in Prospective QSAR Predictions. *Journal of Chemical Information and Modeling, 52*(3), 792–803. doi:10.1021/ci200615h PMID:22360769

Chen, C. C., & Tseng, Y. D. (2011). Quality evaluation of product reviews using an information quality framework. *Decision Support Systems, 50*(4), 755–768. doi:10.1016/j.dss.2010.08.023

Chen, C. P., & Zhang, C. Y. (2014). Data-intensive applications, challenges, techniques and technologies: A survey on Big Data. *Information Sciences, 275*, 314–347. doi:10.1016/j.ins.2014.01.015

Chen, C., Jafari, R., & Kehtarnavaz, N. (2015, September). UTD-MHAD: A multimodal dataset for human action recognition utilizing a depth camera and a wearable inertial sensor. In *2015 IEEE International conference on image processing (ICIP)* (pp. 168-172). IEEE. 10.1109/ICIP.2015.7350781

Chen, G., & Hou, R. (2007). A New Machine Double-Layer Learning Method and Its Application in non-Linear Time Series Forecasting. *Proceedings of the 2010 International Conference on Mechatronics and Automation (ICMA)*. 10.1109/ICMA.2007.4303646

Chen, H., Sun, M., Tu, C., Lin, Y., & Liu, Z. (2016). Neural sentiment classification with user and product attention. *Proceedings of the 2016 conference on empirical methods in natural language processing*, 1650-1659. 10.18653/v1/D16-1171

Chen, J. C., & Chen, J. C. (2005). An artificial-neural-networks-based in-process tool wear prediction system in milling operations. *International Journal of Advanced Manufacturing Technology*, 25(5-6), 427–434. doi:10.100700170-003-1848-y

Chen, J., & Zhu, W. (2010). A hybrid genetic algorithm for VLSI floorplanning. *IEEE Conference on Intelligent Computing and Intelligent Systems (ICIS)*, 2, 128–132.

Chen, T.-C., & Chang, Y.-W. (2006). Modern floor planning based on B* tree and fast simulated annealing. *IEEE Transactions on Computer-Aided Design of Integrated Circuits and Systems*, 25(4), 637–650. doi:10.1109/TCAD.2006.870076

Chen, T., Xu, R., He, Y., & Wang, X. (2017). Improving sentiment analysis via sentence type classification using BiLSTM-CRF and CNN. *Expert Systems with Applications*, 72, 221–230. doi:10.1016/j.eswa.2016.10.065

Chen, W., Ma, C., & Ma, L. (2009). Mining the customer credit using hybrid support vector machine technique. *Expert Systems with Applications*, 36(4), 7611–7616. doi:10.1016/j.eswa.2008.09.054

Chen, W., Zhang, X., Wang, T., Yang, B., & Li, Y. (2017). Opinion-aware knowledge graph for political ideology detection. *Proceedings of the Twenty-Sixth International Joint Conference on Artificial Intelligence (IJCAI-17)*, 3647-3653. 10.24963/ijcai.2017/510

Chen, X., Vorvoreanu, M., & Madhavan, K. (2014). Mining social media data for understanding students learning experiences. *IEEE Transactions on Learning Technologies*, 7(3), 246–259. doi:10.1109/TLT.2013.2296520

Chickering, D. M. (1996). *P Learning Bayesian networks is np-complete. In Learning from data* (pp. 121–130). Springer.

Chitra, P., & Vijaya, K. (2016), Evidence Based Health Care System. *Conference on Advances in EEICB*.

Cho, K., Merrienboer, B., Gulcehre, C., Bahdanau, D., Bougares, F., Schwenk, H., & Bengio, Y. (2014). *Learning Phrase Representations using RNN Encoder-Decoder for Statistical Machine Translation*. arXiv e-prints, arXiv:1406.1078

Choi, H. J., & Park, C. H. (2019). Emerging topic detection in Twitter stream based on high utility pattern mining. *Expert Systems with Applications*, 115, 27–36. doi:10.1016/j.eswa.2018.07.051

Cho, M., Liu, C., Kim, D. H., Lim, S. K., & Mukhopadhyay, S. (2011). Pre-Bond and Post-Bond Test and Signal Recovery Structure to Characterize and Repair TSV Defect Induced Signal Degradation in 3-D System. *IEEE Transactions on Components, Packaging, and Manufacturing Technology*, 1(11), 1718–1727. doi:10.1109/TCPMT.2011.2166961

Chopra, S., Auli, M., & Rush, A. M. (2016, 6). Abstractive Sentence Summarization with Attentive Recurrent Neural Networks. *Proceedings of the 2016 Conference of the North American Chapter of the Association for Computational Linguistics: Human Language Technologies*, 93-98. 10.18653/v1/N16-1012

Cho, S., Binsaeid, S., & Asfour, S. (2010). Design of multisensor fusion-based tool condition monitoring system in end milling. *International Journal of Advanced Manufacturing Technology*, 46(5-8), 681–694. doi:10.100700170-009-2110-z

Chris. (2011). The google self-driving car project. *Talk at Robotics: Science and Systems*.

Chung, J., Gulcehre, C., Cho, K., & Bengio, Y. (2014). *Empirical Evaluation of Gated Recurrent Neural Networks on Sequence Modeling*. arXiv e-prints, arXiv:1412.3555

Clinchant, S., & Gaussier, E. (2011). Retrieval constraints and word frequency distributions a log-logistic model for ir. *Inf. Retr.*, *14*(1), 5–25. doi:10.100710791-010-9143-7

Clough Bruce T. Metrics. (2002), Schmetrics! How The Heck Do You Determine a UAV's Autonomy Anyway? *Air Force Res. Libr.* Retrieved from http://www.dtic.mil/dtic/tr/fulltext/u2/ a515926.pdf

Collobert, R., Weston, J., Bottou, L., Karlen, M., Kavukcuoglu, K., & Kuksa, P. (2011). *Natural Language Processing (almost) from Scratch.* arXiv e-prints, arXiv:1103.0398

Collobert, R., & Bengio, S. (2004). Links between perceptrons, MLPs and SVMs. In *Proceedings of the twenty-first international conference on Machine learning (ICML '04)*. ACM. 10.1145/1015330.1015415

Conti, M., Dehghantanha, A., Franke, K., & Watson, S. (2018). Internet of Things security and forensics: Challenges and opportunities. *Future Generation Computer Systems*, *78*(Part 2), 544–546. doi:10.1016/j.future.2017.07.060

Corazza, A., Di Martino, S., Maggio, V., & Scanniello, G. (2011). Combining Machine Learning and Information Retrieval Techniques for Software Clustering. In A. Moschitti & R. Scandariato (Eds.), *Eternal Systems. EternalS, Communications in Computer and Information Science, 255* (pp. 42–60). Berlin, Heidelberg: Springer.

Cortés, G., Benitez, C., García, L., Alvarez, I., & Ibáñez, J. (2016). *A Comparative Study of Dimensionality Reduction Algorithms Applied to Volcano-Seismic Signals.* Academic Press.

Cote, D. (2018). Using Machine Learning in communication networks. *Journal of Optical Communications and Networking*, *10*(10), D100–D109. doi:10.1364/JOCN.10.00D100

Cruz, E. (2018). A Comprehensive Survey in Towards to Future FANETs. IEEE Latin America Transactions, 16(3), 876-884. doi:10.1109/TLA.2018.8358668

Cui, J. (2018). The application of machine learning in mmWave-NOMA systems. *IEEE Vehicular Technology Conference*, 1–6. 10.1109/VTCSpring.2018.8417523

Cunningham, H., Tablan, V., Roberts, A., & Bontcheva, K. (2013). Getting more out of biomedical documents with gate's full lifecycle open source text analytics. *PLoS Computational Biology*, *9*(2), e1002854. doi:10.1371/journal.pcbi.1002854 PMID:23408875

Currie, G., & Delles, C. (2018). Precision medicine and personalized medicine in cardiovascular disease. In *Sex-Specific Analysis of Cardiovascular Function* (pp. 589–605). Cham: Springer. doi:10.1007/978-3-319-77932-4_36

da Silva, N. F. F., Hruschka, E. R., & Hruschka, E. R. Jr. (2014). Tweet sentiment analysis with classifier ensembles. *Decision Support Systems*, *66*, 170–179. doi:10.1016/j.dss.2014.07.003

Danassis, P., Siozios, K., & Soudris, D. (2016). ANT3D: Simultaneous Partitioning and Placement for 3-D FPGAs based on Ant Colony Optimization. IEEE Embedded Systems Letters, 8(2).

Dang, Y., Zhang, Y., & Chen, H. (2009). A lexicon-enhanced method for sentiment classification: An experiment on online product reviews. *IEEE Intelligent Systems*, *25*(4), 46–53. doi:10.1109/MIS.2009.105

Dasgupta, A., & Deb, S. (2008). Telemedicine: a new horizon in public health in India. *Indian Journal of Community Medicine*, *33*(1), 3–8.

Dash, R., Risco-Martín, J. L., & Turuk, A. K. (2017). A Bio-Inspired Hybrid Thermal Management Approach for 3-D Network-on-Chip Systems. IEEE Transactions on Nanobioscience, 16(8).

Dashboards definition (DD). (n.d.). Retrieved from https://searchcio.techtarget.com/definition/dashboard

Das, S., & Pawar, C. S. (2016). Machine learning based algorithm for high efficiency video coding. Int. *Journal of Advances in Electronics and Computer Science*, *3*(7), 92–95.

Data analytic definition (DAD). (n.d.). Retrieved from https://www.techopedia.com/definition/26418/data-analytics

Data analytics (DA2). (n.d.). Retrieved from https://www.kdnuggets.com/2017/07/4-types-data-analytics.html

Data analytics applications (DAA). (n.d.). Retrieved from https://www.simplilearn.com/big-data-applications-in-industries-article

Data analytics definition (DAD2). (n.d.). Retrieved from https://searchbusinessanalytics.techtarget.com/definition/data-visualization

Data analytics importance (DAI). (n.d.). Retrieved from https://www.digitalvidya.com/blog/ reasons-data-analytics-important/

Data analytics importance (DAI2). (n.d.). Retrieved from https://peterjamesthomas.com/2017/01/10/alphabet-soup/

Data analytics in healthcare (DAH). (n.d.). Retrieved from https://www.healthcareitnews.com/news/5-ways-hospitals-can-use-data-analytics

Data analytics in retail (DAR). (n.d.). Retrieved from https://www.ibm.com/blogs/insights-on-business/consumer-products/2-5-quintillion-bytes-of-data-created-every-day-how-does-cpg-retail-manage-it/

Data analytics purpose (DAP). (n.d.). Retrieved from https://www.quora.com/What-is-the-purpose-of-data-analytics

Dave, K., Lawrence, S., & Pennock, D. M. (2003, May). Mining the peanut gallery: Opinion extraction and semantic classification of product reviews. In *Proceedings of the 12th international conference on World Wide Web* (pp. 519-528). ACM. 10.1145/775152.775226

David, R. (2014). Truth About Driverless Vehicles. *BBC*. Retrieved from http:// www.bbc.com/future/story/20141013-convoys-of-huge-zombie-trucks

Day, M. Y., & Lee, C. C. (2016). Deep learning for financial sentiment analysis on finance news providers. *2016 IEEE/ ACM International Conference on Advances in Social Networks Analysis and Mining*, 1127-1134. 10.1109/ASONAM.2016.7752381

De la Pena, D., Lara, J. A., Lizcano, D., Martínez, M. A., Burgos, C., & Campanario, M. L. (2017, May). Mining activity grades to model students' performance. In *2017 International Conference on Engineering & MIS (ICEMIS)* (pp. 1-6). IEEE. 10.1109/ICEMIS.2017.8272963

De Regge, M., Decoene, E., Eeckloo, K., & Van Hecke, A. (2019). Development and Evaluation of an Integrated Digital Patient Platform During Oncology Treatment. *Journal of Patient Experience*.

Dekhil, O., Hajjdiab, H., Shalaby, A., Ali, M. T., Ayinde, B., Switala, A., ... El-Baz, A. (2018). Using resting state functional MRI to build a personalized autism diagnosis system. *PLoS One*, *13*(10), e0206351. doi:10.1371/journal.pone.0206351 PMID:30379950

Demestichas, P., Georgakopoulos, A., Tsagkaris, K., & Kotrotsos, S. (2015). Intelligent 5G networks: Managing 5G wireless/mobile broadband. *IEEE Vehicular Technology Magazine*, *10*(3), 41–50. doi:10.1109/MVT.2015.2446419

Demir, S., El-Kahlout, I. D., Unal, E., & Kaya, H. (2012). *Turkish Paraphrase Corpus*. LREC.

Deng, X., Liu, Q., Deng, Y., & Mahadevan, S. (2016). An improved method to construct basic probability assignment based on the confusion matrix for classification problem. *Information Sciences*, *340*, 250–261. doi:10.1016/j.ins.2016.01.033

Department for Transport (DfT) and Centre for the Protection of National Infrastructure (CPNI). (2017). *The key principles of cyber security for connected and automated vehicles*. Technical report.

Department of Motor Vehicles (State of California). (2017). *Testing of Autonomous Vehicles*. Retrieved from https://www.dmv.ca.gov/portal/dmv/detail/vr/autonomous/testing

Derlatka, M., & Bogdan, M. (2015). Ensemble kNN classifiers for human gait recognition based on ground reaction forces. In *Human System Interactions (HSI), 2015 8th International Conference on* (pp. 88–93). IEEE. 10.1109/HSI.2015.7170648

Descriptive analytics (DA). (n.d.). Retrieved from https://www.investopedia.com/terms/d/descriptive-analytics.asp

Deshkar, S., Thanseeh, R. A., & Menon, V. G. (2017). A Review on IoT based m-Health Systems for Diabetes. *International Journal of Computer Science and Telecommunications, 8*(1), 13–18.

Dessì, D., Recupero, D. R., Fenu, G., & Consoli, S. (2019). A recommender system of medical reports leveraging cognitive computing and frame semantics. In *Machine Learning Paradigms* (pp. 7–30). Cham: Springer. doi:10.1007/978-3-319-94030-4_2

Devarakonda, M., & Tsou, C. H. (2015, March). Automated problem list generation from electronic medical records in IBM Watson. *Twenty-Seventh IAAI Conference*.

Devasia, T., Vinushree, T. P., & Hegde, V. (2016, March). Prediction of students performance using Educational Data Mining. In *2016 International Conference on Data Mining and Advanced Computing (SAPIENCE)* (pp. 91-95). IEEE. 10.1109/SAPIENCE.2016.7684167

Devijver, P. A., & Kittler, J. (Eds.). (2012). *Pattern recognition theory and applications* (Vol. 30). Springer Science & Business Media.

Dey, L., Chakraborty, S., Biswas, A., Bose, B., & Tiwari, S. (2016). *Sentiment analysis of review datasets using naive bayes and k-nn classifier.* arXiv preprint arXiv:1610.09982

Dey, N., Ashour, A. S., Shi, F., Fong, S. J., & João, M. R. S. (2018). Tavares, Medical cyber-physical systems: A survey. *Journal of Medical Systems, 42*(4), 74. doi:10.100710916-018-0921-x PMID:29525900

Dhunay, N. (n.d.). *Deep Learning and the human brain: Inspiration, not Limitation.* Retrieved from https://www.imaginea.com/sites/deep-learning-human-brain-inspiration-not-imitation/

Di Huang, Y. (2018). A Machine learning approach to MIMO communications. *IEEE Int. Conf. on Communications (ICC),* 1-6. 10.1109/ICC.2018.8422211

Diaz, F., Mitra, B., & Craswell, N. (2016). *Query expansion with locally-trained word embeddings.* arXiv preprint arXiv:1605.07891

Dietterich, T. G. (1998). Approximate statistical tests for comparing supervised classification learning algorithms. *Neural Computation, 10*(7), 1895–1923. doi:10.1162/089976698300017197 PMID:9744903

Dimla, D. E. Jr, Lister, P. M., & Leighton, N. J. (1997). Neural Network solutions to the Tool Condition Monitoring Problem in Metal cutting – A critical review of methods. *International Journal of Machine Tools & Manufacture, 37*(9), 1291–1241. doi:10.1016/S0890-6955(97)00020-5

Diomaiuta, C., Mercorella, M., Ciampi, M., & De Pietro, G. (2017, July). A novel system for the automatic extraction of a patient problem summary. In *2017 IEEE Symposium on Computers and Communications (ISCC)* (pp. 182-186). IEEE. 10.1109/ISCC.2017.8024526

Dix, A. (2009). Human-computer interaction. In *Encyclopedia of database systems* (pp. 1327–1331). Springer.

Dixit, V. V., Chand, S., & Nair, D. J. (2016). Autonomous vehicles: Disengagements, accidents and reaction times. *PLoS One*, *11*(12), 1–14. doi:10.1371/journal.pone.0168054 PMID:27997566

Doan, T., & Kalita, J. (2015). *Selecting Machine Learning Algorithms Using Regression Models*. Academic Press.

Dobrovsky, A., Borghoff, U. M., & Hofmann, M. (2019). Improving Adaptive Gameplay in Serious Games Through Interactive Deep Reinforcement Learning. In *Cognitive Infocommunications, Theory and Applications* (pp. 411–432). Cham: Springer. doi:10.1007/978-3-319-95996-2_19

Dolan, W. B., & Brockett, C. (2005, October). Automatically constructing a corpus of sentential paraphrases. *Proc. of IWP*.

Domingos, P., & Pazzani, M. (1998). *On the Optimality of the Simple Bayesian Classifier Under Zero-One Loss* (Vol. 29). Academic Press.

Dong, X., Xu, Y., Xu, Z., Huang, J., Lu, J., Zhang, C., & Lu, L. (2018). A Static Hand Gesture Recognition Model based on the Improved Centroid Watershed Algorithm and a Dual-Channel CNN. In *2018 24th International Conference on Automation and Computing (ICAC)* (pp. 1–6). IEEE. 10.23919/IConAC.2018.8749063

Donsa, K., Spat, S., Beck, P., Pieber, T. R., & Holzinger, A. (2015). Towards personalization of diabetes therapy using computerized decision support and machine learning: some open problems and challenges. In *Smart Health* (pp. 237–260). Cham: Springer. doi:10.1007/978-3-319-16226-3_10

Dornfeld, D. A. (1986). Acoustic Emission Monitoring for Untended Manufacturing. *Proceedings of Japan / USA Symposium on Flexible Automation.*

Drucker, H., Shahrary, B., & Gibbon, D. C. (2002). Support Vector Machines: Relevance Feedback and Information Retrieval. *Information Processing & Management*, *38*(3), 305–323. doi:10.1016/S0306-4573(01)00037-1

Du, Y., Cui, S., & Guo, S. (2009). *Applying Machine Learning in Game AI Design*. Retrieved from http://cs229.stanford.edu/proj2009/DuCuiGuo.pdf

Du, J., Xu, H., & Huang, X. (2014). Box office prediction based on microblog. *Expert Systems with Applications*, *41*(4), 1680–1689. doi:10.1016/j.eswa.2013.08.065

Du, P., Qu, X., Wei, T., Peng, C., Zhong, X., & Chen, C. (2018). Research on Small Size Object Detection in Complex Background. In *2018 Chinese Automation Congress (CAC)* (pp. 4216-4220). IEEE. 10.1109/CAC.2018.8623078

Duro, J. A., & de Oliveira, J. V. (2008, June). Particle swarm optimization applied to the chess game. In 2008 IEEE Congress on Evolutionary Computation (IEEE World Congress on Computational Intelligence) (pp. 3702-3709). IEEE.

Dykes, B. (2016). *Actionable Insights: The Missing Link Between Data And Business Value*. Retrieved from https://bit.ly/2WFek2z

Ecommerce (ECOM). (n.d.). Retrieved from https://www.linkedin.com/pulse/role-analytics-ecommerce-industry-gauri-bapat

Edla, D. R., Tripathi, D., Cheruku, R., & Kuppili, V. (2018). An efficient multi-layer ensemble framework with BP-SOGSA-based feature selection for credit scoring data analysis. *Arabian Journal for Science and Engineering*, *43*(12), 6909–6928. doi:10.100713369-017-2905-4

Education (EDU). (n.d.). Retrieved from https://pdfs.semanticscholar.org/67a4/28c6764c7ece121dcd0c196f9541c7b2d9f2.pdf

Education (EDU2). (n.d.). Retrieved from https://dzone.com/articles/how-is-big-data-influencing-the-education-sector

Education (EDU3). (n.d.). Retrieved from https://www.allerin.com/blog/4-ways-big-data-is-transforming-the-education-sector

EHR. (n.d.). Retrieved from https://www.techopediaa.com/definitionn/153337/electronic-health-record-ehr

EHR2. (n.d.). Retrieved from https://www.cmss.gov/Mediccare/EHealthRecords/index.html

El Ayadi, M., Kamel, M. S., & Karray, F. (2011). Survey on speech emotion recognition: Features, classification schemes, and databases. *Pattern Recognition, 44*(3), 572–587. doi:10.1016/j.patcog.2010.09.020

Elbamby, M. S., Perfecto, C., Bennis, M., & Doppler, K. (2018). Toward low-latency and ultra-reliable Virtual Reality. *IEEE Network, 32*(2), 78–84. doi:10.1109/MNET.2018.1700268

Elbestawi, M. A., & Dumitrescu, M. (2006). Tool Condition Monitoring in Machining – Neural Networks, In IFIP International Federation for Information Processing, Volume 220, Information Technology for Balanced manufacturing Systems(pp 5-16). Boston: Springer.

Elbestawi, M. A., Dumitrescu, M., & Ng, E.-G. (2006). Tool Condition Monitoring in Machining. In Condition Monitoring and Control for Intelligent Manufacturing (pp 55-82). Springer-Verlag London Limited. doi:10.1007/1-84628-269-1_3

Eriksson, L., Jaworska, J., Worth, A. P., Cronin, M. T., McDowell, R. M., & Gramatica, P. (2003). Methods for Reliability and Uncertainty Assessment and for Applicability Evaluations of Classification and Regression-Based QSARs. *Environmental Health Perspectives, 111*(10), 1361–1375. doi:10.1289/ehp.5758 PMID:12896860

Erin, H. (2004). *A Survey of Thinning Methodologies.* College of Engineering and Computer Science, University of Central Florida.

Erturk, E., & Sezer, E. A. (2015). A comparison of some soft computing methods for software fault prediction. *Expert Systems with Applications, 42*(4), 1872–1879. doi:10.1016/j.eswa.2014.10.025

Esteva, A., Kuprel, B., Novoa, R., Ko, J., Swetter, S., Blau, H. M., & Thrun, S. (2016). Dermatologist Level Classification of Skin Cancer. *Nature.*

ETSI ENI ISG (2019). *Experiential Networked Intelligence Industry Specification Group.* Author.

Everingham, M., Van Gool, L., Williams, C. K., Winn, J., & Zisserman, A. (2010). The pascal visual object classes (voc) challenge. *International Journal of Computer Vision, 88*(2), 303–338. doi:10.100711263-009-0275-4

Fader, A., Zettlemoyer, L., & Etzioni, O. (2013). Paraphrase-driven learning for open question answering. *ACL 2013 - 51st Annual Meeting of the Association for Computational Linguistics, Proceedings of the Conference, 1,* 1608-1618.

Fadlullah, Z. M., Tang, F., Mao, B., Kato, N., Akashi, O., Inoue, T., & Mizutani, K. (2017). State-of-the-art Deep Learning: Evolving machine intelligence toward tomorrow's intelligent network traffic control systems. *IEEE Communications Surveys and Tutorials, 19*(4), 2432–2455. doi:10.1109/COMST.2017.2707140

Fan, W., & Bifet, A. (2013). Mining big data: current status, and forecast to the future. *ACM SIGKDD Explorations Newsletter, 14*(2), 1-5.

Fan, R. E., Chang, K. W., Hsieh, C. J., Wang, X. R., & Lin, C. J. (2008). LIBLINEAR: A library for large linear classification. *Journal of Machine Learning Research, 9*(Aug), 1871–1874.

Fernández-Gavilanes, M., Álvarez-López, T., Juncal-Martínez, J., Costa-Montenegro, E., & González-Castaño, F. (2016). Unsupervised method for sentiment analysis in online texts. *Expert Systems with Applications, 58,* 57–75. doi:10.1016/j.eswa.2016.03.031

Fernando, S., & Stevenson, M. (2008, March). A semantic similarity approach to paraphrase detection. In *Proceedings of the 11th Annual Research Colloquium of the UK Special Interest Group for Computational Linguistics* (pp. 45-52). Academic Press.

Ferreira, R., De Souza Cabral, L., Lins, R. D., Pereira, E., Silva, G., Freitas, F., ... Favaro, L. (2013). Assessing sentence scoring techniques for extractive text summarization. *Expert Systems with Applications, 40*(14), 5755–5764. doi:10.1016/j.eswa.2013.04.023

Fiaz, A., Devi, N., & Aarthi, S. (2013). *Bug tracking and reporting system.* arXiv preprint arXiv:1309.1232

Fiore, U., Palmieri, F., Castiglione, A., & De Santis, A. (2013). Network anomaly detection with the restricted Boltzmann machine. *Neurocomputing, 122*, 13–23. doi:10.1016/j.neucom.2012.11.050

Fister, I. Jr, Perc, M., Ljubič, K., Kamal, S. M., Iglesias, A., & Fister, I. (2015). Particle swarm optimization for automatic creation of complex graphic characters. *Chaos, Solitons, and Fractals, 73*, 29–35. doi:10.1016/j.chaos.2014.12.019

Foroutan, B. (2015). Personalized medicine: A review with regard to biomarkers. *Journal of Bioequivalence & Bioavailability, 7*(06), 244–256. doi:10.4172/jbb.1000248

Franke, K., & Srihari, S. N. (2008, August). Computational forensics: An overview. In *International Workshop on Computational Forensics* (pp. 1-10). Springer.

Freitas, M. L. B., Mendes, J. J. A., Campos, D. P., & Stevan, S. L. (2019). Hand Gestures Classification Using Multichannel sEMG Armband. In *XXVI Brazilian Congress on Biomedical Engineering* (pp. 239–246). Springer. 10.1007/978-981-13-2517-5_37

Freund, Y., & Schapire, R. E. (1996, July). Experiments with a new boosting algorithm. In ICML (Vol. 96, pp. 148-156). Academic Press.

Freund, Y., & Schapire, R. E. (1995). A decision-theoretic generalization of on-line learning and an application to boosting. *Proceedings of the Second European Conference on Computational Learning Theory*, 23–37. 10.1007/3-540-59119-2_166

Freund, Y., & Schapire, R. E. (1996). Experiments with a new boosting algorithm. In *Proceedings of the 13th International Conference on Machine Learning*. Morgan Kaufmann Press.

Friedman, J., Hastie, T., &Tibshirani, R. (2001). *The elements of statistical learning* (Vol. 1, No. 10). New York: Springer Series in Statistics.

Friedman, N., Geiger, D., & Goldszmidt, M. (1997). Bayesian network classifiers. *Machine Learning, 29*(2-3), 131–163. doi:10.1023/A:1007465528199

Fritzke, B. (1994). A Growing Neural Gas Network Learns Topologies. *Advances in Neural Information Processing Systems, 6*, 625–632.

Fritzke, B. (1994). Growing Cell Structures – A Self organizing network for Unsupervised and Supervised learning. *Neural Networks, 7*(9), 1441–1460. doi:10.1016/0893-6080(94)90091-4

Fu, J., Hou, L., Lu, B., & Wang, J. (2014). Thermal analysis and thermal optimization of through silicon via in 3D IC. *12th IEEE International Conference on Solid- State and Integrated Circuit Technology (ICSICT) 2014*, 1–3. 10.1109/ICSICT.2014.7021445

Fu, H., & Qiu, G. (2012). Fast Semantic Image Retrieval Based on Random Forest. *Proceedings of the 20th ACM International Conference on Multimedia*, 909-912. 10.1145/2393347.2396344

Furno, A., Fiore, M., & Stanica, R. (2017). Joint spatial and temporal classification of mobile traffic demands. *IEEE INFOCOM 2017 - IEEE Conference on Computer Communications*, 1-9.

Gabutt, A. C. (2015). *Using deep learning to analyze genetic mutations: an interview with Brendan Frey*. Retrieved from https://bit.ly/2Uolrz4

Gaglio, S., Re, G. L., & Morana, M. (2015). Human activity recognition process using 3-D posture data. *IEEE Transactions on Human-Machine Systems*, *45*(5), 586–597. doi:10.1109/THMS.2014.2377111

Ganapathiraju, A., Hamaker, J., & Picone, J. (2000). Hybrid SVM/HMM architectures for speech recognition. *Sixth international conference on spoken language processing*.

Gandomi, A., & Haider, M. (2015). Beyond the hype: Big data concepts, methods, and analytics. *International Journal of Information Management*, *35*(2), 137-144. doi:10.1016/j.ijinfomgt.2014.10.007

García-Cumbreras, M. Á., Montejo-Ráez, A., & Díaz-Galiano, M. C. (2013). Pessimists and optimists: Improving collaborative filtering through sentiment analysis. *Expert Systems with Applications*, *40*(17), 6758–6765. doi:10.1016/j.eswa.2013.06.049

García, S., Ramírez-Gallego, S., Luengo, J., Benítez, J. M., & Herrera, F. (2016). Big data preprocessing: Methods and prospects. *Big Data Analytics*, *1*(1), 9. doi:10.118641044-016-0014-0

Gautam, G., & Yadav, D. Sentiment analysis of twitter data using machine learning approaches and semantic analysis. In *2014 Seventh International Conference on Contemporary Computing (IC3)*. IEEE. 10.1109/IC3.2014.6897213

Ge, X. (2018). Distinguished capabilities of Artificial Intelligence wireless communication systems. *Computing Research Repository*. (preprint)

Geiger, J., Leykauf, T., Rehrl, T., Wallhoff, F., & Rigoll, G. (2014). The robot ALIAS as a gaming platform for elderly persons. In *Ambient Assisted Living* (pp. 327–340). Berlin: Springer. doi:10.1007/978-3-642-37988-8_21

Genomic analytics (GA). (n.d.). Retrieved from https://www.intel.com/content/www/us/en/healthcare-it/genomic-analytics-overview.html

Genomic analytics (GA2). (n.d.). Retrieved from https://www.intel.in/content/www/in/en/healthcare-it/solutions/documents/genomicanalytics-speed-time-to-insights-brief.html

Gers, F. A., Schmidhuber, J., & Cummins, F. (2000). Learning to Forget: Continual Prediction with LSTM. *Neural Computation*, *12*(10), 2451–2471. doi:10.1162/089976600300015015 PMID:11032042

Ghaffarian, S. M., & Shahriari, H. R. (2017). Software vulnerability analysis and discovery using machine-learning and data-mining techniques: A survey. *ACM Computing Surveys*, *50*(4), 56. doi:10.1145/3092566

Ghiassi, M., Skinner, J., & Zimbra, D. (2013). Twitter brand sentiment analysis: A hybrid system using n-gram analysis and dynamic artificial neural network. *Expert Systems with Applications*, *40*(16), 6266–6282. doi:10.1016/j.eswa.2013.05.057

Girija, D. K., & Shashidhara, M. S. (2012). Classification of Women Health Disease (Fibroid) Using Decision Tree algorithm. *International Journal of Computer Applications in Engineering Sciences*, *2*(03), 205–209.

Girshick, R. (2015). Fast r-cnn. In *Proceedings of the IEEE international conference on computer vision* (pp. 1440-1448). IEEE.

Global Data on Visual Impairments. (2010). Available online: http://www.who.int/blindness/

Glover, F., & Laguna, M. (1998). Tabu search. In *Handbook of combinatorial optimization* (pp. 2093–2229). Boston, MA: Springer. doi:10.1007/978-1-4613-0303-9_33

Go, A., Bhayani, R., & Huang, L. (2009). Twitter sentiment classification using distant supervision. CS224N Project Report, 1(12).

Goller, C., & Kuchler, A. (1996, June). Learning task-dependent distributed representations by backpropagation through structure. In *Proceedings of International Conference on Neural Networks (ICNN'96)* (Vol. 1, pp. 347-352). IEEE. 10.1109/ICNN.1996.548916

Gómez-Bombarelli, R., Wei, J.N., Duvenaud, D., Hernández-Lobato, J.M., Sánchez-Lengeling, B., Sheberla, D., … Aspuru-Guzik, A. (2018). Automatic Chemical Design Using a Data-Driven Continuous Representation Of Molecules. *ACS Central Science, 4*(2), 268-276.

Google Trends. (2017, September 20). Retrieved from https://trends.google.com/trends/

Google Trends. (2017, September 27). Retrieved from https://en.wikipedia.org/wiki/Google_Trends

Gori, M., Cappagli, G., Tonelli, A., Baud-Bovy, G., & Finocchietti, S. (2016). Devices for visually impaired people: High technological devices with low user acceptance and no adaptability for children. *Neuroscience and Biobehavioral Reviews, 69*, 79–88. doi:10.1016/j.neubiorev.2016.06.043 PMID:27484870

Goswami, A., & Kumar, A. (2017). Challenges in the Analysis of Online Social Networks: A Data Collection Tool Perspective. *Wireless Personal Communications, 97*(3), 4015–4061. doi:10.100711277-017-4712-3

Goudas, T., Louizos, C., Petasis, G., & Karkaletsis, V. (2014). Argument extraction from news, blogs, and social media. In A. Likas, K. Blekas, & D. Kalles (Eds.), Lecture Notes in Computer Science: Vol. 8445. *Artificial Intelligence: Methods and Applications. SETN 2014.* Cham: Springer.

Gracia Nirmala Rani. (2013). A survey on B*-Tree-based evolutionary algorithms for VLSI floorplanning optimization. India. *International Journal of Computer Applications in Technology, 48*(4).

Gracia Nirmala Rani, D., & Rajaram, S. (2011). Performance driven VLSI floor planning with B*Tree representation using differential evolution. *Communications in Computer and Information Science, 197*, 456–465. doi:10.1007/978-3-642-22543-7_45

Grant, R. N., Kucher, D., León, A. M., Gemmell, J. F., Raicu, D. S., & Fodeh, S. J. (2018). Automatic extraction of informal topics from online suicidal ideation. *BMC Bioinformatics, 19*(8), 211. doi:10.118612859-018-2197-z PMID:29897319

Graves, A., Jaitly, N., & Mohamed, A. R. (2013, December). *Hybrid speech recognition with deep bidirectional LSTM. In 2013 IEEE workshop on automatic speech recognition and understanding* (pp. 273–278). IEEE. doi:10.1109/ASRU.2013.6707742

Grimaldi, M., & Kokaram, A. (2006). Discrete wavelet packet transform and ensembles of lazy and eager learners for music genre classification. *Multimedia Systems, 11*(5), 422–437. doi:10.100700530-006-0027-z

Grimmer, J., & M. Stewart, B. (2013). *Text as Data: The Promise and Pitfalls of Automatic Content Analysis Methods for Political Texts* (Vol. 21). Academic Press.

Gromski, P. S., Muhamadali, H., Ellis, D. I., Xu, Y., Correa, E., Turner, M. L., & Goodacre, R. (2015). A tutorial review: Metabolomics and partial least squares-discriminant analysis–a marriage of convenience or a shotgun wedding. *Analytica Chimica Acta, 879*, 10–23. doi:10.1016/j.aca.2015.02.012 PMID:26002472

Grover, V., Adderley, R., & Bramer, M. (2007). *Review of Current Crime Prediction Techniques.* Paper presented at the Applications and Innovations in Intelligent Systems XIV, London, UK.

Gu, Y., Chen, T., Sun, Y., & Wang, B. (2016). *Ideology detection for twitter users with heterogeneous types of links.* ArXiv:1612.08207

Guan, S., & Zhang, X. (2008). *Networked Memex Based on Personal Digital Library. In Encyclopedia of Networked and Virtual Organizations* (pp. 1044–1051). IGI Global. doi:10.4018/978-1-59904-885-7.ch136

Guan, W., Wen, X., Wang, L., Lu, Z., & Shen, Y. (2018). A service-oriented deployment policy of end-to-end network slicing based on complex network theory. *IEEE Access: Practical Innovations, Open Solutions, 6*, 19691–19701. doi:10.1109/ACCESS.2018.2822398

Guan, Z., Chen, L., Zhao, W., Zheng, Y., Tan, S., & Cai, D. (2016). *Weakly-Supervised Deep Learning for Customer Review Sentiment Classification.* IJCAI.

Guarin, C. E. L., Guzman, E. L., & Gonzalez, F. A. (2015). A model to predict low academic performance at a specific enrollment using data mining. *IEEE Revista Iberoamericana de tecnologias del Aprendizaje, 10*(3), 119-125.

Gui, G., Huang, H., Song, Y., & Sari, H. (2018). Deep learning for an effective Non-Orthogonal Multiple Access scheme. *IEEE Transactions on Vehicular Technology, 67*(9), 8440–8450. doi:10.1109/TVT.2018.2848294

Guimarães Pedronette, D. C., Calumby, R. T., & Torres, S. (2015). A semi-supervised learning algorithm for relevance feedback and collaborative image retrieval. *EURASIP Journal on Image and Video Processing, 27*(1). doi:10.118613640-015-0081-6

Gulshan, V., Peng, L., Coram, M., Stumpe, M. C., Wu, D., Narayanaswamy, A., ... Kim, R. (2016). Development and Validation of a Deep Learning Algorithm for Detection of Diabetic Retinopathy in Retinal Fundus Photographs. *Journal of the American Medical Association, 316*(22), 2402–2410. doi:10.1001/jama.2016.17216 PMID:27898976

Gupta, R., Sahu, S., Espy-Wilson, C., & Narayanan, S. (2018). *Semi-supervised and transfer learning approaches for low resource sentiment classification.* arXiv:1806.02863

Guyon, I., Weston, J., Barnhill, S., & Vapnik, V. (2002). Gene selection for cancer classification using support vector machines. *Machine Learning, 46*(1-3), 389–422. doi:10.1023/A:1012487302797

Guzdial, M., & Riedl, M. (2016). *Toward game level generation from gameplay videos.* arXiv preprint arXiv:1602.07721

HaCohen-Kerner, Y., Gross, Z., & Masa, A. (2005, February). Automatic extraction and learning of keyphrases from scientific articles. In *International Conference on Intelligent Text Processing and Computational Linguistics* (pp. 657-669). Springer.

Hagenau, M., Liebmann, M., & Neumann, D. (2013). Automated news reading: Stock price prediction based on financial news using context-capturing features. *Decision Support Systems, 55*(3), 685–697. doi:10.1016/j.dss.2013.02.006

Hailong, Z., Wenyan, G., & Bo, J. (2014, September). Machine learning and lexicon based methods for sentiment classification: A survey. In *2014 11th Web Information System and Application Conference* (pp. 262-265). IEEE. 10.1109/WISA.2014.55

Hall, M. A. (1999). *Correlation-based feature selection for machine learning.* Academic Press.

Hall, M. (2000). Correlation-based feature selection for discrete and numeric class machine learning. *Proceedings of the 17th International Conference on Machine Learning,* 359–366.

Hamel, P., & Eck, D. (2010). Learning Features from Music Audio with Deep Belief Networks. *Proceedings of International Society for Music Information Retrieval Conference*, 339–344.

Hammouri, A., Hammad, M., Alnabhan, M., & Alsarayrah, F. (2018). Software bug prediction using machine learning approach. *International Journal of Advanced Computer Science and Applications, 9*(2).

Han, W., Chan, C. F., Choy, C. S., & Pun, K. P. (2006, May). An efficient MFCC extraction method in speech recognition. In 2006 IEEE international symposium on circuits and systems (pp. 4-pp). IEEE.

Hanohano, C. J. O. (2017). *Physical Assault, Perceived Stress, Coping, and Attitudes toward Assault Experienced by Psychiatric Nurses and Their Intent to Leave* (Doctoral dissertation). Azusa Pacific University.

Hansen, J. (2005). *Using SPSS for windows and macintosh: analyzing and understanding data*. Academic Press.

Hansen, L. K., Lehn-Schiøler, T., Petersen, K. B., Arenas-Garcia, J., Larsen, J., & Jensen, S. H. (2007). Learning and Clean-up in a Large Scale Music Database. *2007 15th European Signal Processing Conference*, 946-950.

Harrington, P. (2012). *Machine learning in action* (Vol. 5). Greenwich: Manning.

Hastie, T., Tibshirani, R., Friedman, J., & Franklin, J. (2005). The elements of statistical learning: Data mining, inference and prediction. *The Mathematical Intelligencer, 27*(2), 83–85. doi:10.1007/BF02985802

Hatzivassiloglou, V., & McKeown, K. R. (1997, July). Predicting the semantic orientation of adjectives. In *Proceedings of the 35th annual meeting of the association for computational linguistics and eighth conference of the european chapter of the association for computational linguistics* (pp. 174-181). Association for Computational Linguistics.

Haykin, S. (1998). *Neural Networks – A Comprehensive Foundation*. New York: Macmillan College Publishing Company.

Haykin, S. S., Haykin, S. S., Haykin, S. S., Elektroingenieur, K., & Haykin, S. S. (2009). *Neural networks and learning machines* (Vol. 3). Upper Saddle River, NJ: Pearson.

Hbase. (n.d.). Retrieved from https://www.ibm.com/analytics/hadoop/hbase

Health care (HC). (n.d.). In *Wikipedia*. Retrieved from https://en.wikipedia.org/wiki/Health_care_analytics

Health care analytics (HCA). (n.d.). Retrieved from https://www.infosys.com/data-analytics/verticals/Pages/healthcare.aspx

Healthcare process (HP). (n.d.). Retrieved from https://www.omicssonlineq.org/a-hoppital-health-care-system--2157-7420.1000121.php

Hecht-Nielsen, R. (1992). Theory of the backpropagation neural network. In *Neural networks for perception* (pp. 65–93). Elsevier. doi:10.1016/B978-0-12-741252-8.50010-8

Helgeson, J., Rammage, M., Urman, A., Roebuck, M. C., Coverdill, S., Pomerleau, K., ... Williamson, M. P. (2018). *Clinical performance pilot using cognitive computing for clinical trial matching at Mayo Clinic*. Academic Press.

Herrera, J., Poblete, B., & Parra, D. (2018). Learning to Leverage Microblog Information for QA Retrieval. In *European Conference on Information Retrieval*. Springer. 10.1007/978-3-319-76941-7_38

Herzig, K., Just, S., & Zeller, A. (2013). It's not a bug, it's a feature: how misclassification impacts bug prediction. *Proceedings of the 2013 international conference on software engineering.* 10.1109/ICSE.2013.6606585

He, Y., Yu, F. R., Zhao, N., Yin, H., Yao, H., & Qiu, R. C. (2016). Big Data Analytics in Mobile Cellular Networks. *IEEE Access: Practical Innovations, Open Solutions, 4*, 1985–1996. doi:10.1109/ACCESS.2016.2540520

Hinton, G. E., Osindero, S., & Teh, Y. W. (2006). A Fast Learning Algorithm for Deep Belief Nets. *Neural Computation,* *18*(7), 1527–1554. doi:10.1162/neco.2006.18.7.1527 PMID:16764513

Hinton, G. E., Osindero, S., & Teh, Y.-W. (2006). A fast learning algorithm for deep belief nets. *Neural Computation,* *18*(7), 1527–1554.

Hinton, G., Deng, L., Yu, D., Dahl, G., Mohamed, A. R., Jaitly, N., ... Sainath, T. (2012). Deep neural networks for acoustic modeling in speech recognition. *IEEE Signal Processing Magazine,* 29.

Hondori. (2014). A review on technical and clinical impact of Microsoft kinect on physical therapy and rehabilitation. *Journal of Medical Engineering.*

Hoogeveen, D., Bennett, A., Li, Y., Verspoor, K. M., & Baldwin, T. (2018). Detecting Misflagged Duplicate Questions in Community Question-Answering Archives. *Twelfth International AAAI Conference on Web and Social Media.*

Hore, S., & Bhattacharya, T. (2019). Analyzing Social Trend Towards Girl Child in India: A Machine Intelligence-Based Approach. In *Recent Developments in Machine Learning and Data Analytics* (pp. 43–50). Singapore: Springer. doi:10.1007/978-981-13-1280-9_4

Hossain, Kuchukulla, & Chowdhury. (2018). Failure Analysis of the Through Silicon Via in Three-dimensional Integrated Circuit (3D-IC). *2018 IEEE International Symposium on Circuits and Systems (ISCAS).*

Hossan, M. A., Memon, S., & Gregory, M. A. (2010, December). A novel approach for MFCC feature extraction. In *2010 4th International Conference on Signal Processing and Communication Systems* (pp. 1-5). IEEE. 10.1109/IC-SPCS.2010.5709752

Ho, T. K. (1995, August). Random decision forests. In *Proceedings of 3rd international conference on document analysis and recognition* (Vol. 1, pp. 278-282). IEEE. 10.1109/ICDAR.1995.598994

Ho, T. K. (1998). The random subspace method for constructing decision forests. *IEEE Transactions on Pattern Analysis and Machine Intelligence,* *20*(8), 832–844. doi:10.1109/34.709601

Hua, Y., Guo, J., & Zhao, H. (2014). Deep belief networks and deep learning. *Intelligent Computing and Internet of Things (ICIT), 2014 International Conference on,* 1-4.

Huang, C. L., & Dun, J. F. (2008). A distributed PSO–SVM hybrid system with feature selection and parameter optimization. *Applied Soft Computing,* *8*(4), 1381–1391. doi:10.1016/j.asoc.2007.10.007

Huang, J. (2017). A big data enabled channel model for 5G wireless communication systems. *IEEE Communications Magazine,* *55*(9), 150–157.

Huang, R., Pedoeem, J., & Chen, C. (2018, December). YOLO-LITE: A Real-Time Object Detection Algorithm Optimized for Non-GPU Computers. In *2018 IEEE International Conference on Big Data (Big Data)* (pp. 2503-2510). IEEE. 10.1109/BigData.2018.8621865

Hu, M., & Liu, B. (2004, August). Mining and summarizing customer reviews. In *Proceedings of the tenth ACM SIGKDD international conference on Knowledge discovery and data mining* (pp. 168-177). ACM.

Humphrey, W. S. (1989). *Managing the software process* (Vol. 1). Addison-Wesley.

Humphrey, W. S. (1995). *A discipline for software engineering.* Addison-Wesley Longman Publishing Co., Inc.

Hunicke, R., & Chapman, V. (2004). *AI for Dynamic Difficulty Adjustment in Games.* Retrieved from https://users.cs.northwestern.edu/~hunicke/pubs/Hamlet.pdf

Hussain, A., & Cambria, E. (2018). Semi-supervised learning for big social data analysis. *Neurocomputing, 275*(31), 1662–1673. doi:10.1016/j.neucom.2017.10.010

Hyken, S. (2008). Four Ways Self-Driving Cars Will Improve Customer Service. *Forbes.*

Iam-On, N., & Boongoen, T. (2017). Generating descriptive model for student dropout: A review of clustering approach. *Human-centric Computing and Information Sciences, 7*(1), 1. doi:10.118613673-016-0083-0

Ibnkahla, M. (2018). Applications of neural networks to digital communications – A survey. *Signal Processing, 80*(7), 1185–1215. doi:10.1016/S0165-1684(00)00030-X

Ibrahim, O. A. S., & LandaSilva, D. (2014). A new weighting scheme and discriminative approach for information retrieval in static and dynamic document collections. *Proceedings of the 14th UK Workshop on Computational Intelligence,* 1–8.

Ilinska, L., Ivanova, O., & Senko, Z. (2016). Teaching Textual Analysis of Contemporary Popular Scientific Texts. *Procedia: Social and Behavioral Sciences, 236,* 248–253. doi:10.1016/j.sbspro.2016.12.020

Importance of health care (IHC). (n.d.). Retrieved from http://www.keyush.com/blogs/files/ Importance of Analytics 2020 in Healthcare.pdf

Indeed Reviews. (2017, September). *Reviews from Indeed.* Retrieved from https://www.indeed.co.in/

Introduction to Support Vector Machines. (2017, August 29). Retrieved from http:// www.svms.org/introduction.html

Ioffe, S., & Szegedy, C. (2015). *Batch normalization: Accelerating deep network training by reducing internal covariate shift.* arXiv preprint arXiv:1502.03167

ITU-T Focus Group. (2019). *Machine Learning for Future Networks including 5G.* no Author.

Iverson, J. M., & Goldin-Meadow, S. (2005). Gesture paves the way for language development. *Psychological Science, 16*(5), 367–371. doi:10.1111/j.0956-7976.2005.01542.x PMID:15869695

Jacob, S., & Menon, V. (2019). *MEDICO-A Simple IoT Integrated Medical Kiosk for the Rural People.* Preprints.

Jaderberg, M., Simonyan, K., Vedaldi, A., & Zisserman, A. (2016). Reading Text in the Wild with Convolutional Neural Networks. *International Journal of Computer Vision, 116*(1), 1–20. doi:10.100711263-015-0823-z

Jaimes, A., & Sebe, N. (2007). Multimodal human–computer interaction: A survey. *Computer Vision and Image Understanding, 108*(1), 116–134. doi:10.1016/j.cviu.2006.10.019

Jain, A. K., Duin, R. P. W., & Mao, J. (2000). Statistical pattern recognition: A review. *IEEE Transactions on Pattern Analysis and Machine Intelligence, 22*(1), 4–37. doi:10.1109/34.824819

Jain, A. K., Mao, J., & Mohiuddin, K. M. (1996, March). Artificial neural networks: A tutorial. *Computer, 29*(3), 31–44. doi:10.1109/2.485891

Jain, D. K., Jacob, S., Alzubi, J., & Menon, V. (2019). An efficient and adaptable multimedia system for converting PAL to VGA in real-time video processing. *Journal of Real-Time Image Processing,* 1–13.

Jain, R. K. (2009). *Engineering Metrology.* New Delhi: Khanna Publishers.

Jaiswal, A., & Malhotra, R. (2018). Software reliability prediction using machine learning techniques. *International Journal of System Assurance Engineering and Management, 9*(1), 230–244. doi:10.100713198-016-0543-y

Jaiswal, G., Sharma, A., & Yadav, S. K. (2019, July). Analytical Approach for Predicting Dropouts in Higher Education. *International Journal of Information and Communication Technology Education*, *15*(3), 89–102. doi:10.4018/IJICTE.2019070107

James, J. (2014). *Data Never Sleeps 2.0*. Retrieved from https://www.domo.com/blog/data-never-sleeps-2-0/

Javaid, A., Quamar, W. S., & Alam, M. (2016). A deep learning approach for network intrusion detection system, In *Proceedings of the 9th EAI International Conference on Bio-inspired Information and Communications Technologies (formerly BIONETICS)*, (pp. 21-26). ICST (Institute for Computer Sciences, Social-Informatics and Telecommunications Engineering). 10.4108/eai.3-12-2015.2262516

Javaid, N., Sher, A., Nasir, H., & Guizani, N. (2018). Intelligence in IoT-based 5G networks: Opportunities and challenges. *IEEE Communications Magazine*, *56*(10), 94–100. doi:10.1109/MCOM.2018.1800036

Javed, K., Maruf, S., & Babri, A. (2015). A two-stage Markov blanket based feature selection algorithm for text classification. *Neurocomputing*, *157*, 91–104.

Jean-Louis, M., Audrey, L., & Bernard, L. (2011). Pedestrian Injury Patterns According to Car and Casualty Characteristics in France. Academic Press.

Jeong, G., Kim, S., & Zimmermann, T. (2009). Improving bug triage with bug tossing graphs. *Proceedings of the the 7th joint meeting of the European software engineering conference and the ACM SIGSOFT symposium on The foundations of software engineering*. 10.1145/1595696.1595715

Jesse, L., Jake, A., Jan, B., Jennifer, D., David, H., & Soeren, K. (2011). Towards Fully Autonomous Driving. *Systems and Algorithms. In Intelligent Vehicles Symposium.*

Jha, A., Dave, M., & Supriya Madan, D. (2016). *A Review on the Study and Analysis of Big Data using Data Mining Techniques* (Vol. 6). Academic Press.

Jhamtani, H., Suleep Kumar, B., & Raychoudhury, V. (2014). *Word-level Language Identification in Bi-lingual Code-switched Texts*. Academic Press.

Jiang, H., & Learned-Miller, E. (2017, May). Face detection with the faster R-CNN. In *2017 12th IEEE International Conference on Automatic Face & Gesture Recognition (FG 2017)* (pp. 650-657). IEEE. 10.1109/FG.2017.82

Jiang, L., Wang, D., & Cai, Z. (2012). Discriminatively weighted naive Bayes and its application in text classification. *International Journal on Artificial Intelligence Tools, 21*(1).

Jiang, L., Wang, S., Li, C., & Zhang, L. (2016). Structure Extended Multinomial Naive Bayes. *Information Sciences, 329*, 346–356.

Jiang, W., Strufe, M., & Schotten, H. D. (2017). SON decision-making framework for intelligent management in 5G mobile networks. *IEEE Int. Conf. on Computer and Communications (ICCC)*, 1-5.

Jiang, Y., He, X., Liu, C., & Guo, Y. (2015). An Effective Analytical 3D Placer in Monolithic 3D IC Designs. *IEEE 2015 IEEE 11th International Conference on ASIC(ASICON)*. 10.1109/ASICON.2015.7517146

Jiang, C., Yhang, H., Ren, Y., Han, Z., Chen, K.-C., & Hanzo, L. (2017). Machine Learning paradigms for next-generation wireless networks. *IEEE Wireless Communications*, *24*(2), 98–105. doi:10.1109/MWC.2016.1500356WC

Jiang, L., Cai, Z., Zhang, H., & Wang, D. (2013). Naive Bayes text classifiers: A locally weighted learning approach" in J. *Exp. Theor. Artif. Intell.*, *25*(2), 273–286. doi:10.1080/0952813X.2012.721010

Jiang, L., Zhang, H., Cai, Z., & Wang, D. (2012). Weighted average of one-dependence estimators" in J. *Exp. Theor. Artif. Intell.*, *24*(2), 219–230. doi:10.1080/0952813X.2011.639092

Jiang, X., Wells, A., Brufsky, A., & Neapolitan, R. (2019). A clinical decision support system learned from data to personalize treatment recommendations towards preventing breast cancer metastasis. *PLoS One*, *14*(3), e0213292. doi:10.1371/journal.pone.0213292 PMID:30849111

Jianqiang, Z., & Xiaolin, G. (2017). Comparison research on text pre-processing methods on Twitter sentiment analysis. *IEEE Access: Practical Innovations, Open Solutions*, *5*, 2870–2879. doi:10.1109/ACCESS.2017.2672677

Jianqiang, Z., Xiaolin, G., & Xuejun, Z. (2018). Deep convolution neural networks for Twitter sentiment analysis. *IEEE Access: Practical Innovations, Open Solutions*, *6*, 23253–23260. doi:10.1109/ACCESS.2017.2776930

Jian, W. S., Wen, H. C., Scholl, J., Shabbir, S. A., Lee, P., Hsu, C. Y., & Li, Y. C. (2011). The Taiwanese method for providing patients data from multiple hospital EHR systems. *Journal of Biomedical Informatics*, *44*(2), 326–332. doi:10.1016/j.jbi.2010.11.004 PMID:21118726

Jiman, K., & Chanjong, P. (2017). End-to-End Ego Lane Estimation based on Sequential Transfer Learning for Self-Driving Cars. *IEEE Conference on Computer Vision and Pattern Recognition Workshops.*

Jin, Kim, & Kim. (2014). Decision factors on effective liver patient data prediction. *International Journal of Bio Science and Bio-Technology, 6*(4), 167-178. doi:10.14257/ijbsbt.2014.6.4.16

Jin, K., Dashbalbar, A., Yang, G., Lee, J.-W., & Lee, B. (2016). Bug severity prediction by classifying normal bugs with text and meta-field information. *Advanced Science and Technology Letters*, *129*, 19–24. doi:10.14257/astl.2016.129.05

Ji, W., Xu, J., Qiao, H., Zhou, M., & Liang, B. (2019). Visual IoT: Enabling Internet of Things visualization in Smart Cities. *IEEE Network*, *33*(2), 102–110. doi:10.1109/MNET.2019.1800258

Ji, X., Chun, S. A., Wei, Z., & Geller, J. (2015). Twitter sentiment classification for measuring public health concerns. *Social Network Analysis and Mining*, *5*(13).

Joachims, T. (1998). *Text categorization with support vector machines: Learning with many relevant features.* Paper presented at the European conference on machine learning. 10.1007/BFb0026683

Joachims, T. (2006, August). Training linear SVMs in linear time. In *Proceedings of the 12th ACM SIGKDD international conference on Knowledge discovery and data mining* (pp. 217-226). ACM.

Johnson, A. E., Pollard, T. J., Shen, L., Li-wei, H. L., Feng, M., Ghassemi, M., ... Mark, R. G. (2016). MIMIC-III, a freely accessible critical care database. *Scientific Data*, *3*(1), 160035. doi:10.1038data.2016.35 PMID:27219127

Kacur, J., Vargic, R., & Mulinka, P. (2011, June). Speaker identification by K-nearest neighbors: Application of PCA and LDA prior to KNN. In *2011 18th International Conference on Systems, Signals and Image Processing* (pp. 1-4). IEEE.

Kakkanatt, C., Benigno, M., Jackson, V. M., Huang, P. L., & Ng, K. (2018). Curating and integrating user-generated health data from multiple sources to support healthcare analytics. *IBM Journal of Research and Development*, *62*(1), 2–1. doi:10.1147/JRD.2017.2756742

Kalra, Anderson, & Wachs. (2009). *Liability and regulation of autonomous vehicle technologies.* Rand Corp.

Kambatla, K., Kollias, G., Kumar, V., & Grama, A. (2014). Trends in big data analytics. *Journal of Parallel and Distributed Computing*, *74*(7), 2561–2573. doi:10.1016/j.jpdc.2014.01.003

Kanakaraj, M., & Guddeti, R. M. R. Performance analysis of Ensemble methods on Twitter sentiment analysis using NLP techniques. In *Proceedings of the 2015 IEEE 9th International Conference on Semantic Computing*. IEEE. 10.1109/ICOSC.2015.7050801

Kanavos, A., Perikos, I., Hatzilygeroudis, I., & Tsakalidis, A. (2017). Emotional community detection in social networks. *Computers & Electrical Engineering, 65*, 449–460. doi:10.1016/j.compeleceng.2017.09.011

Kang, H., Yoo, S. J., & Han, D. (2012). Senti-lexicon and improved Naïve Bayes algorithms for sentiment analysis of restaurant reviews. *Expert Systems with Applications, 39*(5), 6000–6010. doi:10.1016/j.eswa.2011.11.107

Kang, S. (2018). Personalized prediction of drug efficacy for diabetes treatment via patient-level sequential modeling with neural networks. *Artificial Intelligence in Medicine, 85*, 1–6. doi:10.1016/j.artmed.2018.02.004 PMID:29482961

Kang, S. K., Huang, W. C., Elkin, E. B., Pandharipande, P. V., & Braithwaite, R. S. (2019). Personalized Treatment for Small Renal Tumors: Decision Analysis of Competing Causes of Mortality. *Radiology, 290*(3), 732–743. doi:10.1148/radiol.2018181114 PMID:30644815

Kanimozhi, S., & Padmini Devi, B. (2018). A Novel Approach for Deep Learning Techniques Using Information Retrieval from Big Data. *International Journal of Pure and Applied Mathematics, 118*(8), 601–606.

Kapetanovic, I. M. (2011). *Drug Discovery and Development: Present and Future*. Rijeka, Croatia: InTech. doi:10.5772/1179

Karayiannis, N. B. (1999). Reformulated Radial basis neural networks trained by Gradient descent. *IEEE Transactions on Neural Networks, 10*(3), 657–671. doi:10.1109/72.761725 PMID:18252566

Kauer, T., Joglekar, S., Redi, M., Aiello, L. M., & Quercia, D. (2018, September/October). Mapping and Visualizing Deep-Learning Urban Beautification. *IEEE Computer Graphics and Applications, 38*(5), 70–83. doi:10.1109/MCG.2018.053491732 PMID:30273128

Kaur, K., & Jain, N. (2015). Feature Extraction and Classification for Automatic Speaker Recognition System-A Review. *International Journal of Advanced Research in Computer Science and Software Engineering, 5*.

Kaur, A., Gupta, P., & Singh, M. (2019). Hybrid Balanced Task Clustering Algorithm for Scientific Workflows in Cloud Computing. *Scalable Computing: Practice and Experience, 20*(2), 237–258.

Kaur, N., & Solanki, N. (2018). Sentiment Knowledge Discovery in Twitter Using CoreNLP Library. *8th International Conference on Cloud Computing, Data Science & Engineering (Confluence)*. 10.1109/CONFLUENCE.2018.8442439

Kauter, M. V., Breesch, D., & Hoste, V. (2015). Fine-grained analysis of explicit and implicit sentiment in financial news articles. *Expert Systems with Applications, 42*(11), 4999–5010. doi:10.1016/j.eswa.2015.02.007

Kavitha, R. (2012). Healthcare Industry in India. *International Journal of Scientific and Research Publication, 2*(8), 1–4.

Kean, S., Hall, J., & Perry, P. (2011). *Meet the Kinect: An introduction to programming natural user interfaces*. Apress. doi:10.1007/978-1-4302-3889-8

Kendon, A. (2004). *Gesture: Visible action as utterance*. Cambridge University Press. doi:10.1017/CBO9780511807572

Khan, A., Doucette, J. A., Cohen, R., & Lizotte, D. J. (2012). Integrating Machine Learning Into a Medical Decision Support System to Address the Problem of Missing Patient Data. *Machine Learning and Applications (ICMLA), 2012 11th International Conference on, 1*, 454-457. 10.1109/ICMLA.2012.82

Khan, W. A., Idris, M., Ali, T., Ali, R., Hussain, S., Hussain, M., . . . Lee, S. (2015, October). Correlating health and wellness analytics for personalized decision making. In *2015 17th International Conference on E-health Networking, Application & Services (HealthCom)* (pp. 256-261). IEEE. 10.1109/HealthCom.2015.7454508

Khan, F. H., Bashir, S., & Qamar, U. (2014). TOM: Twitter opinion mining framework using hybrid classification scheme. *Decision Support Systems*, *57*, 245–257. doi:10.1016/j.dss.2013.09.004

Khan, F. H., Qamar, U., & Bashir, S. (2017). A semi-supervised approach to sentiment analysis using revised sentiment strength based on SentiWordNet. *Knowledge and Information Systems*, *51*(3), 851–872. doi:10.100710115-016-0993-1

Kibria, M. G., Nguyen, K., Villardi, G. P., Zhao, O., Ishizu, K., & Kojima, F. (2018). Big data analytics, machine learning and artificial intelligence in next-generation wireless networks. *IEEE Access: Practical Innovations, Open Solutions*, *6*, 32328–32338. doi:10.1109/ACCESS.2018.2837692

Kim, Y. (2014). *Convolutional neural networks for sentence classification.* arXiv preprint arXiv:1408.5882

Kim, A., & Cho, S. (2019). An ensemble semi-supervised learning method for predicting defaults in social lending. *Engineering Applications of Artificial Intelligence*, *81*, 193–199. doi:10.1016/j.engappai.2019.02.014

Kim, J., Mastnik, S., & André, E. (2008). EMG-based hand gesture recognition for realtime biosignal interfacing. In *Proceedings of the 13th international conference on Intelligent user interfaces* (pp. 30–39). ACM. 10.1145/1378773.1378778

Kim, S. B., Han, K. S., Rim, H. C., & Myaeng, S. H. (2006). Some effective techniques for naive Bayes text classification. *IEEE Trans. Knowl. Data Eng.*, *18*(11), 1457–1466. doi:10.1109/TKDE.2006.180

Kim, S. B., Rim, H. C., & Lim, H. S. (2002). A new method of parameter estimation for MNB text classifiers. In *Proceedings of the 25th annual international ACM SIGIR conference on Research and development in information retrieval*. ACM.

Kim, Y., Seo, J., & Croft, W. B. (2011). Automatic Boolean Query Suggestion for Professional Search. *Proceedings of the 34th International ACM SIGIR Conference on Research and Development in Information Retrieval*, 825–834. 10.1145/2009916.2010026

Kittler, J., Hater, M., & Duin, R. P. (1996, August). Combining classifiers. In *Proceedings of 13th international conference on pattern recognition* (Vol. 2, pp. 897–901). IEEE. 10.1109/ICPR.1996.547205

Klaine, P. V., Imran, M. A., Onireti, O., & Souza, R. D. (2017). A survey of machine learning techniques applied to self-organizing cellular networks. *IEEE Communications Surveys and Tutorials*, *19*(4), 2392–2431. doi:10.1109/COMST.2017.2727878

Klautau, A. (2018). 5G MIMO data for machine learning: Application to beam-selection using deep learning. Proc. Information Theory and Applications Workshop (ITA), 1-9.

Klein, D. (2004). Lagrange multipliers without permanent scarring. University of California at Berkeley, Computer Science Division.

K-nearest neighbors (k-nn) classification – Intro. (2017, August 29). Retrieved from https:// www.solver.com/k-nearest-neighbors-k-nn-classification-intro

Kolchyna, O., Souza, T. T. P., Treleaven, P., & Aste, T. (2015). *Twitter sentiment analysis: Lexicon method, machine learning method and their combination.* arXiv preprint arXiv:1507.00955

Kori, K., Pedaste, M., Altin, H., Tonisson, E., & Palts, T. (2016). Factors That Influence Students' Motivation to Start and to Continue Studying Information Technology in Estonia. *IEEE Transactions on Education*, *59*(4), 255–262. doi:10.1109/TE.2016.2528889

Kresge, N. (2015). *Smart Self-Driving Cars Still Need to Factor in Human Error.* Bloomberg.

Kronish, I. M., Cheung, Y. K., Shimbo, D., Julian, J., Gallagher, B., Parsons, F., & Davidson, K. W. (2019). Increasing the Precision of Hypertension Treatment Through Personalized Trials: A Pilot Study. *Journal of General Internal Medicine*, *34*(6), 839–845. doi:10.100711606-019-04831-z PMID:30859504

Ktoridou, D., & Epaminonda, E. (2014, April). Measuring the compatibility between engineering students' personality types and major of study: A first step towards preventing engineering education dropouts. In *2014 IEEE Global Engineering Education Conference (EDUCON)* (pp. 192-195). IEEE. 10.1109/EDUCON.2014.6826089

Kukkar, A., Mohana, R., Nayyar, A., Kim, J., Kang, B.-G., & Chilamkurti, N. (2019). A Novel Deep-Learning-Based Bug Severity Classification Technique Using Convolutional Neural Networks and Random Forest with Boosting. *Sensors (Basel)*, *19*(13), 2964. doi:10.339019132964 PMID:31284398

Kumar, P., Biswas, A., Mishra, A. N., & Chandra, M. (2010). *Spoken language identification using hybrid feature extraction methods.* arXiv preprint arXiv:1003.5623

Kumar, S., Sharma, B., Sharma, V. K., & Poonia, R. C. (2018). Automated soil prediction using bag-of-features and chaotic spider monkey optimization algorithm. *Evolutionary Intelligence.*

Kumar, S., Sharma, B., Sharma, V. K., Sharma, H., & Bansal, J. C. (2018). Plant leaf disease identification using exponential spider monkey optimization. *Sustainable Computing: Informatics and Systems.*

Kumar, J., Prabhakar, O. P., & Sahu, N. K. (2014). Comparative Analysis of Different Feature Extraction and Classifier Techniques for Speaker Identification Systems: A Review. *International Journal of Innovative Research in Computer and Communication Engineering*, *2*(1), 2760–2269.

Kumar, J., Ye, P., & Doermann, D. (2012). Learning Document Structure for Retrieval and Classification. *Proceedings of the 21st International Conference on Pattern Recognition*, 1558-1561.

Kumar, L., Sripada, S. K., Sureka, A., & Rath, S. K. (2018). Effective fault prediction model developed using least square support vector machine (LSSVM). *Journal of Systems and Software*, *137*, 686–712. doi:10.1016/j.jss.2017.04.016

Kumar, S., Morstatter, F., & Liu, H. (2014). *Twitter data analytics.* New York: Springer. doi:10.1007/978-1-4614-9372-3

Kumar, S., Sharma, B., Sharma, V. K., & Poonia, R. C. (2018). Automated soil prediction using bag-of-features and chaotic spider monkey optimization algorithm. *Evolutionary Intelligence*, 1–12.

Kumar, S., Sharma, B., Sharma, V. K., & Poonia, R. C. (2018). Automated Soil prediction using bag-of-features and chaotic spider monkey optimization algorithm. *Evolutionary Intelligence*. doi:10.100712065-018-0186-9

Kumar, S., Sharma, B., Sharma, V. K., & Poonia, R. C. (2018). *Automated soil prediction using bag-of-features and chaotic spider monkey optimization algorithm. In Evolutionary intelligence* (pp. 1–12). Springer.

Kuncheva, L. I., Rodríguez, J. J., Plumpton, C. O., Linden, D. E. J., & Johnston, S. J. (2010). Random subspace ensembles for fMRI classification. *Medical Imaging. IEEE Transactions On*, *29*(2), 531–542. PMID:20129853

Kuo, M. H., Chrimes, D., Moa, B., & Hu, W. (2015, December). Design and construction of a big data analytics framework for health applications. In *2015 IEEE International Conference on Smart City/SocialCom/SustainCom (SmartCity)* (pp. 631-636). IEEE. 10.1109/SmartCity.2015.140

Kureshi, N., Abidi, S. S. R., & Blouin, C. (2014). A predictive model for personalized therapeutic interventions in non-small cell lung cancer. *IEEE Journal of Biomedical and Health Informatics*, *20*(1), 424–431. doi:10.1109/JBHI.2014.2377517 PMID:25494516

Lai, K., Konrad, J., & Ishwar, P. (2012). A gesture-driven computer interface using Kinect. In *Image Analysis and Interpretation (SSIAI), 2012 IEEE Southwest Symposium on* (pp. 185–188). IEEE. 10.1109/SSIAI.2012.6202484

Lam, A. N., Nguyen, A. T., Nguyen, H. A., & Nguyen, T. N. (2015). Combining Deep Learning with Information Retrieval to Localize Buggy Files for Bug Reports (N). *2015 30th IEEE/ACM International Conference on Automated Software Engineering (ASE),* 476-481. 10.1109/ASE.2015.73

Lamkanfi, A., Demeyer, S., Giger, E., & Goethals, B. (2010). *Predicting the severity of a reported bug.* Paper presented at the Mining Software Repositories (MSR), 2010 7th IEEE Working Conference on. 10.1109/MSR.2010.5463284

Lamkanfi, A., Demeyer, S., Soetens, Q. D., & Verdonck, T. (2011). *Comparing mining algorithms for predicting the severity of a reported bug.* Paper presented at the 2011 15th European Conference on Software Maintenance and Reengineering. 10.1109/CSMR.2011.31

Lample, G., & Chaplot, D. S. (2017, February). Playing FPS games with deep reinforcement learning. In *Thirty-First AAAI Conference on Artificial Intelligence.* AAAI.

Laney, D. (2001). 3D data management: Controlling data volume, velocity and variety. *META Group Research Note, 6*(70), 1.

Laney, D. (2001). *3-D Data Management: Controlling Data Volume* (Vol. 6). Velocity, and Variety.

Lange, B., Koenig, S., McConnell, E., Chang, C. Y., Juang, R., Suma, E., . . . Rizzo, A. (2012, March). Interactive game-based rehabilitation using the Microsoft Kinect. In *2012 IEEE Virtual Reality Workshops (VRW)* (pp. 171-172). IEEE. doi:10.1109/VR.2012.6180935

Lange, B., Flynn, S., Proffitt, R., & Chang, C. Y., & Rizzo, A. (2010). Development of an interactive game-based rehabilitation tool for dynamic balance training. *Topics in Stroke Rehabilitation, 17*(5), 345–352. doi:10.1310/tsr1705-345 PMID:21131259

Lan, M., Tan, C. L., & Su, J. E. A. (2009). Supervised and traditional term weighting methods for automatic text categorization. *IEEE Trans. Patt. Analy. Mach. Intell., 31*(4), 721–735. doi:10.1109/TPAMI.2008.110 PMID:19229086

Laptev, I., & Caputo, B. (2004, August). Recognizing human actions: a local SVM approach. In null (pp. 32-36). IEEE.

Larsen, M. E., Boonstra, T. W., Batterham, P. J., O'Dea, B., Paris, C., & Christensen, H. (2015). We feel: Mapping emotion on Twitter. *IEEE Journal of Biomedical and Health Informatics, 19*(4), 1246–1252. doi:10.1109/JBHI.2015.2403839 PMID:25700477

Latah, M., & Toker, L. (2018). *Artificial intelligence enabled Software Defined Networking: A comprehensive overview.* IET Networks.

Lau, R. Y., Li, C., & Liao, S. S. (2014). Social analytics: Learning fuzzy product ontologies for aspect-oriented sentiment analysis. *Decision Support Systems, 65,* 80–94. doi:10.1016/j.dss.2014.05.005

Lavner, Y., & Ruinskiy, D. (2009). A decision-tree-based algorithm for speech/music classification and segmentation. *EURASIP Journal on Audio, Speech, and Music Processing,* (1).

Le Cessie, S., & Van Houwelingen, J. C. (1992). Ridge estimators in logistic regression. *Journal of the Royal Statistical Society. Series C, Applied Statistics, 41*(1), 191–201.

Lee, Y.-M., Pan, K.-T., & Chen, C. (2017). NaPer: A TSV Noise-Aware Placer. IEEE Transactions on Very Large Scale Integration (VLSI) Systems, 25(5).

Lee, C. C., Mower, E., Busso, C., Lee, S., & Narayanan, S. (2011). Emotion recognition using a hierarchical binary decision tree approach. *Speech Communication*, *53*(9-10), 1162–1171. doi:10.1016/j.specom.2011.06.004

Lee, C. H., Su, Y. Y., Lin, Y. C., & Lee, S. J. (2017). Machine learning based network intrusion detection. *Proceedings of the 2017 2nd IEEE International Conference on Computational Intelligence and Applications (ICCIA)*, 79–83. 10.1109/CIAPP.2017.8167184

Lee, H.-K., & Kim, J.-H. (1999). An HMM-based threshold model approach for gesture recognition. *IEEE Transactions on Pattern Analysis and Machine Intelligence*, *21*(10), 961–973. doi:10.1109/34.799904

Lee, H., Largman, Y., Pham, P., & Ng, A. Y. (2009). Unsupervised Feature Learning for Audio Classification Using Convolutional Deep Belief Networks. *Advances in Neural Information Processing Systems*, 1–9.

Lee, T. S., & Chen, I. F. (2005). A two-stage hybrid credit scoring model using artificial neural networks and multivariate adaptive regression splines. *Expert Systems with Applications*, *28*(4), 743–752. doi:10.1016/j.eswa.2004.12.031

Lesser, V., Horling, B., Klassner, F., Raja, A., Wagner, T., & Zhang, S. X. Q. (2000). BIG: An agent for resource-bounded information gathering and decision making. *Artificial Intelligence*, *118*(1), 197–244. doi:10.1016/S0004-3702(00)00005-9

Lewis, D. D., & Gale, W. A. (1994). *A Sequential Algorithm for Training Text Classifiers*. Paper presented at the SIGIR '94, London, UK.

Lewis, D. D. (1998). Naive (Bayes) at Forty: The Independence Assumption in Information Retrieval. *European conference on machine learning*, 4-15. 10.1007/BFb0026666

Li, J., Ritter, A., & Hovy, H. E. (2014). Weakly supervised user profile extraction from twitter. *Proceedings of the 52nd Annual Meeting of the Association for Computational Linguistics*, 165–174.

Li, R., Zhao, Z., Sun, Q. I., C-Lin, Q., Yang, C., Chen, X., Zhao, M., & Zhang, H. (2018). Deep reinforcement learning for network slicing. Academic Press.

Li, Y. (2017). *Deep reinforcement learning: An overview*. arXiv preprint, arXiv:1701.07274

Li, Y., C., L., & M., C. S. (2012). Weighted naive Bayes for text classification using positive term-class dependency. *Int. J. Artif. Intell. Tools, 21*(1).

Liang, R.-H., & Ouhyoung, M. (1998). A real-time continuous gesture recognition system for sign language. In *Automatic Face and Gesture Recognition, 1998. Proceedings. Third IEEE International Conference on* (pp. 558–567). IEEE.

Liang, S., & Dornfeld, D. A. (1989). Tool wear detection using time series analysis of acoustic emission. *ASME J. Eng. Ind. Trans., 111*(3), 199–205. doi:10.1115/1.3188750

Liddell, S. K., & Johnson, R. E. (1989). American sign language: The phonological base. *Sign Language Studies*, *64*(1), 195–277. doi:10.1353ls.1989.0027

Li, K. A., Baudisch, P., & Hinckley, K. (2008, April). Blindsight: eyes-free access to mobile phones. In *Proceedings of the SIGCHI Conference on Human Factors in Computing Systems* (pp. 1389-1398). ACM.

Lim, S., Tucker, C. S., & Kumara, S. (2017). An unsupervised machine learning model for discovering latent infectious diseases using social media data. *Jouranl of Biomedical Information*, *66*, 82–94. doi:10.1016/j.jbi.2016.12.007 PMID:28034788

Lin & Yang. (2017). Routability-Driven TSV-Aware Floor planning Methodology for Fixed-Outline 3-D ICs. IEEE Transactions on Computer-Aided Design of Integrated Circuits and Systems, 36(11).

Lin, B. S., Lee, C. C., & Chiang, P. Y. (2017). Simple smartphone-based guiding system for visually impaired people. *Sensors (Basel)*, *17*(6), 1371. doi:10.339017061371 PMID:28608811

Lin, T. Y., Maire, M., Belongie, S., Hays, J., Perona, P., Ramanan, D., ... Zitnick, C. L. (2014, September). Microsoft coco: Common objects in context. In *European conference on computer vision* (pp. 740-755). Springer.

Lin, W. Y., Chen, C. H., Tseng, Y. J., Tsai, Y. T., Chang, C. Y., Wang, H. Y., & Chen, C. K. (2018). Predicting post-stroke activities of daily living through a machine learning-based approach on initiating rehabilitation. *International Journal of Medical Informatics*, *111*, 159–164. doi:10.1016/j.ijmedinf.2018.01.002 PMID:29425627

Lin, Z., Yan, Z., Chen, Y., & Zhang, L. (2018). Yan, Y. Chen and L. Zhang, "A Survey on Network Security-Related Data Collection Technologies. *IEEE Access: Practical Innovations, Open Solutions*, *6*, 18345–18365. doi:10.1109/ACCESS.2018.2817921

Li, R., Zhao, Z., Zhou, X., Ding, G., Chen, Y., Wang, Z., & Zhang, H. (2017). Intelligent 5G: When cellular networks meet artificial intelligence. *IEEE Wireless Communications*, *24*(5), 175–183. doi:10.1109/MWC.2017.1600304WC

Li, S. T., Shiue, W., & Huang, M. H. (2006). The evaluation of consumer loans using support vector machines. *Expert Systems with Applications*, *30*(4), 772–782. doi:10.1016/j.eswa.2005.07.041

Litman, D., & Forbes, K. (2003). Recognizing emotions from student speech in tutoring dialogues. In *2003 IEEE Workshop on Automatic Speech Recognition and Understanding (IEEE Cat. No. 03EX721)* (pp. 25-30). IEEE. 10.1109/ASRU.2003.1318398

Liu, H., Li, X., Xie, G., Du, X., Zhang, P., Gu, C., & Hu, J. (2017). Precision Cohort Finding with Outcome-Driven Similarity Analytics: A Case Study of Patients with Atrial Fibrillation. In MedInfo (pp. 491-495). Academic Press.

Liu, Y., & Zheng, Y. F. (2005, July). One-against-all multi-class SVM classification using reliability measures. In *Proceedings. 2005 IEEE International Joint Conference on Neural* Networks, *2005* (Vol. 2, pp. 849-854). IEEE.

Liu, Y., Wang, Y., Kosorok, M. R., Zhao, Y., & Zeng, D. (2016). *Robust hybrid learning for estimating personalized dynamic treatment regimens.* arXiv preprint arXiv:1611.02314

Liu, B., Hu, M., & Cheng, J. (2005, May). Opinion observer: analyzing and comparing opinions on the web. In *Proceedings of the 14th international conference on World Wide Web* (pp. 342-351). ACM. 10.1145/1060745.1060797

Liu, C.-L., Nakashima, K., Sako, H., & Fujisawa, H. (2003). Handwritten digit recognition: Benchmarking of state-of-the-art techniques. *Pattern Recognition*, *36*(10), 2271–2285. doi:10.1016/S0031-3203(03)00085-2

Liu, L., Cheng, Y., Cai, L., Zhou, S., & Niu, Z. (2017). Deep learning-based optimization in wireless network. *2017 IEEE International Conference on Communications (ICC)*, 1-6.

Liu, Q., Li, P., Zhao, W., Cai, W., Yu, S., & Leung, V. C. M. (2018). A Survey on Security threats and Defensive Techniques of Machine Learning: A Data Driven View. *IEEE Access: Practical Innovations, Open Solutions*, *6*, 12103–12117. doi:10.1109/ACCESS.2018.2805680

Liu, W., Wang, S., Chen, X., & Jiang, H. (2018). Predicting the Severity of Bug Reports Based on Feature Selection. *International Journal of Software Engineering and Knowledge Engineering*, *28*(04), 537–558. doi:10.1142/S0218194018500158

Liu, Y. (2016). Fairness of user clustering in MIMO non-orthogonal multiple access systems. *IEEE Communications Letters*, *20*(7), 1465–1468.

Liu, Y., Logan, B., Liu, N., Xu, Z., Tang, J., & Wang, Y. (2017, August). Deep reinforcement learning for dynamic treatment regimes on medical registry data. In *2017 IEEE International Conference on Healthcare Informatics (ICHI)* (pp. 380-385). IEEE. 10.1109/ICHI.2017.45

Liu, Y., Loh, H. T., & Sun, A. (2009). Imbalanced text classification: A term weighting approach. *Expert Syst. Appl.*, *36*(1), 690–701.

Liu, Z., Li, Z., Wu, K., & Li, M. (2018, July/August). Urban Traffic Prediction from Mobility Data Using Deep Learning. *IEEE Network*, *32*(4), 40–46. doi:10.1109/MNET.2018.1700411

Li, X., Nsofor, G. C., & Song, L. (2009). A comparative analysis of predictive data mining techniques. *International Journal of Rapid Manufacturing*, *1*(2), 50–172. doi:10.1504/IJRAPIDM.2009.029380

Li, Y. (2012, June). Hand gesture recognition using Kinect. In *2012 IEEE International Conference on Computer Science and Automation Engineering* (pp. 196-199). IEEE. 10.1109/ICSESS.2012.6269439

Li, Y. II., & Jain, A. K. (1998). Classification of text documents. *The Computer Journal*, *41*(8), 537–546. doi:10.1093/comjnl/41.8.537

Li, Y. M., & Chen, C. W. (2009). A synthetical approach for blog recommendation: Combining trust, social relation, and semantic analysis. *Expert Systems with Applications*, *36*(3), 6536–6547. doi:10.1016/j.eswa.2008.07.077

Li, Y. M., & Li, T. Y. (2013). Deriving market intelligence from microblogs. *Decision Support Systems*, *55*(1), 206–217. doi:10.1016/j.dss.2013.01.023

Li, Y., Li, H., Guan, C., & Chin, Z. (2007). A Self-Training Semi-Supervised Support Vector Machine Algorithm and Its Applications in Brain Computer Interface. *Proceedings of the IEEE International Conference on Acoustics, Speech, and Signal Processing.*

Londhe, A., & Rao, P. P. (2017). Platforms for big data analytics: Trend towards hybrid era. *2017 International Conference on Energy, Communication, Data Analytics and Soft Computing (ICECDS)*, 3235-3238. 10.1109/ICECDS.2017.8390056

Louridas, P., & Ebert, C. (2016, September-October). Machine Learning. *IEEE Software*, *33*(5), 110–115. doi:10.1109/MS.2016.114

Louzada, F., Ara, A., & Fernandes, G. B. (2016). Classification methods applied to credit scoring: Systematic review and overall comparison. *Surveys in Operations Research and Management Science*, *21*(2), 117–134. doi:10.1016/j.sorms.2016.10.001

Lo, Y. C., Rensi, S. E., Torng, W., & Altman, R. B. (2018). *Machine learning in Chemoinformatics and Drug Discovery. In Drug Discovery Today.* Elsevier.

Lo, Y. C., Senese, S., Li, C. M., Hu, Q., Huang, Y., Damoiseaux, R., & Torres, J. Z. (2015). Large-Scale Chemical Similarity Networks for Target Profiling of Compounds Identified in Cell-Based Chemical Screens. *PLoS Computational Biology*, *11*(3), e1004153. doi:10.1371/journal.pcbi.1004153 PMID:25826798

Lu, J., & Keech, M. (2015, September). Emerging technologies for health data analytics research: a conceptual architecture. In *2015 26th International Workshop on Database and Expert Systems Applications (DEXA)* (pp. 225-229). IEEE. 10.1109/DEXA.2015.58

Lu, T., Yang, Z., & Srivastava, A. (2016). Electromigration-Aware Placement for 3D-ICs. *2016 IEEE 17th International Symposium on Qulaity Electronic Design (ISQED).*

Lu, H. E., & Wang, P. S. P. (1986). A Comment on A Fast Parallel Algorithm for Thinning Digital Patterns. *Communications of the ACM, 29*(3), 239–242. doi:10.1145/5666.5670

Luhn, H. P. (1958). The Automatic Creation of Literature Abstracts. *IBM Journal of Research and Development, 2*(2), 159–165. doi:10.1147/rd.22.0159

Lun, R., & Zhao, W. (2015). A survey of applications and human motion recognition with Microsoft kinect. *International Journal of Pattern Recognition and Artificial Intelligence, 29*(5). doi:10.1142/S0218001415550083

Luo, G., & Shi, Y. (2015). An analytical placement framework for 3-D ICs and its extension on thermal awareness. *IEEE Trans. Computer Aided Design. Integrated Circuits Systems, 32*(4), 510–523.

Luong, N. C. (2018). Applications of deep reinforcement learning in communications and networking. *Survey (London, England),* 1–37.

Luu, D. L., Lupu, C., & Chirita, D. (2019). Design and Development of Smart Cars Model for Autonomous Vehicles in a Platooning. *2019 15th International Conference on Engineering of Modern Electric Systems (EMES),* 21-24. 10.1109/EMES.2019.8795199

Lu, Y. C., Wu, C. W., Lu, C. T., & Lerch, A. (2016). An unsupervised approach to anomaly detection in music datasets. *Proceedings of the 39th International ACM SIGIR conference on Research and Development in Information Retrieval,* 749-752. 10.1145/2911451.2914700

Ma, S., Sun, X., Li, W., Li, S., Li, W., & Ren, X. (2018). *Query and Output: Generating Words by Querying Distributed Word Representations for Paraphrase Generation.* arXiv e-prints, arXiv:1803.01465

Ma, Z., & Fokoué, E. (2015). *A comparison of classifiers in performing speaker accent recognition using MFCCs.* arXiv preprint arXiv:1501.07866

Maarek, Y. S., Berry, D. M., & Kaiser, G. E. (1991). An Information Retrieval Approach for Automatically Constructing Software Libraries. *IEEE Transactions on Software Engineering, 17*(8), 800–813. doi:10.1109/32.83915

Maas, A. L., Daly, R. E., Pham, P. T., Huang, D., Ng, A. Y., & Potts, C. Learning word vectors for sentiment analysis. In *Proceedings of the 49th annual meeting of the association for computational linguistics: Human language technologies.* Association for Computational Linguistics.

Machine learning (ML). (n.d.). Retrieved from https://medium.com/@gp_pulipaka/machine-learning-techniques-for-healthcare-data-analytics-part-1-eb5aada5dce5

Machine learning (ML). (n.d.). Retrieved from https://www.xenonstack.com/blog/data-science/preparation-wrangling-machine-learning-deep

Madsen, R. E., Larsen, J., & Hansen, L. K. (2004). Part-of-speech enhanced context recognition. *Proceedings of the 14th IEEE Signal Processing Society Workshop on Machine Learning for Signal Processing,* 635–643. 10.1109/MLSP.2004.1423027

Magdalinos, P., Barmpounakis, S., Spapis, P., Kaloxylos, A., Kyprianidis, G., Kousaridas, A., ... Zhou, C. (2017). A context extraction and profiling engine for 5G network resource mapping. Journal. *Computer Communications, 109,* 184–201. doi:10.1016/j.comcom.2017.06.003

Mahana, P., & Singh, G. (2015). Comparative analysis of machine learning algorithms for audio signals classification. *International Journal of Computer Science and Network Security, 15*(6), 49.

Mahesh, R., Sinha, K., & Thakur, A. (2005). *Machine translation of bi-lingual Hindi-English (Hinglish) text*. Academic Press.

Maimo, L. F. (2017). On the performance of a deep learning-based anomaly detection system for 5G networks. *IEEE SmartWorld, 2017*, 1–9.

Maimo, L. F. (2018). A self-adaptive deep learning-based system for anomaly detection in 5G networks. *IEEE Access: Practical Innovations, Open Solutions, 6*, 7700–7712. doi:10.1109/ACCESS.2018.2803446

Ma, J., Stingo, F. C., & Hobbs, B. P. (2019). Bayesian personalized treatment selection strategies that integrate predictive with prognostic determinants. *Biometrical Journal. Biometrische Zeitschrift, 61*(4), 902–917. doi:10.1002/bimj.201700323 PMID:30786040

Malhotra, R., & Jain, A. (2012). Fault prediction using statistical and machine learning methods for improving software quality. *Journal of Information Processing Systems, 8*(2), 241–262. doi:10.3745/JIPS.2012.8.2.241

Malhotra, R., & Singh, Y. (2011). On the applicability of machine learning techniques for object oriented software fault prediction. *Software Engineering: An International Journal, 1*(1), 24–37.

Malima, A., Özgür, E., & Çetin, M. (2006). A fast algorithm for vision-based hand gesture recognition for robot control. In Signal Processing and Communications Applications, 2006 IEEE 14th (pp. 1–4). IEEE. doi:10.1109/SIU.2006.1659822

Mäntylä, M. V., Graziotin, D., & Kuutila, M. (2018). The evolution of sentiment analysis—A review of research topics, venues, and top cited papers. *Computer Science Review, 27*, 16–32. doi:10.1016/j.cosrev.2017.10.002

Manyika, J., Chui, M., Brown, B., Bughin, J., Dobbs, R., Roxburgh, C., & Hung Byers, A. (2011). *Big data: The next frontier for innovation, competition, and productivity*. Academic Press.

Mao, B., Fadlullah, Z. M., Tang, F., Kato, N., Akashi, O., Inoue, T., & Mizutani, K. (2017, November 1). Routing or Computing? The Paradigm Shift Towards Intelligent Computer Network Packet Transmission Based on Deep Learning. *IEEE Transactions on Computers, 66*(11), 1946–1960. doi:10.1109/TC.2017.2709742

Mao, F., Xu, N., & Ma, Y. (2009). Hybrid algorithm for floor planning using B*-tree representation. *IEEE Third International Symposium on Intelligent Information Technology Application, 3*, 228–231.

Mao, K. Z., Tan, K. C., & Ser, W. (2000). Probabilistic neural-network structure determination for pattern classification. *IEEE Transactions on Neural Networks, 11*(4), 1009–1016. doi:10.1109/72.857781 PMID:18249828

Mao, Q., Hu, F., & Hao, Q. (2018). Deep Learning for intelligent wireless networks: A comprehensive survey. *IEEE Communications Surveys and Tutorials, 20*(4), 2595–2621. doi:10.1109/COMST.2018.2846401

Maragos, K., Siozios, K., & Soudris, D. (2015). An Evolutionary Algorithm for Netlist Partitioning Targeting 3-D FP-GAs. IEEE Embedded Systems Letters, 7(4). doi:10.1109/LES.2015.2482902

Marnewick, A., & Pretorius, J. H. C. (2016, October). Master's of Engineering Management: Graduation rates lagging behind growth rate. In 2016 IEEE Frontiers in Education Conference (FIE) (pp. 1-8). IEEE.

Marquez-Vera, C., Morales, C. R., & Soto, S. V. (2013). Predicting school failure and dropout by using data mining techniques. *IEEE Revista Iberoamericana de Tecnologias del Aprendizaje, 8*(1), 7–14. doi:10.1109/RITA.2013.2244695

Massa, P., & Bhattacharjee, B. (2004, March). Using trust in recommender systems: an experimental analysis. In *International conference on trust management* (pp. 221-235). Springer. 10.1007/978-3-540-24747-0_17

Mathur, S., & Sutton, J. (2017). Personalized medicine could transform healthcare. *Biomedical Reports, 7*(1), 3–5. doi:10.3892/br.2017.922 PMID:28685051

McBride, N. (2016). The ethics of driverless cars. *SIGCAS Comput. Soc.*, *45*(3), 179–184. doi:10.1145/2874239.2874265

McCallum, A., & Nigam, K. (1998). A comparison of event models for naive Bayes text classification. In *Working Notes of the 1998AAAI/ICML Workshop on Learning for Text*. AAAI Press.

McClure, E. (1995). Duelling languages: Grammatical structure in codeswitching. In *Carol Myers-Scotton* (Vol. 17). Academic Press.

McNab. (2007). Network Security Assesment (2nd ed.). Academic Press.

McNemar, Q. (1955). *Psychological statistics*. Academic Press.

Medhat, W., Hassan, A., & Korashy, H. (2014). Sentiment analysis algorithms and applications: A survey. *Ain Shams Engineering Journal*, *5*(4), 1093–1113. doi:10.1016/j.asej.2014.04.011

Mehta, N., & Pandit, A. (2018). Concurrence of big data analytics and healthcare: A systematic review. *International Journal of Medical Informatics*, *114*, 57–65. doi:10.1016/j.ijmedinf.2018.03.013 PMID:29673604

Meier, P., Castillo, C., Imran, M., Elbassuoni, S. M., & Diaz, F. (2013). Extracting information nuggets from disaster-related messages in social media. *10th International Conference on Information Systems for Crisis Response and Management*, 1-10.

Mel'čuk, I. A., & Polguere, A. (1987). A formal lexicon in the meaning-text theory:(or how to do lexica with words). *Computational Linguistics*, *13*(3-4), 261–275.

Melville, J. L., Burke, E. K., & Hirst, J. D. (2009). Machine Learning in Virtual Screening. *Combinatorial Chemistry & High Throughput Screening*, *12*(4), 332–343. doi:10.2174/138620709788167980 PMID:19442063

Melville, P., & Mooney, R. J. (2003, August). Constructing diverse classifier ensembles using artificial training examples. *IJCAI (United States)*, *3*, 505–510.

Memon, Q. (2016). Self-driving and driver relaxing vehicle. *2016 2nd International* Conference on Robotics and Artificial Intelligence *(ICRAI)*, 170-174. 10.1109/ICRAI.2016.7791248

Mendoza, M. (2012). A new term-weighting scheme for naïve Bayes text categorization. *Int. J. Web Inf. Syst.*, *8*(1), 55–72. doi:10.1108/17440081211222591

Meng, X., Wei, F., Liu, X., Zhou, M., Xu, G., & Wang, H. (2012, July). Cross-lingual mixture model for sentiment classification. In *Proceedings of the 50th Annual Meeting of the Association for Computational Linguistics: Long Papers-Volume 1* (pp. 572-581). Association for Computational Linguistics.

Mengke, Y., Xiaoguang, Z., Jianqiu, Z., & Jianjian, X. (2016, March). Challenges and solutions of information security issues in the age of big data. *China Communications*, *13*(3), 193–202. doi:10.1109/CC.2016.7445514

Menon, V. G. (2017). Analyzing the Performance of Random Mobility Models with Opportunistic Routing. Advances in Wireless and Mobile Communications, 10(5), 1221-1226.

Menon, V. G., & Prathap, J. (2018). Vehicular Fog Computing: Challenges Applications and Future Directions. Fog Computing: Breakthroughs in Research and Practice, 220-229.

Menon, V. G., & Prathap, P. M. (n.d.). Moving from Topology-Dependent to Opportunistic Routing Protocols in Dynamic Wireless Ad Hoc Networks: Challenges and Future Directions. In *Algorithms, Methods, and Applications in Mobile Computing and Communications*. IGI Global.

Menon, V.G., & Prathap, P.J. (n.d.). Opportunistic routing with virtual coordinates to handle communication voids in mobile ad hoc networks. In *Advances in Signal Processing and Intelligent Recognition Systems* (pp. 323-334). Springer.

Menon, V. (2019). *Optimized Opportunistic Routing in Highly Dynamic Ad hoc Networks*. Preprints.

Menon, V. G. (2017). Moving from Vehicular Cloud Computing to Vehicular Fog Computing: Issues and Challenges. *International Journal on Computer Science and Engineering, 9*(2), 14–18.

Menon, V. G. (2019). *Light Weight Secure Encryption Scheme for Internet of Things Network, Encyclopedia*. MDPI.

Menon, V. G., & Joe Prathap, P. M. (2016). Analysing the Behaviour and Performance of Opportunistic Routing Protocols in Highly Mobile Wireless Ad Hoc Networks. *IACSIT International Journal of Engineering and Technology, 8*(5), 1916–1924. doi:10.21817/ijet/2016/v8i5/160805409

Menon, V. G., & Joe Prathap, P. M. (2016). Routing in highly dynamic ad hoc networks: Issues and challenges. *International Journal on Computer Science and Engineering, 8*(4), 112–116.

Menon, V. G., Joe Prathap, P. M., & Vijay, A. (2016). Eliminating Redundant Relaying of Data Packets for Efficient Opportunistic Routing in Dynamic Wireless Ad Hoc Networks. *Asian Journal of Information Technology, 12*(17), 3991–3994.

Menzies, T., & Marcus, A. (2008). *Automated severity assessment of software defect reports*. Paper presented at the 2008 IEEE International Conference on Software Maintenance. 10.1109/ICSM.2008.4658083

Merletti, R., Parker, P. A., & Parker, P. J. (2004). *Electromyography: physiology, engineering, and non-invasive applications* (Vol. 11). John Wiley & Sons. doi:10.1002/0471678384

Mester, L. J. (1997). What's the point of credit scoring? *Business Review (Federal Reserve Bank of Philadelphia), 3*(Sep/Oct), 3–16.

Meyer, C. F. (2010). *Introducing English Linguistics International Student Edition*. Cambridge University Press.

Michie, D., Spiegelhalter, D. J., & Taylor, C. (1994). Machine learning. *Neural and Statistical Classification, 13*.

Mikolov, T., Sutskever, I., Chen, K., Corrado, G., & Dean, J. (2013). *Distributed representations of words and phrases and their compositionality*. Arxiv:1310.4546

Milgram, J., Cheriet, M., & Sabourin, R. (2006, October). "One against one" or "one against all": Which one is better for handwriting recognition with SVMs? In *Tenth international workshop on frontiers in handwriting recognition*. Suvisoft.

Miller, G. A., Beckwith, R., Fellbaum, C., Gross, D., & Miller, K. J. (1990). Introduction to WordNet: An on-line lexical database. *International Journal of Lexicography, 3*(4), 235-244.

Milovanovic, D., & Bojkovic, Z. (2019a). 5G Ultra reliable and low-latency communication: Fundamental aspects and key enabling technologies. *LNEE Series, 561*, 372–379.

Milovanovic, D., Bojkovic, Z., & Pantovic, V. (2019b). Evolution of 5G mobile broadband technology and multimedia services framework. *LNEE Series, 561*, 351–361.

Ministry of Human Resource Development. (2018). *Educational Statistics at a Glance*. Retrieved fromhttps://mhrd.gov.in/sites/upload_files/mhrd/files/statistics-new/ESAG-2018.pdf

Mishra, B., & Shukla, K. (2012). Defect prediction for object oriented software using support vector based fuzzy classification model. *International Journal of Computers and Applications, 60*(15).

Mishra, M., & Srivastava, M. (2014). A view of Artificial Neural Network. *2014 International Conference on Advances in Engineering & Technology Research (ICAETR - 2014)*, 1-3.

Mitchell, T. M. (2006). *The discipline of machine learning* (Vol. 9). Pittsburgh, PA: Carnegie Mellon University, School of Computer Science, Machine Learning Department.

Moeslund, T. B., & Granum, E. (2001). A survey of computer vision-based human motion capture. *Computer Vision and Image Understanding*, *81*(3), 231–268. doi:10.1006/cviu.2000.0897

Mohammad, Q., & Gupta, M. (2017). *Advances in AI and ML are reshaping healthcare*. Retrieved from https://techcrunch.com/2017/03/16/advances-in-ai-and-ml-are-reshaping-healthcare/

Mohammed, D., Omar, M., & Nguyen, V. (2018). Wireless Sensor Network Security: Approaches to Detecting and Avoiding Wormhole Attacks. *Journal of Research in Business. Economics and Management*, *10*(2), 1860–1864.

Moysen, J., & Giupponi, L. (2018). From 4G to 5G: Self-organized network management meets machine learning. Journal. *Computer Communications*, *129*, 248–268. doi:10.1016/j.comcom.2018.07.015

MPEG. (2019). *Digital representation of neural networks*. MPEG.

Mudinas, A., Zhang, D., & Levene, M. (2012). Combining lexicon and learning based approaches for concept-level sentiment analysis. In *Proceedings of the first international workshop on issues of sentiment discovery and opinion mining*. ACM. 10.1145/2346676.2346681

Mujeeb, S. a. (2015). A Relative Study on Big Data Applications And Techniques. *Int. J. Eng. Innov. Technol*, *4*(10), 133–138.

Mulay, P., & Shinde, K. (2019). Personalized diabetes analysis using correlation-based incremental clustering algorithm. In *Big Data Processing Using Spark in Cloud* (pp. 167–193). Singapore: Springer. doi:10.1007/978-981-13-0550-4_8

Multinominal, N. B. (2017, October 20). Retrieved from http://scikitlearn.org/stable/modules/generated/sklearn.naive_bayes.MultinomialNB.html

Munjal, P., Narula, M., Kumar, S., & Banati, H. (2018). Twitter sentiments based suggestive framework to predict trends. *Journal of Statistics and Management Systems*, *2*(4), 685-693.

Munjal, P., Kumar, L., Kumar, S., & Banati, H. (2019). Evidence of Ostwald Ripening in opinion driven dynamics of mutually competitive social networks. *Physica A*, *522*, 182–194. doi:10.1016/j.physa.2019.01.109

Munjal, P., Narula, M., Kumar, S., & Banati, H. (2018). Twitter sentiments based suggestive framework to predict trends. *Journal of Statistics and Management Systems*, *21*(4), 685–693. doi:10.1080/09720510.2018.1475079

Murillo Piedrahita, A. F., Gaur, V., Giraldo, J., Cárdenas, Á. A., & Rueda, S. J. (2018, January/February). Leveraging Software-Defined Networking for Incident Response in Industrial Control Systems. *IEEE Software*, *35*(1), 44–50. doi:10.1109/MS.2017.4541054

Murphy, J. (2019). *Best Global Brand 2018 Rankings*. Retrieved from https://bit.ly/2O0XCuG

Murphy, G., & Cubranic, D. (2004). Automatic bug triage using text categorization. *Proceedings of the Sixteenth International Conference on Software Engineering & Knowledge Engineering*.

Murphy, J. (2018, January/February). Artificial Intelligence, Rationality, and the World Wide Web. *IEEE Intelligent Systems*, *33*(1), 98–103. doi:10.1109/MIS.2018.012001557

Murphy, K. P. (2012). *Machine learning: a probabilistic perspective*. MIT Press.

Musumeci, Nag, Macaluso, Zibar, Ruffini, & Tornatore. (2018). *An Overview on Application of Machine Learning Techniques in Optical Networks*. Academic Press.

Nabi, J. (2018). *Machine Learning—Text Processing*. Retrieved from https://towardsdatascience.com/machine-learning-text-processing-1d5a2d638958

Naboulsi, D., Fiore, M., Ribot, S., & Stanica, R. (2016). Large-Scale Mobile Traffic Analysis: A Survey. IEEE Communications Surveys & Tutorials, 18(1), 124-161. doi:10.1109/COMST.2015.2491361

Nadeau, D., & Sekine, S. (2007). A survey of named entity recognition and classification. *Lingvisticae Investigationes, 3–26.*

Naeemabadi, M. R., Dinesen, B., Andersen, O. K., Najafi, S., & Hansen, J. (2018). *Evaluating Accuracy and Usability of Microsoft Kinect Sensors and Wearable Sensor for Tele Knee Rehabilitation after Knee Operation*. BIODEVICES. doi:10.5220/0006578201280135

Nagabhushana, T. N. (1996). *Fault diagnosis of AC and AC-DC systems using Constructive Learning RBF Neural Networks* (PhD Thesis). Dept. of High Voltage Engineering, IISc, Bangalore, India.

Naïve Byes. (2017, August 29). Retrieved from http://www.python-course.eu/naive_byes_classifier_introduction.php

Nallapati, R., Zhai, F., & Zhou, B. (2016). *SummaRuNNer: A Recurrent Neural Network based Sequence Model for Extractive Summarization of Documents*. arXiv e-prints, arXiv:1611.04230

Nallapati, R., Zhou, B., Nogueira dos Santos, C., Gulcehre, C., & Xiang, B. (2016). *Abstractive Text Summarization Using Sequence-to-Sequence RNNs and Beyond*. arXiv e-prints, arXiv:1602.06023

Nandhakumar, N., & Aggarwal, J. K. (1985). The artificial intelligence approach to pattern recognition—a perspective and an overview. *Pattern Recognition, 18*(6), 383–389. doi:10.1016/0031-3203(85)90009-3

Narayan, D., Chakrabarti, D., Pande, P., & Bhattacharyya, P. (2002, January). *An experience in building the indo wordnet-a wordnet for Hindi*. In *First International Conference on Global WordNet*, Mysore, India.

National Highway Traffic Safety Administration. (2014). *Traffic safety facts: Alcohol impaired driving*. Author.

Nawir, M., Amir, A., Yaakob, N., & Lynn, O. B. (2019, March). Effective and efficient network anomaly detection system using machine learning algorithm. *Bulletin of Electrical Engineering and Informatics, 8*(1), 46–51. doi:10.11591/eei.v8i1.1387

Nayyar, A., Mahapatra, B., Le, D., & Suseendran, G. (2018). Virtual Reality (VR) & Augmented Reality (AR) technologies for tourism and hospitality industry. *International Journal of Engineering & Technology, 7*(2.21), 156-160.

Nayyar, A. (2018, August). Flying Adhoc Network (FANETs): Simulation Based Performance Comparison of Routing Protocols: AODV, DSDV, DSR, OLSR, AOMDV and HWMP. In *2018 International Conference on Advances in Big Data, Computing and Data Communication Systems (icABCD)* (pp. 1-9). IEEE. 10.1109/ICABCD.2018.8465130

Nayyar, A., Batth, R. S., Ha, D. B., & Sussendran, G. (2018). Opportunistic Networks: Present Scenario-A Mirror Review. *International Journal of Communication Networks and Information Security, 10*(1), 223–241.

Nebhi. (2012). Ontology-based information extraction from Twitter. *Proc. of the Workshop On Information Extraction And Entity Analytics On Social Media Data, 17–22.*

Need of study image (NSI). (n.d.). Retrieved from http://www.techferry.com/articles/images/outcome.png

Need of study in health care (NSHC). (n.d.). Retrieved from https://www.researchregistry.pitt.edu/files/faqs.pdf

Neethu, M. S., & Rajasree, R. Sentiment analysis in twitter using machine learning techniques. In *2013 Fourth International Conference on Computing, Communications and Networking Technologies*. IEEE. 10.1109/ICCCNT.2013.6726818

Neha Garg, D. K. S. (2018). *The Journey of BIG Data Analysis*. Paper presented at the NDIACom-2018, Bhartiya Vidyapth, Delhi, India.

Nenonen, V., Lindblad, A., Häkkinen, V., Laitinen, T., Jouhtio, M., & Hämäläinen, P. (2007, April). Using heart rate to control an interactive game. In *Proceedings of the SIGCHI conference on Human factors in computing systems* (pp. 853-856). ACM. 10.1145/1240624.1240752

Network (Net). (n.d.). Retrieved from https://itl.nist.gov/div898/handbook/eda/section1/eda11.html

Neubeck, A., & Van Gool, L. (2006, August). Efficient non-maximum suppression. In *18th International Conference on Pattern Recognition (ICPR'06)* (Vol. 3, pp. 850-855). IEEE. 10.1109/ICPR.2006.479

Neural network (NN). (n.d.). Retrieved from https://www.techopediaa.com/definition/55967/artificial-neural-network-ann

Nezhad, M. Z., Sadati, N., Yang, K., & Zhu, D. (2019). A deep active survival analysis approach for precision treatment recommendations: Application of prostate cancer. *Expert Systems with Applications*, *115*, 16–26. doi:10.1016/j.eswa.2018.07.070

Nezhad, M. Z., Zhu, D., Li, X., Yang, K., & Levy, P. (2016, December). Safs: A deep feature selection approach for precision medicine. In *2016 IEEE International Conference on Bioinformatics and Biomedicine (BIBM)* (pp. 501-506). IEEE. 10.1109/BIBM.2016.7822569

Nguyen, D. Q., Nguyen, D. Q., Pham, D., & Pham, S. B. (2014). *A Robust Transformation-Based Learning Approach Using Ripple Down Rules for Part-of-Speech Tagging*. arXiv e-prints, arXiv:1412.4021

Nguyen, H. S. (1997). *Discretization of real value attributes, boolean reasoning approach*. PhD Thesis.

Ning, X., & Karypis, G. (2011). In Silico Structure-Activity-Relationship (SAR) Models From Machine Learning: A Review. Drug Development Research, 138-146.

NIRF Ranking 2018. (2018, April 22). Retrieved from https://www.nirfindia.org/2018/Ranking2018.html

Nishani, E., & Çiço, B. (2017). Computer vision approaches based on deep learning and neural networks: Deep neural networks for video analysis of human pose estimation. *2017 6th Mediterranean Conference on Embedded Computing (MECO)*, 1-4.

Noman, F., Salleh, S. H., Ting, C. M., Samdin, S. B., Ombao, H., & Hussain, H. (2018). A *Markov-Switching Model Approach to Heart Sound Segmentation and Classification*. arXiv preprint arXiv:1809.03395

Norasetsathaporn, P. (2002). *Automatic Relevant Documents Selection Using Categorization Technique* (PhD thesis). Kasetsart University.

Norouzi, M., Fleet, D. J., & Salakhutdinov, R. R. (2012). Hamming distance metric learning. In Advances in neural information processing systems (pp. 1061-1069). Academic Press.

O'Leary, D. E. (2013, March-April). Artificial Intelligence and Big Data. *IEEE Intelligent Systems*, *28*(2), 96–99. doi:10.1109/MIS.2013.39 PMID:25505373

O'Shea, T., Hoydis, J. (2018). An introduction to Deep Learning for the Physical Layer. *IEEE Transactions on Cognitive Communications and Networking*, *3*(4), 563-575.

O'Shea, T., & Hoydis, J. (2017). *An introduction to machine learning communications systems*. Computing Research Repository.

Obermeyer, Z., & Emanuel, E. J. (2016). Predicting the future—Big data, machine learning, and clinical medicine. *The New England Journal of Medicine*, *375*(13), 1216–1219. doi:10.1056/NEJMp1606181 PMID:27682033

Oborski, P. (2014). Developments in integration of advanced monitoring systems. *International Journal of Advanced Manufacturing Technology*, *75*(9-12), 1613–1632. doi:10.100700170-014-6123-x

Oja, E. (1997). The nonlinear PCA learning rule in independent component analysis. *Neurocomputing*, *17*(1), 25–45. doi:10.1016/S0925-2312(97)00045-3

Ojha, M., & Mathur, K. (2016, March). Proposed application of big data analytics in healthcare at Maharaja Yeshwantrao Hospital. In *2016 3rd MEC International Conference on Big Data and Smart City (ICBDSC)* (pp. 1-7). IEEE. 10.1109/ICBDSC.2016.7460340

Oliveira, H., Ferreira, R., Lima, R., Lins, R. D., Freitas, F., Riss, M., & Simske, S. J. (2016). Assessing shallow sentence scoring techniques and combinations for single and multi-document summarization. *Expert Systems with Applications*, *65*, 68–86. doi:10.1016/j.eswa.2016.08.030

Oliver, M., Teruel, M. A., Molina, J. P., Romero-Ayuso, D., & González, P. (2018). *Ambient intelligence environment for home cognitive telerehabilitation* (p. 18). Sensors.

Ong, C. S., Huang, J. J., & Tzeng, G. H. (2005). Building credit scoring models using genetic programming. *Expert Systems with Applications*, *29*(1), 41–47. doi:10.1016/j.eswa.2005.01.003

Opitz, D., & Maclin, R. (1999). Popular ensemble methods: An empirical study. *Journal of Artificial Intelligence Research*, *11*, 169–198. doi:10.1613/jair.614

Ordóñez, F., & Roggen, D. (2016). Deep convolutional and lstm recurrent neural networks for multimodal wearable activity recognition. *Sensors (Basel)*, *16*(1), 115. doi:10.339016010115 PMID:26797612

Oreski, S., & Oreski, G. (2014). Genetic algorithm-based heuristic for feature selection in credit risk assessment. *Expert Systems with Applications*, *41*(4), 2052–2064. doi:10.1016/j.eswa.2013.09.004

Oszust, M., & Wysocki, M. (2013). Recognition of signed expressions observed by Kinect Sensor. In *Advanced Video and Signal Based Surveillance (AVSS), 2013 10th IEEE International Conference on* (pp. 220–225). IEEE. 10.1109/AVSS.2013.6636643

Ou, Bedawi, Koesdwiady, & Karray. (2018). Predicting Steering Actions for Self-Driving Cars Through Deep Learning. *IEEE 88th Vehicular Technology Conference (VTC-Fall)*.

Ozel, T., & Karpat, Y. (2005). Predictive modeling of surface roughness and tool wear in hard turning using regression and neural networks. *International Journal of Machine Tools & Manufacture*, *45*(4-5), 467–479. doi:10.1016/j.ijmachtools.2004.09.007

Padmanabha, Ramnaresh, & Obulakonda. (2018). A Study on Medical Imaging Techniques with Metrics and Issues in Security Cryptosystem. *Indian Journal of Public Health Research & Development*, *9*(12), 2544-2549.

Pai, S. (2004). *Acoustic emission based Tool wear monitoring using Some Improved neural network methodologies* (PhD Thesis). Mysore University, Mysore, India.

Pai, S., Nagabhushana, T. N., & Rao, P. K. R. (2003) Tool wear monitoring in face milling using Fuzzy c means clustering techniques. In *Proceedings of National Conference on Advances in Manufacturing Technology, AMT 2003*. NSS Engineering College.

Pai, P. S., Nagabhushana, T. N., & Rao, P. K. R. (2002). Flank wear estimation in Face milling based on Radial Basis Function Neural Networks. *International Journal of Advanced Manufacturing Technology*, 20(4), 241–247. doi:10.1007001700200148

Pak, A., & Paroubek, P. (2010, May). Twitter as a corpus for sentiment analysis and opinion mining. In LREc (Vol. 10, No. 2010, pp. 1320-1326). Academic Press.

Palangi, H., Deng, L., Shen, Y., Gao, J., He, X., Chen, J., ... Ward, R. (2016). Deep Sentence Embedding Using Long Short-Term Memory Networks: Analysis and Application to Information Retrieval. *IEEE/ACM Transactions on Audio, Speech and Language Processing*, 24(4), 694–707.

Paleologo, G., Elisseeff, A., & Antonini, G. (2010). Subagging for credit scoring models. *European Journal of Operational Research*, 201(2), 490–499. doi:10.1016/j.ejor.2009.03.008

Pal, M., Saha, S., & Konar, A. (2014). A fuzzy C means clustering approach for gesture recognition in healthcare. *The Knee*, 1, C7.

Palo, H. K., &Mohanty, M. N. (2018B). Comparative Analysis of Neural Networks for Speech Emotion Recognition. *International Journal of Engineering & Technology, 7*(4.39), 112-116.

Palo, H. K., Chandra, M., & Mohanty, M. N. (2017A). Emotion recognition using MLP and GMM for Oriya language. *International Journal of Computational Vision and Robotics*, 7(4), 426–442. doi:10.1504/IJCVR.2017.084987

Palo, H. K., Chandra, M., & Mohanty, M. N. (2018D). Recognition of Human Speech Emotion Using Variants of Mel-Frequency Cepstral Coefficients. In *Advances in Systems, Control and Automation* (pp. 491–498). Singapore: Springer. doi:10.1007/978-981-10-4762-6_47

Palo, H. K., Kumar, P., & Mohanty, M. N. (2017B). Emotional Speech Recognition using Optimized Features. *International Journal of Research in Electronics and Computer Engineering*, 5(4), 4–9.

Palo, H. K., Mohanty, J., Mohanty, M. N., & Chandra, M. (2016A). Recognition of Anger, Irritation and Disgust Emotional States based on Similarity Measures. *Indian Journal of Science and Technology*, 9, 38.

Palo, H. K., & Mohanty, M. N. (2016). Performance analysis of emotion recognition from speech using combined prosodic features. *Advanced Science Letters*, 22(2), 288–293. doi:10.1166/asl.2016.6855

Palo, H. K., & Mohanty, M. N. (2016B). Modified-VQ Features for Speech Emotion Recognition. *Journal of Applied Sciences (Faisalabad)*, 16(9), 406–418. doi:10.3923/jas.2016.406.418

Palo, H. K., & Mohanty, M. N. (2018C). Wavelet based feature combination for recognition of emotions. *Ain Shams Engineering Journal*, 9(4), 1799–1806. doi:10.1016/j.asej.2016.11.001

Palo, H. K., Mohanty, M. N., & Chandra, M. (2015). Use of different features for emotion recognition using MLP network. In *Computational Vision and Robotics* (pp. 7–15). New Delhi: Springer. doi:10.1007/978-81-322-2196-8_2

Palo, H. K., Mohanty, M. N., & Chandra, M. (2016C). Efficient feature combination techniques for emotional speech classification. *International Journal of Speech Technology*, 19(1), 135–150. doi:10.100710772-016-9333-9

Palo, H. K., Mohanty, M. N., & Chandra, M. (2018A). Speech Emotion Analysis of Different Age Groups Using Clustering Techniques. *International Journal of Information Retrieval Research*, 8(1), 69–85. doi:10.4018/IJIRR.2018010105

Pandarachalil, R., Sendhilkumar, S., & Mahalakshmi, G. S. (2015). Twitter sentiment analysis for large-scale data: An unsupervised approach. *Cognitive Computation*, 7(2), 254–262. doi:10.100712559-014-9310-z

Panda, S. S., Chakraborty, D., & Pal, S. K. (2008). Flank wear prediction in Drilling using Back propagation neural network and Radial basis function network. *Applied Soft Computing*, 8(2), 858–871. doi:10.1016/j.asoc.2007.07.003

Pandey, S., & Solanki, A. (2019). Music Instrument Recognition using Deep Convolutional Neural Networks. International Journal of Information Technology. doi:10.100741870-019-00285-y

Pandey, N., Sanyal, D. K., Hudait, A., & Sen, A. (2017). Automated classification of software issue reports using machine learning techniques: An empirical study. *Innovations in Systems and Software Engineering*, 13(4), 279–297. doi:10.100711334-017-0294-1

Pandey, S., & Solanki, A. (2019). *Music instrument recognition using Deep Convolutional Neural Networks. International Journal of Information Technology*, 1–10.

Pang, B., & Lee, L. (2008). Opinion mining and sentiment analysis. *Foundations and Trends® in Information Retrieval*, 2(1–2), 1-135.

Pang, B., Lee, L., & Vaithyanathan, S. (2002). Thumbs up? Sentiment classification using machine learning techniques. *Proc. of the Conference On Empirical Methods in Natural Language Processing (emnlp), Philadelphia, July 2002, Association for Computational Linguistics*, 79-86.

Pang, B., Lee, L., & Vaithyanathan, S. (2002, July). Thumbs up?: sentiment classification using machine learning techniques. In *Proceedings of the ACL-02 conference on Empirical methods in natural language processing-Volume 10* (pp. 79-86). Association for Computational Linguistics. 10.3115/1118693.1118704

Pan, S. J., Ni, X., Sun, J. T., Yang, Q., & Chen, Z. (2010, April). Cross-domain sentiment classification via spectral feature alignment. In *Proceedings of the 19th international conference on World wide web* (pp. 751-760). ACM. 10.1145/1772690.1772767

Panth, S., & Lim, S. K. (2016). Probe-Pad Placement for Prebond Test of 3-D ICs. IEEE Transactions on Components, Packaging and Manufacturing Technology, 6(4). doi:10.1109/TCPMT.2015.2513756

Papageorgiou, A., Strigkos, M., Politou, E., Alepis, E., Solanas, A., & Patsakis, C. (2018). Security and Privacy Analysis of Mobile Health Applications: The Alarming State of Practice. *IEEE Access: Practical Innovations, Open Solutions*, 6, 9390–9403. doi:10.1109/ACCESS.2018.2799522

Pappas, N., Katsimpras, G., & Stamatatos, E. (2012). Extracting informative textual parts from web pages containing user-generated content. *Proc. of 12th International Conference on Knowledge Management and Knowledge Technologies*, 4, 1–8. 10.1145/2362456.2362462

Parameters. (2017, August 31). Retrieved from https://www.nirfindia.org/Parameter

Pardo, A., Han, F., & Ellis, R. A. (2017). Combining university student self-regulated learning indicators and engagement with online learning events to predict academic performance. *IEEE Transactions on Learning Technologies*, 10(1), 82–92. doi:10.1109/TLT.2016.2639508

Parikh, R., & Movassate, M. (2009). *Sentiment analysis of user-generated twitter updates using various classification techniques*. CS224N Final Report, 118.

Park & Swaminathan. (2016). Preliminary Application of Machine Learning Techniques for Thermal-Electrical Parameter Optimization in 3D-IC. *IEEE International Symposium on Electromagnetic Compatibility (EMC)*.

Park, S. J., Bae, B., Kim, J., & Swaminathan, M. (2017). Application of Machine Learning for Optimization of 3-D Integrated Circuits and Systems. IEEE Transactions on Very Large Scale Integration (VLSI) Systems, 25(6). doi:10.1109/TVLSI.2017.2656843

Parthiban, G., & Srivatsa, S. K. (2012). Applying Machine Learning Methods in Diagnosing Heart Disease for Diabetic Patients. *International Journal of Applied Information Systems*, *3*(07), 25–30. doi:10.5120/ijais12-450593

Parvathi, I., & Rautaray, S. (2014). Survey on Data Mining Techniques for the Diagnosis of Diseases in Medical Domain. *International Journal of Computer Science and Information Technologies*, *5*(1), 838–846.

Patients like me (PLM). (n.d.). Retrieved fromhttps://www.patientslikeme.com/

Pati, K., Gururani, S., & Lerch, A. (2018). Assessment of Student Music Performances Using Deep Neural Networks. *Applied Sciences*, *8*(4), 507. doi:10.3390/app8040507

Paul, P. V., Monica, K., & Trishanka, M. (2017, April). A survey on big data analytics using social media data. In *2017 Innovations in Power and Advanced Computing Technologies (i-PACT)* (pp. 1-4). IEEE.

Paul, P. V., Yogaraj, S., Ram, H. B., & Irshath, A. M. (2017, April). Automated video object recognition system. In *2017 Innovations in Power and Advanced Computing Technologies (i-PACT)* (pp. 1-5). IEEE.

Pearl, J. (1988). Probabilistic Reasoning in Intelligent Systems. Morgan Kaufmann.

Pearl, J. (2014). *Probabilistic reasoning in intelligent systems: networks of plausible inference*. Elsevier.

Pedraza-Hueso, M., Martín-Calzón, S., Díaz-Pernas, F. J., & Martínez-Zarzuela, M. (2015). Rehabilitation using kinect-based games and virtual reality. *Procedia Computer Science*, *75*, 161–168. doi:10.1016/j.procs.2015.12.233

Pennington, J., Socher, R., & Manning, C. (2014). *Glove: Global Vectors for Word Representation* (Vol. 14). Academic Press.

Pennington, J., Socher, R., & Manning, C. (2014, 10). Glove: Global Vectors for Word Representation. *Proceedings of the 2014 Conference on Empirical Methods in Natural Language Processing (EMNLP)*, 1532-1543. 10.3115/v1/D14-1162

Perceptual edge (PE). (n.d.). Retrieved from http://www.perceptualedge.com/articles/ie/the_right_graph.pdf

Perez, J. S. (2017). Machine learning aided cognitive RAT selection for 5G heterogeneous networks. *IEEE Int. Black Sea Conference on Communications and Networking (BlackSeaCom2017)*, 1-5.

Pérez-Romero, J., Sallent, O., Ferrús, R., & Agustí, R. (2015). Artificial intelligence-based 5G network capacity planning and operation. *Int. Symposium on Wireless Communication Systems (ISWCS)*.

Perini, A., Susi, A., & Avesani, P. (2013). A machine learning approach to software requirements prioritization. *IEEE Transactions on Software Engineering*, *39*(4), 445–461. doi:10.1109/TSE.2012.52

Philip, V., Suman, V. K., Menon, V. G., & Dhanya, K. A. (2016). A Review on latest Internet of Things based Healthcare Applications. *International Journal of Computer Science and Information Security*, *15*(1), 248–254.

Pig. (n.d.). Retrieved from https://www.javatpoint.com/what-is-pig

Piscitelli, D. (2016). Motor rehabilitation should be based on knowledge of motor control. *Archives of Physiotherapy*, *6*(1), 5.

Platt, J. (1999). Fast training of support vector machines using sequential minimal optimization. In Advances in Kernel Methods—Support Vector Learning (pp. 185–208). MIT Press.

Platt, J. (1991). A resource allocating network for function interpolation. *Neural Computation*, *3*(2), 213–225. doi:10.1162/neco.1991.3.2.213 PMID:31167310

Polikar, R. (2006). Ensemble based systems in decision making. *IEEE Circuits and Systems Magazine*, *6*(3), 21–45. doi:10.1109/MCAS.2006.1688199

Polikar, R. (2009). Ensemble Learning. *Scholarpedia.*, *4*(1), 2776. doi:10.4249cholarpedia.2776

Pollettini, J. T., Pessotti, H. C., Filho, A. P., Ruiz, E. E. S., & Junior, M. S. A. (2015). Applying Natural Language Processing, Information Retrieval and Machine Learning to Decision Support in Medical Coordination in an Emergency Medicine Context. *IEEE 28th International Symposium on Computer-Based Medical Systems*, 316-319. 10.1109/CBMS.2015.82

Poplack, S., & Walker, J. (2003). Pieter Muysken, Bilingual speech: a typology of code-mixing. Cambridge, UK: Cambridge University Press.

Poria, S., Cambria, E., Hazarika, D., & Vij, P. (2016). *A deeper look into sarcastic tweets using deep convolutional neural networks.*, arXiv preprint arXiv.1610.08815

Poria, S., Cambria, E., Hazarika, D., Majumder, N., Zadeh, A., & Morency, L.-P. (2017). Context-Dependent Sentiment Analysis in User-Generated Videos. *Proceedings of the 55th Annual Meeting of the Association for Computational Linguistics*, 1, 873-883. 10.18653/v1/P17-1081

Porter, M. F. (2006). An algorithm for suffix stripping. *Electronic Library and Electronic Systems*, *40*, 211–218.

Pouyanfar, S., Yang, Y., Chen, S. C., Shyu, M. L., & Iyengar, S. S. (2018). Multimedia big data analytics: A survey. *ACM Computing Surveys*, *51*(1), 10. doi:10.1145/3150226

Praveena, R., Anand Kumar, M., & Soman, K. P. (2017). Chunking based malayalam paraphrase identification using unfolding recursive autoencoders. *2017 International Conference on Advances in Computing, Communications and Informatics, ICACCI 2017*, 922-928.

Predictive analytics (PA). (n.d.). Retrieved from https://www.sas.com/en_in/insights/analytics/predictive-analytics.html

Predictive Analytics Today (2018). *What is Predictive Analytics?* Retrieved from https://www.predictiveanalyticstoday.com/what-is-predictive-analytics

Press, G. (2017). *Top 10 Hot Artificial Intelligence Technologies*. Retrieved from https://bit.ly/2YM2x4H

Pritchard, D. E., Moeckel, F., Villa, M. S., Housman, L. T., McCarty, C. A., & McLeod, H. L. (2017). Strategies for integrating personalized medicine into healthcare practice. *Personalized Medicine*, *14*(2), 141–152. doi:10.2217/pme-2016-0064 PMID:29754553

Priyadharshini, K. (2019). *Machine Learning: What is it and Why it Matters*. Retrieved from https://bit.ly/2ezVTs8

Procházka, A., Charvátová, H., Vaseghi, S., & Vyšata, O. (2018). Machine learning in rehabilitation assessment for thermal and heart rate data processing. *IEEE Transactions on Neural Systems and Rehabilitation Engineering*, *26*(6), 1209–1214. doi:10.1109/TNSRE.2018.2831444 PMID:29877845

Pronoza, E., Yagunova, E., & Pronoza, A. (2016). Construction of a Russian paraphrase corpus: unsupervised paraphrase extraction. In *Information Retrieval* (pp. 146–157). Springer International Publishing. doi:10.1007/978-3-319-41718-9_8

Qing, R. (2018). Deep Learning for Self-Driving Cars: Chances and Challenges. *ACM/IEEE 1st International Workshop on Software Engineering for AI in Autonomous Systems*.

Qiu, G., He, X., Zhang, F., Shi, Y., Bu, J., & Chen, C. (2010). DASA: Dissatisfaction-oriented advertising based on sentiment analysis. *Expert Systems with Applications*, *37*(9), 6182–6191. doi:10.1016/j.eswa.2010.02.109

Quadri, M. M., & Kalyankar, N. V. (2010). *Drop out feature of student data for academic performance using decision tree techniques*. Global Journal of Computer Science and Technology.

Rabiner, L., & Juang, B. (1986). An introduction to hidden Markov models. *IEEE ASSP Magazine, 3*(1), 4–16. doi:10.1109/MASSP.1986.1165342

Rafique, D., & Velasco, L. (2018). Machine Learning for network automation: Overview, architecture, and applications. *Journal of Optical Communications and Networking, 10*(10), D126–D143. doi:10.1364/JOCN.10.00D126

Rahman, M. A., & Wang, Y. (2016, December). Optimizing intersection-over-union in deep neural networks for image segmentation. In *International symposium on visual computing* (pp. 234-244). Springer. 10.1007/978-3-319-50835-1_22

Rai, A. (2018). *These 6 Machine Learning Techniques Are Improving Healthcare*. Retrieved from https://bit.ly/2YJsu4y

Raigoza, J. (2017, October). A study of students' progress through introductory computer science programming courses. In 2017 IEEE Frontiers in Education Conference (FIE) (pp. 1-7). IEEE.

Rajesh, S., Paul, V., Menon, V. G., & Khosravi, M. R. (2019). A secure and efficient lightweight symmetric encryption scheme for transfer of text files between embedded IoT devices. *Symmetry, 11*(2), 293. doi:10.3390ym11020293

Ramesh, M. (2017). Design of efficient massive MIMO for 5G systems - Present and past: A review. *Int. Conf. on Intelligent Computing and Control (I2C2)*, 1-4.

Rao, S., Suma, S. N., & Sunitha, M. (2015, May). Security solutions for big data analytics in healthcare. In *2015 Second International Conference on Advances in Computing and Communication Engineering* (pp. 510-514). IEEE. 10.1109/ICACCE.2015.83

Raufi, B., & Xhaferri, I. (2018). Application of Machine Learning Techniques for Hate Speech Detection in Mobile Applications. *International Conference on Information Technologies (InfoTech-2018)*.

Ray, S. (2014). *7 Types of Regression Techniques You Should Know!* Retrieved from https://www.analyticsvidhya.com/blog/2015/08/comprehensive-guide-regression/

Razia, S., Prathyusha, P. S., Krishna, N. V., & Sumana, N. S. (2017). A Review on Disease Diagnosis Using Machine Learning Techniques. *International Journal of Pure and Applied Mathematics, 117*(16), 79–85.

Reddy, D., & Mathew, S. (2018). *Revolutionizing healthcare analytics through artificial intelligence and machine learning*. Retrieved from https://bit.ly/2JZbc07

Redmon, J., & Farhadi, A. (2018). *Yolov3: An incremental improvement*. arXiv preprint arXiv:1804.02767

Rehorn, A. G., Jinag, J., & Orban, P. E. (2005). State-of-the-art methods and results in tool condition monitoring- A review. *International Journal of Advanced Manufacturing Technology, 26*(7-8), 693–710. doi:10.100700170-004-2038-2

Rekha, R. U., Anand Kumar, M., Dhanalakshmi, V., Soman, K. P., & Rajendran, S. (2012). A novel approach to morphological generator for Tamil, Lecture Notes in Computer Science. LNCS, 6411, 249-251.

Ren, S., He, K., Girshick, R., & Sun, J. (2015). Faster r-cnn: Towards real-time object detection with region proposal networks. In Advances in neural information processing systems (pp. 91-99). Academic Press.

Rennie, J. D., Shih, L., Teevan, J., & Karger, D. R. (2003). Tackling the poor assumptions of naive Bayes text classifiers. In *Proceedings of the Twentieth International Conference on Machine Learning*. Morgan Kaufmann.

Retail (RET). (n.d.). Retrieved from https://www.rishabhsoft.com/blog/retail-store-analytics

Reviews from Careers 360. (2017, September). Retrieved from https://www.careers360.com/

Reviews from College Bol. (2017, September). Retrieved from https://www.collegebol.com

Reviews from College Dunia. (2017, September). Retrieved from https://collegeDunia.com/

Reviews from College Search. (2017, September). Retrieved from https://www.collegesearch.in/

Reviews from Get My Uni. (2017, September). Retrieved from https://www.getmyuni.com

Reviews from Glassdoor. (2017, September). Retrieved from https://www.glassdoor.co.in/index.htm

Reviews from Google Reviews. (2017, September). Retrieved from https://www.google.co.in/

Reviews from Mouth Shut. (2017, September). Retrieved from https://www.mouthshut.com

Reviews from Quora. (2017, September). Retrieved from https://www.quora.com

Reviews from Shiksha. (2017, September). Retrieved from https://www.shiksha.com/

Reviews from Youtube. (2017, September). Retrieved from https://www.youtube.com

Reynolds, D. A., & Rose, R. C. (1995). Robust text-independent speaker identification using Gaussian mixture speaker models. *IEEE Transactions on Speech and Audio Processing, 3*(1), 72–83. doi:10.1109/89.365379

Rhrissorrakrai, K., Koyama, T., & Parida, L. (2016). Watson for genomics: Moving personalized medicine forward. *Trends in Cancer, 2*(8), 392–395. doi:10.1016/j.trecan.2016.06.008 PMID:28741491

Rifaioglu, A. S., Atas, H., Martin, M. J., Atalay, R. C., Atalay, V., & Dogan, T. (2018). Recent applications of deep learning and machine intelligence on in silico drug discovery: Methods, tools and databases. *Briefings in Bioinformatics*, 1–36. PMID:30084866

Rifkin, R. M. (2002). *Everything old is new again: a fresh look at historical approaches in machine learning* (Doctoral dissertation). Massachusetts Institute of Technology.

Rinaldi, F., Dowdall, J., Kaljurand, K., Hess, M., & Mollá, D. (2003, July). Exploiting paraphrases in a question answering system. In *Proceedings of the second international workshop on Paraphrasing-Volume 16* (pp. 25-32). Association for Computational Linguistics. 10.3115/1118984.1118988

Ristevski, B., & Chen, M. (2018). Big Data Analytics in Medicine and Healthcare. *Journal of Integrative Bioinformatics*, 1–5. PMID:29746254

Ritter, A., Clark, S., & Etzioni, O. (2011). Named entity recognition in tweets: An experimental study. *Proc. of the Conference on Empirical Methods in Natural Language Processing (EMNLP 2011)*, 1524–1534.

Rodríguez-Fuentes, L. J., Peñagarikano, M., Varona, A., & Bordel, G. (2018). GTTS-EHU Systems for the Albayzin 2018 Search on Speech Evaluation. In IberSPEECH (pp. 249-253). Academic Press.

Rodriguez, J. J., Kuncheva, L. I., & Alonso, C. J. (2006). Rotation forest: A new classifier ensemble method. *IEEE Transactions on Pattern Analysis and Machine Intelligence, 28*(10), 1619–1630. doi:10.1109/TPAMI.2006.211 PMID:16986543

Rosati, S., Krużelecki, K., Heitz, G., Floreano, D., & Rimoldi, B. (2016, March). Dynamic Routing for Flying Ad Hoc Networks. *IEEE Transactions on Vehicular Technology, 65*(3), 1690–1700. doi:10.1109/TVT.2015.2414819

Rosenthal, S., Farra, N., & Nakov, P. (2017). SemEval-2017 task 4: Sentiment analysis in Twitter. *Proceedings of the 11th international workshop on semantic evaluation (SemEval-2017)*, 502-518. 10.18653/v1/S17-2088

Ross, M., Graves, C. A., Campbell, J. W., & Kim, J. H. (2013). Using Support Vector Machines to Classify Student Attentiveness for the Development of Personalized Learning Systems. *2013 12th International Conference on Machine Learning and Applications*, 325-328.

Rosten, E., Porter, R., & Drummond, T. (2010, January). Faster and Better: A Machine Learning Approach to Corner Detection. *IEEE Transactions on Pattern Analysis and Machine Intelligence, 32*(1), 105–119. doi:10.1109/TPAMI.2008.275 PMID:19926902

RouseM. (2018). *Telemedicine.* Retrieved from https://bit.ly/2Ah4hs1

Roy, S., & Garg, A. (2017, October). Predicting academic performance of student using classification techniques. In *2017 4th IEEE Uttar Pradesh Section International Conference on Electrical, Computer and Electronics (UPCON)* (pp. 568-572). IEEE. 10.1109/UPCON.2017.8251112

Rui, H., Liu, Y., & Whinston, A. (2013). Whose and what chatter matters? The effect of tweets on movie sales. *Decision Support Systems, 55*(4), 863–870. doi:10.1016/j.dss.2012.12.022

Ruiz, M., & Srinivasan, P. (1999). Hierarchical neural networks for text categorization. *ACM SIGIR Conference, Proc. of the 22nd Annual International ACM SIGIR Conference on Research and Development in Information Retrieval,* 281–282. 10.1145/312624.312700

Rush, A. M., Chopra, S., & Weston, J. (2015). *A Neural Attention Model for Abstractive Sentence Summarization.* arXiv e-prints, arXiv:1509.00685

Russell, S., & Norvig, P. (2003). *Artificial intelligence: a modern approach* (2nd ed.). Prentice Hall.

Russell, W. D., & Newton, M. (2008). Short-term psychological effects of interactive video game technology exercise on mood and attention. *Journal of Educational Technology & Society, 11*(2), 294–308.

Russo. (2015). *Big data analytics.* Best Practices Report, Fourth Quarter.

Ryden, F. (2012). Tech to the future: Making a" kinection" with haptic interaction. *IEEE Potentials, 31*(3), 34–36. doi:10.1109/MPOT.2012.2187110

Sadiq, M. (2016). Design partitioning and layer assignment for 3D integrated circuits using tabu search and simulated annealing. *Journal of Applied Research and Technology, 14*(1), 67–76. doi:10.1016/j.jart.2015.11.001

Sagiroglu, S., & Sinanc, D. (2013). Big data. *RE:view.*

Saha, A., Konar, A., Sen Bhattacharya, B., & Nagar, A. K. (2015). EEG classification to determine the degree of pleasure levels in touch-perception of human subjects. In *2015 International Joint Conference on Neural Networks (IJCNN)* (pp. 1–8). IEEE. 10.1109/IJCNN.2015.7280725

Said, A. (2018). *Machine learning for media compression: Challenges and opportunities. APSIPA Trans. on* Signal and Information Processing.

Saini, A., & Verma, A. (2018). Anuj@DPIL-FIRE2016: A Novel Paraphrase Detection Method in Hindi Language Using Machine Learning. Lecture Notes in Computer Science, 10478, 141-152.

Sakr, S., & Elgammal, A. (2016). Towards a comprehensive data analytics framework for smart healthcare services. *Big Data Research, 4,* 44–58. doi:10.1016/j.bdr.2016.05.002

Salama, M. A., Eid, H. F., Ramadan, R. A., Darwish, A., & Hassanien, A. E. (2011). Hybrid intelligent intrusion detection scheme. In *Soft computing in industrial applications* (pp. 293–303). Berlin: Springer. doi:10.1007/978-3-642-20505-7_26

Salgado, C. M., Vieira, S. M., Mendonça, L. F., Finkelstein, S., & Sousa, J. M. (2016). Ensemble fuzzy models in personalized medicine: Application to vasopressors administration. *Engineering Applications of Artificial Intelligence, 49*, 141–148. doi:10.1016/j.engappai.2015.10.004

Salton, G., & Yang, C. S. (1975). A vector space model for automatic indexing. *Communications of the ACM, 18*(11), 613–620. doi:10.1145/361219.361220

Salunkhe, P., Surnar, A., & Sonawane, S. (2017). *A Review: Prediction of Election Using Twitter Sentiment Analysis.* Academic Press.

Samek, W., Stanczak, S., & Wiegand, T. (2017). The convergence of machine learning and communications. ITU Journal, 1-8.

Sammut, C., & Webb, G. I. (Eds.). (2011). *Encyclopedia of machine learning.* Springer Science & Business Media.

Sanchez-Santillan, M., Paule-Ruiz, M., Cerezo, R., & Nunez, J. (2016, April). Predicting students' performance: Incremental interaction classifiers. In *Proceedings of the Third ACM Conference on Learning @ Scale* (pp. 217-220). ACM.

Sanz, R. A., Virseda, J. A. V., Garcia, R. M., & Arias, J. G. (2018). Innovation in the University: Perception, Monitoring and Satisfaction. *IEEE Revista Iberoamericana de Tecnologias del Aprendizaje, 13*(3), 111–118. doi:10.1109/RITA.2018.2862721

Sapountzi, A., & Psannis, K. (2018). Social networking data analysis tools & challenges. *Future Generation Computer Systems, 86*, 893–913. doi:10.1016/j.future.2016.10.019

Saquib, Ashraf, & Malik. (2017). Self Driving Car System Using (AI) Artificial Intelligence. *Asian Journal of Applied Science and Technology, 1*(7), 92-94.

Saraladevi, B., Pazhaniraja, N., Paul, P. V., Basha, M. S., & Dhavachelvan, P. (2015). Big Data and Hadoop-A study in security perspective. *Procedia Computer Science, 50*, 596–601. doi:10.1016/j.procs.2015.04.091

Sarkar, K. (2018). Learning to Detect Paraphrases in Indian Languages, Lecture Notes in Computer Science. LNCS, 10478, 153-165.

Sathya, M., Jayanthi, J., & Basker, N. (2011). Link based K-Means Clustering Algorithm for Information Retrieval. *International Conference on Recent Trends in Information Technology*, 1111-1115. 10.1109/ICRTIT.2011.5972402

Schoettle, B., & Sivak, M. (2015). *Potential impact of self-driving vehicles on household vehicle demand and usage.* Academic Press.

Schuller, B., Rigoll, G., & Lang, M. (2004, May). Speech emotion recognition combining acoustic features and linguistic information in a hybrid support vector machine-belief network architecture. In *2004 IEEE International Conference on Acoustics, Speech, and Signal Processing* (Vol. 1). IEEE. 10.1109/ICASSP.2004.1326051

Schultz, M., & Reitmann, S. (2018). Machine learning approach to predict aircraft boarding. *Transportation Research Part C, Emerging Technologies, 98*, 391–408. doi:10.1016/j.trc.2018.09.007

Schwartz, B., & Jinka, P. (2016). *Anomaly Detection for Monitoring, Publisher.* O'Reilly Media, Inc.

See, A., Liu, P. J., & Manning, C. D. (2017). *Get To The Point: Summarization with Pointer-Generator Networks.* arXiv e-prints, arXiv:1704.04368

Sehrawat, A., & Raj, G. (2018, June). Intelligent PC Games: Comparison of Neural Network Based AI against Pre-Scripted AI. In *2018 International Conference on Advances in Computing and Communication Engineering (ICACCE)* (pp. 378-383). IEEE. 10.1109/ICACCE.2018.8441745

Sengupta, P. P., Huang, Y. M., Bansal, M., Ashrafi, A., Fisher, M., Shameer, K., ... Dudley, J. T. (2016). Cognitive machine-learning algorithm for cardiac imaging: A pilot study for differentiating constrictive pericarditis from restrictive cardiomyopathy. *Circulation: Cardiovascular Imaging*, 9(6), e004330. doi:10.1161/CIRCIMAGING.115.004330 PMID:27266599

Senliol, B., Gulgezen, G., Yu, L., & Cataltepe, Z. (2008, October). Fast Correlation Based Filter (FCBF) with a different search strategy. In *2008 23rd international symposium on computer and information sciences* (pp. 1-4). IEEE.

SENTIWORDNET. (2006). *A publicly available lexical resource for opinion mining.* Andrea Esuli and Fabrizio Sebastiani.

Serafy & Srivastava. (2015). TSV Replacement and Shield Insertion for TSV–TSV Coupling Reduction in 3-D Global Placement. IEEE Transactions on Computer-Aided Design of Integrated Circuits and Systems, 34(4).

Shafi, M. (2017). 5G: A tutorial overview of standards, trials, challenges, deployment, and practice. *IEEE J. Sel. Areas Commun.*, 35(6), 1201-1221.

Sha, K., Wei, W., Andrew Yang, T., Wang, Z., & Shi, W. (2018). On security challenges and open issues in Internet of Things. *Future Generation Computer Systems*, 83, 326–337. doi:10.1016/j.future.2018.01.059

Sharma, R., Nigam, S., & Jain, R. (2014). *Opinion mining of movie reviews at document level.* arXiv preprint arXiv:1408.3829

Sharma, S., Sharma, B., Sharma, V.K., Sharma, H., & Bansal, J.C. (2018). Plant leaf disease identification using exponential spider monkey optimization. Sustainable Computing: Informatics and Systems. doi:10.1016/j.suscom.2018.10.004

Sharma, G., Sharma, S., & Gujral, S. (2015). A novel way of assessing software bug severity using dictionary of critical terms. *Procedia Computer Science*, 70, 632–639. doi:10.1016/j.procs.2015.10.059

Shashua, A. (2009). *Introduction to machine learning: Class notes 67577.* arXiv preprint arXiv:0904.3664

Sheng, Y. C., Mustafa, M. B., Alam, S., Hamid, S. H., Sani, A. A., & Gani, A. (2016, May). Personal CGPA planning system for undergraduates: Towards achieving the first class CGPA. In *2016 Fifth ICT International Student Project Conference (ICT-ISPC)* (pp. 113-116). IEEE. 10.1109/ICT-ISPC.2016.7519249

Shere, A., Eletta, O., & Goyal, H. (2017). Circulating blood biomarkers in essential hypertension: A literature review. *Journal of Laboratory and Precision Medicine*, 2(12).

Shin, B., Lee, T., & Choi, J. D. (2016). *Lexicon integrated cnn models with attention for sentiment analysis.* arXiv preprint arXiv:1610.06272

Shinyama, Y., Sekine, S., & Sudo, K. (2002, March). Automatic paraphrase acquisition from news articles. In *Proceedings of the second international conference on Human Language Technology Research* (pp. 313-318). Morgan Kaufmann Publishers Inc. 10.3115/1289189.1289218

Shlens, J. (2014). *A tutorial on principal component analysis.* arXiv preprint arXiv:1404.1100

Shlien, S. (1990). Multiple binary decision tree classifiers. *Pattern Recognition*, 23(7), 757–763. doi:10.1016/0031-3203(90)90098-6

Shone, Ngoc, Phai, & Shi. (2018). A Deep Learning Approach to Network Intrusion Detection. *IEEE Transactions on Emerging Topics in Computational Intelligence, 2*(1), 41-50. doi:10.1109/TETCI.2017.2772792

Shum, H.-y., He, X.-d., & Li, D. (2018). From Eliza to XiaoIce: challenges and opportunities with social chatbots. *Frontiers of Information Technology & Electronic Engineering, 19*(1), 10-26. doi:10.1631/FITEE.1700826

Sick, B. (2002). On-line and Indirect tool wear monitoring in turning with artificial neural networks: A review of more than a decade of research. *Mechanical Systems and Signal Processing, 16*(4), 487–546. doi:10.1006/mssp.2001.1460

Šilić, A., Chauchat, J.-H., Dalbelo Bašić, B., & Morin, A. (2007). *N-Grams and Morphological Normalization in Text Classification: A Comparison on a Croatian-English Parallel Corpus*. Paper presented at the Progress in Artificial Intelligence, Berlin, Germany.

Simeone, O. (2018). A very brief introduction to machine learning with applications to communication systems. *IEEE Trans. on Cognitive Communications and Networking, 4*(4), 648–664. doi:10.1109/TCCN.2018.2881442

Singh, S. (2018). *Natural Language Processing for Information Extraction*. CoRR abs/1807.02383

Singhal, A. (2001). Modern Information Retrieval: A Brief Overview. *IEEE Data Eng. Bull, 24*(4), 35–43.

Singh, V., Misra, S., & Sharma, M. (2017). Bug severity assessment in cross project context and identifying training candidates. *Journal of Information & Knowledge Management, 16*(01), 1750005. doi:10.1142/S0219649217500058

Sinha, R., & Shahnawazuddin, S. (2018). Assessment of pitch adaptive front-end signal processing for children's speech recognition. *Computer Speech & Language, 48*, 103–121. doi:10.1016/j.csl.2017.10.007

Sinha, U., & Kangarloo, H. (2002). Principal Component Analysis for Content-Based Image Retrieval. *Radiographics, 22*(5), 1271–1289. doi:10.1148/radiographics.22.5.g02se021271 PMID:12235353

Sisodia, D., & Sisodia, D. S. (2018). Prediction of Diabetes using Classification Algorithms. *Procedia Computer Science, 132*, 1578–1585. doi:10.1016/j.procs.2018.05.122

Sivanandam, S. N., & Deepa, S. N. (2011). *Principles of Soft Computing*. New Delhi, India: Wiley.

Skurichina, M., & Duin, R. P. W. (2002). Bagging, boosting and the random subspace method for linear classifiers. *Pattern Analysis & Applications, 5*(2), 121–135. doi:10.1007100440200011

Snoek, J., Larochelle, H., & Adams, R. P. (2012). Practical Bayesian Optimization of Machine Learning Algorithms. *NIPS Proceedings, Advances in Neural Information Processing Systems, 25*.

Snoek, J., Taati, B., & Mihailidis, A. (2012). An Automated Machine Learning Approach Applied To Robotic Stroke Rehabilitation. *2012 AAAI Fall Symp. Ser.*, 38–41.

Socher, R., Perelygin, A., Wu, J., Chuang, J., Manning, C. D., Ng, A., & Potts, C. (2013, October). Recursive deep models for semantic compositionality over a sentiment treebank. In *Proceedings of the 2013 conference on empirical methods in natural language processing* (pp. 1631-1642). Academic Press.

Social media analytics (SMA). (n.d.). Retrieved from https://iag.me/socialmedia/6-important-reasons-why-you-should-use-social-media-analytics

Sohangir, S., Wang, D., Pomeranets, A., & Khoshgoftaar, T. M. (2018). Big Data: Deep Learning for financial sentiment analysis. *Journal of Big Data, 5*(1), 3. doi:10.118640537-017-0111-6

Sokolov Aleksey. (2015). *Movie Reviews Sentiment Analysis*. Author.

Sokolova, M., Japkowicz, N., & Szpakowicz, S. (2006, December). Beyond accuracy, F-score and ROC: a family of discriminant measures for performance evaluation. In *Australasian joint conference on artificial intelligence* (pp. 1015-1021). Springer.

Sokolova, M., & Lapalme, G. (2009). A systematic analysis of performance measures for classification tasks. *Information Processing & Management, 45*(4), 427–437. doi:10.1016/j.ipm.2009.03.002

Solanki, A., & Pandey, S. (2019). Music instrument recognition using deep convolutional neural networks. *International Journal of Information Technology*, 1-10.

Solanki, A., & Pandey, S. (2019). Music instrument recognition using deep convolutional neural networks. *International Journal of Information Technology*, 1–10.

Solanki, A., & Pandey, S. (2019). Music instrument recognition using deep convolutional neural networks. *International Journal of Information Technology*.

Solanki, A., &Pandey, S. (2019). Music instrument recognition using deep convolutional neural networks. *International Journal of Information Technology*, 1-10.

Solanki, A., & Kumar, A. (2018). *A system to transform natural language queries into SQL queries*. International Journal of Information Technology, 1–10. doi:10.100741870-018-0095-2

Somashekhar, S. P., Sepúlveda, M. J., Puglielli, S., Norden, A. D., Shortliffe, E. H., Rohit Kumar, C., ... Ramya, Y. (2018). Watson for Oncology and breast cancer treatment recommendations: Agreement with an expert multidisciplinary tumor board. *Annals of Oncology: Official Journal of the European Society for Medical Oncology*, *29*(2), 418–423. doi:10.1093/annonc/mdx781 PMID:29324970

Song, Y., He, Y., Hu, Q., & He, L. (2015). ECNU At 2015 CDS Track: Two Re-Ranking Methods in Medical Information Retrieval. *Proceedings of the 2015 Text Retrieval Conference*.

Song, S., & Myaeng, S. H. (2012). A novel term weighting scheme based on discrimination power obtained from past retrieval results. *Information Processing & Management*, *48*(5), 919–930. doi:10.1016/j.ipm.2012.03.004

Spark. (n.d.). Retrieved from https://www.ibmbigdatahub.com/blog/what-spark

Specht, D. F. (1990). Probabilistic neural networks. *Neural Networks*, *3*(1), 109–118. doi:10.1016/0893-6080(90)90049-Q PMID:18282828

Sri, R. L., & Muthuramalingam, S. (2016, December). A Novel Summative Grading Assessment Strategy for Improving Students Performance. In *2016 IEEE 4th International Conference on MOOCs, Innovation and Technology in Education (MITE)* (pp. 311-316). IEEE. 10.1109/MITE.2016.068

Srimani, P. K., & Koti, M. S. (2013). Medical Diagnosis Using Ensemble Classifiers - A Novel Machine-Learning Approach. *Journal of Advanced Computing*, *1*, 9–27.

Stan, A., Yamagishi, J., King, S., & Aylett, M. (2011). The Romanian speech synthesis (RSS) corpus: Building a high quality HMM-based speech synthesis system using a high sampling rate. *Speech Communication*, *53*(3), 442–450. doi:10.1016/j.specom.2010.12.002

Stanley, R. P. (2004). An introduction to hyperplane arrangements. *Geometric Combinatorics, 13*, 389-496.

Stanley, K. O., Bryant, B. D., & Miikkulainen, R. (2005). Evolving neural network agents in the NERO video game. *Proceedings of the IEEE*, 182-189.

Statistics (ST). (n.d.). Retrieved from https://explorable.com/branches-of-statistics

Su, C. J. (2013). Personal rehabilitation exercise assistant with kinect and dynamic time warping. *International Journal of Information and Education Technology (IJIET)*, *3*(4), 448–454. doi:10.7763/IJIET.2013.V3.316

Summerville, A., Snodgrass, S., Guzdial, M., Holmgård, C., Hoover, A. K., Isaksen, A., ... Togelius, J. (2018). Procedural content generation via machine learning (PCGML). *IEEE Transactions on Games*, *10*(3), 257–270. doi:10.1109/TG.2018.2846639

Sun, H., Chen, X., Shi, Q., Hong, M., Fu, X., & Sidiropoulos, N. D. (2017). Learning to optimize: Training deep neural networks for wireless resource management. *2017 IEEE 18th International Workshop on Signal Processing Advances in Wireless Communications (SPAWC)*, 1-6.

Sunny, A.D., Kulshreshtha, S., & Singh, S., Srinabh, B. M., & Sarojadevi, H. (2018). Disease Diagnosis System By Exploring Machine Learning Algorithms. *International Journal of Innovations in Engineering and Technology, 10*(2), 14–21.

Sutskever, I., Vinyals, O., & Le, Q. V. (2014). *Sequence to Sequence Learning with Neural Networks.* arXiv e-prints, arXiv:1409.3215

Suuny, S., Peter, S. D., & Jacob, K. P. (2013). Performance of different classifiers in speech recognition. *Int. J. Res. Eng. Technol, 2*(4), 590–597. doi:10.15623/ijret.2013.0204032

Suykens, J. A. K., & Vandewalle, J. (1999). Least squares support vector machine classifiers. *Neural Processing Letters, 9*(3), 293–300. doi:10.1023/A:1018628609742

Taboada, M., Brooke, J., Tofiloski, M., Voll, K., & Stede, M. (2011). Lexicon-based methods for sentiment analysis. *Computational Linguistics, 37*(2), 267–307. doi:10.1162/COLI_a_00049

Takafumi, Tad, & Jaychand. (2018). *Autonomous Driving System based on Deep Q Learnig.* Academic Press.

Tamura, T. (2014). Wearable inertial sensors and their applications. In *Wearable Sensors* (pp. 85–104). Academic Press. doi:10.1016/B978-0-12-418662-0.00024-6

Tang, D., Wei, F., Qin, B., Yang, N., Liu, T., & Zhou, M. (2016). Sentiment embeddings with applications to sentiment analysis. *IEEE Transactions on Knowledge and Data Engineering, 28*(2), 496–509. doi:10.1109/TKDE.2015.2489653

Tang, T. A., Mhamdi, L., McLernon, D., Zaidi, S. A. R., & Ghogho, M. (2016). Deep learning approach for Network Intrusion Detection in Software Defined Networking. *2016 International Conference on Wireless Networks and Mobile Communications (WINCOM)*, 258-263. 10.1109/WINCOM.2016.7777224

Tansel, A. U. (2013). Innovation through patient health records. *Procedia: Social and Behavioral Sciences, 75*, 183–188. doi:10.1016/j.sbspro.2013.04.021

Tan, W., Blake, M. B., Saleh, I., & Dustdar, S. (2013). Social-network-sourced big data analytics. *IEEE Internet Computing, 17*(5), 62–69. doi:10.1109/MIC.2013.100

Ta, V. D., Liu, C. M., & Nkabinde, G. W. (2016, July). Big data stream computing in healthcare real-time analytics. In *2016 IEEE International Conference on Cloud Computing and Big Data Analysis (ICCCBDA)* (pp. 37-42). IEEE.

Tehrani, N. (2018). How Personalized Artificial Intelligence Is Advancing Treatment Of Diabetes. *International Journal of Scientific and Education Research, 2*, 30–33.

Telles, S., Pathak, S., Singh, N., & Balkrishna, A. (2014). Research on traditional medicine: What has been done, the difficulties, and possible solutions. *Evidence-Based Complementary and Alternative Medicine.* PMID:25013445

Tesla Motors. (2017). *Tesla Autopilot.* Retrieved from https://www.tesla.com/autopilot

Thamizhselvan, M., Raghuraman, R., Manoj, S. G., & Paul, P. V. (2015, January). Data security model for Cloud Computing using V-GRT methodology. In *2015 IEEE 9th International Conference on Intelligent Systems and Control (ISCO)* (pp. 1-6). IEEE. 10.1109/ISCO.2015.7282349

Thelwall, M., Buckley, K., Paltoglou, G., Cai, D., & Kappas, A. (2010). Sentiment strength detection in short informal text. *Journal of the American Society for Information Science and Technology, 61*(12), 2544–2558. doi:10.1002/asi.21416

Thomas, L. C., Edelman, D. B., & Crook, J. N. (2002). *Credit scoring and its applications*. Society for industrial and Applied Mathematics.

Tian, L., Ning, H., Kong, L., Chen, K., Qi, H., & Han, Z. (2018). Sentence Paraphrase Detection Using Classification Models, Lecture Notes in Computer Science. LNCS, 10478, 166-181.

Tian, Y., Lo, D., & Sun, C. (2012). *Information retrieval based nearest neighbor classification for fine-grained bug severity prediction*. Paper presented at the 2012 19th Working Conference on Reverse Engineering. 10.1109/WCRE.2012.31

Tie, L., Zheng, N., Hong, C., & Xing, Z. (2003). *A Novel Approach of Road Recognition Based on Deformable Template and Genetic Algorithm*. IEEE.

Timotheou, S., & Krikidis, I. (2015). Fairness for non-orthogonal multiple access in 5G systems. *IEEE Signal Processing Letters*, *22*(10), 1647–1651. doi:10.1109/LSP.2015.2417119

Ting, K. M., & Witten, I. H. (1997). *Stacking bagged and dagged models*. Academic Press.

Toh, Z., & Su, J. (2016). Nlangp at semeval-2016 task 5: Improving aspect based sentiment analysis using neural network features. *Proceedings of the 10th international workshop on semantic evaluation*, 282-288. 10.18653/v1/S16-1045

Tomlin, R. S. (2014). *Basic Word Order (RLE Linguistics B: Grammar): Functional Principles* (Vol. 13). Routledge. doi:10.4324/9781315857466

Tong, R. M. (2001, September). An operational system for detecting and tracking opinions in on-line discussion. In *Working Notes of the ACM SIGIR 2001 Workshop on Operational Text Classification* (*Vol. 1*, No. 6). Academic Press.

Tools. (n.d.). Retrieved from http://bigdata-madesimple.com/top-big-data-tools-used-to-store-and-analyse-data/

Topiwala, P., Krishnan, M., & Dai, W. (2018). Deep learning techniques in video coding and quality analysis. *Int. Conf. SPIE Applications of Digital Image Processing*. 10.1117/12.2322025

Torun & Swaminathan. (2017). *Black-Box Optimization of 3D Integrated Systems using Machine Learning*. School of Electrical and Computer Engineering, Georgia Institute of Technology.

Touyz, R. M., & Burger, D. (2012). Biomarkers in hypertension. In *Special issues in hypertension* (pp. 237–246). Milano: Springer. doi:10.1007/978-88-470-2601-8_19

Tran, G. K. (2018). Architecture of mmWave Edge cloud in 5G-MiEdge. *IEEE Int. Conf. Communications Workshops*, 1-6.

Tran, D. D., Ha, D. B., & Nayyar, A. (2018). Wireless power transfer under secure communication with multiple antennas and eavesdroppers. *Proc. Int. conference on Industrial Networks and Intelligent Systems, Springer LNICST*, 208-220.

Trankler, H. R., & Kanoun, O. (2001, May). Recent advances in sensor technology. In *IMTC 2001. Proceedings of the 18th IEEE Instrumentation and Measurement Technology Conference. Rediscovering Measurement in the Age of Informatics (Cat. No. 01CH 37188)* (Vol. 1, pp. 309-316). IEEE. 10.1109/IMTC.2001.928831

Tran, S. N., & d'Avila Garcez, A. S. (2018, February). Deep Logic Networks: Inserting and Extracting Knowledge From Deep Belief Networks. *IEEE Transactions on Neural Networks and Learning Systems*, *29*(2), 246–258. doi:10.1109/TNNLS.2016.2603784 PMID:27845678

Tripathi, D., Cheruku, R., & Bablani, A. (2018). Relative Performance Evaluation of Ensemble Classification with Feature Reduction in Credit Scoring Datasets. In *Advances in Machine Learning and Data Science* (pp. 293–304). Singapore: Springer. doi:10.1007/978-981-10-8569-7_30

Tripathi, D., Edla, D. R., & Cheruku, R. (2018). Hybrid credit scoring model using neighborhood rough set and multi-layer ensemble classification. *Journal of Intelligent & Fuzzy Systems*, *34*(3), 1543–1549. doi:10.3233/JIFS-169449

Tripathi, D., Edla, D. R., Cheruku, R., & Kuppili, V. (2019). A novel hybrid credit scoring model based on ensemble feature selection and multilayer ensemble classification. *Computational Intelligence*, *35*(2), 371–394. doi:10.1111/coin.12200

Tripathi, D., Edla, D. R., Kuppili, V., Bablani, A., & Dharavath, R. (2018). Credit Scoring Model based on Weighted Voting and Cluster based Feature Selection. *Procedia Computer Science*, *132*, 22–31. doi:10.1016/j.procs.2018.05.055

Tripathy, A., Agrawal, A., & Rath, S. K. (2015). Classification of Sentimental Reviews Using Machine Learning Techniques. *Procedia Computer Science*, *57*, 821–829. doi:10.1016/j.procs.2015.07.523

Tripathy, A., Agrawal, A., & Rath, S. K. (2016). Classification of sentiment reviews using n-gram machine learning approach. *Expert Systems with Applications*, *57*, 117–126. doi:10.1016/j.eswa.2016.03.028

Trivedi, C. (2018). *Building a Deep Neural Network to play FIFA 18*. Available Online at: https://towardsdatascience.com/building-a-deep-neural-network-to-play-fifa-18-dce54d45e675

Tsai, C. W., Lai, C. F., Chao, H. C., & Vasilakos, A. V. (2015). Big data analytics: a survey. *Journal of Big data*, *2*(1), 21.

Tsai, C. F., Lin, Y. C., Yen, D. C., & Chen, Y. M. (2011). Predicting stock returns by classifier ensembles. *Applied Soft Computing*, *11*(2), 2452–2459. doi:10.1016/j.asoc.2010.10.001

Tsai, C.-W., Lai, C.-F., Chiang, M.-C., & Yang, L. T. (2014). Data mining for Internet of Things: A survey. *IEEE Communications Surveys and Tutorials*, *16*(1), 77–97. doi:10.1109/SURV.2013.103013.00206

Tsatsaronis, G., Varlamis, I., & Nørvg, K. (2010). An experimental study on unsupervised graph based word sense disambiguation. *Computational Linguistics and Intelligent Text Processing, LNCS*, *6008*, 184–198. doi:10.1007/978-3-642-12116-6_16

Tulyakov, S., Jaeger, S., Govindaraju, V., & Doermann, D. (2008). Review of classifier combination methods. In *Machine learning in document analysis and recognition* (pp. 361–386). Berlin: Springer. doi:10.1007/978-3-540-76280-5_14

Tummel, A. A. D. J. C., & Richert, S. J. A. (2015, December). Sentiment Analysis of Social Media for Evaluating Universities. In *The Second International Conference on Digital Information Processing, Data Mining, and Wireless Communications (DIPDMWC2015)* (p. 49). Academic Press.

Turney, P. (2000). Learning algorithms for keyphrase extraction. *Information Retrieval*, *2*(4), 303–336. doi:10.1023/A:1009976227802

Turney, P. D. (2002, July). Thumbs up or thumbs down?: semantic orientation applied to unsupervised classification of reviews. In *Proceedings of the 40th annual meeting on association for computational linguistics* (pp. 417-424). Association for Computational Linguistics.

Twomey, N., Diethe, T., Fafoutis, X., Elsts, A., McConville, R., Flach, P., & Craddock, I. (2018, June). A comprehensive study of activity recognition using accelerometers. In Informatics (Vol. 5, No. 2, p. 27). Multidisciplinary Digital Publishing Institute. doi:10.3390/informatics5020027

Types of analytics (TA). (n.d.). Retrieved from https://www.scnsoft.com/blog/4-types-of-data-analytics

U.S. Department of Transportation. (2017). *Automated Driving Systems - A Vision for Safety*. Retrieved from: https://www.nhtsa.gov/sites/nhtsa.dot.gov/files/documents/13069a-ads2.0_090617_v9a_tag.pdf

Uan Sholanbayev. (2016). *Sentiment Analysis on Movie Reviews*. Author.

Uhrig, R. E. (1995). Introduction to artificial neural networks. *Proceedings of IECON '95 - 21st Annual Conference on IEEE Industrial Electronics*, 33-3. 10.1109/IECON.1995.483329

Van Gestel, T., Baesens, B., Suykens, J. A., Van den Poel, D., Baestaens, D. E., & Willekens, M. (2006). Bayesian kernel based classification for financial distress detection. *European Journal of Operational Research*, *172*(3), 979–1003. doi:10.1016/j.ejor.2004.11.009

Van Poucke, S., Thomeer, M., Heath, J., & Vukicevic, M. (2016). Are randomized controlled trials the (g) old standard? From clinical intelligence to prescriptive analytics. *Journal of Medical Internet Research*, *18*(7), e185. doi:10.2196/jmir.5549 PMID:27383622

Vapnik, V. (2013). *The nature of statistical learning theory*. Springer science & business media.

Vapnik, V., Guyon, I., & Hastie, T. (1995). Support vector machines. *Machine Learning*, *20*(3), 273–297. doi:10.1007/BF00994018

Vasilis, F., Pavlidis, G., & Friedman. (2009). Three Dimensional Integrated Circuit Design. Elsevier Inc.

Vateekul, P., & Koomsubha, T. (2016). A study of sentiment analysis using deep learning techniques on Thai Twitter data. *2016 13th International Joint Conference on Computer Science and Software Engineering*, 1-6. 10.1109/JCSSE.2016.7748849

Venu, S.H., Annie, A.X., & Mohan, V. (2016). *Sentiment Analysis Applied to Airline Feedback to Boost Customer's Endearment*. Academic Press.

Vermeer, S. A. M., Araujo, T., Bernritter, S. F., & Noort, G. (in press). Seeing the wood for the trees: How machine learning can help firms in identifying relevant electronic word-of-mouth in social media. *International Journal of Research in Marketing*. doi:10.1016/j.ijresmar.2019.01.010

Vijay, A., Menon, V. G., & Nayyar, A. 2018, November. Distributed Big Data Analytics in the Internet of Signals. In *2018 International Conference on System Modeling & Advancement in Research Trends (SMART)* (pp. 73-77). IEEE.

Vijayaraj, J., Saravanan, R., Paul, P. V., & Raju, R. (2016, November). A comprehensive survey on big data analytics tools. In *2016 Online International Conference on Green Engineering and Technologies (IC-GET)* (pp. 1-6). IEEE. 10.1109/GET.2016.7916733

Vila, M., Rodríguez, H., & Martí, M. A. (2015). Relational paraphrase acquisition from Wikipedia: The WRPA method and corpus. *Natural Language Engineering*, *21*(03), 355–389. doi:10.1017/S1351324913000235

Vinoj, P. G., Jacob, S., Menon, V. G., Rajesh, S., & Khosravi, M. R. (2019). Brain-Controlled Adaptive Lower Limb Exoskeleton for Rehabilitation of Post-Stroke Paralyzed. IEEE Access. doi:10.1109/ACCESS.2019.2921375

Vinoj, P. G., Jacob, S., & Menon, V. G. (2018). Hybrid brain actuated muscle interface for the physically disabled. *Basic & Clinical Pharmacology & Toxicology*, *123*, 8–9. PMID:29345051

Wadawadagi, R. S. & Pagi, V. B. (in press). An enterprise perspective of web content analysis research: *A strategic roadmap. International Journal of Knowledge and Web Intelligence*. doi:10.1504/IJKWI.2017.10010794

Wadawadagi, R. S., & Veerappa, B. (2019). A multi-layer approach to opinion polarity classification using augmented semantic tree kernels. *Journal of Experimental & Theoretical Artificial Intelligence*, *31*(3), 349–367. doi:10.1080/0952813X.2018.1549108

Waibel, A., Hanazawa, T., Hinton, G., Shikano, K., & Lang, K. J. (1990). Phoneme recognition using time-delay neural networks. In *Readings in speech recognition* (pp. 393–404). Elsevier. doi:10.1016/B978-0-08-051584-7.50037-1

Waldrop, M. M. (2015). Autonomous vehicles: No drivers required. *Nature, 20*(3). PMID:25652978

Wale, N. (2011). *Machine Learning in Drug Discovery and Development*. Wiley. doi:10.1002/ddr.20407

Waltl, B., Bonczek, G., & Matthes, F. (2018). Rule-based information extraction: advantages, limitations, and perspectives. *Jusletter IT, 22*.

Wan, X. (2012, December). A comparative study of cross-lingual sentiment classification. In *Proceedings of the 2012 IEEE/WIC/ACM International Joint Conferences on Web Intelligence and Intelligent Agent Technology-Volume 01* (pp. 24-31). IEEE Computer Society. 10.1109/WI-IAT.2012.54

Wang, J. (2017). Spatiotemporal modeling and prediction in cellular networks: A big data enabled deep learning approach. *IEEE INFOCOM 2017 - IEEE Conference on Computer Communications*, 1-9.

Wang, Q. (2017). Multimedia IoT systems and applications. *Global Internet of Things Summit (GIoTS)*.

Wang, Y. (2016). Deep reasoning and thinking beyond deep learning by cognitive robots and brain-inspired systems. *2016 IEEE 15th International Conference on Cognitive Informatics & Cognitive Computing (ICCI*CC)*, 3-3.

Wang, Y. (2017). Cognitive foundations of knowledge science and deep knowledge learning by cognitive robots. *2017 IEEE 16th International Conference on Cognitive Informatics & Cognitive Computing (ICCI*CC)*, 5.

Wang, Y., Yang, C., Wu, X., Xu, S., & Li, H. (2012). Kinect based dynamic hand gesture recognition algorithm research. In *Intelligent Human-Machine Systems and Cybernetics (IHMSC), 2012 4th International Conference on* (Vol. 1, pp. 274–279). IEEE. 10.1109/IHMSC.2012.76

Wang, C., Zhou, J., Weerasekera, R., Zhao, B., Liu, X., Royannez, P., & Je, M. (2015, January). BIST Methodology, Architecture and Circuits for Pre-Bond TSV Testing in 3D Stacking IC Systems. *IEEE Transactions on Circuits and Systems. I, Regular Papers, 62*(1), 139–148. doi:10.1109/TCSI.2014.2354752

Wang, F. (2015). Adaptive semi-supervised recursive tree partitioning: The ART towards large scale patient indexing in personalized healthcare. *Journal of Biomedical Informatics, 55*, 41–54. doi:10.1016/j.jbi.2015.01.009 PMID:25656756

Wang, G., Ma, J., Huang, L., & Xu, K. (2012). Two credit scoring models based on dual strategy ensemble trees. *Knowledge-Based Systems, 26*, 61–68. doi:10.1016/j.knosys.2011.06.020

Wang, J., Guo, K., & Wang, S. (2010). Rough set and Tabu search based feature selection for credit scoring. *Procedia Computer Science, 1*(1), 2425–2432. doi:10.1016/j.procs.2010.04.273

Wang, J., Wu, Q., Deng, H., & Yan, Q. (2008, March). Real-time speech/music classification with a hierarchical oblique decision tree. In *2008 IEEE International Conference on Acoustics, Speech and Signal Processing* (pp. 2033-2036). IEEE. 10.1109/ICASSP.2008.4518039

Wang, L., & Xie, X. Q. (2014). Computational Target Fishing: What Should Chemogenomics Researchers Expect For the Future of in Silico Drug Design and Discovery? *Editorial Special Focus: Computational Chemistry, 6*(3), 247–249. PMID:24575960

Wang, M., Cui, Y., Wang, X., Xiao, S., & Jiang, J. (2018). Machine Learning for Networking: Workflow, Advances and Opportunities. *IEEE Network, 32*(2), 92–99. doi:10.1109/MNET.2017.1700200

Wang, S., Jiang, L., & Li, C. (2014). A cfs-based feature weighting approach to naive Bayes text classifiers. In *Proceedings of the 24th International Conference on Artificial Neural Networks*. Springer. 10.1007/978-3-319-11179-7_70

Wang, S., Jiang, L., & Li, C. (2015). Adapting naive Bayes tree for text classification. *Knowledge and Information Systems, 44*(1), 77–89. doi:10.100710115-014-0746-y

Wang, T. (2019). Machine learning for 5G and beyond: From model-based to data-driven mobile wireless networks. *Journal. China Communications*, *16*(1), 165–175.

Wang, W. M., Li, Z., Wang, J. W., & Zheng, Z. H. (2017). How far we can go with extractive text summarization? Heuristic methods to obtain near upper bounds. *Expert Systems with Applications*, *90*, 439–463. doi:10.1016/j.eswa.2017.08.040

Wang, W., Zhu, M., Zeng, X., Ye, X., & Sheng, Y. (2017). Malware traffic classification using convolutional neural network for representation learning. *2017 International Conference on Information Networking (ICOIN)*, 712-717. 10.1109/ICOIN.2017.7899588

Wang, X., Jiang, W., & Luo, Z. (2016). Combination of convolutional and recurrent neural network for sentiment analysis of short texts. *Proceedings of COLING 2016, the 26th International Conference on Computational Linguistics: Technical Papers*, 2428-2437.

Wang, X., Li, X. M., & Leung, V. C. (2015). Artificial intelligence-based techniques for emerging heterogeneous network: State of the arts, opportunities, and challenges. *IEEE Access: Practical Innovations, Open Solutions*, *3*, 1379–1391. doi:10.1109/ACCESS.2015.2467174

Wang, Y. Y., & Acero, A. (2007, December). Maximum entropy model parameterization with TF* IDF weighted vector space model. In *2007 IEEE Workshop on Automatic Speech Recognition & Understanding (ASRU)* (pp. 213-218). IEEE. 10.1109/ASRU.2007.4430111

Wang, Y., Li, P., Jiao, L., Su, Z., Cheng, N., Shen, X. S., & Zhang, P. (2017). A data-driven architecture for personalized QoE management in 5G Wireless Networks. *IEEE Wireless Communications*, *24*(1), 1–9. doi:10.1109/MWC.2016.1500184WC

Wang, Y., & Valipour, M. (2016). Formal Properties and Mathematical Rules of Concept Algebra for Cognitive Machine Learning (I). *Journal of Advanced Mathematics and Applications*, *5*(1), 53–68. doi:10.1166/jama.2016.1091

Wang, Y., Wu, P., Liu, Y., Weng, C., & Zeng, D. (2016, October). Learning optimal individualized treatment rules from electronic health record data. In *2016 IEEE International Conference on Healthcare Informatics (ICHI)* (pp. 65-71). IEEE. 10.1109/ICHI.2016.13

Wani, G. P., & Alone, N. V. (2015). Analysis of Indian Election using Twitter. *International Journal of Computer Applications, 121*(22).

Wan, X. (2009, August). Co-training for cross-lingual sentiment classification. In *Proceedings of the Joint Conference of the 47th Annual Meeting of the ACL and the 4th International Joint Conference on Natural Language Processing of the AFNLP* (pp. 235-243). Association for Computational Linguistics.

Wan, Y., & Gao, Q. (2015). An ensemble sentiment classification system of twitter data for airline services analysis. *IEEE International Conference on Data Mining Workshop (ICDMW)*, 1318–1325. 10.1109/ICDMW.2015.7

Warburton, D. E., Bredin, S. S., Horita, L. T., Zbogar, D., Scott, J. M., Esch, B. T., & Rhodes, R. E. (2007). The health benefits of interactive video game exercise. *Applied Physiology, Nutrition, and Metabolism*, *32*(4), 655–663. doi:10.1139/H07-038 PMID:17622279

Ward, M. J., Marsolo, K. A., & Froehle, C. M. (2014). Applications of business analytics in healthcare. *Business Horizons*, *57*(5), 571–582. doi:10.1016/j.bushor.2014.06.003 PMID:25429161

Wasserman, P. D. (1993). *Advanced Methods in Neural Computing*. New York: John Wiley & Sons, Inc.

Wavestone. (2017) Rectrieved from https://www.wavestone.com/en/insight/driverless-car-reality-making/

Waymo, L. L. C. W. (2017). *Self-Driving Car Project*. Retrieved from:https://waymo.com

Waymo. (2017). *Waymo's fully self-driving vehicles are here.* Retrieved from: https://medium.com/waymo/with-waymo-in-the-drivers-seat-fully-self-driving-vehicles-can-transform-the-way-we-getaround-75e9622e829a

Webb, G. I. (2000). Multiboosting: A technique for combining boosting and wagging. *Machine Learning, 40*(2), 159–196. doi:10.1023/A:1007659514849

Webb, G., Boughton, J., & Wang, Z. (2005). Not so naive Bayes: Aggregating one- dependence estimators. *Mach. Learn., 58*(1), 5–24.

Wehrmann, J., Becker, W., Cagnini, H. E. L., & Barros, R. C. (2017). A character-based convolutional neural network for language-agnostic Twitter sentiment analysis. *2017 International Joint Conference on Neural Networks (IJCNN),* 2384-2391. 10.1109/IJCNN.2017.7966145

Weinberg, G. M. (1993). Quality software management. New York: Academic Press.

Weinberger, K. Q., Blitzer, J., & Saul, L. K. (2006). Distance metric learning for large margin nearest neighbor classification. In Advances in neural information processing systems (pp. 1473–1480). Academic Press.

Weng, C. G., & Poon, J. (2008). A new evaluation measure for imbalanced datasets. *Proceedings of the 7th Australasian Data Mining Conference-Volume 87.*

Wen, J., Li, S., Lin, Z., Hu, Y., & Huang, C. (2012). Systematic literature review of machine learning based software development effort estimation models. *Information and Software Technology, 54*(1), 41–59. doi:10.1016/j.infsof.2011.09.002

Werbos, P. J. (2011). Computational intelligence for the smart grid: History, challenges, and opportunities. *IEEE Computational Intelligence Magazine, 6*(3), 14–21. doi:10.1109/MCI.2011.941587

West, D. (2000). Neural network credit scoring models. *Computers & Operations Research, 27*(11-12), 1131–1152. doi:10.1016/S0305-0548(99)00149-5

Whitehead, S. D., & Ballard, D. H. (1991). Learning to perceive and act by trial and error. Machine Learning, 7(1), 45-83. Retrieved from . doi:10.1007/BF00058926

Will the NIRF ranking help students choice of courses & colleges? (2018 May 1). Retrieved from http://www.educationtimes.com/article/93/2018041120180411122852781d9010d4f/ Will the-NIRF-ranking-help-students-choice-of-coursescollege.html

Williams, S. (2015). *The Drug Development Process: 9 Steps From the Laboratory to Your Medicine Cabinet.* Retrieved from https://bit.ly/2Ebgfrr

Williams, J. J., & Katsaggelos, A. K. (2002). An HMM-based speech-to-video synthesizer. *IEEE Transactions on Neural Networks, 13*(4), 900–915. doi:10.1109/TNN.2002.1021891 PMID:18244486

Williams, R., & Wright, J. (1998). Epidemiological issues in health needs assessment. *BMJ (Clinical Research Ed.), 316*(7141), 1379–1382. doi:10.1136/bmj.316.7141.1379 PMID:9563997

Witten & Tibshirani. (2013). *An Introduction to Statistical Learning with Applications in R.* Academic Press.

Witten, I. H., Frank, E., & Hall, M. A. (2011). Data Mining: Practical Machine Learning Tools and Techniques (3rd ed.). Morgan Kaufmann.

Wongchinsri, P., & Kuratach, W. (2017, June). SR-based binary classification in credit scoring. In *2017 14th International Conference on Electrical Engineering/Electronics, Computer, Telecommunications and Information Technology (ECTI-CON)* (pp. 385-388). IEEE.

Woodland, P. C. (2001). Speaker adaptation for continuous density HMMs: A review. *ISCA Tutorial and Research Workshop (ITRW) on Adaptation Methods for Speech Recognition.*

Wright, J., Williams, R., & Wilkinson, J. R. (1998). Development and importance of health needs assessment. *BMJ (Clinical Research Ed.), 316*(7140), 1310–1313. doi:10.1136/bmj.316.7140.1310 PMID:9554906

Wu, J., & Cai, Z. (2014). A naive Bayes probability estimation model based on self-adaptive differential evolution. *Journal of Intelligent Information Systems, 42*(3), 671–694. doi:10.100710844-013-0279-y

Wu, X., Jiang, M., & Zhao, C. (2018). Decoding optimization for 5G LDPC codes by machine learning. *IEEE Access: Practical Innovations, Open Solutions, 6*, 50179–50186. doi:10.1109/ACCESS.2018.2869374

Xia, X., Lo, D., Qiu, W., Wang, X., & Zhou, B. (2014). *Automated configuration bug report prediction using text mining.* Paper presented at the 2014 IEEE 38th Annual Computer Software and Applications Conference. 10.1109/COMPSAC.2014.17

Xiang, Y., Chen, Q., Wang, X., & Qin, Y. (2017). Answer Selection in Community Question Answering via Attentive Neural Networks. *IEEE Signal Processing Letters, 24*(4), 505–509. doi:10.1109/LSP.2017.2673123

Xiao, Liang, Wan, Lu, Zhang, & Wu. (2018). *IoT Security Techniques Based on Machine Learning.* CoRR abs/1801.06275

Xiao, W. B., & Fei, Q. (2006). A study of personal credit scoring models on support vector machine with optimal choice of kernel function parameters. *Systems Engineering-Theory & Practice, 10.*

Xiaoli, L. (2002). A brief review: Acoustic emission method for tool wear monitoring during turning. *International Journal of Machine Tools & Manufacture, 42*(2), 157–165. doi:10.1016/S0890-6955(01)00108-0

Xie, Q., Faust, K., Van Ommeren, R., Sheikh, A., Djuric, U., & Diamandis, P. (2019). Deep learning for image analysis: Personalizing medicine closer to the point of care. *Critical Reviews in Clinical Laboratory Sciences, 56*(1), 61–73. doi:10.1080/10408363.2018.1536111 PMID:30628494

Xie, T., & Yu, Z. (2017). N-of-1 Design and its applications to personalized treatment studies. *Statistics in Biosciences, 9*(2), 662–675. doi:10.100712561-016-9165-9 PMID:29225716

Xin, Y., Kong, L., Liu, Z., Chen, Y., Li, Y., Zhu, H., ... Wang, C. (2018). Machine Learning and Deep Learning Methods for Cybersecurity. *IEEE Access: Practical Innovations, Open Solutions, 6*, 35365–35381. doi:10.1109/ACCESS.2018.2836950

Xu, B., Lo, D., Xia, X., Sureka, A., & Li, S. (2015). *Efspredictor: Predicting configuration bugs with ensemble feature selection.* Paper presented at the 2015 Asia-Pacific Software Engineering Conference (APSEC). 10.1109/APSEC.2015.38

Xu, Z., Wang, Y., Tang, J., Wang, J., & Gursoy, M. C. (2017). A deep reinforcement learning based framework for power-efficient resource allocation in cloud RANs. *IEEE Int. Conf. on Communications (ICC)*, 1-6. 10.1109/ICC.2017.7997286

Xue, M., & Zhu, C. (2009). A Study and Application on Machine Learning of Artificial Intelligence. *2009 International Joint Conference on Artificial Intelligence*, 272-274. 10.1109/JCAI.2009.55

Xu, Q., Chen, S., & Li, B. (2016). Combining the ant system algorithm and simulated annealing for 3D/2D fixed-outline floor planning. *Applied Soft Computing, 40*, 150–160. doi:10.1016/j.asoc.2015.10.045

Yang, C. S., & Shih, H. P. (2012). A Rule-Based Approach For Effective Sentiment Analysis. In PACIS (p. 181). Academic Press.

Yang, C.-Z., Chen, K.-Y., Kao, W.-C., & Yang, C.-C. (2014). *Improving severity prediction on software bug reports using quality indicators.* Paper presented at the 2014 IEEE 5th International Conference on Software Engineering and Service Science. 10.1109/ICSESS.2014.6933548

Yang, H. C., & Lee, C. H. (2006). Mining Unstructured Web Pages to Enhance Web Information Retrieval. *International Conference on Innovative Computing, Information and Control*, 429-432.

Yang, M. C., & Rim, H. C. (2014). Identifying interesting Twitter contents using topical analysis. *Expert Systems with Applications*, *41*(9), 4330–4336. doi:10.1016/j.eswa.2013.12.051

Yang, M.-H., Ahuja, N., & Tabb, M. (2002). Extraction of 2d motion trajectories and its application to hand gesture recognition. *Pattern Analysis and Machine Intelligence. IEEE Transactions on*, *24*(8), 1061–1074.

Yang, W. S., & Dia, J. B. (2008). Discovering cohesive subgroups from social networks for targeted advertising. *Expert Systems with Applications*, *34*(3), 2029–2038. doi:10.1016/j.eswa.2007.02.028

Yang, Y., Li, Y., Li, K., Zhao, S., Chen, R., Wang, J., & Ci, S. (2018). DECCO: Deep-learning enabled coverage and capacity optimization for massive MIMO systems. *IEEE Access: Practical Innovations, Open Solutions*, *6*, 23361–23371. doi:10.1109/ACCESS.2018.2828859

Yang, Y., & Pedersen, J. O. (1997). A comparative study on feature selection in text categorization. In *Proceedings of the 14th International Conference on Machine Learning*. Morgan Kaufmann Publishers.

Yao, K., Zhang, L., Luo, T., & Wu, Y. (2018). Deep reinforcement learning for extractive document summarization. *Neurocomputing*, *284*, 52–62. doi:10.1016/j.neucom.2018.01.020

Yao, X. (1999, September). Evolving artificial neural networks. *Proceedings of the IEEE*, *87*(9), 1423–1447. doi:10.1109/5.784219

Yazti, D. Z., & Krishnaswamy, S. (2014). Mobile Big Data Analytics: Research, Practice, and Opportunities. *2014 IEEE 15th International Conference on Mobile Data Management*, 1-2.

Ye, C., Fu, T., Hao, S., Zhang, Y., Wang, O., Jin, B., ... Guo, Y. (2018). Prediction of incident hypertension within the next year: Prospective study using statewide electronic health records and machine learning. *Journal of Medical Internet Research*, *20*(1), e22. doi:10.2196/jmir.9268 PMID:29382633

Ye, H., & Li, G. Y. (2018). Deep Reinforcement Learning for Resource Allocation in V2V Communications. *2018 IEEE International Conference on Communications (ICC)*, 1-6. 10.1109/ICC.2018.8422586

Ye, Q., Zhang, Z., & Law, R. (2009). Sentiment classification of online reviews to travel destinations by supervised machine learning approaches. *Expert Systems with Applications*, *36*(3), 6527–6535. doi:10.1016/j.eswa.2008.07.035

Yingwei, L., Sundararajan, N., & Saratchandran, P. (1998). Performance evaluation of a Sequential Minimal Radial Basis Function (RBF) Neural network learning algorithm. *IEEE Transactions on Neural Networks*, *9*(2), 308–318. doi:10.1109/72.661125 PMID:18252454

Yogesh, S., Bhatia, P., & Omprakash, S. (2007). *A review of studies on machine learning techniques* (Vol. 1). Academic Press.

Yoon, J., Davtyan, C., & van der Schaar, M. (2016). Discovery and clinical decision support for personalized healthcare. *IEEE Journal of Biomedical and Health Informatics*, *21*(4), 1133–1145. doi:10.1109/JBHI.2016.2574857 PMID:27254875

Young, T., Hazarika, D., Poria, S., & Cambria, E. (2017). *Recent Trends in Deep Learning Based Natural Language Processing*. arXiv e-prints, arXiv:1708.02709

Young, T., Hazarika, D., Poria, S., & Cambria, E. (2018). *Recent Trends in Deep Learning Based Natural Language Processing* (Vol. 13). Academic Press.

You, X., Zhang, C., Tan, X., Jin, S., & Wu, H. (2019). AI for 5G: Research directions and paradigms. *Science China. Information Sciences*, *62*(2), 1–13. doi:10.100711432-018-9596-5

Yuan, P., Zhong, Y., & Huang, J. (2015). *Sentiment Classification and Opinion Mining on Airline Reviews*. Academic Press.

Yu, D. N., Chen, F. J., Fu, B., & Qin, A. (2017). Constrained NMF-based semi-supervised learning for social media spammer detection. *J. Knowledge-Based Systems*, *125*, 64–73. doi:10.1016/j.knosys.2017.03.025

Yue, Hang, & Christian. (2019). Test Your Self-Driving Algorithm: An Overview of Publicly Available Driving Datasets and Virtual Testing Environments. *IEEE Transactions on Intelligent Vehicles, 4*(2).

Zeng, Z. Q., Yu, H. B., Xu, H. R., Xie, Y. Q., & Gao, J. (2008, November). Fast training support vector machines using parallel sequential minimal optimization. In *2008 3rd international conference on intelligent system and knowledge engineering* (Vol. 1, pp. 997-1001). IEEE.

Zeng, W., Jiang, X., & Blunt, L. (2009). Surface characterization-based tool wear monitoring in peripheral milling. *International Journal of Advanced Manufacturing Technology*, *40*(3-4), 226–233. doi:10.100700170-007-1352-x

Zhang, D., Han, X., & Deng, C. (2018). Review on the research and practice of deep learning and reinforcement learning in smart grids. CSEE Journal of Power and Energy Systems, 4(3), 362-370.

Zhang, J., & Wang, F. (2019). Signal identification in cognitive radios using machine learning. In Applications of Machine learning in wireless communications, IET Telecommunications series, (pp. 159-96). Academic Press.

Zhang, X., Xu, C., Cheng, J., Lu, H., & Ma, S. (2009). Effective annotation and search for video blogs with integration of context and content analysis. *IEEE Transactions on Multimedia, 11*(2), 272-285.

Zhang, Y., Liu, B., Liu, Z., Huang, J., & Sun, R. (2019). WristPress: Hand Gesture Classification with two-array Wrist-Mounted pressure sensors. In *2019 IEEE 16th International Conference on Wearable and Implantable Body Sensor Networks (BSN)* (pp. 1–4). IEEE.

Zhang, C., Ouyang, X., & Patras, P. (2017, November). Zipnet-gan: Inferring fine-grained mobile traffic patterns via a generative adversarial neural network. In *Proceedings of the 13th International Conference on emerging Networking EXperiments and Technologies* (pp. 363-375). ACM. 10.1145/3143361.3143393

Zhang, C., Patras, P., & Haddadi, H. (2018). Deep Learning in mobile and wireless networking: A survey. *IEEE Communications Surveys and Tutorials*, 1–67.

Zhang, S., Zhang, S., Huang, T., & Gao, W. (2017). Speech emotion recognition using deep convolutional neural network and discriminant temporal pyramid matching. *IEEE Transactions on Multimedia*, *20*(6), 1576–1590. doi:10.1109/TMM.2017.2766843

Zhang, T., Yang, G., Lee, B., & Chan, A. T. (2015). Predicting severity of bug report by mining bug repository with concept profile. *Proceedings of the 30th Annual ACM Symposium on Applied Computing*. 10.1145/2695664.2695872

Zhao, S., Liu, T., Yuan, X., Li, S., & Zhang, Y. (2007). *Automatic Acquisition of Context-Specific Lexical Paraphrases* (Vol. 178921794). IJCAI.

Zhao, X., Jiang, J., He, J., Song, Y., Achanauparp, P., Lim, E., & Li, X. (2011). Topical keyphrase extraction from Twitter. *Proc. of the 49th Annual Meeting of the Association for Computational Linguistics: Human Language Technologies*, 379–388.

Zhao, X., Zhao, C., Zhu, Y., Tang, M., & Wang, J. (2018, September). Improved Single Shot Object Detector Using Enhanced Features and Predicting Heads. In *2018 IEEE Fourth International Conference on Multimedia Big Data (BigMM)* (pp. 1-5). IEEE. 10.1109/BigMM.2018.8499089

Zhou, G., Hansen, J. H., & Kaiser, J. F. (1998). Linear and nonlinear speech feature analysis for stress classification. *Fifth International Conference on Spoken Language Processing.*

Zhou, L., Lai, K. K., & Yen, J. (2009). Credit scoring models with AUC maximization based on weighted SVM. *International Journal of Information Technology & Decision Making*, 8(4), 677–696. doi:10.1142/S0219622009003582

Zhuang, B., Liu, L., Li, Y., Shen, C., & Reid, I. (2017). Attend In Groups: A Weakly-Supervised Deep Learning Framework for Learning from Web Data. *Proceedings of the IEEE Conference on Computer Vision and Pattern Recognition*, 1878-1887. 10.1109/CVPR.2017.311

Zhu, L. (2014). Tripartite graph clustering for dynamic sentiment analysis on social media. *Proc. ACM SIGMOD International Conference on Management of Data (SIGMOD 14)*, 1531-1542. 10.1145/2588555.2593682

Zhu, M., Cheng, L., Armstrong, J. J., Poss, J. W., Hirdes, J. P., & Stolee, P. (2014). *Using Machine Learning to Plan Rehabilitation for Home Care Clients: Beyond "Black-Box" Predictions*. Berlin: Springer.

Zhu, M., Zhang, Z., Hirdes, J. P., & Stolee, P. (2007). Using machine learning algorithms to guide rehabilitation planning for home care clients. *BMC Medical Informatics and Decision Making*, 7. PMID:18096079

Zimmermann, T., Premraj, R., Bettenburg, N., Just, S., Schroter, A., & Weiss, C. (2010). What makes a good bug report? *IEEE Transactions on Software Engineering*, 36(5), 618–643. doi:10.1109/TSE.2010.63

Zoph, B., & Le, Q. V. (2016). *Neural architecture search with reinforcement learning.* arXiv preprint arXiv:1611.01578

Zumel & Mount. (2014). *Practical data science with R.* Manning Publications.

About the Contributors

Arun Solanki is working in the Department of Computer Science, Gautam Buddha University, Greater Noida, India where he has been since 2009. He has worked as member examination, admission, sports council and other university teams from time to time. He received M. Tech. from YMCA University, Faridabad, Haryana India. He received his Ph.D. in Computer Science and Engineering from the Gautam Buddha University in 2014. More than 50 M.Tech. dissertations are submitted under his guidance. His research interests span Expert System, Machine Learning and Search Engines. He has published many research articles in SCI/Scopus indexed International journal. He has participated in many international conferences. He has been technical and advisory committee members of many conferences. He has organized several FDP, Conferences, Workshops, and Seminars. He has chaired many sessions at International Conferences. Arun Solanki is working as Associate Editor in International Journal of Web-Based Learning and Teaching Technologies (IJWLTT) IGI publisher. He has been working as Guest Editor for special issues in Recent Patents on Computer Science, Bentham Science Publishers. He is the editor of many Books with a reputed publisher like IGI Global, CRC and AAP. He is working as the reviewer in Springer, IGI Global, Elsevier, and other reputed publisher journals.

Sandeep Kumar is an Assistant Professor in Department of Computer Science and Engineering at Amity University Rajasthan, Jaipur. Dr. Sandeep Kumar has received his B.E. in Computer Science and Engineering from Engineering College Kota in year 2005 and M.Tech. in Computer Science and Engineering from RTU Kota in year 2011. He qualified UGC-NET in June 2012. Dr. Sandeep Kumar has obtained his Ph.D. in field of Nature Inspired Computing. He has 10 year teaching experience. His area of interest is theoretical computer science, swarm intelligence and evolutionary computing. Currently he is working on Artificial Bee Colony algorithm, Differential Evolution and Spider Monkey optimization algorithms. He has published more than 50 research papers in various SCI/SCOPUS/ESCI journals/conference proceedings and authored two books and 4 book chapter. He has supervised two Ph.D. thesis and 4 are in progress.

Anand Nayyar received Ph.D (Computer Science) from Desh Bhagat University in 2017 in the area of Wireless Sensor Networks. He is currently working in Graduate School, Duy Tan University, Da Nang, Vietnam. A Certified Professional with 75+ Professional certificates from CISCO, Microsoft, Oracle, Google, Beingcert, EXIN, GAQM, Cyberoam and many more. Published more than 300 Research Papers in various National & International Conferences, International Journals (Scopus/SCI/SCIE/SSCI Indexed). Member of more than 50+ Associations as Senior and Life Member and also acting as ACM Distinguished Speaker. He has authored/co-authored cum Edited 25 Books of Computer

Science. Associated with more than 400 International Conferences as Programme Committee/Advisory Board/Review Board member. He has 2 Patents to his name in the area of Internet of Things, Speech Processing. He is currently working in the area of Wireless Sensor Networks, MANETS, Swarm Intelligence, Cloud Computing, Internet of Things, Blockchain, Machine Learning, Deep Learning, Cyber Security, Network Simulation, Wireless Communications. Awarded 20+ Awards for Teaching and Research—Young Scientist, Best Scientist, Young Researcher Award, Outstanding Researcher Award, Indo-International Emerging Star Award (to name a few). He is acting as Editor in Chief of IGI-Global Journal titled "International Journal of Smart Vehicles and Smart Transportation (IJSVST)".

* * *

PapaRao A. V. Assistant professor of Mathematics working in the university college of engineering Vizianagaram A.P India. He has 17 years of teaching experience and 11 years of research experience. Presently five scholars are working under his guidance. His research interest in ecology, epidemiology, and medicine. His focus on apply machine learning algorithms to find the best solutions for models.

Anu G. Aggarwal is working as Professor in the Department of Operational Research, University of Delhi. She obtained her Ph.D., M.Phil and M.Sc. degrees in Operational Research from the University of Delhi in year 2007, 1999 and 1996, respectively. She has published several papers in the area of Marketing Management and Theory of Reliability. Her research interests include modeling and optimization in Consumer Buying Behavior, Innovation-Diffusion modeling and Soft Computing Techniques. She has reviewed many research papers for reputed journals including IEEE Transactions on Engineering Management, International journal of System Science, Int. J. of Production Research, Int. J. of Operational Research etc.

Janet B. is an Assistant Professor in the Department of Computer Applications, NIT, Tiruchirappalli for over 10 years. She has received honours that include University Rank, NET for Lectureship by UGC and deployed a honeypot sensor as part of National Cyber Coordination Centre Project for Cyber Threat Intelligence Generation. She has published 10 papers in International Journals and made 20 International Conference presentations. She has set up the first of its kind Information Processing and Security Laboratory with Industry involvement. She is a champion of open source technology. Her areas of specialization are Information Processing and Security, Internet of Things, Application Development and Deep Learning.

Santhi B. has 26.5 years of teaching experience. Five Ph.D guided and currently guiding five. Funded project two completed. Area of specialization: Image Analysis, Wireless Sensor Network, Machine Learning, and Deep learning.

Anu Bajaj received the B.Tech. and M.Tech. degree in Computer Science and Engineering from the Guru Jambheshwar University of Science and Technology (GJU S&T), Hisar, Haryana, India, in 2012 and 2014, respectively, where she is currently pursuing the Ph.D. degree in computer science and engineering. She was a Junior Research Fellow with GJU S&T, from 2016 to 2018, where she is a Senior Research Fellow.. Presently she is pursuing a Ph.D. in Computer Science and Engineering, and also working as Senior Research Fellow in GJU S&T, India. Earlier to this, she has worked as a Junior

Research Fellow from 2016-2018 in GJU S&T, India. Her current research interests are within software engineering topics and include software testing, software maintenance and evolution, search-based software engineering, computational intelligence, and soft computing.

Zoran S. Bojkovic is full professor of Electrical Engineering, University of Belgrade. He is a permanent visiting professor at the University of Texas at Arlington, TX, USA, EE Department, Multimedia Systems Lab and Life Senor Member of IEEE. He also, coauthored textbooks/chapters in multimedia communications published by Prentice Hall (2000, 2002), Wiley (2005), CRC Press (2009, 2019), Springer-Verlag and IGI Global. Prof. Zoran Bojkovic is an active researcher in wireless multimedia communications.

Ghanshyam S. Bopche received his B.Sc. (Electronics) and Master of Computer Applications (MCA) degree from the Nagpur University, India in 2007 and 2010 respectively. He received his Ph.D. degree in Computer Science from Institute for Development and Research in Banking Technology, an associate institute of University of Hyderabad (UoH), India in 2017. He was exchange research scholar at the Center for Unified Biometrics and Sensors (CUBS), State University of New York (SUNY) at Buffalo, NY, USA during 2015. Currently he is working as an Assistant Professor at the Department of Computer Science & Engineering in Madanapalle Institute of Technology & Science, Andhra Pradesh, India. His current research interests include Computer and Network Security, Information Assurance, Insider Threats, Digital Forensics, Machine Learning & Data Analytics.

Pradeep Reddy C. H. is currently working as a Professor in VIT-AP University, Amaravati, India. He has a total of thirteen years experience in both teaching and research. He received his B.Tech in Computer Science and Engineering from PBR VITS, JNTU Andhra Pradesh, India and M.Tech in Computer Science and Engineering from VIT University, Vellore, India. He did his PhD in Computer Science and Engineering from VIT University, Vellore. He has published various journals and served as reviewer and editor for reputed journals. His research interests include Wireless Networks, IoT, Security systems and Cloud computing.

Niranjan Chiplunkar is working as Principal and Professor in the Department of Computer Science and Engineering at NMAM Institute of Technology, Nitte, India. He is a Fellow of Institution of Engineers (India) and member of several other Professional bodies like IEEE, CSI, and ISTE. His research interests include Data Mining, CAD for VLSI, and Big Data Analytics.

Gracia Nirmala Rani D. received B.E. degree in Electronics and Communication Engineering from Madurai Kamaraj University (2004) and M.E. degree in VLSI Design from Anna University (2007), Chennai, India. She has awarded Ph.D. degree in Information and Communication Engineering at Thiagarajar College of Engineering (Under Anna University, Chennai) (2014), Madurai, India. Her research interests include RFIC Design, Low power design optimization, Physical Design and VLSI architecture design.

Roshan Fernandes is working as Associate Professor in the Department of Computer Science and Engineering at NMAM Institute of Technology, Nitte, India. Her research interests include Natural Language Processing, Machine Learning, and mobile web services.

Neha Garg is currently working as an Assistant Professor, Manav Rachna International Institute of Research and Studies, Faridabad, India (around 10 years teaching experience), M. Tech from Banasthali Vidyapith, Near Niwai, Rajasthan and Ph. D. pursuing in Computer Science and Engineering from MRIIRS, Fraidabad, India. She has recently published a book "Analysis and Design of Algorithms- a Beginner Hope" with BPB Publication House. She has supervised and Guided research projects of B.Tech She has published research papers in field of Big data, and Data Mining. Her research interests are in the area of "Big Data Analytics" and "Machine Learning".

Bharathi N. Gopalsamy is working as Associate Professor in department of Computer Science Engineering at SRM Institute of Science and Technology, Chennai. She has good knowledge to work with embedded system in addition to computer science engineering concepts. She was awarded with a Ph.D. degree in computer science in 2014 from SASTRA University, having 15 years of work experience as an academician and one and half years of industrial experience in ARM platform with ubuntu OS. She studied her M.Tech in Advanced computing in SASTRA University and done her M.Tech project internship at Center for High Performance Embedded System (CHiPES), Nanyang Technological University (NTU), Singapore. She was completed her B.E in computer science engineering in 2002 at SASTRA University. She published approximately 18 research papers in reputed journals and conferences, guided many of the B.Tech. and M.Tech. students in various domains of computer science engineering and embedded systems.

Vishal Gupta is currently undertaking a bachelors degree course at NITW in Electronics and Communication Engineering Department, NITW. With their recent advent of interest in the domain of deep learning, they started to work on the computer vision-based application using deep learning.

Mohammad Farukh Hashmi received his B.E in Electronics & Communication Engineering from R. G. P. V. Bhopal University in 2007. He obtained his M.E. in Digital Techniques & Instrumentation in 2010 from R. G. P. V. Bhopal University. He received Ph.D. at VNIT Nagpur under the supervision of Dr. A. G. Keskar. He has published up to 50 papers in National/International Conferences/Journals. He has a teaching experience of 7 years. He is currently an Assistant professor at Department of Electronics and Communication Engineering, National Institute of Technology, Warangal. His current research interests are Image Processing, Internet of Things, Embedded Systems, Biomedical Signal Processing, Computer Vision, Circuit Design, and Digital IC Design etc. Mr. Mohammad F. Hashmi is a member of IEEE, ISTE, and IAENG.

Shanthi J. received B.E. degree in Electronics and Communication Engineering at Mepco Schlenk Engineering College from Madurai Kamaraj University (2004) and M.E. degree in Embedded System Technologies from Anna University (2010), Tirunelveli, India. She is currently pursuing Ph.D. degree in Electrical Engineering at Thiagarajar College of Engineering (Under Anna University, Chennai), Madurai, India. Her research interests include Embedded System Applications, Physical Design and VLSI architecture design and optimization algorithms.

Garima Jaiswal is currently pursuing her Ph.D. in the Department of Information Technology from Indira Gandhi Delhi Technical University for Women (IGDTUW), Delhi. Her areas of interests include Machine Learning and Data Mining. She has published 3 papers in International and national conferences and 3 papers in peer reviewed journals.

K. Jayakumar received the B.E. degree in Computer Science and Engineering from M.K. University, Madurai, Tamilnadu, India in 2002, M.E. degree in Computer Science and Engineering from Anna University, Chennai, India in 2005 and Doctorate degree in Computer Science and Engineering from Anna University, Chennai, India in 2018. He is currently working as an Associate Professor at the School of Computer Science and Engineering, VIT University, Vellore, Tamil Nadu, India. His current research interests include Intrusion Detection, Data Mining and, Soft Computing Techniques. He is a Life Member of Indian Society for Technical Education.

Pooja Jha has submitted her PhD in computer Science. She holds her Masters degree in IT. Her interest areas are Software Engineering, Metrics, Reliability and Robotics. She has a work experience of 12 years.

Nimmi K. is currently pursuing her Ph.D. in the Department of Computer Application in National Institute of Technology-Tiruchirappalli. She has completed her M. E in Computer and Engineering from Anna university-Tiruchirappall and holds an MBA in Human Resource Management from Madras University. She received Promising young women award by IIM Calicut in the year 2012. Her research interest includes mobile device security, Deep Learning and Machine learning.

Surinder Khurana is an Assistant Professor at the Centre for Computer Science & Technology, Central University of Punjab, India. He completed his Master's degree from PEC University of Technology. His research areas cover a wide range of issues related to network security and machine learning.

Dragan D. Kukolj is Professor of computer-based systems with Dept. of Computer Engineering, Faculty of Engineering, University of Novi Sad. His main research interests include digital signal processing, video processing and machine learning techniques. He has published over 200 papers in referred journals and conference proceedings. Dr. Kukolj is the coordinator of Intellectual Property Centre of University of Novi Sad.

Akshi Kumar is an Assistant Professor in the Department of Computer Science & Engineering at Delhi Technological University (formerly Delhi College of Engineering). She has been with the university for the past 10 years. She has received her doctorate degree in Computer Engineering in the area of Web Mining, from Faculty of Technology, University of Delhi in 2011. She completed her M.Tech (Master of Technology) with honours in Computer Science & Engineering from Guru Gobind Singh Indraprastha University, Delhi in 2005. She received her BE (Bachelor of Engineering) degree with distinction in Computer Science & Engineering from Maharishi Dayanand University, Rohtak in 2003. Dr. Kumar's research interests are in the area of intelligent systems, social media analytics and soft computing.

Jayakumar Loganathan received his B.Tech degree in Information Technology from Anna University, Chennai, India and the M.Tech degree and Ph.D in Computer Science and engineering from Pondicherry Central University, Puducherry, India, in 2012 and 2019 respectively. He is currently working toward his research on cognitive radio spectrum management schemes at Department of Computer Science, Vel Tech Rangarajan Dr. Sagunthala R&D Institute of Science and Technology, Avadi, Chennai, India. His current research interests include resource management algorithm designs for wireless communication systems, opportunistic spectrum access schemes, multi criteria decision making schemes.

Anand Kumar M. is working as an Assistant Professor in the Department of Information Technology, National Institute of Technology-Karnataka. His area of interest includes Natural Language Processing, Machine Translation System for Indian Languages, Machine learning and Deep Learning for Natural Language Processing and Text Analytics.

Srivani M. is pursuing her Ph.D. in Information Science and Technology, College of Engineering Guindy, Anna University, Chennai under the guidance of Dr. T. Mala, Associate Professor, Department of IST, CEG, Guindy. She has completed M.Tech (IT) with First Rank and Gold Medalist in College of Engineering Guindy, Anna University, Chennai from 2015-2017. M.Tech project was selected as Technology Innovative Project in 2017. She has completed B.Tech (IT) with Gold Medal and sixth rank out of 9939 students. Her areas of interest include Machine Learning, Artificial Intelligence and Cognitive Computing. There are about 5 publications to her credit.

Varun G. Menon is currently working in Department of Computer Science and Engineering, SCMS School of Engineering and Technology. After obtaining his Masters in Computer and Communication with University First Rank, he completed his PhD in Computer Science and Engineering. He is currently serving in the Editorial and Review Boards of many High Impact Factor Journals including IEEE Transactions on Vehicular Technology, Ad Hoc Networks-Elsevier, Computer Communications Journal-Elsevier, Journal of Organizational and End User Computing-IGI Global, International Journal of Distributed Sensor Networks-Sage, International Journal of Communication Systems, etc. He has served in the Technical Program Committee of many prestigious International Conferences. He has also a Masters degree in Applied Psychology and an MBA degree in Human Resources Management. He is also a Life skills and Personality Development Trainer. His research interests include Mobile Ad Hoc Networks, Opportunistic Routing, Underwater Sensor Networks, Educational Psychology, Cyber Psychology, Evaluation Methods in Education, Training and Development, Internet of Things, Fog Computing and Networking.

Dragorad A. Milovanovic received the Dipl. Electr. Eng. and Master of Science degree from The University of Belgrade, Republic of Serbia. From 1987 to 1991, he was a Research Assistant and PhD researcher from 1991-2001 at the Department of Electrical Engineering, where his research interest includes analysis and design of digital communications systems. He has been working as R&D engineer for DSP software development in digital television industry. He is serving as an ICT lecturer and consultant in digital media and medicine/sports for implementation standard-based solutions. He participated in numerous scientific projects and published more than 200 papers in international journals and conference proceedings. He also, coauthored textbooks/chapters in multimedia communications published by Prentice Hall (2002), Wiley (2005), CRC Press (2009, 2019, 2020), Springer-Verlag (2016, 2017, 2018, 2019) and IGI Global (2017). Present projects include adaptive coding of 3D video, immersive media, 5G wireless technology and ultra-low latency services.

Abirami Murugappan is working as Assistant Professor in Department of Information Science and Technology, College of Engineering, Guindy, Anna University. Her areas of interest include Artificial Intelligence, Video Analytics, Image Processing, Text Mining, NLP, Databases, Multimedia and Big Data. She acted as a Principal Investigator for UGC major project research scheme from 2013-2017 and for Centre for Technology Development and Transfer (CTDT) project from 2012-2013. Acted as a mentor for nearly 7 projects under CTDT Students Innovative Projects Scheme. Received CTS Best Young Faculty Award, for the year 2017 and mentor award for the best project in 2016 from CTDT, Anna University. Currently she is guiding 6 PhD candidates and finished one candidate to her credit. She has published more than 113 publications consisting various journals, conferences and book chapters to her credit.

Neha Neha is a Ph.D. scholar in the Department of Operational Research, University of Delhi, India. She has done her M.Phil. degree in Operational Research from University of Delhi and has done her M.Sc in Applied Operational Research, Department of Operational Research, University of Delhi. Her research area is Software Reliability and Operational Research.

Mala Nehru is working as Associate Professor in Department of Information Science and Technology, College of Engineering, Guindy, Anna University. Her areas of specialization are Computer Graphics, Natural Language Processing, Multimedia Systems and Cloud computing. Four candidates completed PhD under her supervision and currently guiding six candidates. There are about 28 International Journal publications and 50 International Conference publications to her credit. She has coordinated and conducted more than twenty faculty development programs, Workshops and seminars. Author of the Lab manual "Graphics and Multimedia" for MCA degree distance education programme in Anna University, Chennai. Author of Book titled "Computer Graphics" for MCA students of Tamil Nadu Open University. Attended and presented papers in International Conferences conducted in "University of Cologne", Germany, "University of Pennsylvania", USA and "University of Malaya", Malaysia. Acted as co coordinator for research Projects worth Rs 75 Lakhs received from various funding agencies.

Srinivasa Pai P. completed his Bachelors degree in Industrial Production Engineering in 1993 from Mangalore University, M.Tech in Maintenance Engineering in 1996 and PhD in Mechanical Engineering in 2004 from University of Mysore. He is currently working as Professor in the Dept. of Mechanical Engg. at NMAM Institute of Technology. His areas of interest include tool condition monitoring, high speed machining, artificial neural networks, signal processing, surface integrity studies etc. He has more than 40 publications in refereed international journals and more than 100 publications in conference proceedings. He has successfully guided 4 research scholars and another 4 are pursuing under him. He has executed several research projects funded by agencies like AICTE, New Delhi, IE(I), Kolkata, TEQIP, etc.

Veerappa B. Pagi has completed his M. E from Bangalore University and Ph. D in Computer Science and Engineering, from Visvesvaraya Technological University, Belagavi, Karnataka, India. Currently, he is working as Professor in the Department of Computer Science and Engineering, at Basaveshwar Engineering College, Bagalkot, Karnataka, India. Earlier he served as a faculty of Computer Science in Sir M. Visvesvaraya Institute of Technology, Bangalore. He has published over 30 papers in International journals and conferences.

Hemanta Kumar Palo completed his A.M.I.E. from Institute of Engineers, India in 1997, Master of Engineering from Birla Institute of Technology, Mesra, Ranchi in 2011 and Ph.D. in 2018 from the Siksha 'O' Anusandhan (Deemed to be University), Bhubaneswar, Odisha, India. He is having 20 years of experience in the field of Electronics and Communication Engineering from 1990 to 2010 in Indian Air Force. Currently he is serving as an Associate Professor in the department of Electronics and Communication Engineering in the Institute of Technical Education and Research, Siksha 'O' Anusandhan

University, Bhubaneswar, Odisha, India. He had been an Assistant Professor in Gandhi Academy of Technology and Engineering, Odisha, in the Department of ECE from 2011 to 2012. He is the life member of IEI, India and has published around 45 research papers in reputed international and national highly indexed journals and conferences and is an organizing member of a number of such conferences. His area of research includes signal processing, speech and emotion recognition.

P. Victer Paul is working as Assistant Professor in the Department of Computer Science and Engineering at Indian Institute of Information Technology Kottayam, Kerala, India, an Institute of National Importance of India. He has completed his Ph.D. in the Department of Computer Science (2015) from Pondicherry Central University, Pondicherry, India. He has done his B.Tech. in Information Technology (2007) from SMVEC and M.Tech. in Network and Internet Engineering (2011) from Pondicherry Central University, Pondicherry, India. He is a recipient of eminent INSPIRE fellowship from Department of Science and Technology, New Delhi. He is a University Gold medalist and University Rank holder in M.Tech and B.Tech studies respectively. He has also received "TCS Best Student Award 2010" from TCS for academic excellence at Pondicherry Central University, Puducherry. He has 7 I years of academic & industrial experience and published over 90 research articles in various International Journals & Conferences. Currently, he is working in the fields of Optimization algorithms, Cloud Computing and Data Analytics.

Janjanam Prabhudas is currently a full-time research scholar from VIT-AP University, Amaravathi under the guidance of Dr Pradeep Reddy CH. He completed his B-tech in VVIT, JNTU Andhra Pradesh and Masters from VRSEC JNTU Andhra Pradesh. His research interests are Machine Learning, Natural Language Processing Deep Learning IoT.

B. Ramachandra Reddy is working as a Senior Assistant Professor in the Department of Computer Science and Engineering at Madanapalle Institute of Technology & Science, Madanapalle, India. He received Ph.D. from PDPM IIITDMJ, Jabalpur. His research interests are Machine Learning, Data Mining, Software Metrics and Software Quality.

Anisha Rodrigues is working as Assistant Professor in the Department of Computer Science and Engineering at NMAM Institute of Technology, Nitte, India. Her research interests include Natural Language Processing, Machine Learning, and Big Data Analytics.

Karpagam S. received the BE degree in computer science and engineering from Anna University, Chennai, India in 2005 and the ME degree in computer science and engineering from Anna University, India in 2010. Currently, she is working as an programmer at Spectrum Info Tech, Virudhunagar, India. She has presented and published 3 papers in Conferences. Her current research interests include: Data hiding, data mining, neural networks and genetic algorithm. She is a Life Member of Indian Society for Technical Education.

Rajaram S. was born in Mamsapuram near Rajapalayam in the year 1973. He received a Bachelor's degree in Electronics and Communication Engineering in 1994 from the Thiagarajar College of Engineering, Madurai and a Master's degree with Distinction in Microwave and Optical Engineering from Alagappa Chettiar College of Engineering and Technology, Karaikudi in 1996. Dr.S.Rajaram holds a PhD degree in VLSI Design from Madurai Kamaraj University. He Completed his Post Doctoral Research in 3D wireless system at Georgia Institute of Technology, Atlanta, USA during 2010-2011. Current service details Since 1998, he has been with Thiagarajar College of Engineering, Madurai. Currently he holds the post of Associate Professor in the department of Electronics and Communication Engineering, Thiagarajar College of Engineering. Any extras such as specializations, papers published, programs conducted, etc. He is a former Member of Academic Council of Thiagarajar College of Engineering and Member of Board of Studies for several educational Institutions. His fields of interest are VLSI Design and Wireless Communication. He is one among the Senior Resource persons in Thiagarajar College of Engineering for conducting faculty development programs. Under his guidance ten research scholars have already obtained PhD degrees in the area of Applications of VLSI Design for wireless Communication systems. He has Published around 170 Papers in reputed Journal and Conferences. He was the recipient of Young Scientist Fellowship From TNSCST, BOYSCAST Fellowship from DST and Cambridge International certificate for Teachers and Trainers. Other qualifications and ex-officio posts held Dr. S. Rajaram is also the principal investigator for several projects funded by AICTE, DST and DRDO. He has established several Research Centres at Thiagarajar College of Engineering such Altera VLSI Design Centre, ASIC Tools Laboratory and TIFAC Core in wireless Technologies in collaboration with Industries and Government Agencies. He is a senior member of the Institute of Electrical and Electronics Engineers (IEEE,USA), Life member of Indian Society of Technical Education, and member of VLSI society of India. He has visited USA for Post doctoral research work and conferences.

Sriparna Saha received her B.Tech. degree from RCC Institute of Information Technology, Kolkata, India and her M.E. and Ph.D. degrees from Electronics and Tele-Communication Engineering department of Jadavpur University, Kolkata, India. She is currently an Assistant Professor in the Department of Computer Science and Engineering of Maulana Abul Kalam Azad University of Technology, West Bengal, India. Prior to that, she was associated as a faculty with Jadavpur University and two other institutions. Her research area includes artificial intelligence, image processing, and robotics. She has over 70 publications in international journals and conference proceedings including IEEE, Elsevier, Springer, etc. She is the author of a book on Gesture Recognition published by Studies in Computational Intelligence, Springer, currently available in many online book retailers. She is also the reviewer for many international journals. Recently, her major research proposal is accepted for Start Up Grant under UGC Basic Scientific Research Grant. She is the member of Board of Studies for Maulana Abul Kalam Azad University of Technology and also the member of Governing Body of IDEAL Institute of Engineering.

Om Prakash Sangwan received his Ph.D. in Computer Science and Engineering and M.Tech. degree in Computer Science and Engineering with distinction in research work from Guru Jambheshwar University of Science and Technology, Hisar, Haryana, India. He is also CISCO Certified Network Associate (CCNA) and CISCO Certified Academic Instructor (CCAI). His area of research is software engineering focusing on planning, designing, testing, metrics and application of neural networks, fuzzy logic and neuro-fuzzy. He has number of publications in International and National journals and conferences. He is presently working as Professor, Department of Computer Science and Engineering, Guru Jambheshwar University of Science and Technology, Hisar, Haryana, India. Before joining the current assignment, he worked as Assistant Professor, Department of Computer Science and Engineering, School of Information and Communication Technology, Gautam Buddha University, Greater Noida, Uttar Pradesh. Earlier to this, Dr. Sangwan has worked as Dy. Director with Amity Resource Centre for Information Technology and Head, Cisco Regional Networking Academy, Amity Institute of Information Technology, Amity University, Uttar Pradesh. He is also a member of Computer Science Teacher Association (CSTA), New York, USA, International Association of Engineer (IAENG), Hong Kong, IACIST (International Association of Computer Science and Information Technology), USA, professional member of Association of Computing Machinery, IEEE and life member of Computer Society of India, India.

Lokanath Sarangi has completed Ph.D. in 2018 from the Siksha 'O' Anusandhan (Deemed to be University), Bhubaneswar, Odisha, India. He is having a vast industrial and teaching experience in the field of Electronics and Communication Engineering. Currently he works as an Associate Professor in the department of Electronics and Communication Engineering, College of Engineering, Bhubaneswar, BPUT Odisha, India. He has published many research articles in both international and national journals and conferences. His area of research includes biomedical signal processing, smart health care system.

Reetl Sarup is a final year engineering student pursuing Information Technology at Indira Gandhi Delhi Technical University for Women (IGDTUW). She holds a pre-placement offer for a full-time employee from the business and financial software company- Intuit, where she explored the use of publish-subscribe messaging system- Kafka during her role as a summer intern with QuickBooks team. She has won prizes in various technical hackathons such as Smart India Hackathon 2018 and Intuit Interns Hackathon 2018. Her special interests include coding in C++, Java and Python as well as exploring the domains of machine learning, artificial intelligence, cloud computing and web development. Being enthusiastic about technology, she pro-actively worked as the Chapter Secretary of ACM Student Chapter as well as Campus Leader at Lean In IGDTUW.

Arun Sharma completed his Ph.D. Degree from Thapar University, Patiala India in 2009. Currently he is working as Associate Professor and Head of the Department - IT at Indira Gandhi Delhi Technical University for Women (IGDTUW), Delhi. His areas of interests include Machine learning, Software Engineering, Soft Computing and Big Data. Under his guidance, 6 students have completed their PhD degree. He has published more than 70 papers in international SCI/SCIE/SCOPUS and other journals and conferences. He is a Senior Member-IEEE and Life Member- CSI.

Deepak Kumar Sharma received the B.Tech. in computer science from G. G. S. Indraprastaha University and M. E. in Computer Technology and Applications from University of Delhi, India. He is presently working as Assistant Professor in the Division of Information Technology, Netaji Subhas Institute of Technology, University of Delhi, India since February, 2011. From July 2004 to January 2011, he worked as a Senior Lecturer at Maharaja Agrasen Institute of Technology (MAIT), Delhi, India. His current research interests include opportunistic networks, wireless ad hoc networks, and sensor networks.

Kamlesh Sharma is currently working as a Associate Professor, MRIIRS, Faridabad, India (more than 12 years teaching experience). MCA, M. Tech from MDU University and Ph. D. in Computer Science and Engineering from Lingaya`s University, India. She is Supervising 2 Ph. D. scholars. Supervised and Guided research projects of M. Tech, B.Tech and application based projects for different competitions. She is also associated with two research projects related to health recommender system and NLP. She has published more than 40 research papers in field of NLP, IOT, Bigdata, Green Computing and Data Mining. Her research area "Natural Language Processing" is based on innovative idea of reducing the mechanized efforts and adapting the software to Hindi dialect. Adopted innovative teaching methodology like role play, case studies, simulation, presentations, live projects, smart classrooms technologies and combined these with regular lecture method to make the overall teaching learning process more effective.

Tamanna Sharma is doing Ph.D. in Computer Science and Engineering from Guru Jambheshwar University of Science and Technology, Hisar, Haryana and completed her Master of Technology in Computer Science and Engineering from Banasthali University, Rajasthan. Her area of research is software engineering with machine learning, mining software repositories, software reliability engineering and Automated Software Debugging.

Alok Kumar Shukla is an Assistant Professor in VNR VJIET, Hyderabad, India. He holds B.Tech degree in Computer Science and Engineering from UPTU University, an M.E. degree in Information Technology from DAVV University, India, and Ph.D. in Evolutionary Computation at NIT Raipur, India. His research is centered in bioinformatics, network security, and machine learning domains.

Simran Sidhu received her Masters in Computer Science and Technology from the Central University of Punjab in 2018. She completed her Bachelors in Computer Science and Engineering from GZS Campus of Punjab Technical University, Jalandhar in 2016. She was a first ranker in all the eight semesters of her Engineering degree, winning gold medals in every semester and hence stood first in the overall order of merit and was thus conferred with the college Roll of Honour. She stood third at the National Level in a technical essay writing competition organised by Indian National Academy of Engineering (INAE) in August 2017. She was inducted as a Student Member of the Indian National Academy of Engineering in December 2017. Her research interests include Artificial Intelligence, Machine Learning, Natural Language Processing, Soft Computing, Computer Networking and Digital Security.

Vaithehi Sinthiya was an assistant professor in the department of English in Karunya institute of technology and sciences, Coimbatore from 2017 July to 2019 April. She had research experience in Amrita Vishwa Vidhyapeetham, Coimbatore. Though, she did her previous dissertation in literature, the research experience changed her plan. In future, she is holding the dream of doing her research in computational linguistics field.

Ashok Suragala is currently working as Assistant Professor in department of CSE in JNTUK-University College of Engineering, Vizianagaram, India. He currently working on ICU Mortality Prediction using computational techniques access the real data from Physionet MIMIC 3 Clinical Database. He is very much interested in clinical data analysis and make predictions. For this he used various Statistical and Inference techniques and build basic and deep models using Statistical programming language like R. He presently Pursuing Micro masters course on Statistics and Data Science from MIT,USA. He also Completed Professional Certification in "Data Science and Big Data Analytics:Making Data-Driven Decisions" from Massachusetts Institute of Technology, Cambridge, Massachusetts, USA.

Nagabhushan Tagadur from SJCE, Mysuru in Electrical Engineering and completed his M.E and PhD degree from Indian Institute of Science, Bengaluru. He is currently the Principal of SJCE, Mysuru and has 33 years of teaching, research, industry and administration experience. He has published more than 20 publications in journals of repute and presented in more than 40 prestigious conferences. His research interests include machine learning, artificial neural networks, computer networks etc. He has successfully guided 9 PhD students and 3 are pursuing under his guidance.

Diwakar Tripathi received BE degree in computer science and engineering from Institution of Electronics and Telecommunication Engineering, New Delhi, India, in 2009, ME degree in computer engineering (software engineering) from the Institute of Engineering and Technology, Devi Ahilya Vishwavidyalaya, Indore, India, in 2014 and Ph. D. from National Institute of Technology Goa, India in 2018. Currently, he is working as senior assistant professor at Madanapalle Institute of Technology & Science Madanapalle A.P. India. His current research includes fraud detection and data mining.

Vibha Verma is a PhD Scholar in the Department of Operational Research, University of Delhi, India since 28 September 2017. She obtained her MSc and MPhil in Operational Research from the University of Delhi, in 2015 and 2017, respectively. She has completed her Bachelors in Mathematics. She has written few research papers which have been published in some international journals and conference proceedings. Her research area is software reliability.

Ramesh S. Wadawadagi has completed his M. Tech in Computer Science and Technology, from University of Mysore, Mysore, and pursuing his Ph. D. at Visvesvaraya Technological University, Belagavi, Karnatak, India. Currently, he is working as an assistant professor at Basaveshwar engineering college, Bagalkot, Karnataka, India.

Index

Ensure Quality Research is Introduced to the Academic Community

Become an IGI Global Reviewer for Authored Book Projects

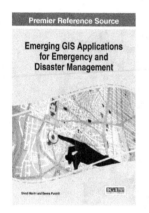

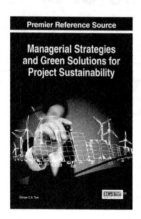

The overall success of an authored book project is dependent on quality and timely reviews.

In this competitive age of scholarly publishing, constructive and timely feedback significantly expedites the turnaround time of manuscripts from submission to acceptance, allowing the publication and discovery of forward-thinking research at a much more expeditious rate. Several IGI Global authored book projects are currently seeking highly-qualified experts in the field to fill vacancies on their respective editorial review boards:

Applications and Inquiries may be sent to:
development@igi-global.com

Applicants must have a doctorate (or an equivalent degree) as well as publishing and reviewing experience. Reviewers are asked to complete the open-ended evaluation questions with as much detail as possible in a timely, collegial, and constructive manner. All reviewers' tenures run for one-year terms on the editorial review boards and are expected to complete at least three reviews per term. Upon successful completion of this term, reviewers can be considered for an additional term.

If you have a colleague that may be interested in this opportunity, we encourage you to share this information with them.